to the Ft. until sometime after day-light
and the attack was not made until at
least one hour after sun-rise. The fight
continued on the left-wing until late in
the evening. We drove the enemy from their
position & gained at this point a signal
victory, which if it had been followed
up would have resulted in a complete
rout of the enemy. While they were retreating & just as they were about crossing the
ridge leading into the central valley, a battery
& several reg'ts came to their aid. The battery
opened upon us, & caused our troops to
falter. At this point our forces were ordered to fall back into the fort. Late in
the evening the enemy charged our works
on our right — and succeeded in getting
possession of them. The fight here was
long & terrible resulting in an immense loss of life on their side. Our
forces finally succeeded in driving them
back. The firing from the batteries was
kept up very briskly on both sides until
after dark. As soon as the firing ceased
I got on my horse & rode into Dover to
learn the result of the day's work. Knowing

Pen and Sword

Lt. Col. Randal W. McGavock,
C. S. A.

Pen and Sword

THE LIFE AND JOURNALS OF

COLONEL, C.S.A.

The Biography — HERSCHEL GOWER

The Early Journals — 1848-1851
HERSCHEL GOWER, EDITOR

The Political and Civil War Journals — 1853-1862
JACK ALLEN, EDITOR

TENNESSEE HISTORICAL COMMISSION - NASHVILLE 1959

Library of Congress Catalog Number: 60-9243

Printed by McCowat-Mercer Press, Inc.
Jackson, Tennessee, U.S.A.

CONTENTS

CONTENTS (cont'd)

ILLUSTRATIONS

ILLUSTRATIONS (cont'd)

The Life of Randal W. McGavock

By Herschel Gower

INTRODUCTION AND ACKNOWLEDGEMENTS

In prefacing the journals of Randal William McGavock with a biography, I have had more than one purpose in mind. First: Randal William McGavock's forebears were an exemplary Scotch-Irish family, who, as members of the great migration from Ireland in the eighteenth century, contributed in heroic measure to the dramatic settlement of the Old Southwest of the United States. Since research on the family brought this pattern of migration into focus and furnished details of movement and settlement too often lacking in the annals of similar Scotch-Irish families, it seemed to me worthwhile to present an archetypal narrative while introducing the young man of the journals.

Second: the members of this large family connection frequently appear in the early journals which I have edited and in those published simultaneously under the editorship of Dr. Jack Allen. Therefore, the preliminary chapters of the biography are an introduction to a number of notable citizens of early Virginia and Tennessee.

Third: in writing the biography I have attempted to chart, as accurately as I could, those years of McGavock's life not recorded by his own pen. That is, I have tried to supplement his journals, and complete a full account of his thirty-six years, with the hope that the biographical narrative may provide a more intimate understanding of this young Tennessean against the cross currents of his age.

A number of people have faithfully assisted me in the task of editing the journals and collecting materials for the biography. Foremost thanks are due Miss Margaret Lindsley Warden for her kind permission to publish the manuscripts of her great-uncle and for giving me access to other private papers relating to the McGavock, Grundy, and Lindsley families of Tennessee.

Much of the history of the early McGavocks of Virginia was communicated by the late Mrs. Jouet McGavock Boyd of Wytheville. Teacher, historian, and family chronicler, Mrs. Boyd graciously gave the editor a full week from her last summer, sharing records collected during a lifetime of research.

I also acknowledge the considerable help of Miss Mary B. McGavock and Jacob McGavock of Wythe County, Virginia.

To these I add a number of individuals in Nashville who have offered much information and several suggestions during the preparation of the manuscript: Mrs. George A. Frazer and Miss Mary Washington Frazer; Dr. William T. Alderson, Mrs. Frank L. Owsley, Dr. Dan M. Robison, Dr. Robert H. White, Mrs. Gertrude Parsley, and Mrs. Hermione Embry of the Tennessee State Library and Archives; Miss Clara Mae Brown, Dr. Henry L. Swint, and Miss Josephine Murphey of Vanderbilt University; Mrs. Henry Dickinson and General Jacob McGavock Dickinson; Carl R. Phillips, Lanier Merritt, William Waller, and Dr. Richmond C. Beatty.

For the use of their notes and for their transcripts of the later journals, I am particularly indebted to Dr. Jack Allen and Dr. A. L. Crabb of George Peabody College for Teachers.

A Fulbright Grant to Scotland, under the auspices of the United States Educational Commission in the United Kingdom, made it possible for me to visit Ireland briefly in 1956 and complete the necessary research for the opening chapters of the biography. This assistance, along with the help and hospitality of George McGavock of Carnlough and the Reverend George Jackson of Glenarm, is gratefully acknowledged. A faculty summer grant from Vanderbilt University in 1958 provided the opportunity for further research in Washington and Boston.

To Mr. Max H. Straw of the Metropolitan District Commission of Boston I express my appreciation for making possible a pleasant visit to abandoned Fort Warren in Boston Harbor. To staff members at the Boston Public, Athæneum, and Harvard Libraries I am grateful for much courteous assistance.

For their abstracts of several court records and other pertinent data in East Tennessee, I am indebted to Mrs. Arthur H. Moser and Miss Pollyanna Creekmore of Knoxville. Friends and fellow members of the Confederate Historical Study Club of Nashville have contributed much information and a warm interest in this book from its inception.

For their personal interest I mention with gratitude Marie Hudson Gower, Isabel Howell, and Robert L. Welker.

HERSCHEL GOWER

Vanderbilt University
October 1, 1959

CHAPTER I

James McGavock Marks Off An Empire

The northeast coast of County Antrim rises quickly from the Irish Sea. Almost at once the hills begin. If the traveller follows the coast road ambling north from Belfast, he sees misty mountains rising in the west, and the road seems commanded from these high craggy places. At Ballygalley Head this same road curves abruptly, as if sidestepping the sea, and then moves northwest again. Gradually the eye falls on Knock Dhu, Ballygilbert, and Slievebane in the distance—Celtic place names assigned to the heights of Antrim.

Only here and there does the visitor see parcels of level land suitable for cultivation; for either the terrain slopes upward, where the soil is thin, or declines to boggy marshes, which furnish peat for the hearth but which require backbreaking labor to be reclaimed for agriculture. To be made arable, this brackish bogland must first be drained by a wide ditch, then made level and given time to dry, and then sweetened by lime and enriched by manure. After this, one may hope to produce a few barrels of potatoes or a few bushels of oats.

In the mid-eighteenth century, when James McGavock of County Antrim ditched the bogland and farmed the sullen slopes, potatoes and oats were the chief crops—with half the land planted in wheat or flax in alternate years. At that time the country was divided into small holdings, most of them from five to thirty acres, and the tenant paid a yearly rent of about five shillings per acre.[1] But lease agreements between the small farmers and their landlords were often in a state of flux, the rent increasing if the tenant improved the land to any considerable degree, and the meager security of the farmer from year to year was at best uncertain.[2]

Such was the status of young James McGavock, his brother Randal, and their widowed mother, living together at Carntown near the village

---

1 Arthur W. Hutton, ed. *Arthur Young's Tour in Ireland,* 2 Vols., (London: George Bell and Sons, 1892), I, 159.

2 J. C. Beckett, *A Short History of Ireland* (London: Hutchinson House, 1952), pp. 114-115.

of Glenarm in Tickmacrevan Parish, where the name McGavock is first recorded. They were members of a family of small farmers generally bearing an excellent character of good sense, honesty, and industry. Some time during the late seventeenth century their McGavock forebears had immigrated to the coastal areas of County Antrim with other Scottish settlers. Here they took up farmlands along the slopes overlooking the Bay of Glenarm and established homesteads on bracken-covered hills, from which they could look eastward across the Irish Sea and trace the coastline of Scotland on a clear summer's day.

The early McGavocks are presumed to have been Scottish Highlanders who first migrated to the richer lands of Galloway, in southwest Scotland, where county chronicles show the presence of the name McGuffock in the first decades of the seventeenth century.[3] There is good authority for our believing that McGuffock is the Scottish spelling and McGavock the Irish for the same family name.[4]

So the Scottish forefathers of James and Randal McGavock moved west across the twenty-five miles of sea channel that divides Scotland from Ireland. They followed the pattern of migration common to many of their countrymen from the time of James I of England, who sent colonies of Scottish farmers and English overlords in the first decades of the seventeenth century to the Ulster lands wrenched away from the Irish Celts. James I hoped that each fiery Scot would kill off two Irish Papists and subdue the country for the English Crown. Consequently with these Scots came Presbyterianism to a country loyal to Rome and determined, in spite of edict and bloodshed, to keep the Catholic faith.

In addition to the religious conflicts between their neighbors and themselves, the McGavocks of Antrim experienced the acute cultural differences that clearly marked the Gaelic-speaking Irish, the Lowland Scot settlers, and the English rulers. Three cultural traditions were thrown together to create an inharmonious climate of misunderstanding and distemper. Historically the Lowland Scot had seldom been on sympathetic terms with his Highland countryman, the Scottish Celt, for all the centuries they had lived side by side in Scotland. The same lack

---

[3] P. H. MacKerlie, *History of the Lands and their Owners in Galloway,* 5 Vols. (Edinburgh: W. Patterson, 1870-79), *passim.*

[4] For these notes on the Gaelic etymology of the name I am indebted to James Ross, School of Scottish Studies, Edinburgh: "McGavock is derived from the Scottish Gaelic and means literally *Son of David.* In its uncorrupted form it is MacDaibhidh. But the form which has come into common usage is from an early diminutive, *Dhabhog,* pronounced Davok. The initial *d* is mutated in the genitive case and is therefore rendered *g.* In fact, this mutation from *d* to *g* is very common in the Anglicization of Gaelic names. Thus the source of McGavock can be taken as MacDhabhog, where the *dh* is a voiced velar fricative becoming *g.*" Also see "MacGuffock" in G. F. Black, *The Surnames of Scotland* (New York: The New York Public Library, 1946).

of understanding was conspicuous in the Lowland Scot's relations with the Irish Celt, whose land he occupied at the bidding of an English king.

These religious and cultural differences were reported in the statistical account of Ardclinis Parish, near Glenarm, as late as the year 1832:

> By the census of 1831, the population of the Parish amounted to 1716, of which there are 6 Protestant, 12 Methodist, and 24 Presbyterian families, the remainder are Roman Catholics. Here is no established house of worship . . . the Protestants congregate in Drumnasole school house, the Presbyterians in Glenarm, the Methodists in Carnlough school house, and the Roman Catholics in Layd Chapel . . . The language of the inhabitants is a compound of English, Irish, and Gaelic; though few of them speak either in purity.[5]

Thus acute political, religious, and cultural differences were still sharply felt two hundred years after the bitter Irish rule of Oliver Cromwell.

The Irish Gael clung resolutely to his ingrained traditions, and so did the Scottish settlers in his midst—the transplanted Presbyterians who came to be called the Scotch-Irish. These inheritors of the ancient Angle speech, as distinguished from the Saxon dialect in the South of England, brought to Ireland an oral literature common to Lowland Scotland.[6] Their *braid Scots* diction spread to Northeast Donegal, Tyrone, Londonderry, Antrim, and eastern County Down—all the areas which received large numbers of colonizing Scots.[7]

The circumstances of the early McGavocks' removal from Galloway and the exact date of their arrival in County Antrim are not recorded, but there is no evidence to contradict thinking of them as typical Scottish farmers seeking a better livelihood on lands made available by the English occupation of Ireland. The tract of land which James and Randal McGavock inherited and farmed, called a *townland* in Ireland, and on which they lived with their mother in a simple but substantial stone farmhouse of two rooms with a thatched roof, lies about one mile south of Glenarm Bay.

This homestead at Carntown (also spelled Carnton) sits high above the shoreline and affords a splendid view of the bay and the sea beyond. Near the house still stand several farm buildings, also of stone, having thatched roofs. These structures probably date back to the occupancy of James McGavock in the eighteenth century. They were used as stable, byre, pig sty, and fowl house—an indication that the McGavocks were

---

[5] "Statistical Account of Ardclinis Parish, 1832," Microfilm A/15, Queens University Library, Belfast.

[6] For a more detailed treatment of Scottish cultural importations to Ireland, especially the Scottish ballads and folksongs, see the author's dissertation, "Traditional Scottish Ballads in the United States," Vanderbilt University, 1957.

[7] G. B. Adams, "An Introduction to the Study of Ulster Dialects," *Proceedings of the Royal Irish Academy,* LII (1948), 45-46.

better off than the poorer farmers who brought their animals into the house in winter.[8]

It is reckoned that the McGavock townland comprised about thirty acres of land and was fertile enough to provide a small family with ample subsistence in ordinary times. Certainly it was one of the respectable tenant farms in the district and the McGavocks might have been reasonably prosperous if rents remained stable and famines held off.

Close by there were a few other resources which the hand of nature provided these upland tenants near the village of Glenarm. In the river there were salmon and trout; grouse could be found in the hills; and there were usually rabbits and hares for the hunter. In addition, the younger children could help the crops by trudging to the beaches and collecting seaweed, which they could bring back to the sloping farm, dry, and use as fertilizer for the potato patches.

Among their neighbors along the coast were the Antrim fishermen, who cured their catches of salmon and herring in salt, sold them to the villagers, or shipped them to Belfast. Another source of revenue for the enterprising was the deposit of lime near Carnlough. This was dug out of the ground and shipped to Scotland, where it was bartered to the Scots for coal.

But minerals were scarce and manufactured articles must be imported all the way from Belfast. Except for the weaving of flax in the small cottages, between seasons of harvest and the next year's planting, there was no industry and little cash with which to meet the lean years of famine and plague. There simply was not enough land to sustain a large family and provide a reserve against hard times. The acreage allotments were generally so meager that the head of a house was known to divide a farm of six acres among his several sons, further reducing the portion of food for each mouth. "The least accident, such as the death of a cow, etc., reduces them to want, so that neither rent nor any common obligation can be paid. They are likewise obliged, in order to make their little patch come near to their support, to crop it every year with oats, till the land become almost a *caput mortuum* . . ."[9]

It was, in all, a life of hazard and general unrest, often attended by illness and contagion. It is no wonder that emigration from Ireland to America became a booming business between 1717 and 1775 and that British authority was constantly disturbed at the depopulation of the

---

[8] These descriptions of Carntown at the present time were furnished by George McGavock of Carnlough, County Antrim, and John R. Heller III, Kensington, Maryland. For other notes on the McGavocks of County Antrim I am indebted to the Reverend George Jackson of Glenarm.

[9] Hutton, *op. cit.*, I, 150.

Protestant areas in the Ulster counties. One writer has estimated that in 1718 "forty-two hundred of the Scotch-Irish left for America, and that after the famine of 1740 there were 12,000 who departed annually."[10] Finally the exodus was held temporarily in check by the occurrence of the American Revolution.

Young James McGavock, born in 1728, familiar with famine and hardship, grew to maturity at Carntown and learned the ways of farm life from his father.[11] He doubtless roamed the craggy hillsides as a youth, scaling the heights of Binnagee and Eagle Craig further up the coast. Perhaps he followed the rapids of Carnlough River down to the sea, and listened to the stories of the fishermen along the quays in Glenarm and Carnlough, and at some point began to think of travelling himself. He was a tall youth with long legs suited to quick movement and easy strides. He had good arms and broad shoulders with ample strength in them. In all, he had the fiber to help hew down a wilderness and put in order the frontiers of a new world.

As this James McGavock approached his twenty-first birthday, there was resounding talk about America circulating through the Glens of Antrim and in the villages of Ulster; everywhere one saw broadside notices that advertised sailings from Belfast and Londonderry to Philadelphia and Newcastle. The emigration fever had risen to a pitch during 1740 and 1741, when most of Ireland experienced a famine, and by 1750 James had seen many of the young men from his own parish leave for the Ulster ports of embarkation. From his own neighborhood went the Craigs, the Wilsons, the McGehees, and the Kirks—young men like himself who sold off their shares at home, or worked out their passages as indentured servants under a five-year bondage once they arrived in America.[12]

Another stimulant to emigration was the dangerous "land reform" which threatened to destroy the agricultural system of the small farmer. By 1750 landlords began to favor the raising of sheep, because the smuggling of wool to France was a flourishing business, and they started the practice of turning arable acres into grazing pastures, driv-

---

10 Henry P. Fairchild, *Immigration, A World Movement and Its American Significance* (New York: Macmillan Company, 1930), p. 41.

11 Because of the fairly regular practice in the McGavock family of naming the oldest son Hugh, in both America and Ireland, I conjecture that the father of James McGavock was Hugh. There is no information about the mother of James, except that she was a widow and remained in Ireland, presumably at Carntown, with her son Randal and his family after James came to America.

12 See Abbott E. Smith, *Colonists in Bondage* (Chapel Hill: University of North Carolina Press, 1947).

ing off the families who had reclaimed the slopes and tilled them for generations. Landlords also enclosed the common lands with stone dikes and hedgerows, a practice that deprived the small farmer of his common grazing privileges and provided increased acreage for the sheep belonging to the landlord.[13]

So James McGavock, the young man with a lean frame and solid jaw, with the strength of his convictions and a searching Presbyterian conscience, sometime after 1750 decided to sell out his holdings at Carntown to his brother Randal. With a determined countenance he explained his intentions to his mother, and, not looking back, he headed for the first America-bound ship leaving Londonderry or Belfast.

The exact year that he departed, the vessel which brought him across the Atlantic, and the cash that he had in his pocket are all unrecorded details. We know that he left the green, boggy shores of Ireland, the turmoil and conflicts of a stricken land, and the company of family and friends behind him—forever.

Family tradition has preserved several stories about James's arrival in Philadelphia and the hardships the youthful Irishman encountered during his first days in the New World. His great-grandson, Randal William McGavock, began a family chronicle in 1853 with this account:

> He landed at Philadelphia with four young Irishmen who were unable to pay their passage money and were about to be sold when he volunteered to part with all his means save one pound rather than see his companions *en voyage* subjected to the humiliating alternative of servitude. Reduced to a small pittance he resolved to make his way in the New World by the strength of his arms and accordingly went out into the country and proposed to do manual labor for an old Dutch farmer. The old man told him that his son was threshing wheat in the barn and if he would thresh as much as his son he would give him five shillings for the day. With a stout heart and determination to do or die, he accepted the proposition and for the first time in his life raised a flail for dear life. After working several hours he became tired and was willing to give it up but was too proud and held on until the young Dutchman proposed to stop. He replied that if he was tired he would blow him awhile, after which they worked more leisurely. He remained with the Dutchman until all of the grain was threshed and then left with a high recommendation and commenced ditching.[14]

In this ditching job James was temporarily at home; he had the advantage of having worked in bog and marsh at Carntown; he could turn sour land into sweet by draining away the muckish waters. He also knew how to save his wages and keep an open eye for opportunity. "At [ditching] he acquired enough money to purchase a wagon and

[13] Beckett, *op. cit.*, p. 117.

[14] Randal W. McGavock, "Genealogical Notes on the McGavock Family to the Year 1853." Microfilm of McGavock Papers, Manuscript Section, Tennessee State Library and Archives, Nashville. Hereinafter cited as McGavock Papers.

team, with which he hauled provisions for the army at Braddock's Depot," wrote his great-grandson.

Perhaps James realized for the first time in the summer of 1755, during the ill-fated expedition that General Edward Braddock made against the French at Fort Duquesne, that everywhere on this new continent there was land for the taking—unclaimed hills and mountain forests in the wilds of Pennsylvania, broad fertile valleys as far as the eye could see down the Wilderness Road in Virginia, and still more land along the rich river bottoms of Kentucky, Tennessee, and Ohio.

Moreover, what James McGavock saw of virgin timberlands in 1757 when he went west with Colonel Francis Nash to Ohio against the Shawnee Indians[15]—what his calculating eye surveyed in the dark backwoods when he led a company of volunteers into the disputed regions along the Ohio River—caused him to believe that he could hew his own empire out of the wilderness.

Still sturdy of frame and strong of muscle, now nearly thirty years old and for five years the target of wintry winds and burning summers, James McGavock on March 17, 1757, acquired by deed from Samuel McDowell and Mary, his wife, a tract of land in Augusta County, Virginia, for the sum of fifty pounds. He thus set his aims in the backcountry on the far side of the Blue Ridge Mountains and thereafter became a Virginia farmer, frontier tradesman, and public-spirited citizen.

In 1760 James McGavock courted and married Mary Cloyd, the daughter of his neighbor, David Cloyd of Rockbridge County, whose lineage was Scotch-Irish like his own and whose family had first come to Pennsylvania from Londonderry, North Ireland. Mary has been described as a sturdy woman of "clear intellect, untiring industry, and strong willpower; characteristics which doubtless greatly aided her husband in his business affairs wherein he was so successful."[16] A good manager and capable mother, Mary Cloyd McGavock bore ten children and brought them all to maturity amid the hardships of the Virginia frontier.

Randal William wrote of James's middle years: "He was a great land locator and his descendants now live upon the various tracts of fine lands in Virginia, Tennessee, and Kentucky that his foresight made

[15] William A. Crozier, *Virginia Colonial Militia, 1651-1776* (New York: The Genealogical Association, 1905), p. 52.

[16] Robert Gray, *The McGavock Family* (Richmond: W. E. Jones, 1903), p. 155. Although Randal William McGavock adopted *Mac* instead of *Mc* in signing his name after 1853, I have used the traditional American spelling of the name throughout.

certain would at no distant day be immensely valuable." Some of his property lay beside that owned by Thomas Jefferson at Natural Bridge; another tract he acquired on New River from one William Herbert; then he purchased Fort Chiswell, the frontier outpost, from John Easdale. Soon after, about 1772, he moved his family from Rockbridge to Fort Chiswell—up the Valley of Virginia far into the forest. This rough fort of block houses that became their home was surrounded by a log stockade and was situated at that strategic point in southwest Virginia where the Richmond Road met the Wilderness Road and crossed the waters of New River. Here James McGavock settled for good after nearly a quarter of a century in America, and here he brought up his children in a fertile valley at the gateway to the great American West.

Fort Chiswell was the last frontier outpost on the Wilderness Road before pack-horse and wagon train heading for Kentucky and Tennessee crossed Cumberland and New Found Gaps in the direction of the Old Southwest. It was the center from which expeditions were sent out, a trading post for white man and Indian, and it was for James McGavock a business venture which he had no cause to regret.

Nearby were the lead mines discovered in 1757 by Colonel John Chiswell, a partner of William Byrd III, for whom Fort Chiswell was named. These mines brought traffic and industry to the lower part of Fincastle County and provided bullets for the guns of the Virginia Militia. The fort also was to become the first seat of government for Montgomery County, for here the magistrates met on the first Tuesday of each month and sat in judgment on "such colonial misdemeanors as hog stealing, cattle rustling, raising false rumors, and counterfeiting."[17] Here was a microcosm of frontier bustle and commerce far removed from the plantation life of the Tidewater Coast and the polite society of cavalier and aristocrat.

James McGavock could hold his own in these surroundings, for he stood six feet tall and had "great vivacity of temper," wrote Randal William. He was a fearless citizen beholden to none. Under his ownership the old fort and stockade were enlarged—about twenty log buildings in all—to provide a more commodious stopping place and better supply depot for the stream of traffic moving west. In the arsenal lead was stored and bullets cached; in another building small articles of crude manufacture, greatly cherished on the frontier, were brought

[17] Two works by Lewis Preston Summers have been helpful: *History of Southwest Virginia, 1746-1786* (Richmond: J. L. Hill, 1903); and *Annals of Southwest Virginia, 1769-1800* (Abingdon, Virginia: Published by the Author, 1929).

from forge and smithy to be sold or swapped to hunters and trappers from the nearby hills.

Here James was granted a license to operate an ordinary, at which he agreed to provide "good, wholesome and cleanly lodging and diet for travellers and stableage, fodder and provender or pasturage, as the season shall require, for their horses . . ." He also agreed, under the same license, that he would not "suffer or permit any unlawful gambling in his house, nor on the Sabbath Day suffer any person to tipple or drink any more than is necessary."[18]

At the same time that James McGavock was operating Fort Chiswell and buying adjacent lands for his five sons, he began to turn to public affairs. He was concerned with the promotion of law and order in a community where men were rough-hewn and quick to bargain with bullets. James accepted appointments as a Justice of the Peace in each of four counties—Botetourt, Fincastle, Montgomery, and Wythe—as each splintered off from a larger territory and formed its own government. On January 20, 1775, he was one of fifteen freeholders who signed the historic Fincastle Resolutions, in which he and fellow colonists "expressed in writing a determination to resist by force of arms the aggression of the British Government."[19] Within a year their dissatisfaction with British rule caused them to bear arms and stand up to their resolves.

In the course of the Revolution the Virginia lead mines were vital to the colonial insurgents, and Fort Chiswell became for six years a supply depot for the Revolutionary Army. Forthwith James McGavock was commissioned a Militia Captain and served as a commissary and recruiting officer; his oldest son, Hugh, served as quartermaster of the Western Battalion and as a captain under Colonel Joseph Crockett in his expedition against the Shawnee Indians at the Falls of the Ohio. Another son, James, Jr., also bore arms.[20]

Always at Fort Chiswell there was the threat that the Tories operating in the Southwest would capture the lead mines for the crown and wreck the supply of precious metal to General Washington's hard-pressed army. As a member of the Safety Committee for Fincastle County in 1775 and 1776, James McGavock helped direct the volunteer defenders of the mines—against the Tory plotters who openly vowed to get the "scalps of James McGavock and William Preston."[21]

---

[18] Jouet McGavock Boyd Papers, Wythe County, Virginia.
[19] *Ibid.*
[20] *Ibid.*
[21] *Ibid.*

The first courts of Fincastle County had been conducted in a log structure not far from the mining operation, a few miles from Fort Chiswell. In 1778, the year after Montgomery County was formed from a corner of Fincastle, James McGavock, Gentleman, was instrumental in establishing the first courthouse of Montgomery County—for he donated to the public interest twenty acres of land and "the use of the spring" immediately adjacent to his Fort Chiswell holdings. It has been suggested that the land and "use of the spring" were a somewhat calculated gesture inasmuch as the courthouse was located practically in the shadow of the tavern (part of the old fort) where James did a flourishing business in provisions and whiskey.[22] Moreover, it is a matter of record that James helped establish soon after the first county jail.

Once the Revolution was over, McGavock gave time and money to the founding of two other institutions—a church and a school. He had been able to give all of his ten children "a good English education" because he had acquired wealth enough to put them under the instruction of a tutor. As early as 1774 he had brought Alexander Balmaine, an Episcopal minister and teacher, into his house to instruct the younger children. Afterwards his son Randal was sent to Carlisle, Pennsylvania, for a "collegiate education." But soon there were grandsons and granddaughters coming along every year, almost as fast as they could be counted, and the country was growing as fast as the McGavocks. So James helped frame the following instrument in the cause of local education:

> We whose names are subscribed here unto do undertake & promise that if an Act of the General Assembly shall be procured at the next session establishing an Academy at Wythe Courthouse, and incorporating Trustees thereof, we will severally pay to the said Trustees for the use of the said Academy the sums of money in Virginia currency prefixt to our respective names. July 1792. James McGavock. £10-0-0.[23]

As teacher for the fall session the Reverend Thomas E. Burch, a classically-educated Episcopal minister, was brought to Wythe County and established in the "Anchor and Hope" Academy, located between Fort Chiswell and Max Meadows. Also during that same year, 1792, the Anchor and Hope Presbyterian Church was founded, with a single structure serving as academy and meeting house. James subscribed to this religious institution without ever finding time to join as a member.[24]

So by the end of the century old James McGavock had helped bring the ornaments of civilization—courthouse, jail, church, and schoolhouse

---

[22] Mary B. McGavock, Max Meadows, Virginia, in a letter to the author, May 22, 1958.
[23] Jouet McGavock Boyd Papers.
[24] *Ibid.*

—to the wilderness reaches of southwest Virginia, where trail and river intersected, and mountains divided east from west, and stories trickled back to fort and cabin of even richer lands beyond.

There was no use stopping now, he said, although he knew that he himself could go no farther into the hickory forests, nor defend with his own sinew the unspoken-for meadows of Kentucky bluegrass, nor drive out the Cherokees from the Tennessee river bottoms. His own days with ax, musket, shovel, and pick must end in Wythe County, for the old hands were weakening and the shoulders growing bent. Aye, he said, with traces of Lowland Scots still in his speech, this is no time to stop—when a man has five braw lads to keep the wheels in motion and stake out his claims.

So he sent David and Randal over the mountains to the Cumberland Settlement at Nashborough, where James Robertson had built a fort in 1780. There the boys could find plenty of work and a lot of land that they could speak for and defend in the name of James McGavock.

CHAPTER II

Jacob Follows the Trail to Tennessee

Hugh, the eldest son of James and Mary Cloyd McGavock, was born in Rockbridge County in 1761, the year after his parents' marriage; he was eleven when James and Mary moved south to Fort Chiswell.[1] The boy was his father's right hand and his mother's guardian, for upon the eldest son devolved duties of family and hearthside. As a growing lad he learned to dig out stumps for new ground and to plow a straight furrow when his father rode off to business; he was taught to hoe, ditch, and harvest; he also learned to drive a good bargain when it came to making a trade, whether the trade meant land or merchandise. He knew from the time that he could remember that women had to be protected, for his mother's mother and his uncle John Cloyd were killed by the Indians in 1764.[2] Growing up with stories of hardship and bloodshed, he could never forget the need for wariness and vigilance.

In 1779 Hugh was serving with Colonel Joseph Crockett's regiment of the Virginia State Line. During 1780 he was promoted to quartermaster of the regiment and he helped guard the Convention Prisoners at the barracks in Albermarle County, Virginia, and at Frederickstown, Maryland. From there, in 1781, Crockett's troops joined those commanded by George Rogers Clark, and Hugh McGavock went with them to Pittsburgh in the expedition against the Shawnee Indians.[3]

Like his father, Hugh was tall and fleet, and he learned about the back country as a quartermaster for the armies of the Revolution. After the war, he returned to Fort Chiswell and settled on the Upper Marks Meadow tract of land that his father had purchased—near the present village of Max Meadows—and here he brought his wife, Nancy Kent. To them were born twelve children in the log house that Hugh built between the sloping hills west of Fort Chiswell.[4] Primarily a farmer, he was also Deputy Sheriff of Montgomery County and Collector of

[1] Gray, *op. cit.*, pp. 9, 11-12.
[2] *Ibid.*, p. 154.
[3] Jouet McGavock Boyd Papers.
[4] Gray, *op. cit.*, pp. 11-12.

Revenue for Wythe County, when the latter was formed in 1790. Some years later, on February 7, 1815, when James Monroe was Acting Secretary of State, Hugh was appointed by President James Madison to the office of Principal Assessor and Collector of the First District of Virginia.[5]

Among the papers left by this Hugh McGavock of Max Meadows is a diary in which he systematically recorded the natural wonders of his age:

> On this morning a most remarkable phenomenon was witnessed in the falling of the stars. The scene was awfully sublime. They descended in such profusion as to resemble a heavy fall of snow and continued until the darkness which rendered them visible was dispelled by the break of day, producing great alarm in the minds of all who beheld it.[6]

And later, in June, 1830, he wrote:

> Snow deep enough to track a deer. The corn has rotted in the ground and they have to list off a field and plant it again. I think we are threatened with famine. May our heavenly father forbid, although our rebellion deserves it.[7]

Hugh was a God-fearing, righteous man. He instructed his children in the principles of a Christian life and taught them to fear the Almighty Lord of the Old Testament. He did not go west, but his beliefs were carried there by his sons.

Now too weak for prolonged labor, nagged by diabetes and the infirmities of old age, James McGavock turned over to young James, his third son, the operation of Fort Chiswell, and to Joseph he gave the use of the Lower Marks Meadow tract. With more land than he could have walked over during the twelve remaining years of his life, old James retired to the "Mansion House" at Max Meadows, a comfortable, two-story log structure near his son Hugh and a dozen grandchildren.[8] Here he was relieved of the heavy duties at Fort Chiswell, but he was close enough to keep his eye on its affairs and give his sons guidance. Here also he could wait for news from David and Randal, the sons out in Tennessee; they had talent for choosing good land and the kind of nerve to forge order in the wilderness.

---

[5] See the seven letters and "Circulars" to Hugh McGavock, Collector of Revenue, Wythe County, Virginia, from James McDowell, Inspector, Sixth Survey District, written during 1799-1800. McGavock Papers.

[6] Quoted in a letter from Jacob McGavock, Wytheville, Virginia, to the author, July 12, 1958.

[7] *Ibid.*

[8] Jouet McGavock Boyd Papers.

In the family chronicle Randal William wrote these notes on his great-uncle David, second son of old James:

> David . . . had extraordinary mathematical talent and acted a long time as a surveyor in Virginia. He came to Nashville in 1786 and gave seven negroes to James Freeland for the tract of land below Nashville upon which stood Freeland's Fort. He raised corn on this tract and returned every winter to Virginia until the fall of 1796 when Tennessee was made a state and he considered it safe to move his family. In 1806 he was elected by the Legislature Register, which office he retained until his death. He also acted as Commissioner to settle conflicting land claims. When he first came to this country he exposed himself so much in hunting the wild beasts of the wilderness that he brought on rheumatism which rendered him almost helpless in his later days.[9]

In his own name and in his father's, this David brought into family possession "2,240 acres of the best land he could find in Davidson and Williamson Counties," and he remained in the position of Register of the Land Office in Tennessee until 1838.[10] When Old James died in 1812, he willed part of this Tennessee land to this son David, the surveyor of Nashville, who had pushed the family fortunes further west.[11]

The old man bequeathed to his fourth son, Randal, who followed David to Nashville in 1796, "two tracts of land adjoining each other on Big Harpath [*sic*], a branch of Cumberland River containing each six hundred and forty acres, a tract of three hundred and twenty acres purchased of William Gellespie, lying in Sumner County on Houns lick creek, and my negro boy Jacob."[12]

This Randal, named for old James's brother in County Antrim, was the first Randal McGavock in Tennessee. His great-nephew, another Randal, wrote about him:

> Randal was educated in Carlisle, Pennsylvania, and came to Tennessee in 1796 . . . appointed clerk of the Old Supreme Court of Mero District, which he held until . . . 1810 . . . appointed clerk of the Circuit Court of Davidson County . . . appointed Clerk of the Supreme Court of Errors and Appeals. He was also elected Mayor of Nashville [1824-25] and alderman on several occasions. He afterwards moved to Williamson County where he farmed until the day of his death.[13]

Prepared by a "collegiate education" for positions in court and legal chamber, this Randal McGavock married into a distinguished Kentucky

---

[9] Randal W. McGavock, "Genealogical Notes on the McGavock Family to the Year 1853." McGavock Papers.

[10] Gray, *op. cit.*, p. 12.

[11] "Will of James McGavock," in Jouet McGavock Boyd Papers.

[12] *Ibid.* At the time of his death James McGavock was the subject of a long elegy in verse written by the Reverend Thomas E. Burch, the Episcopal minister who taught at Anchor and Hope Academy. A handwritten copy from the text printed in an unidentified newspaper is in the Jouet McGavock Boyd Papers.

[13] Randal W. McGavock, *loc. cit.*

family—for his wife was Sarah Dougherty Rodgers, sister of Mrs. Felix Grundy. Their daughter, Elizabeth, was married in 1840 to General William G. Harding, the Middle Tennessee agriculturist and builder of the Belle Meade Mansion near Nashville. Randal's son John McGavock married Caroline Winder and lived at "Carnton," the Williamson County estate that perpetuates in Tennessee the name of the McGavock homestead in Ireland.[14]

But Middle Tennessee was hardly a district of fine brick homes or porticoed Georgian mansions when David and Randal arrived in the late eighteenth century. Most of these were to be built by the next generation—after the country was tamed by bullet and ax and brought under cultivation by plowpoint and harrow. Even their father James, for all his thousands of acres in Virginia, Kentucky, and Tennessee, lived and died in a log house.[15] Even though he was one of the wealthiest landowners in the Southwest and willed fourteen slaves to his wife and children, Old James lived in simple pioneer frugality, a frontiersman till his death, in 1812, at the log "Mansion House" in the little settlement of Max Meadows.

From Tennessee both David and Randal faithfully reported to James the life they encountered in the West and the condition of the lands they had acquired in his name. Their letters, several of them preserved, are filled with notes on the raising of crops, the exploitation of the salt licks around Nashville, and the payment of taxes. There is also mention of lawsuits over disputed holdings and the sons' plans for further expansions.

A typical letter is the one David wrote to his father on May 3, 1801:

> The prospects of our obtaining in this Country the necessary comforts of life, upon moderate terms, by an exchange of the products of labor, such as Cotton, Hemp, Tobacco, flour, etc. give rise to much conversation & joy among us. Our traders are beginning to think of establishing Houses at Natchez & Orleans for the reception of produce from this country.[16]

Then David discussed his own affairs:

> From my last years experiment at the cotton business, I find that, to the making of money very fast, nothing is lacking but an additional number of hands.[17]

That was the general cry. Send us more people, they said. We need hands to clear the fields and plant the crops and help with the harvest. *Send us more hands.*

---

[14] Gray, *op. cit.*, pp. 15, 33, 34.
[15] Jouet McGavock Boyd Papers.
[16] *Ibid.*
[17] *Ibid.*

Apparently the plea was heard in the East, for when David wrote his father on April 17, 1807, he reported: "The Country is filled with new emigrants. They have been arriving every day since October last." Overland they came from Kingsport and Knoxville; by raft they came down the Tennessee River, or found the headwaters of the Cumberland and drifted down to Nashville; they streamed by Fort Chiswell, promising to deliver news from one McGavock to another McGavock.

Old James saw, heard, and remembered. Only the incurable infirmities of old age kept in check his insatiable yearning for more land: deep dirt and tall trees that reached to the sky; the sounds of progress that went with ax, musket, surveyor's chain, and powder-horn; the displays of order that accompanied the sound of the judge's gavel and the charging of a jury and the turning of a key in a jailhouse lock. All these he willed to his sons, along with his land and his fourteen slaves, when he passed on at the age of 84. Old "Dada," as the children called him, had made his mark.

James McGavock of Ireland and Virginia had seventy-two grandchildren, many of whom he never saw. In addition to the McGavock lines, there were the children of the two daughters who married Gordon and David Cloyd; and another daughter married Joseph Kent.[18] The eldest grandsons usually remained at home, and the younger boys were sent west to work with uncles or older cousins or migrating neighbors. Virginia was hardly big enough to hold them all; nor could she have done so if she wished, for the young men had travelling in their heads and the cry was "Come West."

Among these grandchildren was Jacob, the third son of Hugh, who was born at Max Meadows in 1790. According to his son, young Jacob also received "an English education," probably at Anchor and Hope Academy under the Reverend Thomas E. Burch. Then he went to Tennessee at seventeen, where his two uncles, David and Randal, needed a scribe in their office.[19] There were opportunities in abundance in Nashville, and Randal McGavock wrote to his brother Hugh describing them on April 16, 1807.

You have mentioned the intention of your Son James to visit this Country for the purpose of getting into some business that may prove profitable to him. His wish is certainly laudable, and if he is of an enterprising turn, there are but few

---

[18] Gray, *op. cit., passim.* By 1903, James McGavock's descendants in America numbered 1,583—living and dead.

[19] Randal W. McGavock, *loc. cit.*

places, in which such young men could settle, superior to this Country. If James is, or would soon make, an active, accurate Surveyor, I think he might be well employed in this Country, & should he determine on coming, nothing in my power shall be wanting to promote his welfare & interest. Take the mass of the people in the western Country, and they are much more keen and enterprising than in the Eastern.

If you will send Jacob here I think he will improve faster than there where good teachers are so seldom procured. There is at this time in Nashville, a School kept by a man of talents, and will, no doubt, be continued until our College gets into operation. A large elegant building is now going on, & which is to be compleated in less than two years. This College is well endowed & will certainly flourish.[20]

So James and Jacob, younger sons of Hugh, both moved to Tennessee in 1807 and received the protection and counsel of their uncles in the new country.

Apparently Jacob cared more for his work in the Register's Office than for the life of the college student, or else he was kept too busy to attend to studies. For after his apprenticeship, he took the position of clerk in the Superior Court of the Mero District and remained with the court until 1812.[21]

A few of the letters from Jacob to his father in Virginia have survived, and they reveal a young man with good descriptive powers, interested in the life and the people around him, eager to report what he saw during a busy life away from home. The example which follows is typical:[22]

November 10th 1812.

Dear Father

Since I wrote to you last I have visited the greater part of Kentucky. I spent about three weeks in traveling through different parts of that State. My business principally led me to Bairdstown and Springfield with Miss Rogers, sister to Aunt Sally, and a daughter of Mr. Grundys, who were on a visit to some of there relations. I am much pleased with some parts of Kentucky about Lexington and Danville is as handsome a Country as I ever saw, the land lies well and is very rich. Lexington is really a beautiful town and a place of more business than I ever saw, it surpasses my idea of its importance a great many ways, it must be as great an inland town as any in the union. While I was at Lexington I went to see old Unkle Joseph Crockett, and spent two days and nights with him, he expressed great pleasure on finding who I was, being the first of the new race he had ever seen. I was very much pleased with the old gentleman and his family, during my stay I was treated with the greatest attention and kindness, there are but two of his family living with him, Patsey and Eliza, both of them fine agreeable girls, well accomplished and tolerable handsome. Two of his sons are

---

20 Letter owned by Jacob McGavock, Wytheville, Virginia.
21 Randal W. McGavock, *loc. cit.*
22 Letter owned by Mrs. Henry Dickinson, Nashville.

married, Robert and John. Robert is Marshall of that State, his son Joseph is single, and in the practice of physic. Robert and John were both in the Northern army as volunteers, therefore I did not see them. In all life I never heard or read of, in any country, such a spirit of patriotism prevailing, as there is at this time in Kentucky. It appears as if the whole State was dreaned of its male population, all ages and conditions appear to be seized with the same zeal, and it is not confined to the males alone, for the females take a very active part, in providing clothing, to shield the poor soldiers from the piercing blasts of the North who have turned out in defence of their Country, and to protect the defenceless women and children from the savage tomahawk and scalping knife, almost every house I visited I found the females employed in making garments of one description or other for the soldiers, elegant and well accomplished young ladies, (who in some Countries would have spurned at the like,) with their delicate fingers employed in sewing or knitting for to clothe the soldiers who are fighting in the most noble cause. O how I was delighted to see it.

It is rumored in town that the Governor has received orders from the Secretary at war to order out 1,500 of the militia of this State to New Orleans and Florada, the particulars of which I have not yet heard, but I think from every appearance we shall have orders to march or desend the river in a short time. We have not had any recent account of the movements of the Northwestern army, Genls Harrison and Winchester were at fort Defiance and Genl Hopkins and his army were still at fort Harrison, and Hopkins continually in a state of intoxication, so much so that he was entirely incapable of commanding.

The weather has been remarkably cloudy and wet for some time, slight shocks of the earthquake continue to be felt at times. Unkle Randal and Aunt went last Sunday to Brother James's to spend some days. Cousin James has not yet recovered from the hurt he received by the horse running off with the gig sometime since, which I presume you have heard of before this time. Polly has recovered. Write to me, for I am anxious to hear from you all. We are all well.

Remember me to Mother and the family also Grand Mother and all relations.

I am your affectionate Son

Jacob McGavock

Addressed to:

Mr. Hugh McGavock
near Wythe Ct. House
Virginia

By Mail [From Nashville—postage .20]

Another letter[23] from Jacob to Hugh was written when Robert McGavock, Jacob's younger brother, came to Nashville to attend Cumberland College:

Monday night. June 14th. 1813

Dear Father

Brother Robert arrived here yesterday about eleven oclock. He stood his journey very well, and nothing happened [to] him on his journey. He intends spend-

[23] Owned by Jacob McGavock, Wytheville, Virginia.

ing this week in visiting his relations. we were at Unkle Davids last evening, and he is at this time at cousin James McGavocks. I will go with him some time this week to see brother James. And it is probably [that during] the ensuing week, he may be able to make at [*sic*] start to the College. he will stand in need of some things in order to fix him up in the College; from what I have learnt from Robert he appears not to wish to take a regular course. And as I mentioned in my last letter to you, no young man is admitted to go, unless he intends taking a regular education. I have known several young men, who came from a distance, with the intention of studdying the sciences and because they would not learn the lattin were not admitted. In consequence of which, a board of the Trustees convened a few weeks since to devise some mode by which such as did not wish to learn the dead languages might be admitted. what the result of their deliberations have been I do not know but I think such an arrangement has or will take place. I will go with him when he stats [*sic*] to the College and If no such regulation has or is likely to take place I think it will be best for him to take a regular course, when that takes place I will write you the result. he appears willing to learn the lattin. We have not much knews here excepting that of our fighting amongst ourselves. Nashville is at this time in considerable commotion, in consequence of an affair of honor that took place this morning between two of its citizens, Mr. Carroll and Mr. Benton (both young men) the result of which was Carroll had his left thumb shot off, and Mr. Benton his antagonists ball went through his body. I heard from him a few hours ago, he was then out of his head, and but little hopes entertained of his recovery, poor young man I feel very sorry for him, and more for his poor old Mother who I am told depended on him entirely for her support. It seems there is no law that our legislature can pass is severe enough to put a stop to the horrid practice of dueling. And our injured Country cannot afford its young men enemies enough to show their valor in a more noble cause, but they must lavish their spleen upon one another. We are all well. Cousin Polly had a fine daughter a week or so ago.

Remember me to Mother and the family also Grand Mother, & Grand Mother Kent when you see her.

I remain your most affectionate son

Jacob McGavock

N.B. In hast excuse all mistakes.

That same year, 1813, Jacob went as a volunteer to the Creek War with Andrew Jackson, having enlisted with Captain David Deadrick's Company.[24] He was twenty-three at the time—a young man with steel grey eyes, reddish hair, and the ruddy complexion of his Scotch-Irish forebears.[25] The activity which he observed in Kentucky and which impressed him as he passed through the country districts, caused him to decide to take arms against the Indians aroused by the British to the south. At Nashville he left behind a sweetheart aged fifteen—Louisa Caroline Grundy, "a daughter of Mr. Grundys," whom he mentioned in

---

[24] Randal W. McGavock, *loc. cit.*

[25] Portraits of Jacob McGavock are owned by Margaret Lindsley Warden and Mrs. Henry Dickinson, both of Nashville.

his letter to his father. She was a comely girl with a serious face and thoughtful eyes.[26]

When Jackson's men fought the Creeks at Enotochopco on January 24, 1814, Jacob McGavock was wounded in battle and "conveyed in a litter to Huntsville, Alabama, where he remained for some time," according to the account written by his son.[27] Several weeks later he was moved to Nashville, where he slowly regained his strength during the following months and eventually resumed his pen in the office of the Superior Court.

At Nashville Jacob learned the news of Jackson's victory over the British at New Orleans and helped the jubilant citizens of Old Hickory's home district celebrate the end of the war. His admiration for Jackson as a military leader and his staunch respect for him as a friend continued for thirty years after. As a pallbearer and one of Jackson's former comrades-in-arms, Jacob helped bury the Old Warrior beneath the garden trees at the Hermitage.[28]

Another letter from Jacob to his Uncle Joseph McGavock at Max Meadows shows the young man as a town booster proud of the growing city of Nashville. On January 7, 1816, he reported that there were "fifty dry good stores, all in full operation, in addition to several grocery stores and other smaller shops." Real estate values had risen; property that during the previous year had brought $450 to $500 was selling for $800; cotton was bringing $21 and $22 a hundred; tobacco was rising to $5 a hundred. Moreover, the winter was mild and there was grain in abundance.

As for the social activities of Nashville, Jacob spoke of the recent session of the Presbyterian Church of Virginia, which had met in the city; he commented on the number of pretty Virginia girls who had attended the meeting. "They had on their best bib and tucker," he said, "but I escaped."[29] This is the kind of sly comment that either Jacob or his son Randal was capable of making, for both of them had appreciative eyes for pretty girls.

In 1816 Jacob made another professional advancement when he was appointed Clerk of the Circuit Court of Davidson County by Judge Searcy.[30] Here he often saw Felix Grundy, the meteoric, red-haired Kentuckian who had sat as a judge on the Supreme Court of Errors and

---

[26] A portrait of Louisa Grundy McGavock is owned by Mrs. Spence McGavock, Nashville.

[27] Randal W. McGavock, *loc. cit.*

[28] Unidentified newspaper clipping in the papers of Louise Grundy Lindsley.

[29] A copy of this letter was furnished by Mary B. McGavock, Max Meadows, Virginia.

[30] Randal W. McGavock, *loc. cit.*

Courtesy
Library of Congress

James Knox Polk
(1795-1849)

Courtesy Library of Congress

Sarah Childress Polk
(1803-1891)

Courtesy Whitefoord R. Cole, Jr.

Felix Grundy
(1777-1840)

Courtesy Whitefoord R. Cole, Jr.

Ann Rodgers Grundy
(1779-1847)

Courtesy Mary B. McGavock

James McGavock
(1728-1812)

Courtesy Mary B. McGavock

Mary Cloyd McGavock
(1741-1827)

Courtesy Margaret Lindsley Warden

Jacob McGavock
(1790-1878)

Courtesy Mrs. Spence McGavock

Louisa Grundy McGavock
(1798-1878)

Appeals, had been elected Congressman from Tennessee in 1811 and again in 1813, and who was known as "indefatigable Felix" to both his political friends and his political opponents. Jacob's Aunt Sally, the wife of his Uncle Randal, was Mrs. Felix Grundy's sister. So by marriage the Grundy and the McGavock families were already "related," in one sense of the word. Then Jacob met them often at the Presbyterian Church, where Mrs. Felix Grundy—not without opposition—started teaching the first Sunday School in Nashville. The two families, long associated, were united when Jacob McGavock put his courage to the test, walked up the Grundy steps, and asked Judge Grundy for Louisa's hand in marriage.

The news went back to Virginia, in May of 1819, that Hugh's boy Jacob had married well.

CHAPTER III

A Red-Haired Scion Is Born on Cherry Street

When Louisa Grundy was married to Jacob McGavock in 1819, her father had already achieved a notable reputation in Kentucky and Tennessee as one of the most successful criminal lawyers in the West. "If Grundy can't save you, nobody can," was one of the slogans.[1] His powerful, stocky figure and square-cut jaw were familiar in the western courts, and his political oratory had carried him successfully from one public office to another.[2]

In Kentucky Felix Grundy had been elected to the State Legislature in 1800; he had been appointed a judge of the Court of Appeals in 1806; then he was commissioned Chief Justice of Kentucky in 1807 by Governor Christopher Greenup.[3] When he left the bench and moved to Nashville in 1808 to resume the practice of law, he brought his family with him and started a second, even more brilliant, career. For example, out of a total of 106 cases of capital indictment which he represented during his practice in the courts, Felix Grundy lost only one case.[4]

His rising popularity in Tennessee decided him to stand for Congress in 1810, only two years after he settled in the state, and he was elected Representative for two successive terms as a "War" Democrat during the second conflict with Great Britain.[5] At that time the opponents of the war cried loudly that James Madison and Felix Grundy were leagued with the Devil as warmongers leading the country to ruin. Grundy's supporters retorted just as loudly that for once the Devil was in good company.[6]

Mrs. Felix Grundy took an active interest in Nashville's social and religious life. The mother of twelve children, she was an indefatigable

---

[1] Orval W. Baylor, "The Career of Felix Grundy, 1777-1840," *The Filson Club History Quarterly,* XVI (1942), 98.

[2] Portraits of Grundy are owned by General Jacob McGavock Dickinson, Jr., Mrs. Henry Dickinson, Whitefoord R. Cole, Jr., and the Tennessee Historical Society.

[3] Joseph Howard Parks, *Felix Grundy: Champion of Democracy* (Baton Rouge: Louisiana State University Press, 1940), p. 31.

[4] Baylor, *loc. cit.,* 98.

[5] Parks, *op. cit.,* p. 34.

[6] *Ibid.,* p. 42.

in church affairs as her husband was in state and national politics.[7] In 1820 she resolved to start the first Sunday School in Nashville, against which there was immediate opposition from her own church, the Presbyterian, and the other religious sects in the city. At a time when Nashville had no public schools, Mrs. Grundy reasoned that the poor children must first learn to read the Bible for themselves before they could understand it. So she began her Sabbath School in a small, ramshackle house set in the middle of a thicket between Spring (Church) and Broad Streets. She and three fellow teachers, Mrs. Mittie Moore, Nathan Ewing, and Samuel P. Ament, taught spelling and reading on Sunday mornings before the regular services were conducted in the Nashville churches. A few years later, after her determination finally won the support of several Nashville congregations, Mrs. Grundy was honored as the Mother of Nashville's Sunday Schools.[8]

In 1820, the year that Felicia, the Grundys' twelfth child, was born, Louisa McGavock gave birth to the Grundys' first grandchild, a little girl named Ann Eliza. Both girls were reared in a city increasing by leaps and bounds, and both had the advantage of being daughters of first citizens. The Grundys lived at "Grundy Hill," one of the finest brick houses in the city, situated between present Church and Union Streets in the block bordered by Seventh and Eighth Avenues. (This was the house which James K. Polk purchased in 1849 when he returned to Nashville to spend the last few months of his life with his fellow Tennesseans; it remained the home of his widow until her death in 1891.)

Jacob and Louisa McGavock lived three blocks away at 16 Cherry Street in a pleasant town house described later by a granddaughter, Louise Grundy Lindsley:

> The house was a large, two-story brick with an attic almost a full story. It was built as many houses of that period were—opening on the street, the wide stone steps reaching to the pavement. The windows were protected by green shutters or blinds. You entered the double front door into a wide hall which extended the length of the two spacious parlors and entered into a cross hall. It was not a double house, for as you entered on the right hand there were the parlors, on the left the broad stairway.
>
> The sitting room was large with two windows on the north side overlooking the garden, which contained trees and flowering shrubs. I remember especially the altheas, crepe myrtle, and lilacs. The grape arbor extended over a brick pavement with a border of flowers on each side. The two south windows of this room opened upon the porch. This sitting room was always attractive—

[7] "Grundy Family," MS. Notes, Tennessee State Library.
[8] Margaret Lindsley Warden, "Mrs. Grundy Approved," *Nashville Tennessean Magazine*, June 17, 1951, pp. 8-10.

cool and inviting in summer and in winter welcomed you with its bright fire. It was my grandmother's sitting room and she was the center of all activity, social and domestic.

Leaving this room you entered the dining room, which was large and airy, two of its windows overlooking the garden. Under the table was a drugget of three-ply carpet or of Brussels carpet. There was a large sideboard with silver and cut glass and Bohemian decanters. There were two serving tables. This dining room furniture was mahogany. There was no drapery at these windows, but the Venetian blinds were used. Adjoining this room were the pantry, store room, and serving room. General and Mrs. Jackson were guests in this dining room on many a Saturday, he to attend court, and she to visit and shop with the ladies.

Like many of the homes at that period the kitchen was in the basement. There was a large staircase and a dumb waiter leading into the serving room of the dining room. This was large and airy and a full story, as the ground sloped back. There was the coffee grinder screwed to the wall or table into which were dropped whole beans of coffee. This kitchen filled the pantry with preserves, pickle, catsup, sauce, jellies, blackberry wine and cordial, brandy peaches and brandy cherries, as at that period all these things were made in the home. The head cook, Aunt Charlotte, had her assistant, frequently a man cook, and several scullions. She was never happier than when she was preparing a big dinner for her distinguished guests, as she always spoke of them.

Adjoining the kitchen was an L which contained a sewing room—all work done by hand, there being no machines—laundry, and quarters for the house servants. There was a broad, brick pavement in front of the kitchen and L. This was under a covered way and in summer was a delightful place for preparing vegetables.

The carriage house was in the back opening off the alley. Above there were rooms for the men servants. There was a brick wall on each alley side.

The garden on this side contained two large apple trees, grass, and many flowering shrubs. This was a large establishment and required a retinue of servants. The system was well mapped. The mistress had her assistant housekeeper who superintended the servants, men and women, in the house. The head laundry-woman had her assistants, the head sewing woman hers; there was a head nurse who was as competent as many professional nurses today. There was a man nurse for the men. Girls nursing men made their advent with the trained nurse. These servants were experts, being trained by the older ones to take their places in the house. After they were free, many remained with the family—as many as could be supported there. Mammy Dicie, the head nurse, became a professional nurse and made a good living, but returned when the family needed her.

Cherry Street from Cedar Street to Broad was one of the fashionable residence streets. There were many fine homes with their small, beautiful gardens.

When the folding doors between the parlors were folded back the two rooms became a long, imposing drawing room. A mirror over each mantel and a pier mirror between the two front and two back windows increased the apparent size of these rooms.

Lace curtains and crimson brocatelle draped the windows. There was an eight-inch gilded cornice which held these in position. The furnishings of these rooms were rosewood and mahogany. The floors were covered with flowered velvet Brussels carpet.

In the parlor were musical instruments and rare books on the tables. They were a gay family, fond of singing and dancing. Jacob McGavock was an expert dancer and so was Andrew Jackson.

On the second floor there were many bedrooms furnished with fourposter beds, half-canopy beds, and single French beds. Each room had its dresser, wash-stand, and wardrobe, some with mirrored doors, as there were few closets in rooms at this period. There were two rooms in the attic completely furnished for the boys and the overflow company.

In summer mosquito bars were hung over each bed. Remember that there were no screens at the windows and doors to keep out mosquitoes and bugs which followed light into the rooms. There was a feeling of security when you were under the bars and well tucked in and heard a bat or a large bug hit the ceiling. You fell asleep to the hum of the mosquitoes knowing that they could not harm you.

My grandmother had her special little maid who was really a privileged character. She ran her errands, always knew where her palmleaf fan was, and found her glasses, and announced visitors to her. She had her special seat in the sitting room with her work basket and primer, for she had to prepare her daily lessons.

Many distinguished visitors to the city were entertained at the McGavock home. The young people from the country around, found their way to this house and there danced, sang, and discussed the current events.[9]

After the birth of Ann in 1820, a second daughter was born to the Jacob McGavocks the next year. Named Margaret Jane, she lived only eighteen months. In 1823 their first son was born and was proudly named for his two grandfathers—Felix Hugh. This child died at the age of fourteen months. The following year another son was born; he also was named for his two grandfathers—Hugh Felix—but he lived barely nine months. So within a span of three years Jacob McGavock buried three infants, including his first two sons.[10]

It is no wonder that he and Louisa anticipated the arrival of their next child at the end of summer. Little Ann would be six years old; she needed a younger child for company in the big house. Besides, Jacob longed for a male heir to carry on his name, and the Grundys looked forward to a male grandchild. Louisa Grundy McGavock spent the summer of 1826 hopefully.

The fifth child, a son, arrived on August 10, 1826, amid the blazing heat of a Tennessee summer and the rejoicing of two families on Cherry and Vine Streets. Kicking and screaming, displaying stout limbs and

[9] Louise Grundy Lindsley, "The Home of My Grandparents, Mr. and Mrs. Jacob McGavock." Typescript owned by Mrs. George A. Frazer, Nashville.

[10] Gray, *op. cit.*, 21.

healthy lungs, he entered the world with admiring approval heaped on his well-shaped head with its carrot-colored down.

This new son was named Randal William for Jacob's brother of Max Meadows and for his Uncle Randal, recently Mayor of Nashville. The name had been handed down from the Randal McGavock who remained in Ireland when James immigrated to America and was a popular name with the McGavock family on both sides of the Atlantic.[11]

The baby's red hair was also an object of family satisfaction, for both the McGavock and Grundy families boasted of red-haired men with ruddy Scotch-Irish complexions. So this little boy, with smiling gray eyes and a thin, unpredictable mouth, was from the first the esteemed scion of a large connection. In fact, no child born in the State of Tennessee in 1826 could have come into the world under better patronage, with the lavishing of more affection, and with more favorable prospects ahead of him than did Randal William McGavock. Nor, on the other hand, could a child have been born at a more opportune time to experience in full force the bitterest three decades in the history of the United States.

As he lay there in a tiny crib, protected by mosquito netting and watched over by an attentive nurse, rocked gently and sung to by an admiring sister, and pointed at with pride by Judge Grundy, this baby Randal—the son of Jacob, the grandson of Hugh, the great-grandson of Old James—seemed to sleep peacefully and snugly. And for weeks the family, the servants, and a host of visitors tip-toed through the McGavock house on Cherry Street. They did not want to awaken the young man who slept quietly in the upstairs nursery.

Young Randal doubtless awoke to the world about him in the usual ways that children reach awareness; he was a normal child who got his fingers scorched trying to grab at stray sparks on the sitting room hearth; or he first felt the coolness of fresh well water as it trickled down his chin when he tried drinking from a man-sized cedar dipper; or he experienced the sharp pain of a hickory switch when Louisa found him, dirty and bruised, returning from a forbidden excursion down the alley that separated the McGavock house from the back gardens and stables on College Street.

In other ways he became aware of the world around him—on those occasions when his parents entertained and he was presented to the

---

[11] Four days after the birth of Randal William McGavock in Nashville, an Irish cousin of County Antrim met with a strangely violent death. On his tombstone in the Presbyterian churchyard at Glenarm, Tickmacrevan Parish, is the following inscription: "John McGavock son to Hugh McGavock late of Scarryhill who was barbarously and inhumanely murdered without any known cause by a combined banditti near Bellisky Chapel on his way from Cushendal on the 14th day of August 1826 in the 29th year of his age."

company of guests in the front parlor and was rehearsed beforehand in manners and deportment. His hair combed back, his best shoes on, young Randal might have chafed and squirmed in a freshly starched collar and felt immensely uncomfortable when first meeting the stern countenance of President Andrew Jackson or the penetrating eyes of Governor James K. Polk.

On the other hand, he might have learned about the "cruel" world when he was denied the privilege of staying up at night when there was an evening party in his home to celebrate some special event like the soirée described by Miss Jane Thomas when his grandfather was elected Senator to Washington in 1829:

> Mrs. Jacob McGavock, Judge Grundy's daughter, and her husband gave the legislators a party after her father was elected Senator. The supper excelled anything I have ever seen in Nashville . . . They went to New Orleans and got a French confectioner to prepare the supper. The table was set up-stairs in the room over the parlor. The folding doors were open, and the table extended from one room to the other. At each end the table was set in the shape of a cross, and where the table went through the folding doors there was a large pyramid, which was at least three feet high, made of beautiful jelly put in glasses. Dispersed all over the tables were vases of beautiful artificial flowers, with glass globes over each vase. The candlesticks were of silver, and each one held three beautiful wax candles. Long leaves were cut out of tissue-paper, dipped in spermaceti, and covered with isinglass, which made them look like crystallized candy. These were put around each candle, and hung down over the candlestick. On the tables were all kind of large and small cakes, confectionery, and fruits. They had dancing down-stairs.[12]

So young Randal McGavock was to know about the social life of Nashville in his own home.[13]

His earliest reading and ciphering were learned from his mother, for Louisa McGavock was a good student herself, having received in 1813 three certificates of merit as a schoolgirl of fifteen under Miss Louisa Keets, and a "Leaving Certificate of Merit" when she was graduated from Miss Keets's classes on February 10, 1814.[14] Randal began to read the Bible when he was seven or eight; he was probably reading selections from Shakespeare before he went to school, two years later.

---

[12] Jane H. Thomas, *Old Days in Nashville, Tennessee* (Nashville: Publishing House Methodist Episcopal Church, South, 1897), p. 57.

[13] The earliest reference I have found to McGavock as a child is contained in a letter which his mother wrote from Nashville to Maria Reed McGavock of Wythe County, Virginia, on August 8, 1828. The little boy was almost two at the time and obviously much protected. "I have just returned from Franklin. I have been to visit our little Randal who has been there for the last six weeks. We intend him to remain there untill the sickly season among Children is over here." Letter owned by Jacob McGavock of Wytheville, Virginia.

[14] McGavock Papers.

At the age of ten or eleven, the boy was sent to the private academy which Professor Moses Stevens conducted in Nashville under the impressive name, The Classical and Mathematical Seminary.[15] Here he studied Greek, Latin, geography, and mathematics in preparation for the university. Moses Stevens, a forthright New England schoolmaster, had come south several years before. His son assisted him in teaching the young boys, but after the father's death in 1844, the school was discontinued and the Stevens family returned to Salem, Massachusetts. Randal McGavock was a member of one of the last classes graduating from the Classical Seminary and he looked back, in later years, with fondness for the time when he declined Latin nouns for Old Stevens and puzzled over the Greek of the New Testament.[16]

His grandfather Grundy had shown an interest in higher education in Nashville and was chiefly responsible for bringing Dr. James Priestly, Grundy's old principal at Salem Academy, Bardstown, Kentucky, to the city as President of Cumberland College in 1809.[17] David McGavock, Randal's great-uncle, served as a member of the Board of Trustees of Cumberland before the college changed its name to the University of Nashville in 1826.[18] So it was fitting that young Randal, at age seventeen, matriculate at the local University and that Jacob and Louisa McGavock support a hometown institution. At this time the University was presided over by the distinguished Presbyterian minister, Dr. Philip Lindsley, who resigned as acting President of Princeton University to bring higher education to the "less cultivated" Southwest.[19] Lindsley hoped that Nashville might eventually become a seat of learning like Oxford or Cambridge.[20]

In the autumn of 1843 there were three McGavock cousins attending lectures: John Harding, David H., and Randal William.[21] Randal was

---

[15] A. L. Crabb, "The Forties—Nashville's Decade of Self Discovery," *Peabody Reflector and Alumni News,* XII (1939), 409-411; XIII (1940), 4-6.

[16] Cf. Journal of Randal William McGavock, July 23, 1862. (Hereinafter cited as *Journal.*)

[17] A. L. Crabb, *The Genealogy of George Peabody College for Teachers* (Nashville: n. p., 1935), p. 14.

[18] Acts of Tennessee, 1826, Chapter 47. Also see Nell Savage Mahoney, "The University of Nashville," *Nashville Tennessean Magazine,* Part I, December 2, 1951, pp. 30-32; Part II, December 9, 1951, pp. 26-29.

[19] For a brief but stimulating discussion of letters and learning in early Nashville, see John Thompson, "Frontier Appraisal," *Nashville Tennessean Magazine,* June 13, 1948, p. 4.

[20] J. E. Windrow, "George Peabody College and the Lindsley Family," *Peabody Reflector and Alumni News,* VI, No. 9 (October, 1933), 287. In 1829, when delivering a baccalaureate address, Philip Lindsley said: "In casting my eye over the map of Tennessee, it struck me from the first that this was precisely the place destined by Providence for a great university, if ever such an institution were to exist."

[21] *Catalogue of the Officers and Graduates of the University of Nashville,* Nashville, 1850. By 1850 five McGavocks had been graduated from the university.

just entering the three-year course that would bring him to the A. B. degree and prepare him for the study of law. He was the tallest of the three and still growing taller, although he already measured six feet and needed new clothes every year.

At the university he was invited to join the Agatheridon and the Erosophian Societies, rival debating clubs which convened on Saturday mornings.[22] Randal pledged membership with the Agatheridons in December of 1843 and his first subject for debate was "Should foreign emigration to the United States be prohibited?" He was given the affirmative side of the question against the negative argument of his cousin John. The club minutes do not disclose which side won the debate, but the day itself marked the beginning of a career in which speaking became a graceful accomplishment for Randal McGavock.

The Agatheridons took their rules and by-laws seriously; members were fined for negligence or ungentlemanly deportment. The act of spitting on the floor was punished by the forfeiture of 10c; throwing coal brought a fine of 15c; but "reading instead of speaking [an] oration" was a major offense which called for the penalty of a quarter. Moreover, any president who failed to deliver an inaugural address at the time of entering office, or a valedictory upon retiring, was charged the heavy fine of one dollar.[23]

In July of 1844, at the age of eighteen, Randal was unanimously elected president of the Agatheridons; later the same year he was elected secretary, recording the minutes of the meetings and signing his name in a bold scrawl.[24] During that year, on the eve of the War with Mexico, the students found lively debate in such topics as "Would the annexation of Texas to the U. S. be politic?" They also debated broader philosophical questions like "Which is capable of exerting the most influence on mankind, wealth or intellect?" There is no evidence that young McGavock was ever asked to forfeit any of his college allowance for failing to speak. In fact, one incident in his university career indicates that on occasion he may have been inclined to speak too freely.

The professors were beset with disciplinary problems ranging from minor misdemeanors to drunkenness and dueling. The boarding students at the university, many of them away from home for the first

---

22 Beginning as the DeWitt Clinton Society on July 16, 1825, the club changed to Agatheridon on September 18, 1827. The name was compounded from the Greek *agathos* and *eris,* meaning "good contention or good debating." The Erosophian Society (formerly the Carroll Literary Society, founded May 6, 1825) was reorganized on September 14, 1831. Also from the Greek, the name is translated as "lovers of wisdom or knowledge."

23 "Minutes of the Agatheridon Society," April 4-May 9, 1836. Peabody College Library vault.

24 *Ibid.,* (1843-1848).

time, were generally the worst offenders. In fact, the staid townspeople of Nashville and the landladies who provided a roof for the out-of-town boys rather expected them to be a little "wild."[25]

But the "Affair of Chatham Roberdeau Wheat and Randal McGavock" in 1845 involved two town boys of good family and reputation. Their breach of the peace brought a convening of the Board of Trustees, considerable chagrin to President Philip Lindsley, and a conditional suspension for both Wheat and McGavock.

Roberdeau Wheat was the son of John and Selina Patten Wheat. Born on April 9, 1826, he was about four months older than McGavock. The Reverend Mr. Wheat, his father, was rector of Christ Church Episcopal in Nashville and had seven other children, Rob being the oldest.[26] Rob's parents had enrolled him in 1841, at age 15, at Episcopal High School, Washington. While he was there, he was often moody and fault-finding and inclined to blame others for his adolescent discontentments.[27] Then his parents entered him at the University of Nashville as a candidate for the A. B. degree, a year before McGavock matriculated.

The origin of the dispute between Rob Wheat and Randal McGavock was not disclosed in the official notes kept by President Lindsley. Apparently the two boys maintained some kind of running feud during early July, 1845. Then on Tuesday, July 15, "between 3 and 4 o'clock P.M., McGavock assaulted Wheat in one of the college entries or passages & injured him badly."[28] Wheat's battered condition was reported to the college faculty and immediately a hearing was held. Both boys were suspended from the university until a more complete investigation could be made by the President and the Board.

On the following Monday, July 26, at five o'clock, the Board of Trustees met in solemn session to hear the testimony presented. Among the members sitting in judgment were Return Jonathan Meigs, Tennessee jurist and Attorney General; Dr. Boyd McNairy, venerable Nashville physician; Dr. Felix Robertson, the sixth son of General James Robertson, the founder of Nashville, and the first white child born in Davidson County; and the Honorable Edwin H. Ewing, who had just

---

[25] Crabb, "The Genealogy . . . ," p. 23.

[26] Charles L. Dufour, *Gentle Tiger: The Gallant Life of Roberdeau Wheat* (Baton Rouge: Louisiana State University Press, 1957), p. 3.

[27] *Ibid.*, pp. 12-13.

[28] McGavock Papers. There is a note on the flyleaf of the official account which reads: "Paper used by the President in announcing the decision in regard to Wheat & McGavock to the students in the Chapel on Tuesday evening, July 29th, 1845." Below this is a subscript: "This paper was found by Dr. J. B. Lindsley in his father's papers. R. W. McGavock."

delivered the chief address at the laying of the cornerstone of the new state capitol. Another trustee who found the hearing particularly embarrassing was John M. Bass, lawyer, banker, and planter, who was married to McGavock's aunt, the former Malvina Grundy. The minister's son with his abusive language, and Judge Grundy's grandson, with his equally sharp invective, had given the Nashville gossips and the student body choice grist for their mills.

The gentlemen of the Board, after reviewing the testimony in full, reached the following conclusions:

1st. That the irritating or insulting or provoking language used by the parties, previous to the assault, was about equal.

2nd. That the assault does not appear to have been premeditated.

3rd. That no unlawful or deadly weapon was used, but only a common walking stick.

4th. That, apart from the previous insulting language, (of which the Board could form no correct judgment or rather no other judgment than as exposed above,) Wheat was not culpable as he acted only on the defensive & had not even a stick in his hand.

With these facts before them, the Board resolved that "Messrs Wheat & McGavock be not permitted to rejoin the college until they give satisfactory evidence that they will prosecute the quarrel no further, [and] preserve the peace in future. . . ." At the same meeting the Board appointed Dr. McNairy and Dr. Robertson as a committee to call upon the two students and to take steps toward effecting a reconciliation. The committee was asked to report the results to the College Faculty.

The two youths seem to have regretted the incident, at least outwardly, for they both gave solemn promises to Drs. McNairy and Robertson that they would refrain from further demonstrations. Therefore, on July 28, the Board recommended their restoration to the college. President Lindsley personally extracted "the pledge that the quarrel was ended & that in future they would keep the peace." He also reprimanded McGavock "for violating the Laws in assaulting Wheat."[29]

Thus the incident passed. In a few weeks Rob Wheat was graduated from the university and left Nashville for New Orleans. He went south still bearing a few of the bruises which Randal had put on his moody, aristocratic head. It is not likely that the two men ever met again or ever publicly referred to their altercation. Wheat's movements thereafter were far removed from Nashville. In the next few years, as a gentleman-soldier and hired revolutionary, he fought with Lopez in

[29] *Ibid.*

Cuba, with Carvajal and Alvarez in two Mexican revolutions, with William Walker in Nicaragua, and with Garibaldi in Italy. His death in 1862, at the Battle of Gaines' Mill, brought to an end a colorful and brilliant military career.[30]

The twenty-first commencement exercises of the University of Nashville were held with appropriate ceremony on October 7, 1846. Several visitors to "college hill" arrived from neighboring southern states; the conferring of degrees was presided over by the dignified Philip Lindsley. A large number of Nashville citizens, including the civic, professional, and educational leaders of the city, came to hear and judge the seven speakers announced on the program. It was a day of general festivity in the little metropolis of 9,000 people; it was also a day of oratory, sentimentalism, and conspicuously big dinners.

In the McGavock household there were six children, other than Randal, who felt the tremors of excitement. This was the day their older brother was to sit on the speakers' rostrum and deliver his commencement address. Sister Ann was married to Judge Henry Dickinson and living in Columbus, Mississippi, but she sent Randal her congratulations in a long letter which predicted for him a happy future as a lawyer. His brother Edward, a first-year student at the University, and his sister Sallie attended the exercises with their parents. Introduced as the grandson of the late Felix Grundy, Randal displayed his oratorical gifts when he spoke on "The Government of States and Character of Statesmen" to an audience already kindly disposed toward the prepossessing young man.[31] They liked his manner, his occasional flashes of fire, and his touches of humor. They said he would make a fine courtroom lawyer with a little age.

Afterwards Jacob McGavock probably observed to his wife that their son spoke like the Grundy side of the family, but that he looked every inch like a McGavock. Louisa smiled in agreement and could hardly have been more pleased.

---

30 Dufour, *op. cit., passim.*
31 A copy of the program is included in the microfilmed McGavock Papers.

CHAPTER IV

A Southerner Learns Law at Harvard

Randal McGavock left no record of his movements from October, 1846, when he received the A. B. degree at the University of Nashville, until September 1, 1847, when he entered the Harvard Law School. It is likely that he began reading law in the office of one of his father's friends in Nashville. He may have spent the year studying Felix Grundy's library and briefing some of his grandfather's most successful cases. In 1846 Jacob McGavock was Clerk of the Circuit and District Courts of the United States for the Middle District of Tennessee,[1] so it was appropriate that he bring his son into his own office and give him practice in writing out depositions and keeping the records of the court.

There were other affairs to keep the eldest son of a large family occupied. Some of the land which Felix Grundy had taken up in Arkansas, and which had been owned jointly by Grundy and his son-in-law, Jacob McGavock, was now, after Grundy's death, under McGavock's ownership.[2] So Jacob took Randal with him on the steamboat to Pecan Point in Arkansas to look over the plantations there, help with the accounts, and supervise the planting of cotton. It was no small operation to hire competent and honest overseers, provide enough slave labor, and look after property that stretched out on the other side of the Mississippi.

Therefore Randal learned from his father about the value of land, the buying of seed, the breeding of stock, and the way to plan a harvest. He learned, too, what only a farmer knows—the disappointments and fatigue that come with a bad year, or the losses inflicted by the hand of nature when the farmer least expects them. Jacob was a quiet, patient man; like a conscientious father he tried to tell his eldest son everything he could about the rich but sullen, unpredictable earth that would one day pass from his hands to his son's.

---

[1] Randal W. McGavock, "Genealogical Notes on the McGavock Family to the Year 1853." McGavock Papers.

[2] "Will of Felix Grundy," McGavock Papers.

Perhaps this same year Randal was given a trip by steamboat to New Orleans. After 1843 the journey one way could be made in five days and nineteen hours if one took the fast-moving *Talleyrand* from the Crescent City back to Nashville,[3] and certainly New Orleans held immeasurable attractions for the many Tennesseans who traveled to the fashionable city at the mouth of the Mississippi. It is clear from the references that he made later in his journals that Randal was a visitor to New Orleans on at least one occasion. Very probably he went there for part of the winter of 1846-47, stopping to visit his Aunt Martha and his several cousins on the Van P. Winder plantation in Louisiana; for Martha Grundy Winder, his mother's younger sister, often entertained members of the family who were en route to New Orleans for shopping tours and the attractions of the St. Charles Hotel and the French Opera.[4]

To be sure, New Orleans was the most inviting place in the South of the 1840's for a young man just turned twenty to begin seeing the wonders of a cosmopolitan city. It is likely that he went there for the winter season, enjoyed the gay revels of the Mardi Gras, engaged a tailor, and came back to Nashville with the clothes that he would need at Harvard. His cousin John Harding McGavock had just returned from Harvard and was full of salutary advice for young Randal, who, already attracted to the stimulation and excitement of travel, awaited with impatience his first trip to New England.

Three weeks after he reached his twenty-first birthday, on September 1, 1847, Randal registered at the Harvard Law School. Six days after his matriculation an eccentric, bearded New Englander by the name of Henry David Thoreau, who had spent two years in seclusion on the banks of Walden Pond, brought his deliberate idyll and his fronting of "the essential facts of life" to a close and returned to nearby Concord Village as a more or less permanent resident.

Although Thoreau's friend and mentor, Ralph Waldo Emerson, was leaving for a lecture tour in England, Emerson's essays and the writings of the Transcendentalists were shaping the ideas of the Massachusetts intellectuals in September of 1847 and drawing occasional fire from the South because of the strong attacks these writers made on slavery in the Southern States. This was also the year which saw the height of the Mexican War and the internal disputes provoked by that war.

---

[3] A. L. Crabb, "The Forties—Nashville's Decade of Self Discovery," *Peabody Reflector and Alumni News,* XII (1939), 409-411; XIII (1940), 4-6.

[4] Louise Grundy Lindsley, "The Home of My Grandparents, Mr. and Mrs. Jacob McGavock." Typescript owned by Mrs. George A. Frazer, Nashville.

Emerson had written in his journal that Mexico, when conquered by the United States, "will poison us." He complained that the South was pressing the war upon the rest of the country. He believed that the South's motive was the acquisition of more territory for future slave-holding states:

> The Southerner is cool and insolent. "We drive you to the wall, and will again." "Yes, gentlemen, but do you know why Massachusetts and New York are so tame?—it is because we own you, and are very tender of our mortgages which cover all your property."[5]

Thus sectional differences had already begun to sting the sober mind of New England's foremost philosopher.

Yet Thoreau might never have been obliged to spend two years of isolation in the Walden woods if his own society had remained primarily agrarian—as society still was in the South, free of the woes of mushrooming Massachusetts mills. Emerson might never have committed the tactlessness of speaking in terms of "owning you" and "holding a mortgage" on the south if his own vision of society had not been conditioned by the prevailing self-righteousness shared by other New Englanders. Their society and that which had nurtured three generations of McGavocks had grown asunder by the autumn of 1847.

Moreover, Emerson seemed determined to dislike Southerners as individuals, for he wrote in his journal on October 8, 1837, ten years before McGavock arrived in Cambridge:

> The young Southerner comes here a spoiled child, with graceful manners, excellent self-command, very good to be spoiled more, but good for nothing else,—a mere parader. He has conversed so much with rifles, horses, and dogs that he has become himself a rifle, a horse and a dog, and in civil, educated company, where anything human is going forward, he is dumb and unhappy, like an Indian in a church. Treat them with great deference, as we often do, and they accept it as their due without misgiving. Give them an inch, and they take a mile. They are mere bladders of conceit.[6]

Thus run the recorded impressions of the philosophical Emerson, who seeming to base his generalizations about Southerners on a few instances, eventually joined the abolitionist ranks, and in 1865 objected that Grant's terms of surrender to Robert E. Lee were "a little too easy."

At Harvard the catalogue for the academic session of 1847-48 announced a roster of forty-two "Officers of Instruction and Govern-

---

[5] Edward W. Emerson and Waldo E. Forbes, eds. *Journals of Ralph Waldo Emerson, 1820-1872,* 10 vols. (Boston: Houghton Mifflin Company, 1909-1914), VII, 206.

[6] *Ibid.,* IV, 312, 313.

ment" for the 268 students in the college proper. Among the distinguished names were Edward Everett, Henry W. Longfellow, O. W. Holmes, Louis Agassiz, Francis Child, and Evangelinus Sophocles. At the law school Jared Sparks, Joel Parker, and Theophilus Parsons lectured in the recently remodeled Dane Hall, the two-story Georgian building on Harvard Square just south of Massachusetts Hall.

Law students came to Cambridge from all the New England States, from the South, and from as far west as Ohio.[7] The course required eighteen months of residence and the number of students attending classes at one time totalled about 125. With numbers this large, the embryonic barristers made their presence felt in the Harvard Yard and in the social life of the university.[8] Again the Southerners, whose numbers were proportionately high because of the scarcity of law schools in the South, were noted for their lack of what Thomas Wentworth Higginson called "moral improvement":

> There were, by the catalogue of 1845-46 . . . in the Law School . . . 57 [students] from the Slave States; and these few dozen unquestionably exceeded, in capacity of disorder, the whole 3,000 of the present day [1896]. They indeed introduced, unaided, more elements of marked variety into Cambridge society than is now obtainable in the whole university. . . . These young men from Georgia and Mississippi had almost always fashionable clothes and attractive manners, were often graceful dancers, and took the lead in society; but they were very apt to be indolent, dissipated, quarrelsome, and sometimes they were extremely ignorant. They were attracted by the wide fame of Judge Story, and disappeared with the Civil War. There seemed to be no discipline in the Law School,—people spoke of "reading law," but not of studying law,—and the students of this description did very much as they pleased.[9]

So ran the estimate of another New England observer, a student himself in Harvard College during the pre-war "reign of terror" when Southerners were credited with scandalizing the "established morality" of Massachusetts Avenue and Brattle Street.

Some years after Higginson graduated, he returned to a quieter, less colorful Cambridge and remarked to his friend Alderman Chapman "that there were no longer any street fights, as formerly, between the students and the young mechanics of the town."[10] The Alderman is reported as replying: "Those things stopped when the Southern law students disappeared. Hot-headed fellows; always getting into fights.

---

[7] *Quinquennial Catalogue of the Law School of Harvard University, 1817-1924,* (Cambridge: Harvard Law School, 1925), pp. 40-43.

[8] *Centennial History of the Harvard Law School* (Cambridge: Harvard Law Association, 1918), p. 24.

[9] Thomas W. Higginson, "Life in Cambridge Town," in *The Cambridge of Eighteen Hundred Ninety Six,* ed. Arthur Gilman (Cambridge: Riverside Press, 1896), pp. 38-39.

[10] *Ibid.,* 39.

Widener Library Archives

Dane Hall, Harvard Law School, as it looked during McGavock's residence in Cambridge.

Felicia Grundy Eakin (1820-1889), McGavock's Aunt Felicia. Widow of William Eakin, she later married Dr. Robert M. Porter.

Courtesy Margaret Lindsley Warden

"Carnton," Williamson County, Tennessee, built by Randal McGavock (1766-1844), a great-uncle of the diarist. The estate was named for the McGavock townland in County Antrim, and to the back porch were brought the bodies of five Confederate Generals (Adams, Cleburne, Gist, Granbury, and Strahl) after the Battle of Franklin.

Courtesy Margaret Lindsley Warden

Randal W. McGavock
(circa 1850)

I was in some of those fights myself." Perhaps the Alderman was replying to the staid Mr. Higginson with a twinkle in his eye. However, these denunciations by Emerson and Higginson are typical of the judgments put upon the heads of Southerners attending Harvard before the Civil War.

When Randal McGavock entered the law school there were at least two other graduates from the University of Nashville attending classes —Abner Green Gale of Mississippi and John Goff Ballentine of Pulaski, Tennessee.[11] As McGavock's journal verifies, these boys saw each other frequently but did not conspire with other Southerners to form a clique. They mixed freely with other students from New England and the West and spent their leisure smoking an occasional "segar," playing whist, or calling in twos and threes on fashionable young ladies in Cambridge and Boston. They were a gregarious lot who thought girls were better beautiful than brainy and should be kept behind guarded doors for graceful courting. They also believed true masculine hearts would eventually win fair ladies.

These young men who day after day occupy much of Randal McGavock's journal were not essentially different from other youths of twenty-one at the middle of the nineteenth century. They were romantic Victorians, representative of their age and typical of their culture. To denounce the Southerners categorically is hardly to make a fair evaluation.

McGavock's diary, without intending to do so, presents a more accurate account of Southern students at Harvard than the sources most often quoted. His informal chronicle reports misdemeanors, to be sure, and he would have recorded others if he had had cases before him; for nowhere do his diaries retreat from the facts that he met with during the next fourteen years. As a record keeper he was conscientious. As a diarist he has refuted a myth that arose from misunderstanding, sectional egotism, and smugness.

As a twenty-one year old student whose parents were intimates of President and Mrs. Polk, McGavock brought with him letters of introduction to a number of Boston's best families, in whose homes he was entertained; like his grandfather, the late U. S. Attorney-General Felix Grundy, he had a ready wit and was a fluent speaker when the after-dinner toasts were proposed. He was quite acceptable socially, even in Boston.[12]

---

[11] *Quinquennial Catalogue,* pp. 40, 44.

[12] The Brahmans and "Barons" of Beacon Hill and environs with whom McGavock consorted have been identified in footnotes accompanying the journal.

He read his Bible daily, went to church on Sunday (sometimes twice), and reflected much of the stern Presbyterianism of his pioneer forebears in Virginia. As a student he faithfully attended lectures in the law school and went to others in the college when he wanted to learn about American History and Anatomy. He was hardly brilliant, all told, but neither was he indolent in study or disrespectful of learning. His reading list of nineteenth century fiction and poetry was notable.

He drank occasionally, gambled once in a while for small stakes, and frequented the theatre. From time to time he went into Boston and visited *ladies*. He was no thin-blooded Puritan with self-righteous conceits. Moreover, despite what the New England critics have attempted to infer, it cannot be said that it was the patronage of the Southerners at Harvard that kept Boston's brothels from closing their doors.

But perhaps most damning of all was the charge that Southerners as a whole were belligerent and hot-headed—that they began to stir up a fight. There is no hint of this attitude, no goading of the New Englander, no harping on sectional prejudices in the journal kept at Harvard. There is one reference to "Yankee" materialism; one to midwestern "greeness"; but neither of these comes under more than a passing criticism from McGavock's pen.

The longest text is against the Abolitionists, whom McGavock denounced on several occasions. He did not believe, however, that Garrison, Birney, and Pillsbury were representative of the sane New England outlook or could ever reflect the wishes of the whole North. Even after observing an impassioned Abolitionist meeting at the Legislative Hall, McGavock was not incited to settle one of the great questions of the day by recourse to arms.[13]

But Emerson went on with his journal and took another text on Southerners in politics—at the time when Daniel Webster displeased him and much of the North by subscribing, in a conciliatory move, to the Fugitive Slave Law. Bemoaning "the misfortune of New Egnland," Emerson thought the Southerners always managed to get the upper hand in Washington:

> The Southerner has personality, has temperament, has manners, persuasion, address, and terror. The cold Yankee has wealth, numbers, intellect, material power of all sorts, but has not fire or firmness, and is coaxed and talked and bantered and shamed and scared till he votes away the dominion of his millions at home! He never comes back [from Washington] quite the same man he went; but has been handled, tampered with.[14]

[13] *Journal,* March 17, 1848.
[14] *Journals of Ralph Waldo Emerson,* VIII, 100-101.

Here Emerson pits northern "material power" against southern "persuasion"; he juxtaposes "intellect" and "temperament"; he is afraid of losing ground, of being "handled, tampered with," of losing his "Yankee" grip on the affairs of the country at large. This was the growing fear that was finding louder and louder voices in the Northeast when McGavock, a Southwesterner, sat down to classes in the law school on Harvard Square.

The first notice of his attendance at lectures and his participation in the meetings of the Kent Club is given in the journal of his New Hampshire friend Mellen Chamberlain under Thursday, October 14: "Kent Club. Some very fine speeches from Parker, McGavock, Gwathmey, Watson, Kirkpatrick."[15] This first reference, written six weeks after McGavock matriculated, indicates that he was already on the rostrum making speeches—"some very fine speeches." Apparently he was not reluctant, as was his classmate Chamberlain, to enter the contests of wit and oratory which the Kent Club fostered. Chamberlain experienced fear and trembling on these occasions. In another entry he mentioned "most splendid speeches" and confessed "It quite discourages me to hear G[wathmey] & W[atson] speak so finely."[16]

So during the autumn of 1847 McGavock spent many of his evenings preparing debates and studying the legal commentaries on his reading table. He also found time to write courtly letters to Miss Lemira Ewing, the first young lady mentioned as a romantic attachment.

Miss Ewing was living in New Haven with her mother and brother, although her family were Tennesseans. Letters passed between her and McGavock in swift order; they seem to have made the most of the postal services between Boston and New Haven. But apparently Lemira Ewing was engaged at the same time in a correspondence with William S. Eakin, a Tennessean living in New York and working for the firm of W. and T. Eakin.

Affairs grew more and more complicated. During the autumn months of 1847 Miss Ewing was pressed to make a decision and the end of her courtship with McGavock is recorded in the first part of the extant journals. As soon as they had returned their respective bundles of letters, Randal heard that Lemira was married to Eakin. What he confided to his journal was: "Woman, O Woman, thy vows are traced in sand."[17]

[15] Mellen Chamberlain, "Diary and Commonplace Book, 1839-1849." Unpublished. Rare Book Room, Boston Public Library.
[16] *Ibid.*
[17] *Journal,* March 3, 1848.

This affair with Lemira Ewing was Randal's only attachment during the Harvard year. Perhaps his later interest in Miss Maria A. Gould was more fanciful than genuine, for Miss Gould was considered the most beautiful girl in New England. He was understandably filled with curiosity.

The *Boston Bee* in its report of the closing ball at Newport in 1848 stated that "Miss Gould was acknowledged to be the most lovely girl present."[18] Perhaps McGavock was offered more competition than he liked, for the lady had many suitors and was apparently a kind of pin-up attraction—in the Victorian sense—in the rooms of McGavock's classmates. John Noyes Meade, a freshman in the college, reported that he "went into Pope's room and saw a portrait of Miss Gould, the celebrated beauty."[19] Another reference describes the lady as she presided over the fair in City Hall:

> Miss Gould is certainly one of the handsomest girls that I have ever seen: there is no intellectual beauty, but her features are very regular, her hair beautiful, her teeth regular and white, and her skin and complexion faultless; perhaps paint does something for the latter.[20]

Perhaps McGavock was put off by the paint and the swelling ranks of competition.

Nevertheless, the eighteen months he spent at Cambridge were socially stimulating and relatively carefree. Members of his family and other Tennesseans called on him from time to time. He took them to Mount Auburn Cemetery, Fresh Pond, and on circular tours of Boston. He visited his professors and their families in the evenings; he attended celebrations of Christmas and the Fourth of July in the homes of wealthy Boston merchants who maintained lavish establishments on Park Street, Beacon Hill, and Tremont Street. In September he squired the rich Madame Octavia Walton LeVert of Mobile on a sight-seeing trip to Lowell, then to the Boston Athæneum to view the paintings on exhibit in that aloof establishment, and topped the day off having supper with Madame LeVert and her party in the drawing room of the Revere House.[21]

His attitude toward this stunning young widow (whose "name now fills every paper about her outrage at Newport") was not entirely worshipful. As a young man of twenty-two he was curious about the publicized lady of fortune who made her annual progress to Washington,

---

[18] Boston *Bee,* September 1, 1848, p. 1.

[19] John Noyes Meade, "Journal, 1847-1850." Unpublished. Widener Library Archives, Harvard University.

[20] *Ibid.*

[21] *Journal,* September 4, 1848.

New York, Saratoga, Newport, and Boston. She was the darling of the society columnists and her arrival in Boston in 1848 was duly noted by the *Bee:* "Mrs. LeVert, of Mobile, whose wit and accomplishments made her the 'bright, particular star' of the Newport Ball, is at present at the Revere House."[22] An announcement of this kind, in combination with everything else that had been written about "the Belle of Saratoga," was enough to cause any young bachelor to be struck with awe.

As a matter of record, the closing ball at Newport, five days before her arrival in Boston, was Madame LeVert's particular triumph of the 1848 season. It was also one of the most lavish social displays of the 1840's. The *Boston Daily Times* devoted three and one half columns to "the most splendid fete ever given in this country" and sounded a barrage of complimentary adjectives for the "elegant and youthful Madame LeVert, of Alabama, who was 'born to be gay, and was determined to fulfill her destiny'."[23]

The *Boston Daily Evening Transcript* was agog over the personalities who showed up for the affair:

> I must tell you of John Sullivan, the poet, musician, and orator, the Crichton of fashionable society, whom a pair of ruby lips called "a perfect jewel of a man." Between himself and Madame LeVert there was a delightful rencontre . . . The thousand words of real wit that delighted us, I fain would tell, but they were so beautiful and delicate, the spirit passes e'er my little pen can immortalize them.[24]

But the most dazzling report was yet to come. Convinced that the affair had not received all the coverage that it deserved and that Madame LeVert's costume had not been described in words that its "oriental magnificence and Eastern splendor" demanded, the correspondent, who signed his article "Timon," tried to outdo all the rest in adjectival exaggeration:

> Mrs. LeVert was a radiant blaze of richest jewels . . . the Houris of Mahomet's Paradise seemed realized. "By Jove," exclaimed a gay knight as she entered by the side of Colonel Duncan, the noble, brave, gallant hero of many battles, "she looks like a goddess, and she moves a queen." She wore a bodice fitting her beautifully developed form. Over this gracefully fell a network of large pearls "as white as monumental alabaster." Around her delicate waist was a castus or girdle of jewels; there blazed the topaz, the amethyst, emerald, diamond, and turquoise in beautiful harmony . . . The short dress was of rich white satin embroidered with pearls and silver; over this was a tunic of silver lace elegantly embroidered. The trousers were of satin clasped around the fairy like ankles,

---

[22] Boston *Bee,* September 4, 1848, p. 1.

[23] Boston *Daily Times,* September 1, 1848, p. 3.

[24] Boston *Daily Evening Transcript,* September 2, 1848, p. 2.

with silver anklets . . . Her smallest of small wrists were covered with costly and lovely bracelets . . . She had a gorgeous bouquet and jewelled fan. . . .[25]

"Timon" went on to report other features of this dazzling costume of "Nourmahal, the light of the Harem," for he said it needed "new-coined words to do justice to its perfection." At the end he confided to his readers that good judges had estimated the value of the creation to have been between six and eight thousand dollars and that he did not consider these figures an exaggeration.[26]

With this lady McGavock spent the better part of two days, accompanied by his friend Saunders of Alabama and the "agreeable" Miss Bacon; he had an opportunity to make an appraisal of the flamboyant, witty, glittering Mrs. LeVert. What he really thought of her he did not confide at length to his journal. It is significant that he simply referred to her display at Newport as an "outrage" and that he did not stoop to further elaborations ill befitting a gentleman.

At what date Randal McGavock began writing a journal is a question for which there is no exact answer. Very likely he started it at Harvard on the first day of September, 1847. It is probable that having arrived at Cambridge he decided to keep a personal record of his life and movements after his twenty-first birthday. That his earliest extant journal (beginning January 2, 1848) is also his first is hardly to be believed, for it begins as though it were merely a continuation of an earlier journal, now lost.

Unfortunately the book he used provided scant space for his crowded schedule. Measuring 4 x 6½ inches, this diary was entirely too cramped; each page was divided into three days, thus allowing a mere two inches for a single day's entry. Even by reducing his normal handwriting to a feather-line script, McGavock was hard pressed to put everything down. As a result, he often wrote vertically across a page after filling it up horizontally.

More than that, the cramped space very surely affected his style. Although most sentences are complete with subject and verb, the writing tends to be short and choppy in effect. There is not this characteristic in his travel book *A Tennessean Abroad* and in much of the later journal, particularly that section dealing with Fort Warren, when McGavock provided himself with larger pages that were not divided in advance. After keeping a journal during 1848 and 1851, he learned that a "commercial" diary was a cramped affair; therefore all the later

[25] Boston *Daily Mail,* September 4, 1848, p. 2.
[26] *Ibid.*

volumes—beginning in 1855—were standard notebooks which provided more freedom.

One can imagine McGavock sitting up late, wishing for a brighter lamp, wrestling with his memory to recall in sequence the events of a busy day. Certainly writing was not easy for him. He complained once about the time it took and the agony it brought to his soul when he was sending dispatches from Europe. He also remarked that he was sorry he ever agreed to write for publication. But somehow, with whatever determination, labor, and persistence writing required of him, he kept on with the journals.

Beginning in 1848 and ending abruptly in 1862, they were assuredly not written with an audience in mind or to engender public praise for the author. And surely he could not believe that 110 years after he walked briskly up the steps of Dane Hall, or a century after he solemnly swore to the oath of office as Mayor of Nashville, his daily reflections on the world in which he lived would interest readers who otherwise would never have heard of him.[27]

Yet doggedly, and not without denial of vainer pleasures, he wrote. The young orator of 1848 had now become a writer. And in the halls of oratory and letters the combination has always been exceedingly rare.[28]

---

[27] That McGavock was popular as a student is clear. On April 12, 1848, he was elected Marshal of the Law School; then Chief Marshal of Harvard University for the procession to Faneuil Hall when President Edward Everett delivered his eulogy on John Quincy Adams. Cf. *Journal* of this date.

[28] If he wishes to follow the chronology of McGavock's life in detail, the reader may turn to that part of the *Journal* embracing the months at Harvard.

CHAPTER V

A Youth With Long Strides Sees the World

After spending eighteen months in Cambridge, with the exception of two holidays in Washington and Canada, Randal McGavock completed the residence requirements for a Harvard law degree on February 21, 1849.[1] Very probably he stopped in Washington on his way back to Nashville, for there on the fourth of March General Zachary Taylor was inaugurated as the twelfth President of the United States and the attendant festivities were perhaps too attractive for McGavock to pass up with good conscience. If he continued his diary during 1849 and 1850, it has since been lost, and his movements for these years must be documented from other sources or arrived at by conjecture.

It is certain, however, that he was back in Nashville again by April of 1849 when President Polk, now a private citizen, arrived with Mrs. Polk to take possession of "Grundy Hill," thereafter called "Polk Place." In April Randal formally petitioned Litton Bostick, Esquire, for a license to practice law "in the several courts of this state," and Bostick in turn endorsed the application and presented it at the next term of the Davidson County Court.[2] Then on May 10, 1849, Thomas Maney and William K. Turner, Judges of the Circuit Court and Criminal Court of the State of Tennessee, issued, "in the 73rd year of American Independence," a handwritten license granting Randal William McGavock the freedom "to practice as an Attorney, Solicitor, and Counsellor in the several courts of Law and Equity in this State."[3]

At this time James K. Polk had less than five weeks to live; his death came on June 15 in Nashville. Thus was removed from action the third member of the Democratic Triumvirate composed of Grundy, Jackson, and Polk, who had together brought the backwoods democracy of Tennessee to prominence in national affairs.

---

[1] The degree was not awarded, however, until the end of the college year, July 18, 1849. "Commencement Programs, 1849-1869." Harvard Law School Treasure Room.

[2] McGavock Papers.

[3] *Ibid.*

Lawyer McGavock had much to live up to if he followed in their footsteps. Nor was returning to Nashville an easy course for this young man of twenty-two. After eighteen months in the cultivated Northeast, he was deprived now of the gayeties of New York, Boston, Saratoga, and Washington. Nashville was indeed dull to him by comparison.

There is not any evidence that he immediately had many cases in the courts or that he made much money as a practicing attorney. Nashville was bulging with lawyers who had grown up the hard, practical way—which meant that they had read law in some established lawyer's office until the courts granted them a license to practice. Randal returned from Harvard with a degree but no experience. A few minor cases came his way, with a handful of clients trickling into the office he maintained on Cherry Street; like other young lawyers, he experienced the usual starvation period in his profession.

At the same time, however, his father kept him occupied with family business and began to shift to Randal some of the responsibilities of the McGavock property in Arkansas, Tennessee, and Kentucky. The years 1849 and 1850 were not idle, but neither were they as profitable as McGavock might have hoped or as exciting as a young man anticipates.

He might have settled down more earnestly to business in the courts if his affair with Fanny Jane Crutcher in 1850 had ended in matrimony instead of disappointment. All that is known of their relationship is what McGavock wrote about it in his journal of 1851, after the affair was over, but even these few references indicate that he could not forget "Miss *C*—" with the same resignation that followed his courtship of Lemira Ewing. At Christmas, 1850, he reflected moodily on the fact that he had lost his one great chance for happiness;[4] he was restless and discontent at the beginning of 1851. So he decided, "having no entangling alliances or particular object" to bind him to Nashville, "to visit the ancient world."[5]

Undoubtedly, this decision was precipitated by Miss Crutcher's refusal to marry him; but it was also a result of his "longing desire" to explore for himself the wonders of the Old World. For Randal, the son of Jacob, stood in a pivotal position in the history of the McGavock family. For three generations sons and grandsons had migrated westward, turning their backs upon the East; cousins in Tennessee had lost communication with cousins in Ireland; the Carntown boys descended from Randal McGavock of County Antrim had married local girls with

---

[4] Cf. *Journal,* December 25, 1851.
[5] *Journal,* March 20, 1851.

Irish names—Catharine Kane, Mary Wharry, and Mary Darragh[6]—and no longer kept in touch with their American cousins.

Randal was the first member of the McGavock family to turn eastward again and explore the Old World tradition. He might easily have followed the established direction of family migration; he might have forgotten Miss Crutcher by extending the McGavock holdings to Texas or California. Instead, the red-haired young man doubled himself up in a short, narrow bunk on the river packet that left from the foot of Broad Street on March 20, 1851, and started on his journey.[7] On that same evening the first entry of the European journal was written in a leather-bound volume that would survive the decades to come.

The journal reflects the enthusiasm which Randal felt for travel and the almost indefatigable physical capacity that he had for crowding every day with sight-seeing. As Old James could leap across boggy ditches at Glenarm and stride over the mountains of Virginia, as David McGavock could stay long in the Tennessee forests hunting deer and wild game, Randal at age twenty-four, fully grown to six feet two and one-half inches, put his long legs into motion to retrace the footsteps of his forebears. There are occasional glimpses of him making long strides in Europe and startling the villagers to a recognition of the tall man from the American West. At Hucknall he reported that "the natives of this town followed us all over the streets, being attracted by a colored servant in our party and my great height and red whiskers."[8]

Later we see him in the Swiss Alps, making the climb to Mt. Righi, fully equipped for his pedestrian journey:

> Our first care was to procure a knapsack similar to those used by our volunteers in the Mexican War, in which we placed a change of garments and sundry little requisites, such as Murray's hand-book and Kelley's road map of Switzerland; in addition to which we were provided with waterproof coats, double-soled shoes filled with hob-nails, a flask to hold brandy or krischwasser, and an alpenstock, all of which are indispensable upon mountain journeys.[9]

Another glimpse catches Randal and his American companions in Greece as they ride out to the field of Marathon on horseback and recall the ancient battle that they learned about as schoolboys:

> The mounds where the Persians, Athenians, and Miltiades were buried are still plainly visible. Sharp and myself had a race from Vrana to the tomb of the

---

[6] "Pedigree of the Family of Randal McGavock of County Antrim," MS. notes by James Hannah, Agent to the Earl of Antrim, January 4, 1859. McGavock Papers.

[7] *Journal,* March 20, 1851.

[8] *Journal,* May 15, 1851.

[9] Randal W. McGavock, *A Tennessean Abroad* (New York: Redfield, 1854), p. 151. (Hereafter abbreviated as *ATA.*)

Athenians. His horse fell just before reaching the mound, and I won the champagne.[10]

And thus continued the locomotion eastward—Damascus, St. Petersburg, and Moscow—through the shrines of the Holy Land and on to Constantinople.

In Ireland he was not successful in finding members of the McGavock Family. "I have heard Irishmen say that they knew the name about Belfast," he wrote in 1853, after his return from abroad, "but when I was in Ireland in 1851 I took particular pains to search out the name and failed."[11] Nevertheless he felt an affinity for "the land of potatoes and poverty" and for the rest of his life thought of himself as an Irish-American, a transplanted Son of Erin.

He made a point to contrast the Protestant counties of Ulster, from which his great-grandfather had emigrated, with Celtic Ireland :

> After a tour through the southern counties of Ireland, where desolation and want meet the view on every side, one feels, as he passes along the highly cultivated fields of the north, as if he were transported into another land, among a different race of people. Here there is comparatively no beggary or misery. . . . The question naturally suggests itself to the mind as to the causes. . . . Those that inhabit this [northern] section of Ireland are descended principally from the Scotch, and have inherited to a considerable degree their habits of industry and frugality. . . .[12]

McGavock also contrasted American institutions—particularly those of politics and government—with their counterparts abroad. He was so clearly pro-American that he often criticized those European governments which he considered degenerate or overbearing.

He did not approve of the extravagances of monarchy as exhibited by Queen Victoria's mews at Windsor Castle:

> The Queen has in all about three hundred horses, many of which are very superior. What sense can there be in having so many carriages and horses for the use of one little woman and her children, when one third of the number would answer every purpose? But in monarchies the whims and caprices of the sovereign must be indulged . . . at the expense of the *democracy,* the fruits of whose labors are applied to uphold the false dignity of the nation.[13]

He also commented after a noisy visit to the French National Assembly: "My opinion of the French is that they are totally unfit for a republic."[14] A few months later his views seemed justified when he

---

[10] *Ibid.*, p. 323.
[11] Randal W. McGavock, "Genealogical Notes on the McGavock Family to the Year 1853." McGavock Papers.
[12] *ATA,* p. 90.
[13] *Ibid.*, p. 54.
[14] *Journal,* July 18, 1851.

heard the news that the French Republic had fallen under the coup of Louis Napoleon.

Nor did McGavock fail to criticize the Italians who vexed him on more than one occasion with their mercenary tactics and whetted his distaste for the Latin temperament. When the party of Americans, including Henry Maney of Nashville, visited the Columbaria on the Appian Way, Randal's patience finally was exhausted. His friend Henry Maney wrote:

> We had a custode in our company here, who demanded on our parting a most exhorbitant fee for his trouble in showing us around. This we decided not to pay; but gave him, as we drove off, what we deemed a sufficient bonus for his services. With all the energy of Italian gesticulation, he insisted on a greater remuneration, and fretted himself into a towering rage, which was increased to fever heat by McG—'s performing that expressive gyration of the thumb from the tip of the nose at the scamp, as our carriage rattled away.[15]

One also sees McGavock in a lighter mood. At Narni, Maney reported, Randal "had in tow a good-natured Italian youth as a guide, and took great delight in making him dance and turn somersets—for which the promise of a few coppers was ample inducement."[16]

A serious incident, which might have become an international tempest but which ended merely as a diplomatic embarrassment, occurred during the latter part of December when the American party started up the Nile. A tribe of Arabs attempted to waylay the boat hired by the Americans, and hand-to-hand fighting took place on the banks of the river.[17]

The American Consul General at Alexandria, reporting to Daniel Webster, Secretary of State, described the incident as a "serious affray . . . between a party of six American travellers . . . and the native population":

> Mr. [Edwin H.] Ewing in endeavoring to menace [i.e. hold off] the Arabs (about 20 in number) with his gun, was seized by the latter, thrown down and disarmed; when they commenced beating him with their huge sticks (5 feet long & 1½ inches thick) his servant Frank Parish rushed in to save his master. His pistol having been struck from his hand & seized by an Arab, he was shot through the neck and about the same time, among other blows, he received a severe contusion on his head, from which his life was for several days placed in imminent danger.[18]

---

[15] Henry Maney, *Memories Over the Water* (Nashville: Toon, Nelson and Company, 1854), pp. 244-245.

[16] *Ibid.*, p. 203.

[17] Cf. *Journal*, December 24-31, 1851; *ATA*, pp. 218-219.

[18] D. S. McCauley, Report No. 32, January 15, 1852, in Dispatches from Egypt, Jan. 29, 1849-Nov. 17, 1853, State Department Papers. National Archives: Foreign Affairs Section.

The report went on to list the travelers by name and to give a specific account of damages:

Edwin H. Ewing of Tennessee—many severe contusions on the limbs and body.

Frank Parish, his servant, many contusions on the limbs and body and one particularly severe one on the head—shot through the neck.

Randal McGavock of Tennessee—many contusions on the limbs and body; his left hand nearly beat to a jelly in defending his head from the blows of the Arabs.

John Bridge of New York
Lewis Bridge do several contusions.[19]

The Consul General recommended the following procedures:

1st That a demand be made that the ringleaders . . . be . . . arrested for trial.

2nd That the gun and pistol carried off by the Arabs should be restored, otherwise their value taxed on the village and paid over to the travellers.

3rd That satisfactory evidence be given that the Nazeer of the village was not directly or indirectly concerned in exciting the aggressors and that he exerted his authority to quell the disturbance. . . .[20]

These terms seem to have been met, more or less, and the passengers continued on their way to the cataracts of the Nile.

The end of the incident, or at least the last reference to it, came some days later when the supposed marauders were rounded up by the authorities and given their punishment. McGavock and his party were making preparations to leave Egypt and visit the Holy Land when the American Vice-Consul, a native of Cairo, requested their presence at "the punishment and exile of nine poor creatures who participated in the battle on the Nile," McGavock wrote, ". . . but I had not the heart to witness the severity of the Egyptian bastinado, with the knowledge that it was inflicted partly on my own account."[21] So despite his first anger toward the Arabs and his denunciations of the Pasha's slip-shod courts of justice, McGavock finally left Egypt in a more compassionate frame of mind.

He also described another adventure occasioned by his lack of patience while crossing the desert. He and an American friend decided to race ahead of their dromedary caravan, thinking their companions would later overtake them:

We moved on charmingly and at a rapid pace for about two hours, when all of a sudden the bright orb of day became obscured, the whole heavens darkened, and the wind commenced blowing most furiously. It was evidently a *simoon,*

---

[19] *Ibid.*
[20] *Ibid.*
[21] *ATA*, p. 238.

and our only hope of escape was in Him who rules the storm and directs the whirlwind. The sand drifted in such quantities that our track soon became obliterated, and our eyes perfectly blinded. Thirst came upon us, and our only refuge from famishing was a small canteen filled with a mixture of brandy and water. Making our dromedaries kneel down close together, we ensconced ourselves behind them, and waited for the storm to subside. Five long hours, which appeared like so many days, passed away, and still we were alone in the desert waste, without guide, compass, or direction. At last the wind became more calm, the atmosphere clearer, and our hopes brighter. Mounting the camels once more, we pursued our course in the direction that we thought right; and while groping in darkness, we fortunately discovered in the dim distance the form of a man. That form I shall never forget. It was one of the Hadjis on the look-out for us, and without his exertions we would have had to pass the night alone in the broad desert. He informed us that the caravan was ahead, and with his guidance we overtook our friends just as they were pitching their tents. As soon as they discovered us, joy unspeakable burst from their lips; the ladies were particularly delighted, so much so, that they gave utterance to their emotions by a flood of joyful tears. They had given us up as lost, or murdered by the Bedouins. . . .[22]

Thus the spirited adventurer admitted that he had almost gone beyond the limits of a good frolic.

At Florence Henry Maney visited the Imperial Gallery and found McGavock "gazing on the Venus di Medici" in rapt admiration.[23] At the first distant view of Rome, which he beheld from the foothills of the north, McGavock himself wrote:

It is impossible to describe my emotions as we neared the city of so many historical recollections. I thought of its antiquity, its renown, its glory, and its present lowly state. Even my own brief history involuntarily passed before my mind's eye—the past fruitful in its recollections of pleasures and pains. Collegiate days glowing with Roman story, professional trials and juvenile troubles, all came up and suggested thoughts at once pleasing and painful.[24]

The same recollections, with a touch of humor, were called forth on the Plains of Marathon:

While gazing on this renowned spot, I was strongly reminded of my Greek Professor in the Nashville University, who endeavored to impress upon the class the dates of the two great battles of Marathon and Salamis. Every day the question was asked, and we invariably missed. At last we wrote them on the wall of the recitation room, where they can be seen, probably, to this day.[25]

His preparation for visiting Greece was broad, if not always profound. Certainly his reverence for the Holy Land is clearly stated in his dispatches from Palestine.[26]

---

[22] *Ibid.*, p. 246.
[23] Maney, *op. cit.*, pp. 188-189.
[24] *ATA*, p. 181.
[25] *Ibid.*, p. 323.
[26] Cf. *ATA*, pp. 237-282.

There was also a more recent literary influence—the poetry of Lord Byron. During his year and a half at Harvard, McGavock read Byron and reviewed the ancient world through the verse of Byron the poet-revolutionary. Byron was the writer who interpreted antiquity for him in modern terms. It was Byron's last line in the little poem "To Woman" that McGavock quoted—"Woman, thy vows are traced in sand"—when the Lemira Ewing affair was over. It was Byron's poem "Maid of Athens" that McGavock recalled when he conversed with the celebrated maid herself at a party at Piræus.[27]

Then at Athens McGavock saw, in a brief encounter, the girl who seemed to him the contemporary ideal of Grecian beauty:

> . . . we had the pleasure of meeting a number of American and English families, several old Greek Senators and their daughters, besides a number of strangers from different countries. Among the guests was the daughter of a Swedish Count, who married an Athenian woman. This young lady was just sweet sixteen, and without exception the most beautiful and fascinating creature that my eyes ever rested upon. Her form and features were Grecian, with the fair complexion and vivacity of the Swede. She spoke six languages with great fluency, and was just making her debut in society. I fell desperately in love *of course*—and what was a little strange, my friend Johnstone, of South Carolina, found himself in the same interesting situation . . . [he] seemed so in earnest in his attentions that I yielded the field to him, and passed most of the evening with the adopted daughter of Mr. Hill . . . who is not quite so beautiful in person, but in point of intellect and qualities of the heart, she has no superior. Hereafter, when I think of the classic city, the images of these two bright creatures, will come vividly before me, and I will long to be once more in Greece.[28]

Written with a pen dipped in the purple ink of romanticism, these lines reflect a young man's notion of love for the sake of love. When McGavock confessed "I fell desperately in love *of course,*" he was fooling no one in this matter, least of all himself. This Byronic convention he enjoyed to the fullest for the remainder of his youthful years.

Not only did McGavock keep a full diary while he travelled abroad, he also wrote seventy letters (varying in length from 1,500 to 4,000 words) which were dispatched to the *Daily Nashville Union* and printed upon arrival. Each report carried the signature *"Tennessean"* and the first such letter was published by the *Union* on June 3, 1851, about two months after McGavock and his party sailed from New York. The editors introduced the first offering under "Correspondence of the Union" with this headnote:

> The following letter is, as we conjecture, from the pen of one of the gentlemen of the party which left our State and city a few weeks since to proceed to

[27] *Ibid.*, p. 325.
[28] *Ibid.*, pp. 325-326.

England and the Continent. Our readers will perceive that it is numbered as the *third* letter of a series. Numbers *one* and *two* have not yet reached us. We trust that our correspondent will continue his interesting contributions to our columns.[29]

As the other dispatches were received, they too were printed, thus enabling Tennessee readers to enjoy the places of antiquity which McGavock visited and the vicarious acquaintance of personalities—who included Charles Dickens, the Duke of Wellington, the younger Johann Strauss, and other notables—with whom McGavock rubbed elbows in his travels. For the first time in the history of Tennessee, newspaper readers were able to look at the fashionable, cosmopolitan world through the eyes of a native son. For at age twenty-five McGavock was Tennessee's first foreign correspondent.[30]

The method he used in writing the dispatches for the *Union* was fairly straightforward. He kept the journal in daily installments, only occasionally getting behind and having to catch up a week's writing. Then as he found time for an afternoon or evening of leisure, or could stall off the more exciting diversions of travel, he referred to the journal to refresh his memory. From these notes he wrote the letters which he sent to the newspaper, sometimes expanding, sometimes omitting negligible details, and sometimes quoting from *Murray's Handbook,* or whatever tourist guide he carried at the time.[31]

Often the letters and the journal offer interesting points for comparison. The letters are frequently adorned with "polite" prose and circumlocutions that never appear in the quickly written, economical journal. When writing consciously for an audience and aware that he would have readers at home, Randal was usually guarded. Therefore, the journal is the more intimate of the two accounts. It is also, as is to be expected, the more autobiographical. For example, McGavock did not write an account for the newspaper of his visit with President and Mrs. Fillmore when he stopped in Washington en route to Europe.[32] He undoubtedly considered his dinner at the White House a private affair—not the kind of occasion one reports to the public. So were it not for the journal his description of sitting down to a "table of repub-

[29] *Daily Nashville Union,* June 3, 1851, p. 2.

[30] I base this assertion on the fact that McGavock's letters from abroad were published while the author was en route. Coming a close second was Henry Maney, who wrote articles on Europe for the Nashville papers *after* his return, but who published *Memories Over the Water* in 1854, a few months before McGavock's *A Tennessean Abroad* appeared.

[31] McGavock used several volumes of *Murray's Handbook* as guides during his travels. The quotations, appropriately designated, on pages 138-139 in *A Tennessean Abroad* are from *Murray's Handbook for Belgium and the Rhine* (London: John Murray, 1850), pp. 129, 131.

[32] *Journal,* April 2, 1851.

Courtesy Margaret Lindsley Warden

Randal W. McGavock in Alpine walking suit, Geneva, 1851. The leather-bound European Journal is in his right pocket.

Courtesy Mrs. Theresa McGavock Smiser

Edward Jacob McGavock
(1828-1880)

Courtesy Mrs. Henry Dickinson

Ann McGavock Dickinson
(1820-1868)

Courtesy Margaret Lindsley Warden

Sarah McGavock Lindsley
(1830-1903)

Courtesy Mrs. Spence McGavock

Felix Grundy McGavock
(1832-1897)

Courtesy Margaret Lindsley Warden

Mary McGavock Todd
(1838-1908)

Courtesy Margaret Lindsley Warden

Hugh Albert McGavock
(1842-1854)

lican simplicity" bearing "just such a dinner as I would expect at a respectable friend's house at home" would not be available today.

With the exception of a handful of letters written during the next decade to Nashville newspapers, usually of a political nature, and the municipal report which he published upon leaving the office of mayor in 1859, McGavock's only formal writing is represented by his dispatches to the *Union,* which in 1854 were published in book form as *A Tennessean Abroad.* All the rest of his extant prose is contained in the journals.[33]

It is difficult to judge what distinctions he might have achieved in his more mature years if he had continued to write for an audience and if he had disciplined his energies to serious writing. Certainly he was a better prose stylist than his friend Henry Maney, whose *Memories Over the Water* abounds in Victorian circumlocutions and sentimentality. In this passage, which undoubtedly had appeal for many contemporary readers, Maney tells of the mood he experienced as his ship was about to sail for Europe:

> It were hard to describe the contending emotions that now swelled the heart, as we trod the deck of a noble vessel, bound direct for foreign shores. . . . The good ship "Asia" was crowded with passengers, and a great number had come to witness the departure of relatives and friends, while many a thoughtful, anxious face, and many a moistened eye, told how the floodgates of the heart were unlocked, and its deep fountains stirred at the thought that they were parting, and perhaps forever. But for us no eye was dimmed, no loved voice trembled in the fond farewell! for we were alone, without a friend, an acquaintance, or one familiar face, with whom we could claim an adieu.[34]

Perhaps Maney's youthfulness—the writer was only twenty-two when *Memories Over the Water* was published—can be offered as an excuse for his sentimentality; on the other hand, Maney was characteristically given to subjective fancies that McGavock usually subdued when writing for publication.

However, both men were like many of their contemporaries in the South during the next decade when writers turned to oratory and political defense. Maney became a newspaper editor and devoted his energies to politics and political writing until his death in 1858.[35] McGavock entertained the same ambitions and almost bought the Nashville *Daily News* on October 14, 1859. He also began negotiations with the owners

---

[33] The complete journals amount to about 1,500 pages in the original MSS.

[34] Maney, *op. cit.*, p. 27.

[35] Maney was editor of the *Nashville Gazette* from 1854 to 1856; then he was elected to the Tennessee Legislature.

of the *Union and American* on June 1, 1860, with the idea of buying an interest in their paper.[36]

Like other young Southerners with his same background and social position, McGavock became an orator, statesman, and soldier instead of a professional writer. For a man of action there is no time for imaginative flights of fancy or sustained writing when the world in which he lives is threatened. Like his contemporaries, McGavock saw the practical need to defend his political concepts and his institutions at home; therefore he is a case in point of the turn Southern Letters took during the two decades preceding the Civil War. The heat of politics superseded the quieter fervor of the creative spirit.

In 1852, his European travels at an end, McGavock wrote the concluding letter of the series and made a firm avowal of his belief in the preservation of American democracy:

> With such a country, and so much to make one happy, how can any sensible American ever wish to abandon it? Let those who speak of disunion, who have sectional prejudices, or who are blindly led by party rule, make the tour of the Old World, and if I am not greatly mistaken they will return home with national ideas, national love, and national fidelity.[37]

To him *disunion* and *secession* were words he had heard from the Massachusetts Abolitionists when he was a student at Harvard. They did not reflect the political beliefs of the Union-minded young man who returned to Nashville just in time to vote for General Franklin Pierce in the presidential election of November, 1852.

Perhaps his homecoming could not have been better timed; his family and friends welcomed him again after twenty months away and his Democratic friends were anxious to hear about his interview in New Hampshire with General Pierce. On the evening of his arrival in Nashville he joined the torchlight procession and "responded to the call" for a speech in behalf of the Democratic candidates. Two days later, with victory assured and the unity of the nation temporarily secure, there was another procession which called for McGavock at his father's house and again asked him for a speech.

"I responded to their call," he wrote later, "in a few brief and appropriate remarks."[38] The young man of the world had come home again, had rolled up his sleeves, and was ready to take his stand in the political arena of Jackson, Grundy, and Polk.

---

[36] Cf. *Journal* for these dates.
[37] *ATA,* p. 398.
[38] *Journal,* "Resume of Activities, 1851-1854."

CHAPTER VI

Matrimony, the Mayorship, and Party Politics

Once the election excitement was over, Randal McGavock, traveller and correspondent, was feted by his Nashville cousins and the social leaders of the city. He was invited to sumptuous dinners and asked to speak to the guest company about his experiences in Europe and Asia. Toasted and lionized, he was the city's most eligible bachelor and enjoyed a social position second to none.

Yet those months in other parts of the world had not settled his restlessness or halted his long strides. Nor had they completely put at ease the remembrance of love unrequited. In April, 1851, about the time he was sailing for Europe, Fanny Jane Crutcher was married to Dr. David W. Yandell. When McGavock returned in November of 1852, he read, not without a tinge of bitterness, this daily advertisement in the *Union:*

> Dr. David W. Yandell, offers his professional services to the citizens of Davidson County.—Residence on Gallatin Turnpike, four miles and a half from Nashville, at the place formerly owned by the late Josiah Williams, Esq.[1]

And although he wore a beard now, clipped close and snugly following the contour of his chin,[2] and though his family and friends made many comments on the changes that had taken place in his person and manners since he left Nashville,[3] he knew himself that he was little changed.

The journal itself bears witness:

> In the latter part of Feb. 1853 I concluded that I would like to return once more to Europe, and accordingly made up my mind to apply to President Pierce for the Secretaryship to the Legation at Paris, London, or Madrid.[4]

All members of the Tennessee delegation except one wrote flattering letters commending him to the President. William Cullen, a Whig, "refused to recommend any man to Franklin Pierce," a Democrat.[5]

---

[1] *Nashville Union,* November 3, 1852.
[2] McGavock grew a beard during his travels and wore it for the remainder of his life.
[3] *Journal,* "Resume of Activities, 1851-1854."
[4] *Ibid.*
[5] *Ibid.*

Randal's friend Mrs. James K. Polk wrote a formal note in a small, spidery hand on white bond edged in black:

Mrs. Polk takes pleasure in presenting to the *consideration* of President Pierce, *her friend,* Mr. R. W. McGavock, of Nashville, Tennessee.

Mr. McGavock is a highly educated gentleman, has spent much time traveling in Europe, & is the Grand Son of the late Hon. Felix Grundy.

Will the President be pleased to accept Mrs. P.'s assurances of respect.—
Polk Place
Nashville, Tenn.
Feb. 19, 1853.[6]

The other letters speak of McGavock as "a gentleman of finished education" with a "social position not inferior to that of any man in the State," and as a young man who would be a "useful and popular representative abroad" and whose appointment "would be extremely gratifying to the democracy in Tennessee."[7]

Randal went hopefully to Washington for interviews with Pierce and members of his cabinet. After three weeks at the capital he was offered a post in Central America by William L. Marcy, the Secretary of State. This he refused, and held out for Europe.[8] He came back to Nashville to wait, still hopeful. "Time rolled on," he wrote later, "and I never heard a word more about the matter. Office seeking I regard as utterly disreputable to a gentleman and this experiment has taught me a lesson that I will not soon forget. Hereafter offices may seek me, I will never seek them."[9] Instead he started negotiations with publishing houses for *A Tennessean Abroad* and remained in Nashville not at all pleased with his unsuccessful mission to Washington.[10]

On August 10, 1853, he reached his twenty-seventh birthday and the event must have given him pause, for he was approaching what his contemporaries considered old bachelorhood. In mid-August he went down to Catoosa Springs, a fashionable watering place in northern Georgia, and enjoyed a ten-day visit in the company of several eligible young ladies who frequented the springs. "While there I appeared at a Grand Fancy Ball as the Sublime Porte. My costume was the finest in the room and attracted most attention. I brought it from Constantinople," he wrote in the journal. "Here I met a beautiful black eyed girl

---

[6] Her letter is quoted in full and is without salutation or signature. "File on Randal W. McGavock," National Archives: Foreign Affairs Section. (Hereinafter cited as "File.")

[7] *Ibid.*

[8] *Journal,* "Resume . . . 1851-1854."

[9] *Ibid.*

[10] *Ibid.*

from Macon named Ophelia Nisbet, daughter of Judge Nisbet. With this lady I had quite a flirtation."[11]

There were other young ladies with whom he flirted or who struck his fancy to such a degree that he thought seriously of marriage. He was charmed by his cousin Annie Grundy of Kentucky and made excuses to visit her; in Washington he "passed many happy hours" with Sallie Faulkner of Virginia, daughter of Congressman Charles J. Faulkner; at home he courted Lizzie Bonner of Fayetteville and Lydia Smith of Nashville.

In the spring of 1853, shortly after his disappointing trip to Washington, he met for the first time Miss Seraphine Deery,[12] the eighteen-year-old daughter of Mrs. William Deery and the late Mr. Deery of Sullivan County. The meeting very probably took place in Nashville, for Mrs. Deery and Seraphine (after having moved from East Tennessee to Williamson County a few years earlier) frequently came to Nashville on the train, often remaining at the City Hotel or the Saint Cloud for performances of music and theatre.[13] Nashville was attractive to them because it offered Seraphine an opportunity to enjoy the social life which a city could provide. Here she could meet the daughters of Nashville's gentry and the young men of Davidson County. She could also attend the Jackson Day Balls and look for a husband. Randal first refers to Miss Deery in his journal as "a very beautiful and interesting lady . . . whom I found a congenial spirit and with whom I have passed many happy days."[14] Nevertheless, his earliest attraction to her was hardly a case of overpowering infatuation.

The Deery family had risen rather spectacularly in the world since William, Seraphine's father, had emigrated to America from County Derry, North Ireland. From Baltimore William Deery hauled goods and small manufactured articles to the villages and settlements in East Tennessee and eventually settled in Sullivan County at the suggestion of Walter James, an early resident there who took the young Irishman under his wing.[15]

---

[11] *Ibid.*

[12] *Ibid.* The name was pronounced Ser-a-phi-na—four syllables. Born in Sullivan County in 1835, she died 83 years later in Nashville.

[13] Jane H. Thomas, *Old Days in Nashville, Tenn.* (Nashville, 1897), p. 98. Herself a boarder at the St. Cloud from 1851 to 1854, Jane Thomas remembered the Deerys but misspelled the name: ". . . Mrs. Dairy and her daughter . . . boarded there while I was there."

[14] *Journal,* "Resume . . . 1851-1854."

[15] *History of Tennessee . . . Together with an Historical and Biographical Sketch of from Twenty-five to Thirty Counties of East Tennessee* (Chicago and Nashville: Goodspeed Publishing Co., 1887), p. 915. (Hereinafter cited as Goodspeed.)

After a few years of close bargaining and hard work, William Deery became a leading citizen of Blountville, a successful and wealthy merchant, and a large landowner. He was married to Elizabeth Allison and they had three sons and two daughters. The sons first went into business in Knoxville and moved, about 1850, to Williamson County to build a textile mill which manufactured cotton goods and heavy cloth bags. The site of the mill and the surrounding property was named Allisona in honor of their mother's forebears, particularly Robert Allison, their grandfather, who fought in the Continental Army.[16] James and William Deery, the brothers of Seraphine, also owned the steamboat "Cassandra," the only craft of its kind ever to enter Sullivan County.[17]

As Seraphine reached womanhood, Shelbyville was the only nearby town; Allisona was barely a village. Soon Seraphine outgrew them both and went frequently to Nashville, where she bought new clothes and attended many of the gala balls. At age eighteen she was five feet two inches tall and had light brown hair with gold tints. Her blue eyes might have been colored for a china doll. She was little and graceful, and her dresses were bright-colored.

As she and her mother walked across the street from the St. Cloud Hotel to the First Presbyterian Church on Sundays, Seraphine attracted the gazes of the young men in the congregation, and she was aware that the Nashville boys talked about her beauty. As she sat down she was always careful to fuss with the ruffles on her wide hoop skirt and to keep flouncing the petticoats into place long after Mrs. Deery had settled heavily into the pew.

For Seraphine had a charming way of always seeming in distress, both in and out of church, and of running a series of little crises from one day to the next. She felt more at home in the public parlors of the St. Cloud or the City Hotel than she did anywhere else, for here she could entertain without having the responsibility of her own house, and she was never lonely here as she was in the country. In all she was a winsome girl who enjoyed the adulation of the young men who called at the hotel in their fathers' carriages to drive her out to visit the Weavers at "Kingsley" or the Acklens at "Belmont" or the Hardings at "Belle Meade." When she took the train to Allisona in the spring of 1853 to spend the summer once again in the country, she was noticeably unhappy. Her bright eyes fretted tearfully when she said goodbye to Randal McGavock, and she asked him to come to Allisona to see her brothers' mill.

---

16 Through this forebear, also spelled Alison, Seraphine was admitted to membership in the D. A. R. in 1906.

17 Goodspeed, p. 915.

To Randal, towering head and shoulders above this petite girl, Seraphine seemed dainty and defenseless. In his journal that summer he wrote: "From Catoosa I returned to Nashville, stopping at Look Out Mountain, Allisonia (the home of Miss Deery) and War-trace."[18]

He made other visits to Allisona during the next two years, and he saw Seraphine at concerts and public entertainments in Nashville. But, as his journals verify, he had many girls. Seraphine was one name among several. Then in 1854 he became engaged to Miss Lizzie Bonner of Fayetteville.[19] This arrangement was apparently quite informal; there were no definite plans made between the two parties because at twenty-eight Randal was at an age to consider consequences.

On the other hand he was growing tired of some of the drawbacks that bachelorhood imposed, of being "on the carpet" too long, as the old folks said, of hearing jokes faintly behind his back. In January of 1855 he decided definitely to marry Miss Lizzie Bonner. She was an engaging young woman—always mild and genteel in manner, a charming hostess when he visited Fayetteville, and always a good listener. Her father was a wealthy man and a leading citizen in the community. She would make a good wife for an aspiring young politician. But he also found Miss Lydia Smith of Nashville a delightful girl, even though Mrs. Smith had asked him not to flirt with her daughter and he had promised solemnly to comply with her wishes.[20]

So his resolves toward Miss Bonner did not stand firm very long, and on January 10 he had a note from Miss Deery asking him to come to see her.[21] After this, there was an understanding between Randal and Seraphine which the journals do not make clear.

But on February 8 he wrote in his journal: "Received a letter this morning from Miss Bonner which is without exception one of the most beautiful and touching love epistles I ever read." Now a decision was more difficult for Randal than ever. So the rest of that day was spent "reflecting over the strange situation that I now occupy toward several young ladies."

In April Seraphine was back in Nashville again, chaperoned by her sister Martha Eleanor, the wife of William Churchwell of Knoxville, and Randal was not sure that he was pleased. He went around to the hotel, however. "Called on Miss Deery this morning and while there Miss Lytton came in and I drove off with her. Attended the Criminal

[18] *Journal,* "Resume . . . 1851-1854."
[19] The exact date is not given in the journals.
[20] *Journal,* April 2, 1855.
[21] *Ibid.,* January 10, 1855.

Court. Accompanied Miss Deery [in the evening] to the Theatre after which we returned to the Hotel where I witnessed an oft repeated scene with her."[22] During that spring there were other tense moments between the two lovers, for Randal was the kind of over-grown boy who liked to tease his girls and see tears welling in their eyes before he soothed and petted. Seraphine was jealous because she knew about his other flirtations, and she was also bored when he talked about the law courts, or his travels in Europe, or the approaching political campaigns.

On these occasions she had a way of patting her foot beneath the long skirts of her red taffeta dress. She tried hard to listen when Randal spoke of politics and political strategy, but over and over she traced the azure ribbons that tied love-knots in the parlor wallpaper and fixed her blue eyes on the tints of gold in the yellow paper butterflies that seemed to dart back and forth between the lace curtains.

Yet at age twenty this diminutive "Seraph," a wisp of a girl with slender waist and tiny feet, could not only call forth the protective instincts in her beaux but could make them feel happily accomplished when they took her to an evening party. Tennessee boys, reluctant as they often were to attend social affairs, always made a better thing of it when Seraphine was there to respond to the usual small talk. When their other girls stumbled through awkward pauses, Seraphine glided smoothly along. She was glib and companionable with the ladies, sedately flirtatious with the old men, who looked for yet another wink from her china-blue eyes, and in all she glittered as pleasantly as any girl they knew.

Randal McGavock liked these accomplishments in a young lady and he admired beauty. Moreover, he felt sure that Seraphine was in love with him. Or why did she pout so often and so prettily at the smallest misunderstanding between them? Yes, that was it. She was in love with him. He remembered the way they had parted and were reconciled on that blustering, hot-and-cold day in March:

> Called to see Miss Deery this morning and had a long conversation about our affair. She looked blue and little disposed to credit me. . . . At 11 o'clock [in the evening] I walked down to the depot and found Miss Deery in the waiting room. I went into the cars with her and just as I was leaving she said she would not go and I returned with her to the hotel.[23]

He remembered how finally she had forgiven him, and how small and demure she had looked that evening against the massive angels on the hotel staircase.

---

[22] *Ibid.*, April 3, 1855.
[23] *Ibid.*, March 17, 1855.

In the summer of 1855 as he approached his twenty-ninth birthday, Randal was struck with the notion that he must choose a wife and start a family before he grew any older. His younger brother Grundy had been married early in January of that year to Manoah Bostick; the family looked with interest to the time when Randal would make his own selection from the young ladies whose names had been linked with his since the end of the Crutcher affair. His decision, sudden and precipitous, came in August when he proposed to Seraphine Deery. On the twenty-third of that month, less than two weeks after his twenty-ninth birthday, they were married at the Deery home in Allisona, from whence they departed at once for a wedding trip to the East.

For those who knew them both the news was received with incredulity. Randal's friends were thunderstruck at his sudden decision and frankly doubtful of his choice. Then as the year closed, with the honeymoon over and the wedding calls all made, Randal himself took cognizance. "I cannot as yet see what is to be the result of my actions this year—they are in the womb of the future." So at this period in his life, as the journal verifies, he went wholeheartedly into politics with all vigor and might. He strove now, for the first time, to achieve success in some quarter of human affairs.

He made up his mind to fill speaking engagements in behalf of the Democratic ticket in the villages and small towns that surrounded Nashville. He decided to show his serious intentions to the older members of the party before trying to win party nominations. At political rallies he gained a round of cheers in Stewart, Cheatham, and Montgomery Counties during July and August, 1856.

He also filled speaking dates at crossroad stops in Davidson County against his Harvard classmate, Michael Vaughn, a talented young orator who stood firmly in the Whig ranks. The canvass that summer took him to Yellow Creek, Dog Creek, Goodlettsville, Harris' Springs, and Dover. He rode on horseback over rough roads and found his way from one community to the next in Stewart County by following the notches cut on trees to guide the unfamiliar traveller.[24]

He was elated when the Democrats won the state elections and James Buchanan was elected president. ". . . we carried the State by a large majority which compensated me amply for my humble labors in the canvass."[25] He believed Buchanan would be able to put in check the forces that were creating dissension in the country. "His election caused

[24] *Ibid.*, July 31, 1856.

[25] *Ibid.*, "Summary," September 7, 1856.

every patriot in the land to rejoice, because they believe it saved the Union from the wreck of sectional agitation."[26]

McGavock also saw in the triumph of the Democrats another opportunity to apply for a foreign post. So he put aside his old resolve to let public offices "seek me" and went to Washington to petition President Buchanan for an appointment to a European court. His credentials were now clearly impressive, for he had travelled abroad and published a book on Europe and the Near East; he had the support of the Tennessee Delegation in Congress and a testimonial signed by the Democratic State Central Committee of Tennessee.[27] In addition, he could point to the fact that he was a member of the Democratic National Committee.[28]

The letters recommending him speak of his efforts in "battling against Know Nothingism"; they commend him as the young man who exposed "the great fraud attempted to be perpetrated in the garbled publication of Gen. Jackson's letter to Maj. Lewis, and who brought out . . . the true sentiments of the old hero, as expressed in that letter."[29] In all, there was a more solid basis for the appointment than there had been four years earlier. But again he came home to wait, and again he was disappointed. The fierce scramble in Washington, during which other less well qualified men received their spoils, passed him by without a nod. So once again he turned to local affairs.

He began to study the Tennessee statutes and started work on revising them.[30] He spoke at the celebration that the Swiss immigrants of Tennessee held on the Fourth of July and reviewed for his foreign-born friends the principles of American democracy.[31] He was invariably popular with immigrants, particularly the Irish, who rallied to his speeches and christened him a Son of Erin. As an unofficial representative of the Irish laborers who had flocked to Nashville in the '40's and '50's, he helped with their citizenship papers and urged them to exercise their franchise. Soon they learned that when the occasion demanded Randal McGavock, Esquire, knew well enough how to pass the flagon and swap the blarney.

This stood him in good stead in September of 1858 when he decided to run for the mayorship of Nashville. In the course of a week he marshalled his forces, managed his own campaign, and strode ahead to

---

[26] *Ibid.*, March 4, 1857.

[27] "File."

[28] He represented Tennessee at the meetings held at the Burnet House, Cincinnati, June 6-11, 1856. Printed circular, dated June 12, 1856, in McGavock Papers.

[29] "File."

[30] *Journal*, April 30, 1857.

[31] This address, the only complete text of a McGavock speech the editor has been able to find, was reprinted in *Nashville Daily Gazette*, July 10, 1857.

victory. His own account of these few days of heated activity is recorded in the journal.[32]

At one rally during the campaign McGavock was being introduced by a particularly long-winded supporter who elaborated at tiresome lengths on Randal's qualifications and achievements. In overblown oratory the speaker reviewed the advantages of ancestry and travels abroad. "And when this candidate as a youth visited the sunny shores of Italy, so perfect were his features and so commanding his physical endowments that he was followed in the streets. Struck by his fine pair of grey eyes and his titian beard, awed by his kind, benevolent features, the citizens of Italy began to chant in his wake, 'Il Cristo, Il Cristo.' Yes, ladies and gentlemen, they were so struck by your candidate that they called him the Christ. . . ."

At this point the speaker was interrupted by a raucous voice at the rear of the audience. A drunken supporter of the opposition struggled to his feet and roared out in the direction of the platform: "If this man be the Christ, let him be crucified on election day."[33]

Quickly the speaker was silenced and the heresy stalled. Nor was McGavock "crucified" on election day; he polled 93 votes more than his nearest opponent and took the oath as Mayor on October 1, 1858, a few weeks after his thirty-second birthday. The Nashville citizenry looked on in approbation and the German Band serenaded the mayor and his wife at their home on Cherry Street, where they lived in the big house with Randal's mother and father. Later the press commented on the widespread indications of progress:

> Thirty-four years ago [1824] Randal McGavock was Mayor of Nashville—a village containing about 4,500 persons, without even a turnpike approaching it. Now, his grand nephew, Randal W. McGavock, is Mayor of Nashville—a city with 30,000 inhabitants, approached at three points by railroads, and with several others in contemplation. What Nashville may be thirty-four years hence, none of us can realize, in our highest anticipation of progress.[34]

And like his father and uncles, the new mayor was an intrepid citizen and a good town booster. Moreover, he added a becoming dignity to the mayor's social and official duties.

In 1858 Nashville was governed by one board of eight aldermen and another of sixteen councilmen; the mayor sent the two bodies recommendations and presided over their joint meetings. By his election McGavock was the official head of the city, but he had no power to

---

[32] *Journal,* September 17-25, 1858.

[33] For this anecdote I am indebted to General Jacob McGavock Dickinson, Jr., a great nephew of Randal McGavock.

[34] *Nashville Daily News,* December 12, 1858.

make contracts in the name of the municipal government. This authority resided with the chairmen of the various committees. For years the office of mayor had been considered a part-time affair, leaving the incumbent time for other pursuits. McGavock himself practiced law during his term of office, but he saw that the mayor's duties were growing heavier and more time-consuming and that the small salary should be increased to compensate for the amount of work required.[35]

During his tenure in office he filled the journal with notes on daily affairs: street improvements, the building of Howard Public School, railroad development meetings, church services at the new workhouse, planning the Maxwell House Hotel, and providing for the poor and needy. He took a compassionate interest in the unfortunates at the city workhouse and tried as best he could, and as far as funds would allow, to improve their miserable living conditions:

> At the beginning of the present municipal year the Work House was an institution not at all creditable to the city. The prisoners of the city, amounting sometimes to forty or fifty, were crowded, without respect to sex or color, into two small rooms badly ventilated. During the present year [under McGavock's administration] an establishment has been erected, equal, if not superior, in all its appointments, to any similar institution in the country. The sexes are now kept in different apartments, and ample provision made to protect all the inmates during inclement weather while at their work. Every Sabbath afternoon divine service is held in the prison by preachers of the different denominations, and its effects have proved beneficial.[36]

McGavock occasionally suffered the drawback of being an easy mark for the professional imposters and gentlemen beggars or the loose women who arrived in Nashville looking for a handout from public funds.

His reputation for benevolence made some days particularly annoying:

> Occupied most of the day in Corporation affairs. An Irish woman from Me. called at my office with a boy of six years old who could not speak or walk. She wanted him provided for, stating that she was unable to do so. A young man who called with a bone fellon on his thumb . . . wanted me to send him to Cincinnati.[37]

Yet he heard the complaints with sympathy, and administered to the deserving as charitably as he knew how.

In a variety of ways Randal McGavock was a popular representative of the people. He raised funds for the Mechanics Association of Nash-

---

[35] Randal W. McGavock, *Communications from . . . the . . . Mayor R. W. McGavock* (Nashville, 1859), p. 19.

[36] *Ibid.*, p. 10.

[37] *Journal*, April 27, 1859.

ville by lecturing on "Walks About Jerusalem" when he returned from abroad.[38] He was the founder and first president of the Robertson Association, a group of twenty gentlemen who helped the poor and distressed during times of drouth, flood, and epidemic before Nashville had any organized charity.[39] He also became a member and supporter of the Historical Society of Tennessee, to which he presented Felix Grundy's portrait at the public ceremonies held in the capitol building on May 2, 1859.[40] He held office in Phoenix Lodge, Number 131, Free and Accepted Masons, and participated in the rowdy ceremonies of the A. O. M. C., an order requiring membership in Freemasonry as a prerequisite for initiation. The A. O. M. C. members indulged in masculine antics and horseplay, from time to time, and they paraded in the streets bedecked in cowls and mystical robes during colorful torchlight processions.[41]

In 1859 the Chatham Artillery of Savannah, Georgia, visited Nashville as guests of the City of Nashville and were entertained by Mayor and Mrs. McGavock. The round of festivities—including an official banquet, a trip to the Hermitage on two steamers lashed together, the illumination of the capitol building, and numerous fired salutes—caused McGavock to conclude that the visit marked "a succession of the most pleasant entertainments that we have ever had here in Nashville."[42] In appreciation of the hospitality, the corps of Georgians remembered the young mayor with a handsome silver pitcher[43] inscribed:

1786
The Chatham Artillery
of
Savannah
to
R. W. McGavock
Mayor of the City of Nashville
June 1859

[38] A handbill (among the McGavock Papers) announced the lecture for October 18, 1854.

[39] *Journal,* February 15, 1856.

[40] *Ibid.,* May 2, 1859.

[41] A. O. M. C. probably stood for "Ancient Order of the Mystic Cowl," but this identification is not certain. Cf. notice in the *Nashville Gazette,* October 2, 1859; *Journal,* October 3, 1859.

[42] *Journal,* June 16-18, 1859.

[43] Now owned by Margaret Lindsley Warden, Nashville.

At the end of his tenure McGavock wrote and published a detailed report of twenty-four pages that set forth the state and condition of the city of Nashville on October 1, 1859. He divided the affairs of the corporation into the following departments: Finances, Engineer's Department, Water Works, Work House, Police, Fire Department, Market Places, Hospitals, City Property, Poor of the City, Free Negro Population, and Sanitary Department. He accompanied his communication with reports from the Recorder's and Treasurer's offices and gave an itemized statement of the municipal debt.[44] In its way this well-organized report was a landmark in the history of Nashville, for no other mayor had exerted this much effort to inform the citizens about municipal affairs.

In July of 1859, three months before his term was to be completed, a letter signed by "P." appeared in the *Gazette* and exhorted the citizens of Nashville to re-elect Randal McGavock for a second year—if he would run. The correspondent went on to say that in his judgment "there has never been one more anxious and thoughtful for the welfare and improvement of the city than Mr. McGavock."[45]

Randal considered the call to run again, but decided against it finally on September 14:

> Today there was another call upon me to run again for Mayor, and numerous persons of the opposition party have solicited me to run, but after weighing the whole matter deliberately, I resolved not to become a candidate.[46]

Neither publicly nor in his journals did he ever make clear the reasons for his decision. Perhaps he wanted to devote more of his energy to national politics, for certainly this is what he did during the two years between his term as mayor and the outbreak of the Civil War. He saw clearly the forces that openly threatened disunion in 1859, and he began to gird himself for the political struggles ahead.

As the new candidates for mayor started their rounds of speeches, Randal, like a public-minded citizen went to hear them. "While Hollingsworth was speaking," he wrote in the journal, "a man on the opposite side of the street called for me and said that I had made the best Mayor Nashville ever had, and he intended voting for me anyhow."[47] So that night he went home renewed in spirit, heartened by the shouts of "the democracy" ringing in his ears.

---

[44] Randal W. McGavock, *op. cit.,* pp. 21-24.

[45] *Nashville Gazette,* July 1, 1859.

[46] *Journal,* September 14, 1859.

[47] *Ibid.,* September 16, 1859.

Yet personal crises during these same years contrasted sharply with the interludes of public acclaim. With his marriage in 1855 McGavock had acquired responsibilities that could not be set aside. He was to learn, with some vexation, that marriage brought a number of restrictions. His remarks on New Year's Day, 1856, reveal his reflections on the changes:

> On last new years day I was a single man and occupied the day in visiting my friends but today I drank wine only at three places—so much for getting married.[48]

One of the worries he experienced during these months was the settlement of his wife's share in the estate left by William Deery, Seraphine's father. When the mill at Allisona burned in the fall of 1856, the Deery brothers suffered a loss of several thousand dollars, for the mill was not fully covered by insurance. Seraphine's inheritance from her father had been invested in the business, which was now totally destroyed. After seeing the ruins, McGavock wrote: "Such is life—today we are in abundance—tomorrow in poverty."[49]

Seraphine petitioned her brothers, as trustees of her share in the estate, to turn the remainder of her holdings over to her husband. They apparently refused to do so, and McGavock enjoined them, on December 3, 1856, from making any disposition of the property. Complicating the settlement were the claims of Seraphine's sister, Martha Eleanor, whose husband, William Montgomery Churchwell of Knoxville, acted as trustee for his wife. Another hindrance to settlement was the illness of James A. Deery, Seraphine's brother, who could not properly attend to business for several weeks before his death on January 17, 1857.[50]

There was considerable bitterness on three sides, and McGavock was plagued by what he called "Deery rascality."[51] William M. Churchwell's own fortune was wrecked in December, 1856, when the Bank of East Tennessee failed and creditors sued for settlement; so Churchwell in turn sued McGavock for the amount of $10,000, which Churchwell alleged McGavock had drawn from the insurance company for the benefit of the Deery brothers after the fire.[52] Further accusations passed between the several parties and the courts finally ordered a sale of Deery properties and real estate in Allisona, Winchester, Blountville, and Bristol.

These proceedings were time-consuming and expensive at the same time that they were disagreeable. McGavock travelled to East Tennessee,

---

48 *Journal*, January 1, 1856.
49 *Ibid.*, "Summary," September 7, 1856.
50 *Ibid.*, January 14-20, 1857; *Nashville Union*, January 24, 1857.
51 *Journal*, November 5, 1857.
52 *Ibid.*, October 29, 1857.

hired counsel, and spent several weeks trying to protect his wife's inheritance. Finally he bought an interest in the Deery farm on Beaver Creek, near Bristol, at the public sale on September 17, 1857, and owned it jointly thereafter with W. H. Gordon. The year was filled with vexations and strained family finances; Seraphine behaved badly on occasion and grew hysterical in the midst of the court hearings. The McGavocks and the Churchwells continued to disagree and were not able to reach an amicable settlement during several months of litigation.

Moreover, McGavock and William M. Churchwell were sharply contrasting personalities. The husbands of sisters, both were born in 1826 and were lawyers with political ambitions. Churchwell had risen rapidly in East Tennessee politics in 1851 when he was elected Congressman from the Third District at the age of twenty-five.[53] Two years later, after the reapportionment of the congressional districts, he was elected Representative from the Second District by a considerable majority. At the same time he was a large stockholder in the East Tennessee and Virginia Railroad Company. When he declined in 1854 to run for a third term in Congress, he was elected president of the Knoxville and Kentucky Railroad.[54] In November of that same year, with his rather remarkable talents for financial maneuvering, he became president of the Bank of East Tennessee.[55]

Many of the transactions in which Churchwell was involved seemed sound to his investors at the time; in fact his success as a young man was extraordinary. But by the time he reached his thirtieth birthday, he had extended his resources too far and his finances began to tumble.[56] By 1857 he was a spectacular failure, all but bankrupt, and looked upon with mounting suspicion by his fellow Tennesseans.

Churchwell is also believed to have squandered considerable amounts of money on Miriam Florence Follin of New York, the actress who later became Mrs. Frank Leslie. He is supposed to have bought Miss Follin a house on Seventh Street in New York City for $9,000 and to have been engaged with her in a tempestuous love affair.[57] If McGavock had any notion of these illicit arrangements he failed to make direct reference to them in the journals. He may have been suspicious, however, after making the entry on March 25, 1857, when he was trying to locate Churchwell in New York:

---

[53] *Biographical Dictionary of the American Congress,* p. 976.

[54] Ruth Osborne Turner, "The Public Career of William Montgomery Churchwell," Master's Thesis, University of Tennessee, Knoxville, 1954, p. 41.

[55] *Ibid.,* p. 48.

[56] *Journal,* December 17, 1856.

[57] Madeleine B. Stern, *Purple Passage: The Life of Mrs. Frank Leslie* (Norman: University of Oklahoma Press, 1953), pp. 23-24, 212.

I went to all the principal hotels this morning to see if I could find Churchwell. He has either left the city, or [is] stopping at some private home.

About one month from this date, on April 29, 1857, Churchwell made arrangements to buy the house on Seventh Street to which actress Miriam Follin moved a few weeks later.

Yet the banker and ex-Representative from Tennessee still commanded enough influence in Washington to be sent on a secret mission the following year when President Buchanan needed a political observer in Mexico. Churchwell went to Vera Cruz "for the purpose of inquiring into the state and prospects of its [Mexico's] various parties and factions, and of reporting" to the Secretary of State the result of his observations.

Paid at the rate of $10 a day, in addition to travel expenses, Churchwell journeyed to Mexico City and other points in the revolution-torn republic.[58] His secret dispatches with their descriptions of the several changes in government, his interviews with Juarez and members of the cabinet, and his recommendations to the State Department in Washington are sufficient evidence that he worked hard, accurately evaluated the political trends in Mexico, and understood the foreign influences at work there.[59]

Yet it has been suggested that Churchwell schemed, while acting as American agent, to collect personal remuneration from the Liberal Party (the Juarez Government) for procuring Juarez' recognition by the United States. The epithet of "swindler" that he acquired in his bank dealings in Tennessee, his defunct financial status upon leaving for Mexico, and his rather ominous appearance in Vera Cruz "as soon as the liberal armies entered the city," all point to this possibility.[60] In fact his biographer has stated that such unscrupulousness was probable, although the evidence is not entirely conclusive.[61]

So the contrasts between Churchwell and McGavock are all the more pronounced when the careers of the two men are compared. To all outward appearances Churchwell was a successful representative of the United States to Mexico; certainly he remained popular enough with professional politicians to be nominated by President Buchanan as min-

[58] Letter from Lewis Cass, Secretary of State, to William M. Churchwell, December 27, 1858. National Archives: Foreign Affairs Section.

[59] Dispatches from Churchwell to Cass, written from Mexico, January 21, 1859, to March 8, 1859, in "Special Agents, 1858-1862," XXI, National Archives: Foreign Affairs Section.

[60] Paul Murray, "Tres Norteamericanos y su Participacion en el Desarrollo del Tratado McLane-Ocampo, 1856-1860," *Estudios Historicos* (Mexico City), VIII (April, 1946), 26-34. This article is quoted in Turner, *op. cit.*, p. 73.

[61] *Idem.*

ister to Guatemala and Honduras in 1860, although he declined the appointment.[62]

McGavock, on the other hand, was always shuffled aside by the politicians when he sought a post in Europe. Churchwell was twice elected Congressman from Tennessee; McGavock, who considered running for office several times, was never able to gain the nomination of his party. But McGavock was utterly scrupulous; he prided himself, with justification, that there was no stain on his escutcheon.[63] It is little wonder, therefore, that he and Churchwell were never very good friends.

At the Democratic State Convention in Nashville on January 18, 1860, McGavock was elected one of ten vice-presidents. In February he was placed on the Democratic Central Committee and remarked in his journal that the appointment meant "I must work myself to death, and receive no pay or thanks for it."[64] In April of 1860 he went as a delegate to the disastrous Democratic Convention at Charleston and saw eight Southern States solemnly withdraw their members from party prceedings. Two months later he experienced the bitterness that marked the Baltimore Convention and stated early after his arrival in the city that he saw "no hope of harmonious action."[65]

Sectional differences between North and South were seemingly irresolvable and political ideologies were so much in conflict that all attempts at reconciliation seemed likely to be swept away in the face of the mounting storm. But national issues and politics in Tennessee still kept him occupied throughout the summer of 1860; he was more often in the Democratic Committee Room in Nashville than anywhere else. Yet slowly his confidence in the nation to preserve its integrity began to fade into disillusionment.

Exactly what his reflections were from October 1, 1860, until the resumption of the journal on February 4, 1862, is no longer a matter of record. This section of the narrative with its comments on the nation's domestic cleavages was "captured" at the fall of Fort Henry when Colonel McGavock and his men retreated under fire to Fort Donelson. His account of these seventeen months covering the secession of South Carolina, the formation of the Confederacy, the withdrawal of Tennessee from the Union, and his personal decision to bear arms against the "old government" of the United States must be conjectured from sources other than McGavock's private record.

[62] *Ibid.*, p. 79.
[63] *Journal,* August 10, 1856.
[64] *Ibid.*, February 3, 1860.
[65] *Ibid.*, June 19, 1860.

CHAPTER VII

The Colonel's Coat Is Lined With Scarlet

After her seven children had reached maturity, it was customary for Mrs. Jacob McGavock to accompany her husband to the plantations in Arkansas several times each year, for the McGavocks looked upon the Arkansas holdings as a joint responsibility. They were bound to the land and the people they had put upon it—including their sons Edward and Grundy, an overseer, and several slaves. Consequently they left Nashville by steamboat on December 12 to spend Christmas and the last weeks of 1860 at Pecan Point.[1] At this time Jacob was seventy years old and Louisa sixty-two.

At home they left Randal and Seraphine in the town house on Cherry Street to attend to end-of-the-year business and provide Christmas for the servants. John Berrien Lindsley, who had married Randal's favorite sister Sally in 1857, noted in his engagement book on Christmas Day, 1860: "Dinner with Sister Seph."[2] The Lindsleys enjoyed dining with Randal and Seraphine because the two families had always been on the best of terms and because little Louise Lindsley, nearly three, was the delight of her Uncle Randal, still childless after nearly six years of marriage.

But in spite of the sumptuous fare and the gayety that distinguished Randal as a host, there was a cautious tone to the conversation on that last peaceful Christmas in the McGavock household. As afternoon callers moved into the double parlors and warmed themselves before the open fire, the talk that followed was chiefly political. Randal and the visitors speculated on the effects of South Carolina's secession, which had taken place five days before; they discussed whether or not Tennessee would sever itself from the federal government. Opinions were sharply divided and there were strong currents of disagreement.

---

[1] John Berrien Lindsley, "Memoranda, 1856-1866," p. 86. MS. owned by Margaret Lindsley Warden, Nashville. By the Census of 1860, Jacob McGavock owned real estate amounting to $258,800; his personal estate was valued at $224,600. The same census lists Randal W. McGavock with real estate valued at $50,000 and a personal estate of $20,000.

[2] *Idem.*

During that cloudy Christmas afternoon the soft-spoken, scholarly Dr. Lindsley presented a logical analysis of the course South Carolina had taken and cautioned his friends of the dangers that lay ahead. "Separate secession by South Carolina is treason to the slaveholding sister states as well as to the Federal Union, which as yet has not given cause for revolution, whatever party leaders have threatened," he said. "There is every reason to be assured that the *united action* of the Southern States, authoritatively announced, would secure from the Free States the faithful execution of the fugitive slave law, and the acknowledgment of the right to create new slave states. It is remarkable in how many papers, Northern as well as Southern, the ground is taken that it would be bad policy to use force to compel such a state [South Carolina] to come back; and that if let alone returning reason and the inconvenience of being *out* would bring it back again."[3]

Lindsley had many friends in Nashville of the same optimistic view; they hoped still that the Union could be preserved. But other visitors on that Christmas afternoon listened politely and were not convinced. They firmly believed that the Abolitionists would never leave the South alone until the Negroes were emancipated and the economy of the South was totally destroyed. Lincoln was a name they heaped with abuse after the new president-elect had swept aside the two Democratic nominees, John C. Breckenridge and Stephen A. Douglas, in the November elections.

Randal McGavock had campaigned all during the autumn for Breckenridge, only to experience overwhelming defeat. Now he saw the rapid crumbling away of a nation that he had loved all his life with fervor and patriotism because of his dedicated belief in American Democracy. Whatever the turn of future events, he could now believe, with conviction, only in the democracy of the South, which guaranteed States Rights and the continuance of state sovereignty.

So during January and February of the new year McGavock turned his energies to the work of the Southern Rights and Anti-Coercion Association; he addressed public meetings in Nashville and urged the citizens of Middle Tennessee to go to the polls and vote for "Convention"—to call duly elected representatives of the people to consider secession from the government of the United States.[4] When the election was held on February 9, the "Convention" candidates were solidly defeated by 11,877 votes and it was not until June that Tennessee for-

[3] John Berrien Lindsley, "Thoughts and Hints, 1860-1862," p. 1. MS. owned by Margaret Lindsley Warden. (Written on November 9, 1860, this quotation seems to me to reflect Lindsley's views at the end of the year.)

[4] *Nashville Union and American,* Jan. 27; Feb. 3; Feb. 14, 1861.

mally joined the other seceding states and adopted the Constitution of the Confederacy.

During those bitter winter months McGavock also continued the humane work of the Robertson Society. In February he arranged a benefit concert by the Nashville Philharmonic Society in the new Masonic Hall, the proceeds from which were used for the poor of the city.[5] In March his brother Edward's young wife died suddenly in Arkansas, leaving three children under four years of age. So Randal took his mother to Pecan Point to stay with Edward and minister as best they could to the needs of the younger brother.[6]

A few days after they returned to Nashville the shocking news of Fort Sumter was flashed to every corner of the nation. Three days later, on April 15, 1861, President Lincoln sent out a call to Tennessee to join with other states of the Union in raising seventy-five thousand militia for ninety days' service. The effect of these events, portending disaster for the American nation, was to bring four additional states into the Confederacy and cause McGavock to take up arms for the State of Tennessee against the nation whose President was Abraham Lincoln.

By April no less than sixteen companies of volunteers had been organized in the city of Nashville; the newspapers ran advertisements of Southern Flags "made to order" at Singer's Sewing Machine office on College Street; Seraphine McGavock joined other Nashville women, including Mrs. James K. Polk and Mrs. Joseph Acklen, in the Ladies' Soldiers Friend Society for the purpose of "aiding our volunteers in any manner that may be necessary."[7] Randal McGavock spent his evenings studying military manuals and his days recruiting young Irishmen of the city for his "Sons of Erin" Company, which mustered at Cheatham's store on College Street and drilled each afternoon at five o'clock to the fife of Jimmy Morrissey and the drum of Pat Griffin.[8]

As a unit of the Tennessee Home Guard, the "Sons of Erin" elected ex-Mayor McGavock their Captain when they were sworn into volunteer service for a period of twelve months on May 9, 1861.[9] This was one month before Tennessee voters ratified the ordinance of secession. On May 25, McGavock took his men by river on the steamer *B. M.*

[5] *Ibid.*, Feb. 17, 1861.

[6] Lindsley, "Memoranda," p. 88.

[7] *Nashville Union and American*, April, 1861, *passim.*

[8] Patrick M. Griffin, "The Famous Tenth Tennessee," *Confederate Veteran*, XIII (1906), 553.

[9] *Journal*, May 9, 1862. On April 17, 1861, Gov. Isham G. Harris replied to Lincoln's call for Tennessee troops: "Tennessee will not furnish a single man for coercion, but 50,000 if necessary for the defense of our rights, and those of our Southern brothers." On May 1, the Tennessee Legislature in extra session authorized Governor Harris to enter into a military league with the Confederate States.

Runyon to Dover, Tennessee, to begin building Fort Donelson and Fort Henry—the two fortifications designed to resist the invasion of Federal gunboats from the north, if necessary, and to protect Tennessee from Union armies.

This was no small assignment, and the men under McGavock's command seemed to take their job seriously. One fact is certain; they were devoted to the tall, red-haired Captain whom they called "God's own gentleman." As his drummer Pat Griffin remembered him, McGavock was "a clean, strong, brave man, a noble soldier, a loyal friend . . ." He worked them hard by day, but winked at their off-duty diversions, which took the form of stag-dances by moonlight and visits to Lady Peggy's saloon across the Tennessee River from Fort Henry.[10]

Apparently McGavock travelled often between Dover and Nashville during the summer of 1861. He came home to recruit more men for the Tenth Tennessee Infantry, to petition the generals for more supplies and better equipment—both sorely needed—and to put his personal affairs in order. On June 11 he hastily wrote out his will[11] and signed it in the presence of his friends F. B. Fogg and J. B. Knowles:

I Randal W. McGavock, do make and publish this as my last will and testament hereby revoking and making void all other wills by me at any time made. First—I direct that my funeral expenses and all my debts be paid as soon after my death as possible, out of any moneys that I may die possessed of, or may first come into the hands of my executor. Secondly—I give and bequeath to my dearly beloved wife all my real estate wherever situated, also all notes or moneys of every kind that I may be possessed of—and my personal estate excepting that hereinafter innumerated. I leave my gold watch and chain to my brother Jno. McGavock—also all jewelry of my own use. My library I leave to be distributed between my brothers Grundy and Edward. My paintings I wish divided between my nieces and nephews. Lastly—I do hereby nominate and appoint my brother in law Jno. Berrien Lindsley my executor. In witness whereof I do to this will set my hand and seal.

This eleventh day of June 1861
Signed and published in presence of

F. B. Fogg
J. B. Knowles

R. W. McGavock

As the summer wore on and the news of victory at Manassas thrilled the hearts of the volunteers at Forts Henry and Donelson, the construction work moved at a faster pace. In May the Tenth Tennessee, Irish, had been organized at Fort Henry; in September McGavock and his

---

[10] Griffin, *loc. cit.,* 553. See also Charles Moss, "Forgotten Fort Heiman, Land of Late Victory," Reprint from *Nashville Banner,* 1957.

[11] County Court Clerk's Office, Davidson County Courthouse, Nashville. The will was probated in the January term, 1865, and recorded on April 18, 1865.

"Sons of Erin" became Company H of that Regiment, changing their status from Home Guards to Confederate soldiers and officially joining the larger unit.[12] Serving as Colonel of the Tenth was Adolphus Heiman, a well-known Nashville architect and native of Prussia; Captain Randal McGavock was elected Lieutenant-Colonel and second in command by popular vote of the men. While Heiman directed the construction of Fort Henry and drew the plans for another fortification on the west side of the Tennessee River—named officially Fort Heiman—McGavock was given temporary command at Fort Donelson, the Cumberland outpost a few miles east of Fort Henry in the neck of land between the two rivers.

Part of McGavock's duties involved raising new companies to man the fort and strengthen the defenses against the inevitable attack from the north. On September 21, 1861, he wrote W. W. Mackall, A. A. G., that he had just mustered one new company into the Confederate service, had succeeded in raising another from Stewart County, but needed at least three additional companies as soon as possible.[13] By October, the necessity for additional troops became more urgent; the enemy's gunboats were reported at Eddyville, with 750 infantry and 250 cavalry. So McGavock sent a messenger to Colonel Heiman at Fort Henry requesting as many reinforcements as could be spared, for in the event of an attack the position at Donelson was untenable. "I have but few guns," he wrote to Heiman on October 27, "and the companies all raw and unfit for an engagement. Come yourself if possible."

Another letter written by McGavock to Heiman, dated the following day, asked that Heiman "urge Gen. Polk to send a regiment here [Fort Donelson] at once. The Cumberland is in a defenseless condition." The urgency which McGavock felt (and which was justified by the events at Fort Donelson three months later) is expressed in his letter to General Leonidas Polk:

Fort Donelson Near Dover
Nov. 3rd/61

To
Gen L. Polk
Dear Sir

Agreeable to an order from you I have been here for several weeks past forming a regiment. I now have five companies in Camp, but can get no more in this region, as it is exhausted. The remaining five companies will have to come from some other quarter. The companies here are but indifferently armed. If you could furnish us with better arms, I would be much pleased. We have enough cavalry and artillery for the present, *but we must have a well drilled*

---

12 Confederate Archives, Chap. I, No. 92, p. 63. National Archives, Washington, D. C.
13 Letters in McGavock's "War Service Jacket," National Archives.

and armed Regiment here at once. Col Thornton's Reg that was ordered here by you has never arrived. The work of sinking the boats below Line Port has been completed. The gun boats came up to the lower blockade very soon after our boat left, and sent a skiff up to make examination. They then threw shell all round through the country, without doing much damage. I think the sinking of the boats will invite attack, and certainly will be of no use in high water. We have many friends on the river in the counties below this in Ky, who are begging for protection. We are losing ground in this part of Kentucky simply because they are afraid to move. Hundreds will flock to our standard as soon as we make a forward movement. The two hundred Mississippians that Gen Alcorn sent me from Hopkinsville returned last week.

Please inform me by letter through Capt. Dixon how the Field officers of this reg are filled, whether by election or appointment, and how vacancies in companies are filled.

Yours Very Truly
Lt Col R W McGavock
Commanding at Ft. Donelson

The messages between McGavock and his superior officers help piece together part of the biographical data which was lost when the journal of these months was confiscated by Union forces overrunning Fort Henry on February 4, 1862. These official letters reflect the concern McGavock felt as he attempted to fortify the borders of Tennessee against the anticipated attack by Federal forces; they also show the labor he expended in making himself a competent field officer. Now face to face with the realities of preparing himself and his men for their first battle, he looked straight at the grim countenance of war and saw his native soil converted to a battlefield. By Christmas, 1861, the young politician who had canvassed Stewart County five years earlier for the Democrats had become a patriot in uniform, willing to defend with blood and sinew the rights of sovereignty at home.

In another corner of Tennessee his brother-in-law Colonel William M. Churchwell was building the Confederate defenses at Cumberland Gap to protect East Tennessee from invasion.[14] Jacob McGavock, his father, at age seventy-one had transferred his allegiance to the Confederacy and was continuing his duties as Clerk of the Confederate Circuit and District Court of Tennessee under Judge West H. Humphreys, who directed that the old Federal seal be altered for the newly-formed government.[15] Another brother-in-law, Dr. John Berrien Lindsley, had gone to Richmond to offer his services as a volunteer surgeon in July, 1861, but returned to Nashville convinced that volunteer surgeons were

[14] Churchwell, "War Service Jacket," National Archives.

[15] An account of Humphreys' impeachment trial in Washington, to which Jacob McGavock as Humphreys' clerk was subpœnaed, is reported in *The Daily Globe,* June 27, 1862. Humphreys had escaped to the south and was impeached *in absentia,* "36 yeas and 0 nays."

not welcome in the Confederate Armies and thus decided to continue as President of the University of Nashville. Lindsley, who was both a physician and ordained Presbyterian minister, spent the years of confusion and trouble preaching to troops, acting as post surgeon of hospitals before the fall of Nashville, and protecting the buildings and library of the struggling little university from the ravages of war.[16]

The last section of Randal McGavock's journal—from February 4, 1862, until October 8, 1862—is so richly detailed and so carefully set down that there is little need to review this period of his life in a biography intended to be read in connection with the journals. These eight months covering the blunders of Fort Donelson, his imprisonment at Fort Warren, and the reorganization of his regiment in Mississippi are the most dramatic and compelling pages of the narrative. But they need little interpretation here. In the throes of war McGavock found time to record his impressions at length and to present a testimony of the losses he sustained during the last months of his life.

Sometimes with wry, ironic humor and sometimes with bitterness—but never with despair—his daily entries are a sober catalogue of deprivations and disappointments. At the beginning of the war he was separated from the company of his wife and family in Nashville. At Fort Henry, when he retreated with his men under fire, he noted that the Federals "rifled my trunk, drank my whiskey . . . plundered me of everything . . . and will, I suppose, publish my journal, and sell it to help pay the expenses of the war."[17] They also took his horse "Tenth Legion," which he loved with much attachment. When he discovered the loss he went directly to General U. S. Grant to register his complaint with the commander who was enjoying his first major victory and was destined to command all the Union Forces.[18]

Other humiliating losses were reported to him in letters from home while he was a prisoner at Fort Warren on George's Island in Boston Harbor. Here he learned about the Federal occupation of Nashville—the city where he was born, where three years before he had been mayor, where now the leading citizens, including his father, were forced to pledge their allegiance to a hostile government.

He also learned about personal disloyalty in those whom he had

---

16 Lindsley, "Memoranda," *passim.*

17 *Journal,* February 4, 1862.

18 *Ibid.,* February 16, 1862. "Tenth Legion," a chestnut colt, was sired by *Albion and foaled in 1859 by Polly Elliott, the chestnut mare of Col. George Elliott. Polly Elliott was sired by *Leviathan, first dam Caledonia, etc. "Tenth Legion" was therefore a half-brother to Suwarrow, by *Albion, that was ridden by Capt. John Overton, Jr., of Forrest's Cavalry and figures in the saddle-bred stock of "Traveler's Rest," Nashville. These notes were furnished by Gen. Jacob McGavock Dickinson.

trusted. "I received a letter today from my mother in which she states that my negro man, Martin, had left Nashville and gone with the Fed. army."[19] With stinging insult he read in the *New York Herald* that the company flag of his "Sons of Erin" had been delivered as a trophy, with elaborate ceremony and speechmaking, to the Sixty-Ninth New York Regiment. Henceforth his banner, carrying an Irish harp against a background of emerald green and spelling the motto "Sons of Erin, Go Where Glory Waits You," would be carried by an enemy regiment poised to invade the South.[20]

Yet the months that McGavock spent as a prisoner were not without their compensations. His father was allowed to visit him in July. He enjoyed good food, packages from sympathetic friends in New England, and the boost to his morale that came with a new suit from his old Boston tailor. He was permitted to receive drafts from home to buy articles difficult to come by in the blockaded Confederate States and he took delight, as the journal makes clear, in reading current newspapers and periodicals that were not available when he was in the field at the head of his regiment.

After nearly five months at Fort Warren, McGavock was exchanged for three Union prisoners: 1st Lt. W. H. Eldridge, 4th New York Volunteers; 1st Lt. J. W. Adams, 4th U. S. Infantry; and 2nd Lt. C. H. Hatch, 4th New York Volunteers.[21] With other Confederates he was sent on the *Ocean Queen* to Fortress Monroe and thence to Richmond, capital of the Confederacy. The register of prisoners' receipts and disbursements kept at Fort Warren shows that Lt.-Col. McGavock left the military prison with cash amounting to $17.00,[22] which was doubtless the total amount of money he had in hand when he arrived at Richmond on August 5, 1862. Three days later he drew back pay in Confederate money for seven months and eight days—the time since his last payment—at the rate of $170.00 per month, or a total of $1,235.33.[23] With this he started south on his thirty-sixth birthday.

At Max Meadows he stopped overnight for a brief reunion with his father's brother, Randal McGavock of Max Meadows, the uncle for whom he was named; he also had what was to be his last visit with Mrs. Thomas Cloyd, his father's elder sister, a particularly favorite relative because she reminded Randal of his father.

---

[19] *Ibid.*, June 9, 1862.
[20] *Ibid.*, May 15, 1862; *New York Herald*, May 14, 1862, p. 3.
[21] *Official Records*, Ser. II, Vol. 4, p. 443.
[22] Auxiliary Register, No. 3, Military Prison, Fort Warren, Massachusetts. National Archives.
[23] McGavock, "War Service Jacket," National Archives.

He noted in his journal that the lead mines of Montgomery County, which his great-grandfather James McGavock had guarded during the Revolution, were producing eight thousand pounds of lead each day for the use of Confederate Armies. He also noticed the good stands of corn and hay and the prospects for a bountiful harvest.[24] It seemed to him that there was hope as long as one stayed on the land.

At Tunnel Hill, Georgia, seven miles from Dalton, he was reunited with his wife for the first time in seven months. With her family Seraphine had joined other refugees from Tennessee and was "comfortably situated" in a private boarding house where vestiges of the carefree life could still be enjoyed a few months longer. After one week at Tunnel Hill, without hearing from any of his own family at Nashville, Randal left the Deerys and Seraphine and journeyed by train to Clinton, Mississippi, to begin reorganizing his regiment.

The last pages of the journal are filled with these activities during September and October: the reunion of officers and men after separation and imprisonment; the reelection of Colonel Heiman and Lt.-Col. McGavock to their former positions of trust as field officers in the Tenth Regiment; the hustle of men at drill and the foraging for supplies in a nation ravaged and weakened by eighteen months of aggression by land and blockade by sea.

Suddenly, without signature or post script, the journal comes to a close with the entry of October 8, 1862. The personal narrative that McGavock had begun fourteen years earlier at Harvard was suddenly broken off. Now the young lawyer, world traveller and correspondent, author and diarist, was swallowed up in the duties of total war.

When he wrote the last entry his regiment was ordered to Holly Springs to join General John Gregg's Brigade. Then they were sent to Water Valley, where they were reviewed by President Jefferson Davis. During the next few weeks they marched to Tippah Ford, back to Holly Springs, to Waterford, Oxford, and Grenada.[25]

On November 6, after a few weeks of illness and failing strength, Colonel Adolphus Heiman died in a military hospital at Jackson, just before his elevation to Brigadier General.[26] To fill the vacancy Randal McGavock was promoted to Colonel and given command of the Tenth Regiment under General Gregg. Then at the end of December, Gregg was ordered to Vicksburg, where the Confederates encountered Sher-

---

[24] *Journal,* Aug. 11-12, 1862.

[25] Lewis R. Clark, "Tenth Tennessee Infantry," in *Military Annals of Tennessee, Confederate,* ed. John Berrien Lindsley (Nashville: J. M. Lindsley & Co., 1886), p. 285. (Hereinafter abbreviated *Military Annals.*)

[26] Heiman, "War Service Jacket," National Archives.

man's forces at the Battle of Chickasaw Bayou, during which Gregg's men were briefly engaged.

Next they were sent to Port Hudson, Louisiana, on January 6, 1863, making the journey from Vicksburg by transport. Many years later Pat Griffin recalled an incident aboard the boat:

> When we reached Port Hudson, the boat was minus all its mirrors, knives, forks, spoons, blankets, and rations. The captain of the transport reported the matter to Col. McGavock, who ordered his men to fall into line, spread their knapsacks on the ground and open them out, and also to turn their pockets inside out. Col. McGavock, the officers of the regiment, and the captain of the boat went from one end of the line to the other, but not one thing could they find that belonged to the boat. After the search was completed, Col. McGavock made a speech to the captain of the transport, in which he eulogized his regiment, saying that it was made up of honest and brave men, and that, as a matter of course, it must have been some other soldiers or thieves that had ransacked the transport. However, Col. McGavock went to the commissary and drew rations to supply the captain and his crew until they got back to Vicksburg.[27]

Griffin's anecdote illustrates the confidence and respect shared by Randal McGavock and the men under his command.

After three months of building and improving the earthworks at Port Hudson, the "Bloody Tinth" was bombarded on March 13 by a fleet of Federal mortar-boats, gunboats, and men-of-war. Pat Griffin's stirring account of this river engagement brings the scene to focus:

> On the night of the bombardment we had a pyramid of pine knots built up about a mile below the port, right opposite where the gunboats were anchored. We had orders to set fire to the pine knots when the first boat advanced. Two forty-five-gun frigates started up the river at nightfall. The pine knots were ablaze instantly, and every movement of the fleet was seen by the gunners at the port. The first frigate succeeded in getting past, but she was battered up considerably. The second frigate made an effort to compel the port to surrender, but we poured shot into her at such a rapid rate that she ran out the white flag. We ceased firing at once; and when her commander saw that we had stopped, they began firing on us again. Then the captain commanding the battery ordered the boys to "give 'em red-hot shot." The order was obeyed, and the red-hot shot set fire to the frigate, her machinery stopped, and she began to swing round and round. The crew jumped overboard, and we could hear the cries and groans of the wounded and dying. . . . Directly the fire reached their ammunition, when bombshells and cartridges began to explode in a grand fusillade. She floated down the river, and the boats of the fleet moved hurriedly in order to give her plenty of room to pass. Several miles below the magazine exploded, and we knew that the end had come for that frigate. It was a wonderful sight. The port lay in the shadow, and below it the Mississippi stretched away a veritable stream of fire.[28]

It was on this occasion, according to Griffin, that Colonel McGavock

---

[27] Griffin, *loc. cit.*, 554.
[28] *Ibid.*, 555. See also Clark, *loc. cit.*, 285.

"must have had some premonition of his death, for he told me that he was afraid that he would never get back home."

Two months later, with the Federal seige of Vicksburg, General Gregg's Brigade was ordered to Jackson. The imminent danger of losing Jackson and Vicksburg to Federal forces was shaping into a decisive battle; thus the Confederate leaders saw need of as many well-trained troops as could be quickly brought to the defense of the line. They believed that Gregg could drive the invaders back. On May 2, with "some three thousand three hundred . . . well armed, drilled, and disciplined" men, Gregg started for Jackson.[29]

At this time three of his Tennessee regiments were the 3rd, 10th, and 30th, commanded by Colonel Calvin H. Walker of Giles County, Colonel Randal McGavock, and Colonel J. J. Turner of Gallatin.[30] The Assistant Quartermaster of the 30th, Captain S. R. Simpson, hastily scribbled in his diary an account of the long march from Port Hudson to Jackson:

Sat. 2 May — We had orders to march at ten o'clock, we left old Port Hudson & marched to Mrs. Flukers 7 miles & halted, nothing transpired on the route. The weather was very warm & the boys had a hard time of it. . . .

Sun. 3 — Very warm, the boys are getting along tolerable well. Some of their feet are blistered very badly. We passed pine grove meeting house today & saw some young ladies, we passed over the Amite river today. The soil is thin. We encamped at Clinton.

Tues. 5 — We stopped 7 miles from Osika & camped, the night was very cool.

Thurs. 7 — Fine cool day, we started early and marched to the town of Magnolia on the N. O. & Jackson railroad. We went four miles out of town and camped for the night.

Sat. 9 — We started at 5 o'clock & walked 6 miles to Brookhaven & there we took the cars & rode to the city of Jackson. We passed through some fine little towns & the ladies thronged the stations to see & cheer us on our way. We arrived in Jackson about six o'clock in the evening & went out beyond the city to camp, the night was cool & pleasant.

Mon. 11 — Very warm, we had orders to march at day light . . . & we marched 21 miles to the town of Raymond, Hinds Co., Miss. The citizens were overjoyed to see us as the enemy had been in the neighborhood for two weeks burning & destroying everything in their way, we arrived at Raymond about dark. . . .[31]

---

[29] J. J. Turner, "Thirtieth Tennessee Infantry," in *Military Annals,* p. 448.

[30] Also with Gen. Gregg at Raymond were the following: 1st Tennessee Battalion; 41st and 50th Tennessee Regiments; 7th Texas; and the Missouri Battery under Capt. H. M. Bledsoe. As commander of Hood's Texas Brigade, Gregg later served under Robert E. Lee in Virginia and was killed in action on October 7, 1864, near Richmond.

[31] S. R. Simpson, "Diary," MS. in Manuscript Section, Tennessee State Library and Archives.

On the other side of the town of Raymond was assembled a Union force estimated at 11,569 men and composed of the Third and Seventh Divisions under the command of Major General John A. Logan, who was serving under Major General James B. McPherson. Preparations were under way to engage the Confederates at Raymond and take Jackson as quickly as possible. At nightfall Logan's troops outnumbered Gregg's about four to one.

Tired after ten days of marching over dusty roads in scorching sun, deserving a respite from fatigue, the Tenth Tennessee camped on the east side of Raymond on the night of May 11. On the following morning, between eight and nine o'clock, the hungry men marched through the town and were met by the grateful citizens with food and fresh drinking water and loud cheering.[32] At the head of the regiment rode Colonel McGavock in a gray coat with scarlet lining, his sabre belted at his left side. He sat the horse well even though the stirrup straps were too short for his gangly, boyish legs. As the ladies of Raymond waved their handkerchiefs the thirty-six-year-old colonel acknowledged their salutes with a smile and a nod; the children would remember the gray-blue eyes that winked from behind the heavy auburn beard. In a few minutes the Irish regiment from Tennessee had won the admiration of the dusty little town. Then at 9:30 they marched to the outskirts and turned southeast down the Gallatin Road.[33]

Quartermaster Simpson observed in his diary that by mid-morning the sun was bright and warm and that company cooks were preparing two days' rations. "The birds are singing, the sun shining & everything looks gay, we are ready for the fight or the march . . ." Then about a mile from Raymond, Gregg ordered his men to leave the Gallatin Road and proceed for about half a mile through the woods lying between the Gallatin and Utica Roads. As soon as the enemy was sighted in the woods opposite, across a large open field, the companies were immediately formed in the line of battle. There they waited and heard the opening fire of the artillery.

The official report of Colonel J. J. Turner, 30th Tennessee, recounts the action that followed:

> While thus posted, the artillery was still engaged, and I could distinctly hear the commands of the Federal officers, some 400 yards to our left in the direction of the Gallatin Road. After remaining there for some fifteen minutes, we were ordered to move to the left about 600 yards, which we did at double quick, and we then formed in line in the edge of a dense woods, a large field being in our

[32] Griffin, *loc. cit.*, 555.

[33] Official Records, Ser. I, Vol. XXIV, Part I, "Reports," 740.

rear. I ordered forward a company of skirmishers in our front, and immediately I heard the engagement open between the enemy and the Third Tennessee and Seventh Texas. At this juncture we received an order leaving it discretionary whether to attack the enemy or not. After waiting a few minutes the skirmishers were withdrawn, and we moved rapidly by the right flank for about 500 yards, and reached a position near that of the Third Tennessee, and after seven of the consolidated companies had filed into the field, the whole command changed direction by the left flank and moved forward rapidly in line. As soon as those in the field reached the crest of the hill, the enemy opened upon us from the front and right, and Colonel McGavock ordered a charge, which was responded to with alacrity by all the command.[34]

With McGavock's orders to charge, the fury of combat began. The Colonel from Tennessee, his long coat swung over his left arm and his sabre unsheathed in his right hand, led the four hundred men of his regiment forward at about eleven o'clock to meet the destructive fire of the enemy, who were strongly posted in the woods ahead.

At the crest of a little hill, fully in the open, the tall red-haired figure cheered his men to the fight. They followed him without pause as the staccato gunfire from both sides increased in volume and intensity. Towering above his men on high ground, the bright sun marking his forehead and highlighting the vivid hair and beard, McGavock stood a sure target for the enemy.

Three versions, varying somewhat in detail, recount what followed during the next few moments. Colonel J. J. Turner officially reported:

Colonel McGavock, in a few seconds after ordering the charge, while gallantly leading his men, fell, mortally wounded, and some 5 commissioned officers of the Tenth Tennessee were wounded about the same time. The firing thus continued for about half an hour without intermission on either side.[35]

Another witness wrote to McGavock's family:

Colonel McGavock, seeing reinforcements coming, ordered his brave men to charge, he himself taking the lead, being some 20 yards in front of his regiment . . . He had not proceeded far before he was pierced through the heart by a minnie ball. Turning, he called upon Lt. Col. Grace to rally his men, being the last words spoken by as brave a man as ever drew sword in a holy but fruitless cause. His men charged up, got his body, and carried it to Raymond, where several ladies took charge of it and had him interred in a private enclosure. The citizens of Raymond will ever revere him as the brave and gallant spirit that fell in the defense of their homes. His coat had 8 bullet holes through it.[36]

Forty-three years later, "Captain" Pat Griffin as an old man reconstructed from memory the death of his commander:

---

[34] *Ibid.*, 741.

[35] *Ibid.*

[36] Author unidentified. Folio in McGavock Papers.

> We had marched up on a rise and were out in the open, and they were in the woods about one hundred yards in our front when they began to fire on us . . . We had been under fire about twenty minutes, when I heard a ball strike something behind me. I have a dim remembrance of calling to God. It was my colonel. He was about to fall. I caught him and eased him down with his head in the shadow of a little bush. I knew he was going, and asked him if he had any message for his mother. His answer was "Griffin, take care of me! Griffin, take care of me!" I put my canteen to his lips, but he was not conscious. He was shot through the left breast, and did not live more than five minutes.[37]

So in the shadow of a scrub bush on a hot Mississippi hillside, during the heat of a brief, almost inconsequential battle, the thin features, hardened by strain and fatigue, settled quietly at noon to a final repose. Heartbeat and sinew were now no longer charged with the old restlessness. The long legs, stiff and unmoving, lay twisted in a last awkward stride.

Observing a custom of the day, young Griffin took his colonel's handkerchief from the left hip pocket and dipped the white linen in McGavock's still warm blood. This was for "Miss Louisa" McGavock, his colonel's mother. Then he collected the personal effects: a signet ring, gold watch, and a few papers—among them the last journal.

The next day Pat Griffin, prisoner of war, was given a brief parole to bury his commander in Raymond, where a rough wooden coffin was hastily nailed together and loaded on a hired wagon.[38] Accompanying the little procession of townspeople to the grave was a ragged squad of Confederate prisoners guarded by a detail of their Yankee captors.

---

[37] Griffin, *loc. cit.*, 555.
[38] *Ibid.*, 556.

CHAPTER VIII

Post Script: An Old Lady Wears Her Diamonds

When General John Gregg's Battalion fell back from Raymond after two hours of fighting on May 12, 1863, the retreat was covered by the Third Kentucky Infantry. Among the losses were Colonel Randal McGavock and eight other Confederate officers who were killed or mortally wounded. Major General John A. Logan, with two divisions opposing Gregg, lost seven Union officers during the same engagement.

Four days later, on Sunday afternoon, John Berrien Lindsley and his brother-in-law, the Reverend J. W. Hoyte, were returning home from a walk in the country near occupied Nashville, which Federal forces were fortifying heavily against a possible attack by the Confederates. As they crossed the Franklin Pike they met a boy selling the *Louisville Democrat,* which Dr. Hoyte bought and began reading as they walked along.[1] Turning to the telegraphic column, he stopped short.

That same evening Dr. Lindsley recorded the melancholy news in his own war diary:

> I stepped up, and he pointed out the announcement. "Colonel McGavock of the 10th Tennessee killed." We hastened home. Soon as we reached the house Fanny told me that master Randal was killed. Nelson had just come from Pa's with the newspaper. Mrs. L. deeply affected. After a cup of coffee we hastened to Pa's. Found him and Ma in deep distress. Randal was their oldest son and the pride of the whole family. I consider the news probable, but still by no means certain, and endeavor to comfort them accordingly. Such is war.[2]

For a few weeks the family hoped that there had been a mistake, that the first report was somehow in error.

On June 15, a month after Raymond fell, they received a letter from Grundy McGavock of Arkansas, Randal's younger brother, who had seen Pat Griffin. Griffin had escaped from the Federals when the boat carrying Confederate prisoners north had stopped at Memphis; he found

[1] Lindsley, "Memoranda, 1856-1866," MS., p. 131.
[2] *Idem.*

Grundy McGavock and turned over to him the colonel's personal effects. So Lindsley wrote in his diary: "Letter from brother Grundy, Memphis, June 3rd, brings certain intelligence of Brother Randal's death. States that he has his seal ring and knows where he is buried."[3]

Randal's sister Ann and her husband, Judge Henry Dickinson, went to Raymond a few weeks later and found the grave which Pat Griffin had described. They arranged to have the remains brought to their home at Columbus, where funeral services were held on July 29.[4] Then Randal was interred in the Dickinson graveyard until the war was over.

Nearly three years later he was brought home—after two nations had settled their disputes on the battlefields of Atlanta, Franklin, and Nashville. The *Nashville Dispatch* ran a notice on March 16, 1866:

> Yesterday evening the remains of our late fellow-citizen, R. W. McGavock, who was a Lieutenant Colonel in the Confederate army, and was killed in one of the engagements with Gen. Grant's forces a little before the taking of Vicksburg, were brought to this city for re-interment. Col. McGavock was Mayor of Nashville in 1858, and filled the office with signal ability. He was a citizen widely known and highly esteemed.

The same edition devoted a long editorial to McGavock's public life and military career.

On page five his mother and father inserted a funeral notice framed in bold black lines:

> NOTICE
>
> **The friends of Mr. and Mrs. Jacob McGavock are requested to meet on Saturday, the 17th inst., at 11 o'clock, at their residence to convey the remains of their son, the late Col. Randal W. McGavock, to the family vault at Mount Olivet.**

On that St. Patrick's Day, 1866, the newspapers reported "a large concourse of citizens" was present at the last rites and followed the hearse to Mount Olivet. The Phoenix Lodge, Free and Accepted Masons, gave the body burial with "Grand Honors."[5] The Irish of the city stood quietly in little groups and talked again of "God's own gentleman," their leader and friend. The solemn men with rough hands and ruddy faces stated confidently they would never see his like again.

---

[3] *Ibid.*, p. 132.

[4] Alfred L. Crabb, "Lines to A Trustee," *Peabody Reflector and Alumni News,* VI, (June, 1933), 178.

[5] *Nashville Dispatch,* March 18 and 21, 1866.

Already a widow for three years, Seraphine returned to live with the McGavocks for several months in their new house on Spruce Street.[6] From time to time she helped Dr. and Mrs. Lindsley entertain the members of the Robertson Association when the group was reorganized after the war and Lindsley succeeded his brother-in-law as president.[7]

Seraphine was still beautiful in 1868 when she married Connally F. Trigg of Knoxville in the Lindsley's parlor on University Place. She was thirty-three years old at the time, and Trigg was fifty-eight. A native of Virginia and a distinguished lawyer, Trigg moved from Abingdon to Knoxville in 1856 and was an outspoken opponent of secession in 1861.

When Knoxville was occupied by Union troops in 1863 and the city was under military rule, Trigg was appointed judge of the district court of the United States for the eastern district of Tennessee. He held this office at the time of his marriage to Seraphine McGavock, and before him were arraigned, during the period of Reconstruction, a number of Southerners charged with treason for having supported the Confederacy.[8]

At Judge Trigg's death in 1880, Seraphine became a widow again at age forty-five. She lived with her sister, Mrs. William M. Churchwell, also a widow, for the next few years in Bristol. Both were handsome but childless women living off Seraphine's diminishing income; for William M. Churchwell, after losing a considerable fortune before 1861, had died in 1862 of typhoid fever in Knoxville while serving as

---

[6] When Jacob McGavock died in 1878, his will contained the following special bequest: "I give and bequeath to my grandson Randal, son of John J. McGavock, my lot on Summer Street, number 33 in Barrow Grove Place. . . . This is a gift to my said Grandson for his name after my son Randal who is dead. It is not to be counted as any part of his father's share of my estate, but is an independent gift to him." County Court Clerk's Office, Davidson County, Tennessee.

[7] Unidentified newspaper clipping in the Lindsley Papers.

[8] Knoxville *Weekly Whig and Chronicle,* May 5, 1880. When Trigg married Seraphine McGavock he was a widower with four living children (Rachel Trigg McClung, wife of Rufus McClung, Lilburn, Rosalie, and Josephine) and one dead son, Edward. To protect her properties from Trigg's creditors, present and future, a deed of trust was drawn up on the eve of their marriage in which Seraphine conveyed to Godfrey M. Fogg of Nashville, as trustee, all her real estate inherited under the provisions of McGavock's will. This instrument also states that in the event of Trigg's death or the dissolution of the marriage, Fogg would re-deed her the property—which he did after Trigg died in 1880. Soon after, however, several lawsuits were heard over Trigg's property. From 1881 to 1883 Sullivan County records show that Seraphine put up for surety farm animals and household goods (including china and a carriage) and that she pledged a crop of wheat from the farm. Some of these suits were carried to the Supreme Court sitting in Knoxville. After Mrs. Churchwell's death another suit involving Elizabeth A. Deery, daughter of Seraphine's brother William Bruce Deery, was not concluded until 1908. So from 1856 until her old age Seraphine's inheritance was the object of much litigation. These notes through the courtesy of Mrs. Arthur Moser, Knoxville.

Provost Marshal of East Tennessee in the Confederate Army.[9] His death had left his wife nearly penniless.

After Mrs. Churchwell died in 1897, Seraphine married again for the third time. At age sixty-three she was courted by Augustus Herman Pettibone, an Ohioan who had settled in Greeneville after the war. Also a lawyer by profession, Pettibone had first come south in 1863 as a major with the Twentieth Regiment of Wisconsin Infantry. As a soldier he fought under Major General Gordon Granger in Mississippi, Texas, and Alabama until 1865.[10]

After practicing law in Greeneville during the years immediately following the war, Pettibone was elected on the Republican ticket as Representative from East Tennessee to the 47th, 48th, and 49th Congresses. He was an eloquent speaker at the height of his career and even defeated the silver-tongued Bob Taylor in the 1880 campaign for Congress.[11]

So Seraphine Trigg and Augustus Pettibone were married just as the twentieth century brought to Tennessee a new era determined to forget the mistakes and relics of the past. By 1900, therefore, Major Pettibone had lost his political following in East Tennessee, and thereafter his fortunes followed a steady decline. Too old to practice law any longer, he accepted an appointment as government inspector in the Department of Agriculture in 1905 and came to Nashville to spend his last years.[12] With a white, unkempt beard stained by tobacco juice, he was a familiar figure in the streets and saloons of the state capital.

With him came Seraphine, returning to the city where half a century before she had been the mayor's wife and first lady. Now aged and corpulent, she seemed unable to forget that once in these same streets she had been beautiful. As an old woman she wore bright satin dresses and covered the lines in her cheeks with layers of rouge and powder.[13] On Sundays she walked unsteadily on tiny feet down the aisles of the First Presbyterian Church on the arm of Major Pettibone. Her eyelids

---

[9] Knoxville *Daily Register,* August 20, 1862.

[10] A. H. Pettibone, "War Service Record." National Archives, Washington. At the time of their marriage on November 21, 1898, Pettibone was also sixty-three and had been twice married and widowed. His first wife was Sarah Young of Twinsburg, Ohio, whom he married in 1863 and brought to Greeneville after the war. She died there in 1867. The following year he married Mary Speck, daughter of Thomas A. Speck, a merchant tailor once associated with Andrew Johnson. They had one son, Herman, born on October 2, 1875, who was therefore twenty-three at the time of his father's third marriage. These notes through the courtesy of Mrs. Arthur Moser, Knoxville.

[11] *Biographical Dictionary of the American Congress; Nashville Banner* and *Nashville Tennessean,* November 27, 1918.

[12] *Ibid.*

[13] These descriptions of Mrs. Pettibone were furnished by a number of Nashvillians—her surviving acquaintances and relatives.

still fluttered—now from behind the screw curls on a brown wig—and she still enjoyed a young girl's fanciful diversion of trying on the hats in front of her in church. By 1915 only a few people remembered that the matching diamonds she wore had been a wedding gift from Randal McGavock.

When the Mexican War ended in 1848, Seraphine Deery was thirteen years old. She was eighty-two in 1917 when she stood on the steps of Mrs. J. D. Waller's boarding house on Seventh Avenue and watched volunteer companies from Nashville, bound for France, march down the street to the Union Station.

That same winter she suffered two severe attacks of the grippe and was confined to her room for three months, nursed by Mrs. Waller and too ill to see infrequent callers who left their cards at the boarding house door. By January she was not strong enough to attend the Jackson Day Ball, the chief social event of her last years.

Old and unloved, a butterfly to the last, she died on March 20, 1918.[14] Neither of her obituaries in the Nashville papers recalled the fact that she had been married in 1855, at age twenty, to Randal William McGavock.

---

[14] *Nashville Banner,* March 20, 1918; *Nashville Tennessean,* March 21, 1918.

THE EARLY JOURNALS

Herschel Gower, Editor

HARVARD JOURNAL, 1848

EUROPEAN JOURNAL, 1851

CHAPTER IX

"I hail the new year with bright prospects." (January-April, 1848)

Born on August 10, 1826, Randal William McGavock was twenty-one and a half years old when he wrote the first entry in the Harvard Journal. Away from home for eighteen months of residence in Cambridge, separated for the first time from family and friends in the Southwest, he moved easily and gracefully in the urban society of mid-century Boston. Sociable, inquisitive, unrestrained in his interests, he has left a record of a Southerner at Harvard that characterizes both the young man and the society. The daily narrative which follows is in his own words and retains the original spelling; the punctuation has occasionally been modernized for the convenience of the reader.

Jan. 2. Rose 8:00. Ret. 12:00. Yesterday was the beginning of a new year, a day on which many solemn and salutary resolutions are formed, but to be broken. However, I hail the new year with bright prospects and a firm determination that I shall live a happier and more useful life. The past year has been fraught with many great events in the affairs of government, and also in my domestic affairs I have experienced in its revolution many happy and sad times.

Jan. 3. Rose 7:30. Ret. 12:00. After breakfast Rogers[1] and myself walked out to Mount Auburn for exercise. I then set about reading the eighth chapter of the third book of Blackstone and attended the lecture, which was very fine. In the afternoon I was busily employed in reading the law on charter parties, preparatory to my debut before the Moot Court. After tea I smoked a segar with Guild of Dedham, Massachusetts.[2]

---

[1] A fellow student, Robert Lyon Rogers of Carroll County, Maryland, Ll. B. 1848.

[2] Another student, George Dwight Guild.

Jan. 4. Rose 7:30. Ret. 11:00. This morning I read several chapters in the book of Second Samuel, when Webster[3] called, and we chatted until 10:00. I attended Professor Sparks'[4] last lecture on American History for this term; the subject of his lecture was upon the treaty of peace, and the acknowledgment of our independence by England. At 11:00 I attended Mr. Curtis'[5] lecture on Contracts. In the afternoon my case in Moot Court was argued, and decided in our favor. I made a short speech that caused the Judge to laugh and the court to applaud.

Jan. 5. Rose 8:00. Ret. 12:00. After breakfast I read several chapters in the Bible and Blackstone until 12:00 and attended the lecture. In the afternoon I read law and several of Cicero's orations. At the supper table I was highly complimented upon my effort in the Moot Court on yesterday, whether it was merited I am not able to say. I then attended a lecture on Astronomy at the Lyceum by Professor Nichol of Edinburgh.[6] It was very fine.

Jan. 6. Rose 8:00. Ret. 12:00. This morning I called on Nevins to ask him to accompany me to Boston. He declined and I walked in alone. After shopping an hour or so, I went up to the legislative hall and saw the Solons of the Old Bay State. The body are much more dignified than those in the Southwestern country. I also attended several of the courts. This evening I presided over the Kent Club.[7] I received a letter from Lemira E[wing] at New Haven that settled the affair between us.[8]

Jan. 7. Rose 8:00. Ret. 12:00. This morning I returned all my text books to the library and settled all my debts in Cambridge. Attended Professor Greenleaf's[9] lectures on Equity and Blackstone. Being the

[3] Isaac Warren Webster of Kingston, Massachusetts.

[4] Jared Sparks (1789-1866), McLean professor of Ancient and Modern History, was elected President of Harvard in 1849. Earlier he was an ordained Unitarian minister, editor of the *North American Review,* and lecturer. He is best remembered as a pioneer American historian of the Revolutionary period, with many editions to his credit. His course at Harvard on the American Revolution was open only to upperclassmen and law students.

[5] George Ticknor Curtis (1812-1894) was a lawyer and part time lecturer; brother of Benjamin R. Curtis, a justice of the U. S. Supreme Court; and author of several volumes on the history of the American Constitution.

[6] John Pringle Nichol (1804-1859), Regius Professor of Astronomy at the University of Glasgow, author of numerous articles and books, and lecturer on Astronomy during the winter of 1848-49 in the United States.

[7] At this time McGavock was probably temporary chairman of this debating club. There were frequent meetings with scheduled subjects for debate. During the next term he was elected secretary, then president unanimously.

[8] This is the first of several affairs mentioned in the existing journals. None of the letters which passed between McGavock and the young ladies to whom he was attracted seems to have been preserved. For Lemira Ewing, see also footnote 19, following.

[9] Simon Greenleaf (1783-1852), who with Justice Joseph Story was credited with bringing Harvard to its eminent position among law schools in the United States. At this time he held the Dane professorship.

last day of the term, the old gentleman made a very affecting and happy speech. In the afternoon I received a long letter from Father and Mother,[10] containing much good advice and a check on New York for $150 to carry me to Washington City. Supped at Mr. Hooper's[11] with DeBlanc, Wade, Andrews, and Webster.[12] Wrote a letter home.

Jan. 8. Rose 8:00. Ret. 12:00. This is the day on which the Battle of New Orleans was fought. The yankees do not celebrate it like the Southerners. Immediately after breakfast I went into Boston and occupied all forenoon in shopping. At 1:00 I called on Miss Hammond. At 2:00 Bratton[13] of S. C. and myself went to Mr. Amos Lawrence's[14] to dine agreeable to invitation. There we met Mr. Appleton and lady,[15] Mr. Means and Miss Means. We remained until 5:00 and had a very agreeable time. Mr. Lawrence presented me a copy of President Hopkins' lectures on the evidences of Christianity.[16]

Jan. 9. Rose 9:00. Ret. 12:00. This morning Mr. Parker[17] called to see me and sat until 11:00. He gave me a letter to Mr. James Barrow of New Haven that he might show me the curiosities of that place. I then set about writing a letter to Father and Mother. In the afternoon and evening I was employed with reading and conversing with my friends. All the law students are leaving Cambridge for home or places of attraction—many for Washington.

Jan. 10. Rose 7:00. Ret. 2:00. This morning was employed in making preparations to visit Washington. At 4:00 Nevins[18] and myself

---

[10] Jacob and Louisa Grundy McGavock were prosperous Nashvillians with a fine residence on Cherry Street (now the McGavock Block of buildings on Fourth Ave.). Of their thirteen children, seven lived to maturity. The McGavocks were married in 1819 after Jacob had seen service with Andrew Jackson in the Creek War. Besides owning extensive lands in Kentucky, Tennessee, and Arkansas, he held office as County, Circuit, and U. S. Circuit Court Clerk for half a century.

[11] Probably Samuel Hooper (1808-1875), Boston merchant, shipper, legislator, and reputedly one of Boston's wealthiest citizens. He was a partner in William Appleton and Co., which became Samuel Hooper and Co. in 1862.

[12] These were friends and classmates of about the same age: Charles De Blanc of New Orleans; Oliveira Andrews of Norfolk, Virginia; Henry Adams Wade of Elizabethtown, Pennsylvania.

[13] William Means Bratton, a classmate, killed at the Battle of Frazier's Farm in Virginia, 1862.

[14] Amos Lawrence (1786-1852), brother of Abbott and William Lawrence, was a wealthy merchant and philanthropist. In 1821 he was married for the second time to Mrs. Nancy Means Ellis of New Hampshire.

[15] Probably William Appleton (1786-1862), importer, banker, philanthropist, and Whig representative from Massachusetts from 1851 to 1855, and again in 1861.

[16] Mark Hopkins (1802-1887), president of Williams College, theologian, and author, published *Lectures on the Evidences of Christianity* in 1846. At the time a popular success, it was again published in 1909 as the first volume of lectures of the Bross Foundation.

[17] Probably Edward Griffin Parker of Boston, member of the senior law class when McGavock was beginning the course.

[18] William Russell Nevins, a native of New York City, who died at Rochester in 1881.

left Boston, and after a very cold and disagreeable ride we reached New Haven where I stopped and put up at the Fortress House. The object of my stopping here was to see Nathan Ewing who is still in prison for an inditement of assult with intent to kill.[19]

Jan. 11. Rose 10:00. Ret. 11:00. At 11:00 I called on Lemira Ewing and stayed about two hours and dined with her. Our meeting was peculiar unpleasant, considering the connection that hitherto existed between us. In the afternoon I called on Mrs. Ewing. She seemed more cheerful than I anticipated and evinced great fortitude in her misfortune. Lemira and myself called at the prison to see her brother. He was not in the common gaol, but under a keeper.

Jan. 12. Rose 7:00. Ret. 12:00. Last night I crossed the sound and reached New York at 6:00. A Mr. ———[?] from St. Vincent's and myself put our baggage at Lovejoy's and remained in the city until 4:00 this afternoon. During the day I employed my time in visiting places of curiosity, viz. [Hiram] Power's celebrated Greek Slave, the Five Points, and the New Custom House—all well worth seeing. Reached Philadelphia at 9:00 and took supper with Sam Ewing at the Columbia House.

Jan. 13. Rose 7:00. Ret. 11:00. At 8:00 I left Jones Hotel for Baltimore, where I dined. At 4:00 I took the cars for Frederick, which is about 60 miles from Baltimore and is one of the oldest towns in Maryland. Here I remained all night. Feeling very much fatigued from railroad travel I slept soundly. The road that I traveled over today is the oldest in this country and cost an enormous sum of money. It could now be better built for one third the amount.

Jan. 14. Rose 8:00. Ret. 10:00. At 10:00 I hired a buggy and set out for St. Mary's College about 20 miles from Frederick. I reached there at 7:00 where I found Edward[20] looking better than I ever saw him. I occupied the remainder of the day in going about the college and conversing with the faculty and Edward. The college is situated in a very retired place and seems to be a good institution. Everything is carried on systematically.

Jan. 15. Rose 6:00. Ret. 2:00. At 10:00 I left St. Mary's and reached Baltimore for tea, where I remained until 11:00 and set out for Washington in company with several students from Cambridge. We

---

[19] Nathan Ewing was the son of Henry Ewing (1802-1847) and Susan Grundy, whose brother was Felix Grundy. Thus the Mrs. Ewing mentioned later was McGavock's great aunt, his grandfather's sister. Lemira and Nathan were McGavock's second cousins. See Presley Kittredge Ewing and Mary Ellen (Williams) Ewing, *The Ewing Genealogy with Cognate Branches,* Houston, Texas; Hercules Printing and Book Company, 1919.

[20] His brother, Edward Jacob McGavock (1828-1880), two years his junior.

reached the City about 2:00 and put up at Willard's Hotel, which is situated beneath the shadow of the White House, it being the most fashionable house in the city this winter.

Jan. 16. Rose 10:00. Ret. 12:00. This morning Bostick[21] and myself went to Dr. Price's church opposite the White House. Here we found all the elite of the City, composed of distinguished statesmen, politicians, foreign ministers, and curious visitors. In the afternoon I strolled down Pennsylvania Avenue where I met Messers Winthrop, Bell, Barrow, Haskell,[22] and several other acquaintances. After tea I called on Mrs. Barrow with Major Graham. She was quite agreeable and exceedingly kind in her attentions.

Jan. 17. Rose 8:00. Ret. 12:00. Immediately after breakfast Churchill[23] and myself walked round the White House and met the President. He recognized and invited me to call and see his lady.[24] At 11:00, agreeable to engagement, I accompanied Mrs. Barrow and Mr. Dayton of New York to the Senate Chamber where we heard Mr. Barton of S. C. speak on the Ten-Regiment Bill.[25] The remainder of the day was employed in looking about.

Jan. 18. Rose 8:00. Ret. 12:00. This morning I was in both houses of Congress but as nothing of much interest was going on there, I repaired to the Supreme Court room, where I heard Dan Webster make a speech. He is the most extraordinary looking man I ever saw. His very appearance indicates greatness. At 12:00 Bostick and myself called on Mrs. Polk.[26] She was dressed splendidly and received company with great dignity and grace.

Jan. 19. Rose 7:00. Ret. 12:00. At 6:00 this morning Bostick came in my room and bid me farewell. I attended the Senate, House, and Supreme Court. At 5:00 I went to the White House and dined there.

---

21 John Litton Bostick was a Nashville friend and Harvard law student. He died at Griffin, Georgia, in 1864.

22 Robert Charles Winthrop (1809-1894) of Boston, at this time Speaker of the Thirtieth Congress. John Bell (1797-1869), Senator from Tennessee, who in 1826 had defeated McGavock's grandfather, Felix Grundy, for Congress. Washington Barrow (1807-1866), Whig Congressman from Tennessee, former minister to Portugal, editor of the Nashville *Republican Banner* from 1845 to 1847. William T. Haskell (1818-1859) young Whig Congressman from Jackson, Tennessee.

23 Charles Marshall Spring Churchill, a law student from Milton, Massachusetts.

24 As a young man James K. Polk read law in the office of Felix Grundy, McGavock's grandfather, who was appointed Attorney-General of the U. S. by Van Buren. Both Polk and Grundy enjoyed the friendship and political support of Andrew Jackson, and Randal's father, Jacob McGavock, was a pallbearer at Jackson's funeral.

25 A bill to raise, for a limited time, an additional military force of ten regiments.

26 Sarah Childress Polk (1803-1891), wife of the eleventh president, was a friend and confidant of McGavock after she and the President returned to Nashville in 1849 and McGavock began the practice of law.

I met old Ritchie,[27] Crittenden,[28] and many other distinguished men with their ladies and daughters. The dinner was splendidly served, and the President and lady performed the honors with becoming style.[29] At 11:00 I attended an Assembly Ball at Jackson Hall. It was well gotten up and was really a brilliant affair. All the beautiful ladies and distinguished characters of the city were in attendance.

Jan. 20. Rose 12:00. Ret. 12:00. This morning I was aroused by a servant with a note from Mrs. Knox Walker[30] inviting me to go out visiting with her at 1:00. I accepted the invitation and we set out in the executive carriage and called on Bodisco, the Russian minister, Vice-President Dallas' daughters, and several others. I then took dinner with Alexander Barrow and lady at Brown's Hotel. After tea I called on Miss Underwood of Kentucky and Mrs. Gentry of Tennessee.[31]

Jan. 21. Rose 8:00. Ret. 12:00. Owing to the death of one of the members, nothing was done in either house today. I occupied several hours in visiting the patent office, which is the greatest curiosity in Washington. Here is to be seen a collection of all things patented, and many other curious things—such as Egyptian mummies, geological specimens, antique paintings, and many other things worthy of one's attention.

Jan. 22. Rose 9:00. Ret. 11:00. Today I visited the Post Office Department and called on Cave Johnson,[32] who was exceedingly polite. At noon the avenues were filled with persons to witness the funeral procession of Colonel [William M.] Graham, who was killed in Mexico. He was interred with military honors. The Executive and his Cabinet were in the procession. After tea I left Willard's and went to Miss Polk's, near the Capitol, where several of my Cambridge friends were boarding.

Jan. 23. Rose 7:00. Ret. 12:00. This morning I wrote a long letter to Father. In the afternoon I went to St. John's Church, where I heard a most excellent sermon from Dr. Price. On my return I met Benson, who presented me to several Tennesseans. After tea I left Miss Polk's for Brown's Hotel, not liking a private house, particularly one occupied by such a stack of old maids.

---

[27] Thomas Ritchie (1778-1854), a journalist and politician of Richmond, Virginia, who in 1845 established the *Union,* a paper reflecting the views of Polk and his administration. He was affectionately dubbed "Father Ritchie" by admiring Virginians.

[28] John Jordon Crittenden (1787-1863), at that time Senator from Kentucky, later Governor. He served as U. S. Attorney-General under both Harrison and Fillmore.

[29] This dinner is noted in Polk's diary on January 20, 1848.

[30] Mrs. John Knox Walker, whose husband was private secretary to President Polk.

[31] Probably a daughter of Senator Joseph R. Underwood of Bowling Green, Ky.; and probably the wife of Representative Meredith P. Gentry of Franklin, Tennessee.

[32] Postmaster-General under Polk, from Clarksville, Tennessee.

Jan. 24. Rose 7:00. Ret. 12:00. This morning I went to the Senate Chamber and heard Mr. Hale of N. H. speak on the Ten-Regiment bill. Mr. Barrow spoke in the House, but I did not hear him. He was followed by a Mr. Featherstone from Mississippi in a very ranting style, which is quite the go in the House. I walked from the Capitol with a lady from Illinois whose name I did not hear when I was presented by Mrs. Barrow.

Jan. 25. Rose 8:00. Ret. 12:00. This morning I spent a short time in the Supreme Court and heard B. F. Hallett of Boston speak on the Rhode Island case, as it was called. I then went into the Senate and listened to Mr. Clarke of N. J., but he was so dry I left and called on Cave Johnson's family, Miss Ritchie, and Miss Dallas. When I returned to my hotel I found a young cousin from Virginia (Robert Kent) who has been going to Georgetown College, but was on his way to Princeton. Parker of Boston[33] supped with me, after which I called on Judge Catron,[34] Miss Underwood, and Haskell. I also went to the theatre and was most awfully bored.

Jan. 26. Rose 9:00. Ret. 12:00. After breakfast I walked up to the Patent Office with William Campbell.[35] At 11:00 four of us, viz. Parker, Warren, Dunwoody,[36] and myself went to the arsenal, where we heard Col. Fremont conclude his defense on the charges of mutiny before the Court Martial.[37] We then went to the Senate Chamber, where we heard James A. Dix of New York make a very able speech on the Ten-Regiment bill. When I returned to my hotel I found Edward, my brother, who became dissatisfied with St. Mary's and left. Tonight Edward and myself attended a levee at the President's. It was very grand.[38]

---

33 Either Edward Griffin Parker or Jonathan Mason Parker, both of whom were from Boston and attending Harvard law school in 1848.

34 John Catron (1778-1865), a jurist from Nashville; at this time an associate justice of the U. S. Supreme Court.

35 William Bowen Campbell (1807-1867), Colonel of the First Tennessee Volunteers during the Mexican War; Governor of Tennessee (1851-53); Brigadier-General in the Union Army (1862-63).

36 Three Harvard law students.

37 John Charles Fremont (1813-1890), explorer, politician, and soldier was found guilty of mutiny, disobedience, and conduct prejudicial to order while in California during the Mexican War. President Polk remitted the penalty recommended by the court-martial and public sentiment exonerated him from the charges.

38 Polk described this open house in his diary: "This evening I held a levee or general drawing room. The East room and all the parlours were opened and brilliantly illuminated. The Marine band occupied the outer Hall. Hundreds of persons, ladies and gentlemen, attended. The evening was wet, but notwithstanding that, the parlours, including the East room, were all occupied, though not so much crowded as I have seen them on similar occasions." Jan. 26, 1848.

Jan. 27. Rose 7:00. Ret. 12:00. Immediately after breakfast Edward and myself went round to see the various departments. At 11:00 I called on the President to procure a letter of introduction for S. A. Ewing to Edward Everett,[39] at the request of his mother. I then went to the Capitol where I heard Mr. Webster in the Rhode Island case. His argument was very fine. I also heard S. S. Phelps of Vermont in the Senate. At 7:00 I called on Miss Wilson of New York City at Senator Dix'.[40] After tea I went to see Dr. Collyer's model artistes.[41] Called on General Sam Houston. Wrote a letter to Mrs. Dickinson.[42]

Jan. 28. Rose 7:00. Ret. 3:30. After breakfast Edward and myself called at the Treasury Department to see Major Graham, who gave him some state bonds to carry home. I then walked through the Naval Department and at 1:00 I called on the President and conversed socially about one hour. He gave me a letter of introduction to Edward Everett for S. A. Ewing at the request of his mother. Then went to the Supreme Court and heard Clifford the Attorney-General make a speech. Walked out to the Congressional Cemetery. It is a poor affair. Attended a very brilliant party at old father Ritchie's. . . .

Jan. 29. Rose 5:00. Ret. 3:30. At 5:00 Edward and I left Washington and parted at the Relay House, he for home and I for Cambridge. I reached Baltimore very early and spent the day in writing to Father and visiting the curiosities of the city. Among other things the Washington monument, Phoenix Shot tower, and cathedral, and so forth. Baltimore is a handsome city. At 8:00 I left for Philadelphia and after seven hours' ride reached Jones Hotel, where I found a nice bed, which is very acceptable to a fatigued traveler.

Jan. 30. Rose 9:00. Ret. 2:00. This morning I went to Dr. Bethune's church,[43] where I found Uncle Eakin[44] and Julia, his neice.

---

[39] At this time Edward Everett was President of Harvard.

[40] John Adams Dix (1798-1879), Senator from New York (1845-49), railroad president, later Major-General in the Federal Army, U. S. Minister to France, and Republican Governor of N. Y.

[41] Dr. Collyer's *Model Artistes,* brought to America from the Royal Academies of London and Paris, were twenty in number, and represented "exact and faithful personifications of paintings and sculptures of the Great Masters" in tableaux on the stage of Odd Fellows Hall. See *National Intelligencer,* January 29, 1848.

[42] His sister, Ann McGavock Dickinson (1820-1868), who was the second wife of lawyer Henry Dickinson of Columbus, Mississippi. Ann was the oldest McGavock child to reach maturity, Randal being the second and the first son. In later entries he calls her Sister Ann, but always refers to his brother-in-law, who was twenty years his senior, as Judge Dickinson. Their son, Jacob McGavock Dickinson (1851-1928), was Secretary of War in the Cabinet of William Howard Taft.

[43] George Washington Bethune (1805-1862), noted for his pulpit eloquence, turned from the Presbyterian to the Reformed Dutch Church and preached in Philadelphia from 1843 to 1848.

[44] William Eakin, a prosperous Nashville merchant, was born at Muff, County Londonderry, Ireland, in 1810. With his father and mother, John and Jane Rodgers Eakin, and

I dined with him at the U. S. Hotel and remained with him the greater part of the afternoon. I called on Susan McGavock at Mrs. Lamb's, but did not see her. After tea a fire broke out on Chestnut, and I had an opportunity of seeing the mob firemen display their extinguishing skill. At 11:00 Horace Berry and myself called on Mastin, Clay, and Nichol. I met several Nashville acquaintances today.

Jan. 31. Rose 6:00. Ret. 1:00. At 7:00 I left Philadelphia for New York, by way of Camden and Amboy, which is the cheapest and most preferable route. I reached N. Y. at 12:00 and put up at the City Hotel. Here I found Major McCullough of the Texian Rangers, and Thomas, William [S.], and Argyle Eakin.[45] After tea William Eakin invited me to go to the Astor Place Opera. I accepted and several of us set out together. The opera was Romeo and Juliet. The house is the finest in the U. S. I witnessed more display and rich dressing among the ladies and gentlemen than I ever expect to see again. I was highly pleased with the performance.

Feb. 1. Rose 9:00. Ret. 8:00. After breakfast Dunwoody[46] and myself started to take a walk up Broadway. Our attention was attracted by an auction of watches. We stepped in, with no intention of bidding, but I was induced to make a bid, in which I was most shamefully swindled. Forever it will be a good lesson to me *in future*. At four Dunwoody and myself left New York for Boston on the steamer Massachusetts, by way of Stonington [Connecticut]. Coming from the South I felt the cold on the Sound very perceptibly.

Feb. 2. Rose 2:00. Ret. 10:00. This morning as I stepped out of the car, I was much surprised to find the snow eight inches deep. We took breakfast at the Revere and then went out to Cambridge which appeared almost deserted. I immediately went to Rogers' room in Graduates Hall, he and I having agreed to room together. After dinner I

---

six brothers and sisters, William immigrated to Shelbyville, Tennessee, in 1822. There this large family joined William's two older brothers, John, Jr., and Spencer Eakin, who had arrived in 1817 and 1820, respectively, and were rapidly acquiring fortunes in various business interests, chiefly mercantile. In 1842, twenty years after he had arrived in Tennessee as an immigrant lad of twelve, William Eakin married Felicia Ann Grundy, youngest daughter of Felix and Ann Rogers Grundy. He died in 1849, leaving his wife with two daughters and a considerable fortune. His MS. memoirs have been microfilmed and are on deposit at the Joint University libraries, Nashville, with other Eakin papers.

45 Thomas, Argyle Pearson, and William S. Eakin were the sons of John Eakin, Jr., the founder of mercantile businesses in Shelbyville and Nashville. Their mother was Lucretia Pearson of the Flat Creek community, near Shelbyville. Argyle was married in 1846 to Miss Louise Phoebe Wright, adopted daughter of Mr. and Mrs. John Melchour Hill of Nashville, and they lived in New York, where Argyle, William S., and Thomas were representatives of W. and T. Eakin and Co. William S. married Lemira Ewing, who had been the object of McGavock's attention until January 1848.

46 Henry Macon Dunwoody of Roswell, Georgia, Harvard law student, who was killed at the battle of Gettysburg, July 2, 1863.

went round to see Ballentine,[47] who had been sick for several weeks. The remainder of the day was employed in recounting my adventures in Washington.

Feb. 3. Rose 7:30. Ret. 12:00. After breakfast I called on Ballentine, then returned to my room and wrote a long letter to Mother, another one to Lemira Ewing, which I enclosed with her letters, and sent them to her as our previous connection with each other had been dissolved. I then took up my Blackstone and resumed my reading again. After tea I looked over some of my old newspapers that I found in my bag in the postoffice.

Feb. 4. Rose 7:30. Ret. 10:00. This morning we had a very good sample of what is termed a Northern winter. It was cold and snowing very fast. Everyone that could command a horse and sleigh were out, but I preferred to remain in my room and con the pages of the Blackstone. After dinner Gale came to our room and we occupied several hours in conversing.[48]

Feb. 5. Rose 7:30. Ret. 11:00. The weather continues cold and snow is still falling. Today I have employed my time in reading Congressional speeches and a little law. In the afternoon Gale called round and he and Rogers had a long discussion as to the propriety of ministers preaching in roabes and behind pulpits. Rogers contended that it was all nonsense. After tea I commenced to read, but felt so very sleepy that I dozed away in my chair for two hours.

Feb. 6. Rose 8:00. Ret. 11:00. This morning we had a Miss Fisher at our table, being quite good looking. We had to be on our P's and Q's. We then called on Ballentine and set until 11:00. The remainder of the day was employed in reading several articles in the Massachusetts Quarterly Review. One on the Mexican War was well written but breathed the spirit of unpatriotism and fanaticism that seems to pervade the whole community.

Feb. 7. Rose 7:30. Ret. 11:00. Nearly the whole of the forenoon was employed in writing a letter to Anna Waters in answer to a very lengthy one received from her. In the afternoon I read a portion of Blackstone on the origin and prerogatives of the various courts of England, and some letters written about ten years ago written by E. C. Hines descriptive of Boston and its environs.

---

[47] John Goff Ballentine of Pulaski, Tennessee. Ill at Harvard, he survived all the members of his class but one and died at Pulaski on November 23, 1915.

[48] Abner Green Gale of Nashville. He and McGavock were both graduated from the University of Nashville in 1846, and both received the Ll. B. from Harvard in 1849.

Feb. 8. Rose 7:30. Ret. 9:30. At 10 Rogers and I set out in a beautiful sleigh and splendid horse on a pleasure excursion. We went through Lexington and Concord; here we saw the monuments erected on the two battlegrounds. We then returned through Lincon, Western Waltham, Watertown, Roxbury, Brookline, Dorchester, and Boston—a distance of at least sixty miles, being the most extensive sleigh ride that I ever took.

Feb. 9. Rose 7:00. Ret. 11:00. I employed the forenoon in writing a letter to Sister Ann describing my visit to Washington. In the afternoon I went to see Gale. After tea I paid a visit to Ballentine who was quite sick. There I found Fillmore[49] and we took a game of Faro. The remainder of the evening was occupied in reading the comments of the Washington Union upon Mr. [John] Bell's anti-war speech. It was very tart.

Feb. 10. Rose 8:00. Ret. 11:00. After breakfast I read over the Boston papers, then finished writing a long letter to Sister Ann. The remainder of the day was employed in reading Blackstone and Pope. Some friends dropped in during the day and we had a very agreeable conversation. The weather continues very cold and the sleighs are running at a furious rate.

Feb. 11. Rose 7:30. Ret. 10:00. All the forenoon was occupied in reading Blackstone. In the afternoon I read Mr. Webster's celebrated speech in reply to Mr. Hayne of S. C. on the resolution offered by Mr. Foot, of Connecticut, relative to the public lands. It is certainly one of the most masterly efforts that ever issued from the American press.

Feb. 12. Rose 7:30. Ret. 11:00. This forenoon was employed in reading and writing. After dinner Gale and myself walked into Boston and attended the Museum. The Enchanted Horse was played, the scenery in it is said to excell anything ever presented on a Boston stage. It was truly magnificent. We then walked round to Little and Brown's to look at some London editions of Shakespeare. The evening was spent in Mr. De Blanc's room.

Feb. 13. Rose 7:30. Ret. 11:00. After breakfast I walked round and set a few hours with Ballentine. The remainder of the day was employed in reading and writing a letter to Jas. McNutt.[50] After ten I dressed up and went with Mr. Upham to Misses Uphams'. Here I found

---

[49] Millard Powers Fillmore, Jr., of Buffalo, N. Y., whose father was to become thirteenth president upon the death of Zachary Taylor in 1850.

[50] James A. McNutt (1826-1874) of Wythe County, Virginia. The son of Margaret McGavock and the Reverend Samuel McNutt, he was a first cousin of Randal McGavock.

several agreeable young ladies. Miss Fisher from Oswego, N. Y., played and sang beautifully on the piano-forte.

Feb. 14. Rose 8:00. Ret. 10:00. Immediately after breakfast I went into Boston and spent the whole day in visiting. I called on Mr. Amos Lawrence, Mrs. Appleton, Mr. Greenleaf, Mrs. Frothingham,[51] Miss Hammond. I went into the Legislative Hall and heard several speeches. There are about six hundred members. They carry on their business much more expeditiously than with us. This is Valentine's Day.

Feb. 15. Rose 7:30. Ret. ——. After breakfast I called on Ballentine. The whole forenoon was spent in finishing my letter to McNutt. After dinner I rigged up and went into Boston to fulfill an engagement to ride with Mrs. Appleton in a sleigh. We rode to Lexington and returned through Cambridge. The lady proved agreeable, and I had a pleasant time of it. I returned to Cambridge and spent the evening in reading.

Feb. 16. Rose 7:30. Ret. 11:00. After setting a few hours with Ballentine and reading the Boston papers, I commenced reading a new and very popular novel called Jane Eyre. Not that I expected to derive much information from it, but merely to render myself sufficiently acquainted with it to carry on a conversation about it.

Feb. 17. Rose 7:30. Ret. 10:00. Immediately after breakfast I resumed reading Jane Eyre, and finished it about six o'clock. It was much better than the works now daily thrown from the press, being well written and interesting. After tea I took a game of whist at Ballentine's room, and devoted the rest of the evening to reading.

Feb. 18. Rose 7:30. Ret. 11:00. The forenoon was employed in writing and reading Blackstone. After dinner Rogers and myself went out to Fresh Pond to witness the process of taking ice. This pond is very large, and surrounded by immense ice houses which contain enough to supply a very large demand. They ship it to almost every port in the world. It is the largest export of the State. Their manner of taking it very ingenious and curious. It is cut out with ploughs drawn by horses and put into the houses by steam power.

Feb. 19. Rose 8:00. Ret. 12:00. The whole of this day has been spent in my room, reading newspapers, etc. In the evening I went round and paid several visits. There was quite an excitement in Cambridge today, occasioned by a difficulty between two Irishmen, in which one of them was stabbed. Anything of the kind always arouses this peaceful community.

[51] Probably Mrs. Samuel Frothingham of Boston.

Feb. 20. Rose 8:00. Ret. 11:00. This forenoon was occupied in reading Jared Sparks' Life of Ben Franklin, and conversing with Rogers and Gale. At 12:00 I went over to Divinity Hall to see Mr. Miller from New York. After dinner I wrote a letter to Father, giving him an account of Edward's departure from St. Mary's College. After tea I read several newspapers.

Feb. 21. Rose 7:30. Ret. 10:00. After breakfast Gale and myself went to the Law Library and took out our text books for next term. We then went over to Gore Hall and spent several hours in looking at the books and some beautiful paintings of every species of American fouls by Audubon. These paintings cost $1,000. We then went to Sparks' room and set until dinner time. After dinner I promised myself several hours' reading, but Gale came and set until tea.

Feb. 22. Rose 8:00. Ret. 11:00. After breakfast Miller[52] and De Blanc insisted that I should go out skating with them. I consented and we went out to Fresh Pond and spent the whole forenoon. In the afternoon I commenced reading Graham's[53] History of the U. S. One thing I did not exactly admire in his memoir, viz. his notions of slavery in this country. After tea Gale, Sparks, and myself took a game of cards at Gordon's room from New Orleans.[54] Returned to my room and read until bedtime.

Feb. 23. Rose 8:00. Ret. 10:00. This morning I spent about half hour in Ballentine's room. I then repaired to my books, read first chapter in the Book of Kings, and Blackstone on cognizance of private wrongs. In the afternoon I went out to Mt. Auburn more for exercise than anything else and employed the rest of the day in reading and talking with my friends.

Feb. 24. Rose 7:30. Ret. 11:00. This morning was occupied in reading a little history and law. In the afternoon and evening I remained in my room doing first one thing then another. I received a letter today from Mrs. Waters in which I received the sad intelligence of the death of my friend F. B. Fogg.[55] He was a very great loss.

Feb. 25. Rose 7:30. Ret. 2:00. The greater part of this day was spent in my room. Henry Fogg called to see me, much distressed about the death of his brother. He said that he would go home tomorrow.

---

[52] William Frederick Miller of Buffalo, N. Y.

[53] James Grahame (1790-1842), *The History of the United States of North America,* London, 1827.

[54] William Alexander Gordon.

[55] Francis Brinley Fogg, Jr., of Nashville, graduate of Nashville University (1843) and Harvard Law School (1846), who died on February 13, 1848.

After tea I attended a party at Mr. Hammond's in Boston, which I found very agreeable. At one I started on foot to Cambridge.

Feb. 26. Rose 8:00. Ret. 11:00. After breakfast Gale and myself went into Boston. I called on Mr. Frothingham and got him to go my security on a bond given to the college. At three o'clock I went to see Mr. Bayn's [?] panoramic picture of a voyage to Europe. It comprises views of Boston and its harbor, Halifax, the River Mersey, Liverpool, London from the Thames, and both sides of the Rhine. It is evidently the work of a finished artist and one who is imbued with the poetry of art, as well as thoroughly versed with its rules and technicalities.

Feb. 27. Rose 8:00. Ret. 11:00. I employed the whole of this morning in my room, reading the Bible and some other things. In the afternoon I wrote a letter to Mrs. Eakin.[56] After tea I called to see Ballentine, who was talking about going home as usual. His brother had just arrived and was exceedingly desirous that he should go, thinking that it would improve his health.

Feb. 28. Rose 7:30. Ret. 12:00. Today is the beginning of a new term. Mr. Greenleaf and Mr. Parker were both in their seats. Greenleaf begun with a few congratulating remarks, and reading the rules of the initiation. He also gave out several Moot Court cases and placed me on one for the fourth of April. Mr. Parker then made a short address to us. He said that he had been connected with the law for many years, but that this was a new sphere to him. He hoped that our mantle of charity would be broad enough to cover all his deficiencies.[57]

Feb. 29. Rose 8:00. Ret. 11:00. After breakfast I read the lecture in Kent on the sources of the Municipal Law upon which Mr. Parker lectured. He opened by giving a brief sketch of the author and eulogizing him very highly. He promises to be a good lecturer, although he is [not] very fluent. In the evening I read a speech of John Bell in the Senate on the Ten-Regiment bill. It is an able document. Notwithstanding I differ with him in some of his premises.

Mar. 1. Rose 7:30. Ret. 12:00. Commenced reading Cruise Digest of the English Laws. It is regarded by many as being very dry and difficult to comprehend, but to be a good lawyer it is necessary to be

[56] His aunt, Mrs. William Eakin of Nashville, the former Felicia Ann Grundy. A prominent social leader of the city, she later married Dr. Robert Massengill Porter.

[57] Joel Parker (1795-1875) resigned as Chief Justice of the New Hampshire Superior Court to accept the Royall Professorship at Harvard in 1848. He is reported as saying, after a few months of lecturing, that he would have gladly gone back to New Hampshire on his hands and knees, had such been possible. But he remained in the chair until 1868. He is remembered as a precise, exact teacher and a careful logician, taking such pains in handing down decisions in Moot Court cases that students might have thought they involved final judgments in actual litigation.

acquainted with it. Mr. Greenleaf's lecture upon this morning was very fine. After tea I read Graham's History until twelve. This morning Rogers, Gale, Sergeant, Lippitt,[58] and myself left Mr. Upham's where I have boarded ever since I have been here and formed a club.

Mar. 2. Rose 7:00. Ret. 10:30. After breakfast Rogers and I took a short walk. I then returned to my room and read Kent on the Report of Judicial Decisions, attended Mr. Parker's lecture, returned to my room and read until two o'clock. After dinner I attended the Kent Club, was elected Secretary, and appointed to open the debate. I then called on Ballentine, took a game of whist. After tea I wrote out the proceedings of the Club.

Mar. 3. Rose 7:00. Ret. 11:00. Read Cruise's Digest until 11:00, and Professor Greenleaf's lecture upon it. I then read newspapers until 2:00. After dinner Nevins told me that William [S.] Eakin had married Lemira Ewing, an event that caused a feeling of disgust to gush from my bosom and to exclaim: Woman, O Woman, thy vows are traced in sand. After tea I paid Gale a visit. The balance of the evening was devoted to reading.

Mar. 4. Rose 7:00. Ret. 11:00. After breakfast Nevins called in for a short time. The whole forenoon was employed in reading law. After dinner I went round to Sergeant's room and spent several hours. The remainder of the day was spent in reading Graham's History of the Early Colonists. This portion of our history is very interesting. It shows what privations and many unsuccessful efforts those daring spirits underwent in their endeavors to populate a New World.

Mar. 5. Rose 7:00. Ret. 11:00. This morning Rogers and I walked into Boston to hear old Father [Edward T.] Taylor preach, a man that founded the Sailors' Bethel. He was sick and we were disappointed. We then went to the Melodeon to hear Theodore Parker, a celebrated abolitionist, preach.[59] He delivered a sermon on the life and character of Mr. [John Quincy] Adams to an immense audience. We had an unpleasant walk out; a northeaster was blowing. In the evening I wrote a letter to Father.

Mar. 6. Rose 7:00. Ret. 10:00. This morning I read several chapters in the Bible and Cruise on Fee Simple, and attended the lecture. In the afternoon I read Blackstone and Graham's History. After tea I

[58] Henry Sargent of Byfield, Massachusetts, after his graduation in 1849 private secretary to Daniel Webster. John Lippitt of Cranston, Rhode Island.

[59] Theodore Parker (1810-1860), Unitarian clergyman, abolitionist, incendiary. He made anti-slavery speeches in Faneuil Hall, aided the escape of fugitive slaves, and published *A Letter to the People of the United States Touching the Matter of Slavery* (1848).

read the Union. Rogers informed that I was elected a member of "The Club," which is devoted to the discussion of legal topics. I think it will prove beneficial.

Mar. 7. Rose 7:15. Ret. 11:00. Read Kent on Civil Law and attended the lecture upon it by Judge Parker. He is not as good a lecturer as Professor Greenleaf. He lacks that perspicuity and ease which distinguish Greenleaf. In the afternoon I attended the Moot Court where I heard one or two very good speeches. After tea I read Kent until ten, then paid a short visit to De Blanc.

Mar. 8. Rose 7:00. Ret. 11:00. Read Cruise Digest and attended the lecture, which was the best Professor Greenleaf ever delivered on the subject. The rest of the day was employed in reading law and history. In the afternoon Rogers and I took a stroll round Cambridge for exercise. The ice on the ground rendered it disagreeable.

Mar. 9. Rose 7:15. Ret. 10:00. Read Kent until 10:00, and heard a lecture upon it. In the afternoon I attended the Kent Club. One of the gentlemen that was appointed to open the debate was absent and the President appointed me to supply his place. Although it was a subject to which I had given some attention, yet I was unprepared to speak.

Mar. 10. Rose 7:30. Ret. 11:30. Read the lecture in Kent, but did not attend the lecture room. At 12 o'clock Rogers and I went into Boston to witness the reception of John Q. Adams' remains. The day was very bad, being muddy and rainy, yet there was a large concourse of people thronging the streets to see the last of a man they idolized. The body was deposited in Faneuil Hall, where everyone went to see it. The curiosity to look at the coffin was so great that they rushed over the police. The hall was splendid, heavy in mourning, and the music was very fine. Major Quincey received the Congressional Delegates that attended the remains from Washington in a very appropriate speech. After tea I went to hear Horace Greeley lecture on his favorite theme. I then called at the Tremont to see Colonel Gentry of Tennessee.[60] Left my card.

Mar. 11. Rose 7:15. Ret. 11:00. The entire day has been spent in my room reading Kent's second volume. I am very much pleased with his style. It is easy, chaste, and intelligible. Although this work stands high, yet I think it has not attained near the reputation it merits and must eventually possess. I sent Governor A. V. Brown [of Tennessee] a copy of the statistics of the railroads in Massachusetts. Received a letter from Judge Dickinson and Sister Ann.

---

[60] Meredith P. Gentry (1809-1866), of Williamson County, Tennessee, Representative to the Thirtieth Congress.

Mar. 12. Rose 8:00. Ret. 11:15. This is a beautiful morning, being clear and mild. This morning I read my Bible until 11, when Eugene Batchelder[61] came in and set till dinner. He gave me a description of a pedestrian tour he made to Mt. Washington and gave me an insight into some of the peculiarities of Yankims. In the afternoon I wrote a letter to Mrs. Bass,[62] and paid a visit to Ballentine. After tea Nevins called on me and we had a social chat.

Mar. 13. Rose 7:15. Ret. 11:00. This morning I read and attended the lecture on Cruise. After the first lecture the death of Henry Wheaton, the Professor of International and Civil Law in this institution.[63] I then devoted several hours to the investigation of a case in Moot Court. In the afternoon and evening I read Kent and Graham's History. I received a letter from Father this morning.

Mar. 14. Rose 7:30. Ret. 11:00. Read and attended the lectures on Kent and Abbott's Shipping. In the afternoon Rogers and I walked into Boston and called on General [Sam] Houston. At 7:00 we attended a Houston meeting at the Tremont Temple. It was the greatest sea of human beings that have assembled in Boston for years. The General spoke an hour and a half amid the constant applause of an audience curious to see the hero of San Jaciento. Mr. Kaufman, member of Congress from Texas, spoke.[64] He is rather a weak vessel.

Mar. 15. Rose 7:30. Ret. 11:00. This is one of the coldest days that I have felt this winter. Read and attended the lecture on Cruise. During the lecture, Professor Greenleaf read a letter from a Mr. Lee who graduated from here in 1842 and is now Chief Justice in the Sandwich Islands, and appointed to write a code of laws for their government.[65] Professor G. said that the responsibilities of graduates here are very great and admonished us to make ourselves masters of our profession. In the afternoon I read law and called on Nevins.

Mar. 16. Rose 7:00. Ret. 11:30. This morning I read and attended the lecture on Kent, after which I read several newspapers on the subject of the war. In the afternoon I attended the Kent Club where we had a very spirited and instructive debate on the war question.

---

[61] Eugene Batchelder of Cambridge, Massachusetts, who entered the law school in 1844 and received the Ll. B. in 1845.

[62] His aunt, Malvina Grundy, who was married to John M. Bass of Nashville.

[63] Thus reads the original.

[64] David Spangler Kaufman (1813-1851), representative from Texas to the Thirtieth Congress.

[65] William Little Lee of Sandy Hill, N. Y., who was graduated in 1844 (instead of 1842) and who died in Honolulu, H. I., on May 28, 1857.

Chamberlain[66] and myself opened the discussion and made two speeches each. Several of the gentlemen spoke. After tea our table club went to hear the Harmonians in the Lyceum. This time I consider lost. I neither derived pleasure nor benefit.

Mar. 17. Rose 7:00. Ret. 11:00. This morning I read Cruise on Life Estate and attended the lecture at 11:00. Went into Professor Parker's room to consult him on a point in law. He was very polite and offered to lend me any assistance in his power. In the afternoon I went to the Legislative Hall to hear Mr. [Wendell] Philips, a Boston lawyer and abolitionist, speak on the propriety of Massachusetts seceding from the Union. I had often heard of the vituperations heaped upon the Southern slave holders by the Abolitionists and fanatics of New England. But I never fully realized the extent of their folly and gasconading presumption until I listened to Mr. Philips and Garrison,[67] two of their able and devoted advocates. These two men addressed a Committee (appointed by the Legislature) in behalf of certain petitioners praying that Massachusetts should quietly secede from the Union. Their speeches were disgraceful to themselves, the State, and to the party to which they belong. They were filled with abuse of the most vile and atrocious character. They said that the Union was founded in blood and associated with blood, that the Constitution was leagued with death and a covenant with hell. It was rubber for one portion of the Union and wrought iron for the other—and like expressions. Fortunately for the country, these men are not allowed to participate in our councils, because they refuse to take the oath to support that instrument which every true patriot holds dear and sacred. But it is really alarming to see how rapidly they increase. Some years ago their petitions were not noticed or listened to. But now they hold their meetings and petition for a dissolution of our Union with impunity.

Mar. 18. Rose 7:30. Ret. 2:00. This morning I read Graham's History and some law. In the afternoon Nevins called and set several hours. After tea I paid several visits, among others [to] Thomas Sparks of Louisiana. Here I found six or eight gents drinking and card playing.

---

[66] Mellen Chamberlain (1821-1900), autograph collector, historian, and librarian, was born in Pembroke, N. H. After graduating from Harvard Law School in 1848, he was admitted to the Boston Bar, married Martha Ann Putnam, and lived in Chelsea. During the Civil War he was elected to the Massachusetts Senate and later served in various other public offices. In 1878 he became librarian of the Public Library of Boston, wrote historical studies, and collected MSS. relating to New England history.

[67] Wendell Phillips (1811-1884), orator and reformer, who said in Faneuil Hall on October 30, 1842, "My *curse* be on the Constitution of these United States." Both he and William Lloyd Garrison (1805-1879) demanded a division of the Union. Unable to record his full impression of these two incendiaries in a few words, McGavock turned to a blank page at the back of his journal and thus completed the longest single entry of 1848.

I joined and came out $4.00 winner, the first money I ever won by cards. The Cambria brought news of the Revolution in France and abdication of the throne for Count de Paris.

Mar. 19. Rose 7:30. Ret. 11:00. After breakfast I wrote a long letter to Father. In the afternoon I went to church in Cambridge Port and heard a very good sermon on the duties of a Christian. I then called on Herndon of Alabama[68] and Dunwoody of Georgia. After tea I read several chapters in the Bible, when Jenness of New Hampshire[69] came in and set a while. I have suffered today with a soar throat and bad cold.

Mar. 20. Rose 7:30. Ret. 11:00. This morning I received a long letter from Mother who had just returned from New Orleans. It contained much salutary advice. Read Cruise and attended the lecture. In the afternoon I went to Lippitt's room and set a while. After tea I attended a law club and heard a very good argument by Messers Roosevelt and McCarthy.[70] Read History until bedtime.

Mar. 21. Rose 7:30. Ret. 12:00. This morning I read Kent on Divorce and attended the lecture, returned to my room and read an article in the Washington Union in vindication of the Mexican Treaty. In the afternoon I was engaged in looking out some authorites on a Moot Court case. After tea I read Graham's History on Bacon's Rebellion, the Colonial administration of Sir William Berkeley and the author's views of slavery in the U. S.

Mar. 22. Rose 7:30. Ret. 11:00. Read three chapters in the book of Kings, Cruise on Estates for life, and attended the lecture. In the afternoon I attended the Kent Club and listened to an argument upon the propriety of allowing persons to give evidence in their own case. After tea I searched out authorities in my Moot Court case until nine, then read newspapers and Graham's History. Received a long letter from Anna Waters.

Mar. 23. Rose 7:30. Ret. 10:00. Read and attended the lecture on Kent and spent several hours in searching authorities. After dinner I attended the Moot Court. The argument was better than usual—Messers Crocker[71] and Lippitt. Smith[72] and Nevins were the counsel. After tea I attended a lecture on elocution by C. P. Bronson, who professes to

---

68 Thomas Hord Herndon of Eutaw, Alabama.

69 John Scribner Jenness of Portsmouth, New Hampshire.

70 Robert Barnwell Roosevelt (1829-1906), Democrat, reformer, a writer on outdoor life, and uncle of President Theodore Roosevelt. John Francis McCarthy of Washington, D. C., who died in New Orleans in 1858.

71 Timothy Doane Crocker of Cleveland, Ohio.

72 William Henry Leland Smith of Lowell, Massachusetts.

teach Dr. Rush's admirable system of throwing the voice from the abdomen.

Mar. 24. Rose 6:00. Ret. 12:15. This morning I read Kent and attended the lecture, after which I searched the reports for adjudicated cases on delivery of personal property. In the afternoon Nevins, Rogers, Lippitt, and myself walked into Boston and promenaded Washington Street until dark. Lippitt and I then called on some *ladies*. Returned at 12:00. Received a letter from J. A. McNutt today. A convention was held in Boston today to take into consideration the propriety of abolishing the Sabbath.

Mar. 25. Rose 7:30. Ret. 11:00. This morning I spent in the library scanning authorities, etc. In the afternoon I read several papers and walked out to Mt. Auburn with Mr. Force,[73] who took tea with me. After tea I went to his room and set a time. I then called on De Blanc. The remainder of the evening was spent in reading Graham's History of this country.

Mar. 26. Rose 9:00. Ret. 12:30. After breakfast I went round to Wilson's[74] room and set a hour. Gale and I then went to church and heard a very good sermon. In the afternoon I read some law, etc., etc. After tea Rogers and I walked in and from Boston. He went to see a lady in Charlestown, and I called to see *one* in the City.

Mar. 27. Rose 8:00. Ret. 10:30. Read several chapters in the Bible. Went to the library and spent the whole day in searching out authorities for a Club case. After tea I made a speech before the Club on a case involving a nice distinction in the Conflict of Laws. I then read Graham on the character of the Puritans. Called on Chamberlain who opposed me in the case above alluded to.

Mar. 28. Rose 6:00. Ret. 10:00. Read three chapters in the book of Second Kings before breakfast. I then accompanied several friends into Boston to hear Daniel Webster speak before the Supreme Court, but owing to the illness of his daughter, Mrs. Appleton, the case was postponed. However, we remained and heard several speeches from lesser lights. Feeling rather poetical today, I purchased the works of Shakespeare, Milton, and Byron. The people are in perfect extacies today about the news brought by the Caledonia confirming the previous news that France was a Republic.

---

[73] Manning Ferguson Force of Washington, D. C. He later moved to Cincinnati, Ohio, became a Lt. Col. in the Federal Army in 1862, and died in Sandusky on May 8, 1899. McGavock was his prisoner for a brief time after the fall of Fort Donelson. See the entry for February 27, 1862.

[74] Eliel Soper Wilson of Ann Arundel County, Maryland.

Mar. 29. Rose 7:30. Ret. 12:00. Read Cruise and attended the lecture, also paid some attention to my Moot Court case. In the afternoon I read the glorious news from France, whose success in establishing republicanism on a firm basis is hailed with joy and hope by every American. She aided us in our struggle for liberty and it is but natural that we should sympathize with her in her hour of trial.

Mar. 30. Rose 7:30. Ret. 10:00. This morning I read and attended the lecture on Kent. In the afternoon several of us walked into Boston to hear Mr. Choate[75] speak before a Committee of the Legislature on the boundary line between Massachusetts and Rhode Island, which has been in dispute for many years. After tea I read until 10:00.

Mar. 31. Rose 7:30. Ret. 10:00. This forenoon was occupied in reading the lectures, etc., etc. In the afternoon I read some authorities on a Moot Court case. After tea I read the correspondence between N. P. Trist and Mr. Buchanan.[76] It shows conclusively to my mind that Trist was unworthy of such an important trust, viz. to negotiate a treaty between two belligerent nations. The appointment was an unfortunate one.

Apr. 1. Rose 8:00. Ret. 10:00. I spent all of this morning in the library searching over those old, musty tomes for ideas expressed ages ago. In the afternoon I took a long walk, returned to my room and spent the evening in reading Graham's History on the colonization of New England, which I found exceedingly interesting.

Apr. 2. Rose 8:00. Ret. 11:00. This morning I dressed up and went to church, where I heard a Mr. Allbrook preach upon the sinfulness of our race, which proceeded from the disobedience of our first parents. He drew a beautiful picture of the Fall of Eden, but not so touching as Milton. In the afternoon, I wrote a long letter to Mother.

Apr. 3. Rose 7:00. Ret. 11:00. Immediately after breakfast several of us walked into Boston to hear Dan Webster speak in the Supreme Court. But we were disappointed. He did not speak. We remained an hour or so and listened to Judge Shaw, who is regarded as the soundest judge in New England, read one or two opinions. In the afternoon I was engaged in my Moot Court case. After tea I attended the law club and listened to a very able argument by Day and Smith.

---

[75] Rufus Choate (1799-1859), native of Massachusetts, lawyer and statesman. After practising in Danvers, he served short terms in both houses of the Massachusetts Legislature; afterwards he was Congressman (1831-1834), and Senator (1841-1845) in Washington.

[76] Nicholas Philip Trist (1800-1874), Virginia lawyer, assistant secretary of state under Polk, and peace commissioner to Mexico in 1848. He negotiated and signed the treaty of Guadalupe Hidalgo. James Buchanan (1791-1868), fifteenth president of the U. S.

Apr. 4. Rose 7:00. Ret. 12:00. Read and attended the lecture on the subject of Dower in Cruise. Had our Moot Court case postponed in order to enable the students to hear Dan Webster, who spoke before a Committee of the Legislature on a railroad question. He had a large crowd to hear him, but I thought he was not as animated as usual, being much distressed about his son who died in Mexico and the indisposition of his daughter.[77] After tea I read his great speech in the Senate on the .... bill. Also wrote a long letter to Sister Ann and Judge [Dickinson].

Apr. 5. Rose 7:30. Ret. 11:00. Read and attended the lecture on Kent. In the afternoon I attended a very interesting and exciting debate in the Kent Club on the all-absorbing question of the day, viz. the French Revolution. The ardent and patriotic sympathized with the people, while the others contended that the people of France were too fickle and unstable for a Republic. Wrote a letter to Sister Ann.

Apr. 6. Rose 7:30. Ret. 11:00. This is the day set apart by the Governor for fasting and prayer. All the business houses are closed and the people flock to the various churches. In the forenoon I paid a visit to Nevins and Ballentine. In the afternoon Mr. Russell of Plymouth[78] and I walked into Boston. After promenading around the Common and through Washington, Hanover, and Ann Streets, we repaired to the Melodeon, where we heard Garrison, Quincy, Philips, Channing, Parker, etc., the most rabid abolitionists in Massachusetts, speak on the Revolution in France.

Apr. 7. Rose 7:45. Ret. 10:30. This morning I read and attended the lecture on Slaves and Servants in Kent. In the afternoon and evening I was occupied in one of Scott's novels called The Heart of Midlothian, which Judge Kent says every lawyer should read. I also read a long and interesting letter in the Washington Union from Paris, giving an account of the recent events that have transpired in that City.

Apr. 8. Rose 7:00. Ret. 11:00. This forenoon was occupied in reading The Heart of Midlothian, in which I became much interested. It is not my practice to read novels, but when one peruses a book of this character, he is not only highly interested but edified. The remainder of the day was employed as usual.

Apr. 9. Rose 8:30. Ret. 2:00. This is one of the most delightful morns that we have had this Spring. After breakfast Nevins, Gale, and

---

[77] Major Edward Webster died in Mexico of typhoid fever on January 23, 1848. Julia Webster, the wife of Samuel Appleton Appleton of Boston, was a victim of consumption. She died on April 28, 1848, and was buried on May 1. Her brother's body arrived from Mexico and was buried four days later.

[78] Thomas Russell of Plymouth, Massachusetts, who died in Boston in 1887.

myself walked out to view the beauties of J. P. Cushing's villa.[79] Beautiful towers, slopes, swells, velvet lawns, majestic groves, winding paths, and charming vistas are a part only of the many attractions. Read in the afternoon. After tea Mr. Rich[80] and I called on Judge Parker and lady,[81] whom we found very agreeable. I then called on Professor Greenleaf and his family. Returned to my room and wrote a long letter to Anna Waters.

Apr. 10. Rose 7:45. Ret. 11:00. This morning I read and attended a very difficult lecture on Jointure in Cruise. Read law until two. In the afternoon I attended the Moot Court, heard a very able and reputable speech from Mr. Ayer[82] of New Hampshire. Then took a walk with De Blanc to Brighton. After tea I presided as Judge on a case in our law club. Ayer and Rogers were the counsels in the case.

Apr. 11. Rose 8:00. Ret. 12:00. Read Kent and attended the lecture. The remainder of the day was occupied in reading law, etc. After dinner I spent an hour or so at Lippitt's room and walked over to Brighton to see Winship's nurseries, but was disappointed, having missed the way. This has been a delightful day.

Apr. 12. Rose 8:30. Ret. 12:00. Read Cruise and attended the lecture. At one o'clock the students had a meeting to receive the report of a Committee appointed to inquire about their having a place assigned them in the procession to attend the eulogy on Mr. John Q. Adams by President Everett next Saturday. I was appointed unanimously Chief Marshal of the Law School. Quite an honor. We had a most enthusiastic meeting of the Kent Club this afternoon. I made a speech on the French Revolution.

Apr. 13. Rose 7:30. Ret. 12:00. Read and attended the lecture on Kent, after which I read newspapers until the dinner hour. I then went into Boston for the purpose of seeing Mr. Devins, Chief Marshal of

---

[79] John Perkins Cushing (1787-1854), Boston merchant and philanthropist, erected in 1830 a handsome mansion on Summer Street, surrounded by a wall of Chinese porcelain. The house was kept, to the amazement of Boston society, by a staff of Chinese servants. The place to which McGavock refers here was the celebrated "Belmont," at Watertown, where Cushing erected numerous plant and fruit houses, lavished great expenditures on horticultural specimens, and maintained a large conservatory of exotic and native plants.

[80] William Alexander Rich of Washington, D. C.

[81] Professor Joel Parker was married to Mary Morse of Keene, New Hampshire. Their home in Cambridge was always open to students and McGavock recorded several visits there. S. Arthur Bent in "Personal Recollections," *New England Magazine,* XLVII, p. 244, described Parker as a man of constant hospitality. "He was never so much at home as when entertaining in his charming house a few members of the school. I can see him now holding to his critical and appreciative eye his Rhine wine in its Bohemian or Venetian glass." For opinions of Parker, at the time McGavock was a prisoner at Fort Warren, see the entry for March 14, 1862.

[82] Benjamin Franklin Ayer of Manchester, New Hampshire.

the procession to attend Mr. Everett's eulogy, about the order of the day, which he politely gave. Went to the Exchange and looked over the papers. Returned to Cambridge.

Apr. 14. Rose 8:00. Ret. 10:00. Read and attended the lecture in Cruise. Called a meeting of the Law students and took the vote as to whether they would attend the procession on tomorrow or no. They voted Yes! Made a speech in a Moot Court case which was received with applause. Ballentine made a good speech in his way. After tea I paid several visits.

Apr. 15. Rose 6:30. Ret. 12:00. Immediately after breakfast I went into Boston to discharge my duties as Marshal of the Law Students. After I had formed them in the procession I was appointed Chief Marshal of Harvard University. We marched through the principal streets to Faneuil Hall where there was a great rush. I suppose there were 8,000 persons under the roof! The Honorable Edward Everett delivered the Eulogy upon John Q. Adams in a very happy style. His gestures were perfect but I was disappointed in the speech. It was simply a narrative of Mr. Adams' life. After he concluded, all the Marshals repaired to the Tremont House where we had a splendid dinner. Late in the afternoon I called on the Misses Hammond, Mr. Amos Lawrence, and the Misses Clarke.

Apr. 16. Rose 7:30. Ret. 11:00. This forenoon was occupied in talking and laughing over the scenes witnessed on yesterday. In the afternoon I wrote a long letter to Father. After tea I read some in Graham's History and Blackstone's Commentary. This has been a delightful day—just like a southern spring day.

Apr. 17. Rose 7:00. Ret. 12:00. Read three chapters in the Book of Kings. Read and attended the lecture in Kent on Corporations. In the afternoon I attended the Moot Court, but the speeches of the council were so dry and uninteresting that I left. After tea I attended the law club and read the life of William Shakespeare. It is really wonderful that so little should be known of the life and character of that great man.

Apr. 18. Rose 7:00. Ret. 11:00. Read Mr. Clay's letter to the public consenting to allow his name to be presented to the National Convention as a candidate for the Presidency. To what lengths will inordinate ambition lead a man! If he should be nominated again, defeat is inevitable. Read and attended the lecture on Kent. In the afternoon, I went to Gore Hall and examined the John James Audubon celebrated paintings of American birds, which are really exquisite.

Apr. 19. Rose 8:00. Ret. 10:00. This morning the ground was covered with snow, something unusual at this season of the year. Read the lecture on Cruise, but owing to Professor Greenleaf's indisposition, we had no lecture. In the afternoon, I attended the Kent Club and was unanimously elected President. I declined, but they refused to receive my resignation. The evening was spent in reading.

Apr. 20. Rose 7:00. Ret. 11:00. Read and attended the lecture on Cruise. The remainder of the day was spent in reading and writing an opinion on a law case. At 9:00 o'clock Mr. Force and myself went to a party at President Everett's given to Judge Parker and lady. Here I was presented to Mr. Longfellow and lady, Miss Palfrey, and several others. I was much pleased with Mr. Everett and his family. He has a splendid bust of himself taken by [Hiram] Powers.

Apr. 21. Rose 7:00. Ret. 12:00. Read and attended the lecture in Kent. The balance of the day was spent in reading and writing. In the afternoon I was tempted by unusual pleasantness of the weather to take a long stroll. Called on Ballentine and De Blanc. Russell called to see me after tea and gave me a long account of news of the disturbance in Great Britain and almost every European power. It seems that the days of kings are few and sorrowful. This is certainly the most outstanding year in the political affairs of the world since the birth of Christ. The spirit of Liberty is now spreading over the European continent with such astonishing rapidity as even to alarm its most sanguine sympathizers as to its probable durability.

Apr. 22. Rose 8:00. Ret. 2:00. This forenoon was spent in library writing and looking up cases. In the afternoon I completed the life of Shakespeare. After tea I called on Mrs. Sparks; and set to a late hour playing cards with Gordon [and] De Blanc. It is very interesting for a time, but it soon becomes a bore to me.

Apr. 23. Rose 8:00. Ret. 12:00. After breakfast I went to Nevins' room and smoked a segar, then returned to my room and read till dinner hour, after which I escorted the Misses Clark to church in Cambridge Port. When we returned I took a walk round to Warren's room from Ohio.[83] After tea I wrote a long letter to John A. McEwen of Nashville.[84]

Apr. 24. Rose 8:00. Ret. 11:00. Read and attended the lecture on Kent, after which I read the Washington Union. In the afternoon, I

[83] Samuel Mills Warren of Cincinnati.

[84] John A. McEwen, a leader in the establishment of public schools in Nashville, was editor of the *Nashville Gazette* in 1851 and a member of the first Board of Education in 1854.

was engaged in looking up a case which I had to debate in "The Club." After tea I went to the club and read a decision on a case discussed the previous meeting. I then proceeded to discuss it without any previous investigation, and of which I knew nothing, a practice that is both foolish and ruinous.

Apr. 25. Rose 7:30. Ret. 12:00. Received a letter from Mother and Sally Bass, giving an account of the burning of L. McGavock's house, and other things that had happened at home.[85] Read and attended the lecture on Kent's Commentary during the afternoon. At 5:00 Rogers, Russell and I walked into Boston and attended an Abolition meeting in Faneuil Hall. The object of the meeting was to raise funds to bail those three men imprisoned in Washington City for decoying and stealing some 70 slaves belonging to citizens of the District. The meeting was full and addressed by Messers Clapp, two Channings, and several others.

Apr. 26. Rose 8:00. Ret. 11:00. Read and attended the lecture in Cruise on the subject of Insurance, which I find quite difficult to understand. Read law until dinner time. At 3:00 I attended the Kent Club. Heard a very excellent discussion from E. G. Parker upon the perpetuity of the English government. Roosevelt, the secretary, gave a very humorous and poetical description of the previous meeting, in which he complimented my humble self upon my popularity in being unanimously elected President of such a literary club. He also described my speech to [the] club in very high terms. The evening was occupied in my room.

Apr. 27. Rose 8:00. Ret. 10:00. Read and attended the lecture on Cruise. Also read the Washington Union, in which I found a most disgraceful discussion on the slavery subject produced by a bill introduced in the Senate by Mr. Hale of N. H. After early dinner Ballentine and I procured fine horses and rode to Charlestown, thence to Chelsea beach, which is truly beautiful. Here we had a splendid view of Old Ocean, upon whose bosom might be seen a hundred vessels. Our horses were so fleet and the beach so level and smooth that we could not forego the pleasure of having a race. We run and I beat. We then returned through Charlestown, Boston, Roxbury, Brookline, Brighton, back to Cambridge—a very long and to me delightful ride.

Apr. 28. Rose 8:00. Ret. 11:30. This morning I felt very sensibly the effects of my ride yesterday afternoon. Attended the lecture on

---

[85] Lysander McGavock (1800-1855) was Jacob McGavock's first cousin and lived at "Midway," Williamson County, Tennessee. His account books and other papers have been microfilmed and are on deposit at the Joint University Libraries, Nashville.

Cruise and read the history of Charles 1st until two. After dinner I attended Dr. Wyman's lecture in the College on Anatomy.[86] It was very interesting and instructive. I learned many things of importance. I then read the English Encyclopædia and Macaulay on the Life of Charles First. I also read the Honorable Edward Everett's Eulogy on the life and character of John Q. Adams, which I consider very fine. Sent John A. McEwen a copy.

Apr. 29. Rose 9:00. Ret. 11:00. The whole day has been employed in reading and writing in regard to the justice of the execution of Charles 1st as a revolutionary measure. I think it may have been expedient. Considered as a judicial act it seems to have been a flagrant violation of the most sacred principles of law and justice. The evening was spent in social conversation at Gale's and Lippitt's rooms. The arrival of the steamer America today brought news of the suppression of the Chartists in England and all things on the continent now appear to work well. The suppression of the rebellion in England caused a considerable increase in the market.

Apr. 30. Rose 7:30. Ret. 11:00. Was occupied in my room until twelve, then called on Herndon and Dunwoody. In the afternoon I attended church in the chapel, where I heard a very excellent Sermon. I then wrote a long letter to Mother. After tea I called on Miss Everett. She was very agreeable and intelligent, but remarkably homely. I also saw Mrs. Everett.

[86] Jeffries Wyman (1814-1874), Professor at Harvard, lecturer on Comparative Anatomy, and President (1856) of the Boston Society of Natural History.

CHAPTER X

"The President would have granted my request." (May-August, 1848)

The following entries show clearly that McGavock, a Democrat, studied objectively the platforms of the various political parties of 1848 and that he closely observed the leading candidates in the presidential election. His own gift for vigorous oratory and political debate distinguished him as a student at the Harvard Law School and won him a cordial esteem with professors and fellow students.

May 1. Rose 7:30. Ret. 10:00. Read several chapters in the book of Kings and the lecture in Cruise. Mr. Greenleaf looked very feeble this morning. His health is very delicate. Read Mr. Everett's eulogy upon John Q. Adams. It is not as fine as I anticipated. The evening was occupied in my room.

May 2. Rose 6:00. Ret. 11:00. This being Exhibition Day in the College proper, there were no lectures in the Law School. I attended the Exhibition where I heard some very good speeches. Mr. Tiffany of Maryland and Mr. Young of Boston, I thought excelled. The afternoon and evening were spent in reading law, Byron, and conversing with Rogers.

May 3. Rose 7:00. Ret. 11:00. Read three chapters in the Bible and the lecture on Cruise. Rogers left this morning for Lowell, to be absent for several weeks. In the afternoon I presided over the Kent Club. The discussion was unusually animated. The question was this: Is the Wilmot Proviso Unconstitutional?[1] Being a question in which my feeling was enlisted, I declined giving an opinion. I took the vote of the Club and they decided almost unanimously that it was.

[1] The Wilmot Proviso was an amendment proposed by David Wilmot, Representative from Pennsylvania, which would have prohibited slavery in any territory which the United States should acquire through a peace treaty with Mexico. Passed by the House, it was never acted on by the Senate.

May 4. Rose 7:00. Ret. 10:00. Read and attended the lectures in Kent and Abbott on Shipping. Abbott Lawrence, Jr., called on me for the first time today and invited me to dine at his father's on Saturday. I brought a letter of introduction to Mr. Lawrence and this is the first notice he has taken of it. Of course I will send my apology.[2] Read a letter from General Taylor defining his position in politics.

May 5. Rose 7:00. Ret. 10:00. Read and attended the lecture on Kent. Also read Cruise on the subject of Insurance, which I find quite difficult. In the afternoon I attended Dr. Wyman's lecture on Anatomy. Here I learned many things about the human frame that I was in total ignorance of. The evening was employed in conversing.

May 6. Rose 6:30. Ret. 10:30. After breakfast Sargent and I walked into Boston. I went into the Municipal Court and heard the Clerk read fifteen or twenty indictments. I then called on Miss Hammond. At her suggestion we called on Miss Merrill, whom I found quite pretty and agreeable. We then called on Miss Morton at Judge Shaw's. Went to the Museum. Walked out. After tea I called on the Misses Clarke.

May 7. Rose 7:30. Ret. 11:00. This forenoon was occupied in reading and talking. After dinner I went to church and employed my time until tea in reading Shakespeare. After tea I spent about half an hour in a most unhappy state of mind, caused by reflections upon some of my past career. Force called to see me this evening. Finished The Tempest.

May 8. Rose 6:00. Ret. 12:00. Read and attended the lecture on Kent, after which I read a pamphlet published in Boston some years ago on the history of the political parties of this country. After dinner Nevins, Gale, and I walked out to Porter's where we witnessed a trotting match. After tea I read Cruise on the subject of Uses.

May 9. Rose 6:30. Ret. 10:00. Read and attended the lecture on Kent, which was very dull. I then read my newspapers. In the afternoon, I read Cruise upon Uses. After tea I called on Joyes[3] of Kentucky and Ballentine. Mr. Williams, one of the old students and a clever fellow, staid all night with me.

May 10. Rose 6:00. Ret. 7:00. This morning Williams and I took a walk to Mount Auburn, something unusual for me. Read and attended the lecture on Cruise. After dinner I presided over the Kent Club.

[2] McGavock and the Lawrences met on more friendly terms later, especially in 1851 in London, when Abbot Lawrence, Sr., was U. S. Minister to Britain.

[3] Patrick Joyes of Louisville, Kentucky.

Owing to the Dudlean lecture the club adjourned until tomorrow afternoon. After tea I was engaged in writing.

May 11. Rose 8:00. Ret. 10:00. This being a cold and inclement day, I remained in my room and read law all the forenoon. After dinner I presided over the Kent Club, where we had a very interesting and animated discussion whether the general government ought to assume the debts of those States that repudiate.

May 12. Rose 7:30. Ret. 11:00. Read and attended the lecture on Cruise. Mr. Greenleaf introduced to the students a gentleman from Norway sent to the U. S. by his government to examine our system of trial by Jury. He can't imagine how twelve men, ignorant of the law, can administer Justice properly. In the afternoon I attended Dr. Wyman's lecture on Anatomy, which was very interesting. I consulted Dr. Wyman about my health.

May 13. Rose 7:00. Ret. 12:00. This forenoon was occupied in reading speeches on the propriety of the national government assuming the debts of the States that repudiate. In the afternoon I went into Boston with some friends. Attended the Museum and walked about the City in a very unprofitable and to me uninteresting way.

May 14. Rose 7:30. Ret. 11:00. This morning I remained in my room reading the Washington Union and some other papers. In the afternoon I wrote a letter to Father. After tea I paid a visit to Gordon, Joyes, Woolley, Hamilton,[4] Sargent. Returned to my room and read a few pages in Childe Harrold.

May 15. Rose 7:30. Ret. 10:00. Read and attended the lecture on Cruise. Returned to my room and papers. After dinner I was engaged in reading, etc. This has been a delightful day for outdoor excursions. The streets are filled with Bostonians riding in buggies and on horseback.

May 16. Rose 7:00. Ret. 11:00. Read several chapters in the Book of Chronicles. Also read and attended the lecture on Cruise, which was more interesting than usual. In the afternoon I was engaged in writing an opinion on the Kent Club question. After tea I paid a visit to Force, and read until bedtime.

May 17. Rose 8:00. Ret. 2:00. Read and attended one of Mr. Parker's dull lectures on Kent's Commentary. I was then occupied until four in writing out my opinion on the following question: Ought the General Government to Assume the State Debts in Case They Repu-

---

[4] Robert Wickliffe Woolley and James Fletcher Hamilton were both from Lexington, Kentucky.

diate? I decided that it was unjust, inexpedient, and unconstitutional. Mr. Force read a beautiful oration about the Politicians. Russell and I walked into Boston and attended a frenological [phrenological] lecture in the Tremont Temple, after which we promenaded and called on some *ladies*.

May 18. Rose 9:00. Ret. 2:00. Read and attended the lecture on Kent. Also read several papers. In the afternoon I took a short nap and read several pages in Kent. After tea I called to see Ballentine, and found him quite ill. Set up with him until two o'clock, then retired to bed in Wilson's room, where I slept soundly and sweetly.

May 19. Rose 6:30. Ret. 1:00. Took a short walk before breakfast, arranged some papers, and attended the lecture on Kent. In the afternoon I attended Dr. Wyman's lecture on Anatomy, in which he showed the differences between the bones of animals and human beings. Attended the Moot Court, but it was so very hot that I left. The thermometer stood at 94°.

May 20. Rose 7:30. Ret. 11:00. Immediately after breakfast Nevins and I went into Boston. I called on Mrs. Appleton, Mr. Frothingham, Misses Merrill and Hammond — also Mr. Amos Lawrence. Took dinner at Parker's.[5] In the afternoon we went to the Museum and saw Moll Pitcher played.[6] It was written in Boston and has references to scenes about Nahant.

May 21. Rose 8:00. Ret. 10:00. After breakfast I went to Lippitt's room and set a while, then called on Ballentine and set until dinner time. In the afternoon I visited Nevins, read the life of James Gibson, a Boston merchant who was at the siege of Louisburg [?]. I then read Cruise until bedtime. Mr. May of Virginia called on me today. The weather is damp and disagreeable.

May 22. Rose 6:30. Ret. 12:00. Read and attended the lecture on Cruise. The afternoon was occupied in reading. Today the Democratic National Assembly meets at Baltimore to nominate their candidates for President and Vice-President. There will doubtless be some dissention, but I hope differently.

May 23. Rose 8:00. Ret. 12:00. Read and attended two lectures in Kent. In the afternoon I attended the Moot Court. After tea I examined the subject of Divorce and wrote one or two pages upon the subject.

---

[5] Harvey D. Parker began operating a restaurant in 1832 under Tudor's Building in Court Square. He founded the famous Parker House Hotel at School and Tremont Streets in 1854.

[6] Based on incidents in the life of Mrs. Mary Ludwig Hays McCauley (1754-1832), *Moll Pitcher* was written by J. S. Jones and first produced in New York in 1841, featuring Rosetta Clark.

The telegraphic dispatch from Baltimore is that Mr. Stevenson of Virginia was elected President of the Convention. Hannegan and Houston were addressing the [Convention.][7]

May 24. Rose 8:00. Ret. 12:00. Read several chapters in the Bible and several pages in Cruise when [Henry] Fogg and M. Vaughn reached here from Nashville. They dined with me and I succeeded in procuring rooms for them. The greater part of the day was employed in conversing with them about matters at home. After tea I read some letters, Governor Jones' speech in favor of Mr. Clay for the Presidency, also one lecture in Kent.

May 25. Rose 7:00. Ret. 10:00. Read and attended the lecture on Kent and also read several chapters in the Bible. In the afternoon I read until five o'clock, then took a walk out to Mount Auburn with M. Vaughn and showed him the principal tombs in the cemetery. After tea I read law until bedtime.

May 26. Rose 7:30. Ret. 11:00. Attended the lecture on Cruise, and read The Two Gentlemen of Verona, one of Shakespeare's best productions. In the afternoon I attended Dr. Wyman's lecture on the human muscles, which I found very instructive. The evening was spent in my room.

May 27. Rose 8:00. Ret. 11:00. This morning I read some law and several newspapers. After dinner Lippitt and I walked into Boston, attended the Museum, and walked about until 10 o'clock. Today we received the news of General Cass's and Butler's nominations by the Baltimore Convention, a very good ticket considering the great rage for military men.[8]

May 28. Rose 7:30. Ret. 11:00. Read several chapters in the Book of Chronicles, then attended the Unitarian Church, where I heard an excellent sermon from the first chapter and twenty-fifth verse of Acts. In the afternoon I wrote a letter to Mother. After tea Gale and myself paid a visit to Judge Parker and lady. We passed a delightful evening.

May 29. Rose 7:00. Ret. 10:00. Read three chapters in the Bible and one chapter on Trusts in Cruise. Attended the lecture. After dinner Fogg called and set until three o'clock. I then attended Dr. Wyman's

[7] Andrew Stevenson (1784-1857), Democratic Congressman, Speaker of the House of Representatives (1827-1834), Minister to Great Britain (1836-1841), and gentleman farmer of Albermarle County, Virginia. Edward Allen Hannegan (1807-1859), Democratic Congressman from Indiana, Senator, and U. S. Minister to Prussia.

[8] Lewis Cass (1782-1866), statesman, Senator, Secretary of State under Buchanan, diplomat, and unsuccessful candidate for president in 1848. William Orlando Butler (1791-1880), aide-de-camp to General Andrew Jackson (1816-17), Congressman from Kentucky, major-general of volunteers during the Mexican War, and unsuccessful Democratic candidate for vice-president in 1848.

lecture upon the abdomen, which was exceedingly interesting. After tea I felt so drowsy that I retired quite early.

May 30. Rose 7:00. Ret. 12:00. Read Kent and attended the lecture. In the afternoon I attended the Moot Court and heard a very interesting argument on Assault and Battery, after which Miller of N. Y.[9] and I rolled nine pins until six o'clock. After tea I read Cruise until twelve o'clock, being somewhat behind in the lectures. This has been a very damp and disagreeable day.

May 31. Rose 7:00. Ret. 12:00. Read and attended the lecture on Cruise. In the afternoon Lippitt and I walked into Boston. After making some purchases, we called on a *woman,* then returned to Cambridge. News reached Boston today of another revolution in France. The radicals headed by Rollin attempted to overthrow the Lamartin party, but were suppressed by the National Guard.[10] After tea I read Cruise on the subject of Mortgages.

June 1. Rose 7:00. Ret. 12:00. Read and attended the lecture on Kent. Also read a sketch of General Cass's life in the Washington Union. In the afternoon I attended Moot Court. After tea several of us walked into Boston and went to the Abolition Convention in Faneuil Hall. Here I saw Birney[11] that ran for president. He is a tall, slim man with long beard and hair that is red. I heard a negro speak, also Pillsbury,[12] Garrison, and Philips, etc. The meeting was very disorderly.

June 2. Rose 7:00. Ret. 10:00. Read several chapters in the Bible and Kent's Commentaries. Attended the lecture. In the afternoon I attended Dr. Wyman's lecture on the structure of the heart, which was peculiarly interesting. The right hand side of the heart is termed the Venous side and the left the Arterial side. After tea I read a pamphlet on the causes of the War of 1812 by George M. Dallas.[13]

June 3. Rose 7:30. Ret. 10:00. This morning I read a little law and several papers. In the afternoon I went to Nevins' room and whiled away a few hours. We then took a walk up to the observatory where we had a splendid view of Boston, Bunker Hill, Roxbury, and the sur-

[9] William Frederick Miller of Buffalo, N. Y.

[10] Alexander August Ledru-Rollin and Alphonse de Lamartine.

[11] James Gillespie Birney (1792-1857), Kentucky-born anti-slavery leader, editor of the *Philanthropist,* secretary of the American Anti-Slavery Society, and one of the founders of the Liberty Party, which nominated him in 1840 and 1844 for president. He spent the later years of his life residing in the North and lecturing against slavery.

[12] Parker Pillsbury (1809-1898), Congregationalist minister of Concord, New Hampshire, joined the anti-slavery forces of William Lloyd Garrison and lectured in New England and the West. His recollections, *Acts of the Anti-Slavery Apostles,* were published in 1883.

[13] George M. Dallas (1792-1864), Vice-President under Polk.

rounding towns. The environs of Boston excell any in this country for beauty. Read the life of William O. Butler and F. P. Blair.[14]

June 4. Rose 8:00. Ret. 12:00. After breakfast I went to Nevins' room and set until church time. Attended Church and then went to DuPont's room and set until dinner,[15] after which I remained in my room and read my Bible and Childe Harrold's Pilgrimage. Byron's description of the ruins of Athens and the beauties of those regions through which he passed are really sublime.

June 5. Rose 7:00. Ret. 12:00. After breakfast I called on Ballentine whom I engaged in a game of whist. Read a few pages in law. There was no lecture today, it being according to custom to set apart a day for the President and Honorable .... to hold their election. It is a custom that has been in existence ever since the Revolution. Nevins and I went into Boston to see ...., but were ill paid for our trouble. Today was cold, damp, and dreary. News reached Boston today that a peace had been concluded with Mexico. This evening we went to the opera Ernani, which was played admirably. Truffi the prima donna was admirably suited in every respect to sustain the character of Elvira.[16]

June 6. Rose 8:00. Ret. 11:30. This morning I read and attended the lecture on Kent. In the afternoon I attended Moot Court where I listened to a very interesting speech from Mr. Sears.[17] Judge Parker declined giving an opinion until he could investigate it more thoroughly. After tea I read 8 or 10 pages on Pleading.

June 7. Rose 7:30. Ret. 10:30. The National Whig Convention meets today at Philadelphia. It is generally believed that General [Zachary] Taylor will receive the nomination. Then what a battle we should have on the great political checkerboard between the Generals.[18] Read a chapter in Cruise on Mortgages and attended the lecture on Kent. In the afternoon I attended Moot Court. After tea read a paper. This has been a very unpleasant day.

June 8. Rose 6:30. Ret. 10:00. Read several chapters in the Bible and the first chapter in Cruise on Mortgages. Attended the lecture. In the afternoon I attended the Moot Court. The news reached here this evening by telegraph of the nomination of General Taylor and Millard

---

[14] Francis Preston Blair (1791-1876), journalist and politician who supported Van Buren and Free-Soilism in 1848.

[15] Victor du Pont of Wilmington, Delaware.

[16] Teresa Truffi, popular soprano who sang with various New York and Boston opera companies.

[17] Philip Howes Sears of Boston.

[18] That is, between Generals Lewis Cass and Zachary Taylor.

Fillmore for the offices of President and Vice-President. Being both popular men, I fear they will succeed.

June 9. Rose 8:00. Ret. 10:00. Read three chapters in the second book of Chronicles. Attended the lecture on Cruise. This morning all the students were talking about the nomination. Some approved it, but the New England men do not like it. In the afternoon I attended a very interesting lecture by Dr. Wyman on the circulation of the blood. Also attended Moot Court.

June 10. Rose 6:30. Ret. 11:00. Read the correspondence between General Cass and Dan Webster on the Quintuple Treaty in 1842.[19] They evinced great personal spleen on both sides. In the afternoon I read Cruise on the subject of Mortgages. After tea Mr. Farnum of Boston called to see [me]. Read several pages in Cruise on Mortgages.

June 11. Rose 7:30. Ret. 12:00. This morning I read some in Allison's Europe.[20] In the afternoon I attended church in the Chapel. Dr. Walker preached from first verse of the forty-sixth Psalm. After tea Nevins and I walked out to Fresh Pond. Returned to my room and wrote a letter to Father, one to John H. McGavock,[21] and one to J. L. Bostick.

June 12. Rose 7:30. Ret. 11:00. This morning I read several pages in Cruise on the subject of Deeds and attended the lecture. It was announced today that Professor Greenleaf had resigned his professorship, much to the regret of all the students. After tea I attended a Democratic meeting in Faneuil Hall called to ratify Cass and Butler's nomination. It was very enthusiastic. Messers Hallett and Green addressed the meeting.[22]

June 13. Rose 7:30. Ret. 10:00. Attended the lecture on Deeds. In the afternoon I attended Moot Court and wrote a letter to J. B. Southall.[23] The evening was employed in reading one thing and another. Being somewhat unwell, I retired quite early.

---

19 The Webster-Ashburton Treaty, negotiated by Daniel Webster and Lord Alexander Baring Ashburton, contained five provisions, among which was the settlement of the long disputed boundary between Maine and Canada.

20 Sir Archibald Alison, *History of Europe. . . .* New York: Harper and Brothers, 1842-43, 4 vols.

21 John Harding McGavock (1824-1861) was a second cousin. He also attended the University of Nashville and was graduated from the Harvard Law School in 1847.

22 Benjamin Franklin Hallett (1797-1862), native of Barnstable County, Massachusetts; editor, and politician. He wrote extensively, especially in pamphlet form, including speeches, letters on politics, and Fourth of July orations. C. J. Greene of Massachusetts, a delegate to the Baltimore Convention.

23 Joseph Branch Southall was married to Mary Cloyd McGavock, a first cousin of McGavock's father.

June 14. Rose 7:30. Ret. 11:00. This morning I attended the lecture on the subject of Deeds and read some little law. In the afternoon I attended Moot Court and Dr. Wyman's lecture on Anatomy. In the evening I read some in Byron's Child Harrold.

June 15. Rose 8:00. Ret. 12:00. Read several pages in Kent and attended the lecture in Cruise on Deeds. In the afternoon I attended Moot Court where I listened to a very interesting argument by Day[24] and Jenness on a case where a lawyer refused to defend his client because he believed him guilty. Professor Greenleaf delivered his last opinion today, which was really splendid. After tea I attended the opera of Il Giuramento. Truffi did splendidly in the dying scene.

June 16. Rose 7:30. Ret. 12:00. Attended the lecture on Deeds. This is the last lecture that Mr. Greenleaf will ever deliver in Dane Hall. The parting scene was very affecting. Everyone seemed to be parting with their best friend. The school and the profession will feel his loss very much. Today I was elected Marshal on the Jury Case. After tea I attended the largest Whig meeting that I ever saw in Faneuil Hall. Messers Choate, Gaines of Kentucky, and Lunt made speeches for Old Zack.[25]

June 17. Rose 8:00. Ret. 11:00. This morning I read several papers and a little in Child Harrold, which I admire very much. Rogers staid with me last night and we made a settlement of our accounts today. I think I shall never go in the same room with any body again. I have done but little today. After tea I read some in Kent and Byron.

June 18. Rose 8:00. Ret. 10:00. Read several chapters in the Bible and attended church in the Chapel. Dr. Walker[26] preached a splendid sermon on the subject of honor, showing conclusively that true honor was to be cherished and admired, while false honor should be condemned. In the afternoon I wrote a long letter to Father.

June 19. Rose 8:00. Ret. 12:00. Read my Bible, also read and attended the lecture on Story's Commentary of the Constitution, after which the students had a meeting to finish electing counsel for the Jury Cases. I resigned the office of Marshal, but they refused to accept it. In the afternoon I took a long nap. At 11:00 Jenness, Vaughn, De Blanc, and myself went in bathing in the River Charles.

---

[24] Henry Day of West Springfield, Massachusetts.

[25] John Pollard Gaines (1795-1857), Whig Representative from Kentucky to the Thirtieth Congress. George Lunt (1803-1885), author, Massachusetts Legislator, editor of the Boston *Courier* (with George S. Hillard). He wrote poetry, social tracts, political sketches, and strongly supported Taylor for president.

[26] James Walker, D. D. (1794-1874) was at this time Alford professor of natural religion, moral philosophy, and civil polity at Harvard. A leading expounder of the metaphysics of Unitarianism, he was President of Harvard from 1853 to 1860.

June 20. Rose 6:30. Ret. 12:00. Read and attended the lecture in Kent on Bailments. Read the General Tracts between the U. S. and the Republic of New Granada. After tea I read twenty or thirty pages in Story's Constitutional Law, also eight or ten pages in Shakespeare. This has been a warm, damp, and unpleasant day.

June 21. Rose 7:00. Ret. 12:00. Read and attended the lecture on Bailments, after which the students had a meeting and elected me counsel on the Jury Case, which I resigned together with the Marshalship. In the afternoon I attended an exceedingly interesting lecture on the brain by Dr. Wyman. In the evening attended the Kent Club and heard a beautiful speech from Russell, and I was elected the next orator. Mrs. Clark, our boarding house keeper, told us this evening that she could not entertain us any longer. I will therefore have to catch my dinner tomorrow where I can. Took a walk this evening to Fresh Pond with Woolley and De Blanc. After tea I read Shakespeare, etc.

June 22. Rose 7:00. Ret. 12:00. Read a few chapters in the Bible, also read and attended the lecture on Story's Commentary on the Constitution. The afternoon was employed in reading one thing or another. After, I attended the opera in company with several friends. *Today I changed my boarding place from Mrs. Clark's to the Misses Uphams'.*

June 23. Rose .... Ret. 9:00. Read and attended the lecture, and read newspapers until dinner time, after which I went to Nevins' room and set until four o'clock, then attended Moot Court. Mr. Parker gave an opinion on a case that he deferred and gave a lecture on the manner of proceeding in a Jury Trial, which I found very instructive to me, knowing but little about it.

June 24. Rose 7:00. Ret. 12:00. This morning I read some newspapers when Fillmore called and occupied the whole morning. In the afternoon I received a long letter from Sister Ann. After tea I went in bathing in the River Charles with several friends, also read the latter part of Shakespeare's Two Gentlemen of Verona. I do not admire it much.

June 25. Rose 7:00. Ret. 10:00. Read several chapters in the Bible. Attended church this morning in the Chapel. Dr. Walker gave a beautiful discourse on the object and efficacy of prayer. He was unusually happy. In the afternoon I remained in my room reading, etc. After tea I made several calls.

June 26. Rose 6:30. Ret. 2:00. Read and attended the lecture in Kent on the subject of Bailments. Then went into Boston and called on

Governor Jones of Tennessee,[27] also on Miss Hammond. At three I returned to Cambridge, dressed, and attended the opera with Hammond. The audience was the largest and most select that I have had the opportunity of meeting at the Howard. Truffi and Benedetti excelled themselves.

June 27. Rose 7:00. Ret. 10:00. Read several chapters in the Bible. Also read and attended the lecture on Story's Constitutional Law. In the afternoon I attended Moot Court, where I heard one of the most ludicrous speeches that was ever delivered in Dane Hall, by Smith of Ohio.[28] It was a real specimen of Western greeness and self-confidence.

June 28. Rose 8:00. Ret. 11:00. Read and attended the lecture on the Constitution, then summoned twelve members of the Senior Class to serve as jurors on a case to be argued next Monday in the Moot Court. It was quite an amusing task. In the afternoon I attended Dr. Wyman's lecture on the eye, which was very interesting. He dissected several balls and explained the entire operation of that most important member. I then attended the Kent Club and heard Smith of Ohio for about two hours. Mr. and Mrs. Gale reached Cambridge this morning. The disaffected Whigs had a meeting at Worcester this morning and nominated delegates to attend at Buffalo, N. Y.

June 29. Rose 7:00. Ret. 10:00. Read a speech of S. A. Douglas of Illinois, delivered the eighth of this month at a Democratic Meeting at New Orleans. Also one by the Hon. Pierre Soule.[29] Ballentine returned this morning and gave me an interesting account of his tour north. Attended the lecture on Story's Constitutional Law. In the afternoon I read a little in law. In the evening I read Shakespeare's comedy of the Twelfth Night.

June 30. Rose 6:30. Ret. 11:00. This morning I read my Bible, also read and attended the lecture on Constitutional law. In the afternoon I attended Dr. Wyman's lecture on the reproductive organs, after which I attended the Moot Court. The evening was passed in my room, reading, etc.

July 1. Rose 6:30. Ret. 12:00. This morning I received a letter from Mother approving my wishes to apply to the President for an appointment to some of the European Courts. At twelve I went into

[27] James Chamberlain Jones (1809-1859), Governor of Tennessee, U. S. Senator, and president of the projected Memphis and Charleston Railroad. The first native Tennessean to be elected Governor, he defeated James K. Polk for the office in 1841 and 1843.

[28] Ypsilanti Alexander Smith of Findlay, Ohio.

[29] Pierre Soule (1801-1870), native of Bordeaux, France, practised law in New Orleans, and was Senator from Louisiana in 1847 and again in 1849-1853. A States Right Democrat, he served on General Beauregard's staff during the defense of Charleston and was made Brigadier-General for special service to the Confederacy.

Boston and called on Mr. Gale and Lady. At three I dined with B. F. Hallett. Met a beautiful lady and spent an agreeable time.

July 2. Rose 7:00. Ret. 10:00. After breakfast I called at Nevins' room and set until twelve, then called on Woolley of Kentucky, Joyes, Rich, etc. In the afternoon I wrote two long letters to Mother and Sister Ann. Then attended church in the chapel. Dr. Walker preached a fine sermon from the seventh chapter, seventh verse, of St. Matthew.

July 3. Rose 7:00. Ret. 12:00. Read several chapters in the Bible, attended the lecture on Kent's Commentary. This morning Gale brought some of his things to my room and left Cambridge for Boston. In the afternoon the Jury Trial came off in Dane Hall. Bartlett, Soule, Chamberlain and Bryant[30] were the counsel. I acted as Marshal with an old sword on; Ayer Deputy-Marshal; and Ballentine Cryer. It passed off very well. Judge Parker was highly delighted. After tea Nevins and Ballentine called to see me.

July 4. Rose 5:00. Ret. 12:00. This is the seventy-second anniversary of American Independence, a day that gave birth to the greatest nation in the world. Since the last 4th of July we have seen the thrones of Europe totter and fall, and [other nations] are now endeavoring to emulate our institutions. The Bostonians celebrate this day more handsomely than we do. This morning Mr. Joyes and I went into Boston to witness the Floral Procession, [and] the Military, and heard an oration by Mr. Giles. In the afternoon we took an excursion among the islands in Boston Bay. We had a large crowd and a band of music on a steamer called the Charter Oak. After tea, according to invitation, I went to Mr. Williams' house on the Common, from the roof of which I had a splendid view of the fireworks.[31]

July 5. Rose 8:00. Ret. .... After witnessing so many beauties yesterday, I feel little like work this morning. Last night I fortunately met Mr. Geddis and Lady from New Orleans, two of my particular friends. This morning I attend[ed] the lecture on the Constitution, then the remainder of the day was spent in reading Shakespeare and other reading.

July 6. Rose 6:30. Ret. 11:00. This morning I attended the last lecture of this term on Constitutional law. It was one of the best lectures that Judge Parker has delivered. He examined the Constitutionality of slavery and he was opposed to the institution—thought it uncivil, etc. In the afternoon Mr. Geddis and lady and a Miss Feasenton called

---

[30] John Harriman Bartlett of Concord, New Hampshire. Augustus Lord Soule of Exeter, New Hampshire. Napoleon Bonaparte Bryant of Andover, New Hampshire.

[31] Compare this entry with those of July 4 and 5, 1862.

in a carriage for me to accompany them to Mt. Auburn and Mr. Cushing's place. I went to Boston with them and took tea.

July 7. Rose 6:30. Ret. 10:00. This morning at nine o'clock, the Jury Trial came off, and at the instance of the counsel I officiated as Marshal in place of Lippitt, who was elected. The speeches of counsel were very good and the trial was well conducted. The jury failed to make a verdict. After tea I called on Professor Greenleaf and family.

July 8. Rose 7:00. Ret. 11:00. At ten o'clock Moale [?] from Baltimore and myself took a drive in a buggy through Brighton to Jamaica Plains, which is one of the most beautiful places in New England. We then drove into Boston. I dined at the Revere with Mr. Dunn and lady. Called on Mr. Geddis and lady, Mr. and Mrs. Gale, Mr. Amos Lawrence. Boston is now filled with strangers, principally southerners.

July 9. Rose 6:30. Ret. 10:00. This morning after reading several chapters in the Bible, [I] then attended church in the Chapel. Heard an excellent sermon from Dr. Walker, whom I consider one of the most powerful Divines that I ever had the pleasure to listen to. I fully intended hearing his sermon this afternoon, but was asleep when the hour arrived. After tea I attended church, but felt so drowsy that I could not hear it out.

July 10. Rose 7:00. Ret. 12:00. This morning I called on Professor Greenleaf and obtained a certificate that I have attended the law lectures two terms. Then read several Washington papers and one or two political speeches. After dinner I went to sleep and awoke at five o'clock. After tea took a walk with Herndon, and wrote a letter to Father, and Mrs. F[elicia] Eakin.

July 11. Rose 6:30. Ret. 11:00. This forenoon has been occupied in my room, reading [Robert C.] Winthrop's speech at the laying of the cornerstone of the Washington Monument. It is a fine production and well worthy of its distinguished author. In the afternoon I paid several visits and took a bath in the River Charles. After tea I read until bedtime.

July 12. Rose 6:30. Ret. 11:00. Immediately after breakfast I attended the exhibition of the Junior Class. I heard several very good speeches, but I am convinced that the North cannot compete with the South in fine orators. They lack the first element of an orator, viz. Action, Action, Action. In the afternoon I went into Boston to *see a lady.*

July 13. Rose 6:30. Ret. 1:00. This has been the most agreeable day that I have passed in Cambridge. At 11:00 the members of the Senior Class formed in procession, preceded by Kendle's [?] splendid band. We marched to the Chapel, where Mr. Tiffany from Maryland delivered a beautiful and affecting valedictory to his classmates. Mr. Clark read a beautiful poem portraying in living colors the collegiate life. We then repaired to Harvard Hall, where was prepared a most .... collation. At four they assembled on the green and danced several sets, then went into one of the halls and danced until six. The class then formed in procession and again marched round all the Halls, giving each three hearty cheers. After tea I went to a levee given by President [Edward] Everett to the class.

July 14. Rose 7:00. Ret. 12:00. This morning I remained in my room, reading Byron and other things. After dinner I read some little law and talked to some of my visitors. After tea I walked round to see Vaughn and set until eleven, talking to Miss Sallie McGee and several other girls of the same stripe, which time I considered thrown away.

July 15. Rose 8:00. Ret. 12:00. This morning I remained in my room doing one thing and another. I read the first two chapters in the third book of Blackstone. After dinner I went into Boston, paid a visit to Mr. Amos Lawrence, and to Miss Feasenton of Cincinnati. Met with P. Smith of Nashville, who told me that Frank McGavock was at Cape May.[32]

July 16. Rose 8:00. Ret. 10:00. Read several chapters in the Bible, a portion of Don Juan, and twenty pages in Blackstone's Commentary. Woolley called to see me this morning and set several hours. In the afternoon Lippitt called and we took a walk together. I endeavored to read Byron tonight in bed, but as usual dropped to sleep.

July 17. Rose 5:00. Ret. 12:00. I was much more industrious this morning than usual, having done some reading before breakfast, after which I wrote several letters to Frank McGavock, directing them to different places. I received a letter from my old friend Rogers, which I answered immediately. In the afternoon I did not do much of anything. After tea I paid visits to Herndon and Lawrence.[33] Read Byron, etc.

July 18. Rose 7:00. Ret. 12:00. Read the morning papers and three chapters in the book of Esther. Woolley of Kentucky then called and set until twelve o'clock. I then commenced reading Don Juan. The

---

[32] Francis McGavock (1794-1866), first cousin of Randal's father, formerly in charge of the Tennessee office for the registration of lands, clerk of the Chancery Court at Nashville, and owner of real estate in Davidson and Cheatham Counties.

[33] Isaac Lawrence of New York City.

reviews all regard this production of Byron very licentious, but all agree in acknowledging the great genius displayed in every line of it. After tea I went round to Jones' room.[34] He was madly drunk. He threw his books all over the room and played a little hell. He took his trunk and went into Boston in spite of our persuasions. [James Semple] Christian and [Oliveira] Andrews went with him. Returned to my room and read Don Juan until twelve o'clock.

July 19. Rose 7:00. Ret. 12:00. Immediately after breakfast Lippitt and I went into Boston and spent the day. Called on Mr. Frothingham, Mr. Geddis and lady. Dined at the Revere with Dr. Lindsley, Jr.[35] Came out late in the afternoon and called on Herndon and Vaughn. Fogg staid with me all night. Read the Nashville Union, etc., etc.

July 20. Rose 7:00. Ret. 10:00. After breakfast I went round to see Lindsley and Vaughn off for the White Mountains, after which I done some little reading. In the afternoon I read some in Don Juan, which I like very much notwithstanding it's a little smutty. After tea I hired a horse and rode out to Watertown, then to Brighton, then to an encampment where the returned volunteers [from the Mexican War] were encamped. They were as dirty a looking set of fellows as I ever saw, the result of sheer laziness and nothing else.

July 21. Rose 8:00. Ret. 12:00. This morning I remained in my room reading my Bible, Byron, etc. This day has been so very warm and sultry that I have not been able to do much of anything. My room has been like an oven. After tea Jones and myself went in bathing, then called on Herndon, and set until a late hour.

July 22. Rose 6:00. Ret. 11:00. At eleven o'clock I went into Boston to witness the reception of the returned volunteers. The City Military turned out in large numbers and the dinner at Faneuil Hall was a grand affair. Being one of the invited guests, I had a fine seat on the stand, where I saw and heard everything. The speech of Col. [Thomas] Childs, who rallied the Indiana volunteers, was very fine. And all the speeches were well received except General [Caleb] Cushing's, who was booed [?] by the volunteers as well as other persons. He seems to

---

[34] William Chamberlayne Jones of Tuscumbia, Alabama.

[35] John Berrien Lindsley (1822-1897). His unpublished diary provides notes about this journey from June to September, 1848, from Nashville through the Northern and Middle States, with his own approximation of the miles: "Steamboat, 5,000; Railroad, 1,650; Canal, 390; Stage, 920; Foot, 1,040 = 9,000 miles." The Revere House, built in Bowdoin Square in 1847, was a fashionable hotel often patronized by celebrities visiting Boston. Dr. Lindsley married Sarah McGavock (see footnote 44) and became one of Tennessee's most distinguished educators. Consult his biography by John Edwin Windrow, Chapel Hill, 1938.

be very unpopular indeed. Received a letter from Judge [Henry] Dickinson today.

July 23. Rose 8:00. Ret. 11:00. This morning I read several chapters in the book of Job and some eight or ten pages in Byron. In the afternoon I wrote a long letter to Judge Dickinson and read several chapters in the fourth book of Blackstone. In the evening I paid a visit to Herndon and several other fellows.

July 24. Rose 6:30. Ret. 11:00. Received a letter from Mrs. Bass.[36] Read two cantos of Don Juan and several pages in law. The afternoon was employed in reading newspapers and other things. Went in bathing with Jones and Christian, went to Jones's room and set until a late hour.

July 25. Rose 6:30. Ret. 12. This morning I was so vexed because I did not receive a letter containing a draft that I could not read with any pleasure. However, I managed to read a little law and Don Juan. At three o'clock I went into Boston and met Frank McGavock, two daughters and son. He said that my money had been mailed at the Astor House. I immediately sent a telegraphic dispatch to learn if it had been sent. Went back to the Revere and set in the parlor with the girls and a Miss Mason from Holly Springs.

July 26. Rose 6:30. Ret. .... At 9:30 I went into Boston and accompanied Mr. Mason and Sister, David McGavock and two Sisters,[37] through the villages that environ Boston, showing them everything of interest. I remained with them until 10:00. Received an answer to my dispatch yesterday, that there was no letter there. Read some little after I returned from Boston.

July 27. Rose 7:00. Ret. 10:00. This morning I packed up my things and set off at 10:00 for Boston. Went to see Mr. Samuel Frothingham, from whom I borrowed $150.00 to travel upon, being disappointed in receiving a draft from home. Wrote a letter to Father. Bid Cousin Frank farewell and left Boston for New York, by way of Fall River, on the splendid steamer Bay State. This I consider the most agreeable route at this season of the year. It was a little rough round Point Judith, but not unpleasant. We stopped at Newport a few minutes. It is a pleasant place. There is a large company there now.

July 28. Rose 2:00. Ret. 3:00. Reached New York at 7:00, and started for Philadelphia at 9:00. Dined at the U. S. in Philadelphia, met Billings, Berry, and Smith of Nashville. At 3:00 I started on a boat for

---

[36] Mrs. John M. Bass, the former Malvina Grundy, was a sister to McGavock's mother.

[37] David H., Susannah Elizabeth, and Amanda McGavock were the children of Francis "Frank" McGavock and Amanda P. Harding of Nashville. Thus they were his second cousins.

Baltimore, by way of New Castle. It is preferable to riding in the cars. Reached Baltimore [at] 9:00 and started for Washington. Put up at Willard's Hotel.

July 29. Rose 7:30. Ret. 11:00. This morning I felt quite unwell, produced by eating crabs last night. Called on Major Graham and Knox Walker. I wished to see Mr. Polk, but being Cabinet Day I was denied the opportunity. Went up to the Capitol and heard Benton, Bell, Niles and several other members speak. In the afternoon I took a nap, then called on Mr. Force, etc.

July 30. Rose 7:30. Ret. 11:00. This morning I occupied my time in talking and walking about the hotel. Went to Benson's room and set awhile. In the afternoon I walked toward the Capitol and nearly every man I met was a military character. This City is filled with them. After tea I read General Pillow's defense before the Court Martial.

July 31. Rose 8:00. Ret. .... At 11:00 I called on the President and applied to him for a foreign mission, but I was disappointed. There was no vacancy either in the Legations or charges d'affaires. The President would have granted my request if there had have been.[38] During the day I called on Mr. Winthrop and went up to the Capitol. In the afternoon I left Washington for New York.

Aug. 1. Rose .... Ret. 12:00. This morning I feel much fatigued from travelling all night. Reached New York after a delightful trip from Philadelphia and put up at the Astor House. Here I met F. B. Fogg and lady and daughter,[39] also John Lawrence, who accompanied me to the Bowery Theatre, where I saw some of the roughest specimens of nature in the shape of humans that my eyes ever rested upon. It was filled with what's termed the Bowery boys and girls. There was a fight about every three minutes among them and such a noise I never heard. I was glad I went for it is improving to see humanity in all its various complements.

---

[38] This was the first of three unsuccessful attempts to secure a foreign post. Other overtures were made to President Pierce in 1853 and to President Buchanan in 1857. President Polk was daily plagued by office seekers during this his last year as president. He recorded in his diary on July 31, 1848, the day of McGavock's visit: "I had a throng of visitors this morning . . . Maj'r Gen'l Worth . . . Maj'r Gen'l Butler and his wife . . . other ladies and gentlemen . . . It gave me pleasure to see these gallant officers. . . . I cannot say as much for the herd of persons who called to importune and annoy me about offices in the course of the morning. I have a great contempt for professional office seekers. . . ." McGavock was the son of family friends from Tennessee, and not yet 22 years old; so he was hardly a professional office seeker. Even if a foreign post had been available, Polk would probably have advised him to return to Harvard and complete his law education.

[39] Francis Brinley Fogg (1795-1880) was a native of Brooklyn, Connecticut, who settled in Nashville where he practised law for half a century, and for twenty-five years as a partner of Ephraim Foster. He took an active part in the deliberations of the Constitutional Convention in 1834, aided in inaugurating a system of internal improvements in Tennessee, and helped establish free schools in Nashville.

Aug. 2. Rose 8:00. Ret. 12:00. This morning I called on the Eakins and [Millard] Fillmore [Jr.]. The remainder of the day was occupied in walking through the streets, particularly Broadway, looking at the thousand and one curiosities that attract a stranger's eye. In the evening I went into the drawing [room] to see Judge Guion and daughter. Found them quite agreeable.

Aug. 3. Rose 5:00. Ret. 10:00. Left New York at 7:00 for Catskill Mts. The scenery on the Hudson River certainly excells anything in this country. It is grand beyond description, and to the lover of the picturesque, it offers a treat. Left the Hudson at Catskill for Pine Orchard in the stage. The ascent to the mountain is very steep, but the road is very good. After tea I went into the parlor, but the company was excessively dull and uninteresting. The house on this mountain is very fine and well kept.

Aug. 4. Rose 5:30. Ret. 12:00. Rose early to see the sunrise, which is said to be very beautiful. But its beauties were obscured this morning by the clouds. The view from this great elevation is the grandest that I ever beheld, and will repay one for the visit. Left the mountain at 10:00 for Albany, which I reached at 3:00. The scenery on the Hudson excells anything I ever saw. It is one continual succession of beauties from its mouth to its source. In the afternoon I walked about the City and viewed its public buildings, the most attractive of which is the Capitol, State House, Museum, Exchange, and one or two hotels. After tea I went to the Museum and saw New York As It Is played most admirably.[40]

Aug. 5. Rose 8:00. Ret. 10:00. This morning I walked about Albany, looking at the City. Went to see the great canal basin where the boats receive and discharge freight. The public buildings of Albany are quite handsome and without doubt it is a flourishing place. At 2:00 I took the cars for Utica, where I stopped to see the Trenton Falls.

Aug. 6. Rose 6:30. Ret. .... After breakfast I went with several gentlemen in a hack to Trenton Falls, which is about fifteen miles from Utica. The falls and the scenery about them are certainly very beautiful and grand and quite equal to my expectations. Returned to Utica in the forenoon. Utica is situated in Mohawk Valley and is a beautiful and prosperous City.

Aug. 7. Rose .... Ret. 11:00. Started at 1:00 this morning for Buffalo. The cars were so much crowded with persons going to the

[40] *New York As It Is* was written by Ben Baker. The first New York production starred Frank Chanfrau in 1848.

Buffalo Convention that I had to take a freight car with others to Syracuse, where I took breakfast. Here I saw the celebrated salt works. Stopped a few minutes at Auburn and saw the state prison. Dined at Rochester where I met [Robert Barnwell] Roosevelt of New York, who brought me a message from Miss Crowder and Miss Foster from the Cave. Reached Buffalo at 7:00 and put up at the American hotel. The country about this place is better than any portion of the North that I have seen; that is, the lands are more fertile, judging from the growth and fine crops of wheat.

Aug. 8. Rose 7:00. Ret. 12:00. This whole day has been employed in visiting the docks, looking at the different buildings, none of which are very striking, and listening to the Free Soil men talk about their views of the Presidency.[41] After tea Harvey,[42] a Cambridge friend, and myself went over to hear the Free Soil men speak. The crowd was quite large and enthusiastic. Several speeches were made by Messers Grover, N. Y., Chase, Ohio, and a fugitive slave from Detroit. I met several acquaintances here today, which made it more pleasant than it would have been otherwise.

Aug. 9. Rose 8:00. Ret. .... The speaking commenced this morning at daylight. The Convention was called to order at 12:00, and Sawyer of Ohio appointed President *pro tem.* Preston King of New York then introduced several resolutions that were agreed upon by committees, which were received almost unanimously. A committee was then appointed, consisting of one from each State represented, to erect a platform, after which they adjourned until 3:00.

Aug. 10. Rose 7:00. Ret. 12:00. This is my birthday and I am resolved to live a better man henceforth and intend to do more than I have done in any previous year. No place is more auspicious for forming such resolutions than this great and wonderful Niagara, where the hand of Divinity is seen in one of its grandest pictures. No language of mine can begin to portray its mightiness. Suffice to say that I was perfectly charmed. This morning I went in company with a friend from Boston to see the falls from Goat Island, from which many of the best views of this mighty cataract are to be had.. We went down Bidell's stairway and into the Cave of the Winds, where I got a good shower bath from the spray. In the afternoon I went in company with Mr.

[41] The Free Soil Party (1848-55) was made up of members of the old Liberty Party and the "Conscience Whigs" of Massachusetts. They favored the Wilmot Proviso, abolition of slavery, and Van Buren for president. The 1848 motto was "Free Soil, Free Speech, Free Labor, and Free Men."

[42] Alexander Whitelaw Harvey of Peacham, Vermont.

Johnstone, lady,[43] and Miss Elliott from S. C. to the Canada side, from which the falls are better viewed. Crossed the great bridge.

Aug. 11. Rose 7:30. Ret. 11:00. This morning the news reached Niagara that the Convention at Buffalo had nominated Van Buren and Charles F. Adams as candidates for President and Vice-President, which with the Democrats and Whigs will probably create some difficulty between the two geographical sections of the country, which is much to be deplored. This morning I wrote letters to Mother and Sarah.[44] In the afternoon walked down to the Pagoda [?] ballroom and danced with a lady from New York City. It was a very dull affair.

Aug. 12. Rose 6:00. Ret. 11:00. The greater part of the forenoon was spent in Cataract [?] house. Mr. Tide [?] from Troy and myself walked down to the Whirlpool, but was not repaid for the walk and the 25 cents we paid to view it. At two o'clock I left Niagara for Montreal on the splendid steamer Ontario. At the mouth of the Niagara River I saw many things to interest me. Bidell's Monument is in ruins, having been blown up by someone hostile to Her Majesty's rule. Immediately at the mouth of the Niagara is to be seen Fort George on the Canadian side and Fort Niagara on the American. The most beautiful and astonishing thing to be seen after you enter the lake is the spray rising from the falls.

Aug. 13. Rose 7:00. Ret. 12:00. The whole of this day has been spent on Lake Ontario. In the morning we stopped at Oswego which is a very handsome and flourishing town. There are many flour mills in this place. Voorhies of Tennessee, who I met at Niagara, got out here. The boat docked during the day at Kingston, which is very strongly fortified. The market house there cost 30,000 pounds and is a very handsome building. We stopped at several places during the day, on both sides. The lands in some places on this lake are good, but generally very poor. During the day I had an opportunity of hearing Charles Sumner and Tilden of New York discuss the free soil question. After tea we landed at Odgensburg, where we lay all night. Carmack [?] of Mississippi, Lawton of Georgia, and Ogston of Maryland and myself went [to see] the spray rising from the falls.

---

43 Probably relations of William C. Johnstone of "the Santee Country" in South Carolina. Young Johnstone traveled in Europe with McGavock in 1851-52.

44 Sarah Malvina Bass McGavock (1830-1903), often called Sister Sallie, was his favorite sister. Married in 1857 to Dr. John Berrien Lindsley, she inherited many of Brother Randal's personal effects, including these journals. Her daughters, the late Louise Grundy Lindsley and Annie Lindsley Warden, preserved the journals for half a century, after which they became the property of Miss Margaret Lindsley Warden, whose kind permission has made their publication possible.

Aug. 14. Rose 7:00. Ret. 12:00. This morning I left Ogdensburg on the steamer British Empire and went down the St. Lawrence to La Chine. Here I took the first cars I saw for Montreal. The scenery on the river is very fine, and the rapids are really frightful. But the boat glides over them very safely. After tea Ogston of Maryland and myself went to the theatre to see the Ballet Company dance. The parquett was full, but the boxes quite empty. The house is very fine.

Aug. 15. Rose 7:30. Ret. 11:00. After breakfast Ogston and myself procured a Phaeton and two Canadian ponies and started out to see the curiosities of Montreal, but we had hardly ascended the mountain before a rain came up and compelled us to return. We got wet and muddy all over. But we determined not to be outdone, so we went to see the celebrated cathedral, which is supposed to be the largest church on this continent. Its exterior is very imposing, but I do not admire the inside. At 5:00 in the afternoon Mr. Sorel [?] and daughter of Georgia, Lawton and lady of Georgia, Fisher and lady, and Ogston [and I] started for Quebec. The view of Montreal as we left the quay was very imposing.

Aug. 16. Rose 7:00. Ret. 11:00. This morning we woke up and found ourselves in the lofty citadel of Quebec. We ascended the hill in carriages through narrow and tortuous streets. Entered at Biscet [?] gate and put up at the Albion House. After we got our breakfast we started out to see the City. We visited the Cathedral, Citadel, the Barracks, the Plains of Abraham, and everything worth a stranger's attention. This is the strongest fortified city in America and appropriately called the Gibraltar of America. The Citadel and fortifications look very curious to me, never having seen a fortified city before. All this work might have withstood the soldiery of the last century, but not the present mode of warfare. At five we left Quebec for Montreal on the same boat.

Aug. 17. Rose 8:00. Ret. 11:00. This morning I visited the House of General Assembly, the interior of which is fitted off in some stile. I saw the portrait of the Queen in full length taken by her artist. I also saw the Mace, and took a seat in the Governor General's chair. One expression fell from our guide, which attracted my attention. He said that it was expected the Northern and Southern portions of this Union would separate and that the North would become annexed to Canada. I thought myself that it would be just the reverse in less than ten years. Montreal is a beautiful city and the most flourishing one in Canada. In the afternoon I left Montreal for St. Johns, where I remained all night.

Aug. 18. Rose 7:00. Ret. 8:00. This morning I came down Lake Champlain, which I consider very beautiful. The shores are elevated and in a high state of cultivation. Burlington, in Vermont, is in a high, beautiful place. In the afternoon I came down Lake George, which is renowned in story. The scenery on this lake is surprisingly beautiful, but today was so inclement and disagreeable that I could not enjoy its beauties as I could have wished. When I reached Caldwell at the head of the Lakes, I was quite unwell. Here I remained all night in a comfortable bed.

Aug. 19. Rose 7:00. Ret. 12:00. This morning I left Caldwell in a stage for Saratoga Springs. On the route we saw Glen Falls, Fort William Henry, and Fort George. Having gone ten miles in the stage, we took the cars, went two miles when the passenger car became detached from the locomotive and went ten miles before the engineer knew it. Reached Saratoga at 3:00. Ogston and myself then procured a buggy and went to a trotting match. Here we saw Lady Suffolk and several other fine trotters. We then went to Saratoga Lake. After tea I went into the U. S. Hotel ballroom, but saw but little beauty.

Aug. 20. Rose 7:30. Ret. .... Before breakfast I walked down and drank freely of the celebrated Congress water, which I relish very much. The forenoon was occupied in walking about and talking to acquaintances. After dinner I wrote a letter to Sister Ann. The evening was passed away in walking about the hotel, conversing first with this man and that one.

Aug. 21. Rose 8:00. Ret. 12:00. Walked down to the Spring and drank of its exilirating waters. In the afternoon Ogston, Parker, Reynolds, and myself took a drive to Saratoga Lake where we had some refreshments. This lake is a beautiful sheet of water and much resorted to by pleasure parties. After tea we went into the ballroom where we saw two New York exquisites dance the Polka. We then rolled nine pins and tried our luck at roulette. I won $2.00.

Aug. 22. Rose 7:00. Ret. 10:00. Left Saratoga at 9:00 and reached Troy at 11:00. Here I stopped and dined. Troy is situated at the head of tide water on the Hudson. It is well layed out and has many fine buildings. I think it the most beautiful town in New York. Left Troy at 2:00 for Greenbush, opposite Albany, from which I saw the burnt district. Some 500 houses were destroyed. The fire originated from an old washerwoman's cap [?] that took fire. At 3:00 I left Greenbush for Springfield, where I remained all night.

Aug. 23. Rose 7:00. Ret. 10:00. Left Springfield at 9:00 and reached Cambridge just in time to see President Everett confer degrees on a number of young gentlemen, after which they had a collation but I did not attend. In the afternoon I was busily engaged in setting my room in order and preparing for study again.

Aug. 24. Rose 8:00. Ret. 11:00. This morning I looked over some papers that I found in my box and read some letters. In the afternoon I went into Boston, paid some visits, and done some shopping. After tea I called to see Miss Tip [?], but she was absent, and I amused myself talking to others.

Aug. 25. Rose 8:00. Ret. 11:00. This forenoon I finished arranging my room and procured all my text books. I saw our new Professor today at the dinner table. Mr. Parsons[45] seems to be a very affable man and I think he will please the students very much. In the evening I read a portion of J. C. Calhoun's speech on the Oregon Bill.

Aug. 26. Rose 9:00. Ret. 11:00. This morning I footed up some of my accounts and finished reading J. C. Calhoun's speech on the Oregon Bill, which I consider a masterly effort. In the afternoon I went into Boston where I remained until 10:00. Called on Mr. [F. B.] Fogg with whom I had a long conversation about home affairs. Rolled ten pins with Fillmore, Ogston, and Parker.

Aug. 27. Rose 8:00. Ret. 10:00. After breakfast I called to see Gale, who was complaining of fever. I then called and set awhile with Fillmore. Then read several chapters in the book of Job. After dinner I commenced to read, but felt so somnambulent that I laid down and slept all the afternoon.

Aug. 28. Rose 7:00. Ret. 12:00. Read Benton's speech in the Senate upon General Henry's [?] appointment to Brevet Major General. It is very abusive and shows what a revengeful spirit he has. Today is the beginning of a new Term in the Law School and I hope to do more work than I did last term. Professors Parker and Parsons made very good introductory lectures. The courses of study and the examinations are changed somewhat from last term. At 7:00 I went into Boston to see Mr. Frothingham about a draft that I transferred to him. Saw Mr. Fogg and Ogston off for Newport. After tea I wrote a letter to H. L.

---

[45] Theophilus Parsons (1797-1882), whose father had been Chief Justice of the Supreme Judicial Court of Massachusetts. The son was known for his abilities as an effective speaker and as a conversationalist using rich allusions and anecdotes. He remained at the Harvard Law School until 1870, fully supported the so-called war powers exercised by the Union during the Civil War, and gained popular local support for his arguments.

Hallett [46] giving an account of the lecture today. Read the introduction to Blackstone.

Aug. 29. Rose 6:00. Ret. 12:00. This morning I read the Introduction to Blackstone and the commentary on Marshall upon which Mr. Parsons our new Professor lectured. His style is easy, fluent, and pleasant, evincing much humor and pathos. The students gave close attention to his lectures and all seemed highly pleased. He bids fair to be a popular lecturer. In the afternoon I read some law and one or two political speeches.

Aug. 30. Rose 6:00. Ret. 11:00. Read and attended the lecture on Story's Agency by Judge Parker, after which the members of the Kent Club met and reorganized. I submitted the following question for discussion, among others, which was adopted: Was Ireland Justifiable in Her Recent Rebellion? In the afternoon Jones of Alabama and myself took a bath in the Charles. Read Agency until bedtime.

Aug. 31. Rose 6:30. Ret. 12:00. This morning I read and attended the lectures on Blackstone and Insurance. Remained in my room all afternoon and read law. After tea several of us law students went to a [Zachary] Taylor meeting in Cambridge Port. It was a dull affair. Few there and no excitement whatever.

---

[46] Henry Larned Hallett of Boston, a classmate, who was apparently away from Cambridge during the early lectures of the new term. He received the Ll. B. in 1849 with his class, however.

CHAPTER XI

"I read Blackstone and Shakespeare." (September-December, 1848)

From this period only one letter from McGavock to his family in Tennessee has been preserved. Quoted in part below, it provides an illuminating addendum to the journal of 1848.

Cambridge, Mass.
Aug. 25, 1848

My Dear Father,

On yesterday the Alumni of Old Harvard assembled in the Church, where they were addressed in an able and masterly manner by the Rev. Dr. Bushnell of Ct. I was really surprised to see so many in attendance. There must have been at least 500 and a great many silver locks among them. It is a custom for the Alumni of this institution to assemble once every year to renew early associations, and pledge their love & faith to their Old Alma Mater. It was indeed an interesting spectacle to see with what enthusiasm those old grey headed men entered into the proceedings of the day. You would have judged from their countenances that they were students of yesterday, instead of the last century.

The Deligates to the Buffalo Convention called a meeting in Faneuil Hall on Tuesday evening, for the purpose of ratifying the nominations of said Convention. Charles Sumner, a rabid Abolitionist, presided. The meeting was [not?] very large, but composed of the real fanatics. Van Buren was hailed as their standard bearer with great applause. But it is my impression that he will not receive a real *Whig or* Democratic *vote in the old bay State, and I am confident that he will not get one electoral vote any where, not even in New York.*

I was presented to Preston King of N. Y. at Niagara. He was the father of the Buffalo Resolutions and is now the leader of the Barburners in N. Y. He was the intimate friend of Silas Wright, and acquired his present position because he was presumed to herald the views of that great Statesman. We came down Lake Ontario together and he seemed to be very much of a gentleman; the only objection I had to him was his recent tergivisation in politics. He is very sanguine as to Van Buren's success in N. Y.

I will give in my next a history of my tour. Newport is very much crowded at present. There is to be a grand Fancy Ball there on the 30 inst. Mr. F. B. Fogg is now in Boston.

I believe that I have given you all the news about Cambridge.

Remember me to Mother and all the family.

Your Affectionate son,
R. W. McGavock

Sept. 1. Rose 7:00. Ret. 11:00. Read several chapters in the book of Job and ten pages of law. At 10:00 I attended the first lecture of Professor Franklin Dexter, who was recently appointed to lecture on Constitutional and International law.[1] He made only a few remarks explaining the course that he intends to pursue. He seems fluent, has the reputation of being a man of ability, and will doubtless give satisfaction. After tea I attended a Free Soil meeting in the Port. Stephen Philips[2] made a speech three hours in length abusing the Whigs and Democrats and more particularly their candidates.

Sept. 2. Rose 6:30. Ret. 12:00. Read a new poem called Child Harrold written by a member of the last Senior Class about a foundling placed in the Commons. It is very good and has some merit. Commenced reading Allison's Europe today. It is quite an undertaking, but I must carry it through. At 11:00 Saunders of Alabama and Mr. Atherton of New Orleans called to see me. I went with them to Mount Auburn and Cushing's. After dinner Jones and myself went into Boston, saw a balloon ascension, and took tea with Mrs. LeVert[3] of Mobile and Miss

[1] Franklin Dexter (1793-1857), U. S. District Attorney, prominent member of the Boston Bar, lecturer at Harvard during 1848-49 on Constitutional and International law, the Jurisprudence of the United States, and Patents.

[2] Stephen Clarendon Phillips (1801-1857), Massachusetts Representative to the Twenty-third and Twenty-fourth Congresses and unsuccessful Free Soil candidate for Governor in 1848 and 1849.

[3] Octavia Walton LeVert (c. 1810-1877), socialite, authoress, and world traveler, was the wife of Dr. Henry S. LeVert of Mobile and the granddaughter of George Walton, a signer of the Declaration of Independence. Usually known as Madame LeVert, she kept a French salon where she entertained notables like Henry Clay and Millard Fillmore, could converse brilliantly in four languages, it has been said, and was the symbol of Deep South extravagance, elegance, and refinement. As well known in New York and Washington as in Mobile, she traveled to Europe in 1853 and was received by Queen Victoria, Napoleon III, and the Brownings. This journey was recorded in *Souvenirs of Travel* (1857, 2 vols.). After the Civil War she went to Washington to ask a pardon for her friend General Beauregard and in 1874 made her appearance as a public reader.

Bacon of Kentucky, both very agreeable. The former's name now fills every paper about her outrage at Newport. Received a letter from Rogers.

Sept. 3. Rose 6:00. Ret. 12:00. This morning I read a little in my Bible but was interrupted by Saunders and Jones. Batchelder then came in and bored me until dinner time, after which I wrote a long letter to Mother, giving her a minute account of my recent tour through the North and Canada, knowing that she would feel interested in my travels.

Sept. 4. Rose 6:00. Ret. 11:00. Immediately after breakfast I went into Boston to see Saunders. As soon as I reached there we left for Lowell in company with Mrs. LeVert of Alabama, Mr. and Miss Brown of Kentucky, and Mr. Atwood of Louisiana. We had a very delightful trip to Lowell. On our return we went to see the paintings in the Boston Athaneum and the Greek Slave. I dressed, and supped with this party and set with them in the drawing room at the Revere until nine o'clock, after which Saunders, Jones, and myself called on some *ladies.*

Sept. 5. Rose 7:30. Ret. 10:00. Read three chapters in the Bible, also read and attended the lecture on Blackstone and Insurance. The lectures today were exceedingly interesting and edifying. In the afternoon and evening I remained in my room and read my law books and the introduction to Allison's Europe.

Sept. 6. Rose 7:30. Ret. 12:00. Read and attended Mr. Parker's lecture on Agency. In the afternoon I attended the Kent Club. The question was this: Was Ireland Justifiable in Her Recent Rebellion? The debate was very interesting. After tea I went to Faneuil Hall and listened to Mr. Van Buren speak to about 5,000 Free Soil men. He is a good speaker, but not so finished as I expected to find him.

Sept. 7. Rose 6:00. Ret. 10:00. Read and attended the lectures on Blackstone and Insurance. Dined today with Vaughn at Joslin's. In the afternoon I attended Professor Parson's first Moot Court. The case was not as interesting as usual. News reached here today of the loss of the splendid ship Ocean Monarch with a hundred and eighty lives.

Sept. 8. Rose 6:30. Ret. 12:00. This morning I attended Mr. Dexter's lecture on the Constitution. He gave an account of the relation that exists between the Executive, Legislative, and Judiciary, and the powers of each. In the afternoon Mr. Joslin of Mississippi called on me. After I went with him and his brother's family to see Miss Gould, who is considered the most beautiful lady in New England.

Sept. 9. Rose 7:30. Ret. 11:00. This morning I remained in my room reading law and other things. In the afternoon Gale and myself went into Boston and spent several hours. After tea I attended a Free Soil meeting in the Cambridge Lyceum. Richard H. Dana[4] spoke, but I became so much . . . [This entry was not completed.]

Sept. 10. Rose 6:30. Ret. 10:00. During the forenoon I remained in my room reading the Bible and conversing with some visitors. After dinner I wrote a long letter to my old friend R. L. Rogers of Maryland. I also wrote a letter to Father. After tea I read some in Allison's history of Europe.

Sept. 11. Rose 7:00. Ret. 11:00. This morning I read and attended the lecture on Agency. Mr. Parker put me on a Moot Court case today which is to be argued in the course of several weeks. In the afternoon I remained in my room and read law, etc.

Sept. 12. Rose 6:30. Ret. 10:00. Read and attended the lectures on Blackstone's Commentary and Insurance. Professor Parsons was peculiarly happy today in his expositions of the English Constitution. He said that our Constitution was the only one that deserves the name. I do not think that he done justice to England. He was rather partial to our Constitution.

Sept. 13. Rose 7:30. Ret. 12:00. Read three or four chapters in the book of Psalms. Also read and attended the lecture on Agency. In the afternoon I attended the Kent Club where I heard several speeches on the perpetuity of the Union. In the evening I attended a Taylor meeting in the Cambridge Lyceum. Mr. Lunt[5] of this State made a short and very good speech, considering the cause. Mr. Duncan of Louisiana then spoke for about three hours. I was not at all pleased with either his matter or manner.

Sept. 14. Rose 6:30. Ret. 10:00. After breakfast I read several chapters in Insurance, then went with Fillmore of N. Y. and Shelton[6] of Georgia to the Navy Yard in Charlestown to see the splendid war steamer Vermont launched. She is the largest warship that belongs to the U. S. except the Pennsylvania. Her keel was built in 1817. It was a splendid sight to see her slide off of the stocks so smoothly amid the roaring of cannon and shouts of 100,000 people. After dinner Fillmore and I went out to Mount Auburn to see two ladies, but were foiled in our efforts by Gilbert[7] and Shelton.

---

[4] Richard Henry Dana, Jr. (1815-1882), lawyer, author of *Two Years Before the Mast,* and one of the founders of the Free Soil Party.

[5] George Lunt (1803-1885), author, member of the Massachusetts Legislature, and editor of the Boston *Courier* (with George S. Hillard). He wrote poetry, social tracts, political sketches, and strongly supported Zachary Taylor for President. His notable work about Lincoln and the Civil War is *The Origin of the Late War* (New York: D. Appleton Co., 1866).

[6] Joseph Thomas Shelton of Talbotton, Georgia.

[7] Samuel Henry Gilbert of St. John, New Brunswick.

Sept. 15. Rose 6:30. Ret. 11:00. This morning I attended a very able lecture on the English Constitution by Professor Dexter. He differed very widely from Professor Parsons in his estimate of that instrument. During the remainder of the day I was busily engaged in writing a speech which I have to deliver before the Kent Club next Wednesday.

Sept. 16. Rose 7:00. Ret. 9:00. This morning it was so cold that I had to build a fire. After breakfast I read two very able speeches delivered at the Whig State Convention on Wednesday at Worcester by Rufus Choate and Robert C. Winthrop. Read several chapters in the book of Psalms and committed several pages of my speech. After tea I read some time, but feeling unwell I retired early.

Sept. 17. Rose 6:30. Ret. 8:00. After breakfast I took a long walk on Winter Hill thinking that it would make me feel better, but it done no good. After tea I remained in my room and read some writings of mine. But my illness prevented me from doing much.

Sept. 18. Rose 6:00. Ret. 4:00. This morning I felt extremely ill, occasioned by the sudden inclemency of the weather. So I remained in my room all day long—complaining. One cannot appreciate the value of health until sickness comes upon him. Then he learns its lesson. I saw Mr. Lawton and lady of Georgia this afternoon. They invited me to call and see them.

Sept. 19. Rose 7:00. Ret. 10:00. This morning I rose with a severe headache and cold, which disqualified me for business. So contented myself in reading over and over again the speech which I am to deliver tomorrow. Also read some papers, etc. When I retired I took a dose of pills.

Sept. 20. Rose 6:30. Ret. 12:00. This morning I attended Professor Parker's lecture on Agency. In the afternoon I delivered a speech on the Spirit that now pervades our national politics before the Kent Club. It was well received and I was highly complimented upon my efforts. I then went into Boston, called on Mr. Lawton and lady of Georgia. After tea Christian of Virginia and myself went to see the Viennoise children dance.[8] I was much pleased.

Sept. 21. Rose 7:00. Ret. 10:00. This morning I attended Professor Parson's lectures on Blackstone and Insurance. In the afternoon I went into the Moot Court and listened to several speeches. The judge declined to give an opinion then. He said that he wished to reflect a little more upon it. Being unwell I retired early.

---

[8] Les Danseuses Viennoises were acclaimed in New York during 1846-47. This ballet company of forty-eight young girls, drilled by Madame Josephine Weiss, first appeared there on December 7, 1846, and later toured other American cities.

Sept. 22. Rose 7:00. Ret. 10:00. This morning I attended Mr. Dexter's lecture on the Constitution. He drew a comparison between the English and our own Constitution, showing that the great principles of the latter are derived from the former. Called on Dr. Wyman today and he gave me some medicine to take.

Sept. 23. Rose 7:00. Ret. 8:00. This morning I felt extremely ill, so much so that I could do no business. Remained in my room all day, groaning, etc. I noticed in a Nashville paper this morning that a great conflagration had occurred in Nashville on the 14th and that the First Presbyterian Church was destroyed.

Sept. 24. Rose 7:00. Ret. 10:00. This morning I felt very unwell, so much so that I kept to my room all day. Read several chapters in the Bible, then took my bed. In the afternoon some friends called to see me, and by their agreeable conversation I was cheered up and made to feel better.

Sept. 25. Rose 6:30. Ret. 12:00. Read and attended Professor Parker's lecture on Agency. He commenced lecturing today on Story's Equity Jurisprudence. In the afternoon I read several chapters in Insurance. After tea, Fillmore, Appleton,[9] Shelton, and myself attended the National Theatre where we saw Yankee Hill[10] appear.

Sept. 26. Rose 6:30. Ret. 10:00. This morning I read law until 11:00, then attended the lectures on Blackstone and Insurance. In the afternoon I attended the Moot Court. After tea I went into the Kent Club where I heard Russell speak on the Tariff. The excitement in the club seemed to be wearing away.

Sept. 27. Rose 6:30. Ret. 11:00. Read and attended the lecture on Agency. In the afternoon I remained in my room and read some newspapers, etc. Received a letter from Father and Mother today in which I learned that I was an uncle.[11] I immediately answered the letter. Retired later than usual.

Sept. 28. Rose 6:30. Ret. 10:00. This morning I wrote letters until 12:00, then attended Professor Parson's lecture on Insurance. In the afternoon I attended the Moot Court where I heard a very good argument from Johnson.[12] After, I called on Gale, Swan,[13] and Fillmore, then retired to my virtuous bed.

---

[9] Edward Dawes Appleton of New York City.

[10] George H. Hill (?-1849), actor, "lecturer," and comic entertainer of New York and Boston theatrical companies.

[11] Louise Grundy Dickinson, the daughter of Ann McGavock and Henry Dickinson, was born on September 7, 1848; married Philip Lindsley, nephew of John Berrien Lindsley, on April 28, 1869; and lived in Dallas, Texas, for the remainder of her life.

[12] Henry Augustinus Johnson of New Bedford, Massachusetts.

[13] Otis Dwight Swan of New York City.

Sept. 29. Rose 7:00. Ret. .... Read several chapters in the Book of Psalms, also read some pages in law. Attended Mr. Dexter's lecture on the Constitution. After dinner I remained in my room and read several of Demosthenes' orations against Philip. After tea I called on Judge Parker and lady.

Sept. 30. Rose 7:00. Ret. 12:00. After breakfast I examined the report on a Moot Court case, also read several chapters on Insurance. In the afternoon Gale and myself went into Boston and attended a new theatre just established and called Bland's Lyceum.[14] A play called the Jibbannansy[15] was acted and was a complete humbug. Returned to tea and spent the evening in Shelton's room.

Oct. 1. Rose 8:00. Ret. 11:00. This morning I remained in my room and read Horace Mann's speech on the subject of slavery delivered in Congress last August. It is the most masterly production that I ever read on that side of the subject. Also read Mr. Choate's speech delivered at Salem last week at a Taylor meeting. It is quite eloquent. After dinner I read several chapters in the Psalms. After tea called on Miss Everett and passed a very pleasant evening.

Oct. 2. Rose 7:00. Ret. 10:00. This morning I read and attended the lectures on Agency and Equity. Received a long letter from Judge Dickinson. In the afternoon and evening I was engaged in reading Story on Agency, which I consider very interesting. His works generally are very diffuse.

Oct. 3. Rose 8:00. Ret. 12:00. This morning I read and attended the lectures on Blackstone and Insurance. Mr. Parsons announced that Judge Cushing[16] has been appointed by the board to lecture on Civil Law. In the afternoon I attended Moot Court. After tea attended the Kent Club and made two speeches on foreign emigration. Then read a chapter in Allison's Europe.

Oct. 4. Rose 7:00. Ret. 11:00. Read and attended the lecture on Agency. In the afternoon I read Agency until 4:00, when Mr. Swan of New York City called on me and set until tea time, after which I resumed reading Agency until bedtime. This has been a cold, dark and rainy day.

Oct. 5. Rose 7:00. Ret. 10:00. Read several chapters in the Book of Psalms. Rolled ten pins with Vaughn and Shelton, then read and

---

[14] Under the management of W. H. Bland, this theatre located on the east side of Sudbury Street near Court Street first opened its doors on September 19, 1848.

[15] *Jibbannansy* by George W. Harby was first performed in New York in 1838 and starred "Giant" Porter.

[16] Luther Stearnes Cushing (1803-1856), Massachusetts author and jurist, lectured on Roman Law at Harvard during 1848-49 and 1850-51.

attended the lectures on Blackstone and Insurance. In the afternoon Professor Parsons commenced his new system of Parliamentary discussion. They adopted the rules of the House of Representatives. Several motions and bills were introduced. Professor Parsons, who was chosen Speaker of the House, then gave us a short lecture on the rules of Legislature.

Oct. 6. Rose 7:00. Ret. 12:00. This morning I attended Mr. Dexter's lecture on the jurisdiction of the Supreme Court of the U. S. The lecture was unnecessarily dry, but very important. We then held the second meeting of our Congress. The Speaker appointed the standing committees. I was on one of the committees. Some resolutions were then passed—one limiting the speaker to ten minutes, and another prohibiting applause. After tea Gale and myself went in to the Boston Theatre to hear the Ravel Family.[17]

Oct. 7. Rose 7:00. Ret. 11:00. Went into Boston and called on the following persons: Mr. Winthrop and Mr. Lawrence, Mrs. Hallett, Frothingham, Appleton, and Robinson of Nashville; Misses Williams, Merrill, Hammond, etc. In the afternoon I rode out to Cambridge with the beautiful Miss Gould and called on her after tea and passed a most delightful evening.

Oct. 8. Rose 7:30. Ret. 10:00. Read several chapters in the Bible and then set about writing a long letter to Judge Dickinson, giving him an account of the political movements in the North, and gave him my views on the subject of slavery in the territories. After tea I read some in Allison's Europe.

Oct. 9. Rose 7:00. Ret. 12:00. Read and attended the lectures on Agency and Equity. After dinner I read law until 5:00, when Jones of Alabama called and invited me to go and hear Forrest in Othello. The house was filled to overflow. Forrest did well, as usual. He was well sustained. Iago was splendidly acted by Marshall.[18] In fact it was acted better than I ever saw.

Oct. 10. Rose 8:00. Ret. 12:00. Read and attended the lectures on Blackstone and Insurance. Attended the Moot Court in the afternoon and took notes of the case. After tea I attended the Kent Club where I listened to several good speeches on the subject of the abolition of capital punishment. Read the latter part of Othello.

---

[17] A family troupe of actors, who for two decades performed in New York, often at Niblo's Gardens.

[18] Edwin Forrest (1806-1872), Shakespearian actor born in Philadelphia, rival of England's William Charles Macready (1793-1873). Wyzeman Marshall was a versatile actor in Forrest's company.

Oct. 11. Rose 8:30. Ret. 11:00. This morning I read several chapters in the Book of Psalms. Also read and attended the lecture on Blackstone. In the afternoon I remained in my room and read law. After tea I occupied myself in reading speeches and other miscellaneous readings.

Oct. 12. Rose 8:00. Ret. 10:00. Read and attended the lectures on Blackstone and Insurance. Professor Parsons gave out today that Mr. Choate would lecture tonight at Brookline. I very cooly asked him what was to be the nature of his speech, knowing at the same time that it was politics. The question created a general laugh. In the afternoon I attended the Moot Court. After, I read until bedtime.

Oct. 13. Rose 8:00. Ret. 12:00. Vaughn and myself drew up a report on the Statutes of Tennessee in reference to aliens inheriting real estate. We suggested that the Legislature ought to allow them to inherit it. But as our report was not called up today, we will have more time to prepare ourselves. Attended Professor Dexter's lecture on the Constitution. Our Congress met this morning and we had quite an animated discussion on the bill for abolishing capital punishment in Massachusetts. After tea I had calls from Shelton, Batchelder, and Vaughn. Received a letter from Grundy[19] and Mother.

Oct. 14. Rose 7:30. Ret. 12:30. Called on Gale and read John Bell's speech in Murfreesboro. It is very able, yet I differ with him in many things. Read Byron's Parisina, which I consider very beautiful. Also examined a brief on my Moot Court case. News reached here this morning that Ohio had elected a Democratic governor. In the afternoon I examined a law case. After, I read a chapter in the fourth book of Blackstone. Also read Allison's Europe in reference to the causes of the French Revolution in 1792.

Oct. 15. Rose 8:30. Ret. 1:30. Read five or six chapters in the Book of Psalms, and some of Byron's letters. In the afternoon I wrote letters to Mother, Grundy, and Felecia Eakin. In the evening Vaughn and myself walked out to Fresh Pond where we saw Madam [Josephine] Weiss with her Viennese children. Took tea at Joyslin's. Jones called to see me after tea.

Oct. 16. Rose 8:00. Ret. 12:00. Read several chapters in the latter part of the Book of Psalms. Also read and attended the lectures on Blackstone and Insurance. In the afternoon I read two chapters in Story

---

[19] His younger brother Felix Grundy McGavock (1832-1897), who studied medicine at the University of Nashville, married Manoah Bostick in 1855, and inherited some of the McGavock properties at Shawnee Village near Pecan Point, Arkansas, where he practised medicine.

on Agency. After tea I went to the Boston Theatre to see Forrest in Metamora, but the house was so much crowded that I was compelled to leave. So I went to the Museum where I saw Mrs. Barrett and Warren act as Mr. and Mrs. Teazle in the play called The School for Scandal.

Oct. 17. Rose 8:30. Ret. 11:00. Read Blackstone until 11:00 and then attended an exhibition in the chapel. The performances of the young men were good, but not very interesting. In the afternoon I attended the Moot Court, where I listened to a very able decision of Judge Parker on the jurisdiction of the State Courts over counterfeiters and clippers of the U. S.

Oct. 18. Rose 6:30. Ret. .... This morning I read and attended the lectures on Agency and Equity. In the afternoon I examined one or two points in my Moot Court case. At tea Chamberlain handed me a note from E. G. Parker[20] in which he wishes me to allow him to recede from some bets we made several months ago on the Presidential election. I think it was as cool a specimen of Yankee impudence that I ever saw. After tea I read Allison and Blackstone.

Oct. 19. Rose 7:00. Ret. 1:00. This morning I read and attended the lectures on Equity and Agency. We completed Agency this morning and will now take up Pleading. In the afternoon I answered Parker's note declining letting him off. And at the same time I gave him a piece of my mind about the way he had acted. After tea Gale and I went to hear Forrest in Macbeth, but owing to the indisposition of Mr. Thorne they had to play Damon and Pythias, a play that I do not much admire. Here I met Parker and he alluded to his note.

Oct. 20. Rose 8:30. Ret. 12:00. Read a chapter in Blackstone and the celebrated case of Marbury vs. Madison upon the principles of which Professor Dexter delivered a learned argument. After dinner a class composed of Cassidy of Alabama, Shelton of Georgia, Sargent of Massachusetts, Vaughn of Tennessee, and myself assembled in my room and examined each other on Blackstone, a practice which I find very improving. Late in the afternoon Vaughn and myself took a walk among the tombs at Mt. Auburn. In the evening I read Blackstone and Allison.

Oct. 21. Rose 6:30. Ret. 11:30. This morning Joplin of Mississippi called to see me. At 11:00 I went to Boston and occupied the remainder of the day in looking at books and pricing them. After tea I called on Miss Gould but found her indisposed. I then returned to Vaughn's room and we had a social chat about matters in general.

[20] Edward Griffin Parker of Boston.

Oct. 22. Rose 8:00. Ret. 10:00. Read several chapters in the Book of Psalms and attended the Episcopal church. After dinner I read law and history. In the evening I endeavored to read, but as is frequently the case, my eyes became dizzy and I was compelled to close my books.

Oct. 23. Rose 7:00. Ret. 10:00. Read several chapters in the fourth book of Blackstone. Attended Professor Parsons' lecture on Blackstone. He had a model ship made of mahogony in the lecture room today in order to explain its different parts. In the afternoon and evening I remained in my room reading law and history.

Oct. 24. Rose 7:00. Ret. 10:00. Read some in Allison's Europe and Chitty on Pleading. Attended the lecture on Blackstone. After dinner I walked into Boston to hear Mr. Webster speak in Faneuil Hall. The galleries were crowded with ladies and the lower part filled to sufferea- tion with men. He spoke two hours on the Sub-Treasury and the Tariff.

Oct. 25. Rose 7:00. Ret. 12:00. This morning I went into Boston to witness the grand celebration of the introduction of the Cochituate Lake water into Boston. The procession was the grandest affair I ever saw. It took it four hours to pass any given point. After tea the city was beautifully illuminated and the fireworks on the Common looked very grand. There never was as many persons in Boston as today. The whole city looked like one vast sea of human beings.

Oct. 26. Rose 7:00. Ret. 11:00. Read and attended the lectures on Blackstone and Insurance. After dinner we had a Parliament meeting and quite a discussion about Hallett's motion to vote thanks to General Taylor for his meritous services in the Mexican War. The Speaker at last decided that it involved politics and was not a proper thing to discuss there. After tea I attended a Free Soil Meeting in the Cambridge Lyceum. Charles Sumner[21] spoke and made one of the most eloquent speeches I ever listened to. His figures were really sublime.

Oct. 27. Rose 7:00. Ret. 1:00. This morning I read a chapter in Blackstone and several chapters in the Book of Psalms, then attended Mr. Dexter's lecture on the Constitution. In the afternoon read law. After tea I went down to the Port to hear J. P. Hale[22] of New Hampshire speak to a Free Soil meeting. I was disappointed in him. He advanced two doctrines that I consider very dangerous to the country. One was that the church ought to take hold of this Free Soil movement. The Whigs at Cambridge had a splendid illumination and torch light

[21] Charles Sumner (1811-1874), lawyer, politician, and one of the founders of the Free Soil party. He was Senator from Massachusetts from 1851 to 1874.

[22] John Parker Hale (1806-1873), lawyer, politician, and diplomat; at this time he was Senator from New Hampshire and active in anti-slavery movements.

procession tonight. Went to a party at Mrs. McGee's and had a glorious time. Such kissing and such girls I never saw before.

Oct. 28. Rose 7:00. Ret. 11:00. This morning I read some law and other reading. In the afternoon I went into Boston and purchased eighty-seven dollars worth of law books from Little and Brown through Chamberlain. After tea I read Webster's speech in the celebrated Knapp case.

Oct. 29. Rose 7:00. Ret. 11:00. Read four chapters in the Bible. I then set about writing letters. Wrote one to Aunt Felicia and one to Sister Ann, giving them an account of the great celebration on Wednesday. After tea I called on Shelton and set an hour or so. Returned to my room and wrote this.

Oct. 30. Rose 6:30. Ret. 12:00. Read a chapter in Blackstone and attended the lecture on Pleading. In the afternoon I read Shakespeare's Macbeth which I consider one of his best. At 4:00 Sargent, Shelton, and myself went into Boston to hear Macready in Macbeth. I consider him the very best Tragedian now living. Some give preference to Forest, but I think there [is] no comparison. Macready was well supported by Mr. Wallack, Rider, etc. The Whigs of Boston had a grand torch light procession tonight. Read Louis McLane's letter to the people of Delaware on the qualities of the two candidates for Pres. It was a very good thing.

Oct. 31. Rose 7:00. Ret. 10:00. Read the chapter in Blackstone on Praemunires. Attended lectures on Insurance and Blackstone. Judge Parsons asked me this morning if I would not preside over the Parliamentary meeting Thursday. I told him that I would. After dinner I attended Moot Court. After, I read until 10:00.

Nov. 1. Rose 7:00. Ret. 10:00. Read several chapters in the Bible, also a portion in Chitty on Pleading. Attended both the lectures. In the afternoon I remained in my room, read law, newspapers, etc. After tea I paid some visits to my friends.

Nov. 2. Rose 7:30. Ret. 12:00. Attended the lecture on Insurance, etc. In the afternoon we had a Parliamentary meeting. Judge Parsons called me to the Chair and I presided over this stormy deliberation. Some of the members tried to confuse me by offering amendments, motions, etc., but I stuck to it and out-generaled them at last. Argued a case for the Marshall Club.

Nov. 3. Rose 7:30. Ret. 12:00. We had no lecture today owing to the absence of Mr. Dexter. Remained in my room all day and read. In the evening several of us went into Faneuil Hall to a Whig Meeting.

Mr. Hoffman of New York City spoke. I thought his speech decidedly the best I have heard this campaign.

Nov. 4. Rose 8:00. Ret. 10:00. This morning I remained in my room examining a Moot Court Case. Received a long letter from Mother saying she had not heard from me in six weeks. In the evening I passed away the time in reading and conversing.

Nov. 5. Rose 8:00. Ret. 11:00. Read several chapters in the Book of Psalms. Also some of Byron's letters. Wrote two long letters: one to Mother and another to Edward. In the afternoon I read Werner, which I admire very much. It is a beautiful tragedy, such as Byron alone could create.

Nov. 6. Rose 7:00. Ret. 1:00. Read several chapters in the Bible, a chapter in Blackstone, and attended the lecture on Pleading. After dinner I read Hamlet for the first time in my life. After tea Gale and myself went in to see MacReady act Hamlet. He did his part splendidly. He had a fine house and everyone appeared delighted. Winthrop and Choate spoke for the last time tonight to a large Whig Meeting in Faneuil Hall. The Whigs will make desperate efforts to carry this state. Received and answered a letter from Mother.

Nov. 7. Rose 7:30. Ret. 2:00. This is the day on which the great Presidential election is to be held. Tis for the vox populi to determine whether Taylor or Cass is to be their choice. It is a mighty day. The people from Maine to Texas are all wending their way to the polls. I have no vote in Massachusetts. After tea several of us went into Boston to see how things were going on. There was great excitement in State Street. It was thought that Taylor would not get the popular vote of the state. Boston gave Taylor 35,000 majority over Cass and Van Buren. Received a letter from Father.

Nov. 8. Rose 8:00. Ret. 10:00. Read the Washington Union and listened to some surmises and calculations of different individuals on the results of yesterday's election. Attended the lecture on Pleading by Professor Parker. In the afternoon and evening I remained in my room reading Blackstone, Allison, and Shakespeare.

Nov. 9. Rose 8:00. Ret. 11:00. Read Insurance and Blackstone. Attended lectures on them. In the afternoon I attended Moot Court but was little interested. Read the remainder of the Book of Psalms. The telegraphic dispatches show today that General Taylor is elected beyond all doubt. General Cass has certainly sustained a Buena Vista defeat.

Nov. 10. Rose 6:00. Ret. 10:00. Read a chapter in Blackstone and attended Mr. Dexter's lecture on the treason of Aaron Burr. It was a very able and eloquent lecture. He gave a full history of Burr's life and character. After the lecture we had a Parliamentary meeting. The question as to whether atheists should be allowed to give evidence in courts of justice was discussed. Cassidy of Georgia made a speech which was highly complimented by Judge Parsons. I thought it a rather flimsy affair. He said that owing to the confusion occasioned by the absence of the proper speaker he refrained from speaking the last meeting, which I did not like, being in the chair myself. After tea Swan and myself went to hear MacReady in Henry the Eighth and The Jealous Wife.

Nov. 11. Rose 7:30. Ret. 11:00. From the papers this morning it seems that General Taylor will carry all the South with but few exceptions. Received visits this morning from Fillmore, Jones, Vaughn, and Fogg. In the afternoon I took a long walk through Cambridge Port with Vaughn. After tea I read J. C. Calhoun's speech upon the amendment to the Oregon Bill by the House.

Nov. 12. Rose 8:00. Ret. 12:00. Read three chapters in Proverbs. Wrote a letter to Father. In the afternoon I called on Mr. Joplin and took tea with him. After tea I read a chapter in Blackstone and a chapter in Allison. This morning there was a slight snow and the day looks gloomy, like the faces of the Democrats.

Nov. 13. Rose 7:00. Ret. 11:00. Read and attended the lecture on Pleading and Equity. Also read three chapters in Proverbs. In the afternoon I attended the Moot Court. After tea I read law until bedtime. The State elections in Massachusetts came off today.

Nov. 14. Rose 8:00. Ret. 10:00. Read several chapters in Proverbs and the lectures on Blackstone and Equity. In the afternoon I attended the Moot Court. After tea I called on Swan of New York and smoked a segar, then went to the Kent Club and made a speech on the negative side of this question: "Is the government of England likely to endure?"

Nov. 15. Rose 7:30. Ret. 11:00. Read several chapters in Proverbs and the lecture on Pleading. Attended both of the lectures. After dinner I read the Merchant of Venice. I admire it very much and think it one of Shakespeare's masterpieces of composition.

Nov. 16. Rose 8:00. Ret. 1:00. Read and attended the lectures on Evidence and Criminal Law. In the afternoon I attended Moot Court and listened to two of the greatest boobies in the school, Smith of Ohio and Davis[23] of Massachusetts. After tea Gale and I went to hear MacReady in Shylock. He acted in this play splendidly. The Comedy of the Jealous Wife was also played, in which MacReady and Mrs. Wallack both excelled.

[23] Jerome Davis of Belchertown, Massachusetts.

Nov. 17. Rose 7:00. Ret. 11:00. Read my Bible and a chapter in Blackstone. Attended Mr. Dexter's lecture on the subject of treason. After the lecture we held our usual Parliamentary Meeting, at which several speeches were made. In the afternoon and evening I remained in my room and read one thing or another.

Nov. 18. Rose 7:30. Ret. 12:00. Read law during the forenoon. After dinner I went into Boston and called on Miss Gunn [?], Amos Lawrence, and Mr. Frothingham. After tea Chamberlain and I called on Professor Parsons and family. His wife is a pretty and very clever lady. His daughters are also interesting.

Nov. 19. Rose 8:00. Ret. 1:00. Read my usual number of chapters in the Bible. Also read several of Byron's beautiful letters. After, Vaughn and I went to church in the Port and set in Joplin's pew. They sang the prayer of Moses which I consider very beautiful. After tea I called on Swan and spent three hours in drinking hot punch, smoking, and conversing on politics, etc. Swan and Wetmore[24] had a very warm debate about the difference between the intention and expectation to do an act. The weather has been very cold today.

Nov. 20. Rose 7:30. Ret. 11:00. Rose this morning and found that there had been a heavy snow storm during the night. Found great difficulty in getting to breakfast. Attended the lectures on Pleading and Equity. In the afternoon I read several interesting articles in the Washington Union and the chapter in Blackstone on Homicide. After tea I read Blackstone and Shakespeare. This has been a very disagreeable day.

Nov. 21. Rose 8:00. Ret. 11:30. Read three chapters in the Bible and the lecture on Evidence. Attended the lectures on Evidence and Blackstone. In the afternoon I attended the Moot Court and listened to a very able argument in an Equity case. After tea I attended the Kent Club and listened to a debate on this question: Was the Institution of Chivalry Beneficial to the World?

Nov. 22. Rose 8:00. Ret. 10:00. Read three chapters in Proverbs and several chapters in Pleading. Attended the lecture on Pleading. Mr. Cushing delivered his first lecture on Parliamentary Law this morning. I was much pleased with him. He treated the subject very ably. In the afternoon I read law, etc.

Nov. 23. Rose 8:00. Ret. 11:00. Read four chapters in the Bible. Read and attended the lectures on Evidence and Criminal Law. Received a letter from John H. McGavock. After dinner I went to the general

---

24 William Shepard Wetmore of New York City.

library and spent several hours examining books. In the evening I remained in my room reading law and newspapers.

Nov. 24. Rose 7:00. Ret. 2:00. Read three chapters in the Bible and the Washington Union. Attended Mr. Dexter's lecture on the Constitution. Had a very interesting debate in Parliament today on the system of voting by open ballot in Massachusetts. In the evening we held another meeting and I made a speech in which I paid Cassidy of Georgia in his own coin—about a remark he made in the previous meeting. During my speech Pearsons[25] of Vermont hissed. I thought he hissed at me and thanked him for his trouble. He replied and said he did not hiss at me, but at the applause which was contrary to the rules. After the meeting adjourned I was complimented highly, then went to Shelton's room with some six or eight fellows and we had a jolly time. Got into a difficulty with Elder[26] of Pennsylvania.

Nov. 25. Rose 9:00. Ret. 12:00. This morning I remained in my room reading, etc. After dinner I met Elder and he made an apology for what he said last evening in his room. Russell, Swan, Vaughn, Gale, and I walked into Boston and stayed two or three hours. After tea I called on Miss Gould—she was out. So I talked a while to the old folks. Also called on Cassidy and Jones.

Nov. 26. Rose 8:00. Ret. 12:00. Read several chapters in the Bible and went to the orthodox church where I listened to an able sermon on the efficacy of prayer. In the afternoon I read Kenilworth until four o'clock. Swan and Gale then called and invited me to go with them to Fresh Pond. After tea I read Scott's work called Kenilworth. The story is good and the language fine.

Nov. 27. Rose 7:00. Ret. 11:00. Read Kenilworth until 10. Cassidy and Jones then called and set until 11:00. Attended Professor Parker's lecture on Pleading. Sent Gen. Harding[27] a ticket to go up Salt River on the steamer Free Trade. In the afternoon I remained in my room and read until tea. After tea I attended the Wheaton Club.

Nov. 28. Rose 7:30. Ret. 12:00. After breakfast Gale and I went into Boston and attended an auction of English books, but they went so dear that I made no purchases, but went to Little and Brown's and bought Burke's Works, Graham's N. S. and Don Quixote. Called on

---

[25] William Barron Chapin Pearsons of Hartford, Vermont.

[26] George Wilson Elder of Bellefonte, Pennsylvania.

[27] William Giles Harding, agriculturist and stock breeder, was born near Nashville, Tennessee, in 1808. He was graduated from the American Literary and Scientific Academy at Middletown, Connecticut, in 1829, after which he returned to Nashville and became one of the leading farmers of the state. His wife was Elizabeth I. McGavock, Randal's second cousin. In 1853 he built "Belle Meade" mansion where he died in 1886.

Miss Watson of Tennessee and Miss Hammond and found both out. After tea I called on Miss Gould. She was going to a ball in Faneuil Hall and looked very beautiful.

Nov. 29. Rose 5:30. Ret. 12:00. Read three chapters in the Bible and the lecture on Pleading. Attended the lectures on Pleading and Parliamentary Law. After dinner I resumed reading Kenilworth which I find very interesting. Received several calls from friends. After tea I amused myself talking, reading papers, etc.

Nov. 30. Rose 7:00. Ret. 12:00. This is Thanksgiving Day in Massachusetts. Being no lectures, Gale and I went to church. At two o'clock I set down to a splendid dinner at Misses Uphams' with the Misses Lyman and several others. I had a delightful time with them, so much so that I remained with them until ten o'clock when we were alarmed by the cry of fire. Williams' stables burnt up, together with several horses.

Dec. 1. Rose 8:00. Ret. 11:00. Went round and examined the ruins of the fire last night. Wrote a long letter to Robert Lyon Rogers of Maryland. After dinner I called to see Gale who was somewhat indisposed. Returned to my room and wrote a long letter to Bostick. After tea I read Kenilworth and retired.

Dec. 2. Rose 7:30. Ret. 2:00. After breakfast Russell, Vaughn, Shelton, and myself walked down to East Cambridge to hear Rufus Choate and Dan Webster argue a divorce case. A Mr. Wiatt of Old Cambridge sued for divorce for adultery. The evidence was very rich and obscene. The case will be taken up again on Monday. After dinner I resumed reading Kenilworth and finished it. I think it one of the most beautifully written and best conceived novels I ever read. After tea Jones called to see me. I went to his room and played several games of backgammon and drafts. He is a very good player and I a miserable one.

Dec. 3. Rose 7:30. Ret. 11:00. Called on Gale and set an hour and a half talking with him and Swan of New York about eloquence, etc. Returned to my room and read the first three chapters in Ecclesiastes and wrote a letter to my Mother. In the afternoon and evening I remained in my room reading law, etc.

Dec. 4. Rose 8:00. Ret. 9:00. After breakfast Jones and I walked to East Cambridge to hear the Honorable Rufus Choate and the Honorable Dan Webster speak on a divorce case. Mr. Choate made a very ingenious argument, but was evidently trammeled. Mr. Webster was more animated than usual. He made a splendid argument. In the afternoon I attended the Moot Court. After tea I retired early. I felt very unwell.

Dec. 5. Rose 7:30. Ret. 11:30. Read several chapters in the Bible and the lecture on Evidence. Attended the lectures on Evidence and Blackstone. After dinner the Moot Court. After tea I attended the Kent Club and made a speech on the Wilmot Proviso, then went to Shelton's room and indulged in a game of whist.

Dec. 6. Rose 7:30. Ret. 10:00. Read the remainder of Ecclesiastes and some law. Attended the lectures on Pleading and Parliamentary Law. In the afternoon and evening I remained in my room and read Lord Thomas Erskine's able vindication of the rights of juries in the courts of Kings Bench, Westminster, in the case of the King versus the Dean of St. Asaph.

Dec. 7. Rose 8:00. Ret. 11:00. Read the Song of Solomon. The descriptions of the beauties of the Church are very grand. It is compared to a beautiful woman. Read the lecture on Evidence. Attended the lectures on Evidence and Blackstone. In the afternoon I attended the Parliamentary Meeting. Nothing occurred of interest. Dined at half-past four at my boarding place. We had an extra dinner. After tea I went to Swan's room and had a game of whist, etc.

Dec. 8. Rose 7:30. Ret. 11:00. Read three chapters in Isaiah and three chapters in Blackstone. Attended the lecture of Mr. Dexter on the Constitution and heard Mr. Parker give three opinions on Moot Court cases. In the afternoon and evening I remained in my room reading law and Scott's novel on the Crusades.

Dec. 9. Rose 8:00. Ret. 12:00. Went into Boston about ten and called on Misses Watson and Hammond. Saw a splendid copy of Webster's dictionary made by the publishers to present to Queen Victoria. Called on a *woman,* etc. Supped with Brown[28] of Virginia, after which we called on Mr. Parker and Mr. Parsons. Spent a very agreeable evening. Mr. Parsons presented me with some fine German tobacco.

Dec. 10. Rose 8:00. Ret. 12:00. Read my usual portion in the Bible. Heard two splendid sermons from Dr. Walker. Wrote a long letter to Father. After tea I received visits from Swan, Bostick, Underhill,[29] and Jones. Read a portion of the Pickwick Papers, which are very amusing.

Dec. 11. Rose 7:00. Ret. 11:00. Read several chapters in the Bible. Also read and attended both of Professor Parker's lectures. In the afternoon and evening I remained in my room reading law and other

[28] Henry Benajah Brown of Richmond, Virginia.
[29] Walter Mitchell Underhill of New York City.

matters. I have felt very uneasy all day, fearing that I was going to have a spell of sickness.

Dec. 12. Rose 7:30. Ret. 11:00. This morning I read and attended the lectures on Criminal Law and Evidence. In the afternoon I attended the Moot Court. After tea I employed some time in examining a Moot Court case, and then went into the Kent Club where I heard the following question discussed, viz. Are parties beneficial or not?

Dec. 13. Rose 8:00. Ret. 12:00. Received a letter from Father in which I learned that Carry Winder and John McGavock were married and that several other matches were likely to take place soon.[30] Attended the lectures on Pleading and Parliamentary Law. In the afternoon I went into Boston. At 6 o'clock I supped agreeable to invitation at Mr. S. Frothingham's. After tea some ladies and gents came in and we had a very agreeable party. I was presented to Mr .Woolcot,[31] partner to Abbott Lawrence, who invited me to take a Christmas dinner. Walked out to Cambridge with Mr. Rich.

Dec. 14. Rose 7:30. Ret. 11:00. Read President Polk's long message which measures eighteen feet. It is very good but entirely too long. Read and attended the lectures on Criminal Law and Evidence. At three o'clock my Moot Court case came off. Sears, my opponent, spoke one hour and a half. I spoke about one-half hour. Created a sensation, but lost my case. I was highly complimented for my efforts. Read an opinion in the Wheaton Club after tea.

Dec. 15. Rose 8:00. Ret. 11:00. Attended Professor Dexter's last lecture on the Constitution. His lectures have been very able and I have been much benefited by them. Attended the Parliament and heard a debate on a bill for the abolition of corporal punishment in our Navy. Had a little excitement. Cassidy of Georgia was not allowed to extend his speech beyond ten minutes. Attended Moot Court in the afternoon.

Dec. 16. Rose 7:30. Ret. 12:00. Read the sparring in the Senate between Benton and Calhoun on a petition presented by the citizens of New Mexico for a territorial government. Read several chapters in the Pickwick Papers. After dinner I went into Boston and done some shopping. Called on Parker and received five dollars that I won on the

[30] Caroline E. Winder, born September 9, 1829, in Mississippi, was married in Louisiana on December 6, 1848, to John McGavock (1815-1893) of Williamson County, Tennessee. Their home was "Carnton," named for the home of the McGavocks of County Antrim, North Ireland; it was to this house that the bodies of five Confederate Generals (Cleburne, Adams, Gist, Granbury, Strahl) were brought after the Battle of Franklin; and on part of this property, donated by McGavock, stands the Confederate Cemetery of Franklin.

[31] Joshua Huntington Wolcott, a partner in A. and A. Lawrence and Company, was a wealthy merchant of Boston. He was married to Cornelia Frothingham and lived at 48 Boylston Street, where McGavock took his New England Christmas dinner.

Presidential Election. After tea I attended the grandest concert ever given in Boston. It was given by the Philharmonic Society. There was at least three thousand persons present. Miss Gould was the handsomest lady in the house. I saw Miss Watson of Nashville and escorted her to the carriage.

Dec. 17. Rose 6:30. Ret. 9:00. Read three chapters in the Book of Joshua and then attended church in the Chapel. Dr. Walker preached the most magnificent sermon. I was so much pleased that I went to hear him again at three o'clock, after which Bostick of South Carolina and Swan and Wetmore of New York and myself walked out to Fresh Pond. After tea I wrote a letter to Sister Sarah.

Dec. 18. Rose 7:30. Ret. 11:00. Read three chapters in the Bible. Also read and attended the lectures on Pleading and Equity. At three o'clock I attended Moot Court and noted down the case. After tea I remained in my room and read law.

Dec. 19. Rose 8:00. Ret. 12:00. This morning I remained in my room reading until 11. Attended Professor Parker's lectures on Criminal Law and Evidence. In the afternoon I attended the Moot Court. After tea I went to the Kent Club, was called to the Chair. We had a rich meeting. Smith of Ohio made three of his *big* speeches. The question was whether General Taylor's administration was likely to prove beneficial to the country. This question was gotten up specially for Smith's benefit.

Dec. 20. Rose 8:00. Ret. 11:00. Read until 11:00, then attended Professor Parker's lecture on Pleading and Professor Cushing's lecture on Parliamentary Law. The remainder of the day was occupied in reading Hugh S. Legare's[32] speeches and the Pickwick Papers, etc. From the papers it seems that the gold mania in California is increasing in New York and Boston. A great number of vessels are leaving daily from these ports loaded with provisions and goods and adventurers. The President's message has caused the people to run mad almost about this gold region, which will turn out, I fear, like all such wild schemes.

Dec. 21. Rose 8:00. Ret. 12:00. Read several chapters in the Bible and attended the lectures on Criminal Law and Evidence. At three o'clock I attended the Moot Court and noted the case. Received a letter from Sister Ann. After tea we held our last Parliamentary Meeting for this term. It was a racy affair. Chamberlain was in the chair but was compelled to leave it. Wells was then called to the chair and we had some rich resolutions and speeches. I offered a resolution of thanks to

[32] Hugh Swinton Legare (1797-1843), South Carolina statesman, editor, orator, and Attorney-General under President Tyler.

our Speaker, Judge Parsons, which passed unanimously. If the closing meetings of Legislative Bodies are as rich as this, it is quite a treat to see it. Smith as usual made an ass of himself.

Dec. 22. Rose 5:30. Ret. 11:00. Read Blackstone until 11 o'clock, then attended a splendid lecture by Professor Dexter on the Right of Eminent Domain. After dinner I went to see Gale and Swan, set until four o'clock, then returned to my room and read Pickwick. After tea I read Blackstone on Public Ways. We had a heavy snow storm today, snow about ten inches deep.

Dec. 23. Rose 8:00. Ret. 12:00. Read a while in my room and then went into Boston. After passing the earlier portion of the day in shopping, having my measure taken for shirts, etc., I met with Rider of New York[33] and we went together to Faneuil Hall to see an Abolition Fair. The hall was beautifully decorated with evergreens and flowers, and there were many nice little things for sale. But I was disappointed. It did not come up to my expectations.

Dec. 24. Rose 7:30. Ret. 10:00. Read three chapters in the Book of Isaiah and intended going to church, but some friends called in and I was precluded. After dinner I listened to a splendid sermon from Dr. Walker. After tea I went to Swan's room of New York, where I passed Christmas Eve most delightfully.

Dec. 25. Rose 8:00. Ret. 1:00. This is Christmas morning. How I would like to pass the day at home, surrounded by friends. But if this may not be, I am content to enjoy a New England dinner. I was invited to dine with Joslin but declined on account of a previous engagement with Mr. Woolcot of Boston. At four o'clock Mr. Rich and myself left Cambridge in a hack and reached Mr. Woolcot's at five. We had a splendid dinner and an agreeable party. I set at table with Miss Bigelow. After dinner we had a party composed of the elite of Boston. I was presented to Abbott Lawrence who invited me to call and see him. I danced with his daughter. I made a small speech with Frothingham at the request of Mr. Woolcot.

Dec. 26. Rose 8:00. Ret. 10:00. After the very agreeable evening passed last night, I feel very well. Attended the lectures on Criminal Law and Evidence. After dinner I attended the Moot Court and noted the case. After tea I attended the Kent Club and made a speech on this question: Which furnishes the greater field for eloquence, the pulpit or the bar?

---

[33] Thomas Benjamin Rider of Chatham, New York.

Dec. 27. Rose 8:00. Ret. 12:00. After breakfast I went into the lecture room and read Blackstone until 11 o'clock and then attended the lectures on Pleading and Parliamentary Law. In the afternoon and evening I continued reading Blackstone, wishing to finish it. I received a letter from Rogers. We have another snow today.

Dec. 28. Rose 8:00. Ret. .... Read three chapters in Isaiah and a portion in Blackstone. Attended the lectures on Criminal Law and Evidence. In the afternoon I attended the Moot Court and heard Gale speak.

CHAPTER XII

"In London we met the Duke of Wellington." (March-June, 1851)

The raison d'être *for his journey abroad and the personal curiosity that McGavock felt at age twenty-four when he set out for Europe are expressed in his first letter to the* Daily Nashville Union: *"Some persons are content if they have a well-written history or book of travels over which they can go into ecstasies without the trouble of locomotion, and at the same time enjoy the cozy fireside and perfume of the well-filled meerschaum; but with me it only creates a desire to see with my own eyes, and learn for myself, things I have failed to realize in books."*

A journal of my travels in different parts of the world, taken daily, in short notes, and commenced at Nashville, Tennessee, my place of residence, on the 20th of March, 1851.

RANDAL W. McGAVOCK

The autographs of the officers and passengers on the Waterloo, a Liverpool Packet, on which I sailed from New York on the 12th of April, 1851.

Ship Waterloo

Edmund Harvey, Brooklyn, L. I., Captain
William Richardson, First Mate, Brooklyn, L. I.

List of Passengers

Jas. H. Otey, Columbia, Tennessee
Edwin H. Ewing, Nashville, Tennessee
Benj'm. Litton, Nashville, Tennessee
William Wales, Nashville, Tennessee

Jos. Davies Hamilton, Nashville, Tennessee
James B. Price, Lebanon, Tennessee
Jas. D. Maney, Nashville, Tennessee
Rev'd. H. MacDougall, M. A. Oxon, Brighton, England
Thomas Hill, New York
Adam T. Sackett, New York
Henry L. Patterson, M. D., Philadelphia
Ben Dana, Jr., Watertown, Massachusetts
J. P. Cummins, Toronto
John H. Pratt, Philadelphia
Henry Johnson, Newark, N. J.
Hector Tyndale, Philadelphia
William H. Hull, Baltimore, Md.

Lady Passengers

F. G. Eakin, Nashville, Tennessee
M. L. Bass, Nashville, Tennessee
Helen M. Hill, New York

March 20. Well we are at last off en route for Europe, a trip that I have long had in anticipation and now hope to accomplish satisfactory to myself. Having a longing desire to visit the ancient world I have hit upon this period of my life to perform the tour, believing that I can realize more pleasure and improvement than at any subsequent time, and at the same time I am better able to leave home, having no entangling alliances or particular object to bind me to Nashville. For the last few days I have been leave-taking, which is the most disagreeable part one has to go through. Yet it proves one thing which we all like to know, viz. who really feels an interest in us. Well all is over now—the parting wave of handkerchiefs has ceased to be seen, the last tear has been wiped away, the city is lost in the distance, and the heart is heavy with the thoughts of loved ones left at home. But adieu, a long adieu, to everything behind me. I am determined to be happy and reap the full measure of enjoyment and improvement. We left the warf at Nashville at 6:00 P. M. for Paducah on the Memphis Packet Embassy. Our party consists of Mrs. Wm. Eakin,[1] child,[2] and servant,[3] Miss Maria

[1] Mrs. William Eakin, at this time a widow, was the sister of McGavock's mother. She signed the passenger list as F. G. Eakin, *i.e.* Felicia Grundy Eakin, and is supposed to have been in temperament much like her father, Felix Grundy.

[2] The child was little Willie Eakin, about seven years old, the daughter of Mrs. William Eakin.

[3] McGavock later calls the servant Mary; she was probably the Negro girl Mary Jane whom Felix Grundy left in his will to his daughter Felicia Grundy Eakin.

Bass,[4] and William Wales, Esquire. Feeling much fatigued with the labors of the day, I dropped lazily into my berth, which was more like a Dutch oven than aught else I can liken it. Now for dreams, etc., etc.

March 21. After a restless night I arose and thought we had made a fast run, being in sight of the iron works 100 miles below Nashville. These iron establishments are quite numerous on the river and yield handsomely. If we had slack-water navigation, so as to let boats run at all seasons, the iron interests would be much advanced. There is also many reliable stone quarries which are now being worked for shipment. We reached Smithland just too late to take a packet up the Ohio, and consequently went to Paducah, which is considered a better point to get an up-river boat. There we put up at the Marshall House, where we expect to remain during the [night]. After tea we were entertained by the landlady giving us an account on the village. We also listened to some very good music by her daughters and their beaux. They waltz very prettily, considering, etc. The Magnolia was lying [at] the warf, taking on cotton. She is the most magnificent boat on the western waters. She conveyed the Divine Jenny Lind to St. Louis.

March 22. At 3:00 we were aroused from our peaceful slumber by Turner the porter announcing the arrival of the Belle Key, a very fast Louisville boat. In a few minutes we were in readiness and groped our way in the dark to the boat through mud knee deep. However, we were compensated in getting a good boat. The cabin was full and among others I noticed the father of the famous Sallie Ward. He with other gents of the same stripe sat at the card table all day, betting high.[5] This scenery on the lower Ohio is very like that of the great Mississippi, low banks subject to inundation with a range of lofty hills back. We had quite an amusing scene on board today with a young couple. It appears that a young printer from Cincinnati fell in love with a girl about fifteen from Natchez while at school. He followed her home, run off and married her on the warf boat, and immediately took passage on the Belle Key. She on the fourth day after marriage began to rue her bargain. She said that she repented her conduct and got off of the boat

---

[4] Maria Bass was the daughter of John and Maria Grundy Bass, and was one of McGavock's favorite first cousins. She later married Vernon K. Stevenson, the father of the railway systems in Tennessee, and died of consumption as a young woman in 1859.

[5] Robert J. Ward was a resident of Louisville. His daughter Sallie Ward was one of the most famous Kentucky belles of the era, noted for her personal charms and beauty. On December 5, 1848, Sallie Ward was married in Louisville to Timothy Bigelow Lawrence, son of the wealthy and powerful Abbot Lawrence of Boston, whom McGavock knew casually while at Harvard. The marriage lasted only a few months and was followed by a legal separation. See Robert Means Lawrence, *The Descendants of Major Samuel Lawrence* (Cambridge, 1904).

below Louisville without her husband, saying she would return to her father. What a commentary upon matrimony.

March 23. Reached Louisville too late for the Cincinnati Packet and consequently had to lay over until tomorrow. In the afternoon Mr. Wales and myself left the ladies at the Gault House and went out sight-seeing. The city is larger and more attractive than I had expected. The streets are laid off at right angles, broad and well built up. The churches are large and fine. We dropped in at the Fifth Presbyterian Church and heard a very eloquent sermon from Mr. Robinson of Frankfort. The Catholics are just completing a magnificent cathedral in the city. It is next largest to that at Montreal on this continent. The private dwellings here are very fine and the outgrounds exhibit much taste. After tea we amused ourselves looking at and listening to Miss Page, an old maiden acquaintance of the family who endeavored to make herself very elegant and entertaining.

March 24. At ten o'clock we went to the Cincinnati boat, where we found a number of Dr. Breckenridge's friends assembled to take leave of him previous to his departure to Europe. Here I saw Dr. Yandle, the destroyer of my happiness as I shall always believe. I did not speak to him, but I felt as if I could kill him as I would a dog.[6] But the affair is passed and may all traces of it soon escape my recollection.[7] The boat is very much crowded, but like most crowds I found but very few interesting persons. Miss Coleman, a neice of Mr. Crittenden's, I found to be quite interesting. She was en route to New York, where she purposes going to a French school. I felt all day like Jonah did when the whale swallowed him, viz. rather down in the mouth. Thoughts of the gay deceiver will not down.

March 25. Reached Cincinnati before day this morning, took breakfast at the Burnet House, which is decidedly the most magnificent hotel in the U. S. The whole house is complete. After breakfast we walked through some of the principal streets and then to the Art Union, where

[6] David Wendell Yandell (1826-1898) was a physician and the son of a physician—Lunsford Pitts Yandell (1805-1878). Both were born in Middle Tennesse, became prominent surgeons in Kentucky, and held chairs at the University of Louisville. D. W. Yandell was appointed medical director of the Department of the West at the outbreak of the Civil War and was assigned to the staff of General A. S. Johnston; he later participated in the battles of Shiloh, Murfreesboro, and Chickamauga.

[7] The "affair" which McGavock took so much to heart was between Miss Fanny Jane Crutcher and himself. He apparently declared his matrimonial intentions toward Miss Crutcher, a native of Nashville, and was spurned by her. About April 10, 1851, she was married to Dr. David Wendel Yandell, "the destroyer of my happiness," and they lived on a farm near Nashville before settling permanently in Louisville. McGavock makes another reference to "Miss C—" on April 9, 1851, and refers to "my old flame" on July 1, 1851. Many years later, on August 28, 1858, he refers to Miss Crutcher's mother in a humorous way as "my old mother-in-law, Mrs. Crutcher."

we saw Power's Greek Slave, a statue by Baber and some good paintings. We then went to the Pittsburgh Packet, where we found Mr. Steale and lady, a relative who seemed glad to see us and invited us to remain with them a day or so. Cincinnati is a real go-ahead place; everything is moving and everybody seems busy. It is a great place for manufactures. The river for miles above the city is lined with mills of various descriptions, exhibiting quite a contrast to the other side. We left this place on a fine steamer with a large number of passengers for Pittsburgh.

March 26. After a good night's rest I rose and went out on deck to admire and enjoy the scenery of the upper Ohio, which [is] more beautiful and romantic than that below. The hills on either side are higher and more imposing to the eye. The town and villages on its banks all seem to be flourishing, particularly those on the Ohio side. Having rather a dull and prosy crowd on board, I passed the day in reading Abbott's Summer in Scotland, which I found interesting, but more suited to children than old stagers. In the afternoon I took a long nap and then went out again with the ladies to enjoy the scenery, finding something to interest and amuse us at nearly every view.

March 27. We left home just one week ago today and my thoughts involuntarily turn thither. But away ye gloomy thoughts of the past. The future, the glorious future, contains all that I hope for in this world. About noon we hove in sight of Wheeling, Virginia, where we had a view of the great suspension bridge. It is a beautiful structure built on the same principle of that at Nashville and apparently more substantial. Here we put off some drovers from Indiana [?] with some fine horses going to New York, where they will be scientifically broke and sold at a large profit for northern trotters. Wheeling has improved very much in the last few years. I noticed the operation of several glass, iron, and other factories. There are several towns of importance above Wheeling and the scenery becomes more and more beautiful as you ascend to its source.

March 28. We reached Pittsburgh just before breakfast, where we had some difficulty in determining whether we would take the mountain or canal route. At last we determined upon the latter and made great haste to get to the canal boat, which was to leave at 8:00. After much vexation with baggage, porters, etc., we reached the boat in the nick of time. Pittsburg and all the little towns that surround it exhibit a spirit of activity and enterprise that astonishes a stranger. The whole country for miles is filled with manufacturing mills and the atmosphere is filled with coal smoke, rendering it very disagreeable as a place of residence. Now for the raging [?] canal. Our boat was named Kentucky. It was about 60 feet long and 12 feet broad, and manned just like a steam boat, with the exception of engineers, and capable of accomodating 150 persons. It was really curious to see them stow the passengers away at night on swinging cots suspended from the sides, one above another. I drew the upper shelf and slept surprisingly [well] considering I was compelled to lay in one posture all night. The boat reminded me of Napoleon's carriage, for it contained more in it than the uninitiated would ever dream of. The canal runs along the valleys of the Allegheny, Kiskiminitas, Conemaugh—three beautiful rivers. The valleys are rich and in a high state of cultivation, surrounded by lofty and romantic mountains, filled with beds of coal, iron, etc. The trade on this canal is four or five times as great as that on the Cumberland. Boats heavily loaded are passing continually.

March 29. [No entry for this date.]

March 30. Reached Johnstown yesterday afternoon in time for the Philadelphia cars. The road as far as Harrodsburg [Harrisburg] passes over a mountainous country. We went through a tunnel 101 feet long and up and down 5 inclined plains. The cars are propelled by stationary engines at the top of the mountain, which renders it less dangerous and more expeditious. We breakfasted in Harrodsburg [Harrisburg] and then passed through a beautiful region of country in a high state of cultivation to Philadelphia. After I had dined and brushed up I took a long walk up Chesnut and down Walnut Streets, two of the main streets of the city. On the former the eye of the stranger is first attracted by old Independence Hall, which still stands in its primitive grandeur as a monument of our country's renown.

March 31. Having written a long letter home descriptive of our journey, I took a stroll down Chesnut Street and was very much interested in looking at the fine store houses and richly furnished windows. While out I met with an old Cambridge acquaintance, Eugene Batchelder, who gave me many items of city news and pointed out to me several distinguished characters whom I was glad even to have a sight of, viz. Mr. Tupper, the author of the Proverbial philosophy, who is now on a visit to this country. He is of small statue, with light hair and eyes. There is nothing very striking about him.[8] Also Com. Stockton

[8] Martin Tupper (1810-1889), English poet, lecturer, and "people's philosopher," lectured in America in 1851 and again in 1876. His autobiography is *My Life as an Author* (1886).

and Gen. Riley. They are both large and rather fierce looking.[9] In the afternoon we drove out to Girard College and Laurel Hill, which I had seen before.

April 1. This morning Mr. Wales, Miss Jones [?], Maria, and myself took a drive out to Fair Mount, Girard College, and Laurel Hill, all of which places are ornaments to the city of Philadelphia and visited by every stranger. After dinner I went with Aunt Felicia and Maria Bass to a notary's office to have their descriptions taken and affadavits made in order to procure their passports in Washington, after which we took a walk down Walnut Street and amused ourselves looking at and comparing the fine residences of the wealthy merchants. At 10:00 I left the city in the cars for Washington for the purpose of procuring passports and letters and also to see some old friends.

April 2. Reached Washington this morning for breakfast, after which I strolled up to the State Department in search of my old classmate, Henry Sargent of Massachusetts, who is acting as private secretary to Mr. Webster. I found him pleasantly situated and surrounded by everything to make a young bachelor happy. He was glad to see me and was very kind in aiding me to procure passports and letters. We then went to the White House to search out another Cambridge chum, M. P. Fillmore, the son of the President. He seemed more than happy to meet me, invited us to take seats, and handed round his segars as of old as a prelude to our autobiographies since we last met. After a delightful conversation of some three hours, I got up to start, having several visits to make during the day, when Fillmore insisted that I should call and take a family dinner with him, which I did not feel at liberty to decline. So at 3:30 I found myself seated with the President of the United States, his daughter and sons, at a little round table in the West Room. The dinner was plain yet substantial, just such a dinner as I would expect at a respectable friend's house at home. The President is a fine looking, dignified, and agreeable gentleman, such an one as is well fitted by nature to adorn the highest office in the world. His daughter, of whom I had heard much, struck me agreeably by her suavity of manner and great intelligence. She is not pretty or fine looking, yet possesses a face full of meaning. While seated at this table of republican simplicity my mind was forcibly struck with the contrast between our free institutions and those governments I am about to visit on the other side of the waters.

---

[9] Robert Field Stockton (1795-1866), Naval Commander, hero of the Mexican War, U. S. Senator, and president of the Delaware and Raritan Canal Company. Bennet Riley (1787-1853), General in the Mexican War, distinguished for his fighting at Cerro Gordo and Contreras.

April 3. Left the Capitol this morning at 6:00 in company with my friend Sargent and Miss Webster. Reached the Columbia House before dinner.

April 4. Went to the Old State House this morning to see some of the sharp Philadelphia lawyers. Several courts were in session, but nothing of importance going on in any of them. I saw Merideth, Randal Gilmer, Wharton, and several judges of reputation. Sargent then went with me to see his cousin, Winthrop Sargent, and Burgin, a young lawyer of the city whom we knew at Cambridge. At 3:30 I dined with Sargent at Jones Hotel, agreeable to invitation. At 5:00 I left Philadelphia for New York via N. Brunswick and reached the Irving House about 10:00, where I found my party awaiting my arrival. Having procured very comfortable rooms and made my preparations for a week's stay in this Gotham of America, I retired to pass a night in quietude after two or three week's travel.

April 5. The first night in New York has passed away and I feel ready to begin my operations for the week. This morning I took a walk to the postoffice expecting to find letters from home, but was disappointed. I then proceeded to William [?] Street in search of Messers J. Stuart and Company, who were kind enough to secure our berths and aid me in procuring foreign exchange. Mr. Stuart then went with me to take a look at the ship Waterloo, which was to convey us over the mighty deep. I was much pleased with the appearance of the vessel and think that our voyage will be a pleasant one. It is about 1500 tons burden and very commodious accomodations for cabin passengers. After tea we went to Burton's Theatre and saw a piece played called Love in a Maize, which had a good deal of character, as all that Burton takes in hand usually possesses.[10] After this there was represented a farce called The Tiger, which has had quite a run for weeks past at this popular place of amusement.

April 6. None of the party went to church today, but all remained at the hotel sleeping, reading, and writing letters. In the afternoon, I walked up to Twentieth Street to Mr. Jolin's [?] to see if Bishop Otey had arrived, who constitutes one of our party.[11] Finding that he had

---

[10] *Love in a Maze* by Dion Boucicault was first produced in New York in 1851 and starred John Lester-Wallack.

[11] James Harvey Otey (1800-1863), first Protestant Episcopal Bishop of Tennessee, was a native of Bedford County, Virginia. He was graduated from the University of North Carolina in 1820 and remained there as instructor in Greek and Latin. He was consecrated a bishop in 1834, the duties of which took him by horseback through Florida, Louisiana, Mississippi, Arkansas, the Indian Territory, and Tennessee. He was the originator of the idea and one of the founders of the University of the South at Sewanee, Tennessee.

not yet reached New York, I proceeded down Fifth Avenue, where my eyes rested on marble-fronted palaces of many a wealthy man, exhibiting beauty of architecture and conveniences of every kind.

April 7. This morning Aunt Felicia, Maria, Mr. Wales, Argile Eakin and his wife, and myself drove out in hacks to see High Bridge, about ten miles from the city, and over which the water is conveyed from Croton River, some twenty miles further. This aqueduct is regarded as one of the greatest in the world, equalling in many respects the old Roman aqueducts. The reservoir in the upper part of the city was built at an immense cost and is as ornamental as useful. From its summit one has a fine view of the city. On our return I had an opportunity of seeing portions of New York that I had never seen before. After tea Mr. Wales and myself went to the Broadway Theatre to see a new piece played called The Vision of the Sun, the scenery of which is most gorgeous.[12] On our way to the theatre we had quite an amusing scene. We had scarsely left the hotel when we were caught in a whirlwind which carried my hat in the air out of sight and turned my umbrella, which was new, wrong side out. Determined not to be out done, I told Maria to cling on to my arm and we would go anyhow. So on we went up to the Broadway in the pelting wind and rain without hat or umbrella.

April 8. Today I was occupied visiting some of my old college friends. I saw Nevins, Rider, Jenness, Day, and several other old friends. After dinner I called on Miss Tomes and then returned to write some letters home.

April 9. Was presented by Aunt F[elicia] to Mr. Garven of Louisville, who seemed to take a deep interest in my recent affair with Miss C—, and reprobated her conduct in high terms. Climbed the steeple of Trinity Church today. It is decidedly the best view to be had of New York. From this imminence can be seen the beautiful bay as far out as Sandy Hook, the immense line of vessels of every description that surrounds the city the adjacent towns of Brookline, Harlem, Hoboken, and Jersey City, all of which places possess attractions for the eye of the stranger. In the afternoon we visited the Dusseldorf Gallery, where we saw several very fine paintings.

---

[12] The play which McGavock saw was probably a revival (or a new version) of the play which was first produced in New York in 1825 and featured J. L. Foot in the leading role.

April 10. This morning a party of Tennesseans reached here—consisting of Ed H. Ewing[13] and Frank Parrish,[14] Benj. Litton,[15] Mr. Price,[16] and Jas. Maney.[17] They are all going to Europe on the same vessel that we go in. I went with them to J. Stuart's to make their financial arrangements and also went with them to see the Waterloo. After dinner I took an omnibus and rode up Broadway as high as 24th Street to see Miss Tomes. I did not find her, but took tea with her brother who lives in some style. Saw Mrs. Blood of New Orleans this afternoon, an old acquaintance. She was looking well and has two children. Went to Burton's Theatre tonight and saw a piece called Love in a Maize performed. It is very good and amusing.[18]

April 11. Agreeable to previous arrangement, Miss Tomes, Maria, and myself took a drive through Brookline on Long Island to Greenwood Cemetery, which is rapidly becoming a place of much note about New York. It is beautifully situated on the Bay, surrounded by a fine iron railing and has many very handsome monuments and enclosures in it. One monument attracted my attention above all others by its singularity and magnificence. It was erected to the memory of Miss

---

13 Edwin Hickman Ewing (1809-1902), lawyer and Congressman from Tennessee, was born in Nashville. A popular orator and student of the classics, he was graduated from the University of Nashville in 1827 and admitted to the bar in 1831. He was a member of the State House of Representatives, 1841-42; a Whig in Congress, 1845-47; and a trustee of the University of Nashville, 1839-92. After his return from Europe he wrote the introduction to Henry Maney's *Memories Over the Water,* which was the first travel book by a Tennessean and which preceded the publication of McGavock's *A Tennessean Abroad* by only a few months (1854).

14 Frank Parrish was a mulatto, by trade a barber, who went to Europe as the personal servant of Edwin H. Ewing. He "looked after" the party of Tennesseans, was dubbed "Knight of the Razor," and returned to Nashville as barber and hairdresser at the Nashville Inn, 56 Public Square. He is listed with his own card in the Nashville City Directories of the 1850's, and in 1859 operated a barber shop at the St. Cloud Hotel. Here he kept on display several mementoes from his journey to the Holy Land: (1) A rock from the top of Mt. Sinai; (2) Vial of water from the River Jordan; (3) A paper containing flowers from the Valley of Jehosephat; (4) Another paper containing flowers from the Garden of Eden.

15 Benjamin Litton was a prominent Nashville attorney who was admitted to the Davidson County Bar in 1823. He lived in the 1850's on the Hillsboro Road; part of his property, including his home, later became the southern portion of the Vanderbilt University campus.

16 James Barry Price (1832-1892) was born in Danville, Virginia, and moved to Lebanon, Tennessee, with his parents, Colonel M. A. Price and Marie J. H. Barry Price. His maternal grandfather, Dr. James Barry, was the brother of Sir Edward Barry of London. Young Price, at age 19, was the youngest male member of the McGavock-Otey European party. After his return to Tennessee he was married to Mary Murphy (1843-1870), who was born in St. Mary's Parish, Louisiana. Price died in Denver, Colorado.

17 James D. Maney was born in 1830, the son of Thomas and Rebecca Southall Maney. His younger brother, Henry Baker Maney (1832-1858), was also in Europe in 1851; Henry's letters have been published in part, with a preface, by Alfred Leland Crabb in "Letters Over the Water," *Tennessee Historical Quarterly,* XVI (Sept., 1957), 262-272. In later life, James D. Maney was auditor of the N. C. & St. L. Railroad.

18 Either McGavock liked this play well enough to return for a second performance or else he recapitulated in error the events of his crowded week in New York.

Conda [?], an only daughter of a very wealthy merchant who was killed by jumping from her carriage while the horses were running. She was returning from a very brilliant ball at which she had reigned supreme as the belle of the evening. Brookline is a very quiet place compared with New York, but it is extending very rapidly. The evening was passed with two young friends, Jenness and Rider.

April 12. Well this is the day of our departure for the Old World. Having made all preparations for the voyage we all found ourselves aboard the Ship Waterloo, bound for Liverpool at 10:00 the appointed hour, and surrounded by many friends who came to take leave of us. That I may remember them, I here insert their names: Mr. Stuart, Miss Tomes and her brothers, Jenness, Ryder, Argile Eakin and his lady. At 11:00 the steam tug Achilles came up to tow us out. After taking leave of all and finding the vessel moving from the dock, we looked round to see if all of our party were on board. To our surprise we found two missing, viz. Ewing and Litton, who had gone to buy some books and were left. I went to the captain and told him that two of our party were standing on the dock and he said he would wait half an hour. In a few minutes we discovered them coming to us in a little skiff. I looked at them through the spy glass and laughed most heartily at them. The scenery on the New York Bay is really very beautiful, equal I expect, to any in the world for grandeur and extent. About 5:00 I bid Jenness goodbye, who was kind enough to come outside Sandy Hook to see the last of me. Now the tug has left us and we are all alone on old ocean's broad waves, subject for three weeks or more to the winds and the weather.

April 13. Rose this morning after a good night's rest and found that we had made but little speed, being scarcely out of sight of the Jersey hills, which loom up to the mariner's vision when far out at sea. During the day several vessels came in sight to relieve the monotony of a calm sea. We made but little progress and the day passed heavily. During the afternoon we had two very bloody fights on board between the sailors, who were all drunk, which is generally the case when a vessel starts out on a long voyage. The mates took their liquor away and they soon became pacified.

April 14. The sky indicated this morning the appearance of rough weather, which was soon confirmed by the appearance of many monsters of the deep floating on the surface of the water, which is regarded by sea-faring men as a sure precursor of storms—which was verified. We saw two large whales about a half-mile off, spouting the water high in the air, and about 1000 purpoises swimming with the ship. They are about six or ten feet in length and go in shoals. Some of the passengers amused themselves firing at them with their revolvers, but without any success. During the day many of the passengers became deathly seasick, but I could not sympathize with them, not having experienced the feeling. The steward laid in a full supply of luxuries at New York and furnished an excellent table, but it was all lost to most of the Tennesseans.

April 15. Captain Harvey, thinking that summer had fairly set in, left the stove in New York and the stewardess, thinking likewise, failed to bring out a sufficiency of covering—both of which would have been very acceptable to shivering passengers for two days. But fortunately we struck the Gulf Stream this morning and found the temperature decidedly more agreeable. I was told by Mr. Richardson, the mate, that the difference between the temperature in the Gulf Stream and other parts of the ocean was about 10°. There is something very curious about this stream. Many theories have been advocated for its causes, all of which seem plausible. Its course is from the Gulf, round the coast of the United States, to the banks of Newfoundland, where it strikes and is dessiminated in all directions.

April 16. Rose this morning and found that the weather had moderated considerably. We were all on deck after breakfast and passed what appeared to be the top of a ship's cabin, a melancholy memento of the injury received by some craft in a storm. It was painted white and looked as if new, but the captain said he thought it might have been blown off some time last winter. The passengers all look in better spirits today, and cheerful faces are getting pretty abundant, and backgammon and drafts seem capable at last of absorbing attention—a good evidence of recovery on the part of the invalids. Our fellow companions have proved a very quiet and agreeable company. They improve on acquaintance and evince a degree of sociability and freedom of manner which is always desirable on a long voyage.

April 17. Rose this morning and found that the winds and the waves have subsided and that all on board were decidedly better. Bishop Otey having offering up prayers for our preservation during the first night, etc., we ate a hearty breakfast. We all then went on deck and the Bishop bantered me for a game of chess and beat me so badly that I threw up the board and retreated to my journal. About 4:00 we were all on deck amusing ourselves in various ways—some reading, some playing games, and others conversing—when Ed Ewing who had been awfully seasick ever since the day we started came out, drew a long breath, saying he would like to shout one loud God Dam just for relief.

Bishop Otey was very near and said, "Ewing, I would not say that." Whereupon Ewing commenced making an apology, saying that really he did not know he was in hearing. In a few minutes after this a severe gale sprung up very unexpectedly while we had on a full sail. In a moment it rent in twain our main sail and threw the vessel on her beam end—also carried off the flying gib and boom—much to the consternation of the passengers. I was not frightened because I had seen vessels in a much greater strait. But I was considerably amused at some of our party. Ewing said he was prepared for the worst. Bishop Otey trusted in the saving power of Providence. Hamilton and Wales pulled at the ropes for life and death. Mr. Litton bid farewell to his wife and children. Aunt Felicia gave up the ghost. And our servants rolled into their bunks, where they covered up their heads until the storm had subsided. The excitement occasiond by the gale made all on board feel decidedly better.

April 18. Rose this morning and found ourselves sailing finely under full sail with a new main sail, making about ten knots per hour and 700 miles from New York. The day was pleasant and nearly all were on deck, amusing themselves variously. Nothing occurred of note save our piece of a wreck, which the captain said might have floated about for six months; also a great quantity of seaweed which usually floats in the Gulf Stream. This evening I indulged my fancy in looking at the setting sun, which is very beautiful as it sinks beneath the horizon, reflecting its beams on the broad expanse of water. After tea I was highly interested in a discussion between Ed Ewing and Bishop Otey upon the merits of Macaulay and other historians, after which I was entertained until bedtime by a gent from Pennsylvania who undertook to learn me a game at cards called cribbage, which I found a little more intricate than games generally.

April 19. About 2:00 A. M. this morning, during the still watches of the night, I was aroused from a sweet sleep by the loud and awful cry of "Murder, murder, murder," accompanied by a scuffling on deck as if someone was being stabbed. Thinking it might be a mutiny, I hurried on deck and found that the cry proceeded from a man who had the *mania a potu,* and conceived that they wanted to murder him. The officers immediately had him carried below and all on board was quiet again. A bark under full sail was seen this morning in the distance making its way in the direction of New York. Occupied myself in the afternoon re-reading Messers Hayne and Webster's speeches on Mr. Foot's resolution, which never loses interest. After tea I played whist with some Philadelphians, who proposed after we got through to drink the usual Saturday night toast: "Sweethearts and wives for the bachelors and wives and sweethearts for the married men."

April 20. This is our second Sabbath at sea and one month since we bid goodbye to our friends at home, which appears much longer. At 11:00 Bishop Otey assisted by Mr. Macdougal, an Episcopal clergyman who has been stationed in some of the southern islands, held divine service in cabin. The Bishop had hardly begun his sermon when all on board were alarmed by the cry of man overboard. In an instant I was on deck and found that the man who alarmed us last night by the cry of murder had jumped into the sea. He was sensible in selecting the time, for it was in dead calm and the ship standing perfectly still, having made only three miles in two and a half hours. He swam like a fish until the sailors threw him a rope and drew him up on deck again. After dinner Dr. [William H.] Hull, who is the ship's physician, invited me to visit the steerage passengers with him, where I saw something of the sailor's life and the poor man's way of living on board ship. Their place for sleeping is cramped and filthy, while each one does his own cooking. Nearly all of the sailors have venereal, which is very common. The females in the steerage made loud complaints against the deranged man. One woman said that he pulled her nose during the night.

April 21. We were driven out of our course last night towards the Banks of Newfoundland, which the captain wishes to avoid fearing we may meet ice. We remained in doors during the morning as the rain prevented us from being on deck—except an occasional sally to see the spouting of a large whale. We have made little or no progress during the day. The sails have been flapping against the mast and the ship rolling lazily along, making [us] sick and tired of a calm, which is very desirable on land but anything else on sea. The captain declares that he never had so slow a time of it and thinks there must soon be a favorable change from the appearance of the barometer. The amusements of the day have been of a dull and unexcitable nature, such as sixing [?] cents, crack-loo, urche, etc. Bishop Otey had prayers this evening as usual.

April 22. Last night we made little or no progress but the weather is very cool and rainy and the barometer stands lower than the captain ever saw it. At noon the skies began to lower and the winds to rage, indicating a severe storm. At 3:00 it seemed as if the spirits of the mighty sea were wakened from their dreams. The wind blew a perfect hurricane and the short, high sea was perfectly furious—lashing about in all directions with the madness of a maelstrom and with a violence that apparently nothing could resist. Heavy squalls and thick weather added to the fearful tempest that was raging. The vigilant officers and crew of our noble vessel were all on deck to a man, wrapped in their oilskin dresses and waterproof overcoats, ready to meet the worst. All sails were immediately reefed and we stood full three hours with our head to the wind, buffeting the winds and the waves, which rolled mountains high like a thing of life. Our noble ship stood it well and came out with flying colors. It was truly a magnificent scene, and could we have divested ourselves of its reality, it might have been likened to a fancy picture, in which some strange and curious dance was being represented between the sea and the ship. But our danger was too real for such thoughts. The fact of our being near the Banks of Newfoundland and the region of floating icebergs was too strongly impressed upon our minds to allow any visionary feelings to possess us at the time. The captain says that it was the worst storm that he has seen for three years.

April 23. After rolling about last night from side to side over a heavy sea, we are blessed this morning with a favorable wind which carries us in a southeasterly direction at the rate of ten knots per hour, which will carry us out of the region of floating icebergs, which the captain much feared. Saw a large ship in the distance today going west. Since the above was penned we have seen three icebergs some three miles off, which is as near as I wish to get to them. It is a grand sight to see these immense fields of ice drifting on old ocean's wave with the rays of the sun reflecting upon it. From these crystal plains rise sometimes isolated, sometimes in groups, elevations of thirty feet or more in height. In the spring these fields begin to drift along in solemn procession to the southwest, in which direction they hold their heavy course, whether in calm or, in spite of, adverse winds. We also had a snow storm today. Saw two large ships going our course at dusk, but they were too far off to distinguish them.

April 24. How silent are the winds. No billow roars. But all is as tranquil as Elysian shores. What a vast difference in one's feelings when the ship is almost still and making twelve knots per hour. We have experienced both and can truly say that calm which are [*sic*] so desirable on land are most horrible on sea. We are now on the Banks of Newfoundland where we have been driven by stress of weather out of our natural course. A large iceberg was seen this morning, thirty or forty feet out of water. Passed an English ship today under full sail. During the day we had a very amusing jury trial on deck. Ewing and

Dana[19] were the judges; Wales, Sackett[20] and Hamilton constituted the jury; Maney, the clerk; Patterson, Tyndale, and myself officiated as counsel; Cummins, as sheriff. The case was Pratt vs. Johnson for assault and battery. The trial was regularly conducted and our client found guilty. The verdict of the court was that he should furnish champagne for the party to be drunk at Cape Clear. I was fined three bottles for contempt of court. The speeches of counsel and the whole procedure was exceedingly interesting.

April 25. This morning at 6:00 we spoke a vessel called the Dawcus [?] Prince, eighteen days out from Harve and bound for New York. We have had beautiful weather and a fine sail today, having made about ten knots per hour. Nearly all of the passengers were on deck today enjoying the pleasant weather and playing a game called shuffleboard, which is entirely new to me. I suppose it belongs to the sea for it seems peculiarly adapted to the deck of a vessel. They have a square chalked out on one end of the deck, which is sub-divided into ten parts, which are numbered. They take sides and four blocks on each side of different colors, which they slide along and endeavor to get into this square.

April 26. There was nothing of much interest occurred during the day except that we spoke an English ship called Balona [Balogna?]. It was a really a beautiful sight to see the vessels of two rival nations passing each other on the mighty deep and exchange courtesies by hoisting their flags and giving their longitudes. We were in two hundred yards of her and she seemed to have a large number of emigrants on board, who threw up their hats and shouted most vociferously as the stars and stripes floated from our spanker gaff, showing that they were looking anxiously for the time to arrive for the realization of all their bright anticipations. The day has passed away without knowing exactly how—in a kind of lazy innertness which is unavoidable on shipboard.

April 27. This is the third Sunday since we set sail at New York and the probabilities are that we will have to spend one or two more if the winds do not freshen. The ship rolled so much during the day that we had no sermon, which the captain, mate, and sailors all rejoiced in, saying that we would have favorable winds now. It is really astonishing how superstitious seafaring men are in this advanced age of civilization!

---

[19] Benjamin Dana, Jr. (1830-1898) was the son of a founder and director of the Watertown (Massachusetts) Bank. Young Dana, who never married, went abroad again in 1870 and remained in England until his death.

[20] Adam Treadwell Sackett (1828-1878), only child of Clarence D. and Gertrude Onderdonk Treadwell Sackett of Brooklyn, New York, was a lawyer. He was married in 1854 to Sarah Elizabeth Ostrander and they were the parents of eight children. Later Sackett inherited an estate and resigned from his law practice in the city of New York.

When we set out, the captain remarked that our voyage would not be a prosperous one because we had two Divines on board, all of which he fully believes—notwithstanding he is a very intelligent man. The day has been occupied in reading and conversing, as it was too inclement to go out on deck.

April 28. Nothing occurred today of any note. The weather was pleasant and we amused ourselves on deck playing shuffleboard, etc. One or two sails in view. After tea we had a really jolly time; all of the musical instruments and talent was brought into requisition and we sung comic, sentimental, patriotic, and all kinds of songs. About 11:00 whiskey punch was called for and a good many of the party became highly inspirited and threw out a good deal of wit and humor. They kept it up to a late hour on deck, somewhat to the annoyance of the more sober and serious portion of the passengers. I was greatly amused at a little occurrence on deck between an Englishman and American, both of whom were a little fuddled. The latter commenced singing a Yankee song which related to our struggle with the mother country, and at which the Englishman fired up immediately and evidently showed fight.

April 29. Rose late feeling somewhat unwell from the night's dissipation, but soon became interested in a little book called Now and Then by Warren[21] and forgot my indisposition. The captain succeeded in getting a fine observation at 12:00. We are now 780 miles from Cape Clear, being in Lat 48°, 40, and Long 28°, 15. Nothing has occurred today worthy of note. We have had on all day full sail and averaged only six knots per hour. For the last few days I have stood on deck for hours watching the sun declining below the horizon. The varigated tints which usually adorn the clouds around the sun are really very beautiful. But you may say what you please, but a sunset on land is more attractive to my eye. There has not been a clear sunset since we left New York and the captain says he does not wish to see one, as it usually indicates low winds. The musical fever which prevailed last night exists again tonight.

April 30. This has been a day without incident. Weather fair and progress about six knots per hour. A bark going the same course has been in sight all day, but not near enough to distinguish [to] what nation she belongs. I was quite amused this evening at a discussion between a Philadelphian named Tyndale and an Episcopal clergyman

---

[21] Samuel Warren (1807-1877), English novelist, lawyer, and Conservative member of Parliament. He scandalized the medical profession with *Passages From the Diary of a Late Physician* (1832), and also wrote the sensationally popular *Ten Thousand A Year* (1841).

on the subject of the Unity and Trinity. They became quite heated in debate and finished of course as they began without either being convinced. It is thought that we will reach Cape Clear by Sunday, which will bring us to our place of destination some time during the middle of next week.

May 1. Well this has been a day perfectly barren of incident, nothing having occurred to dispel the monotony, not even the sight of a distant sail, which we have hardly failed seeing any day since our departure. Weather very inclement, wind adverse, driving us some four points out of our course towards the north. This is the first of May, the month of flowers and poetry, but here far away at sea where nought that's green or fragrant greets the eye, one feels quite different to what he usually does on this bright day. How different are my spirits now than this day one year ago. Then I met for the first time one who I loved sincerely and who had just recovered from a severe attack of fever. She looked pale and emaciated but as interesting to me as ever. We met on the street. I gazed on her pallid cheek, pressed her delicate hand, and was happy. But now, oh how changed are my feelings. Through some freak of misfortune we were separated and I have known no happiness since. And today my heart feels sick when I think of the past without any future to cheer me on. This is the fate of man—today all is hope, but before the morrow sun greets his eyes, hope departs him and all his bright anticipations are blasted.[22]

May 2. This morning I rose in time for breakfast and took a promenade on deck. Weather clear and a fine breeze from the coast of France. Several gentlemen at table this morning said they saw a white rat in their stateroom and endeavored to catch it, but it escaped. The mate says that he saw it come aboard at New York on the .... from a China vessel. I think it would [be] quite a curiosity at the World's Fair. According to observation we are 350 miles from Cape Clear. Nothing has transpired today that would either create interest or amusement. I have occupied myself in reducing this journal to a letter form in order to transmit it home to friends.

May 3. During the night we were driven considerably out of our course towards the north of Ireland. At 7:00 the captain had all things ready for tacking toward the south, which course we have been running during the day. If the wind does not veer in our favor we will be driven into the Bay of Biscay. This has been the most disagreeable day we have

[22] This is obviously another reference to Miss Fanny Jane Crutcher and reflects one of young McGavock's gravest moods of melancholia. He writes later (December 25, 1851) that he was miserable on Christmas Day, 1850; thus it can be inferred that the Crutcher affair lasted less than a year.

had since we started. At the tea table Mr. Ewing read a sheet written by Mr. Wales which created much amusement. It has considerable merit. It took off several of the passengers in good style and pictured all the little incidents on shipboard, and was called the Waterloo Budget. We all again assembled around the cheerful board to sing songs and drink for the fourth Saturday night the old toast of sweethearts and wives.

May 4. Wind continued adverse. Our progress during the day was about four knots per hour. During the forenoon while all were out on deck, I concluded to try an experiment and went up the shrouds. Mr. Richardson, in order to have some merriment, called two sailors who came up after me with ropes and lashed me to the riggin, high up in the air. While in this position all of the steerage passengers came out to take a laugh at the lubber in the round top. It is a custom among the sailors to require a treat from the individual who is so unfortunate as to be caught. In the afternoon we spoke an American ship with a black diamond on her sail. She belongs to the Philadelphia line of packets. Feeling dull and disagreeable, I retired—hoping that I would rise in the morning and find the wind change favorable, also find ourselves near Cape Clear.

May 5. The ship rolled very much last night, rendering it very unpleasant. But fortunately the wind was in our favor and we made our way at the rate of 11 knots per hour, making Cape Clear about dusk, being in sight from the top mast at ten minutes past five. It was really cheering to catch a glimpse of old Ireland after four weeks on the sea. The revolving light at Cape Clear was distinctly seen and even the perfume from her shores greeted our grateful noses. At table today another newspaper was read by Dr. Patterson of Philadelphia, called the Stormy Petrel, which afforded much amusement as it really possessed merit. After tea the gentlemen assembled around the table and drank whiskey punch to Old Erin.

May 6. Made a fine sail last night and found ourselves in sight of the highlands of Dungarvan [County Waterford] this morning. We were so far off that I could form no idea of the character of the country, but was told that it was nothing but a rocky shore. About 11:00 the wind subsided and were again blessed with a perfect calm. We stood out in the channel all day turning round and round and making no progress. At three a curious looking steamer passed near us bound for Bristol. She was painted black, with red wheels and chimney, and loaded with fine large cattle. After tea we all assembled on the deck where we amused ourselves by moonlight dancing, waltzing, etc. by the flute and violin, which sounds beautifully on the water. At 11:00 we retired to the cabin where we passed several hours in singing songs, telling anecdotes, and drinking punch. At 12:00 I went out and took a look at Tuskar Lighthouse and then retired.

May 7. When I went on deck this morning I saw about 20 sails, which was really a beautiful sight. We spoke one vessel from New Orleans, which told us that they had been in the channel one week and out 118 days, which was some consolation to us who had been out 26. We saw this morning both sides of the channel opposite Bardsey Island. This portion of Wales and the Irish coast on tother side are very hilly. The shores of Wales are rugged, yet every spot that would bear cultivation seemed to be laid out in small farms enclosed with hedges. About 6:00 we took on a pilot who gave us a paper containing a description of the London fair. At dusk a steamer tug came along side and will remain with us until morning. The sunset this evening, as presented to us, was very beautiful. The reflection on the snow-capped summits of Great Ormes Head, the water and the many sails in sight—all combined to increase its beauty. During the day all has been bustle, making ready to leave the ship. But our hopes were disappointed and we remained another night on the Waterloo.

May 8. Rose at 2:00 in order to see the scenery on the River Mersey and our approach to Liverpool. The whole stream was filled with vessels from every nation and clime, besides some 20 or 30 steam tugs that were going out to tow in ships. The whole atmosphere was filled with coal dust from these boats, rendering it very disagreeable and the prospect indistinct. The approach to Liverpool does not equal my expectations, although the quay gives it an appearance quite different from our American cities. About 6:00 when we had just passed Rock Fort and New Brighton, our captain informed us that he was going ashore to get a customs house officer. I went with him to procure lodging for the party at the Waterloo Hotel. Having succeeded in getting good rooms and a fine breakfast, I returned to the ship after the ladies. After all the baggage and passengers were aboard, we left, giving three hearty cheers for the Waterloo and her crew, which was responded to by the officers and sailors most heartily. I shall always remember with pleasure my voyage in this vessel and her fate will be read with interest.[23] When we landed at the quay our baggage was carried to Prince Dock, where it was examined by the customs house officer. The search was not so close as I had expected from accounts. Everything passed with the exception of some daguerreotypes, for which I had to pay a shilling a piece. After delivering my letters to Messers Stuart, etc., and eating a fine piece of

[23] Strange to say, the *Waterloo* was lost on her next voyage.

English beef, I took a bath and retired feeling very much fatigued from walking during the day.

May. 9. Went this morning with Mr. Litton and Ewing to see Mr. David Stuart, our banker, who I found to be just such a man as his brothers in New York and Philadelphia. Having made all our arrangements with him relative to monetary affairs, I returned to the hotel and accompanied Aunt Felicia and Maria to see some of the public buildings. We went first to the Exchange buildings which are very large and constructed with sandstone. In the square fronting these buildings is the monument to Lord Nelson, which I was disappointed in. It is nothing but a bronze representation, a figure on the top, and [bronze] around the pedestal, which is made of plain stone. It weighs 90 tons and cost £9,000. The next building was the Custom House, which is very massive and handsome. In front is a statue of Huskisson, who represented Liverpool in Parliament and did much towards the improvement of the city by advocating the extension of railways, etc. We then went to see St. Luke's, St. George's, and St. James' churches, which are handsome buildings—also visited St. James cemetery. After dinner we crossed the river to Birkenhead with Mr. Stuart, where we saw one of the largest parks in this portion of England. It contains 1,000 acres and is beautifully laid out with hedges, walks, flower beds, bridges, artificial ponds, etc. After looking at this we went to Mr. Stuart's residence and took tea. We found his family very pleasant. He was particularly polite in showing us his premises, which are very handsome and convenient. Reached our hotel about 10:00.

May 10. This being one of the market days, we visited St. John's market, which is 180 feet in length and has five wide avenues. The beef, mutton, and fish were very fine—particularly the beef. But the vegetable market does not equal those in the U. S. We then went into a little church near St. George's Hall and was ushered by the sexton into the clerk's room, who invited us to be seated, and in a few minutes turned round and asked me if I had my license. "License for what?" said I. "To be married," he replied. We all commenced laughing when he discovered his mistake and said he was expecting a bridal party. In a few moments the party came in and we witnessed for the first time a marriage in Old England. Judging from all appearances they were commoners. We then went into St. George's Hall, which is used by the city as an assembly room. It is said to be the largest room of the kind in the three kingdoms. I was a good deal amused here, when we asked to go in and look at the hall. The boy asked us for our permit. I told him that we were Americans and in a hurry and could not take time to procure a permit. The little fellow hesitated a moment and said, "If you are Americans you can enter." We then examined the docks, which are the greatest works of art and interest in the city. I was amused today at a note received by Bishop Otey from the parson of St. James church calling the Bishop "My Lord," etc., "Your Lordship's Most Obedient and Humble Servant," etc. It pleased the Bishop to the very soul, as he plumes himself considerably upon his office.

May 11. This has been a dull and uninteresting day to me, having rained all day. I remained in my room and wrote a letter to the Nashville Union. This morning the Tennesseans that came over with us started to Ireland and the probability is we will not meet again until we reach Paris. Captain Harvey, the steward, and stewardess called to see us today and bid goodbye before leaving for London. The Bishop invited me to go with him to hear Dr. McNeill preach, but I declined. He has the character of being one of the best preachers in Great Britain. If the climate of England is at all times as variable as it has been during our short sojourn, it must be exceedingly unwholesome and unpleasant. I think it has rained every day since our arrival.

May 12. The steamer came in this morning from New York but I received no letters, which was quite a disappointment. Left Liverpool for Manchester at 12:00. We took the express train which gave me an insight into fast travelling in England. We went at the rate of 60 miles per hour. From Liverpool we passed through a tunnel 1½ miles length. The country between the two places looks very beautiful and seems to be in a high state of cultivation. The farm houses look old and very delapidated. We are now in the greatest manufacturing town in the world and indeed it looks like it, for when one looks upon the great number of chimneys rising to the clouds and the smokey, dingy appearance of the houses, he can fully realize the fact. There is nothing of note here but the mills. I took a circuit this afternoon and saw the Cathedral, Exchange, and Infirmary, which are the only public buildings in the place and not much worth our attention. This evening I met Messers Dana and Sackett who came over with us on the Waterloo.

May 13. After eating a good breakfast, Messers Sackett, Dana, and myself went round to see some of the great mills of Manchester, but we gained admission to but few as the English fear that foreigners will copy their machinery. Saw for the first time several post carriages of the olden times dashing along with a bridal party. Left Manchester at 10:00 for Rousley in Derby, then by post over a good MacAdamized road, passing through a beautiful and romantic county through the towns of Stockport, Buxton, Addlington, Ashford, Bukewell, and the vales of Addington and Miller. We reached Rousley about 4:00 and stopped at the Red Cock Inn, a very old but comfortable house founded by John Stevenson in the year 1652. After dinner, it being a lovely day, we took a walk to Haddon Hall—just one mile distant—the estate of the Duke of Rutland. The view from the Hall tower is truly beautiful, while the old structure possesses many attractions from its associations with Lords and Ladies. It is several centuries old and still contains articles of use while occupied. Saw at the Inn tonight an original letter of Lord Byron's, which is a great relic.

May 14. After breakfast we started in a post carriage to Chatsworth, about three miles from Rousley, the estate of the Duke of Devonshire. We first drove through the park filled with deer and all sorts of game to the little town of Edinsor [?], one mile from Chatsworth. At 11:00 we were ushered in by the porter to the painted hall, where we registered our names, and then went through the entire house and grounds, viewing the statuary, paintings, fountains, grand observatory, waterfalls, and a thousand things that I cannot describe. This is said to be one of the finest places in all England. The day is beautiful and everything combines to render our visit to Chatsworth agreeable. We returned to Rousley, got our dinners, and again started for Newstead Abbey by way of Winfield Manor House, and in sight of Hardwick House, another estate of the Duke of Devonshire. This has been a most charming day and I have seen more than I can possibly describe. On our way I saw a great many old men in shawls [?], who reminded me of the olden times. Last night I went into the bar room of the Inn where I found assembled some of the men of the village of Afferton drinking their *(hale)* ale—as they called it—and telling long fish stories. The old lady of the Inn is very kind in showing us everything and giving a description of the country about Newstead Abbey.

May 15. Left Afferton after an early breakfast and rode 12 miles to Newstead Abbey, the home of Lord Byron. Just before reaching Newstead we passed through Sherwood Forest, rendered notorious for the fact that Robin Hood rode over the ground and lived in the caves round about. The Abbey is now owned by Colonel Wildman, an early friend of Byron's, who purchased it during his lifetime. When Byron wrote his elegy on Newstead it was in a state of ruin. Colonel Wildman, being a man of wealth, has spared no pains or expense in restoring the Abbey as near as practicable to its pristine beauty. The Abbey is a fine specimen of ancient architecture and possesses many attractions to the eye of the stranger aside from the associations. In front is a beautiful lake with pleasure boats upon it. In the Court is a fountain, which looks very curious, playing all the time. We were conducted through the entire Abbey and was shown all the chambers, paintings, sculpture, library, drawing rooms, and dining rooms—also the monument in the parlor to the memory of his dog. Saw the mounted skull and everything pertaining to Newstead. We then went to a little village called Hucknell, about four miles off, to see the church in which Byron is interred. It is altogether a very common place, unworthy to be the resting place of such a man as Byron. The natives of this town followed us all over the streets, being attracted by a colored servant in our party and my great height and red whiskers.[24]

May 16. At Hucknell we took the cars for Nottingham, thence to Derby, and thence to Birmingham, where we remained overnight. Nottingham is the place where stockings are made. There is also the remains of an old castle and a fine cathedral. Derby is a pretty place, rendered important by its centrality. There is a beautiful arboretum in Derby, and it also has one very fine church in which are interred some of the Devonshire family. Stayed all night in Birmingham. Went around this morning and examined some of the manufactures for which this place is so celebrated. We first went to Jennins and Bethridge, where we saw the process of making papier mache work, then to Elkington Masons patented Electro Plate manufactory; then to the glass manufactory. All of these places are well worth seeing. Saw also the monuments to Nelson and Watt. Left Birmingham at 11:00 for Stratford-upon-Avon, the birthplace of Shakespeare, the immortal bard. Stopped en route to see Kenilworth and Warwick castles. Went in the evening to the theatre, but was sadly disappointed. The play was miserably acted and the theatre very small, reflecting no credit upon the birthplace of the great master of the drama in English. I have seen so much today that it is impossible in so short a space allotted in this book to give more than a passing notice of what come [*sic*] under my observation.

May 17. We stayed all night at an Inn called the Red Horse in which Washington Irving wrote his Sketch Book. The name of Red Horse reminds me of the fact that most of the public houses have just such names as White Lion, Great Bear, Pea Cock, etc. We first went this morning to see the house in which Shakespeare was born. It is a small two story frame, built in the olden style with a wooden sign in front: "This is the house where Shakespeare was born." The lower floor is of stone and the fireplace very white. In the room in which the poet was born is to be seen thousands of names written on the wall

---

[24] The prison muster rolls from Fort Warren, George's Island, Massachusetts, give his height as 6 feet 2½ inches.

and the window glass. Among them I saw that of Sir Walter Scott and other great men. We then visited the Stratford church in which the remains of "the sweet swan of Avon" are deposited. His tomb is just without the railing of the chancel between his wife and daughter. It is the plainest in the church and has an inscription as written in the front of this book.[25] At 12:00 we left Stratford for Oxford, the great seat of learning in England. Passed by Blenheim Park, the residence of the Duke of Marlborough granted to the original Duke by Queen Ann for his military services. Reached Oxford about 5:00.

May 18. This morning I was presented to an Episcopal minister from America named Cox. He called on the Bishop and introduced several members of the college who were very polite in procuring us seats in St. Mary's church where I found many students all dressed in their gowns and Oxford capes, which give them a distinction which I admire. In the afternoon we again went to St. Mary's and was fortunate in hearing an excellent sermon from the Archbishop of Canterbury, who is considered one of the greatest men in the Church of England. His sermon was certainly excellent, but it was delivered in a kind of nasal tone of voice, which seems to be general here and exceedingly disagreeable to me. The Bishop was invited and did pronounce benediction in one of the churches this evening. At 9:00 this evening I heard Old Tom, the great bell in Christ Church, toll 101, there being that number of students.

May 19. This morning we attended choral service in Magdalen Chapel. The service was very impressive to me, never having seen it before. We then went round with the President of one of the colleges to see the various college buildings, all of which look old and rusty. There are 20 colleges in Oxford, numbering 5400 members. The students all wear gowns and conduct themselves with great decorum. The Bodeleian Library founded by Sir Thomas Bodley at the close of the 16th century is an interesting place. It contains perhaps the most valuable collection of books and manuscripts in Europe. We saw the cross in the middle of the street marking the spot where Cramner, Ridley, and Latimer were burned and the monument erected to their memory. We also saw the Arundelian Marbles, which are curious specimens of Egyptian antiquation. Oxford is a beautiful place, surrounded by green meadows and fine places for promenading. I should have liked to have passed a week here, but being anxious to see the Great Exhibition, I go to London this evening.

[25] He apparently meant to jot down the quatrain that begins "Good friend, for Jesus sake forebear. . . ." But this does not appear anywhere in the manuscript. It is quoted in full, however, at the end of "Letter Five" in *A Tennessean Abroad.*

May 20. We reached the great city of London via the Great Western railroad last evening about 6:00 and stopped at Miss Lawson's, No. 46 Great Ormand Street, Queen's Square, Bloomsbury. I did not intend going out today, but Captain Harvey in whose ship we came over in called and insisted that I should go with him to see the great exhibition. I acceeded and we drove to Hyde Park where we saw the great Crystal Palace and all that is in it. The building is certainly wonderful, far beyond my concepting, and its contents from the various nations is still more wonderful. To describe what I saw would take volumes, and suffice to say that all of the nations were better represented than our own, which is so well able to furnish articles of attraction. A larger space was appropriated to the U. S. than any other nation, expecting that she would do her best, and the consequence is that it is nearly all vacant. Austria, France, Turkey, and the Indias are particularly well represented. Thus far the Exhibition has reflected honor upon its projectors and will redound to the glory of England.

May 21. I intended going to the Exhibition again today, but learning that the great Derby stake for £5,780 was to run on the Epsom course, I changed my mind and took the cars for Epsom, where I saw the greatest race that has been made in England for years. I had a good stand where I could overlook the entire course and see all that was going on. There was about 6,000 persons present; 33 horses were in the race; and the riders were elegantly dressed; and all in different colors. They run on the turf in England, which they consider better than the prepared tracks. There was three or four races going on during the day, but the Derby seemed to attract all the interest. During the day all sorts of games were carried on for money, just like it is in our country.

May 22. This morning we spent about four hours in the British Museum, which is one of the greatest places of resort and curiosity in Europe. Here I saw specimens of all sorts of relics of antiquity, and specimens of all the different arts are to be seen here in their perfection. I could spend six months here most delightfully, finding something new every visit to interest and instruct. I then called on the Hon. Abbott Lawrence and his family, our minister to this court. He was very polite and furnished me with much information relative to the city and cards to the different public places. Mr. Lawrence lives in great style in Piccadilly, one of the most fashionable parts of the city, in the neighborhood of Apsley House, the residence of the Duke of Wellington.

May 23. Started out very early to see Westminster Abbey, which is the largest, most ancient, and curious building in England. Here is the place where many of the kings, queens, poets, statesmen and other great men of the nation are buried. From Westminster Abbey we crossed over to see the new Houses of Parliament, which are very splendid buildings. From Westminster Bridge we had a fine view of the Thames, which is a very insignificant little stream compared to our rivers and it is wonderful what an amount of commerce is carried on upon it. The bridges over the Thames are very substantial structures but fall short of my expectations as regards beauty, etc. From the bridge we took a cab and rode down the Surrey side to the tunnel, through which we passed. It is a wonderful triumph of art. We then walked through a very low part of the city, by the East India docks, to the London Tower, where we saw the Crown Jewels and many curious things, the cell where Sir Walter Raleigh was confined and wrote his life, the block where Lady Jane Grey and others were beheaded. We then went to St. Paul's Cathedral which, next to the Abbey, is the finest building in the city. We went all over the building, even to the very ball, which is 400 feet high. Here I had a fine view of the great city.

May 24. At 12:00 we all called upon Mr. Lawrence and his family. They received us very kindly and furnished us with cards of admission to many of the places of public resort. We then drove round to Buckingham Palace, which is a beautiful building. Here we saw Her Majesty's stables, which are well worth seeing. We saw the State carriage and all the other carriages, which are very fine—together with 150 splendid horses. From this place we drove through Hyde Park to Regents Park to see the zoological gardens, where we had an opportunity of seeing a great collection of wild animals, birds, reptiles, and every other kind of creeping thing. These gardens are very extensive and beautiful and much resorted to in the afternoons by the best class of people.

May 25. This morning Dr. Brackenridge and Mr. Pickett of Kentucky called and went with Aunt Felicia to hear a Presbyterian preacher. They came home very much put out with the politeness of the Englishmen. They had to stand during the whole discourse and no one offered to give them a seat. Bishop Otey and Maria went to an Episcopal Church. I remained during the entire day in my room writing a description of my travels for the Union, which I find to be no small job. It occupies much time and mental labor, and I almost feel conscious that I will never be remunerated. This afternoon has been very dark and gloomy, which always affects my spirits. I never feel well when the clouds obscure the sun.

May 26. This morning we took the rail for Windsor Castle, one of Her Majesty's country seats, which is about 25 miles from London.

We were conducted through the State Apartments in quick time with a crowd of about 50 persons, many of them French. The situation of the Castle is very commanding, furnishing a survey of many miles. The apartments are well furnished, but not so elegant as I anticipated. I was not near so well pleased with Windsor as I was with Chatsworth. After going hurriedly and unsatisfactorily through the apartments, we went to the top of the tower, which is very high and overlooks the entire place, which is 30 miles in circumference. We also went through the Royal Mews, where we saw some fine horses and any number of carriages. I think it foolish to have so many conveyances which they cannot possibly use. Returned to London about 3:00.

May 27. Went to the Crystal Palace with the ladies and remained until 2:00. This is decidedly the most attractive place about London. I see something new every time I enter the Palace. At three I went to the Houses of Parliament where I had the pleasure of hearing several of England's great men speak. The members all set and lounge about with their heads covered, which I consider very undignified. They nearly all stammer in their speech, and upon the whole I was very much disappointed. The building is very splendid and a great ornament to the city. After seeing the two Houses of Parliament, I went to see an amateur performance at the Devonshire House. Charles Dickens was the principal actor. It wound up with a ball and supper. Here I had a fair opportunity of seeing the ladies of the nobility. As a general thing they are not prepossessing. I was more struck with the daughter of the Duchess of Sutherland than any of the rest. Paid £2 for my ticket and stayed until 2:00. The house was very fine and the Duke very affable and polite.

May 28. This morning we went to Madame Tussaud's and Sons exhibition of wax figures and statuary. It is an attractive place. After seeing this we went down to the Chinese Junk which I had seen before, but wanted the ladies to look at it. Here we saw many Eastern curiosities, such as money, prints, etc. After viewing the Junk we returned to our lodgings on Great Ormand Street where I devoted the afternoon to writing a description of the World's Fair for publication, which I found to be a very difficult task. To condense in the small space of a letter what is to be seen at the Fair would be utterly impossible, so I was compelled to make merely a synopsis of the Exhibition. I regret that I ever commenced writing for the papers, as it occupies much valuable time.

May 29. Immediately after breakfast I walked down to Oxford Street and took an omnibus for the Crystal Palace, but it turned out that

I landed on the opposite side of Hyde Park and had to walk through. But I did not regret this as I saw a regiment of soldiers drilling, and crossed the great Serpentine River. As soon as I reached the Palace I ascertained that the Queen and Royal Family were in—where I had a fine opportunity of seeing Her Majesty walking about and examining the different articles at her leisure. She is a little, short woman, rather heavy, light hair, and eyes rather popped, with a countenance indicative of great purity and benevolence of character. She reminded me very much of John McGavock's wife. When she left the building the people formed a line to get a sight of her as she passed out. She bowed to them, but with little grace. After seeing the queen to my satisfaction, I called at Mr. Lawrence's, the American Minister, and left my passport with Mr. Davis to have it visaed for the different countries on the continent. This evening I carried Aunt Felicia and Maria to the Italian opera in Covent Garden. The opera was Gli Ugonotti[26] and the principal performers were Madame [Giulia] Grisi and Madame [Jeanne Anais] Castallani, Signor [Matteo] Mario and Signor Tagliafico. The queen was present with the Duke of Cambridge and two ladies. The house was crowded and the opera was very magnificent.

May 30. This morning I went to Sir John Soames museum. It is a private collection of Egyptian antiquities and other curiosities well worth seeing. An Egyptian sarcophagus attracted me more than anything else, as it is the most perfect one in England. From this place I visited the Northumberland House in Trafalgar Square, which is considered as a fine specimen of a London Palace. From the palace I crossed over to the National Gallery of paintings and sculpture. In this I was disappointed. There are many excellent paintings here, but not equal to what it should be. I noticed in the collection a full length portrait of John C. Calhoun. In the afternoon I wrote my eighth letter for the Nashville Union. At 10:30 I went with the ladies to a soiree at Mr. Lawrence's, the American Minister. Here we met many of the Lords and grandees of London, among the rest the old Duke of Wellington. He is very old and infirm, but still shows what he once was. In size the Duke is about five feet ten.[27] Also saw the Duke of Rutland, the Marquis and Marchioness of Westminster, the Marquis of Breadalbane, the Marquis of Cranby [?], etc.

---

[26] *Gli Ugonotti,* usually called *Les Huguenots* in America, was first sung on February 29, 1836, in Paris. It has become the most famous and most popular of the operas written by Giacomo Myerbeer (1791-1864).

[27] Born in 1769, Arthur Wellesley, the first Duke of Wellington, died on September 14, 1852, about three and a half months after McGavock met him in London.

May 31. Called on Mr. Taylor and family and Groosbeck [?] of Cincinnati, and then went to the Exhibition and from there to Mr. Lawrence's. In the afternoon I accompanied the ladies to the Royal Botannic Gardens in Regents Park. There is a large collection of American flowers there. It is a pretty place and much resorted to on Saturday, which is fete day. Two fine bands of music are playing during the fete. After seeing the gardens I went very reluctantly, merely to gratify Bishop Otey, and dined with Mr. Anderson. The party was pleasant. About 11:00 Mr. Anderson and myself walked down Regent Street and several other streets to witness the illumination in honor of Her Majesty's birthday. This afternoon I was very much vexed with Mrs. Eakin on account of some unpleasant remarks made to me. I regret exceedingly that I ever offered to come with her. She is cross and huffy and hard to please.

June 1. The day has been occupied almost entirely in writing letters, etc. After dinner Colonel Bigelow Lawrence called and paid a long visit. He seemed to take a great deal of interest in Willie Eakin's ear, being afflicted with deafness himself.[28] Late in the afternoon we drove round to see Mr. David Stuart of Liverpool, but found him out. I then took a long walk all alone through a very dense part of the city and yet I felt lonesome and unhappy—all for what?—merely for a woman who deceived me, who received my addresses that she might crush me. I have endeavored to bury all thoughts of her but I cannot; like Banquo's ghost, it will not down, but haunts me continually and makes me perfectly unhappy.

June 2. This morning Bishop Otey and the ladies went to Great Malvern, where they propose staying until next week. After they left I continued my labors of sightseeing. I first went to the Billingsgate fish market where I had a fine mess of fish for breakfast. This market is exceedingly low and dirty. I then visited Guild Hall, the Post office, Royal Exchange, Bank of England, and Mansion House—also the fire monument and London bridge, where I took a boat for Greenwich, about eight miles below. On my way to Greenwich I fell into conver-

---

[28] Timothy Bigelow Lawrence, son of Abbot and Katharine Bigelow Lawrence, was born in 1826. After his graduation from Harvard in 1846, he served as aide-de-camp on the staff of Governor George Nixon Briggs of Massachusetts. When his father was appointed U. S. Minister to the Court of St. James in 1849, young Lawrence, legally separated from Sallie Ward, went to London as an attache of the American Legation and was popular with Americans visiting the city. He was married for the second time, in 1854, to Elizabeth Chapman of Bucks County, Pennsylvania. During the first year of the Civil War he served in the Union Army, but was obliged to withdraw from active service because of increasing deafness. In 1862 he was appointed U. S. Consul-General in Italy, lived abroad for several years thereafter, and later helped to found the Boston Museum of Fine Arts, to which he gave his collections of armor and wood carvings.

sation with a man whom I afterwards took to be either deranged or drunk. He said that he was a Mason and I replied that I was also. He commenced questioning me. I declined answering his questions. He flew into a great passion and said that I had inveigled him and was no Mason. Seeing his manner was anything but that of a gentleman, I abruptly left him to his own meditations. Received calls today from Mr. Ashbel Smith of Texas[29] and Griffin Taylor, Esquire, of Cincinnati. This evening I went to the Princes[s] Theatre on Oxford Street where I heard Mr. and Mrs. Keane in the Merchant of Venice, the Alhambra by Irving, and a very excellent farce called Lodgers at the Exhibition.[30]

June 3. This morning I visited the coliseum at the instance of some friends and found it to be one of the most interesting places in London. I obtained more insight from looking at the painting representing the city from St. Paul's Cathedral than I could by all the guides and descriptions in Christendom. It is really a wonderful work. The statuary, paintings, artificial scenery, and gardens are well worth seeing—also the caverns. From this place I went to Westminster Hall to witness the proceedings of the different courts. The members of the courts all wear wigs and gowns, which give them a very venerable appearance. The high court of Chancery is held in the House of Lords. Here I met Mr. Stuart and lady, who invited me to go with them to Richmond and Kew. I accepted their kind invitation and passed an exceedingly agreeable day. Richmond is a very beautiful place, remarkable for its scenery. Kew is noted for its botannical gardens. It is royal property. Stopped at Vaux Hall and witnessed the circus, fireworks, concert, dancing, etc.

June 4. Being considerably fatigued from the labors of the last two days I indulged myself and did not rise until 10:00. At 12:00 I set out and visited a Ragged School in Field Lane, which I found to be rather a curious place. Children from two years old up to twenty were there to receive instruction. The teachers were very polite to me. They showed and explained everything. Their institutions are very laudable, for they receive and educate those who would grow up in ignorance and vice were it not for their kind aid and attention. After seeing this school I took a long walk and returned to my lodgings for the day. I then commenced my tenth letter for the Nashville Union—wrote until 12:00.

---

[29] Ashbel Smith (1805-1886), surgeon-general and secretary of state of the Republic of Texas before annexation; Confederate general; legislator and politician.

[30] Charles John Kean (1811-1868) and his wife Ellen Tree Kean (1805-1880). At this time Kean was manager of the Princess Theatre, where he staged a notable series of Shakespearian revivals with careful attention to historical accuracy.

June 5. After completing one or two letters this morning I went to St. Paul's Cathedral where I witnessed a sight nearly equal to the Crystal Palace. It was a celebration of the Charity Schools. There were about 5,000 children and as many spectators. The children were all ranged together on elevated seats near the organ. They sang Old Hundred and several Psalms together most beautifully. The Archbishop of Canterbury delivered a sermon but I was not near enough to hear anything. Here I met Dr. Patterson of Philadelphia, who went with me to see Newgate Prison, Batholomews Hospital, and the Ragged School. While at Newgate we saw them send ten or twelve women to the Pen, and while at the hospital we heard a lecture and went through the sick rooms with the attending physicians and students. Dined with Dr. Patterson and Tyndale on the Strand. After dinner we went to the Haymarket Theatre and then to Evans' Cider Cellar in Covent Garden. This latter place is noted as a place where young men meet to revel at night. They have excellent concerts there.

June 6. After carrying my trunks to Mr. John Miller's in 26 Henrietta Street, I took the Great Western Railroad for Gloucester and thence for Worcester on my way to Great Malvern to join my party. I remained in Gloucester long enough to visit the Cathedral, which is very old, having been built sometime about 1070. During Cromwell's time it was much damaged. The heads of all the figures on the outside of the building were broken off, a sight to be seen in nearly all the Cathedrals of this country. The railroad on this route is very fine. They have both the narrow and wide gauge and the cars are better than the generality of cars on the railroads in England. Every day I am more and more struck with the politeness and cordiality of Englishmen. They have invariably treated me with marked politeness.

June 7. Stayed all night at the Star and Garter in Worcester. When I paid my bill this morning I forgot the waiters and left the house for the coach office. Before I had proceeded very far I was accosted by the boot black, who told me that I had not paid him, and then by the waiter, and lastly by the chambermaid—all of which was very annoying. Upon reaching Great Malvern I found my party, together with Dr. Breckenridge and Colonel Grigsby and lady from Kentucky. They are staying at Dr. Wilson's celebrated hydropathetic establishment and some of them are undergoing the treatments. Bishop Otey is decidedly better than he was when he left London, and I strongly hope that he may receive permanent relief. I put up at a hotel called the Abbey, which is one of the nicest places that I have seen in England. Malvern is beautifully situated on the side of lofty hills with pure air and good water.

June 8. This morning was devoted principally in writing the eleventh letter for the Nashville Union. I then called at Dr. Wilson's establishment and passed an hour or so conversing with Mrs. Grigsby and others, when in stepped Mr. David Stuart and lady of Liverpool, who came by on their way home to see us. Mr. Stuart went with me and explained the entire system of hydropathy, he being a great believer and having been benefitted himself. This afternoon I rode on a donkey with my feet touching the ground and a boy walking behind holding on to the tail and whipping the poor animal along to the top of Malvern Hills, which are 1500 feet high and from which there is one of the most magnificent views in all England. It is different from our wild and romantic scenery in America. There nearly all is forest ground, while here everything is under a fine state of cultivation, lacking only a sheet of water to make it perfect.

June 9. This morning I left Malvern with Aunt Felicia, Maria, Willie and Mary[31] for Wales, Ireland, and Scotland. Bishop Otey's health being exceedingly delicate, he remained at Dr. Wilson's to try more effectually the hydropathic system. I do hope he will be benefitted. We meet again in London. Dr. Breckenridge of Kentucky came with us as far as Worcester. Mr. David Stuart and lady accompanied us on their way home as far as Crewe. We had intended going on as far as Llangollen this evening but the weather is so inclement that we concluded to remain at the Albion Hotel in the ancient town of Chester. The railroads were crowded today with persons going to London to see the World's Fair. This is Whitsuntide week and all the laboring classes have holidays and their employers allow them to go to London. The fares on the roads are reduced for their benefit, which is an unusual privilege in this country. Throughout this country the poorer classes have regular organized clubs formed for the purpose of relieving each other in sickness or distress. They meet once every year and have a dinner, preaching, dancing, drinking, carousing, etc. All the coaches were filled today with men, women, and children—walking, reeling, and going in all kinds of ways to different celebrations.

June 10. This morning we walked round the walls of Chester, visited the Cathedral, barracks, and old houses—all of which are very curious. It is the only walled town now in England. The store houses are arranged both below and above so that one can walk along the

---

[31] Here McGavock gives the name of his aunt's maid, who served as nursemaid for little Willie Eakin.

portico over the lower story and do their shopping in those above without getting wet. The barracks are formed partly out of an old castle that once stood on the spot. Chester is situated on a rocky hill on the banks of the River Dee, over which there is a stone bridge with an arch that spans 200 feet, said to be the largest in England. There is about 400 soldiers at this point and 30,000 stands of arms besides all the necessaries of war. At 11:00 we left Chester for the Llangollen station, where we took a coach for Corwen in Wales, passing through the beautiful vale of Llangollen. Here we dined, and took a post coach for Cape Cerrey, near Snowden mountain, where we now are. The scenery along this route is very beautiful, far surpassing anything to be seen in England and equal in many respects our American scenery. The mountains are high, rugged, and barren. The vales are narrow, deep, and beautiful—filled with cataracts and mountain streamlets filled with trout. The towns that we passed through today are miserable hovels, built of stone and presenting a very unsightly appearance. The homes in the country are very small, built of stone, and look very uncomfortable.

June 11. Last night I was soothed to sleep by the murmuring of the mountain brooks around Cape Cerrey and the dulcet tones of a harp touched by an old Welshman. This morning I arose very early and went angling on Cape Cerrey lake, but as I was pressed for time I did not have an opportunity of ascertaining whether I had any trout luck or not. After a good breakfast we proceeded through a very beautiful mountainous country to the vale of Llanberis at the foot of Mount Snowden. This is a great slate region. There is a very large mine just opposite Victoria Hotel, from which immense quantities of slate is transported by rail to Menai Straits. The whole country in north Wales, which is very mountainous, is filled with slate, lead ore, copper, etc. The houses of the people are very inferior, being built of stone or slate and covered with the same. The people, although industrious, are poor and many in want of the necessaries of life. From Victoria Hotel we proceeded to ascend Mount Snowden on ponies with a guide. It is the highest mountain in Wales, being 3,751 feet high. The path up is very narrow and rugged, but the view which I consider very grand will fully repay the trouble. From this point I could see nearly all of Wales, which is a mountainous and sterile region. From this point we went to the Britannia Tubular Bridge, thence to the Suspension Bridge, and thence to the Belle Vue Hotel on Menai Straits.

June 12. Staid overnight at the Belle Vue Hotel on Menai Straits near Bangor, where we remained until 11:00 today, when we left by rail for Holyhead and thence by boat to Kingstown, and rail again to Dublin, Ireland. On the route we became acquainted with a Dr. Watkins from Troy, N. Y., who had with him a daughter about 22 years of age and a young wife about 20. He is about 60 and married without letting his daughter know anything about it. The mother looks up to the daughter who is the perfect picture of unhappiness. I do really pity all of the party. It shows what fools old men sometimes make of themselves. In crossing the channel nearly everyone was sick. It is said to be much worse than crossing the ocean, being a much shorter run. Stopped at Greshman's on Sackville Street.

June 13. This morning we started out sightseeing in the capital city of Auld Ireland, the land of potatoes and poverty. Near Carlisle bridge is a tall stone pillar to the memory of Nelson and in the Phoenix Park there is a monument called the Wellington testimonial. The custom house, court house, and Trinity College are fine structures—also the Bank of Ireland and the Catholic Chapel. A river called the Anna Liffey flows through the center of Dublin over which there is seven fine bridges. We visited the cemetery in which we saw the vault containing the remains of O'Connell.[32] His heart was left in Italy and his body placed in this vault, where all Catholics love to go and gaze upon the shrine that contains the mortal remains of a man whose memory they worship. In St. Patrick's Cathedral we saw the tomb of Curran [?] and Jonathan Swift, the old Dean.

June 14. Left Dublin this morning on the railroad for the city of Cork in the southern part of Ireland—distance over 160 miles. The country between the two places is rolling and at this time looks well, but the dwellings of the peasantry are miserable hovels, far inferior in point of comfort and cleanliness to our negro cabins. The city of Cork is situated on either side of a river that empties into the harbor and is surrounded by high hills. The streets are narrow and filthy, the houses look old and delapidated, and the population the worst I ever saw. The streets are filled with men, women, and children almost in a state of nudity—and the most filthy beings in the world. The southern part of Ireland is, strictly speaking, an agricultural country, but in truth it may be termed [a] poverty region.

June 15. Last evening Aunt Felicia was quite sick, so much so that she sent for the doctor. This morning she is up and thinks she will be able to proceed tomorrow on our journey. The weather is very inclement today, which prevents our visiting the places in the neighborhood of Cork. Went to Father Matthews' church today. It is rather small and very

[32] Daniel O'Connell (1775-1847), Irish patriot and politician.

plain. This afternoon I took a steamboat for the cove about 8 miles from the city. The scenery on the River Lee is very beautiful. Its banks are filled with villas and bathing houses. Rock Castle is a place of some interest. Here William Penn embarked for the new world. There are several little islands in this stream, upon one there is government naval stores, upon another power, and upon another the prison, which is very strongly fortified. The harbor of Cork is said to be the last in the three kingdoms. The scenery on the river I consider very fine, but the town of Cork I do abominate.

June 16. Left the city of Cork this morning in an Irish jaunting car, which is quite a funny looking vehicle, for the Castle of Blarney, about five miles distant. It is an old ruin resorted to by persons desirous of kissing the Blarney Stone. All of us ascended to the top of a lofty tower on the extreme corner of which we saw and kissed this much celebrated stone, more for the name of the thing than anything else. The country about Blarney is very pretty but not worth going to see. From this point we took the rails for Mallow and thence by coach to the Victoria Hotel on the Lake of Killarney. The poverty in this region of country exceeds anything I ever heard of or saw. The coach as we passed along was thronged on either side with men, women, and children almost in a state of nudity, and the most miserable looking beings I ever saw crying out in the most doleful manner: "Mister, for God's sake, give us a penny. We are starving." Among them we saw many grey-haired men and women just on the verge of the grave crying for bread. The conditions of the people in this portion of Ireland is really deplorable. I took particular pains to inquire into the causes of this wretchedness and was told that it was all owing to the failure of crops and the want of labor.

June 17. After a good night's rest we to[ok] a guide and went through the pass of Dunloc [?] and the three lakes, which are very pretty but far short of my ideas. The scenery is all in miniature and to one accustomed to the grand and wild scenery around the American lakes would think but little of Killarney. We were rowed through the lakes by four stout Irish boys, all of whom told me they were going to America, which seems to be like the Promised Land to all Irishmen. The charges at this place are enormous, quite equal to Niagara. In the Gap of Dunloc [?] we stopped at the old home of Kate Karrey and bought six pence worth of goat's milk and Putteen or mountain dew, as they term it, from Kate's granddaughter. She is better looking than the generality of Irish women. Returned to the Victoria by 3:00 and dined. Left immediately on the same route back to Dublin in order to witness the grand review and celebration of the Battle of Waterloo tomorrow.

June 18. Rode all last night in the cars and consequently felt much fatigued this morning. At 11:00 we took a carriage and drove out to the Phoenix Park to witness the grand review and celebration of the Battle of Waterloo. But the day was so inclement that it was postponed and we were of course disappointed. Returned to Gresham's Hotel and passed the remainder of the day writing letters for the Union and several friends. The city of Dublin is next to London in size, but falls far short in my expectations. The Four Courts, Trinity College, Customs House, Bank of Ireland, and Conciliation Hall are substantial structures, but most of the buildings look old and delapidated. The streets are narrow and dirty and filled with swarms of human beggars, who are not only annoying to strangers but disagreeable to look at.

June 19. This morning we left Dublin by rail for the city of Belfast, which we reached in the afternoon about 7:00 and stopped at the Imperial Hotel. There is nothing of note between the two cities. We passd through several old towns but they were devoid of attractions. The fields around Belfast are filled with linen put out to bleach. The city is by far the most attractive place in Ireland. The streets are wide and well built and the place looks clean and decent. Near the docks I noticed a triumphant arch made of wood, which was erected for the queen to pass through when she visits Ireland. On one side is this inscription in the Irish language: "One hundred thousand welcomes to you," and the other the following, "God Save the Queen." There is a good college and many superior linen manufacturers in Belfast.

June 20. Left Belfast this morning at six for the Giants' Causeway, by way of Antrim and Ballymoney. Reached the Causeway House at 11:00 and immediately procured a guide and started off to this great curiosity of nature. The Causeway itself disappointed me, although it is upon examination a very curious phenomenon of nature. It consists of a series of stone columns of almost every conceivable shape, which are divided into blocks from three to six feet in length fitting into each other as nicely as if done by the hand of art. After walking over the Causeway I left the ladies and took a boat in order to explore the caves, and get a good view of the heights beyond. The caves are all humbug, but the heights are really very grand and well repay one for the visit. The Giants' Organ, the Giants' Eyeglass, and the Spanish Organ are curious places. The guide pointed out to me the high point of land that the Spanish Armada battered down with cannon thinking it was the Castle of Dunlose about five miles off. On these heights the sea gulls and other water fowl build their nests. Last week a young Scotchman about 22 years of age fell from one of these heights into the sea in an attempt to get at the nests of those birds. His brother several days after the occurrence found the body near the spot where it fell. An American vessell loaded with lumber was wrecked last week on this shore. She belonged to St. John's. This coast is considered very dangerous and many wrecks take place. Tourists visiting the Causeway will do well to take a stick or horsewhip along to keep off the swarms of human insects that infest the region round about.

June 21. Left the Causeway House this morning in a post carriage for Coleraine and thence by coach to Londonderry. In Coleraine we stopped at a hotel kept by a man named Davock, who recognized the similarity of my name on the trunk and inquired where my ancestors were originally from. Said his name was originally McDavock and the Mc had been dropped. I inquired if any of his family ever immigrated to America and he told me none ever went to his knowledge. This name comes nearer to mine than any I have ever seen and may be the same altered. Our ancestors originally came from this part of Ireland and I feel a little curious to know if any of the family are living and who they are.[33] We come to Derry to please Aunt Felicia, who desires to visit Muff, a little place about 5 miles distant in which her husband was born.[34]

June 22. All of the party except myself drove out to a little place called Muff about five miles from Londonderry to attend church and see some of Mr. Eakin's old friends. I accepted the invitation of the hotel proprietor and went with him and his lady to the cathedral where I listened to a very excellent discourse from the Archbishop of Derry. After service I returned to the hotel and wrote my thirteenth letter for the Nashville Union. In the evening we went over the River Foyle and took tea with Mrs. Lindsley and family. She had six grown daughters and one son. We were received and entertained with real Irish hospitality. The punch was made and passed around very freely and upon the whole I passed a delightful evening.

June 23. Mr. Garvin of Louisville, Kentucky breakfasted with us this morning. During the day we received several calls from persons to whom we had letters and they pressed us to remain longer. But being anxious to get into Scotland, we were obliged to decline. During the

33 McDavock, McGuffock, and McGavic are variant spellings of McGavock. Eight years later, after corresponding with Forrest Reid of Londonderry, Ireland, McGavock received a pedigree giving the lineage of the Irish members of his family, all of whom were descended from Randal McGavock of County Antrim, a brother of his great-grandfather, James McGavock the emigrant.

34 William Eakin described his early life in Muff and his family's emigration to Tennessee in an unpublished memoir on microfilm at the Joint University Libraries, Nashville.

day I visited the poor house, Gwin's charitable institution, and several other places of the like character, and was much pleased with them all. At 4:00 we left Londonderry (which is the most interesting [place] that I have seen in Ireland) on a splendid boat called the Thistle for Glasgow. She was loaded with cattle, horses, and Irishmen going over to get work. The spire of the cathedral and Walker's monument can be seen for many miles down the Foyle. We run close to the Giants' Causeway and had an opportunity of seeing all of the beautiful scenery on the sea shore.

June 24. Rose about 4:00 this morning and found that we were in the Clyde and very near to Dumbarton Castle. The scenery on the lower Clyde is extremely beautiful, but as you approach the city it becomes very narrow and uninteresting. There is a great deal of traffic carried on in this river and its banks present a busy scene. Manufactories, shipbuildings, etc., are carried on extensively. Upon reaching the Queens Hotel in George Square [in Glasgow] we found that Dr. Watkins and party from Troy, N. Y. had just reached the city. After getting my breakfast I went out sightseeing. In George Square there are several monuments of interest—one to Sir Walter Scott, one to Watt, and one to Sir John Moore. Near this square is the Royal Exchange, which is a very fine building. In front of it is a bronze statue of the Duke of Wellington. The cathedral, infirmary, and public buildings generally are very good. The streets are wide and the city is well kept. In the necropolis, near the cathedral, are several superior monuments. Set up until a late hour running on with Miss Watkins of N. Y.

June 25. After breakfast I went with the ladies to Buchanan Street where we all made purchases of different articles of Scottish plaid. We then took a cab and drove through the West End of Glasgow, where they are very many beautiful buildings of stone. We then went through Argyle Street, the Cross, and other important places. The churches and public buildings of this city are substantial but not at all remarkable. The population of Glasgow is nearly 400,000. It is a manufacturing place and is growing rapidly. While out today I noticed an omnibus with five horses and two tongues, three horses abreast and two in the back. It was divided into three apartments and capable of holding 60 persons. It is running in opposition to the Paisley railroad. Mr. Hugh Elliott of Philadelphia called on us this evening. He is in consumption and travels for his health.

June 26. Left Glasgow at an early hour this morning on an excursion to Ayr, about 42 miles distant. Near this town is the birthplace of the great Scottish poet Robert Burns. We went into the cottage which is now occupied by persons "Licensed to sell beer, ale, and other spiritous liquors." Near the cottage there is a beautiful monument erected by voluntary contributions, and the Brig of Doon, so celebrated in Tam o' Shanter's story. Kirk Alloway is near by and an old Scottish sexton receives the visitor and tells many yarns that would probably interest if one had time to listen. Ayr and Paisley are cities of considerable importance in a manufacturing point of view. Returned to Glasgow about 4:00 and found Dr. Breckenridge waiting at the Queen's Hotel for our return.

June 27. When I asked for my bill this morning I was utterly astounded to find that it amounted for three days board to more than ten pounds. Left Glasgow at 7:00 for Tarbet on Loch Lomond. The Clyde near the city is exceedingly narrow but is being enlarged every day by means of excavation. Thousands of Irishmen (who dealt with the spade) are constantly at work night and day—an undertaking which is a grand one will soon be completed. Dumbarton Castle on the Clyde is one of the four old castles that were stipulated at the union of the two countries to be kept up. Here we took the rails at the foot of Loch Lomond and came in a little steamer to this place. After a good luncheon we procured a carriage and drove to Loch Long and Glenroc [?], which did not come up to my expectations. This afternoon we have been highly amused at the Scottish peasantry. A party came here to see Loch Lomond and have a Pic Nic. They brought a band of music and danced at a high rate. Dr. Breckenridge and myself went bathing in Loch Lomond, but the water was so cold that we soon came out.

June 28. Left Tarbet at 7:00 this morning in a little row boat on Loch Lomond for Invermade [?]. Here we procured a Drosky and rode five miles to Loch Katrine, a beautiful little lake which Sir Walter Scott has rendered celebrated by his poem The Lady of the Lake. Rob Roy's house was pointed out to us. At the extremity of the lake, which is called the Trossachs, the scenery is really beautiful. After dining here at an excellent hotel we proceeded by post coach to Sterling, which is beautifully situated on a lofty eminence commanding a fine view of the river and champagne country around, with the beautiful hills in the background. After viewing the old castle and battlefield of Bannockburn, we took the rail for Edinburgh.

June 29. This morning I went with Dr. Breckenridge and the ladies to hear a sermon from Dr. Candlish, one of the most distinguished divines in Edinburgh. He preached an excellent discourse but delivered it with so much nervousness that it was disagreeable to listen to him.[35] After church I called at the Waterloo House on the Watkins from Troy, N. Y. Dr. Breckenridge and myself walked to the top of Calton Hill, at the head of Princes Street, where we had an excellent view of the city and beautiful country in the environs. Upon the top of this hill there are several monuments—one to Nelson, Stuart, and Burns, besides others of less note. On our return we examined Sir Walter Scott's monument in Princes Street, which is decidedly the most beautiful structure of the kind I ever saw.

June 30. Notwithstanding the excessive heat of the day, we set out about 11:00 this morning in a cab on an excursion of sightseeing. We first went to Holyrood where we saw many things that belonged to Mary Queen of Scots. It is a curious old place and is now used for barracks. We then took the Victoria Drive around Arthur's Seat and Salisbury Craigs. It is a beautiful drive. On our return we saw the old pensioners taking their annual parade. We then visited the Parliament House, John Knox House, and the Regent Moray's House—all places of interest in Scottish history. In the afternoon I took a walk through George Street and Princes Street, which are well built up and look well.

---

[35] Robert Smith Candlish, D. D. (1806-1873) was at this time minister of St. George's Free Church, Edinburgh.

CHAPTER XIII

"I believe the French unfit for self-government." (July-September, 1851)

Interested as he was in European politics, McGavock took every opportunity to observe political institutions abroad and the heads of government that represented them. The pages which follow express his reactions to the governments of France and Italy. These views he summarized in part when he wrote Letter Twenty-Eight to the Daily Nashville Union: *"The more I see of the governments of Europe, the more I admire and appreciate our own; and there is nothing in my opinion so well calculated to make a man patriotic and attached to the union of the States and the perpetuity of our institutions as a tour of observation among the nations of Europe."*

July 1. This morning I received letters from Mother informing me that three of my letters had been published and favorably received as far as she had heard, and that my old flame was not so great a belle as formerly—was growing coarse and ugly. About 10:00 we visited Donelson and Heriot Hospitals, which are very beautiful structures used for the education of boys. We then took a circuit round the old and new parts of the city and I can safely say that take it all in all it is the most beautiful city in the kingdom. The scenery in the suburbs is exquisitely fine. We visited the old castle which is in the very center of the place and termed by Sir Walter Scott the heart of Midlothian. A regiment of soldiers are kept here all the time and the regalia of Scotland is deposited in one room here. The window where Douglas was thrown from the castle after being murdered was pointed out and some curious specimens of old armour. Sir Walter Scott's monument, which is near the center of the place on Princes Street, is without doubt the most beautiful thing of the kind I ever saw. It is very elegant and chaste in all its parts. There are also beautiful memorials to Lord Melville, Bruce, and Nelson.

July 2. Left Edinburgh at 8:00 for Melrose Abbey, so celebrated in Sir Walter's works. The old ruin stands in the midst of a pitiful little town hardly worthy of a name. Here we procured a vehicle and drove out to Abbotsford, about three miles distant. It is a lovely spot, every way worthy to be the home of the great novelist. A Mr. Hope now resides here and deserves praise for keeping the premises in such perfect order.[1] I saw Sir Walter's library, which is extensive and select, his chair, his study, paintings, and museum of ancient trophies. The room in which he died was pointed out and many other interesting things too numerous to mention. After enjoying the beauties of his residence, we proceeded to Dryburgh Abbey, the place where he is interred between his wife and son. The tomb is exceedingly plain and unostentatious, but he needs no sculptured marble to perpetuate his memory. It will live long after all such remembrances moulder to decay. From Dryburgh we went by rail to Berwick-upon-Tweed, and thence in the night to York in England.

July 3. Reached York this morning about 2:00 and put up at the Black Swan. At 10:00 we took a cab and drove through the city and around the walls. It is a very old place, having its existence before the birth of Christ. York Minster is about the only place to induce the stranger to visit the city. It is larger than the Abbey of London and quite as elegant in its finish and proportions. The windows are of stained glass and the entire structure is gotten up on a grand scale. Just as we were leaving York today for London I met my old Cambridge friend, Pat Joyce of Louisville, Kentucky. He was travelling with a young man named Jacobs of the same place. After a fatiguing ride of eight hours we reached London and succeeded in getting rooms in the West End at Miss Ayers on George Street near Hanover Square.

July 4. Went to Mr. Miller's this morning and got our trunks and letters. Here I ascertained that N. S. Brown of Tennessee was in the city and boarding at the same house that we are. Returned to my boarding house and found him. He seems to be in better health than he was when he left Tennessee.[2] The ladies, Governor Brown, and myself then

---

[1] James Robert Hope (1810-1886) was married in 1847 to Charlotte Harriet Jane Lockhart, granddaughter of Sir Walter Scott. At the time of McGavock's visit, Hope was renting Abbotsford from his brother-in-law, Walter Lockhart-Scott, who died in 1853. Afterwards the Hopes took the surname Hope-Scott. Now the descendants of Sir Walter who live at Abbotsford have taken the surname Maxwell-Scott.

[2] Neill Smith Brown (1810-1886) was thirteenth Governor of Tennessee at the age of 38. In 1850 he was appointed Minister to Russia by Zachary Taylor and remained at St. Petersburg until 1853—except for the summer of 1851 when his family joined him in

went to hear Fanny Kemble read the Merchant of Venice, which she done in her usual elegant manner. The house was thin but very respectable. We had quite an American dinner today at our boarding house. The health of the President of the U. S. and Queen Victoria's were offered and drank with great gusto. Several patriotic speeches were also delivered. In the evening Mr. Peabody, a wealthy American merchant, gave a large ball in honor of the memorable 4th.[3]

July 5. After transacting my monied arrangements for the continent, I returned to our boarding house and went with the ladies to see the exhibition, which I found more interesting than when I left the city last month. Very many articles have been placed there that I did not see before. The Queen was present as usual this morning, but the crowd seems to diminish every day. This evening we went to Her Majesty's Opera to see her in State. Governor Brown went with us but was refused admission because he had on a colored cravat. He was of course very much vexed, but returned and put on a black cravat. Four boxes were appropriated by the royal party. The Queen and Prince Albert sat together, and the ladies and gentlemen in the same box were standing during the whole opera. A company of soldiers were stationed at the door of the house to keep order and guard her person as she went in and came out. She was dressed magnificently and returned the applause of her people (who worship her) with becoming dignity. The house was very much crowded and the opera passed off brilliantly.

July 6. After taking [*sic*] the rounds and peeping into some of the churches, I returned as usual to my writing desk where I remained nearly the entire day. In the afternoon Maria and myself took a walk through Hyde Park, which is much resorted to on the Sabbath by the working classes for recreation after the labors of the week. It is a delightful place and the stranger finds much to interest him as he walks through the various footpaths, etc. After tea Gov. N. S. Brown and myself walked through Regent Street for exercise. This is the main street in London where all the fashionable do their shopping. In the evening it is filled with perfect shoals of lewd women who walk to and fro seeking who they may take in. They are much bolder here than any city that I have ever seen. They think nothing of accosting a man on the street and taking him by force of arms to their dens of pollution.

London. See Robert H. White, *Messages of the Tennessee Governors, 1845-1857,* (Nashville, 1957).

[3] George Peabody (1795-1869), American merchant and philanthropist. After acquiring considerable wealth at home, he moved to London and established the banking and mercantile business which bore his name. His gifts to worthy causes ran to 8 or 9 million dollars, part of which bequests later established George Peabody College for Teachers in Nashville.

July 7. After breakfast I walked down to Mr. John Miller's, the American agent, expecting to get letters from the U. S., but was disappointed. Gov. Brown and myself then went to the Burlington Gardens on Regent Street to see a horse 21 hands in height and a hybrid of the deer and pony, both of which were great curiosities. I then called with the ladies on the Lawrences. Miss Kitty has just returned from the continent and looks well.[4] Colonel B[igelow] Lawrence invited me to a party at Mr. Russell Sturgess,[5] one of the partners of the Bairings. I attended and passed the latter part of the evening agreeably. Nearly all of the company present were Americans but had become so English in their appearance and manners that I took them to be residents of London.

July 8. We have now been waiting one week in London for Bishop Otey, who is still at Great Malvern. His health prevents him joining us and we have concluded to go on to Paris and let him follow when he becomes able.[6] Left the Surrey Side of London by rail at 2:00 for Dover, which is about 60 miles. Here we took a boat for Bologne in France. The sea was unusually rough and nearly everyone was sick. For the first time I suffered from this terrible nuisance, more from seeing others vomit than the roughness of the sea. At Boulogne there is nothing of interest to the stranger; it is inhabited principally by fishmongers and English traders. Here our luggage was weighed a second time and we were required to pay an additional charge for freight. Passports examined but being o.k. gave us no trouble.

July 9. Reached Paris this morning about 2:00 and was detained at the Custom House about two hours. They overhauled all of our trunks and made us pay 25 shillings duty on some English satins and Scotch shawls, which vexed me considerably. Found apartments at Hotel Maurice in the third story, retired immediately, and slept until 10:00, and was then roused by the music of the French Military. After breakfast I went down to Livingstone and Wells, the American agents, where I met Dana and Sackett. In a few minutes Mr. Litton and Maney came in, whom I accompanied to their lodgings, where I saw Mr. Ewing, Price, and Frank Parrish. After setting a while with my Tennessee

---

[4] Katharine Bigelow Lawrence (1832-1895) was the youngest child of the Abbot Lawrences. In 1854 she was married to Augustus Lowell, and thus were united two of Boston's most prominent families.

[5] Russell Sturgis, a native of Massachusetts, was a wealthy shipping merchant and the father of Russell Sturgis the architect, art critic, and writer.

[6] Although still not well after several weeks of hydropathic treatments at Dr. Wilson's "hydro" in Great Malvern, Bishop Otey wrote to McGavock on July 7 and stated that he would come ahead to London. The Bishop's letter, now owned by Miss Margaret Lindsley Warden, arrived in London just after McGavock and his party left for Paris.

friends, I called on Mr. Rotch,[7] lady, and sister of Boston, who are staying at the Hotel Bristol. After tea I went to the Circus and Madame Alexander's place of amusement.

July 10. After breakfast I went to the American agent but received no letter. Here I met Mr. Ewing and Litton, who went with me to see Colonel Sanford, the secretary of legation to Mr. Rives. He received us politely and gave us some information relative to passports. We then called on Mr. Howard and lady of Nashville who have just returned from the East and gave us very discouraging accounts of the difficulties to be encountered by tourists. In the afternoon I met Dr. Buchanan of Nashville, who has been here several months purchasing apparatus for the medical school recently established there. He told me that he had been very successful and would start home next week. This evening I went with the ladies to see the Opera Comique, which is one of the favorite places of most on the Boulevard. The acting was good and the singing tolerable.

July 11. Started early this morning with the ladies and a guide named Payne who is an Englishman to see the Louvre, a castle or royal residence at an early period of the monarchy, but now used as a kind of museum or collection of the fine arts, both ancient and modern. It was built by Louis XI and Napoleon, and certainly possesses many things to interest the stranger, aside from the historical associations. The external appearance of the palace is rather poor, but the interior is really elegant and it contains a collection of paintings, sculpture, and antiquities nowhere else to be seen except in Italy. After spending about five hours in the Louvre I accompanied Mr. Eustis of Boston[8] to the Palais Royale, called since the late revolution the Palais Nationale. It is nothing more than an immense block of buildings forming a hollow square, in the middle of which is a garden of very poor merit. There is much, however, to interest the stranger here in the way of shops, cafes, and restaurants. I could spend days within this square in going from one door to another looking at the many little things of curiosity.

July 12. At 8:00 we started on the railroad for Fontainbleau, a little town about 11½ leagues southeast of Paris and containing 8,500 inhabitants. In this town there is a palace or chateau much celebrated in French history as the residence of monarchy. It was in this palace that Napoleon signed his abdication and bid farewell to his soldiers on his departure to Elba. The forest of Fontainbleau contains 35,000 acres and

[7] Benjamin Smith Rotch and his wife, Annie Bigelow Lawrence Rotch, the daughter of Abbot Lawrence.

[8] Probably Henry Lawrence Eustis (1819-1885), engineer, Harvard professor, and brigadier-general in the U. S. Army during the Civil War.

looks very much like the wild regions of my own country. Three large oaks stand near the center, designated as the Bouquet, King, and Queen of the Forest. The pools filled with fish, the fountains, groves, grass plots, vineyards, and gardens make it a spot of real beauty. Dr. Buchanan of Nashville went with us and enjoyed the day finely. In the evening the Doctor and myself went to the Mobile Ball, which is without doubt the most lovely spot I ever beheld. They dance in the open air on the naked ground. The dressing and dancing was magnificent. The garden was lighted up with gas in all the fantastic shapes that one could think of. Refreshments furnished, games of all kinds indulged in, and a woman to go home with you if you choose. Ah, this Paris is a great place. The people live for enjoyment and they will have it in spite of everything.

July 13. This would be called Sunday at home, but here in Paris it is nothing more than any other day in the week. This morning all of the Tennesseans that came over with us took a trip to Versailles and Saint Cloud, places of great celebrity near Paris. At the former place we saw the finest palace in France. It was built by Louis 14th and contains the finest paintings, furniture, and sculpture, etc., to be seen in any other palace about Paris. The outgrounds and fountains surpass anything in the world. Near Versailles are two smaller places elegantly furnished but far inferior to *the* palace. One of them was the last abode of Louis Philippe before going to England. On our return we stopped at Saint Cloud, the summer residence of Louis Napoleon. The palace is small but well furnished. The fountains do not equal those at Versailles but play most beautifully. There was about 10,000 persons at this place enjoying themselves in every conceivable manner—some dancing, some eating and drinking, and some promenading. There is a fine view of Paris from this point. It is estimated that more than two-thirds of the population of Paris are out of the city during the summer months on Sunday. It is a great fete day. The best balls, plays, operas, and amusements of every character is carried on here while the people of our country are worshipping God.

July 14. This morning I walked down to Livingstone and Wells on the Place de la Bourse and looked over the American papers, after which I went to the Exchange, which is a very large, elegant, and costly structure. Here I listened for a while to the chattering of business men in French, all of which was Hebrew to me, and then returned to my hotel by way of the Boulevard, which is the great thoroughfare of Paris. The number of cafes and restaurants on this street is astonishing. In front of each there are rows of tables and chairs, at which are seated gentlemen and ladies eating and drinking at their leisure. The French know nothing about the quietude and happiness of the fireside—nine-tenths of them live in these establishments and seem to care or think of nothing but frolic and fun.

July 15. [No entry for this date.]

July 16. The ladies having shopping engagements this morning, I accepted the invitation of Colonel Bryan and Mr. Masson to visit the palace of the Luxembourg, which is one of the most beautiful and attractive places in Paris. It was at one time used as the residence of royalty, but is at present the depository of the fine arts. I saw here an excellent collection of modern paintings and several pieces of fine sculpture. The exterior of the palace is more imposing than the Louvre and the interior is really elegant. The gardens, groves, and fountains are all in perfect taste and are much resorted to in the summer months by sewing women and persons of leisure. We next visited the Pantheon, which was built for a church but was never used as such. It is the largest and probably the finest structure in Paris. There are three domes on the building, one above the other, and it forms one of the most prominent objects in the city. We then visited the Bibliotheque de St. Genevieve, Hotel Cluny, Garden of Plants, Goblein's Manufactory—all of which are places of great interest. After tea I called on Ewing and party who leave tomorrow for Switzerland.

July 17. About 10:00 I accepted the invitation of Mr. Hugh Elliott and Dungan [?] of Philadelphia and went with them to the Palace of the Tuileries, the place where Louis Philippe abdicated. The room which contains the throne was injured very much and some of the front rooms, but the most of them remain as they were originally. The palace is very extensive and contains many ancient and valuable paintings and some curious works of art. Among other things I noticed a clock that tells the time in any part of the world and another of perpetual motion. There is also a statue of solid silver presented to Napoleon. We then drove up to the Triumphal Arch, which furnishes the best view of Paris. It is a magnificent structure erected to receive the remains of Napoleon when they were brought from the Island of Elba. We then crossed over the way to the Hipperdrome and passed the afternoon very agreeably in looking at the feats of horsemanship and a balloon ascension.

July 18. After breakfast I walked down on Place de la Bourse and got a letter from Bishop Otey dated Cambridge in which he states that he is en route for Scotland and will join us in about ten days if his health permits. At 12:00 I went to the National Assembly, having given 12 francs for a ticket. Here I found stationed at the door about 1200 persons all in a row waiting for the door to open. The building was surrounded by a strong military force which looked rather queer in a republican government. My seat was very high up over the Tribune where I could neither see or hear much. It is a very large body and makes more noise than any set of men I ever saw assembled to legislate for a nation's weal. Lamartine attracted my attention more than any one else. He is rather tall and slender, with sharp visage, fair complection, gray hair and light eyes. He speaks fluently and with dignity. The bill under discussion was one of unusual interest, viz. the revision of the Constitution. The President favors it in order that he may be reelected. My opinion of the French is that they are totally unfit for a republic.

July 19. Started out immediately after breakfast this morning with Mr. Masson, who married old man Grizard's daughter, in sightseeing. We first went to examine some opera glasses at Chevalier's, but they were so dear that I declined purchasing. We then went to Saint Sulpice and Notre Dame, two of the finest churches in Paris. After seeing these buildings we visited the Courts of Justice, Sainte Chapelle, and a place called the Morgue, where they expose to the public gaze the bodies of those persons found in the River Seine every morning. It is a horrid sight that I have no disposition to see again. We next visited the Hotel de Ville and column of July 1830. From this point we went to see Lafayette's Tomb, which is nothing but a plain slab in a small cemetery back of a convent, then to Pere La Chaise, Abbatoir of Popincourt, Hotel Royal des Invalides, artesian well, Chapel of Saint Ferdinand, etc. When we completed this round we stopped at a restaurant on the Champs Elysees and got a good dinner.

July 20. This morning the ladies went out with Colonel Bryan to see the Magdalene Church and cemetery. I remained in my room at the Hotel Maurice writing letters for the Union and one to Father. About 12:00 I called on Austin of South Carolina and endeavored to find Dr. Mercer and daughter of New Orleans, but failed. Every time I turn round in Paris I meet with some acquaintance from the States. It is estimated that there is 8,000 Americans now in Paris, more probably than there ever was at one time before. In the afternoon I took a walk in the Tuileries, which is always crowded during the summer months. Nearly all Paris was out at Versailles today to see the fountains play. They are the finest in the world.

July 21. This morning Colonel Bryan and myself visited the Hotel de Ville, which is now occupied by the Prefect of the Police. It is a very large and costly structure, presenting an imposing appearance externally. The interior is not so rich as I expected. It is undergoing repairs.

Returned to my hotel and passed several hours writing. In the afternoon Bryan and myself walked up to the Triumphal Arch and dropped in, on our return, at the Garden of Flowers, which is a place of the Mobile character. Here I met a number of Americans and among them Messers Garven, Scott, and Humphrey of Kentucky, and Peters of Virginia. The gardens are very beautiful but the women not so attractive as I have seen. On my return to Hotel Maurice I met an old college acquaintance, Whitney of Boston, who informed me of the death of George Gorham Williams, an old friend.[9]

July 22. [No entry for this date.]

July 23. This morning I accompanied the ladies to Saint Denis, about six miles distant from Paris, to see the old cathedral in which the royalty of France have been interred from the days of Dagobert, the first king, down to the beginning of Louis Philippe's reign. The church is very fine and contains many beautiful monuments and old historic paintings. We also visited the chapel erected by Louis Phillipe on the spot where the Duke of Orleans was thrown from his carriage. It is a beautiful little house and contains a marble statue of the Duke in his dying moments, also an excellent painting representing the same melancholy occurence. It is said that the Duke was returning from the house of his mistress in his cups when he was killed. Called on Mr. Rives, the American Minister, and was kindly received. Received a call today from Mr. Sanford, Secretary of Legation. Went with the ladies to the Italian opera, where we saw the Prophete represented most magnificently. Dr. Jourdan of Arkansas paid me a visit today.

July 24. Called this morning on Dr. Mercer and his daughter from New Orleans. The Dr. seems to be an agreeable gentleman and the daughter also. She is in delicate health. Was introduced to Mr. Winthrop of the same city. Called on Colonel Sanford and returned to my room and wrote letters. In the evening I went with Dr. Jourdan of Arkansas to see some ladies, where we remained several hours and returned to our hotel. Received from Colonel Sanford, the Secretary of Legation, a silver medal of admission into the National Assembly, which I will avail myself of tomorrow. The weather here at this season is perfectly delightful, so much so that I would not object to remaining all summer. In the evening the streets of Paris are crowded with persons setting out in the front of cafes eating creams and drinking white wine.

July 25. After passing the morning in looking round among the shops, pricing little articles which I found as dear if not dearer than in

---

[9] Charles Brewer Whitney and George Gorham Williams of Boston, both of whom attended Harvard Law School.

New York, I went with Maria to the National Assembly which met and adjourned in a few minutes. The more I see of this body of men and their manner of conducting business, the more I am inclined to believe them unfit for self-government. It is the most noisy and disorderly set of men I ever saw assembled to legislate for the welfare of a nation. Returned to my hotel and found two letters from home—one from Father and Sallie, and the other from A. G. Gale. Both are dated four or five weeks back. Dr. Jourdan and myself went round to my banker's to make some monied arrangements, and returned by a jeweler's where he purchased a diamond pin for $150.

July 26. Went this morning with Dr. Jourdan of Arkansas to my banker's and succeeded in procuring for him a letter of credit to travel over the continent, and then to the jeweler's with him. The Dr. cannot speak one word of French and consequently makes a bad out of it. Many Americans as well as English travel over the continent without speaking any language but their own. I noticed at the table d'hote today a great number of American faces, among them two or three beautiful faces, but it is almost as difficult to form a female acquaintance here from the States as among foreigners. After tea Dr. Jourdan of Arkansas, Mr. Farrington, and Harrison of New Jersey went to the Bal Mobile. The two last went with girls to a cafe and from there to *their apartments, I suppose.* I went with Peters of Lynchburgh, Virginia, to the Hotel de Paris and occupied Mr. Leggatt's room of the same city.

July 27. [No entry for this date.]

July 28. [No entry for this date.]

July 29. [No entry for this date.]

July 30. This morning I accompanied Colonel Bryan to the galleries of the Louvre, a place of great attraction at all times. The paintings are all excellent and grow upon me every time I look at them. Many artists of both sexes are here every day copying different pieces. Strangers are admitted with passports. When we returned to our hotel we called on the Misses Pennington of New Jersey, whose acquaintance we formed through their brother. After dinner I accompanied the ladies to Franconia's Circus and then went with the brother to the Chateau des Fleurs, which is the most beautiful place in its way I ever saw. Ten thousand gas lights illuminate a garden filled with beautiful flowers and women, making it more like a Fairy scene than anything else. Received letters today from Edward and Mother.

July 31. Passed several hours this morning examining engravings which I found to be inferior to what I expected to find. Called with the ladies to see Miss Mercer of New Orleans, but found her out. After tea I called with Garven to see Miss McMicken of Cincinnati, whom I found to be an agreeable but not handsome lady. We then went to the Mobile Ball and found a very slim number there. These balls are very agreeable for a while, but one of my disposition soon tires. I think I will cease my visits and occupy my evenings hereafter more profitably. Sometimes a man may find a very beautiful and nice woman at such places, but the great majority of them are nothing more than common prostitutes who make their living by entrapping the unwary.

Aug. 1. The whole of Paris is now on the *qui vive* about the Fetes to be given next week in honor of the Exhibition at London and to the honorable commissioners, the Lord Mayor of London, and the Aldermen, together with the Mayors of all the principal cities in Great Britain and many distinguished foreigners. Prince Albert declines coming, but the Lord Mayor has accepted and everything is now making ready for the occasion. All of the hotels are crowded and I hear of nothing else but the Fetes. It is a matter of no little curiosity to see how the citizens of Paris will receive their old enemies the British. This demonstration on the part of the French is the result of the great Exhibition. How it will terminate remains yet to be seen.

Aug. 2. The Fetes opened today with a grand dinner given by the Prefect of the Seine to the Lord Mayor of London and the Honorable Commissioners of the Exhibition. Mr. Berger, the Prefect, made a very appropriate speech, in which he alluded to the relations existing between the nations and the importance of cultivating peace, amity, and concord. He spoke in French, which the Lord Mayor did not understand, but it was translated for him and he made an appropriate answer. Many distinguished men were present and the whole affair went off well. After dinner the company were amused with private theatricals and a magnificent concert over which the celebrated Strauss presided.[10] The Hotel de Ville was elegantly fitted up and illuminated for the occasion.

Aug. 3. Agreeable to arrangement the guests of the city of Paris went out to the Palace of Versailles where they occupied the forenoon in examining the palace and the pictures. After this they were invited into the out-grounds to see the water works. All of the fountains were playing. The day was beautiful and everything looked grand. More than 100,000 persons were present and everyone returned to their homes perfectly delighted with the entertainments of the day. The railway was crowded with trains about half mile in length, each of which had two locomotives attached to them and filled inside and outside with

[10] Johann Strauss, the younger (1825-1899).

persons anxious to witness the Grand Fete. I noticed in the gardens today 700 orange trees and many exotics of rare beauty.

Aug. 4. Colonel Sanford, the American Secretary of Legation, called to see me today and presented me with an invitation to Louis Napoleon's Fete at Saint Cloud. At 3:00, the hour appointed, Bishop Otey, Maria Bass, and myself started in a carriage for Saint Cloud, which is about 4 miles from Paris. The road was crowded with fine equipages and the people assembled to see the invited guests pass. The company was large and composed of some of the first men in France and a number of distinguished foreigners. The President and the Lord Mayor of London with their suites promenaded through the palace and gardens until dinner was announced. Music was playing in different parts of the grounds and the palace, and everything induced to make the entertainment pass off brilliantly. Saint Cloud is smaller than Versailles, but is much more preferable as a place of residence. It was the favorite chateau of Napoleon and is now the residence of the President.

Aug. 5. The British Minister, Lord Normandy, gave a brilliant entertainment to the Commissioners of the Exhibition this evening, after which the *Great Ball* given by Mr. Berger came off at the Hotel de Ville. It was without doubt one of the most magnificent entertainments that was ever given in Paris. Colonel Bryan went with Aunt Felicia and Maria and I went with the Misses Pennington from New Jersey. Every nation in the civilized world were represented on this occasion. The Hotel de Ville was illuminated most brilliantly and the decorations and ornamental display was really elegant. The President of the Republic, the Lord Mayor of London, and the Commissioners were in attendance, besides about 6,000 invited guests, forming a spectacle at once grand and imposing.

Aug. 6. This morning I went down to the French Commissioner's on the Boulevard to procure tickets for the Grand Review on the Field of Mars on the strength of Dr. Breckenridges's commission from the Governor of Kentucky, but failed—all the tickets being disposed of. On my return to Rue de Rivoli I called at Hotel Bristol on Colonel Winthrop and Dr. Mercer of New Orleans. Governor N. S. Brown and lady reached Paris this morning. At 3:00 I went out to the Field of Mars determined to run the chance of getting a seat. When I reached there I found the Field surrounded and the neighboring housetops filled with people anxious to witness the Review and sham fight. At 4:00 about 25,000 troops stationed themselves in the Field and about the same number on the heights beyond the River Seine. Louis Napoleon then rode on the Field escorted by a strong guard of cavalry. Soon after the fight was commenced by the troops in the Field. The bridge was taken by opposite forces who crossed and came over in the field where we had a full view of the entire force, amounting to 50,000 troops, consisting of cavalry, artillery men, and soldiers—all of whom were in full dress, making a scene of surpassing beauty. After the fight was over the entire forces were reviewed by Napoleon in the presence of the Lord Mayor of London and the Honorable Commissioners. I suppose that 800,000 persons were present to witness the occasion. The Fetes wound up this evening with a grand opera. I did not go, being too fatigued.

Aug. 7. This morning I commenced to finish a letter for the Union, but as usual something interferred and it was put off for another day. Governor N. S. Brown and lady arrived last night from London and I called to see them, but found that they had gone to search a lost carpet bag. After dinner I called on the Misses Pennington from New Jersey and passed the evening very agreeably. They have just returned from a continental tour and interested me exceedingly in the sights they had seen and the wonders they had encountered. Our hotel seems very quiet today, as all the English have returned to London to abuse the Fetes of the week and swear that John Bull can beat them.

Aug. 8. [No entry for this date.]

Aug. 9. [No entry for this date.]

Aug. 10. This morning Aunt Felicia and Bishop Otey went to an English chapel in the city and thence to the Hotel des Invalides to see one of Napoleon's old soldiers buried in the place where the Emperor's remains are deposited. Feeling exceedingly unwell I remained in my bed all day, took medicine, and had two chills. In the evening Mr. Taylor of Saint Louis and Governor Brown called to see me and raised my spirits considerably by their lively conversation. The last few days have been anything but agreeable to me, aside from being sick. My spirits have been unusually depressed. Thoughts of home and the reminiscences of the past year force themselves upon my mind and render me perfectly miserable. Language used to me, by one whom I thought incapable of such, also makes me feel unpleasant. I allude to *A F.*[11]

Aug. 11. This morning I rose considerably better than I was last night, the medicine having the desired effect. About 11:00 I ventured out and purchased a carpet bag for the journey, finding that my portmanteau is too small to contain my necessaries. In the evening I took a walk with the Misses Pennington of New Jersey on the Boulevard,

[11] His disagreements with Aunt Felicia, probably occasioned by travel fatigue, were temporary. This entry was written on McGavock's twenty-fifth birthday.

where one always finds something odd to attract their attention. The gentlemen and ladies are strewn along the sidewalks in front of all the cafes, where they have small tables and chairs arranged for sipping wines, coffee, etc. The shop windows on the Boulevards contain generally the contents of the store and it is only necessary for one to stop and look in to see anything he wishes to purchase. Retired early—decidedly better—and hope to be ready to start in the morning for Brussells in Belgium.

Aug. 12. This morning I was up at 6:00, called a cab and drove into Fauberg Saint Germain to see Masson who borrowed my pencil about two weeks ago and never returned it. He was in bed. I asked for the pencil and he produced it, much to my surprise and satisfaction as I valued it highly, being a gift from my Father. After 7:00 o'clock breakfast we left Hotel Maurice and reached Brussells in Belgium at 5:00 in company with Governor N. S. Brown and lady and a young man named Johnston from South Carolina. We stopped at the Belle Vue Hotel, which is situated near the Palace Royal, the residence of Leopold, the present King of the Belgians. The country between the two places is rolling and cultivated in small parcels with one half dozen sorts of grain growing within fifty yards circuit. Received a visit this evening from Dr. Elliott of Kentucky and Colonel Anderson of New Orleans, who start on Thursday for Munich [?].

Aug. 13. Procured carriages this morning and drove out to the Battlefield of Waterloo, which is .... miles from Brussells. Here we hired a Belgian guide who explained to us the positions of the conflicting parties and the monuments erected on the grounds to commemorate the deeds of Englishmen slain in the battle. The Belgians have thrown up a mound 200 feet high on the battlefield and placed a lion in a belligerent attitude looking defiance towards France. The positions of Napoleon and Wellington was pointed out, and, if I am any judge, the English had every advantage. They were protected in front by a thick brick wall and a hill and on the rear by a heavy forest. There can be no doubt that Napoleon would have been victorious had not Blucher proved traitor.[12] All Englishmen visit this spot and boast much of their victory, but in truth they deserve no credit whatever. They had all the advantages, besides being aided by the Allied Powers. We purchased some sticks cut from the battleground and some old balls and pieces of armour picked up off of the field, which they have been selling ever since the battle. *They are said to be* manufactured for the purpose and buried in the ground some time in order to give an old appearance. In

[12] Gebhard Leberecht von Blücher (1742-1819), Prussian field-marshal.

the evening we went to Mr. Baird [?], our charges d'affair, agreeable to invitation. He lives in good style and has an interesting family.

Aug. 14. This morning Bishop Otey and party, together with Governor Brown and lady, went to Aix-la-Chapelle. Wishing to visit Holland I separated from them and come to Antwerp with Mr. William Johnstone of South Carolina, who proposes making the entire tour with me.[13] I hope to rejoin the party on the Rhine. We reached Antwerp in one hour and a half by rail from Brussells, put up at a very good hotel called the .... Grand Laborein. Here we procured a commissioner and started out sightseeing. We first visited the museum or academy of paintings. It contains a great number of pictures brought from supressed convents and churches in the towns and among them several excellent ones of Reubens, Van Dyck, and two Matsys, the blacksmith painter. The two last were natives of this place. We then visited Saint Jacques, the cathedral of Notre Dame and the church of Saint Paul's, or the Dominican Church. In the latter we saw an excellent representation of Christ on Calvary, an artifical eminence raised in a yard attached to the church against the walls, and covered with slag or rock work and planted with statues of saints, angels, prophets, and patriarchs. The cathedral is a very fine structure and can be seen for many miles off from its great height. This evening a young man named Hume from South Carolina came from Brussels to join us, which I regret very much as he is very annoying and disagreeable.

Aug. 15. This is a holyday throughout Belgium, being one of the days set apart by the Catholics for the Fete of the Virgin Mary. The stores in Antwerp were closed and the streets crowded with people from the country, who flocked in to participate in the grand occasion. At 12:00 we left on a steamboat for Rotterdam with a large number of passengers, among whom I was pleased to find Colonel Winthrop and lady and Mr. Falsome [?] and lady of New York. Mr. F. is our consul at the Hague. The scenery on the river between Antwerp and Rotterdam is very uninteresting until you come in sight of latter place, where the eye meets with windmills without number, which are used for various purposes—some for pumping water out of fields, some for grinding, some for sawing lumber, and every other possible use. Families live in these mills and make their living by attending to them. In Holland windmills answer the purpose of steam. Stopped at a hotel called Bath. After tea we went with a commissioner to see a Dutch Fair in the

[13] This decision was undoubtedly wise. The less robust members of the Tennessee party —Bishop Otey, Mrs. Felicia Eakin, Maria Bass, and little Willie Eakin, accompanied by the nursemaid Mary—went their way at their own pace, leaving McGavock and William Johnstone to more vigorous sightseeing.

streets. Here we witnessed a sight well worth seeing. The people crowded the streets looking at puppet shows, making of cakes which they sold at auction, and every other conceivable amusement to amuse the rabble. Rotterdam is the second city in Holland. It is situated on the right banks of the river. Maas is 21 miles from the sea and has a population of 78,000. It consists of as many canals as streets. The houses all lean over the streets, which are very narrow, and look very curious. There is a statue to Erasmus in one of the squares. Rotterdam is strictly a commercial city and has but little to interest the stranger.

Aug. 16. After an early breakfast we took the rails for Delft, eight miles from Rotterdam, where we walked about some time in search of some one who could speak English and direct us to the place where we wished to take the canal for The Hague. While in this dull and uninteresting village we went into an old church and saw the tombs of the Prince of Orange and Grotius. Between Delft and The Hague we had a fine opportunity of seeing life on the Holland canals. Many families live altogether on these canals and we were told that persons were never known to sleep in a house. We saw several large boats drawn by women (who are larger than the men) and dogs. They pull together and look very singular. Dogs are worked here instead of horses. They use them for drawing boats, wagons, and everything else. The Hague is the prettiest city in Holland. It is the seat of government and residence of King William III. We first visited the picture gallery, which contains some of the best paintings in Europe. The most remarkable ones are Paul Potter's Young Bull and Rembrandt's picture of a surgeon attended by his pupils proceeding to dissect a dead body. We next visited the palace of the late King William II, father of the present king. It is a fine building and contains many superior paintings by the Old Masters. Just opposite is the palace of the king, also a fine building. Here we saw the Queen enter her carriage to drive to the Palace in the Wood, several miles out of the city. She is a large Dutch-looking woman with a benevolent countenance. Several statues of the Prince of Orange are scattered through the city. Left The Hague at 4:00 on the railroad for Amsterdam. A party of many soldiers were on the train, which rendered the trip very disagreeable.

Aug. 17. The railroads in Holland are inferior to any that I have yet seen. The cars are very wide and run unsteady. Smoking is allowed and very little order is maintained. The country between Rotterdam and Amsterdam is perfectly flat, filled with dykes and ditches and covered over with thousands of windmills. We reached Amsterdam about dusk last evening and put up at a hotel called Oude Doden, which is very poor and knows how to charge. Met Mr. Ruth and several Americans this morning at the breakfast table. Went out at 10:00 to Haarlem to hear the organ in the great church of San Bavo. It is said to be the largest instrument of the kind in the world and is certainly superior in tone and outward workmanship that I have ever seen. The church is very large and has several things of interest in the way of sculpture. We heard a Dutch sermon, *which was all Dutch to us.* The men all set with their hats on except during prayers, and the women with their short-waisted dresses and gold head bands present a curious spectacle. Returned to Amsterdam and set down to a miserable dinner, after which we visited the zoological gardens, which is not worth seeing after visiting the gardens at London. On our return we stopped to see an establishment belonging to Jews for cutting diamonds. This evening I endeavored to do some writing, but the Dutch made such a noise on the street that I had to give it up. Men and women rove the streets at night and make all sorts of noises—hollowing, singing, etc.

Aug. 18. Amsterdam is the principal city of Holland and is situated at the confluence of the River Amstel and Zuider Zee, called the Y. It has 212,000 inhabitants, is in the shape of a crescent surrounded by a wall, and filled with canals running in every direction and dividing the city into 95 islands traversed by no less than 290 bridges. The houses are all built of brick with leaning fronts and narrow streets, making it one of the most curious cities in Europe. The palace, formerly the Staats Huis, is a vast and imposing building of stone standing on 13,659 piles driven 70 feet in the ground. There are many things of interest too inside the palace. It is chiefly remarkable for one grand hall occupying the center of the building lined with white Italian marble, 120 feet long and 57 feet wide and 100 feet high. The museum or picture gallery contains some good paintings, but there are several private collections in the city far superior. The whole city of Amsterdam, its houses, canals, and sluices, are founded upon piles, which gave occasion to Erasmus to say that he had reached a city whose inhabitants, like crows, lived on the tops of trees. About eight miles from the city is a little village called Brock. It is the neatest place I ever saw. No vehicle is allowed to enter it. The streets are narrow and the whole place fragrant with flowers. On our return we stopped to see a Dutch farmhouse where they made the little round Dutch cheeses so celebrated for their good quality. Left Amsterdam at 6:00 for Arnheim on the Rhine.

Aug. 19. Left Arnheim this morning at 8:00 on a steamer for Duisburg where we took the railroad and reached Dentz on the right bank of the Rhine, connected by a bridge of boats 1,400 feet long, with

Cologne, and strongly fortified as a tête de pont. We put up at Hotel Bellevue, which is the best that I have yet seen since I left Paris. The scenery on the Rhine between the mouth and Cologne is not at all interesting. The banks are low and the villages and farmhouses of a mean description. The boats on the Rhine up to this point are good but nothing extra—not at all to compare with our boats on the Cumberland and Mississippi Rivers. My trunks were not examined by the officers today, while some of the ladies belonging to their own country were shamefully treated. They tumbled their linen about and acted unnecessary strict I thought.

Aug. 20. After breakfast Johnstone, Hume, and myself went over to Cologne and examined the register at Hotel Disch, where we found that Bishop Otey and party had left yesterday morning for Coblenz on the Rhine. Cologne is a walled city with a population of 85,000. The streets are narrow and exceedingly filthy. The place is devoid of interest except a few old churches which contain some curious specimens of antiquity. The cathedral, which is uncompleted for want of means, is the largest and purest specimen of Gothic architecture in Europe. It was begun in 1248 and is still undergoing repairs and approaching completion. Here we were shown a slab in the pavement beneath which the heart of *Mary of Medicis* is buried. The celebrated Shrine of the Three Kings or Magi, who came from the East with presents for the infant saviour. It is made of solid gold and silver plate, richly studded with precious stones. In St. Peter's Church we saw the famous painting representing the Crucifixion of that saint, with his head downwards by Reubens, who presented it to this church in which he was baptized. The priest who exhibited the painting to us requested that we should look at it through our legs, a very ludicrous position, yet it certainly enhanced the effect. We also visited the church of Saint Ursula and of the 11,000 Virgins. Here we saw a large collection of skulls and bones fixed most curiously in the wall and presenting a scene too interesting to be overlooked. Today it was excessively warm, so much so that I became quite sick and returned in a drosky to Hotel Bellevue.

Aug. 21. This morning after paying an enormous bill at Hotel Bellevue and passing some sharp words with the proprietor, we left Dentz in a steamer for Coblenz on the Rhine. When we got aboard we found Mr. Dr. Gailliard and Mr. Porcher of South Carolina, who I found to be agreeable gentlemen. The scenery between Cologne and Bonn is wholly uninteresting, but from this point we had a view of the Seven Mountains which for us was the grand commencement to the beautiful scenery of the Rhine. The most interesting of the group is the famed Drackenfeld (Dragon's Rock) whose precipices rise abruptly from the riverside and [are] crowned with a beautiful ruin. The Rhine is a rapid and muddy stream about the width of the Ohio. The Germans call it Father or King Rhine. The scenery as high up as this place (Coblenz) from Bonn is exceedingly beautiful and fully comes up to my expectations. We reached Coblenz about 4:00 and put up at a comfortable hotel called the Trois Suisses. Coblenz is a strongly fortified but extremely dirty and uninteresting town. After depositing our baggage we walked over the bridge of boats and examined the citadel of Ehrenbreitstein, which renders Coblenz the bulwark of Germany and Prussia on the side of France. It is one of the strongest fortifications in Europe and is capable of containing 100,000 troops. After enjoying a fine view of the Rhine and many miles around, we returned to Coblenz and walked over a stone bridge that spans the Moselle, which empties itself into the Rhine at Coblenz. Saw Bishop Otey and party's names registered on the books and they are just two days ahead of us.

Aug. 22. After a very early breakfast Johnstone, Hume, and myself left Coblenz on the same boat for Mayence and thence to this place (Wiesbaden) the most celebrated watering place in Germany. The scenery on the Rhine between Coblenz and Mayence is beautiful beyond description. The lofty range of hills on either side covered with grape vines and old castles combine to render the Rhine one of the most beautiful rivers in the world. Two or three lines of steamers are constantly going to and fro conveying tourists from all nations who stop here and there to view the river from some high point or examine some interesting old castle connected with some historical event. At Biebrich, just below Mayence, we saw the palace of the Duke of Nassau, which is a very pretty building but nothing extraordinary in appearance, and in the Hotel Brussels where we stopped we had a full view of the Duke himself. He is small, near-sighted, and looks rather insignificant. Mayence is strongly fortified and has several thousand Austrian or Prussian troops stationed there. Wiesbaden is the capitol of the Duchy of Nassau and has 12,000 inhabitants. It is the residence of the Duke and the seat of his government. It is the most fashionable watering place in Europe. It is beautifully situated in a valley surrounded by hills and has a large spring in the center of the town which is hot enough to burn one's fingers, tastes like chicken broth, and has a heavy scum on the surface. Upon the whole Wiesbaden is rather a quiet place except for a large gambling house called the Kursaal, where gentlemen and *ladies* can be seen at any hour in day or night betting high at roulette and other games.

Aug. 23. After a very late breakfast we walked round the colonnades and examined some beautiful ornamental work in buck's horn and ornamental ivory. These colonnades form part of the Kursaal, are lined with gay shops, and serve as a promenade in wet weather and as a sort of bazaar during the whole season. Left Wiesbaden about 2:00 and proceeded by rail in about two hours to Frankfort on the Main, which is a free town and the seat of the German Diet. It has 62,000 inhabitants, of whom 6,000 are Jews. It is one of the most lovely as well as handsome cities in Europe. In the old part of the town the streets are narrow and look very curious. In the new they are wide and the houses very fine. From the cathedral, which we ascended, is the best view of the city and surrounding country. The Town House called Bösner [?], a building of the 15th century, is one of the lions of the place, but is remarkable only for a banqueting room which contains some excellent portraits of the different emperors of Germany. We stopped today at the Hotel d'Angleterre, which is one of the best in the city. After tea we took a walk on the river banks, stopped at a cafe and took some refreshments, and then returned to our hotel.

Aug. 24. Procured a cab and drove soon after breakfast to see Dannecker's statue of Ariadne in the garden of Mr. Bethman, near the Freiburg gate. It is the boast of Frankfort and deserves to be ranked among the distinguished productions of modern art. We then visited the picture galleries which contain many beautiful pieces of modern art, but few belonging to the old masters. The poet Goethe was born here. The house where he lived is still standing and contains over the door his father's coat of arms, bearing the poetical device of three lyres. This was the cradle also of the Rothschild family. Luther also resided here and the house is now marked by his bust and the inscription: *In Silentio et Specrit Fortitude Vestrie.* At 3:00 we separated from Dr. Galliard and Mr. Porcher of South Carolina and left Frankfort by rail for Heidelberg, which is about three hours travel.

Aug. 25. This morning Johnstone and myself walked up to the old castle of Heidelberg which overhangs the town and presents from its summit a beautiful view for miles around. The castle is decidedly the best ruin that I have seen on the continent and contains some curious relics of the past in the interior. Among other things I was struck with the famous Heidelberg Tun, constructed [in] 1751; it is the largest wine cask in the world, 36 feet long and 24 feet high; being capable of holding 800 hogsheads or 283,200 bottles. In former days, when the tun was filled with the produce of the vintage, it was usual to dance on the platform on the top. It has remained empty in the cellar of the castle since 1769, more than half a century. Heidelberg itself is a poor looking place and the hotels are also poor, but the scenery cannot be too highly lauded. It is charmingly situated on the banks of the Neckar, which flows through a cove of great beauty from which there is an extensive view of the Rhine and hills beyond. It is almost limited to one street, which is three miles in length, with a population of 13,000. The university is not so flourishing at present as formerly. The buildings are small and mean looking. The students walk the streets with their pipes and tobacco hanging in the button holes of their coats. They spend a great deal of their time in taprooms and fight duels daily. Johnstone and myself left Mr. Hume, who is generally behind hand, and proceeded to Baden-Baden, the celebrated German watering place which is about three hours ride by railroad from Heidelberg.

Aug. 26. Baden-Baden is embosomed among hills forming an offset or commencement of the Black Forest range, and seated on the banks of the Oos. The town has about 6,000 permanent residents and during the summer is always crowded. The grand focus of attraction about Baden is Conversation Haus, a handsome building with a Corinthian portico surrounded by gardens and pleasure grounds. In this establishment they have their balls and gaming tables, also a theatre, library, and reading room. I saw an old lady from Russia stand at the roulette table this morning for 16 hours and [she] lost 500 francs. She handled money like an experienced gambler and bet with as much coolness as any man could summon. This establishment is let out by the government to a company of speculators who pay 35,000 florin and agree to spend additionally 250,000 fr. on the walls and buildings. I like Baden more than I do Wiesbaden. The water is pretty much the same—warm enough to boil an egg or scald a pig.

Aug. 27. We intended taking the 6:00 o'clock train this morning for Strasburg in France, but was too late and waited until 10:00. Just before starting I saw the Grand Duke of Baden driving in his carriage. He is a good-looking man. Reached Strasburg at 1:00 and put up at Hotel de Paris, which is very excellent. Dined here and then occupied three hours in examining the cathedral and other things. The cathedral is unfinished. It has the highest spire in Europe and a curious clock much noted throughout the world. The spire rises 474 feet above the pavement, 24 feet higher than the Great Pyramid of Egypt and 140 feet higher than Saint Paul's. In Saint Thomas church I saw the monument of Marshal Suze, the masterpiece of the sculptor Pigalle, erected to his memory by Louis XIV, also two bodies said to be of a Count of Nassau Swarwerden and his daughter. They have been preserved for more than a century and present really a disgusting spectacle. The houses about Strasburg are very curious, having more stories in the roof than the main body of the building. I noticed one house with as many as eight stories in the roof. Returned to Kehl on the German side of the Rhine at 4:00 where we had left our baggage and took the rail for Freiburg.

Aug. 28. We stopped last night at a very good hotel called Zehringer Hof. When we arrived the front of the hotel was lined with Baden troops. Upon inquiry I ascertained that it was in honor of the Prince of Prussia's arrival. An excellent band of music played until bedtime. The Prince is a large, fine-looking man and was dressed perfectly plain. After breakfast I went into a shop and paid 20 francs for two German pipes as presents for friends. The cathedral here is very fine and pleases my eye as much as any I have yet seen in Germany. It is the only large Gothic church in Germany which is finished and which has escaped destruction from fire and the violence of war. At 11:00 we started on a heavy lumbering diligence for Schaffhausen in Switzerland, after being considerably annoyed with a valet de place and the loud stir about baggage. We took an outrider seat called the Imperial, but regretted it afterwards, as there came up a heavy rain and we were all completely drenched. Fearing that we might take cold, we stopped at a little village called Neustadt about 20 miles from Freiburg. We changed our clothes and remained here all night. Hume, J[ohnstone] and myself amused ourselves playing polka [*sic*] until 12:00.

Aug. 29. After paying a very high bill we started this morning for Schaffhausen, but ascertained en route that the falls of the Rhine were on this side. We concluded to remain here all night as the Hotel Weber seemed to be better than we were likely to find in the town. No American ought ever to visit these falls, as they are inferior in height and beauty to many waterfalls in the States unknown and unheard of out of their immediate neighborhood. They are 70 feet high, but do not look to be over 20 feet. The country around is quite elevated and from Hotel Weber the view is pretty but nothing more. Like at Niagara the stranger may expect to be fleeced, or else he will bear it. For crossing the river below the falls in a little rowboat we were told that we had to pay one-half franc each, but on our return they demanded one franc each, and at the castle, from which there is the best view, we were required to pay one franc each by a saucy woman, who, if she had been a man, I would have given a sound thrashing. I saw today for the first time two men kiss each other. They both had long moustaches and looked very queer to me, although it is the custom in Germany. Mr. Brooks and party from Boston reached the falls this evening.

Aug. 30. Procured a return carriage and started early this morning for Zurich, the largest manufacturing town in Switzerland. It has a population of 14,500 and is beautifully situated at the north end of the Lake of Zurich and on both banks of the Limmat, just where it issues out of the lake in a rapid and healthful stream, clear as crystal. We reached Zurich about 3:00 and stopped at an excellent house called Hotel Bauer. After dinner we set out and walked round the town and among other sights we were shown in the arsenal a crossbow said to be that with which William Tell shot the apple from his son's head. In the river I noticed several flour mills built on piles and moved by the action of the current, which is very swift. There are no fine buildings in Zurich. The road between this and the falls is very excellent but the scenery very uninteresting. Several things attracted my attention today out of the ordinary way of doing things, viz. an ox and a horse working together in a wagon. This was the only ox I saw. The Swiss usually work milk cows, which are very large and fine looking. They have a light yoke on the neck, which serves as a collar, for [with?] traces made of ropes, which are hitched singletree. The cows here are shod with iron like horses. The taprooms here have the sign of the bottle and glass made of iron and painted to look like wine. In the cemetery of Zurich they have the anchor over the tombs instead of the cross as in Germany.

Aug. 31. This morning is rainy and from the appearance of the clouds I fear that we will be disappointed in our visit to Mount Rigi. Left Zurich in a private carriage at 8:00 for Lucerne, crossing the high chain of the Albis, which intervenes and running nearly parallel with the Lake of Zurich. When we reached the summit we were furnished an excellent view of the town of Zurich and the country for many miles in circumference. The coaches in this country are exceedingly slow. It took us eight hours to make 26 miles, including two hours required to feed. The town of Lucerne contains a population of 8,339, all Roman Catholics except about 200 Protestants. It is the place of the Papal Nuncio and is beautifully situated between the Giant Pilatus and Rigi and in sight of the snowy Alps of Schweitz and Engelberg. It is not a place of any considerable trade and there is nothing here to interest a stranger aside from the beauty of its situation. The hotel of Lucerne called Schweizerhof is very large and well conducted. It is crowded at present with persons waiting for the weather to clear off in order to ascend the Rigi.

Sept. 1. Sent our baggage to Berne this morning by the diligence and proceeded on an excellent little steamer to a little town called Weggis, at the foot of Mount Rigi. Here we ascended an excellent pathway to the summit of the mountain. After walking one hour and a half we found ourselves in deep snow, but we managed to make our way after much difficulty and fatigue to the hotel. Here we procured breakfast, purchased some wooden works, got a tolerable view, and descended with two New Yorkers in time to take the boat for a little town at the head of the lake of the Four Cantons called Fluellen, and walked from thence to an inn nine miles distant called the Swan Arms. Ed Ewing and Price left Mount Rigi this morning for Zurich. I also saw Bishop Otey's name registered on the 25th of August. The scenery on the Lake of the Four Cantons is really very beautiful. Eat our dinner at 7:00 and fell to sleep soon afterwards.

Sept. 2. I saw yesterday in the village of Altdorf the square in which William Tell is said to have shot the apple from his son's head. The place where he stood is marked by a stone fountain surrounded with statues of the dauntless crossbowman and his child. The place where the lime tree stood is marked by another fountain. I slept last night without rocking. This morning we left on the diligence for a little village called Andermatt, passing through scenery of wild and romantic beauty. At the Devil's Bridge, so called from the difficult pass, I was perfectly charmed. It is situated at the head of the most stern and magnificent scenery of the whole pass. The Reuss leaps down into the head of the savage gorge in a lofty cataract and in the very midst of its din and spray two bridges have been thrown across. Walked from Andermatt to Hospital, about two miles off at the foot of Mount Saint Gotthard.

Sept. 3. Hospital, or Hospenthal, is the starting point for pedestrians going to Saint Gotthard's or the Grimsel. At the hotel called the Golden Lion pack horses and guides may be procured on reasonable terms. A large party of French and Germans rested here last night and started this morning in the rain. Six Americans were also here. Owing to the inclemency of the weather and the indisposition of my travelling companion Johnstone, I have concluded to wait until tomorrow. The village of Hospital is very small and filthy. The houses look old and delapidated and the people are evidently in a squalid situation. The pass of Saint Gotthard has been made of late years one of the best in Switzerland and is much used by persons going to Italy. Late this evening Mr. Williams and lady from Boston stopped at the hotel and interested me very much with their lively conversation. It is always agreeable to meet with people from one's own country.

Sept. 4. My friend Johnstone was decidedly better this morning and we started on foot with our *Alpine Sticks* for the Grimsel mountain through the Furca [Furka] Pass. About two hours after leaving the hotel at Hospital, John Onifar, our faithful guide, brought us up in front of an old stone house called The Hospice inhabited by two Capuchin friars who keep an inn. The guide went in and drank some wine, but we remained at the outer door amusing ourselves looking at the friars pecking stone for minerals. Their beards were long and they were appareled in a long gown, over which they had a leather girdle and many beads. On the top of the Furca we found the snow several feet deep. Met three Bostonians here and took goats' milk and cheese from an old woman who occupies a small hut on the summit of the mountain during the summer months. After a walk of five hours through the narrow and difficult mule pass, we came to the beautiful glacier of the Rhone. It was the first glacier that I ever saw and surpassed in beauty all my anticipations. It is several thousand feet high and as clear as crystal. We walked over the lower part of the glacier and was fortunate in having fine weather to see it in all of its glory. The River Rhone rises under this mountain of ice. Reached the rude hotel on Grimsel about 4:00, where found quite a crowd of pedestrians. Late this evening I went out to see the men milking goats, which amused me exceedingly. They had little stools fastened around them with a belt and milked the goats from behind.

Sept. 5. Long before the dawn of day the hospice of the Grimsel was in general commotion. Some were making ready to go one way and some another. After an early breakfast we made a short detour to the glacier of the Aar, which is said to be the largest in Switzerland, being 18 miles in length. The top of the glacier was filled with stones, which destroyed its beauty near the base, but I was told by an Englishman that the further one went the more beautiful it became. Returned to Grimsel, which is 7,000 feet above the sea, and descended the mountain on foot to the village of Meysingin, where we remained all night in an excellent inn called The Baths of Reichenbach, situated on the opposite side of the valley near the falls of the same name. It is about eight hours' walk from Grimsel to Meysingin, and the scenery is extremely beautiful. At Handek, between the two places, are the falls of the Aar, which is considered one of the finest cataracts in Switzerland from its height (more than 200 feet) the quantity and rush of water, the gloom of the gorge into which it precipitates itself, and the wild character of the rocky solitude around it. Retired very early, much worsted from the day's work.

Sept. 6. Woke up this morning and found myself too lame in the knee to travel on foot, so Johnstone and myself procured horses at the rate of 20 francs each and started for Grindelwald, about 16 miles distant over the great Scheideck. It is one of the finest passes in Switzerland. Several glaciers of great beauty are to be seen—one called Rosenlaui, and the others Grindelwald glaciers. The view down the valley of Grindelwald from the top of the Scheideck is very striking. The Wetterhorn (Peak of the Tempest) overhangs the path, an object of stupendous sublimity. Four different avalanches descend from it during the spring, and as we passed we saw the ice and snow falling in immense quantities from its summit. Upon a slope in front of the Wetterhorn is usually stationed an old man who blows the Alpine horn, a rude tube of wood six or eight feet long. The echo is extremely beautiful. Grindelwald is a small village of scattered houses with nothing to recommend it but the scenery. We put up here at a capital inn called the Eagle.

Sept. 7. It was our intention to have visited Wengern Alp this morning, but the weather was so inclement that we abandoned the idea, dismissed our horses, and proceeded in a carriage to Interlaken by way of Lauterbrunnen, where we saw the celebrated Falls of Staubbach, a small body of water falling nine hundred feet and looking for all the world just like the stream from an engine's pipes. We remained at Interlaken but a short time. It is a small place beautifully situated between the two lakes, has two or three good hotels inhabited during the summer months mostly by English. The females in this Canton wear black worked [?] caps on their heads, most of them have goiters, which is a disease of the country, and large heads. At 4:00 we discharged our faithful guide and crossed Lake Thun in an iron steamer for the village of Thun, which is beautifully situated and has an excellent hotel called the Bellevue.

Sept. 8. Left Thun at 6:00 this morning in the diligence and reached Berne at 9:00. The road is excellent and the valley of the Aar very beautiful and well cultivated. Berne is situated very high, commanding an extensive view. It contains about 23,000 inhabitants and is one of the chief cities in Switzerland. The bear is the armorial bearing of the town. Figures of the bear are to be seen in every street and two live ones are kept in the suburbs of the town at the expense of the corporation. During the day we visited the museum where we saw one of the Great Bernard dogs stuffed that saved the lives of 15 persons, also a chamois stuffed with three horns, besides a large collection of animals and birds. The town clock is worth seeing, being similar to the one at the Strasburg cathedral. I noticed during the day several good stone houses, in the windows of which were placed cushions outside the sash to set upon, which seems to be pretty general here. The country houses in this neighborhood are larger than usual, with very broad roofs and eaves almost touching the ground. The farmers here stack their manure with as much pains as they do their hay. Read an account in the Times today of the execution of 50 Americans in Cuba for aiding in revolutionary movements. If true, it will create excitement in the States and probably bring on a war with Spain.

Sept. 9. Left Berne at 8:00 in the diligence for Vevray, passing through Freyburg, Basle, and several other small places. Freyburg is beautifully situated and is surrounded by the Alpine range of mountains. The two suspension bridges and the cathedral are the only objects here worth seeing. One of the bridges is said to be the largest in the world, being 941 feet in length, 180 feet high, 22 feet, 11 inches in breadth. Soon after leaving Basle we met Bishop Otey and party with Henry Fogg and Henry Maney added to it on their way to Berlin and Vienna. I stopped and exchanged a few words with them and while talking the diligence got far ahead of me. An old Swiss came along with his wife in a buggy. I stopped them and asked to ride with them until I overtook the diligence. They readily agreed and I rode five miles in their carriage and walked from there to Vevray. I did not regret this much as I had a fine view of the castle of Chillon and Lake Leman by moonlight. Stopped at L'Hotel des Trois Couronnes.

Sept. 10. Johnstone and I rose early this morning and drove in an excellent carriage to the old castle of Chillon so celebrated in the writings of Byron and Rousseau, the former in his sonnet on Bonnivard and the later his Heloise. The castle is kept in excellent order and is now used as a magazine for military stores. We were ushered through the dungeon where Bonnivard was confined, saw the ring in the pillar to which he was dragged, and also saw the names of Byron, Shelley, Rousseau, Sue, Dana, Peel and others cut in the rock on the pillar to which Bonnivard was chained. Returned to Vevray and took the 10:00 o'clock boat for Lausanne. Lake Leman and Geneva are both very beautiful. The water is as blue as indigo and the scenery very fine. At Lausanne I stopped at Hotel Gibbon where the historian wrote his rise and downfall of the Roman Empire. A portrait taken from the original hangs up in the dining room. Here I found Ewing and Price and made arrangements for going with them into Italy next week. Left Lausanne at 6:00 and reached Geneva at 12:00.

Sept. 11. Stopped last night at the Grand Hotel des Borgues, which is the best in Geneva. From my window I have an excellent view of the lake, Mont Blanc, and the clear waters of the Rhone. Geneva has upwards of 30,000 inhabitants and may be called a pretty city, although it has but few attractions for the stranger. The public buildings are devoid of any architectural beauty. Geneva is the headquarters of strangers visiting Mont Blanc and Italy. Thirty or forty thousand pass through every summer and leave a considerable amount of foreign gold with her citizens. In the manufacture of watches, musical boxes, and all kinds of gold works it has long been celebrated. 100,000 watches are made here annually. Upwards of 50 watch makers and 70 jewellers' workshops are kept in constant employment, and in good years 75,000 ounzes of gold, 5,000 marks of silver and precious stones to the value of a million of francs are used in them. They are very strict in Geneva about passports. I reached here at 12:00 in the night and mine was taken from me. This is Fete Day; all of the stores are closed.

Sept. 12. Rose rather early this morning and went out shopping. Purchased a musical box, some wooden ware, and jewelry. Had my likeness taken by a Daguerreotypist full length in my Alpine costume. The view of Mont Blanc from Geneva is extremely beautiful today. The atmosphere is perfectly clear and the snow-clad peaks rise high up in the heavens far above the neighboring peaks, presenting a view worthy of the poet's pen or the painter's pencil. After enjoying an excellent dinner at my hotel, I wrote a letter to Sister Sallie and Mr. Vaughn. Also wrote No. 22 for the Union, giving an account of Belgium. Here as at almost every place that I have visited in Europe, I find a crowd of Americans.

Sept. 13. This morning I went out shopping and made a pretty big hole in my pocket. I purchased a lady's watch and several little articles necessary for my journey. About 2:00 I met with Mr. Brooks and lady and Miss Winthrop who invited me to go with them to the museum. I did so and found several pieces of painting by modern artists that I consider good. The sculpture room is not worth looking at, being nothing but a collection of plaster pieces and one or two in marble. After dinner Miss Winthrop and myself walked up to the top of our hotel where we had a telescopic view of Mont Blanc, the ranges of the Alps, and Jura mountains. The sunset was clear and the effect of the reflection on the snow-capped peaks was exceedingly beautiful. Wrote letters until 12:00 and retired.

Sept. 14. Well we have another bright and beautiful day and I should have gone to church, but being considerably behind in my correspondence, I occupied the whole day in writing. After dinner I went into Mr. Brooks's room and talked a while with Miss Winthrop. Geneva is the greatest place for firing off guns and popping of whips that I have ever seen. The drivers of every description seem to try which can make the greatest noise, much to the annoyance of the visitors who are unaccustomed to such sounds. On the Lake of Geneva the boats all have satin [?] sails which look very pretty on the water but are not so serviceable as our own. Wrote letters today to Sister Sallie, Vaughn, and the Union.

Sept. 15. Left Geneva at 7:00 this morning in the diligence and reached Hidel Union in Chamonix about 6:00, passing en route through several little villages and a country without any particular interest until we reached Chamonix, which is quite romantic. At Bonneville we crossed the stone bridge at the end of which is a column erected in honor of Carlo Felice, who added to the security of the town by the formation of strong embankments to restrain the furious Arve. Just beyond this we saw a fair in a little village. The collections of black pigs and cattle, sheep, and goats were very large and managed altogether by women, who tie strings about the necks of the animals and examine their parts with as much ease and knowledge as men. Indeed, the women of this country do most of the work. They attend the stock, gather the crops, and do all kinds of work. Many laughable incidents occurred today. Among others I saw a woman riding a hog, and rode myself several miles in a wagon with a very pretty girl who carried a black pig in her lap. Dined at Saint Martin. Passports examined today.

Sept. 16. After an early breakfast the following named Americans left Chamonix with a guide to climb the lofty steeps of Mount Blanc, viz., Johnstone and Hume of South Carolina; P. C. Brooks, wife, and neice, Miss Winthrop; two ladies named Sigonny; Mr. Bemis and a clergyman from Boston. We first went to the Montanvert and saw the Mer de Glace, the enormous glacier which terminates in the Glacier du Bois and the source of the Arvaron in the valley of Chamonix. It is very beautiful but inferior in clearness and formation to the glacier of the Rhone. There is a house called the pavillion at this place where they keep refreshments and curiosities for travellers. After viewing this we descended to the foot of the glacier where the Arvaron issues out, and from thence we ascended a mountain on the opposite [side] of the valley called the Flegere amid clouds so thick that we could hardly see. When we reached the top we ordered dinner, which was pretty good, with the excepting of the manner of changing plates, which was by taking the leavings out with his fingers. After discussing the dinner we looked out and found the lofty snowcapped peaks of Mont Blanc in all grandeur. The sunset on the mountain was magnificent, which contrasted with the impenetrable darkness in the valley rendered [it] extremely beautiful. The mountain peaks of Switzerland differ from those in America in this particular. Here they are sharp and pointed, and there they are round. Quite a singular incident occurred today while we were ascending Mont Blanc. Mr. Bemis of Boston rolled a stone which accidentally struck a cow and which killed the poor creature which started rolling down the mountain.

Sept. 17. Early this morning the owner of the cow (who was a poor man) called on Mr. Bemis the second time and demanded 60 francs for his loss. Bemis thinking it was an exorbitant demand, refused to pay it, whereupon he was told by the hotel keeper that three .... had ordered that he should not leave Chamonix until the money was paid. Rather than have a difficulty Bemis gave him 55 francs and let the matter rest. It was altogether a singular incident. I suppose that one might throw the same rock a thousand times again and do no damage. Chamonix is the starting point for Mont Blanc, has several good inns, and is much visited in the summer. Left early this morning on post for Martiny by the pass called the Tete Noire. It is not so interesting in point of scenery as the Caldo Balme, but a much better and easier road. Distance 90 miles. Passports visaed twice today. Stopped tonight at the Hotel du Particulier. I found Mr. Ewing and Price waiting for me. At 11:00 we left Martiny in the diligence for Italy. *Left Hume thank God in Martiny.*

Sept. 18. After a miserable night's ride in a miserable coach and rainy weather, we reached the station for breakfast, which I found to be as intolerable as the infernal coaches, fit only to convey brutes not men. The pass of the Simplon built by Napoleon is a great triumph of art over nature. It is from 25 to 30 feet in breadth, and the average slope nowhere exceeds 6 inches in 6½ feet. The number of bridges constructed for the passage of the road amounts to 611 in addition to the far more vast and costly construction, such as terraces of massive masonry miles in length; of ten galleries cut out of the living rock; and 20 houses of refuge to shelter travellers and lodge the laborers constantly employed on the road. The hospital on the summit of the pass is a very large stone building under the care of the Soeurs de la Charite and contains many victims of goiter, eretimin [?], the prevailing maladies of the district. It has been snowing all day very hard. The snow in the road is three feet thick and we were compelled to stop and remain overnight on the mountain.

Sept. 19. I slept soundly last night without much rocking, being fatigued by constant travel. The inn on the Simplon is not good or even comfortable. After about two hours' travel we entered Piedmont. Here our passports were visaed and baggage hauled over.[14] At 12:00 we reached Domo d'Ossolo, the first Italian city, where we lost the connection of the diligence and was compelled to remain at the Hotel de la Port until 2:00 tomorrow morning. In this town I observed a striking difference in the appearance of things. Frescoe paintings are visible on the roadside, on the chimneys, in the churches, and everywhere. The interior of the cathedral in this place is quite pretty, presenting a great contrast with the roughness of the exterior. The Hotel de Ville here is also a handsome building.

Sept. 20. Left Domo d'Ossolo at 2:00 in the diligence for Baveno on Lake Maggiore, where we procured a small boat and rowed out to the Borromean Islands. There are two in number. One called Isola Madre and the other Isola Bella. One has a good hotel upon it and both have very pretty gardens. After viewing the islands we crossed over to a little town called Pallanza where we got on the lake steamer for *Sesto Calende* in Lombardy. Here our passports were again taken and luggage overhauled. The officers found a revolving pistol, dirk, and bullets in my trunk, which they took away from me, made much fuss about the matter, and said that I could not carry them into the Dominions of Austria. Not wishing to lose them I gave them in charge of the captain of the boat and directed him to forward them to a hotel in Genoa. This circumstance gave me some annoyance as I knew not what might be the results, two Americans having been imprisoned recently under slight pretences. I kept my ire down, however, and proceeded in the diligence to the city of Milan.[15]

Sept. 21. After surrendering up our passports at the gate of the city and receiving another in return, we entered Milan about 10:00 last night and endeavored to procure apartments at the Hotel de la Ville, but it was crowded and we were compelled to lounge about the streets for two hours and at last procured comfortable rooms at the Hotel Royale. Milan is all excitement today. The Emperor visited the city and reviewed about 50,000 troops in the Piazza d'Armi. It was a fine military display but unequal to the review in Paris. Some of the Austrian troops are good looking and well drilled, but most of them are small and insignificant in appearance.

Sept. 22. The Emperor Francis Joseph is a youth in his twenty-first year, rather tall and awkward. His features remind me much of a young man named Beech in Nashville. Mr. Ewing thinks that he resembles

---

[14] Lombardy (Milan) and Venetia (Venice) at this time were part of the Austrian Empire.

[15] These confiscated arms, later returned, were useful to McGavock and party in Egypt. See entry for December 24, 1851.

John McGavock. After reviewing the troops yesterday he rode on horseback dressed in the Austrian uniform—white coat and blue pants—through the principal street called the Borgi di P[orta] Orientale to the Duomo, which is undoubtedly the finest cathedral that I have yet seen—and probably in all Europe. A description of this building is utterly out of my power. Here the Emperor was conducted and received the sacrament in the presence of an immense assembly. After this ceremony he was received by the city authorities in the Hotel de Ville, then left the place for a little town in the neighborhood. Out of each window in the streets through which he passed they had hung out a red or yellow curtain and in the evening the city was illuminated. Soon after breakfast this morning we reported ourselves according to law at one of the public bureaus and had our temporary passports stamped with the privilege of remaining in Milan four days, after which we must absent ourselves unless they grant a longer indulgence. We then visited the Arco della Pace, which is one of the most beautiful gateways in Europe. We then went to see the celebrated painting of the Last Supper which is almost defaced by time. Here we saw the Emperor again and an exhibition of bombardment on an old house which I thought very poor. The scaling, ladders, and whole affair was managed clumsily. Ascended the spire of the cathedral and obtained a beautiful view of the city, which is perfectly flat, and the distant Alps which relieve the view. Attended an excellent opera this evening.

Sept. 23. Rose at 5:00 and started per railroad for Lake Como, which we accomplished in two or three hours. The city of Como, situated at the foot of the lake, is a pretty place numbering 30,000 inhabitants. The cathedral here is very large and built of white marble. When we reached the lake we were placed on a very inferior steamer ordinarily used for the transportation of merchandise. The good boats were reserved today for the Emperor of Austria, who went up on a visit to one of the palaces. The Lake of Como, called by the ancients, Lacus Larius, is about 40 miles long and is fed chiefly by the Adda. Taken altogether, it surpasses in beauty of scenery and the richness of its almost tropical vegetation any lake that I ever saw. Many villages adorn its banks and several palaces of some notoriety, viz., Villa d'Este, Villa of Count Taverna, Madame Pasta, and Taglioni—the two celebrated singers. All of the railroad stations and villages that we passed through today were decorated to receive the Emperor. Our passports were demanded twice today. Reached our hotel in Milan about 9:00.

Sept. 24. After procuring our passports from the authorities we went round to see the Brera, or Palazzo delle Scienze e delle Arti, which is quite a large building containing a library, gallery of paintings, and statuary of great value. We occupied several hours here and then visited La Scala, the largest theatre in Italy except San Carlo at Naples. The form of the house is semi-circular and is capable of containing 3,600 spectators. Most of the celebrated singers have appeared at La Scala during some portion of their career. Near a church called San Lorenzo in the Corso di P. Titurise [?] stand the Colonna di San Lorenzo, or Temple of Hercules, the only vestiges remaining in Milan of the old Roman architectural magnificence. They are 16 in number, of the Corinthian order, standing upon a continuous basement. Mouldering, fire-scathed, shattered by violence, these relics contrast strangely with the bustle and vivacity of the street in which they stand. On our return from this place my attention was attracted by a Jew with a rail cap selling books by weight near the Duomo. Fruit is also sold in Milan by weight. The females, many of whom are pretty, all wear black veils on their heads in the street.

Sept. 25. Left Milan this morning at 5:00 for Verona in the diligence which was placed on the railroad and conveyed as far as Treviglio, where horses were in waiting. In a few hours we were in Bergamo, a very pretty city containing about 35,000 inhabitants and situated partly on a lofty hill and partly in a valley. From Bergamo we went to Brescia, where we dined. This seems to be a prosperous town and contains upwards of 30,000 inhabitants. After dinner we ran along the base of a range of hills, passing the foot of L. Di Garda, to the city of Verona, which we reached very late in the night. Here our passports were examined for the second time during the day. The country through which we passed today is very beautiful and productive. The vintage has just begun and the grape gatherers are seen in all directions with their baskets filled with excellent grapes.

Sept. 26. Diligence riding in Italy is worse even than in Switzerland. The coaches are cramped, dirty, and uncomfortable. The horses are so poor that they can scarsely drag themselves along, and yet they are forced by the most unmerciful treatment to draw a heavy diligence with weight enough upon it to require a steam engine. Aside from this the postilions are all beggars and hand their hats round to the passengers at every change of horses for *drink money*. Stopped this morning at Hotel Le Duc Torri. Retired immediately and slept until 10:00, when we breakfasted and started out sightseeing. Visited the amphitheatre supposed to have been built between 81 and 117 of our era and contemporary with the Coliseum. The interior is nearly perfect, but the exterior is much delapidated. The walls at this time are 100 feet high and very thick. It is capable of holding 25 or 30 thousand people. The interior of the Duomo is worth seeing as it contains several valuable pictures.

Sept. 27. At 4:00 yesterday afternoon we started on an excellent railroad and reached the city of Venice at 8:00. The country between the two cities is perfectly delightful: two ranges of mountains on either side and a valley filled with grapevines trained on trees and laden with delicious grapes. When we reached the station our passports were demanded but our baggage was passed. When we got our baggage ready it was placed in a long black gondola which rowed us through long narrow streets—if I may so term—to the best hotel in Venice called the Albergo Reale Danieli, beautifully situated on the Riva degli Selinvorri [?]. I have done but little today in the way of sightseeing, but remained mostly in my room reading Murray's description of this ancient and renowned city. It has been cloudy and dismal all day and prospects of fair weather very gloomy.

Sept. 28. The day has been exceedingly inclement, so much so that we confined our work of sightseeing in and about the Piazza of Saint Mark, which is at present the center of business and amusement in Venice. It is one of the most beautiful squares that I have ever seen and would reflect honor upon any city. We first ascended the great Campanile tower which stands near the angle of the Piazza and Piazzetta, where we obtained an excellent view of the city. This tower is perfectly square and is 323 feet high and 42 at the base. The whole is surrounded by a lofty pyramid. A watchman is stationed in the belfrey, who at stated times beats the great bell. It is ascended by a continuous inclined plane and affords a prospect worth the toil of climbing. Venice is emphatically a city of the sea. It is situated on 72 islands and is entirely surrounded by water. The houses are stoutly built and covered with tile. One grand canal divides the city, which is intersected by numerous small canals or streets. Persons may walk over the most of Venice on sidewalks and a few paved streets, but nearly everything is conveyed in gondolas—all of which are painted black, with a cloth covering in the center to protect the passengers from the weather. The gondoliers ply the oar with a great dexterity and turn the corners with great precision and swiftness. There is not a carriage or horse in all Venice. The cathedral of San Marco is one of the most curious structures that I have ever seen. The ceiling is all mosaic and the floors of tissilated marble. The doors and paintings are all very curious and the works of art and beauty here displayed is truly magnificent.

Sept. 29. This morning Colonel [Anthony] Kimmell of Frederick County, Maryland, joined our party and we procured a gondola with two gondoliers and rowed out to the Lido, where Byron used to bathe and ride. The island is devoid of interest and the beach far inferior to many that I have seen. On our return we landed on an island to see the Armenian College, which still flourishes. Byron's old tutor is still there. We then visited some of the churches which are truly magnificent. The palaces of the city all look old and rusty. Some of them contain fine paintings which I have noted in Murray's Handbook. The city was illuminated by the *authorities* (not the people) in honor of Frederick Francis, first Emperor of the Austrian Dominion, who reached here at 12:00 tonight en route for Verona. The Rialto looked pretty, but the reception was very poor.

Sept. 30. After breakfast we went for the second time to the Ducal Palace, crossed the Bridge of Sighs, and examined the dark dungeons and instruments of torture used in ancient times. When we came out we met a procession of priests bearing the cross in front and the Virgin in the rear. As they walked along they were singing and the people fell on their knees. This ceremony is never gone through except by order from the Emperor after praying three days for fair weather. Our guide then conducted us into the Duomo and showed the stone upon which John the Baptist was beheaded. The stone out of which the water gushed when touched by Moses, also a piece of cross and earth containing the blood of Our Saviour. The Emperor visited some of the churches today and left the city in the Trieste steamer this afternoon amid the firing of cannon and shouts of the military.

CHAPTER XIV

"The Arabs are a strange people." (October-December, 1851)

The journal entries for the closing weeks of 1851 run almost double in length those which McGavock made at the beginning of his journey. Each day in Italy and Egypt was so crowded with scenes and associations recalling the ancient world that he expanded his daily record during this period by filling up the unused pages of January and February in the leather-bound diary. Then his narrative reaches a stirring climax with the hand-to-hand fighting on the banks of the Nile as the year closes.

Oct. 1. Agreeable to arrangement, Mr. Flagg of Saint Louis, who is our consul at Venice, and Colonel Kimmell of Maryland, met us at 11:00 at the railroad station and we set off together for Padua, where we got our breakfast and procured a vetturini to carry us to Florence. The college in Padua is small and has lost its ancient renown. The Duomo is large and very fine. Crossed the river Adige about dark on a bridge of boats and reached Rovigo at 8:00, where we remained all night at a tolerable inn. This whole region of country is very low and the banks of the rivers are all levied to the height of from 6 to 20 feet. The white and purple and dark grapes grow in that region in great abundance. The vintage has commenced and the girls may be seen gathering grapes everywhere, and the little low wagons with long casks filled with wine may be seen everywhere.

Oct. 2. Agreeable to arrangement we were waked this morning at 3:00 and left Rovigo for Bologna, in one of the States of the Church.[1] We crossed the River Po and several of the canals. The Po is about the size of the Cumberland—very rapid, and has a high levee on either side to protect the lands from inundation. Breakfasted at Ferrara and reached

[1] Romagna and Umbria were ruled by the Pope, with the government generally in the hands of priests and ecclesiastics.

the Hotel Brun in Bologna at 6:00. The passport system in Italy is exceedingly annoying. Ours were examined and visaed six times today. In the single town of Ferrara we had to submit to three examinations. We fed the custom house officers and our baggage was allowed to pass without examination. The vintage has just begun in Italy and I notice women gathering and men hauling grapes by the cart load. The hotel keepers and everyone that a traveller comes in contact with here must be closely watched, as they will take all sorts of advantages.

Oct. 3. We started early this morning to see the sights of Bologna, the city famed for sausages. From the observatory we obtained a fine view of the city and environs for miles around. The city itself is perfectly level and bounded on one side by beautiful, sloping hills. Lofty leaning towers built of brick are among the peculiar features of the place. The cathedral and galleries of paintings in this city are well worth one's attention. Left Bologna at 12:00, after being almost annoyed to death about our passports. The visa of both the civil and military authority is required, together with the signatures of some half dozen men before we could leave. Reached the summit of the Appenines at 8:00, where we remained all night at an inferior inn.

Oct. 4. Made another early start this morning and run until 11:00 before we could get any breakfast, which was so miserable that I would have preferred not having any at all. While waiting for our horses to baite, we amused ourselves in various ways—some playing with the girls of the house, some laughing at a woman riding straddle on a man's saddle, and some examining the turned-up shoes on the mules, which looked very singular. When we reached the gates of Florence, our passports were examined and our luggage passed by bribing the officers, which is exceedingly wrong but is a necessary evil hard to get rid of. Put up at Hotel York, where we were furnished with an excellent supper, after which we all had a money settlement and some little unpleasant feelings.

Oct. 5. Agreeable to arrangement last night, Colonel Kimmel and myself attended divine service in the English chapel. A youth preached an old man's sermon. Many English people were present and we paid two pasils admission fee at the door, which goes to pay for the church. On our return we met Mr. Bemis and Flagg in one of the churches. Received the letters from home today written by Mother and Sallie in August. They contained a great deal of news which was of great interest to me. The Austrian soldiery are stationed in Tuscany.[2] I saw the fun-

[2] The Grand Dukes of Tuscany (Florence) frequently relied upon Austria for military and police forces.

eral procession of an officer pass the hotel today. The music surpassed any band I ever heard. After tea we walked round to Cafe de Paris where we met some half-dozen Yankees eating bread soaked in coffee, a system of currency that a Southerner would disdain.

Oct. 6. The first thing that I did this morning was to climb the tower of the Duomo which furnishes a beautiful view of the city of Florence and its environs surrounded by hills covered with beautiful villas. The tower is the highest point in the city, and, like the cathedral, it is built of varigated marble which looks like mosaic work. The interior of the building is large but perfectly plain compared to other churches in Italy. We then visited the Galleria Imperiale e Reale, which contains the richest and most varied collection of paintings and sculpture in the world. To give anything like an account of the works of master artists in this collection would require many pages. Those that I admire most I have noted in Murray. We were all accosted this morning by a very pretty flower girl who furnished us with a little bouquet which they expect pay for, either at the time or before your departure from the city. They are generally pretty, wear the broad brimmed Leghorn hat, and dress with taste.

Oct. 7. Mr. Preston of Boston called at Hotel de York this morning and conducted us to the studio of Hiram Powers, the American sculptor. He received us very kindly and seemed quite affable. He looks to be 45 or 50 years of age. He showed us many beautiful works of art, viz. busts of Washington, Franklin, Clay, Webster, Calhoun, and others, also a beautiful statue of a fisherboy and the models of his two pieces called America and California. From the studio we went to Gallileo Tower and to the Palazzo Pitti, now the residence of the Grand Duke and guarded by Austrian troops. It is a very extensive building constructed of heavy, rough stone like the lower part of Dr. Martin's house in Nashville. The rooms are all fitted up in style and adorned with some of the oldest and best paintings in Italy.

Oct. 8. We went to the Pitti Palace again today and walked through the Boboli garden, which is very extensive and elevated, giving a fine view of the city, and filled with statuary of no mean character. The museum connected with the palace is decidedly the finest that I have seen in Europe. The wax figures showing up the human frame in all its parts are unequal anywhere and the collection of birds, minerals, and animals are very extensive and superior. The room recently erected by the Grand Duke and dedicated to Gallileo, who was a resident of Florence, is one of the most exquisite apartments that I ever saw. It contains a statue of the philosopher in one end and busts of his pupils arranged around. The floor is of tesselated marble and the ceiling frescoe representing the life of Gallileo.

Oct. 9. In Florence there is a pretty good reading room where American papers are usually kept. I visited it this morning and occupied several hours in looking over the news of the day. I then visited one or two private palaces on the Arno which are well furnished and contain some excellent paintings. On my return to the hotel I witnessed the ceremony of making a monk, which is rather curious. A procession is formed of monks, all masked, bearing the newly initiated member in a covered hand-barrow or sedan. He is carried to the monastery in this manner, there to remain until he choses to come out again into the .... Met Mrs. Winthrop of New Orleans in the street today who informed me of the death of Miss Mercer of that city. She died in Paris.

Oct. 10. We all started off this morning to finish up Florence. After examining the bridges across the Arno, which is a very insignificant river, we went through several churches and wound up with Santa Croce, the principal church of the Black or Observative Friars in ancient Florence. The exterior of the building is not completed. The interior is very attractive, not so much for any architectural elegance but as the depository of the remains and monuments of the mighty dead. Here I noticed a monument to Michaelangelo, Gallileo, some of the Bonaparte family, and many others of distinction. The practice of burying in churches is not a good one as it is calculated to create disease in the community, but I must say that when I leave this mortal world, I should like to be deposited in the vault of some church.

Oct. 11. The most of this day has been occupied in writing letters for the Union and revisiting objects in the city which I have seen before. In the afternoon I took a long walk with a young lady from England whom I found not only pleasant but particularly agreeable. We met again after dinner on the balcony of the hotel and continued our conversation. About 9:00 I walked round to Cafe de Paris where I met an acquaintance and *accompanied her home.* In the last few days much mirth has been created among the members of our party about the doings of old Colonel Kimmel and Price in their rooms, all of which was an excellent idea considering those concerned. Florence is decidedly a nice place. I like it very much, and would not object to passing the winter here if I had the time.

Oct. 12. This morning Mr. Ewing, Price, Johnstone, and Colonel Kimmel drove out to Fiesole, which is considered one of the beautiful drives about Florence. I remained at the hotel under the pretext of visiting Winthrop of New Orleans, but followed a young lady to church across the River Arno. In the afternoon I joined my friends and rode out with them to Cascine where all the city seemed to be assembled to hear the military band. The Grand Duke, who is an old man, was out among the rest. Two open carriages were along, one with four white and the other with four black horses. A man rode before to announce his approach and clear the way. After dinner I met a young lady from England on the balcony of the hotel and made an arrangement to meet her after going to the opera, an engagement fulfilled to the letter. This night has been the happiest that I have passed in Europe.

Oct. 13. Agreeable to previous arrangement we left Florence this morning for Genoa much against my inclination, as I have just formed an arrangement that would render my stay at Hotel de York very agreeable. We took the rail, however, and in a couple of hours found ourselves in the city of Pisa, renowned for its Leaning Tower, which we ascended and obtained a fine view. The cathedral and cemetery near the Tower are also objects of great interest. The Tower is built of brick and leans over 13 or 14 feet. Seven bells, four large and three small, are on the top of the Tower, one of which is remarkable for its sweetness of sound. Left Pisa at 3:00 for Leghorn, where we took a very good steamer for Genoa, after being vexed almost out of our lives about passports.[3] Leghorn was at one time a place of considerable commerce, but of late years it has fallen off greatly.

Oct. 14. Last night I laid down on a sofa in the cabin of the boat where I fell to sleep and did not wake up until this morning, when I walked out on deck and found that we were standing out in the harbor of Genoa, filled with vessels and presenting a scene of beauty and activity that I no where saw in Italy. The city is in the form of an amphitheatre and rises gradually from the water's edge to the summit of the Appenines which come in to the sea just here. Each peak is surmounted by a strong fortress, making it one of the most formidable cities in the Sardinian Dominion. Stopped at Hotel Fedder where I found a letter informing me that my arms could be had by applying at the diligence office. They were rolled up with great care and I feel much obliged to the captain of the boat of Lake Maggiore for his kindness.

Oct. 15. Started out early this morning with a valet de place to see the sights of Genoa. From the top of one of the churches we had a fine view of the harbor and city, which is situated on the side of the Appenines which commence right at the sea. The panorama is one of the most beautiful that I have ever seen. The streets of Genoa are generally very narrow and nearly everything is carried on the backs of

[3] Genoa was at this time part of the Kingdom of Sardinia.

mules, donkeys, and men. All of the wood used in the city and the gravel used on the streets are carried in baskets on these animals. The women are generally well-looking and wear white veils over their heads. The palaces of Genoa are very fine and show considerably what this city once was. In a business point of view it is at present the most important place in Italy. The streets all present an active appearance and everything seems to be in flourishing condition.

Oct. 16. Procured a carriage and drove out about 5 miles to a place called Villa del Marchesi Ignazio Pallavicino a Pegli, situated on the sea on the road to Nice. There is nothing extraordinary about the building except the extensive marble terraces that surround it, but the grounds, which are elevated high above everything around on a hill, [are] laid out in all the taste that an Italian could bring to bear upon it—observatories, rustic seats, grottoes, artificial caves, waterfalls, romantic bridges, boats, swings, fountains, flower beds, and every nameable thing calculated to beautify and adorn a country seat. It ranks among the first of the places of the kind that I have yet seen. We passed several hours here very delightfully, returned to Genoa, and occupied the evening in discussing the subject of slavery in the Indies with an Englishman.

Oct. 17. There never was a greater truth than the old saying, "We know not what a day may bring forth." Yesterday it was our intention to go to Civita Veccia by steamer and thence to Rome, but this morning we employed a vetturini and started from Genoa to Lucca soon after breakfast. Dined at Rapallo and proposed passing the night at Sestri. The road runs along the shore of the Mediterranean nearly all of the way and is one of the most romantic drives that we have yet had in Italy. On the roadside I notice fig and olive trees in abundance, also a hedge of cactus running along the shore of the sea. The houses in the villages along the route are built principally on arcades, and the people are noted for making light .... chairs, which are not only beautiful but as light almost as a feather. At the dinner table today Mr. Ewing used language to me that was anything but gentlemanly in relation to an affair in Florence. [He] being from the same city and a much older man than myself, I was compelled to pass it over.

Oct. 18. Our hotel keeper at Sestri was an old soldier in Napoleon's wars. He showed us several wounds received in battle. The scenery between Sestri and Levanto is both varied and beautiful. The road leaves the sea and we had only occasional views of the blue water until we neared the Gulf of Spezzia this evening. It is the Gulf where Shelley was drowned and was intended by Napoleon to be the stronghold of Italy on account of the spaciousness of the harbor and the advantages of situation. His plans were frustrated by the French Ministry and it is at present nothing more than a small town of about 8,000 inhabitants. Dined today at Borghetto and was charged four francs for dinner which we demurred and paid three, walked off and received his thanks. Italian hotel keepers as well as shop keepers always charge as much again as they are entitled to, expecting you to object to it. Such a system may suit some persons, but to an American it is exceedingly annoying.

Oct. 19. After being almost worried to death last night by the fleas and mosquitoes we left the Hotel de L'Univers in Spezzia and pursued our journey. The Gulf of Spezzia is very pretty, but small in comparison to what I had expected. Soon after leaving Spezzia we crossed a stream in a ferry boat called Niagara, which is usually fordable but swollen today by the recent heavy rains. Our boat grounded before we reached the opposite shore and we were all carried out on the ferrymen, which created much laughter and amusement. One of the females walked out with a basket on her head, holding her dress high above her middle. At Sarzana we were much amused in observing a custom that seems peculiar to this place, viz. the women wear little straw bonnets on their head not large enough for a doll. At Carrara we dined and visited the quarries which have more celebrity than any in Italy for beauty and texture. We have passed out of Sardinia into Modena and then into Tuscany today, having our passports visaed three times and baggage examined. We are now at the Hotel de la Poste in Pietrasanta [?].

Oct. 20. Made an early start this morning, called at Carrara and visited the celebrated marble quarries, reached Lucca at 12:00 where we dined and started at 4:00 for Florence by way of Pisa. Reached Florence about 9:00 and put up at the Hotel de York where we staid when here before. My room at this hotel is just where I wanted it, being situated conveniently to a certain Lord's apartments from England, whose party is exceedingly agreeable. Coming into Florence tonight our baggage was examined and we were detained some time because we could not speak the language. At last they let us get through—to get rid of us no doubt. The disposition of the Italian race to cheat on all occasions was strongly marked in all of our transactions today.

Oct. 21. This morning I commenced writing my 25th letter for the Union, but was interferred with by a disposition to look at a young lady and laid aside my pen. Walked up to the gallery of paintings where I found Henry Maney of Nashville who informed that Colonel Hart and Grigsby of Kentucky and Henry Fogg were in Florence. I then called with him to see these gentlemen at their apartments on the opposite side of the Arno. Here I learned that Bishop Otey and Aunt Felicia had returned to Paris from Berlin on account of the illness of Willie and a general desire of the party to return. I regret this exceedingly as they will be denied the pleasure of seeing Italy, one of the main inducements of coming to Europe. Heard also today that William Polk had been elected to Congress in opposition to Thomas.[4]

Oct. 22. Received visits this morning from Colonel Hart and Grigsby of Kentucky, and Mr. Grant of Virginia. The last two names are American artists living in Florence. Colonel Hart wished to accompany us tomorrow to Rome, but young Fogg and Maney put in their claims—very much against my wishes—and Hart was compelled to give out going with us, the carriage being too small to carry all of us. Being from the same town, we could not well get over letting the young men go in preference to Colonel Hart. Visited today the Church of San Lorenzo, which contains the chapel of the Medici. The exterior of the building is very rough, but the interior of the chapel is one of the most exquisitely finished rooms in Florence. Saw my *Lord's lady* today and found her exceedingly agreeable. Retired at 2:00.

Oct. 23. We were joined this morning by Fogg and Maney and started from Hotel de York at 6:00 for Rome in a carriage. Feeling much fatigued from the labors of the night, I felt drowsy and slept the greater part of the day. About 2:00 we stopped at a miserable hotel at Montevaroni and procured a dinner fit only for those who made it. Man and beast live under the same roof and enter at the same door. Fleas and other vermin in abundance. The country through which we passed today is not only mountainous and sterile but uninteresting. Stopped tonight at the Hotel Royal in Arezzo, a town containing over 10,000 inhabitants and the birthplace of Petrarch, Meconas [?], Vasari, and Michael Angelo. The latter was born in the neighborhood but attributed his talent to the genial air of Arezzo. Some historical and Etruscan curiosities are seen in this town.

Oct. 24. Left Arezzo at 6:00 and dined at an inn near Cortona, an old Etruscan city situated on a lofty hill. While waiting for our dinner we walked up to the city and examined the museum, which contains many Etruscan relics—among which I noticed an old bronze lamp. In the cathedral we saw the tomb of the consul Flaminius. The present town lies within the ancient circuit and the ancient walls still exist. When we returned to the inn we found a very good dinner served for us. After eating the dinner and while paying the bill, Price stole a kiss

[4] William Hawkins Polk (1815-1862), brother of James K. Polk, was a lawyer, state representative in Tennessee (1842-1845), and Minister to the Kingdom of Naples (1845-1847). He served in the Mexican War and later practised law in Nashville. James Houston Thomas (1808-1876), lawyer and Congressman (1847-1851), until his defeat by Polk.

from the landlady. Proceeded on our journey after dinner and soon reached the shore of Lake Thrasimene, celebrated in history as the place where the great battle of Thrasimene was fought—one of the few defeats, says Livvy, of the Roman people. The lake is 30 miles in circumference and 8 miles wide—without any beauty. We are stopping tonight at a miserable hotel in Passignana fit only for such cattle as inhabit them.

Oct. 25. Started from Passignana at 5:00 this morning in a perfect stew with our vetturini [vetturino] for bringing us at such an hotel, and the hotel keeper for furnishing us with such miserable fare. Reached Perugia at 12:00, where we procured breakfast and occupied about one hour in making a settlement. We then procured a guide and went into several churches and examined the outer walls and gates which still stand as a monument of the past. One mile this side of Perugia is an old Etruscan tomb called the Grotto di Volunni, discovered in 1840 by a peasant. It is approached by a long flight of steps descending to the entrance in the hillside. The tomb consists of ten chambers; the largest, with a beam and rafter roof, is 24 feet by 12 feet, 8 inches [and 16 feet] high. The nine others which open into it are of rather smaller size. Several urns, inscriptions, and curious figures are to be seen here.

Oct. 26. Left Foligno after an early breakfast and passed through the valley of Clitumnus to the town of Spoleto, stopping en route at the little temple supposed to be the one described by Pliny as dedicated to the River God Clitumnus and celebrated by the pen of Dryden, Addison, and Byron. It is quite small and is now used as a chapel dedicated to San Salvadore. At Spoleto we visited the citadel, which is situated on an elevated hill affording one of the best views in Italy. It is now used as a prison and contains 500 convicts at present. There is an acqueduct here worth seeing, said to be built by Theodelapius III, Duke of Spoleto in 604. It serves as an acqueduct and bridge and is a work of considerable magnitude. Leaving Spoleto after a good dinner, we passed through a narrow valley, ascended a lofty hill, and reached the Hotel d'Europa in the town of Terni in time enough for a miserable supper. Had quite a disputation this evening with Mr. Ewing on the propriety of securing the approbation of parents in affairs of matrimony.

Oct. 27. This morning we procured a guide and walked to the Falls of Terni, which are five miles distant from the town of Terni. These are artificial and superior to any cascade in Europe but much exagerated by travellers, Byron, and other writers. The situation is rather romantic. The River Velino that makes the falls is a small stream about 40 or 50 feet in width. There are three successive falls estimated to be between eight or nine hundred feet in height. We were followed nearly the whole way by females with donkeys who insisted on our taking a ride for two francs. Returned to Hotel Europa in Terni and set off for Narni, which we reached about 3:00 and put up at La Campagna. Narni is beautifully situated on a lofty eminence commanding a fine view of the valley of the Nar. The great object of interest in Narni is the ruined bridge, which has for ages been regarded as one of the noblest relics of Imperial times.

Oct. 28. Started at 6:00 from Narni and reached Civita Castellana about noon, where we procured a good dinner at La Porta, and examined some old Etruscan remains in the neighborhood. The road between the two places is exceedingly interesting. It emerges from a great ravine of the Appenine which enters at Spoleto and approaches the broad plains of the Tiber which we crossed over the Ponte Felice built by Augustus in 1798.[5] After dinner we proceeded on our journey and reached a very good inn at Le Sette Vene, 22 miles from the Eternal City. The lands in this portion of Italy are cultivated on a larger scale than any I have yet seen. They are owned by large proprietors who cultivate them through agents. The cattle here, like those in Lombardy, are all white or grey and the hogs perfectly black. Donkeys and mules are generally used for light work and oxen for the heavy.

Oct. 29. Our hotel last night was terribly bad. Fleas, bad coffee, and dishonesty was lavished upon us in abundance. Left early and soon came in sight of the Eternal City. The great dome of Saint Peter's was the first object to attract our attention. It is impossible to describe my emotions as we neared the city of so many historical recollections. I thought of its antiquities, its renown, its glory, and its present condition. Even my own history was brought before my mind's eye. The past, fruitful with its recollections of pleasures and pains, collegiate days, professional trials, and personal troubles—all came up and suggested thoughts at once pleasing and painful. As we advanced, the appearance of the country became more pleasing and the vegetation less scanty. Monte Maria covered with stone, pines, and cypresses was on our right, the hills of Frascati and Albano on our left, and the plains of the Tiber spread out before us. We crossed the Ponte Molle and entered Rome by the Porta del Popolo and put up at the Hotel Europa in the Piazza di Spagna. At the gate we paid 12 pauls for entering the city, a system of bribery that is a shame to the Pope's government. There never was

[5] McGavock's pen slipped here, of course. The editor experienced many difficulties in transcribing the remaining portions of the European Journal. McGavock wrote hurriedly, often horizontally and vertically on the same page; his haste produced careless spelling of Latin and Italian proper names; and the syntax is frequently confusing.

as many Tennesseans in Rome as entered her gates today—six, including Frank Parrish. After dinner I called on Colonel Kimmell and several other Americans at the Hotel d'Angleterre. Learned through a letter from Mr. Stuart that Aunt Felicia sailed on the 15th of this month for home with Mr. Litton. Bishop Otey sailed before her with Dr. Mercer and the corpse of his daughter, who died in Paris. Neither of them have written me a word, which I consider very strange.

Oct. 30. This morning we employed a guide and went out to search for private apartments in order to avoid the expense of staying at a hotel. We entered several houses through narrow and filthy alleys to examine rooms, but none suited us. We then went to the Hotel d'Angleterre where we have some American friends and engaged rooms from tomorrow. This afternoon Mr. Ewing, Fogg, and myself walked through a number of filthy streets to Ponte [San Angelo], which crosses the Tiber opposite the castle of San Angelo. Just beyond is the great church of Saint Peter's. I was disappointed with the magnitude of the building viewing it externally, but when I entered its sacred doors and viewed the interior, it fully equalled and even surpassed my expectations. Externally it is not so fine as the Duomo at Milan, but its internal splendor surpasses all the buildings that I have yet seen. On our return we saw a long procession of monks dressed in their dark brown cloaks and sandals, bearing lighted candles and a bier upon which one of their order was being borne to his long home. We also saw a carriage dashing through the streets filled with young women gaily apparelled with wreaths on their heads, playing tamborines and singing merrily. I did not ascertain its meaning.

Oct. 31. Paid our bill at the Hotel Europa this morning and ordered our baggage to be removed to Hotel d'Angleterre. Walked down to Messers Plowders etc., this morning and read the English papers. This afternoon Mr. Ewing, Fogg, and myself went to the chapel in the Vatican where we saw the Pope and his Cardinals. The Pope is a large and fine looking man with an intelligent face.[6] He was dressed in a white satin robe with a long train spangled with gold. The Cardinals were all men advanced in years and dressed in scarlet robes. The ceremony was very imposing. At the door of the chapel were stationed the Swiss Guard to protect the Pope. They were dressed in a kind of uniform made of black, yellow, and red stripes, giving the exact appearance of a clown in a circus. This uniform is said to have been introduced at the instance of Michael Angelo. After dinner I spent several hours con-

---

[6] Pius IX, elected Pope in 1846, died in 1878.

versing with Hoffman of New York and then finished my 25th letter for the Union.

Nov. 1. At 10:00 I went again to the Capella Sistina, or Sistine Chapel, where I saw the Pope officiate at the celebration of All Saints. The Cardinals were all present, some of whom were dressed, differently from yesterday, in dove color and white robes. After the ceremony I went into Saint Peter's and examined regularly the monuments, statuary, paintings and works of art in the various chapels and aisles. The Baldacchino, or grand canopy, is of solid bronze and the largest and richest that I have ever seen. The bronze statue of Saint Peter stands near the canopy, the toe of which is nearly worn off by the kisses of the people. Behind the canopy and at the extremity of the church, is a large bronze chair inside of which is preserved the wooden chair of Saint Peter. Returning from Saint Peter's I called and was kindly received by Mr. Cass, our Charges d'Affaire. He has a suite of rooms on the Piazza del Popolo well furnished and containing some valuable paintings, statuary, and other relics that he purchased during the seige for a mere song. Mr. Cass is said to be one of the popular foreign ministers in Rome and has a great influence with the government.[7]

Nov. 2. At 10:00 I went with Colonel Kimmel and the Misses Thurston of New York to a little chapel where we heard some excellent singing by the Sisters of Charity. We then took a walk on the Pincian Hill, the favorite promenade of the modern Romans, from which we had an excellent view of Saint Peter's and the Piazza del Popolo. At 11:00 we attended church in a chapel attached to the American Legation. About 25 persons were present and the discourse was delivered by a Mr. Hastings of Michigan. The privilege of preaching in the city of Rome was granted to Mr. Cass, our Charge d'affaires, on account of the interest taken in their troubles in 1849. Tomy Cass is, I am informed, both popular with the government and people of Rome. This afternoon Mr. Cox, an Episcopal clergyman from Connecticut, officiated in the English Church outside the walls in which he prayed for *our Sovereign* Lady the Queen, and that she might have victory over all her enemies. Several Americans were present and all concurred in pronouncing it todyism and bad taste.

Nov. 3. After depositing several letters in the post office at Torlonia's, my banker, I procured a guide and went on the tower of the Capitol, which affords the finest view to be had of the city. Here I occupied about one hour in fixing the Seven Hills and other prominent

[7] Lewis Cass, Jr., was appointed American Charge d'Affaires to the Papal States in 1849, and Minister Resident in 1854.

objects in my mind. On the north I viewed the modern city; on the east the meanderings of the yellow Tiber; on the south the ancient ruins; and on the west the distant range of the Sabine hills. It is impossible to describe the feelings that animated my bosom while gazing on the antiquities of so many ages. I thought of my schoolboy days when I used to con over and recite the writings of Cicero, Cæsar, Virgil, and the other writers. All of my early reading came up fresh in my memory and I felt that I was once more a boy. The day was not clear and I could not see much beyond the campagna, but really I felt as if I could spend the day upon the Tower. Descending the lofty height I proceeded to examine the site of the Roman Forum which joined the Capitol, occupying a space between the Capitoline and Palatine hills. The floor of the Forum is about 20 feet below the level of the earth, but has been excavated mostly and is now plainly seen. Fourteen columns are still standing and the arch of Septimus Severus is almost perfect. From appearances the Forum must have occupied a very large space. Just below is the ruins of the Palace of the Cæsars now covered over with a garden of vegetables, vines, etc. Some of the old arches are used as a depository of hay and as a stable for horses and cows. Passing under the Arch of Titus I came to the Coliseum, which is certainly the most stupendous ruin in the world. It is much larger than the one at Verona but not so perfect, having suffered severely by the desolations of war and time. I then walked round and took a general view of the ruins, intending to return again and examine them more particularly. After dinner I called with some six or eight Americans to see Mr. Chapman, an artist of New York of considerable character.[8] He showed us a beautiful copy of a Bible published by the Harpers and illustrated by himself and also a Madonna intended for the gallery in New York. He is the artist of the painting called Pocohontas in the Rotunda of the Capitol. He has an interesting wife and three little children. There are 20 American artists now in Rome—12 painters and 8 sculptors.

Nov. 4. At 10:00 we left the hotel to see a procession on the Corso and the Festival of San Carlo Borromeo in the Church of San Carlo. The Corso near the church was lined on either side with French soldiers. The Cardinal Senator and the Pope rode in splendid carriages heavily mounted and drawn by elegant black horses. The Pope's carriage was drawn by six horses and had five outriders. When the Pope passed, the soldiers and the people fell upon their knees and he waved his finger first on one side and then on the other. He then entered the church and

---

[8] John Gadsby Chapman (1808-1889), American painter, lived most of his adult life in Rome where he gained a wide reputation.

was carried round it in a large chair borne by the Cardinals with two large fans made of white peacock feathers carried on either side by priests. The ceremony was very imposing and interesting. I noticed in the crowd two priests that were as black as any of our Tennessee negroes. We then visited the Borghese Palace, occupied by a private gentleman.

Nov. 5. This morning I ascended the great dome of Saint Peter's with a party of Americans. There is no place that I have ever been that caused such thrilling emotions. Standing on the oldest, largest, and greatest church in the world and gazing upon a city full of historical interest was well calculated to induce me to linger and drink in the mighty panorama. This dome is upwards of 400 feet in height and reached by an inclined plane as high as the roof and a winding stairway to the summit. We got into the ball, which is capable of holding 16 persons. From this dome the view is superb—just below is the Vatican Palace and the gardens, in front the Tiber Castle of San Angelo and the modern city, to the right the ancient ruins, and in the distance the snow-covered mountains and blue Mediterranean. No one can fully appreciate the immensity of this building until they go on top and walk around it. Here he will see workshops and people living on the roof who are constantly employed in repairing the edifice. When we came down there was service in one of the chapels and we saw a pilgrim leaning upon his staff upon his knees and dressed in the habit of a monk with shells fastened onto the cape. We then went into the Vatican and saw the gallery of paintings, maps, and statuary, also the manner in which they manufacture mosaics. Coming out of the Vatican we found it raining again. We have not had a clear day since we have been in Rome. Italian skies and Italian sunshine I am beginning to regard as all humbug. I have not enjoyed a real pleasant day since I have been in the country.

Nov. 6. This morning we procured a guide and commenced visiting the sights of Rome regularly. We went first to the Custom House near the Corso. It was once an ancient palace. The cornice is very beautiful, but the pillars in front are much mutilated. From the Custom House we visited the church of the Jesuits which is one of the largest and finest in the city. It contains among other things four columns and a ball made of lapis-lazula. Close to this church we saw the Roman College, which is an extensive building with a pole on the roof upon which they hoist a black ball at 12:00 every day, at which time a cannon is fired from the Castle of San Angelo and all the bells in the city are rung. Approaching the Capitol by a lofty flight of steps with huge statues of Castor and Pollux with their horses at the top, we turned to the left and entered the Museum which is exceedingly interesting, although small compared to the one in London and Paris. Among the numerous objects, I was particularly interested in one or two sarcophogus, the Dying Gladiator, Venus Capitol, Agrippina, mother of Germanicus, the Infant Hercules, Statue of the Faun, Antina, and the Amazon. Just opposite the Museum is the Palace of the Conservatory, used for the settings of the Senate. It contains some good paintings and exquisite statuary, particularly those in a room dedicated to Canova, which contains the best of many of the modern artists. From this palace we visited the Tarpeian Rock, which is approached through a small kitchen garden and overlooks a dirty street below. Near the Capitol we went into the prison where Saint John and Saint Peter were confined. The entrance is occupied as a chapel and the dungeon which is two stories underground is reached by narrow stairs. In the floor there is a spring out of which Saint Peter baptized the jailors, and on each side there is a door through which the angel delivered him. Seeing this interesting place we roved about the Coliseum several hours and returned to our hotel.

Nov. 7. Set from 8:00 until 9:00 for my likeness in cameo and then drove with Colonel Kimmel to the church of Saint John Lateran, which is the principal temple of Rome and of the Catholic world. In the Piazza there is one of the largest obelisks in Rome, originally erected at Thebes by Theutruosis [?] II, King of Egypt, as ascertained by the hieroglyphics. It is of red granite and is 33 meters in height, exclusive of base and pedestal. The interior of the church is very fine, particularly the Corsini Chapel built by Pope Clement XII in honor of Saint Andrew Corsini. The palace adjoining the church is the largest in Rome and contains many antique relics and some excellent modern paintings. From the Lateran we went to the Church of Santa Maria Maggiore, situated on the Esquiline Hill near the ruins of the Temple of Juno Lucina. The chapels are very fine in this church, particularly the chapel of the Virgin or the Borghese Chapel. We next visited the Quirinal Hill, also called the Monte Cavallo, which is decorated with two groups of men above 18 feet high taming horses—which are considered masterpieces of Grecian sculpture. In the center is an obelisk of red granite 45 feet high found near the Mausoleum of Augustus and a vase of gray granite about 45 feet in circumference brought from the Roman Forum. Near this is the Pontifical Palace and the Rospigliosi Palace, both of which are large but not very attractive. From this point we went to see the Pantheon, but it was so dark we concluded to visit again. We then called on a magnificent Roman lady and passed several hours most delightfully.

Nov. 8. Visited the Colonna Palace this morning. The picture gallery is the finest hall in Rome, upwards of 150 feet in length. In the rear of the palace the gardens extend to the top of the Quirinal and are remarkable for their pines and for the massive fragments of the supposed Temple of the Sun. Passing the palace of the Popes and the celebrated fountain in the Piazza, we proceeded to the Viminal and the baths of Diocletian, said to have covered many acres. The ruins are now apparent in a portion of the circuit of brick wall, in an immense hall converted into the church of Santa Maria of the Angels, and in other large brick walls and arches. Some of the pillars of the hall—eight in number—still remain and are in the church, occupying there their original position. They are of single pieces of Egyptian granite, 50 feet high and 5 feet through. Everything evinces what tremendous labor was lavished on these baths. Nothing remains to show their *modus operandi* interesting to an antiquary. This church of Santa Maria degli Angeli is a handsome building in an exact Greek Cross. We found the relique room lighted and ready for exhibition. Saw bones of many martyrs, teeth, hearts, heads, some figures like mummies with palms in hand, sleeping martyrs (as it is said). Back of the baths was an open quadrangle with marble colonnade and walls at the sides called barracks of Diocletian. We then went into the studio of Mr. Crawford, an American sculptor. Saw his figure of Patrick Henry. Saw the grounds of the celebrated Pretorian Camp near Porta Pisa. We then visited the garden of Sallust, passed through the Porta Salina, through which the Sabine women entered; and visited the Albano Villa, the stables and out houses of which were thrown down by the French in 1849. It is an exceedingly interesting place and contains many fine paintings, old statuary, and gardens. Returned to the hotel in a heavy rain and abandoned sightseeing for the day.

Nov. 9. This as usual is a very gloomy day calculated to give one the blues and fit only for those who are never effected by inclemency of weather. Italy has the character abroad of having the finest climate in the world. But from my experience it is the worst. It has rained nearly every day since we entered the country. Mr. Ewing and the rest of the party went to hear Mr. Hastings in the American Chapel today, but I remained in my room reading and writing until late in the afternoon when we went to Saint John Lateran's Church to see the *veritable* heads of Saint Peter and Saint Paul exhibited. When we reached the church we found a number of persons assembled doubtless to see the heads, but were disappointed. For some cause or other, which we did not find out, the heads were not exhibited. But we were fully repaid in hearing some excellent music on the organ and the finest singing I ever listened to. The voice of one of the eunuchs certainly excelled anything I ever listened to. It was as soft and as sweet as that of the most beautiful female. It looked very strange to see a large overgrown man with a delicate female voice. These eunuchs are castrated by their mothers during infancy expressly for the choir which all are ambitious to get into. Returned to the hotel, dined, and paid a visit to the Misses Thurston of New York. Here I met a young Italian of high birth who belonged to the Republican party. He spoke very feelingly of the miserable condition of his country, the inefficiency of the government, and the weakness of the Pope. He expressed himself freely and apparently without fear.

Nov. 10. Going to Saint Peter's we found the Tiber raging high and out of its banks among the houses. At Saint Peter's we went into the catacombs, found there many tombs of saints, heroes, popes, especially the Tomb of Saint Peter, where his body is buried, and above which is the church. A hundred lamps are kept burning constantly. A splendid sarcophagus of an ancient Prefect of Rome, named Junius Bassus, in two stones of marble. We then went into the sacristy of Saint Peter's, in which are deposited the robes used on grand occasions. The Vatican being open to the public on Mondays, we repaired hither and examined it thoroughly. The Vatican is a stupendous structure containing 4,422 apartments, 8 grand and 200 smaller staircases. The space it occupies is immense. Its length is said to be 1,151 English feet and its breadth 767 feet. It is rather a collection of separate buildings than one regular structure, and hence its general appearance is anything but prepossessing. We went first into the library and found the rooms beautiful, but were denied all access to the manuscripts without a permission from the Pope. I regretted this much, as there are 23,000 and many of them very rare and ancient. The Sistine Chapel in which we were twice before has the most splendid frescoes by Michael Angelo, among which are the Last Judgment, the masterpiece of Raphael. Four rooms with frescoes we saw today, also the Gobelin tapestries taken from the cartoons of Raphael. The gallery of paintings are small but very select. The collection of statues, busts, etc. are superior to anything of the kind in Europe. I could spend weeks in this department, which is rich beyond description. We then went into a large room where they were making mosaic work for Saint Paul's new church, not yet completed, situated on the Tiber. The Vatican gardens are quite pretty but nothing extraordinary. Strangers can look over them from the windows and from the tops of Saint Peter's, but are not allowed to enter its guarded precincts fearing they may murder the Pope while he is taking his walks. A portion of the Vatican is appropriated for the residence of the Pope and is exempt from inspection. After going through all the various ramifications of this immense building, we took final leave and gazed for the last time on this noble palace and the lofty dome of Saint Peter's. We then examined the Castle of San Angelo, crossed Ponte San Angelo, and penetrated the center of the city where Mr. Ewing and myself called on a Roman lady with whom we passed an hour very pleasantly. Some of the Roman ladies are very large and fine looking, differing materially in appearance from the Venetian, Florentines, and women in other parts of Italy.

Nov. 11. This morning we set out with a guide to visit Saint Paul's new church beyond the Ostia gate.[9] Passing the Capitoline we saw some remains, apparently of the ancient walls of some of its buildings. Came soon upon the theatre of Marcellus, two stories of which for one-third of the way round are complete, but worked in the back Ossian's Palace, remains also of portico placed before it by Augustus, some columns with Corinthian capitols. Shape of the Rome Theatre shown upon the staircase to the museum of the Capitol where there are some of the tablets of a map of Rome, among other things of the theatre of Pompey. Passed a place where the poor all but fighting for soup at a convent in the Jews' quarter from which they are not allowed to go, dirty miserable looking wretches mostly under the water of the Tiber. Crossed bridge of Fabricius to an island on which temple Sarapus formerly existed. Hence on continuation of bridge to the other side of the Tiber. Broken bridge below and bridge Seste above. Island, that of Saint Bartholomew. On the other side of the Tiber we were in the region formerly called *trans Tiberi* and now *trans Tevere,* between Juniculum and the Tiber, where the people are said to retain the features and the customs of the ancient Romans. We saw some Roman noses, nothing else particular. Found on the Tiber at what they call the Port of Rome a number of small sailing vessels and a little steamer about the size of a Dime which runs to Naples. Here crossed from Mount Aventine the Sulliciano on which Codes [?] performed his act of heroism. Crossed river to Eis-Tiber and passing on soon came to the house of Runzi near Aotha bridge, some evidences of antiquity in the lower story. Inscrip-

---

9 Impressed by dramatic scenes of Rome in floodtime and cramped for space in the diary, McGavock wrote this entry in fragmentary sentences which run together in a series of impressionistic images.

tions on a door stone, now broken up. Temple of Vesta—round-shaped with a top like an umbrella—supported on a colonnade of tall Corinthian columns. Small with a round body very well preserved—indeed almost entire. Near is a portion of the Temple of Fortuna turned into a church, no great thing. On the left about 100 yards from these is an arch of Janus. There are no remains of the old Temple of Janus. A huge piece of architecture, probably placed at corner or corners of streets to protect from rain. Its roof rests on four large pieces with niches for statues in them. It was 60 or 70 feet high. Near this is the Cloaca Maxima leading to the Tiber, large enough as someone said for a wagon loaded with hay to pass. We had a bad view of it as the water was in it from some quarter; I suppose the Tiber, though it was clear. It appeared to be a large and exceeding strong work, though but a short distance from the Tiber. Into this all the smaller sewers emptied. Near a small arch of Septimus Severus, Temple of Ceres, and Proserpine, now converted into church of Santa Maria in ...., with pillars worked in and a strange aged piece of marble as large as a cart wheel, about which there is some legend, passed along under the Aventine, and by the Tiber where there were huge masses of brick, said to be barracks, used now as stables for some buffaloes (not bison) used as work animals and a wall under a fortress upon the Aventine where marks of French cannon balls from Mount Juniculum where was the French camp they had destroyed. Palace of Basiline. We were shown where Garibaldi stood. After passing by the pyramid, the tomb of Caius Castrius, we found the road covered with water from the overflow of the Tiber and the people floating about in tubs. Determined not to be outdone, Johnstone and myself hired a cart and rode to Saint Paul's church which is not yet completed. The inside is of beautiful marble.

Nov. 12. This morning four of us took a carriage for Tivoli, 18 miles distant from Rome, passing en route Hadrian's Villa, which was evidently very extensive but at present nothing but a mass of brick and mortar. Just before reaching Tivoli we passed the Lago di Turtaro, so called from the petrifying quality of its waters, which produced the stone called travertine. The margin has been so much contracted by the gradual deposits of the water that the lake is now almost covered by a thick crust of travertine. The sulphurous odor of the pool makes its position known long before the traveller reaches the spot. This lake is drained by a canal into the Arno. Tivoli is a small town situated on the side of the mountain and has nothing to attract one's attention but the falls which are artificial. The view from Villa d'Este, which is now in ruins, is extremely fine. The broad campagna is spread out before the eye with the lofty dome of Saint Peter's looming up in the distance. Tivoli is much resorted to by the Romans in the summer months who wish to avoid the malaria of lowlands. The day being rather cloudy we were compelled to forego the pleasure of making any excursions from Tivoli. Two young Frenchmen with their wives who are quite pretty went out with us and made the day pass away very pleasantly. Mr. Ewing was exceedingly attentive to the ladies, so much so that he afforded the rest of the party considerable food for laughter. Returned to Rome late in the evening and went to hear Madamoiselle Rachel perform. She is decidedly the best actress that I have yet seen on the European stage. The theatre in which she appeared was rather small and not very full. She is tall and rather slender, with fair conplexion, black hair, and piercing black eyes. Her appearance was queen-like.[10]

Nov. 13. Procured a carriage again this morning and drove out on the old Appian Way, stopping to see various places of interest as we passed along. Passing through the Porta Latina we stopped to see several Columbaria (or tombs), among them the Columbarium of the slaves of Augustus, Tomb of the Scipios in a vineyard near the Porta San Sebastiano on the left of the Appian Way, marked by a solitary cypress tree, the most ancient and the most interesting of all the tombs yet discovered. Just beyond, in the church of San Sebastiano, we saw in a glass case an impression of the feet of Christ upon a stone when he visited Saint Peter in Rome, who said to him, "Domine quo vadis?" There is a small church in Rome called by these words for name. Under this church of San Sebastiano are the catacombs, so celebrated as the place of burial and also of assemblage for the meetings of the early Christians. We went under and through them to some extent. Just beyond this church is the Circus of Romulus, son of Magentius, sometimes called the Circus of Caracalla. Examined well and got a good idea of a race course with its goal, its spina, its seats, etc. Near this is the tomb of Cecilia Metella, wife of Crassus. It is a large round structure. But as the custode was imprisoned for theft, we could not get inside of the tomb. We then went to see the fountain or Grotto of Egeria Numa Pompilius on a hill formerly. It must have been very beautiful, paved with serpentine stone and lined with marble, a marble statue recumbent, etc. Returned to Rome by way of the *Nova* Appia where we had a fine view of the old aqueduct, which was an immense undertaking. These aqueducts are built mainly of brick; the base of the columns are of stone. Returned to Rome via the Porta San Giovanni

---

[10] Rachel (1821-1858) was born Elizabeth Felix at Mumpf, Switzerland, and became one of the great tragediennes of the middle 19th century.

near Saint John Lateran, and stopped at the Santa Scala, in which are the marble steps upon which Christ descended when he was sentenced by Pontius Pilate. They have been covered two or three times with wood—worn out by the people who are constantly ascending on their knees—kissing as they go a cross on every step. Price, Maney, and Frank Parrish went up.

Nov. 14. This morning I went to see the Pantheon and found it covered with water from the Tiber to the depth of one foot on the floor. It is the largest dome in the world, being perfectly round, with a massive portico in front. Returned by way of the custom house which is also a very ancient and curious building. The remainder of the day was spent in my room writing letters, etc. My cameo came in today and I think the artist has succeeded admirably in getting a good likeness.[11] Last night an unfortunate diffculty took place between two members of our party, which threatened to separate us, but through the intercession of Colonel Kimmel of Maryland, the whole matter was adjusted and things now move on as before. Called this afternoon on Major Cass, who furnished me with the late papers from the United States and informed me that the Pope and Cardinals had quite a stiff quarrel yesterday. The Pope recommended liberal measures in the administration of the government and was opposed by his advisors, which occasioned the ebullition. Major Cass seems to be quite popular with the government and people of Rome. His collection of antiques are very valuable. I noticed today among other things an old marble statue of Christ on the cross, a portrait of Columbus from life, also one of Americus Vespucius, which he intends presenting to Congress. I should like exceedingly to be in his position for several years just for the purpose of making a handsome collection of antiques.

Nov. 15. The climate of Rome is more disagreeable than any I have yet seen in Europe. RAIN, RAIN, RAIN is expected and duly received every day. Notwithstanding this, the streets are so filthy that I never like to venture outside the door of my hotel. Johnstone, Maney, and myself went out in search of pictures today, but failed in getting what we wanted, viz. a copy of Geode's *Hope* and *Beatrice*. We went into the studios of various artists who are assembled in Rome from all parts of the world to copy the pieces of the old masters and improve their style. With but few exceptions, the collections in Rome are inferior to those in Florence. Take out a few paintings in the Vatican by Raphael and the collections in one or two of the palaces, and Rome has very

[11] This cameo, an excellent piece of craftmanship, is owned now by Miss Margaret Lindsley Warden.

little to boast of, while the public and private galleries of Florence are rich in both ancient and modern paintings. After going through a number of picture shops (nearly every other house in Rome has old pictures for sale) we went to the Spada Palace to see Pompey's statue "at the foot of which Cæsar fell." It is 11 feet high and of Parian marble, holding a globe in one hand. The picture gallery in this palace contains several old and rare paintings of great value. After dinner I called on the Misses Thurston from New York and passed one hour. They are very clever but talk entirely too much. It seems that I would give almost anything to talk to a pretty girl from my own country. I have not met one since I left Paris.

Nov. 16. This morning I wrote letters until about 2:00 and then went with Johnstone to see some paintings, after which we returned to the hotel and received a call from a young man from South Carolina who is in delicate health and out of money. Johnstone loaned him $25, which he said was sufficient to carry him to Leghorn where he could get his passage on an American vessel for New York. It is very bad for one to be without money anywhere, and more particularly away from home and friends. After dinner I occupied four or five days [hours?] in reading the Last Days of Pompeii, which I find exceedingly interesting, particularly as I am about to visit Pompeii and there is no handbook for central Italy.

Nov. 17. This morning I took a carriage and drove to Signor Mazzioni's studio and purchased of him two pictures copied from the originals, viz. *Beatrice Cenci* and *Hope* by Geode.[12] I also purchased some engravings which I left with the paintings at Messers Packenham, Hooker and Company on the Piazza di Spagna, with directions to be forwarded to the care of John A. Underwood, Esq., Merchants Exchange, N. Y. Johnstone purchased a statue today called the Venus of the Shell, which he gave $300 for. It is one of the prettiest pieces of statuary that I have seen in Italy. The day has been occupied in making preparations to leave Rome tomorrow morning after a stay of three weeks, during which time it has rained nearly every day.

Nov. 18. This morning 11 Americans started from Rome for Naples by ventturini, who contracted to furnish us with our lodgings and provisions on the journey, a system very much in vogue throughout Italy. Our party consisted of the following persons: Misses Thurston of New York, and their brother; Colonel Kimmel; Ewing, Price, Maney,

---

[12] The painting of Beatrice Cenci is owned by Miss Margaret Lindsley Warden.

Fogg, Johnstone, and myself.[13] We passed down the Corso probably for the last time, gazed on the Capitol, Forum, and Coliseum once more, and then took leave of the "City of the Soul" via Porta Giovanni from which commences the new Appian Way. We dined at Albano in a hotel which was once a magnificent palace beautifully situated on a lofty hill and commanding a view of the campanga, Pompey's villa, and the sea. Stopped tonight at a hotel in Cisterna, the place where the "Tres Tabernæ" mentioned in the Acts of the Apostles, where the Christians repaired to meet Saint Paul. But the distance from Rome is sufficient to prove that this is an error. The habitations of the peasantry along the road today are made principally of poles fixed in a conical shape and covered with straw, giving it the appearance of a haystack. They have but one aperture serving for a door and build their fires in the center. The stock in this region have the same kind of shelter and man and beast fare pretty much alike. In one place I saw a village built entirely of these haystack habitations. The people in this region are mostly shepherds and spend their lives with their flocks and dogs. We met quite a number of wine carts today carrying the vintage to Rome in small casks. They have high wheels, short shafts, and a round awning on the top to protect the driver from the weather. Small bells are invariably attached to the back of the covering.

Nov. 19. Mr. Ewing being quite unwell today we did not start until the other carriage had started about half hour. We got off, however, in sufficient time to reach Mola, our resting place tonight. Soon after leaving Cisterna we entered the celebrated Pontine Marshes, which in ancient times contained the site of 23 of the most flourishing cities in Italy. These marshes are 24 miles in length and from 6 to 52 miles in breadth. They cover some of the best lands in Italy and only want an enterprising people to reclaim them and make good tillable lands of them. The Italians, however, are such a miserable race that they will never do anything towards improving their country. The road passes in a straight line through the marshes with two rows of elms on either side and a canal filled with water. A chain of the Appenines runs parallel with the road on one side and the sea is not far distant on the other. We dined today at Terracina, a beautiful village situated on the seashore. Here our passport was visaed and the doganna bribed by our *cocher* to let the baggage pass without examination.[14] From our window at the hotel in Mola we have a fine view of the town of Gaeta, the place where Pope Pius IX found refuge during the troubles of 1848

[13] The eleventh American, whom McGavock neglected to call by name, was Frank Parrish, the servant of Mr. E. H. Ewing.

[14] At this point the party was entering the Kingdom of the Two Sicilies.

and was visited by the King of Naples. The landlord of the hotel endeavored to play upon us the same trick that has been attempted on several occasions before in Italy—that of putting us in inferior rooms, reserving the best for the English who travel by post. We gave him a blow-up and were furnished with the best apartments.

Nov. 20. Set out from Mola at 8:00 and reached Capua in the night. It was our intention to go on to Naples, but our horses gave out and the weather is so bad that we concluded to remain tonight at Capua, situated at a distance of three miles from the ancient city and 15 miles from Naples, occupies the site of Casilinum on the Volturno, 12 miles from its mouth. The town is now occupied by the military, which compelled us to seek lodgings in a room some distance from the hotel. Five of us slept in one room, and two of us in one bed. Before retiring we all took seats around a brazier filled with coals and chatted about the inclemency of the weather, the filthiness of Capua, and our eternal horror of all vetturini and Italians generally. Fleas and filth seem to be all the go in Capua. We dined today at Saint Azeta and passed through the little town of Fondi, which contains the most curious looking population that I have ever seen. The men all have a haggard appearance, wear long red cloaks thrown over their shoulders like the Spaniards, and look like they would as soon run a dagger into a man as not. The inhabitants were all out in the street and kept up such a chattering that we could hear nothing that was said by our party. It was about dusk when we passed through Fondi and all the inhabitants seemed to be going into the church to say their evening prayers, I suppose. Poor, ignorant and degraded people. They know nothing of the comforts of life, the beauties of religion, or the duties of man.

Nov. 21. After eating a miserable breakfast in a cafe, we got on the railroad and reached Naples about 10:00. We reached the city in a storm and had great trouble at the depot and reached the Hotel in a heavy rain. We stopped at a Hotel fronting on the bay and called the Hotel de Estrangers. Our sitting room is large and well furnished and some of our bedrooms good. The view is beautiful, embracing the entire bay, the Islands of Capri and Ischia, Mount Vesuvius, the ancient cities of Herculaneum and Pompeii, and a number of small towns that stud the shores of the bay. The bay is terminated by two capes—that of Misenum to the right, and of Minerva to the left—and is closed by the Island of Capri. A part of the city extends to the west in the form of an amphitheatre on the hills of Posilippo, Saint Erno, and Antignano. Another part to the East is a plain covered with villas from the Ponte della Maddalena to Portici and to Vesuvius. Towards the north Naples is surrounded by a ridge of hills which separates it from the Terra di Lavoro or those fertile plains the Campagna Felix, called by the Romans their richest patrimony. The bay of Naples is certainly very beautiful but inferior in my opinion to that of New York. It is large and safe but not so well protected as that of New York.

Nov. 22. This morning Colonel Kimmel and Price came to our hotel, having gone to the Hotel del Universo at first with the Thurstons. This afternoon we took a walk through the gardens of Chiaja [Chiagi?], situated on the Bay and used as a kind of fashionable promenade. We then walked through some of the principal streets to the Palace Royal, a large building used as the residence of the King. From this point we had an excellent view of Vesuvius, which has now been at rest for one year. The summit was enveloped in clouds and if any smoke ascended, we could not discover it. Passing along today, several things attracted my attention, viz. a Greek merchant dressed in his native costume who accosted us in English and invited us into his store where he exhibited a beautiful collection of Turkish articles; the lazaroni in the streets are as numerous as represented, and quite annoying; the cab horses in Naples are driven without bits, but the reins are attached to bands fastened around the nose. I saw the Queen in a carriage today. She is about 40 or 50 years of age. The carriage stopped, she got out and kneeled on a cushion in the center of the street, and [was] surrounded by Lazaroni, who were also on their knees. The meaning of the ceremony was not exactly understood by myself, but I supposed she was religious. At our table d'hote today I counted 14 Americans out of 16 persons. One of the Englishmen evinced his ignorance at the table by asking one of us what the governor of a state meant.

Nov. 23. Well after writing all morning I have succeeded in bringing up this journal which I allowed to get behind at least ten days. Some of the party went to church this morning in the English chapel and returned complaining that they had to pay 50c at the door for entrance money. This afternoon we took a long walk in the gardens fronting on the bay and enjoyed much the splashing of the waves against the shore and the tossing to and fro of a little boat in which were men shooting ducks. This garden stretches along the bay for some distance and contains fine groves and a number of fountains and statuary. It is the favorite promenade in the evening. We met many strangers—and mostly English. This evening we all went to the San Carlo theatre, which is the largest and most splendidly furnished house in Europe. It has six tiers, the fronts of which are beautifully carved and gilded. The boxes are all lined with red velvet and damask curtains. The parquette is so arranged that all can see; the seats are of iron, entire with cushions. The scenes of the stage are gotten up with great taste and the orchestra is very fine. The opera tonight was very good and the ballet superb. In looking round the house I observed but little beauty. Nearly every other man in the house was a soldier; among them I noticed several American officers belonging to the Independence, now lying in the bay under the command of Commodore Morgan. Passing along today I observed some boys playing a game of ball which they rolled on a small stick in their hands through an iron ring fastened in the ground.[15]

Nov. 24. This morning we set out from our hotel to see the Studio (or museum), passing through the Palazza Royal and up a very busy street called the Strada del Toledo. Immediately opposite the palace of the King we went into the church of Saint Francis de Paolo, a modern construction in the form of a circular temple with two rows of semi-circular porticos supported by columns. The interior is decorated with paintings by Camuccini and other modern artists of celebrity. The building containing the museum is one of the largest and finest in Naples. The first room that we entered contains a number of old vases, statues, and mummies taken from the ruins of Pompeii. The second room contains some paintings of an inferior character and a large collection of statuary forming the inheritance of the Farnese family at Rome and those discovered in the excavations of Herculaneum and Pompeii. I noticed in this collection a full-length statue of Cicero and also one of Homer, besides a number of busts of eminent characters of antiquity—such as Lycurgus, Euripedes, Socrates, etc. Several singular figures are in this room made of dark-colored marble with white marble attached for the hands and face, giving them the appearance of clothed figures. There is a large mosaic about 20 feet broad and 16 feet wide found at Pompeii and representing a battle between Alexander and Darius. I observed also a large porphory vase brought by Hannibal from Hadrian's Villa. We then entered a room of bronzes. I saw a bust of Seneca which is the exact image of General [Zachary] Taylor. We were next conducted upstairs in a room containing many fine stones and cameos of antiquity, among which is the finest cameo in the world—belonging to the King of Naples. It was found, according to tradition, in the Tomb of Hadrian by a soldier who sold it for a very small sum. It is now valued at one million of dollars. On one side is represented the head of Medusa and on the other that of Alexander. It is certainly very beautiful. We were also shown in this apartment some bread found in Pompeii with the baker's mark upon it, paints found in a shop

[15] This was probably a kind of croquet or closh.

in Pompeii, and some cloth made out of asbestos and found in Greece. In the picture gallery I observed a beautiful Annunciation by Pinturicchio and some fine paintings by Caracci, Schidone, and Correggio. A picture representing the Three Ages is very fine.—Napoleon as Jupiter, and Josephine, Mary Magdalene by Albano, portrait of Columbus, etc. The next room contained cooking utensils used in Pompeii, an old bell with a flat piece of iron suspended from the thing used in our country to fasten the singletree to the plow and struck with a hammer to make it sound. The papyrus manuscripts found in Herculaneum and Pompeii and the ingenious mechanism employed in unrolling them is here exhibited. The library [is] composed of 150,000 printed volumes and 3,000 manuscripts. A collection, unique for its number and beauty, of vases called Etruscan medals, sculptures, and other objects in bronze, antique glassware, and provisions found in these two cities, paintings from the excavations of those cities, cork models of the ancient theatre of Herculaneum and of the temples at Pestum. This is one of the richest museums in Europe. In walking the streets today, I observed several peculiarities, viz. the figure of Christ and Madonna on the bows of the little boats and on the handles of cooking utensils; women money changers on the street behind a small table filled with coppers, carrying vegetables in large baskets on donkeys from house to house; pimps who annoy strangers to death by asking if you will have a woman, boy, beast or foul. This afternoon I walked down to the light house and saw the Independence at anchor in the bay and the arrival of the French steamer.

Nov. 25. Colonel Kimmel and I called on Mr. Harnet this morning to procure tickets of admission to the palaces and other public places about Naples. He is our consul here and has been in office 40 years. We then went to the museum and examined some of the apartments that we omitted yesterday. The collection of frescoes found in Pompeii are very extensive and curious. The Farnese Bull and the Hercules are two of the finest pieces of statuary in Europe. We then took a carriage and drove out to Campo Santo (or cemetery), one of the most curious places about Naples. It is essentially the city of the dead. Those that are able have private chapels, and are either placed in the wall of the Chapel or in the vault below. Many of these chapels are connected, covering a large space and forming a hollow square which is paved with lava, beneath which are deep pits where the Lazaroni are thrown after death. A Capuchin conducted us over the premises and politely consented to remove the stone that covered one of these pits for us to look into. It was about 50 feet deep and 15 square, containing bodies in various stages of putrification. The effluvia was horrible and the appearance of the bodies sickening. They have 365 vaults of this description (one for each day of the year). The bodies are cast in promiscuously without any garments and a register is kept containing an accurate description of every death. The view from Campo Santo is very fine, commanding Vesuvius, the bay, and the city of Naples. Returning to Naples we drove through many of the streets, which are very narrow, dark, and without sidewalks. Balconies are attached to nearly every window and the houses range from four to eight stories. Passing through the center of the city we went to the Grotto in the west end. It is a road through a hill a third of a mile in length; the length is about 1500 feet and the width sufficient for two carriages to pass; the roads originally passed over the hill. The Grotto was probably made by the Cumacans and Neopolitans in order to facilitate their communication. It was enlarged under Don Pedro di Toledo. Over the entrance of the Grotto is the remains of the tomb called the Tomb of Virgil, said to have been placed here by order of Augustus, who desired the remains of the poet to be interred in Naples, his favorite residence. No traces exist either of the urn or columns. Its external form is that of a tower rendered picturesque by the ways [walks] and plants that surround it. Leaving the tomb we walked through the gardens to our hotel, stopping on the way to examine some coral work and other little ornaments peculiar to Naples. After dinner the party amused themselves as usual narrating adventures and examining stories.

Nov. 26. Left Naples at 9:00 on the railroad for ancient city of Pompeii, about 16 miles distant, passing through several small towns on the bay. The city is situated on an elevation about one-half mile from the base of Vesuvius. The excavation made here in the last few years has brought to light many relics of antiquity that are invaluable. But as I have noted these curiosities in my discussion of the museum, I will merely put down my impressions of the place. The streets are crooked, with sidewalks, and their names [are] cut on the curbstones. The houses are built of small bricks and composed of one or two stories, generally enclosed in a square court surrounded with porticos where the doors are placed. In the center of the court is a well or reservoir of water. The rooms on the ground floor are without internal communication; they are small but lofty; the greater part without windows receive the light from the door; [they] have a ceiling and are paved with mosaics; the walls are covered with figures of various descriptions, and the architectural views on a white, red, or yellow ground. We were conducted first to the house of Arrius Diomedes by a soldier placed there to prevent spoilation and pilfering. This house is situated outside the walls in the suburbs in the direction of Vesuvius. Its interior is a long square surrounded with a portico supported by stuccoed pilasters. In the middle was a small garden with six columns, a basin of white marble, and a well. Some of the rooms are painted on a red ground with figures and arabesques. A skeleton supposed to be that of Diomedes was found here holding in one hand a key, in the other coins and gold ornaments; behind this another holding bronze and silver vases. Under the garden portico is a cellar which contains many of the vases used by the ancients for preserving wine. Two staircases lead to the second story placed in the middle of a covered court with 14 brick stuccoed columns and a mosaic pavement. We then examined the custom house and public granaries which are very small considering the accounts given by historians. In the same street a bake shop was pointed out, which contained an oven very like those used at the present day and one or two grinding machines made of hard stone and made precisely on the same principle of our back mills. The houses of Caius Sallustius, Vettius, and Pressius are along the finest. The rooms are generally small and lewd frescoes are visible on the walls. The temples, amphitheatre, and public houses are all built pretty much on the same principle. The public baths are quite perfect, consisting of a circular apartment with niches and a large marble basin in the center. Warm and cold baths were given as in the present day. Adjoining this was a large room for wiping off and dressing. Places for keeping the perfumes and linens are still to be seen in the side of the wall. The Temple of Isis, Tragic Theatre, and Temple of Music are all interesting ruins from which many valuable curiosities have been taken and deposited in the museum. Many beautiful mosaics and frescoes are still in Pompeii, but are guarded by soldiers to keep persons from taking them. On the front steps of many of the doors I observed either the word *Have* or *Salva,* meaning welcome, in mosaic. After roving about several hours through these old ruins of brick and mortar we returned to the railway station and were highly amused at some rustic music and antics performed by the servile Italians for a few Grannies [?] while we were waiting for the cars. Reached Naples at 6:00—time enough for dinner.

Nov. 27. This morning being rather favorable, a party of ten left the Hotel des Estrangers for the summit of Vesuvius—consisting of an English gentleman and his lady, together with the following persons from America: Mr. Edward Henriques and lady, corner of 13th Street and Fifth Avenue, New York; Colonel Kimmel of Maryland; William C. Johnstone of South Carolina; Edwin H. Ewing, Henry Maney, H. M. R. Fogg, James B. Price, and Frank Parrish of Tennessee. We left the hotel at 9:00 and reached here again at 6:00, after toiling hard all day. As we were going to Vesuvius we stopped and examined the old theatre in Herculaneum, discovered in 1689 by some inhabitants of Resina, having dug to the depth of 65 feet for a well, found remains of valuable marbles and inscriptions relative to Herculaneum. From this point some took horses and others walked to that part of the mountain where the ascent is very abrupt. Here the ladies were carried in a chair, fastened on poles, by four stout Italians. The gentlemen were also assisted by holding on to straps thrown over the shoulders of an Italian. The man who pulled me up did not seem to mind it much, as he carried a basket filled with wine, apples, and eggs on one arm for the use of the party. This part of Vesuvius is exceedingly rough and difficult of ascent, but we tugged on and finally reached the summit, where we looked down to the depth of 600 feet into the burning crater. At times the sulphurous smoke was almost suffocating until a breeze would pass over and relieve us. I eat several eggs roasted on the edge of the crater. While walking down into the mouth of the crater my stick, which happened to sink too deep below the surface, took fire and induced me to return very soon. The views from various points in ascending Vesuvius —of Naples, the bay, and the many little towns along the coast—are really very beautiful. Vesuvius is situated between two mountains, one called the Somma, the other the Ottajano. Though separated, these mountains have a common base. It is supposed that formerly they were united and that their separation is due to an eruption which rendered them craters. Vesuvius has the form of a cone; its perpendicular height is 3,373 feet, the circumference of which the three mountains at the base is 30 miles. Three roads lead to the summit—that of Saint Sebastian to the north, of Ottajano to the east, of Resina, which is the most frequented, to the west. At Resina are conductors who serve as guides to the crater, the circumference of which is 5,624 feet. The form and surface of the crater are sometimes convex, at others concave. The species of crust of which it consists is formed by lava, scoria, sand, ashes, and other volcanic matters. At the periods of eruption the lava spreads over the soil like a torrent, forming small hillocks during its course, and when deprived of its natural heat, it assumes the hardness of marble, in which state it is used for paving Naples and the neighboring towns.

Nov. 28. This morning the same party that ascended Vesuvius made an excursion west of Naples as far as Baiæ, celebrated in ancient times for the number and magnificence of its villas. Horace preferred Baiæ to all other places. Cæsar, Pompey, Marius, and other distinguished public men had villas on this coast, which is very beautiful, surpassing as is thought by *some* the bay of Naples. We saw a great many things today and all I can do is barely to mention their names. The first place after passing the Grotto and Virgil's Tomb was a small lake called Agnano, surrounded with hills formed by the lava and extinct volcanoes. It is about three miles in circumference and is very deep, being the crater of an ancient volcano. In its vicinity are remains of parts of the ancient Thermæ, called the Stuffi di San Germano, consisting of small rooms in which the heat of the vapor rises to 39 and 40° of Reaumur. The lake is in constant ebulition from the vapors below. Near the lake is the Grotto del Cane, mentioned by Pliny and is dug on a sandy soil at the depth of ten feet, a height of nine, and a breadth of four feet. A light inodorous vapor rises about six inches from the soil. The interior of the Grotto is without encrustations or any deposit of saline matter. This Grotto, formerly called the Cavern of Charon, derives its present appellation from the experiments made on a dog who would die at the end of two minutes if not restored to the open air. When we reached the Grotto an old woman was standing at the door with a little dog tied with a string ready to receive us. Between Lake Agnano and Pozzuoli is the Solfatara, called by the ancients *Forum Vulcani,* situated in a narrow plain surrounded by the Monti Lucogei, or Phlegrean Fields, was considered at the time of Pliny and Strabo as a volcano not entirely extinct. Several apertures exhale a heated vapor in which the smell of sulphur and ammonia predominate. Flames are visible during the night, when the fire is also more distinctly heard. The Solfatara appears to have been a mountain, the summit of which fell in by the violent action of a volcano. The noise produced by the rolling of a stone on the surface would indicate that the interior is hollow. Numerous mineral waters exist near this spot represented by the poets of antiquity and that where Hercules fought with the giants. Leaving this place we passed through the town of Pozzuoli, stopping to see the Temple of Serapis and the amphitheatre or coliseum. Going a little farther we passed the lakes of Lucrin and Averno and a little farther towards Baiæ are the ruins of the Temples of Diana, Mercury, Venus, etc. We returned to Naples via the coast and enjoyed a delightful view. When I reached the hotel I found Colonel Bryan of Tennessee, who has been endeavoring to overtake me for some time past. He showed me a New York paper that contained the arrival of Aunt Felicia and party in that city. After dinner we all assembled in our large parlour and had a real American jollyfication.

Nov. 29. This morning I went to the banker's and drew 20 pounds, after which I went among the coral shops looking for ornaments to give to friends at home, and also some lava work, which I think quite pretty.[16] This afternoon Fogg and Maney set off on the Marseilles steamer for Paris and thence home. When our hotel bill was presented, we found a pretty charge for broken furniture, which all considered unreasonable and unjust.[17] The landlord was called up and quite a quarrel ensued which resulted in nine of us leaving the Hotel des Etrangers and coming to the Hotel d'Univers, where we have much better apartments and a finer view of the gardens and the bay. After dinner we called for a pack of cards and had a nice little game of whist. We enjoyed this evening—for the first time—a clear sunset.

Nov. 30. This morning our party joined a part of Baltimoreans staying at the Hotel New York and started out in a small boat to see the American frigate Independence now lying in the bay. Before we reached the vessel we were overtaken by the police, who wished to turn us back intimating at the same time that a little *kelker chose* (quelquechose) would let us pass. Colonel Kimmel was our spokesman on the occasion. Pulling a printed paper out of his pocket resembling a pass, he gave a policeman some of his artillery and ordered the boatman to row ahead. We were too late to hear the sermon performed by the chaplain, but were very kindly received by the officers, conducted over every part of the ship, and made to feel like we were once more in our own happy land. I exchanged cards on board with a young midshipman named T. W. Hester from about Fayetteville, Tennessee, and Joseph M. Bradford from Huntsville, Alabama. Returning to the Hotel New York, we were allowed by the landlord to see the corpse of the Greek Ambassador who died of consumption and was laid out in state. His flesh looked like wax. Returning to the hotel, we walked through the public gardens where we met Robert Hume of Charleston, who travelled with us on the Rhine and in Switzerland. After dinner we went to the opera at San Carlo. It was thinly attended. When the opera was over we went to the Caffe de Europa and got some refreshments and then called with a *man* to see a pretty Italian woman.

Dec. 1. This has been one of the most disagreeable days that I have experienced in Naples. The rain has fallen incessantly, and there is no pleasure in seeing sights in inclement weather. After writing three

[16] A piece of brain coral which McGavock bought in Naples and had shipped home survived the journey and the intervening decades. It is now owned by Miss Margaret Lindsley Warden.

[17] The broken furniture was probably the result of the "American jollyfication" on November 28.

or four hours, I went with Colonel Bryan to his banker's, which I found, like most of the banking establishments in Italy, to be in the sixth story and an out-of-the-way place. When I returned to the hotel I found several American papers, in one of which I noticed the death of my old friend Miss Septima Fogg. Her brother left Naples on Saturday with the view of reaching home before the crisis. She was a lady that I estimated very highly and I lament her early dissolution.

Dec. 2. This morning we got our passports and procured tickets on the French steamer for the island of Malta, for which we paid 24 dollars. We then went through the King's city palace. It is one of the largest, best furnished, and neatest palaces that I have seen in Italy. Many of the rooms are painted in imitation of those in Pompeii. The frescoes and paintings are also very fine. The walls of the throne room are covered with crimson velvet and gold. A strong military force is constantly kept in the palace to guard the royal family. We then took a carriage and drove to another large palace of the King's—on a lofty hill which commands a fine view of the city and bay. Mr. Hester of the Frigate Independence dined with us today.

Dec. 3. This morning was occupied in paying bills and packing trunks. At 12:00 we went to the police office and received a ticket of health, without which we could not get upon the steamer for Malta. At 2:00 the passengers were all assembled and duly counted, and at 3:00 we drew up the anchor and started. Just before leaving we received a note from Mr. Bradford of Huntsville, Alabama, saying that the Independence would salute us as we passed, and all the Americans—twelve in number—were prepared to return the compliment. The steamer ran very close to the vessel; the Stars and Stripes were floating; and the notes of Hail, Columbia! were distinctly heard. We gave them three hearty cheers for America and bid adieu to the beautiful city of Naples and to smoking Vesuvius amid the shouts of our countrymen. The Bay of Naples is certainly beautiful—and more so from the sea. The island of Capri, with the ruins of old Tiberius' palace crowning its summit, the Grotto, the Isle of Ischia, the lofty cone of Vesuvius, surrounded by a field of lava, and the long line of buildings around the bay, render it a magnificent panorana, well deserving the praise of the poet, the pencil of the painter, and the admiration of everyone. Colonel Kimmel, our old travelling companion, starts tomorrow for Rome, Colonel Bryan for home, etc. The following named Americans embarked today on the same steamer for the Island of Malta: Edwin H. Ewing and self and James B. Price of Tennessee; William C. Johnstone of

South Carolina; Brevard of North Carolina; Thurston and his sisters; and two brothers named [John and Lewis] Bridge from New York.

Dec. 4. After an unpleasant night's rest in my clothes, I rose early and found that we were near the island of Strombolli, which rises high in the sea, shaped like a cone. Near it are the islands of Salina, Lipari, Vulcano, Parnaria, and Basiluzzi. In the distance the snowcovered summit of Mount Etna was visible. Etna is much higher than Vesuvius, but not so pretty. About 8:00 we passed through the renowned Scilla and Charibdis. Scilla rises abruptly from the sea on the Italian shore and is now the site of a village of that name. Charibdis, just opposite, looks like a bar extending into the sea. The rock has disappeared. A short distance south of these two celebrated points is the town of Messina, situated on a hillside with a beautiful bay and strong fortifications. The steamer remained in the harbor five or six days [?] and the passengers all went ashore and walked through the town. The church of Saint Gregorini is the finest building in the place. The streets of Messina are very filthy and there is nothing in the town to attract the stranger's attention. There is a considerable trade between Sicily and the U. S., and it increases rapidly. While lying in the harbor another French steamer came alongside and had on board a number of Americans who have been making a pedestrian tour through Sicily. This evening we had a glorious sunset and bid adieu to the shores of Europe with a right good will.

Dec. 5. We entered the harbor of Valletta, the modern capitol of Malta at daylight this morning. After some detention, we procured a boat, came ashore, and put up at a very good hotel on the Strada Reale in the center of the city, kept by Mrs. Dunsford. After breakfast we procured a guide and visited our banker's and made the necessary inquiry relative to the departure of the steamer for Alexandria. This being finished, we commenced the work of sightseeing and done up the town in short order. First of all we went round and examined the fortifications, which are the most extensive and strongest in the Mediterranean. They were built by the knights of old of a soft tertiary limestone. The English church built by Queen Adelaide is quite handsome and the only spire in Valletta. The cathedral dedicated to Saint John the patron of the order is not remarkable or attractive externally. It was built by the Grand Master John de la Cassiere. Some of the bells are said to have been brought from Rhodes. The interior affords a rich field for the study of the art and taste of the 16th and 17th centuries. The floor is a mosaic pavement, chiefly composed of the sepulchral monuments of the knights, whose effigies in full costume are represented in white marble. The Chapel of the Madonna contains some 6 or 8 keys said to be the keys of Jerusalem, Acre, and Rhodes. The railing in front of the chapel is made of solid silver. From the cathedral we went into the Palace of the *Grand Master,* now the residence of the British governor. It contains several fine halls and an armory. In the armory I observed many curious things used by the old knights, and among them a cannon made of rope and lined inside of copper—spurs, swords, and armor used in old times. I tried on the armour of the Grand Master Vignacourt, which is inlaid with gold. From the palace we took a small boat for two shillings and went out into the harbor to see the English Fleet. They have about 10 vessels in the Mediterranean, including her war steamers. We boarded the Queen, one of the ships of the line, and was politely conducted by one of the officers over the vessel, who explained everything. She has 120 guns and 3000 men on board. I do not think that the English keep their decks so clear or that they manage their vessels so well as our American sailors. The Bay of Valletta is well protected from the sea and is formed by a succession of creeks, into which vessels run in perfect safety. The Quarentine harbor is also very safe and convenient. Valletta is noted for the number of its steps, by which communication is kept up from street to street. Several flights must be ascended before reaching the Strada Reale. The women of Malta all wear black silk scarfs over their heads. The Maltese carriage is a heavy, lumbering concern capable of holding 4 persons, drawn by one horse, and with two wheels.

Dec. 6. Valletta is laid off at right angles and built of stone houses with projecting windows. The streets are kept perfectly clean and it is one of the most agreeable places that I have visited since I left Paris. This morning we procured a carriage and drove out to Citta Vecchia on the opposite side of the island, passing through a barren waste of rocks. Citta Vecchia was at one time the chief town of Malta, but has been superseded by Valletta. The catacombs here are very extensive and worth visiting. From the top of the cathedral we had a fine view of the island and Saint Paul's bay, where the Apostle was shipwrecked—also the grotto where he lived as the guest of Publius—Bible, Acts 28. The houses on this place are constructed of tertiary limestone, mostly square, with flat roofs. Beggars very numerous and persevering. Valletta is furnished with water by an aqueduct similar to the old Roman aqueduct from Citta Vecchia. On the road we stopped to see several jackasses so celebrated in America. A jack that would sell for 100 or 150 dollars in Tennessee can be purchased here for 90 or 100. In the royal gardens near Valletta we found a large number of orange trees laden with fruit, of which we tasted and found to be excellent. At 5:00 every evening the military band plays on the square fronting the governor's palace. The music is good but not equal to the bands in Italy and Germany. Had an excellent dinner at 6:00. The fruits were very superior. Melons and green peas were on the table.

Dec. 7. The first thing on docket this morning was to visit the French packet office and take our passage for Alexandria. Fortunately there was but few passengers from Marseilles, and we had no difficulty in procuring good berths. Our passage money was exorbitant, being 280 francs. This steamer brought the news of a dispatch having reached Marseilles from Paris stating that Louis Napoleon had dissolved the National Assembly and proclaimed himself dictator. This same report has been received several times recently, and there is some probability of such an event ultimately taking place.[18] After procuring my passage I returned to my hotel and occupied myself until 4:00 writing a descriptive letter of Switzerland. At 5:00 we went on board the French steamer and set off from Valetta to the ancient city of Alexandria. The news of the death of the King of Hanover, who was the uncle of Queen Victoria, had just been received in Valletta and the flags of the fleet were half mast and all the bells in the city tolling, which produced a fine effect as we were making our way out into the deep blue Mediterranean. The lighthouse at this place is considered one of the best in the Mediterranean and is visible far away, serving as a beacon to guard vessels from her rock-bound coast. The English are particularly fortunate in possessing the little island. It is a kind of key to the Mediterranean and is impregnable to foreign assaults.

Dec. 8. This morning all is beautiful and clear, the passengers all out on deck, talking, walking, and smoking according to their pleasure. Out of 10 first class passengers, I numbered 8 Americans, a Russian Prince, and an Englishman. Among the second class passengers are four Sisters of Charity belonging to the order of Saint Joseph. They are on their way to Jerusalem, where they expect to establish a school for the children of all nations. One of them asked me if I was a Catholic. I replied negatively and she said that if I went to the Holy Land I would certainly go home a good Catholic. She also told Mr. Bridges of New York, who has lost his voice from some bronchial affliction, that Saint Joseph could cure him, etc. Mr. Ewing and Price and myself was all desperately seasick today.

---

[18] The coup d'état which Louis Napoleon Bonaparte effected on December 2, 1851, and the events immediately following brought another Bonaparte to dictatorial power as Napoleon III, and thus began the Second French Empire.

Dec. 9. Finding it rather dull on board I took up Stephen's Travels in Egypt and commenced reading them. They were written in 1835 but are still interesting to one going to that country. Warburton's Travels are also very entertaining. About noon today our captain, who like all Frenchmen is very civil, pointed out to us the low coast of Barbary. We were not sufficiently near to form any idea of the country. Several small schooners passed us today bound towards Malta. The sea in this quarter does not seem to be much traversed by trading vessels. Our steamer is called the *Nil,* belongs to a French company, rolls terribly, and is upon the whole a tolerable boat.

Dec. 10. Among our passengers bound for the Nile is a young Englishman apparently of fortune, but exceedingly verdant as to the ways of the world. He laid in a stock of wine and provisions sufficient to last 6 men up the Nile. He seems to have taken Murray for his guide and every little foolish item that he puts down as requisite the poor young fellow has provided. Among the list of stores I observed 6 dozen bottles of ale, one basket of champagne, one barrel of potatoes, rice, coffee, tea, sugar, etc.—besides a gun, fishing tackle, etc. Nothing has occurred on board today worth noting. The rain rendered it too disagreeable to stay on deck and we were compelled to resort to books or anything else to while away the time.

Dec. 11. Rose early this morning expecting to see the ancient land of Egypt, but was disappointed. No land was yet visible. After walking the deck for several hours, we descried in the dim distance the outlines of Pompey's Pillar, the Pharoahs, and new lighthouse, and the masts of vessels consisting of merchantmen, men-of-war, and other craft. As we neared the harbor the wind was blowing and the rain descending in torrents. We stood out a short time waiting for a pilot, but as none came our captain concluded to venture—and on we came to our place of anchorage near the Pasha's Harem and palace. As soon as the anchor was cast the steamer was surrounded by a number of small boats rowed by half-naked Arabs who wished to carry us ashore. At last 6 of us got into one of the boats, leaving the courier and Frank [Parrish] to take care of the baggage. Before reaching the shore the rascally Arabs demanded their pay, fearing that we would not give them enough and actually dropped their oars and refused to go on. Mr. Ewing and I drew our pistols and told them to carry us ashore or we would shoot them, a threat that soon brought them to their senses. When we reached the shore, each of us mounted a small donkey and rode through the muddy streets and rain to the Hotel Europa, amid the shouts of Arabs and our own loud laughter. On our way Johnstone's donkey fell with him and rolled his new suit of fancy stripes in a mudhole, much to our amusement and his discomfiture.

Dec. 12. We all called this morning on our consul, Mr. McCauley of North Carolina.[19] He is a Democrat and has acted as an officer of the government at different points for the last 20 years. His wife and daughter came into the room. They were very polite and invited us to take a family dinner with them on Sunday. We then returned to our hotel, which is situated on a large and handsome square in the Frank Quarter and procured an omnibus in which we drove to the canal back of the city to look at some Nile boats. Eight or ten were lying together, but none of them equalled my expectations. Returning we passed through a long avenue of trees to Pompey's Pillar, which is a tall round granite column with a Corinthian capitol. It is situated on a slight eminence commanding a view of the city, the sea, and Lake Mareotis. Near Pompey's Pillar is a modern cemetery; over each grave I noticed a brick tomb plastered over, looking like a bake oven, with a small round hole in the top, and an aloe planted in it. Around the Pillar also is a number of small houses built of mud and occupied by a swarm of miserable, sore-eyed Arabs that look more like brutes than humans. We also saw Cleopatra's Needle, which stands near the sea. It is nearly underminded. Some of the characters are nearly defaced by time and some are quite distinct. It stands a venerable monument of the past.[20]

Dec. 13. Rose quite early this morning and took a ride on a donkey through the streets. The little Arab boy who drove the donkey first carried me through a narrow street called the Turkish Bazaar, which was lined with small shops in which there was a large Arab sitting with his legs crossed tailor fashion smoking his pipe leisurely and waiting for customers. I then went to one of the slave markets and found a number of Nubian slaves valued at from 50 to 75 dollars—according to age and looks. When I started out of the establishment, they closed doors upon me and cried out *backshish* (tobacco).[21] Finding that they would not let me out without some trouble, I paid them sixpence and returned to the hotel. After paying the master for the use of his donkey, the little boy who drove me followed on after me begging for money, whereupon his master fell upon him and gave him a severe bastinadoing. After breakfast Mr. McCauley called and set an hour or so. We then agreed to take our Nile boat from this point instead of Cairo, employed a

[19] Daniel Smith McCauley (or McAuley) served as American Consul at Tripoli in 1831 and Consul General at Alexandria from 1845 until his death in 1852.

[20] McGavock bought a two-foot bronze replica of Cleopatra's Needle at some point during his journey; it is now owned by Miss Margaret Lindsley Warden.

[21] In *A Tennessean Abroad,* "backshish" is translated as "gift" by McGavock.

dragoman, selected our boat and drew up the usual contract. Our expenses according to the arrangement will average about 16 shillings each per day. There are many peculiarities to be sure in this city, some of which I will notice briefly: Donkeys answer instead of cabs; Camels for transporting things. We frequently see 8 or 10 tied together and heavily loaded with goods. The military are all black and cut a ludicrous figure on parade. At night every person is required by law to carry a lantern and if he is found without one the guard cries out and he is imprisoned. I have witnessed several funeral processions in the last two days and they are very curious. Little children go before crying out to the top of their voices, then come the men bearing a gaudy-looking coffin on their shoulders, and followed by a number of women with covered faces crying most piteously. The females here all go with their faces covered, with the exception of the eyes, which show through a small aperture in the covering.

Dec. 14. This morning I was aroused by the sound of sparrows and the cries of camel drivers carrying water from house to house on their backs in leather bags, out of which they draw into the skins of hogs or goats instead of buckets. Another odd custom attracted my attention today, viz. a child with its head shaved with the exception of a small patch on top and carried astride of the mother's shoulder. The women and men here shave their privates, so I have been told. The barbers here are also dentists. At 1:00 John Bridge, Johnstone, and myself complied with an invitation to dine with our consul, Mr. McCauley, where we met all of his family, including two sons-in-law, Mr. Moore, an Irishman, and Mr. Longshaw, an Englishman, and Mr. Gilbert, the English consul. We had an excellent dinner and agreeable company. After smoking and chatting a while, we were invited to take a ride on horseback. Accepting, we all mounted very good horses and rode out to the race course, which is about one mile outside the gates of the city. Returning, we went to Mr. Longshaw's house, where we had an excellent supper and passed a pleasant evening with the exception that none of them could pronounce or recollect my name. They were excessively polite, so much so that they furnished us with two guns to use on the Nile and undertook to have made for us an American Flag and Penant. In the course of conversation with Mr. McCauley, the subject of establishing a line of camels between Saint Louis and Santa Fe was introduced. He thought that the government would do well to try the experiment and appropriate $20,000 towards it for military and postal purposes. The fact of the camel being able to go so far and so long without food or drink is decidedly an advantage, and for many reasons stated by him I am disposed to receive the suggestion as a good one. He has communicated with the State Department, but they have taken no action in the matter.[22] We returned to our hotel about 10:00, listened to an Italian grind an organ for a time, and then retired.

Dec. 15. It seems as if the rain will follow us eternally. Ever since we left Martigny in Switzerland, we have had inclement weather with the exception of only a few days. Remained in my room all day and wrote two letters for the Union—one describing Venice and the other Milan. Called on the English consul this afternoon and went with him to see the yacht that was beaten by the American at Southampton. It is a very pretty boat, well fitted out, but not so well suited for just running as our boats. A party of Americans arrived today at our hotel from Constantinople.

Dec. 16. This morning we started to walk to the Pasha's Palace, but finding it rather muddy we mounted donkeys and rode. The exterior of the palace and harem are not very fine, but the interior is fitted up in a style both comfortable and elegant. The walls are covered with figured silk and some of the floors are made of ebony inlaid with ivory. My donkey driver, who could speak a little English, was our interpreter and was allowed to walk on those beautiful floors in his bare and dirty feet. The present Pasha sleeps in a bed, whereas his father and all his predecessors slept on the floor. At present the Pasha is in Cairo. On our return we stopped to see an infant school. The teacher and children were all seated in the Turkish manner, repeating their letters from small boards. The teacher was very polite, invited me to take a seat by his side on his coattail, and offered me a pipe as usual. Coming along a little farther, my little guide showed us a mill where they were grinding wheat. It was exceedingly primitive in its structure and reminded me of our old-fashioned mills in the west. Mr. McCauley sent us our flag and penant today, both of which are very handsome. The most of the day has been occupied in writing a letter upon Milan. Had a game of whist, but was unlucky. Mr. Ewing and I lost every game.

Dec. 17. Today we all went to our consul's and had our contract witnessed, and also closed the contract with the owner of the boat, who

[22] In the National Archives, Washington, D. C., in "Despatches from D. S. McCauley to Daniel Webster, Secretary of State," there is a letter dated May 15, 1851, in which McCauley recommends the introduction of the "Swift Camel" or dromedary "to tie together" the Eastern and Western parts of the United States after the acquisition of New Mexico and California. McCauley enclosed a long, detailed report with drawings. Action was taken about three years later. On March 3, 1855, the Thirty-Third Congress approved a bill directing the War Department to purchase camels for military purposes. A report on this experiment, made while Jefferson Davis was Secretary of War, was published in *Sen. Ex. Doc.* No. 62, 34th Cong., 3d Sess., 1857.

was very kind, leaving us with a small library to use on the Nile. News reached Alexandria today confirming the news brought by the French steamer relative to the dissolution of the Assembly and of Napoleon's having declared himself dictator, and of the imprisonment of Thiers, Dumas and others.[23] The weather has been so bad today that we were compelled to remain indoors. In ancient times, historians say, that it never rained in Egypt. But we can certainly testify to the contrary.

Dec. 18. This morning [I met] Mr. Rice of Mississippi, whose acquaintance I made two winters ago in Columbus. He has a young bride with him and is now en route for Italy. At 3:00 we mounted donkeys and rode down to the Mahmoudieh Canal, where our boat was in readiness to bear us up the current of old father Nile. Several Americans rode down to see us off, and among them was Mr. Rice, Mr. Grafton and his son-in-law, Mr. Riensen of New York City. After chatting some time we bursted several champagne corks and drank to our safe return to the States. Our boats then shoved off and we left the city of Alexandria for Cairo with the Stars and Stripes floating to the breeze and amid the report of guns, pistols, etc. Our boat is named Zeynt al Nile (ornament of the Nile), formerly belonged to the Pasha, and said to be one of the fastest boats on the river. We have on board just 25 persons all told, viz. Mr. Ewing, Price, and myself from Tennessee; Johnstone of South Carolina; John and Lewis Bridge of New York; Teyfel, a courier; and Frank Parrish, a servant of Mr. Ewing's; Camellitti, a Maltese, is our dragoman; one cook and two waiters; besides the Reis,[24] and 13 Arabs to draw and manage the boat. Our provision is ample, having wines and everything suitable for the table, besides good beds and ample room to turn about in.

Dec. 19. This morning we rose after a comfortable night's rest and found that we had run 25 or 30 miles during the night and was near to the town of Atfeh on the banks of the Nile. Here we passed through the lock and purchased some provisions. Atfeh is a small, dirty place devoid of anything to interest the stranger. The homes are built principally of mud hovels, far inferior in appearance and comfort to a pig sty. The Rosetta branch of the Nile is about twice the width of Cumberland river. We passed several villages today, all of them pretty much like Atfeh, with mud houses and mosques towering about them. Pretty fair wind today. Broke one of our masts tonight and laid by.

---

[23] Louis Adolphe Thiers (1797-1877), French statesman and historian, who was exiled to Germany at this time. Probably Jean Baptiste Andre Dumas (1800-1884), French chemist, Minister of Agriculture (1850-51), President of the Paris Municipal Council, and master of the French mint.

[24] The captain of the boat.

Dec. 20. Rose this morning and found the men tracking or towing, a sight both strange and ludicrous to me. They were all stripped stark naked with their heads and privates shaved, excepting a small patch on the back of the head. Each one has a rope tied round their shoulders, which is attached to the main rope. While tracking they generally sing and seem to work cheerfully. After breakfast a brisk breeze came up and we run with one sail as far as a little town on the right bank called Kafr Qayad, where we cast anchor and remained all night. As soon as we landed our guns were brought out and [we] made our first essay after game. While out I noticed a cotton field with stalks six or eight feet in height, and bolls containing very good cotton. Their manner of cultivation is just like ours, except they do not plow so deep. Sugar cane was also growing nearby, but far inferior to ours, and planted differently, being as thick as the wild cane in new ground. After dark we took a couple of lanterns and went into the town where we saw sights both strange and disgusting. The inhabitants were assembled at a dirty cafe, or house of public resort. Two women were hoisted on a kind of platform with their faces covered and beating tambourines for the amusement of a crowd of dirty-looking men and women seated around singing, smoking, and sipping coffee. We went in and were invited by the host to take seats. After drinking a cup of coffee and taking a whiff or so at their pipes, we went out into the street, followed by the women who wanted us to go home with them and give them *backshish.* Disgusted with their obscenities, we returned to the boat and had a game of whist. The scenery of this part of the Nile is precisely like that on the coast of Louisiana, the banks low and caving, and the lands perfectly level. Date and fig trees are the only growth. Camels and buffaloes are used principally for cultivating the land, which taken in connection with the singular appearance of the Arabs forms a picture at once beautiful and unique.

Dec. 21. Made an early start today and with a fair wind moved swiftly along, passing every boat that we came across. Being Sunday and having nothing particular to do, I read Faust, a tragedy by Goethe, which is very much overrated in my opinion. In the afternoon we all assembled on the deck of our little boat and chatted over things in general and the character of the Nile in particular. While on deck I was attracted by some of the crew going through the forms of the Mohemmed religion. They first wash their face, feet, and privates, and then kneel and rise on their feet six times, touching their faces to the ground twice every kneeling. According to the Koran, they are required to wash themselves and pray three times a day—first at sunrise, then at

3:00, and at sunset, always turning their backs to the West. Passing along the Nile hundreds of Arabs can be seen at these hours coming down to the water's edge and going through the forms of their religion. I observed another peculiarity among these people today. Nearly all of the men are deprived of one eye and a forefinger to keep from being taken for soldiers. This cruelty is perpetrated by their parents in infancy. The present Pasha has passed a law requiring all persons so situated to work for the public good, a regulation which may prevent such barbarity.

Dec. 22. This morning Mr. Ewing and myself took a long walk before breakfast. About noon we came in sight of that part of the desert which extends down to the river before reaching the village of Wardan. Just above Wardan we discovered for the first time two of the great Pyramids, which our dragoman said was 30 miles distant. The sand bars this evening were literally covered with wild geese and ducks, at which we made several ineffectual shots. This evening we changed partners and I was again unsuccessful at whist. Several good resolutions were made tonight by some of the party relative to obscene conversation—soon to be broken, I fear.

Dec. 23. We rose this morning and found our boatmen struggling with adverse winds on one side and a sand bar on another, but at last we succeeded in getting off and reached the place where the Damietta branch sets in. The great work of erecting a barrage [or dam of arches] commenced by Mohammed Ali is not yet completed, being several times undertaken and re-undertaken according to the disposition of the Pasha. There is a bridge across each branch built of brick and consisting of a number of well-turned arches about 30 feet in breadth. It is intended to husband the water of the river for irrigating the land in low water. The undertaking is a great one, but I think it will never answer the purposes of its designer. The great difficulty is the want of a sufficient foundation to sustain the presence of the water at high tide. It is a graceful structure and beautiful to look upon, but too light in my opinion for its use. We fully expected to reach Cairo today, but the want of wind has detained us and the probability is that we will not reach Boulak before tomorrow morning. About dusk we all mounted the backs of Arabs and rode out of the boat to the shore where we had a very pleasant walk through a field of wheat about six inches high. The weather here now is precisely like our spring.

Dec. 24. This morning I was aroused by loud cries on board and on shore—near to which we were lying—as if someone was being murdered. Going out I discovered 40 or 50 men armed with long bludgeons and belaboring each other most cruelly. Upon inquiry I ascertained from our dragoman that it was a difficulty between the natives of an adjoining village and our crew about a log of wood that was floating down the stream. I went out to try and quell the disturbance, but the natives were so intent upon beating our crew that my efforts were fruitless. Returning to the boat, one of the crew informed me that they had killed our *Reis* (Captain), but it was a mistake as I saw him brought on board a few minutes after. Our crew then commenced tracking, but were not allowed to proceed by the hostile Arabs. Mr. Ewing then went out with a double barreled gun and Frank Parrish followed him. They endeavored by signs and words to persuade the Arabs to allow us to proceed, but they were bent upon their purpose and refused to let our men go on. One of the Arabs struck Frank with a large stick, which disarmed him; whereupon Mr. Ewing raised his gun to shoot, but was disabled by a large Arab who ran behind him, knocked him down, and took away his gun. When I saw this, I gave the alarm to the rest of the party and rushed to the scene of action with a revolving pistol and dirk knife, followed by Lewis Bridge with a holster pistol. As soon as we reached the top of the bank, which was quite abrupt, 15 or 20 Arabs made at us with their long boat sticks. I fired off my six barrels and Bridge his single barrel, which caused the Arabs to retreat in some cane nearby. Three or four remained and seemed determined to murder us, and came at me all at once, aiming their blows at my head, which I dodged and succeeded in repelling with my knife. At this stage of the game we returned to our boat, which was floating near the shore, and succeeded in saving our lives. The Arabs, which were about 100 in number, were all armed with boat sticks, and seeing that our crew had deserted us, and that our shots were all expended, returned to the bank from the cane and endeavored to draw us back to the shore. But our dragoman cut the rope and we poled to Boulak on the opposite shore. We thought they would pursue us, but they did not. Arrived at Boulak, we sent Frank, who was shot by one of the Arabs with his own pistol in the neck, with the dragoman to Cairo for medical aid. We soon followed on Donkeys and put up at the British Hotel. Here we found two English physicians who extracted the ball from Frank's neck and dressed my arms and hands, which were disabled by the blows received by the sticks of the Arabs. Mr. Ewing also had a blow on his right hand. During the day we called on our vice-consul, who is a native of Cairo, and laid the whole affair before him. He stated to us that the government had just made complaint before him, that many of the villagers had been imprisoned, and some of them badly shot and stabbed. At his instance, we drew up a report or statement of the whole affair and were examined by the Pasha's physician. The excitement throughout the city seems to be very great and the blame laid all at our door. I discovered this evening that I had received two bird shots—one in each leg—which came doubtless from Mr. Ewing's gun taken in the beginning by the wild Arabs.

Dec. 25. This morning I felt quite stiff in the arms and legs. Frank and Mr. Ewing doing well. The current of opinion relative to our difficulty has changed this morning in our favor and the probability is that we will have no further trouble and be allowed to proceed on our voyage up the Nile. Last Christmas was extremely gloomy to me. I was at home but wished at the time that I could transport myself to some other quarter. Today I have remained in the hotel and I may say a prisoner in a foreign land. But let the worst come, I am prepared to meet anything. If the decision of the Pasha be against us, be it so; if in our favor, I will be content.

Dec. 26. Our little (in statue) consul called to see us this morning and gave considerable encouragement relative to the disposition of the Pasha. He says he does not intend sending our statement in, but will let the matter go on as at present, and that we will have no difficulty, can leave when we please, and have a guard if we wish it. This afternoon Mr. Ewing and myself walked round the park upon which the hotel is situated and saw many peculiarities of Eastern life, viz. females riding on donkeys with attendants and large silk robes enveloping their forms entirely and looking like an inflated balloon. Men dressed and seated in the Turkish manner were setting round in cafes made of open cane work, smoking long pipes, and sipping coffee. We also saw the women of the Pasha's harem driving out in carriages drawn by four horses with two Arabs running in front of each carriage with whips in their hands to clear the way. The carriages are European. I noticed some African cows today, which are rather singular in appearance. They are small with a kind of lump just over the shoulders, rather low behind. The climate here is delightful and as soft as a summer's day. Melons, vegetables, etc. are in abundance and one feels like he was at home on a bright and balmy day.

Dec. 27. At 10:00 we all went to our vice-consul's, who is a native of Cairo, and from thence proceeded with him to the office of police, with an Arab walking ahead of us with a mace in his hand and sword fastened around him. We were ushered before the Pasha (or Busharo) and Colonel of Police in great style. We were invited to take seats on a wide lounge upon which they were sitting, and were offered pipes and coffee. After asking me if I was not cold in bad English and looking at the wounds received in the battle, they turned to our consul and talked of our case. Everything was decided in our favor and we were told that we could proceed up the Nile and have any guarantee we liked from the government. There are so many rumors afloat about the number of Arabs wounded in the affray of Wednesday, that I find it difficult to arrive at the truth. I was told today that the one shot in the nose had died, and that four others were wounded with balls. Three of our crew have been imprisoned, but I think they will be released when we start up the river. This afternoon I took a walk through some of the bazaars which are exceedingly narrow and dirty; some of the windows which project from the houses are so close together that they touch each other and it is difficult to see the heavens for the height and narrowness of the streets. Tonight I hear a great noise in the streets, consisting of the beating of drums and the sound of many voices. Our landlord says that it is a marriage celebration.

Dec. 28. This morning Mr. Ewing, Lewis Bridge, and myself rode on donkeys to the Citadel, where we had a fine view of the city, the river, the side of Old Memphis, the Pyramids, and the environs for miles round. The Citadel is situated on a lofty hill and is considered quite strong. Besides the fortification, there is a new mosque commenced by Mohammed Ali. One of the palaces belong to the Pasha and a remarkable well called Joseph's well, which was made by the ancient Egyptians and supplied with water from the Nile by Saladin for the use of the city. Returning to the hotel we stopped and went into the mosque of Sultan Hassan, which is one of the finest in Cairo. Before entering we were required to take off our shoes and put on slippers made of a kind of matting. This mosque is said to be one of the finest specimens of Saracenic architecture in Egypt and consists of an open square without any cover, with a fountain in the center containing water for ablutions, a kind of altar before which they pray, and [a] room containing the remains and relics belonging to Hassan. At our table today I noticed a number of small earthen jars for filtering and keeping cool water, which I consider worthy of being introduced into our country. They are made of simple clay without any polish, and by placing them in a draft, the water can be made as cold as ice. They are made in Upper Egypt and it may be that there is some peculiarity in the clay, but I intend procuring a piece and carry[ing] it home as a specimen.

Dec. 29. At 11:00 we mounted donkeys and rode out to Heliopolis, or the ancient city of On mentioned in Genesis. It is situated about 4 or 5 miles from Cairo and has but few remains of its antiquity. The great obelisk, remains of Sphinxes, mounds of the old town, fountain of the sun, and sycamore of the Holy Family. Returning we passed by one of the Pasha's palaces, the tomb of El Ghoree, now in ruins, tombs of the Memlook Kings. We went out of a gate called the Bab el Fotook and entered through the Bab el Nusz. In winding our way through the narrow streets of Cairo, we came across a drove of slaves. They were all singing, had their hair plaited, were as black as night, and looked perfectly wild. When we reached the hotel we found old Mr. McAuley, our consul at Alexandria, standing on the steps waiting for us. He had received a letter from Mr. Maurey of this place informing him of our difficulty, and had also heard through rumor that the affair was very serious. Deeming it a matter that required his personal attention, the old gentleman hurried down immediately and says that he will open a correspondence with the Pasha—immediately. Our affair has created a great deal of excitement in the country, and they seem to look upon it as something very extraordinary.

Dec. 30. Soon after breakfast we accompanied our vice-consul to the police office to hear the examination of some of the Arabs that were wounded, our Reis, and dragoman. The evidence given by the hostile Arabs was *false* and ridiculous, and no two of them agreed. That given by our *Reis* and dragoman was very much the same. Two of the wounded Arabs were examined, but I did not recognize either of them. The ringleaders of the affair have not yet been taken, having deserted the village and gone to the desert. The mode of conducting the suit was rather singular. No record was kept of the proceedings, except the noting on loose paper of the evidence, by a scribe. Our vice-consul questioned the Arabs, and the Colonel of the Police questioned our side. Coffee was handed round as before, and we were treated with the utmost politeness. They informed us when the evidence was completed that they would furnish us with two of their best *kawasses* [?] to go with us up the Nile. Returned to the hotel and found Mr. McAuley very ill and in bed. After dark Mr. Ewing and myself walked down the street in front of the hotel, where a number of tents are pitched and saw the Dance of the Dervishes, a kind of religious fanaticism similar to that exhibited at our camp meetings in times of great excitement. A number of them stand in a circle and jerk their bodies, first to one side and then the other, uttering singular sounds and completely exhausting themselves.

Dec. 31. Mr. McAuley rested badly last night and is no better this morning. I fear the old man is not long for this world. Johnstone and myself mounted donkeys this morning and rode to Old Cairo, the streets of which are hardly wide enough for two persons to walk side by side. We went into an old Greek Church in the cellar of which a small niche was shown in which, our guide told us, the Holy Family staid while in Cairo. Several old pictures are hanging on the wall representing the Holy Family's flight into Egypt. While here we crossed the canal to the Island of Roda for the purpose of seeing the Nileometer, which is nothing but a large basin into which the water flows and is measured by a wooden pillar in the center and proclaimed by cryers in different parts of the city during the season of inundation. There is a new palace adjoining the Nileometer and beautifully situated on the point of the Island of Roda. Abbas Pasha has considerable taste for fine public buildings and has not only improved but erected new ones. After this we went to see the tombs of the Memlook Kings and of Mohammed Ali and family, which are placed in a house covered with domes. The tombs are constructed of marble and painted over to suit the taste of the people. During the day I observed several things worthy of note, viz. the women, who are perfect nonentities here, generally have their faces, hands, and arms tattooed like the ancient Egyptians; each village (everybody in Egypt lives in villages) has its own distinguishing mark; the donkeys and horses here are generally shaved with the exception of their legs, and sometimes I notice the ends of their tails dyed red with henna. The caravan of pilgrims have just returned from Mecca and they are now making preparations for a grand celebration tommorrow or next day, when a number of *blind* and foolish fanatics will throw themselves down and be ridden over by a shiek on the sacred horse. The Arabs are a strange people and the more I see of them the more curious I become to learn their real character.[25]

* * * * * *

[Note on back flyleaf]

Names of Guides, Dragomen, and Servants of Note that I have met during my travels

John Onifar, Guide in Switzerland

Fanteno Camellitti, Dragoman on the Nile

Antonio Semiana Servant do

---

25 Here ends the last entry of the European journal. With William Johnstone of South Carolina, McGavock remained abroad until September, 1852, visiting the Holy Land, Russia, and Eastern Europe. Although he states later that he kept a daily journal, this portion of his manuscript has not been recovered. The reader may follow his travels through the East by consulting the later chapters of *A Tennessean Abroad*.

The Political Journals
1852 - 1860

The Civil War Journals
1862

Jack Allen, Editor

INTRODUCTION AND ACKNOWLEDGEMENTS

Part One includes the journals of Randal W. McGavock written on two separate occasions. One was during the year 1848, while he was a student at the Harvard Law School. The other was in 1851, while he was traveling in Europe, North Africa, and the Middle East. As he journeyed about the Old World in 1851, McGavock also wrote a series of letters that were printed periodically in the *Daily Nashville Union.* When he returned to America he published a book entitled *A Tennessean Abroad* in 1854.

During the period 1852-1854, while establishing himself as an attorney in Nashville, McGavock apparently kept no daily journal. On January 1, 1855, however, he returned to journal-keeping in earnest, continuing the practice without a break until seven months before his untimely death on May 12, 1863. Before beginning daily entries in his 1855 journal, McGavock used a few pages to summarize his major activities during the years 1852, 1853, and 1854. Only occasionally, after 1855, did circumstances prevent his making daily entries. When such interventions occurred, McGavock was always careful to recapitulate the significant happenings so as to preserve the continuity of his account.

One journal is missing, that encompassing the period from late 1860 to early 1862. McGavock reports having lost it at the fall of Fort Henry. This unfortunate loss constitutes the one significant break in the chain of events which McGavock chronicled.

The journals reproduced in Part Two were written by McGavock in ink on good quality booklets containing lined pages and hard-back covers. The journals are, as a consequence, still in a fair state of preservation. In a few instances there is evidence of mutilation, an entire page or portion of a page having been cut from the journal with a sharp instrument. There is some indication that these deletions may have been material relating to personal family matters, but this is by no means certain. The handwriting throughout is neat and reasonably legible. Often, however, it seems evident that McGavock wrote the entries in haste. Though a well educated man and a fluent writer, he frequently misspelled words and neglected to punctuate properly. No effort has been made to correct misspelling or revise punctuation, but rather to reproduce the journals as precisely as possible. The only exception is the insertion of a bracketed word occasionally to help clarify meaning.

The footnotes constitute a major addition to the journals. More than in most editorial efforts of this character, considerable attention has been given to the identification of individuals. McGavock was a "name dropper" who seemed to know everyone. The journals are filled with personalities of local and national interest. National figures whose biographies are found in standard reference sources are merely identified. Tennessee personalities, particularly those not found in standard reference sources, are dealt with in some detail.

Randal McGavock was a man with a wide variety of interests. This is reflected in his journals. It is difficult, therefore, to generalize about the nature of his daily entries. On occasion, the entries are quite personal, describing his movements and transmitting his feelings. Often they are descriptive of people and places and things. Then, again, McGavock is led to comment on an affair of the moment, be it a session in court, a congressional action, a happening in Europe, or a Civil War military campaign.

The antebellum journals have much of value for the social historian. Repeatedly there are excellent insights into the functioning of mid-Nineteenth Century urban society. These same journals also contain considerable political information. McGavock not only served a term as mayor of his city but also interested himself in state and national politics and participated as a delegate in the Charleston and Baltimore conventions in 1860.

Two aspects of the Civil War journals are of particular significance. The first is McGavock's description of the fall of Forts Henry and Donelson, some really good war reporting. Then there is his account of prison life at Fort Warren. That it was still a "gentleman's war" in 1862 is abundantly illustrated by McGavock's record of his daily activities and those of his fellow Confederate officers on George's Island in Boston Harbor.

The journals in Part Two were first reproduced in typewitten form by the editor in 1941. At that time the original manuscripts were in the possession of Miss Louise Grundy Lindsley, a niece of Randal McGavock. She had received the journals from her father, John Berrien Lindsley. Her graciousness and assistance were of immeasurable value during this first editorial work. After Miss Lindsley's death in 1944 the family papers passed to Miss Lindsley's niece, Miss Margaret Lindsley Warden of Nashville. Miss Warden has shown an equal interest in these materials. It is through her generous consent that the journals are now being published in printed form.

Dr. Alfred Leland Crabb of Nashville was one of the first to recognize the true value of the McGavock journals. It was through his encouragement that the initial editorial task was undertaken. A particular debt is owed Mrs. Cora Wayne Wright who typed the journals from the original. Thanks are also due Mr. Robert N. Bahnsen and Mr. William Louis Patton who were of much assistance in the second editing. The advice and consultation of Dr. William T. Alderson and Dr. Dan M. Robison of the Tennessee State Library and Archives, Dr. Herschel Gower, and Dr. Robert H. White are gratefully acknowledged. Finally to the members of the Tennessee Historical Commission I express appreciation for their interest in publishing these commentaries from the pen of one of the Volunteer State's most exciting young personalities.

JACK ALLEN

George Peabody College for Teachers

CHAPTER XV

"Hereafter offices may seek me, I will never again seek them." (1852-1854)

Randal McGavock kept a daily journal of his activities during a year at the Harvard Law School (1848) and again on a European journey (1851). Upon returning from his travels abroad he apparently discontinued this practice until 1855. Before starting again to write a journal with daily entries, he prepared a resumé of certain major activities which had transpired during the years 1852-1854. It is fortunate that he decided to use the opening pages of his new journal in this manner. For, while the resumé lacks the detail provided by daily entries, it does provide some excellent insights into the man and his times. Here we see an engaging young member of the Southern gentry, seemingly as much at home on the national scene as in the familiar confines of Nashville, Tennessee.

In April 1851 I left the U. S. for the shores of Europe in company with my Aunt Mrs. Eakin (now Mrs. Porter), her little daughter Willie and my cousin Marie Louise Bass, also Bishop Otey, Hon. Edwin H. Ewing, Ben Lytton, James Price, James D. Maney, and Jos. Hamilton of Tennessee. While abroad I visited the most interesting portions of Europe, Africa, and Asia. During my absence I kept a daily journal from which I wrote letters descriptive of my tour for a newspaper published in Nashville called the Union and American.

In Oct. 1852 I landed on the Steamer Pacific belonging to the Collins line at the city of New York. It was in the midst of the Presidential campaigne and the whole country was in a state of excitement on that subject.

After passing a week very pleasantly in New York I went to Boston to see my friends and my old Alma Mater at Cambridge. While in Boston my friends of the democratic party induced me to make a speech in favor of Gen Pierce.[1] It was my first political effort and I felt very thankful that I did not make a failure. I was introduced to the audience by Chas. Woodburry[2] (a son of the Judge) as the grandson of Hon. Felix Grundy[3] which caused me to make a greater effort probably than I would otherwise have done. After passing a few days very pleasantly at the Revere House in company with the Hon. Piere Soulee of La. and the Misses Jarvis of Conn. I proceeded with Charlie Woodburry to Concord N. H. to see Gen. Franklin Pierce then candidate for the presidency against Gen. Winfield Scott.[4] The Gen. received us very cordially at a room in a hotel where we drank champagne and conversed freely on the approaching election and the various subjects that divide the two great political parties. I was much pleased with his frank and open manner but did not form a very high opinion of his abilities as a statesman. I had a letter of introduction to him from the Hon. B. F. Hallett of Boston which induced him probably to devote more attention to me than I deserved. Before leaving Concord I wrote a letter to the Union and American of Nashville describing my interview.

Returning to Boston I took the rail-road for Albany and Buffalo. Here I crossed Lake Erie to Detroit thence across the State of Michigan by rail to the flourishing city of Chicago in Ill. thence down the canal to La Salle on the Illinois river. It was very low and the little boat in which we embarked for St. Louis was so much crowded that a party of us took the stage at Peoria and crossed the pararies to Alton on the Mississippi and thence to St. Louis by boat. I remained one week in St. Louis as the guest of Gen. Harney[5] of U.S.A. St. Louis is the most flourishing city in the west and her geographical position must in a few years render her the great commercial emporium of the mighty west. The society here at present is not so good as in Nashville or Louisville

---

[1] Franklin Pierce (1804-1869), fourteenth President of the United States.

[2] Charles Woodbury and Randal W. McGavock were classmates in the Harvard Law School.

[3] Felix Grundy (1777-1840), lawyer, statesman, was born in Berkley County, Virginia. He began the practice of law in Bardstown, Kentucky in 1797; a member of the Kentucky Constitutional Convention in 1799; served in the Kentucky House of Representatives 1800-1805; a member of the Supreme Court of Kentucky 1806-1807; moved to Nashville, Tennessee in 1807; elected as War Democrat to the Twelfth and Thirteenth Congresses; a member of the Tennessee House of Representatives 1815-1819; served in the United States Senate 1829-1838 and 1839-1840; Attorney General in President Van Buren's Cabinet 1838-1839.

[4] Winfield Scott (1786-1866), one of America's outstanding military leaders.

[5] William Selby Harney (1800-1889), soldier, was born in Haysboro, Tennessee. He entered the army in 1818; fought against the Florida Indians; ranking cavalry officer under General Scott during the Mexican War; brevetted brigadier-general in 1847; suspected of Southern sympathy in 1861 and deprived of his command; brevetted major-general near the close of the war because of his useful services in the past.

owing to the number of foreigners. But in a few years I expect to see St. Louis next to New York among the cities of the Union. If I could cut loose from early associations, and divest myself of the many ties that bind me to Nashville this would be the theatre of my career. Leaving St. Louis on a steamer I decended the Mississippi as far as Cairo thence up the Ohio to Louisville thence by stage to Nashville. It was a happy day to me when I arrived at my native city and received the congratulations of my family and friends after having been a rover so long. All seemed glad to see me, and many comments were made upon the changes that had taken place in my person and manners since leaving. It was the day before the election when I arrived and at the instance of some of my democratic friends I joined the torch light procession and proceeded as far as Broad St. where I responded to the call and made a speech from a carriage. Two days after the election the news by telegraph informed us of the triumph of the democratic party. The democracy of Nashville was highly elated and formed a procession, and waited upon me at my fathers house. I responded to their call in a few brief and appropriate remarks. After the excitement of the election had subsided and I had seen all my friends, I once more resumed the practice of the law. It is no easy matter to settle down to the dull routine of the practice after eighteen months absence. But man without some useful vocation is of but little use to himself or the community. Time drags heavily with him and he becomes restless and impatient to be off again.

In the latter part of Feb. 1853 I concluded that I would like to return once more to Europe, and accordingly made up my mind to apply to President Pierce for the Secretaryship to the Legation at Paris, London, or Madrid. I left Nashville in the stage for Louisville stopping at Bardstown to see my brother Jno. Jacob[6] who was a student at St. Josephs College. In Louisville I met the widow and daughter of Sam Grundy (decd) of Washington Co Ky. I was much pleased with my Cousin Annie who is a gay and interesting woman.

Proceeding up the Ohio as far as Cincinatti I took the rail-road for Washington via Pittsburg and Baltimore. Arrived at the Capitol two days before the Inauguration and found the city crowded with office seakers—and persons who wished to witness the proceedings of the fourth. I stopped at Browns hotel and soon commenced the work of procureing letters of recommendation for the appointment I desired. I at last had my batch prepared, and flattered myself that it contained

---

[6] John Jacob McGavock was born in Nashville, Tennessee, June 3, 1835. For several years he was a wholesale merchant in Nashville. Afterwards he moved to Arkansas where he remained until his death.

an array of names sufficiently formidable and potent to secure almost any office. I had a letter signed by all of the Tennessee delegation except Wm. Cullum[7] who "refused to recommend any men to Franklin Pierce." A private letter to the President from Mrs Jas K Polk—one from the Hon Jas Buchanan[8] of Pa.—Sam Houston[9] of Texas—Cave Johnson of Ten. besides a number of senators and other distinguished men. I remained in the city three weeks during which time I had frequent interviews with the President and the members of his Cabinet. Mr. Marcy[10] offered me the appointment of Sec to Central America which I declined. Learning that the foreign appointments would not be made for several months I determined to leave Washington. The day I left, I called on the President and he informed me that there was no telling what would be the result of my application. When the appointments came up, my claims would be duly considered. Time rolled on, and I never heard a word more about the matter. Office seaking I regard as utterly disreputable to a gentleman and this experiment has taught me a lesson that I will not soon forget. Hereafter offices may seek me, I will never again seek them. While in Washington I had an agreeable time with my friends and the ladies. Among the many female acquaintances that I formed I was more particularly pleased with Miss Sallie Faulkner—daughter of the Hon - Chas- Faulkner[11] of Va. I passed many happy hours with her and separated with some regret.

From Washington I went to New York with the manuscript of my travels abroad with the view of publishing it. I saw Harper—the Appletons and other publishers, but could make no arrangement with them that suited me. Leaving New York I returned to Nashville by way of Washington and Louisville, not at all pleased with my mission.

Soon after my return I met a very beautiful and interesting lady from Franklin Co. Miss Seraphine Deery in whom I found a congenial spirit —and with whom I have passed many happy days. Soon after this my Cousin Annie Grundy visited us—and I was so much pleased with her—

---

[7] William Cullum (1810-1896), Congressman from Tennessee, was born in Monticello, Wayne County, Kentucky. He moved to Carthage, Tennessee; became a member of the State House of Representatives and, later, of the State Senate; a Whig in Congress 1851-1855; Clerk of the National House of Representatives 1855-1857; spent the remainder of his life in the practice of law.

[8] James Buchanan (1819-1868), fifteenth President of the United States.

[9] Samuel Houston (1793-1863), soldier, statesman, was born near Lexington, Virginia. He served in the Creek War; practiced law for a time; Congressman from Tennessee 1823-1827; Governor of Tennessee 1827-1829; Commander-in-Chief of the Texas Army in the Texas War for Independence; first President of the Republic of Texas 1836-1838; again President of Texas 1841-1844; a Democratic representative from Texas in the United States Senate 1846-1859; Governor of Texas 1859-1861.

[10] William Learned Marcy (1786-1861), statesman.

[11] Charles James Faulkner (1806-1884), lawyer, congressman.

that I made an excuse to return home with her. I had business in Ky. but my little Cousin was the real attraction. I went up to Carrollton on the Ohio to attend to the estate of my Uncle Joseph McGavock[12] who died leaving all his property to an entire stranger named Hussby. He was non compus when the will was executed. I contested it before the probate Court but was curt. I then took an appeal to the Circuit Court, and had a Curator appointed to manage the estate. In the month of Aug I visited Catoosa Springs in Georgia where I enjoyed myself very much for ten days. While there I appeared at a Grand Fancy Ball as the Sublime Porte. My costume was the finest in the room and attraced most attention. I brought it from Constantinople. Here I met a beautiful black eyed girl from Macon named Ophelia Nisbet daughter of Judge Nisbet. With this lady I had quite a flirtation. From Catoosa I returned to Nashville stopping at Look Out mountain, Allisonia (the home of Miss Deery) and War-trace.

The remainder of 1853 was occupied in reading and attending strictly to what little business I had in the Courts.

1854

In June 54 I started with Henry Fogg[13] to Charleston S C. but at Atlanta we separated, I wishing to visit some friends in Macon. I remained in Macon three days and was highly delighted with my visit. Several parties were given to me viz Dr Collins, Col DeGraffenreid, Jas Nisbet and Miss Ophelia Nisbet was looking beautiful and contributed greatly to my enjoyment. From Macon I went to Miledgeville where attended with Col De Graffenreid the legislative body—and was presented to Gov Johnson[14] who is a fine looking and affable gentleman. I was not favorably impressed with the legislative body, or the Capitol of Ga. I then visited the village of Sparta in Hancock Co. The object of my visit to this place was to see Dr. Terrell and family whose acquaintance I formed in Paris. Dr. T. is one of the most prominent men in the State, but is a great sufferer, having a cancer on his face. He has only one child, a beautiful and interesting daughter whom I admire beyond measure. I remained in Sparta five days, and was received with all the kindness I could desire. Leaving Sparta I proceeded to Charles-

[12] Joseph McGavock (1787-1853), soldier, was born in Wythe County, Virginia. He moved from Virginia to Tennessee; resided there several years; returned to Virginia; afterwards moved to Carroll County, Kentucky. He was a captain in the War of 1812, and acquired some reputation as a soldier and officer.

[13] Henry Middleton Rutledge Fogg, the son of Francis B. Fogg, was a young Nashville attorney, a law partner of his father. He graduated from the University of Nashville in 1847, entered the Confederate Army in 1861, and was killed in January 1862 at Fishing Creek, Kentucky.

[14] Herschel Vespasian Johnson (1812-1880), twenty-third Governor of Georgia.

ton via Augusta. I stopped at an elegant new hotel called the Truitt Home, where I [met] some friends viz. Seniter Yulee[15] of Fla and lady —Miss May Wickliff of Ky.—Miss Lizzie Sanford of Ala.—Miss Ghist of Fla. and remaining several days in the City I took a small steamer for the Santee country to visit my old friend and travelling companion Wm. C. Johnstone. He recently married a beautiful lady, and seems very happy on his rice plantation. I remained three days with him and then returned to the city in the height of the gay season. I was invited out every evening—and enjoyed myself exceedingly. The South Carolinians are high toned people, and understand entertaining better than any people in the U. S. according to my taste.

Returned to Nashville in March—and was soon after appointed a delegate by Gov. Johnson[16] to the Southern Commercial Convention at Charleston. I did not go, having so recently been there.

In the month of July I lost my youngest brother Hugh Albert—poor little fellow—death was a great relief to him, for his suffering was agonizing. He lay on his back for six weeks with inflamitory fever—and before death his right leg was entirely mortified. He was in his 13th year and decidedly the brightest and most lovely character I ever saw. All who knew him loved and admired him not alone for his extraordinary mind—but great purity. He is gone—and I never expect to see his like again.

Soon after his death I left the City for Catoosa Ga stopping en route at Winchester Springs to see Miss Lizzie Bonner of Fayetteville, and at Alisonia to see Miss Seraphine Deery. At Catoosa I did not participate in the gayeties, but passed most of my time with Miss Nisbet of Macon Miss Pollie Chaire of Fla. and several Nashville ladies viz Miss Corine Hays, Harriett Erwin, Miss Spence. Returning home we visited Look Out again—and I witnessed two rare adventures in which two ladies were thrown in an interesting position from their horses.

Soon after my return I visited Carrollton Ky to attend to a law suit commenced last year. I missed the time, and had to return without accomplishing any thing. Returning to Nashville I complied with a promise, and visited Miss Lizzie Bonner at Fayetteville and also Miss

---

[15] David Levy Yulee (1810-1866), Delegate and Senator from Florida.

[16] Andrew Johnson (1808-1875), seventeenth President of the United States, was born in Raleigh, North Carolina. He served in the Tennessee Legislature for a time; a Democrat in Congress 1843-1853; Governor of Tennessee 1853-1857; United States Senator 1857-1862; appointed Military Governor of Tennessee in 1862; elected Vice President on the National Union ticket in 1864; became President of the United States April 15, 1865, upon the death of President Lincoln; impeached by the House of Representatives in 1868 but acquitted; elected to the United States Senate in 1874, but served only a short period until his death.

Deery at Alisonia. In the month of Oct. I published a book of travels—entitled "A Tennessean Abroad" or letters from Europe, Africa, and Asia. The book has been well received, and highly spoken of by most of the leading Journals of the country.

Death has made his mark in our family this year—first my brother Hugh—then Uncle Tommy Mason of Ark.—then Aunt Sallie McGavock of Williamson Co—then Uncle Winder of La and Mae Mason of Ark.

Indeed this has been a remarkable year in the history of the world—War, pestilence, famine, and hard times have all made their appearance at once. The war now raging in Europe between the Allies and Russia is one of the greatest and most destructive the world has ever seen. The result is yet to be seen.[17] The crops this year are short throughout the whole U S—and hard times is the universal cry.

But notwithstanding all this real estate brings a higher price in this city than ever before. A great number of lots have changed hands, and all brought high prices. I have invested about $5,000 and hope to realize something from it.

The past summer was the longest and hottest that I have ever experienced.

This is the last day of 1854. Gen Sam Houston has just arrived in our city—and I predict that his claims will be strongly urged for the next Presidency.

---

[17] The Crimean War 1854-1856.

CHAPTER XVI

"I have been in quite a stew about an *affaire de coeur.*" (1855)

From New Year's day, 1855, to within seven months of his untimely death, Randal McGavock kept an unbroken series of journals. For the most part these journals contained daily entries. Much that he wrote in 1855 concerns the comings and goings of a gregarious young bachelor, commanding the attention of a succession of Southern belles as he moved along the mainstream of Nashville and Middle Tennessee society. This is accompanied by a seriousness of purpose, however, reflected in his efforts to establish a law practice and in his comments on local and national affairs. His marriage on August 23 was followed by the traditional honeymoon to Niagara Falls. This, in fact, distracted McGavock from his journal for much of the remainder of the year.

1855

Jan. 1st Clear and delightful weather.

The year 1855 opens most auspiciously—the sun is bright, and the air as balmy as a spring morn. May it be as bright and fruitful as it promises. This morning I started out as is my custom to make the compliments of the season to my friends.[1] I first called on Mrs Jas K Polk[2] where I met Gen Sam Houston of Texas who is on his way to Washington. From Mrs Polk's I called on Mrs Russell Houston,[3] Mrs Bankhead, Miss Calls, Mrs Donelson, the Misses Spence of Murfrees-

[1] It was a widely practiced custom among members of the Southern gentry to visit with one's friends on the first day of the new year.

[2] Mrs. Polk was the widow of James Knox Polk (1795-1849), eleventh president of the United States.

[3] Mrs. Houston was the wife of Russell Houston, a Nashville attorney and business executive. Mr. Houston was a director of the Louisville and Nashville Railroad 1862-1869; Vice President 1867-1868; President June 11, 1868-October 8, 1869. He remained as attorney for the railroad until his death in 1895.

boro, Miss Harriett Erwin, Miss Lydia Smith and Mrs. V K Stevenson.[4] At last named place I dined by invitation, and had an excellent piece of venison and other things in keeping. After tea I called on Mrs Donelson by invitation, where I passed an agreeable evening.

Jan. 2nd Clear and pleasant.

The entire morning was occupied in the Criminal and County Court rooms, and attending to some little business. Commenced reading Bancrofts History of the U S today for the second time. After tea I accompanied Miss Lydia Smith to an Amateur Concert for the benefit of Mr Hess in the Christian Church. The music was highly creditable. Among the ladies I recognized Mrs McCragy, Miss Cunningham, Miss Brennon, and Mrs Yeatman.[5] The audience was large.

Jan. 3rd Cloudy and warm.

This day has been occupied in attending the Criminal Court, and reading Harper's Magazine for this month.

Jan. 4th Rain and warm.

At ten [oc] this morning a meeting of the citizens was called at the Court House to make suitable arrangements to receive the remains of Gen Robert Armstrong[6] late proprietor of the Washington Union, who died a short time since in Washington. Resolutions were passed, and pall bearers appointed, and among them my father who was a companion in arms. Gen Armstrong was a citizen of Nashville until appointed Consul to Liverpool by President Polk after which he resided in Washington until his death. He was a bosom friend of Gen Jackson[7]

---

[4] Mrs. Stevenson was the wife of Vernon K. Stevenson, the father of the railway system in Tennessee. As a Nashville merchant Mr. Stevenson became interested in the incorporation of the Nashville and Chattanooga Railroad. His energetic work was largely instrumental in securing appropriations of $500,000 from both Nashville and Charleston, South Carolina, a $250,000 subscription from Augusta, Georgia, and $30,000 from Murfreesboro, Tennessee. The company was organized in 1848 with Stevenson as president. He held this position until the close of the Civil War. He was also instrumental in projecting the Nashville and Northwestern Railroad in 1854.

[5] Mrs. Yeatman was the wife of Thomas Yeatman, an important figure in the business development of Nashville. In 1820 Mr. Yeatman formed a partnership in the commission business with Joseph and Robert Woods. The firm of Yeatman, Woods and Company owned several steamboats and did a large business in cotton and tobacco. The firm made a large fortune in cotton, retired from business, and went into banking. Yeatman was a member of the board of directors of the Nashville Bank in 1821 and of the Board of Public Works about 1830.

[6] Robert Armstrong (1792-1854), soldier, was a native of Abingdon, Virginia, and the son of Trooper Armstrong, a Revolutionary soldier. He enlisted in the War of 1812; was Postmaster of Nashville for sixteen years, being appointed by President Jackson in 1829; Consul at Liverpool 1845-1849. After returning to the United States he became proprietor of the *Washington Union*.

[7] Andrew Jackson (1767-1845), seventh President of the United States, was probably born in the Waxhaw settlement in South Carolina. He was appointed Solicitor of the western district of North Carolina in 1788 and located in Nashville, Tennessee; repre-

and spent the greater portion of his life in the public service. He was a Lieutenant in the Creek war, Brigadier Gen of the Tennessee brigade of Volunteers in the campagne of 1835 against the Creeks and Seminoles. For many years he was Postmaster at Nashville—As a man he was sincere, stern, but kind in his nature—not talented, but possessed of indomitable energy. This is the last day of indulgence on the paper due on the first. The amount of protested notes is unusually large in all the Banks—indicating the pressure of the times. Called after tea on Mrs. Donelson.

Jan. 5th Rain and river very low—but rising.

In the forenoon I attended the Criminal Court, but as nothing of interest was going on I returned to my office and occupied the remainder of the day in reading. About dusk I walked through the mud to the river to see Mrs. Donelson off for La. Spent the evening playing bacgammon with Wm Lawrence.

Jan. 6th. Cloudy and very windy—a little rain.

The Criminal Court adjourned today. Being quite incleamant I remained in my office reading law and history. Called with Rice and Allison[8] after tea to see Miss Lydia Smith where we met W. H. McNairy[9] who is now a clerk in the Navy Department at Washington. We played whist, drank punch, and enjoyed ourselves in conversation until a late hour.

Jan. 7th. Rain in the morning and snow in the evening.

I did not attend Church today, but passed the forenoon with my father's family and the afternoon in my office reading history and after tea . . . .

Jan. 8th. Foggy and drizzly rain all day.

The Circuit Court met this morning, but will adjourn for the celebration of the glorious eighth. The remains of Gen. Robert Armstrong were burried this morning in the city cemetery with appropriate honors.

At 10 oc I started in company with Mr A L P Green, my father, Sister Sallie and Mary to Williamson Co. to attend the wedding of my brother

sented Tennessee in Congress 1796-1797 and in the United States Senate 1797; Judge of the State Supreme Court of Tennessee 1798-1804; served in the Creek War in 1813; major general in the United States Army in the War of 1812; Governor of Florida for a time in 1821; served in the United States Senate 1823-1825; President of the United States 1829-1837.

[8] Samuel P. Allison (1827-1858), lawyer, was a native of Williamson County, Tennessee. He graduated from Yale and studied law at Lebanon, Tennessee. He moved to Nashville to practice law and remained there until his death.

[9] Walter H. McNairy (d. September 3, 1898) was the son of Dr. Boyd McNairy. He graduated in medicine but never practiced. He was a clerk in the Navy Department for many years.

Dr F Grundy MacGavock. We went out the Nolensville turnpike, and reached the place of destination about dark. My brother married Miss Mary Manoah Bostick, daughter of the late Mr Jos Bostick. The family are highly respectable but plain. The young lady is fine looking and very intelligent. I did not enjoy the evening much, particularly as I had to sleep in a feather bed with two other men.

Jan. 9th Foggy and drizzly rain all day.

Most of the company left Mrs. Bostick's last night and this morning before I got up. At 12 oc the bridal party left Mrs. B's and came to my father's where some of the family had assembled to meet them. At a late hour some of Grundy's friends gave him a splendid serenade. Miss Martha Nowelle and Felix Lanier were married tonight.

Jan. 10th Rain all day

Nothing of interest has transpired today the weather is so inclement, and the streets so muddy that I have remained in my office most of the day writing declarations. Rec'd a note from Miss Deery today requesting me to go and see her. . . .

[*One page of the journal has been torn out at this point. The next entry begins in middle of a sentence.*]

. . . but few persons at the church. He requested that no sermon be delivered—and Dr Edgar only prayed and sung. At half past two oc Allison and myself drove out to Gov N S Browns by invitation to dine with the Judges of the Supreme Court (Mr's Caruthers, Joelten and McKinney) also Mr Meigs. The dinner was excellent and I enjoyed the evening. After tea I called on Miss Ophilia Martin and was somewhat disapointed in her.

Jan. 18th Clear and cool.

The entire day has been occupied in the Circuit Court and in reading the proceedings of the Southern Commercial Convention now in session in the city of New Orleans. In the afternoon I met Gov Johnson at the Union office and discussed the propriety of holding a State Convention. He opposes it—but I think it very essential for the democratic party to open the camp with avowed principles,—particularly in these times of know-nothing-ism.[10] Took tea with Rice and Allison.

---

[10] The American (or Know-Nothing) Party was founded in New York in 1849 and enjoyed a meteoric career during the 1850's. It developed as a secret organization, its members being pledged to vote only for native Americans, to work for a twenty-one-year probationary period preceding naturalization, and to combat the Catholic Church. It became perfected as a national organization by 1854 but died out in the heat of the sectional antagonism over slavery.

Jan. 19th Clear and mild.

Passed the day in the Supreme and Circuit Court rooms. After tea I called by request on Miss Bettie Malone of Athens Ala and Mrs Boyd of Clarksville—at Dr Green's

Jan. 20th Clear and mild

This morning I attended the Supreme and Circuit Courts. Occupied the remainder of the day in reading a book written by Henry Wikoff entitled "My Courtship and its Consequences." It is founded on facts, and is truly an interesting work, showing the fickleness of woman and the manouvering of a man in search of the almighty dollar. The scene is laid in Europe, and the affair happened while I was there.

Jan. 21st Severe storm about 10 o'clock this morning and heavy rain. Cleared off—very cold in the eve.

Attended the first Presbyterian Church this morning and heard a sermon by Dr. Edgar.[11] In the afternoon and evening I remained in my office reading. In Nashville Sunday is always a very long and dull day to me. We have no promenades or places of resort and one dislikes the idea of visiting.

Jan. 22nd Clear and cold.

Attended the Courts today. Nothing has transpired of note.

Jan. 23rd. Very cold and snow storm.

At 10 o'clock Edward my brother and myself started in a buggy to Franklin. Stopped and dined at Cousin Lysander McGavock's[12] and passed the night at James McGavock's.

Jan. 24th Cloudy and very cold.

Called this morning on aunt Sally Otey,[13] and Aunt Eliza Ewing in Franklin. On our return to this city we bought two mules for the plantation from a man named Johnson. Mr O B Haynes'[14] two daughters

---

[11] John Todd Edgar (1792-1860), Presbyterian minister, was a native of Delaware. He moved to Nashville, Tennessee, August 4, 1833 and was a pastor of the Presbyterian Church of Nashville for twenty-six years. He was one of the city's outstanding religious leaders and during his pastorate added 897 members to the church rolls. He edited the *American Presbyterian* during its brief publication, January 1835 to December 1836; was a member of the publishing committee which established the *Christian Record* in November 1846; was a member of the editorial committee of the Presbyterian Record 1849-1850.

[12] Lysander McGavock (1800-1855), farmer, was born in Nashville, Tennessee, the son of David McGavock. He had an excellent farm in Williamson County, Tennessee.

[13] Sally McGavock Otey (1805-1872) was the wife of John H. Otey and resided in Williamson County, Tennessee.

[14] Oliver Bliss Hayes (1783-1858), lawyer, Presbyterian minister, was a native of New England. He settled in Nashville, Tennessee in 1808 and began the practice of law. After having developed a successful practice, he retired and was ordained a minister in the Presbyterian Church.

Laura and Corine were married at 4 oc this afternoon and started for New Orleans at 6 oc. Laura married George .... formerly of this city and Corine married Wm L Lawrence of this city. Called after tea with Robt Brown on the Misses Martin of Pulaski.

Jan. 25th Clear and mild. Strong NW wind in the evening.

This morning the Supreme Court decided the great rail-road case which has created so much interest of late. The legislature of [18]51 and [18]52 passed an act authorizing the vote of certain counties in the State to be taken on the subject of taxation for internal improvements. The county of Davidson agreeable to this act voted one million of dollars towards four different roads leading from Nashville. The anti-tax men made a great voice and finally brought suit in the Circuit Court. Being curt in this court they appealed to the Supreme Court of the State where the decision below was confirmed. I have never been fully satisfied as to the constitutionality or policy of this act, as I deem it exceedingly dangerous to submit to the masses the power of voting taxation upon the minority. After tea I called on Miss Malone of Ala Finding her out I called on Miss Lydia Smith where I played whist until 9 oc and then went out to Billy Thompson's by invitation to meet Miss Martin.

Jan. 26th Clear and very cold.

Attended the Circuit Court this morning and occupied the remainder of the day in my office. Received a letter this evening from Judge Dickinson, also a paper containing a complimentary notice of my book.

Jan. 27th Clear and very cold.

The telegraph brought us the news by the Pacific in which it is stated that the Czar[15] has consented to an armistice and accepts the articles of peace offered by the Allies. I cannot believe this until confirmed. Occupied the day in my office.

Jan. 28th Cloudy, snowing and cold.

Occupied the day in my office and with my father's family. After tea I called on Rice and passed one or two hours in agreeable conversation.

Jan. 29th Cloudy, very cold and light snow.

Attended the Circuit Court. Dined today with Mrs Porter, dinner given to Charles Mason, a cousin from Ark, who has just married a Miss Tolbert of Wilson Co. Called after tea on Miss Ophelia Martin.

[15] Nicholas I, Czar of Russia 1825-1855.

Jan. 30th Clear and very cold. River very low.

In the Union and American of this morning I notice a complimentary extract from the Southern Standard of my book, "Tennesseean Abroad."[16] Attended the Circuit Court this morning, and investigated Story's Equity Pleadings on the subject of bills. After tea a drunken fellow named Mason entered my office and asked me to give him a dollar. He said that he was from Va. From his appearance I judged him to be one of the many gentleman beggars who now infest this country. They travel over the land with forged letters of introduction—make it a business before reaching a place to find out certain persons whom they suppose will furnish them money.

Jan. 31st. Clear and very cold.

This morning I read an account of the awful condition of things now in the city of N. Y. It appears that a procession containing 150,000 persons out of employment formed in masses on the 6th instant in that city and demanded support from the Corperation, passed resolutions calling upon Congress to give each of them 160 acres of government land and furnish them implements of husbandry and money to convey them westward. At the same time we see advertisements offering $1.50 per day for labor and no one offers. This mass of beings are composed of both natives and foreigners and evince a spirit of Agrarian-ism that is really disgraceful to our country. This afternoon I called to see Miss Lydia Smith and after tea I went to Dixon Topp's by invitation to meet Misses Martin.

Feb. 1st Clear and pleasant

Nothing of note has transpired today, the river is still low—business dull—and nothing exciting in the society of the place. Attended the Circuit Court today.

Feb. 2nd Clear and pleasant

Occupied most of the day in attending to out-door business. After tea I called with Cox on the Misses Martin.

---

[16] The *Southern Standard* was a leading Mississippi Journal. The following is a portion of the extract:

> The chief merit of this work, consists in the faithful, and accurate account of what was useful and interesting in the different countries which were visited by the travellor. He passed no attractive object of nature or art. The impressions which these objects made upon his mind are conveyed to the mind of the reader in a clear and felicitous style. We regard it therefore as a book of great merit, because it furnishes to the intelligent and inquiring reader much useful information, well arranged, containing nothing superfluous—well written in a chaste and graphic style. . . .

Feb. 3rd Clear and pleasant

Recd a letter this morning from Miss Bonner in which she evinces great impatient in not seeing me. Attend the Circuit Court today.

Feb. 4th Clear and pleasant, very dusty.

Replied in a long letter to Miss Bonner. Attended the first Presbyterian Church this morning. In the afternoon we [received] a visit from Cousin Thos MacGavock[17] of Ky

Feb. 5th Cloudy and warm

Attended the Circuit Court this morning but occupied most of the day in reading Story on Equity Jurisprudence. In the afternoon I walked down to the river to see brother Ed[18] off for Ark. Called on Miss Martin after tea.

Feb. 6th Clear and pleasant

Attended the Circuit Court again this morning. Nothing occured during the day worthy of note. Walked out this afternoon with Miss Smith and took tea with Rice.

Feb. 7th. Cloudy and slight rain.

Attended Supreme Court and Circuit Courts today. Supreme Court adjourned today—being the last day of the term the Judges delivered a number of opinions and among them the Penitentiary case which has attracted some attention on account of its political bearing.

Feb. 8th. Cloudy and cold — a little snow.

Recd a letter this morning from Miss Bonner which is without exception the most beautiful and touching love epistles I ever read. Passed most of the day in my office—reading and reflecting over the strange situation that I now occupy towards several young ladies.

Feb. 9th. Cloudy and cold.

Attended the Circuit Court this morning and occupied the remainder of the day in my office. After tea I attended Miss Jennie Whitfield—daughter of the member of Congress from Kansas[19] to a ball given at Odd Fellows Hall by the Medical Faculty to the Students. It was largely

---

[17] Thomas Cloyd McGavock (1823-1860), son of Robert, was born in Howard County, Missouri.

[18] Edward Jacob McGavock (1828-1880), planter, was born in Nashville, Tennessee. He operated a large plantation at Pecan Point, Arkansas from 1852 until his death, which occurred in New Orleans.

[19] John Wilkins Whitfield (d. 1879) was a native of Tennessee. He represented the Territory of Kansas in Congress from 1854 until the seat was declared vacant in 1856. Later in the same year he returned to Congress. His work during the Civil War caused him to be cited by General Price for "dashing boldness and steady courage." He was commissioned brigadier general in 1863.

attended, and was decidedly the entertainment of the season. I danced until half past two oc.

Feb. 10th Clear and cool.

After my disipation last night I feel somewhat dull today. The Trustees of the University [of Nashville] met today and received the resignation of all the faculty in the College proper. As I anticipated dissension has arose owing to religious differences in the faculty. No preacher ought ever to be permitted to enter the faculty. A committee was appointed to re-organize the faculty. A telegraph dispatch was received here today announcing that the Russians had defeated the Allies—that Breckinridge has declined accepting the appointment to Spain and that Dodge[20] of Iowa was appointed in his place.

Feb. 11th Clear and mild.

Attended the Presbyterian church this morning. After dinner Rice and myself walked out to Miss Jennie Lytton's and remained until 11 30 oc.

Feb. 12th Cloudy and mild rain.

Attended the Circuit Court this morning where I met Gov. Helm[21] of Ky who has recently been elected President of the Nashville and Louisville Rail-road Co. I have been very unhappy today on account of some unpleasant words passed in the family. Wrote one letter to Miss Deery and one to Miss Bonner. Took tea with Jno O Ewing.

Feb. 13th Cloudy and rain.

Attended the Circuit Court this morning. In the afternoon Cox and myself called on Gov Helm's daughter of Ky. After tea called with Rice on Miss Smith.

Feb. 14th. Cloudy, cold and a little snow.

Attended the Circuit Court this morning. Occupied most of the day in my office. In the evening I attended a wedding party Mr Jas Erwin [gave] to Miss McAlister.

Feb. 15th Cloudy and cold.

Attended the Circuit Court today—and occupied most of my time reading in my office.

Feb. 16. Clear and cold.

Attended the Circuit Court today—and occupied most of the day reading in my office.

---

[20] Augustus Cæsar Dodge (1812-1883), statesman.

[21] John Larue Helm (1802-1867), lawyer, Governor of Kentucky, business man.

Feb. 17th. Clear and pleasant.

The Circuit Court adjourned this morning. Gov Helm of Ky made a speech to a large audience in the Court House on the subject of the Nashville and Louisville Rail-road. He advanced nothing new but made a good speech. Took tea with Miss Helm at V. K. Stevensons. An acquaintance named Ramsey who recently married Mr Hawkins daughter was arrested today by the U S Marshall for taking money out of a letter belonging to Nichol and Peacock. I really feel sorry for his wife.

Feb. 18th Clear and pleasant.

Attended the first Presbyterian Church this morning and heard a doctrinal sermon from Mr Carr. Walked out with Miss Helm in the afternoon and called with Merideth after tea on Miss Mary Stevenson of Maury Co.

Feb. 19th Clear and pleasant

Occupied the entire day in my office reading and meditating over certain matters pertaining to myself.

Feb. 20th Clear and pleasant

Dined today with Aunt Felicia. In the afternoon I walked out to see Miss Litton. Attend a delightful party in the evening at Dr David T McGavock's.[22]

Feb. 21st Clear and pleasant.

Rose this morn at 12 oc feeling heavy from the effect of disipation. last night. Remained in my office all day.

Feb. 22nd Clear and pleasant.

Occupied the day reading in my office. After tea I accompanied Miss Lydia Smith to a party at Mr. Jas Erwin's.

Feb. 23rd Warm and rain the morn then snow and cleared off cold

Remained in my office this morning. Attended Ramsey trial before the Magistrate for embezzling money in a letter. He was discharged. After tea Sallie had some half dozen ladies and as many gentlemen to pass the evening with her.

Feb. 24th Cloudy and very cold.

Passed the day in my office, and at the house with the Misses Spence who are passing a few days with Sallie. Provisions and money are unusually high here at present, owing probably to the failure of last years crop and the war in Europe.

---

[22] David Turner McGavock (1813-1886) was born in Nashville, Tennessee. He studied medicine with Dr. Charles Pugsley, an English physician who settled in Nashville about 1830, but did not practice his profession.

Feb. 25th Cloudy and very cold, river still very low.

Attended Dr Edgar's church this morning. In the afternoon Rice and myself called on Miss Lydia Smith. Rice left tonight for Va. and I shall miss him very much as he is very companionable.

Feb. 26th Clear and very cold.

Remained in my office nearly all the day. Started at 11 00 oc for Fayetteville to see Miss Bonner.

Feb. 27th Clear and very cold.

Staid all night at Wartrace. Started early and reached Fayetteville at 4 oc. After tea I called on Miss Bonner.

Feb. 28th Clear and very cold.

Occupied most of the day at Dr. Bonner's. Miss Lizzie seems perfectly delighted to see me. Took tea with her. Fayetteville is a very pretty little village—and some agreeable people live here.

March 1st Clear and cold.

Passed nearly all of the day at Dr. Bonner's and after tea I had an interesting and to me amusing interview with the old folks—all night.

March 2nd Clear and cold.

Started from Fayetteville at 8 o.c. this morning and reached Nashville at 10 00 oc this evening.

March 3rd Clear and cold.

Remained in my office nearly all day reading. Took tea with Miss Lydia Smith and remained there until 12 oc.

March 4th Clear and mild.

Attend the Presbyterian church this morning and walked out to see Miss Jane Litton after dinner.

March 5th Cloudy and very mild, river still very low.

Attended a *small* meeting of the Democrats of Davidson Co this morning for the purpose of appointing deligates to the State Convention on the 27th. I was appointed a deligate

March 6th Cloudy and very mild.

Remained in my office most of the day and attended an agreeable party this evening at Sterling Cockrell's.[23]

March 7th Clear and pleasant.

Remained in my office most of the day, Mather Grundy and his wife reached home today from New Orleans.

---

[23] Sterling Robertson Cockrill (1804-1891) was born in Nashville. He moved to Arkansas and died at Mt. Nebo. He was a trustee of the University of Nashville 1852-1861.

March 8th Clear and pleasant

Nothing has transpired today of moment. Remained in my office reading thru and thru—

March 9th Clear and pleasant.

Remained in my office all day reading. River still low and town dull.

March 10th Clear and very mild.

Quite a number of persons living in Williamson Co came down today on the cars from Franklin and returned after doing their shopping. This is an excellent road—passes through the richest portion of the State and will when completed be of great benefit to this city and the country generally. Called with Henry Fogg on Miss Lydia Smith this evening.

March 11th Cloudy, very warm and a little rain.

Attended the Episcopal Church this morning and occupied the rest of the day reading and conversing with the family.

March 12th Cloudy and very mild. Tornado.

Remained in my office reading most of the day. In the afternoon I had a long conversation with Sterling Cockrell on the subject of a patent that he has recently taken out for a machine for cleaning the leaf and dirt from cotton. If it succeeds it will be equally as important to the interest of the south as the invention of the gin. Just before dusk we had quite a blow & heavy rain and at 11 oc P.M. a Tornado passed over the city and done considerable damage. The copper was torn from the roof of the Capitol, the tin from the roof of the 1st Presbyterian Church, and several large brick houses in the vicinity of the city were entirely demolished.

March 13th Warm and cloudy.

Attended the funeral of Walter Scotts infant this morning. After tea I called to see the Misses Comer of Macon Ga.

March 14th Clear, warm, and windy

Occupied the day in my office. Called in the evening with Comer to see Miss Smith & afterwards his sisters.

March 15th Cloudy and cold, rain.

Walked round to Aunt Felicia's this morning and found her and Miss Ophelia Putnam just starting with a bag of old clothes to trade them off for china. They bantered me to carry the bag. I started with them but did not go far before I threw them down. Called on Miss Saunders in the afternoon and Miss Mary Jones Polk after tea.

March 16th Cloudy and rain very heavy

A telegraphic dispatch reached here this morning that the Emperor Nicholas was dead—of apoplexy. If this be true it will in all probability change the present aspect of affairs in the Crimea. A speedy termination of the war is very desirable for the commerce of the world—and the prosperity of not only Europe but the United States. Miss S Deery arrived at the City Hotel last night. I called this evening but found her out—after which I went up to see Mrs Bankhead where I met Allison who has just returned from Washington.

March 17th Clear and cold.

Called to see Miss Deery this morning—and had a long conversation about our affair. She looked blue & little disposed to credit me. In the afternoon I drove out in a buggy with Celestia Comer of Macon Ga at 11 oc I walked down to the depot and found Miss Deery in the waiting room. I went into the cars with her & just as I was leaving she said she would not go and I returned with her to the hotel.

March 18th Clear and very cold.

Attended the Episcopal Church this morning. In the afternoon I called on Miss Deery but she excused herself. I then walked out to see Jennie Litton and contracted a violent cold.

March 19th. Clear and very cold.

Remained at home all day nursing my cold. Father started this afternoon for the plantation & Comer & sisters for Macon.

March 20th Clear and very cold.

Remained in my office all day—nothing has transpired worthy of note—

March 21st Clear and very cold.

Remained in my office all day reading and doctoring my *ailings*. After tea I went to Mrs Tom Smith's where I passed a very delightful evening. The party was small but agreeable.

March 22nd Clear, very cold and windy.

Remained in my office all day reading a book called Purple Tints of Paris by Bayle St. John.

March 23rd Clear, very cold and windy.

Occupied the day in my office. After tea I went to Mrs. Bankheads where the Musical Club met. Dull evening.

March 24th Clear, mild, very windy and dusty.

Recd a note from Miss Bonner this morning. Remained in my office all day reading Purple Tints of Paris.

March 25th Clear and cold.

I did not go to church today but remained at home reading.

March 26th Clear and very cold.

Nothing has transpired during the day of moment. Attended a Caucus meeting of democrats in the Union Office where I heard Jno K Howard introduce for criticism the Platform to be presented tomorrow.

March 27th Clear and very cold.

At 10 oc this morning the Democratic State Convention assembled at the Court House and nominated by acclimation Gov Andrew Johnson as their candidate for re-election. The Convention was respectable in numbers and the Platform presented by the Committee was cordially adopted. The Resolutions denounced the secret order of Know-Nothings —and re-iterated the main tenance of their ancient principles. They endorsed the Administration of Franklin Pierce. Several speeches were made by A V Brown, Payne of Maury and Jno K Howard of Wilson. Rode out to see Miss Litton in the afternoon and called to see Lydia Smith after tea.

March 28th Clear and very cold.

News by the steamer Atlantic reached here this morning confirming the death of the Emperor Nicholas and the peaceable assension of his son Alexander II[24] to the Throne. Read also an account of a magnificent fete given in Paris by the Americans in that city on the 22nd of Feb in commemoration of Washingtons Birthday. It is discribed as the most brilliant ball of the season. The Nashville Gazette is filled this morning with the creed of the American Party (Know Nothings) as published by the Order in the State of New York. In reading it over I discover some objectionable features and also some features that any patriot must endure.

March 29th Clear and cold.

About 3 oc this morning I was aroused by the fire bells and got up, and found the State Penitentiary in flames. I went out and aided to stay the destroying eliment. The fire originated in the shops all of which were distroyed—also the roof on the walls and the front wing next to town. The prisoners were turned out of their cells and some of them done good work. Many of them were taken outside of the walls to work the engine. They had very little water and of course could do but little except pull down the combustible material before the flames. None of

[24] Alexander II, Tsar of Russia 1855-1881; known as the "Tsar Liberator" chiefly because of his Edict of Emancipation, March 3, 1861, which gave personal freedom to the Russian serfs on the private estates of the nobility.

the prisoners escaped. One poor convict who was an idiot suffocated to death. It is not known how the fire originated. Mrs Bass, two daughters Mary and Mariah and son Jno reached the city [today] from New Orleans. Gov N S Brown[25] called to see me this afternoon and we had a long converstion on Know Nothingism and religion.

March 30th Clear and cold.

Remained in my office all day reading. After tea Sallie and myself called on Miss Maria Washington and Miss Lydia Smith.

March 31st. Clear and pleasant.

Remained in my office all day. Took tea at Mrs. Craighead's with Miss Pattie Paul of Norfolk Va. and Jack Johnson's two daughters who have just returned from Va.

April 1st Clear and pleasant.

Attended the 1st Presbyterian Church this morning. Mr. Rice[26] of Va delivered a very good discourse. Walked home with Miss Deery and her mother. In the afternoon I walked with Miss Lydia Smith.

April 2nd Clear and pleasant.

This morning I passed by Mrs Tom Smiths and she stopped me and said that Lydia was unhappy and thought I was the cause of. She asked me not to flirt with her daughter. I told her I would not. Attended the Criminal Court during the day. Called on Miss Deery and her sister in the afternoon and attended the Theatre this evening.

April 3rd Cloudy and a little rain.

Called on Miss Deery this morning and while there Miss Lytton came in—and I drove off with her. Attended the Criminal Court. Accompanied Miss Deery to the Theatre after which we returned to the Hotel where I witnessed an oft repeated scene with her.

April 4th Hard rain all day.

Attended the Criminal Court today. In the afternoon I walked down to the river and saw Miss Deery off for Memphis.

---

[25] Neill S. Brown, soldier, lawyer, Governor of Tennessee, was born in Giles County, Tennessee in 1810. In 1835 he began his professional career as a lawyer; served as a soldier in the Seminole War in 1836; represented Giles County in the Legislature in 1837; represented Davidson County in the same body in 1855 and was elected Speaker; elected Governor in 1847; served as United States Minister to Russia from 1850 to 1853. He was a successful lawyer for fifty years, and was noted for his constructive support of public education both before and after the Civil War.

[26] John Holt Rice (1818-1878), a native of Petersburg, Virginia. He was licensed by the New Brunswick Presbytery in 1845. He filled pastorates in Louisiana, Florida, Virginia, Kentucky, Mississippi, Alabama, and Tennessee. He was the agent of the Presbyterian Board of Publication in Kentucky and Tennessee about 1855 and, in 1878, was a member of the Southern General Assembly.

April 5th Rained all day.

Attended the Criminal Court during the day. Ben Haley was sentenced 4 years for shooting a man. Called on Miss Bonner at Academy after tea.

April 6th Rain and cloudy all day.

Called on Miss Bonner this morning. Attended the Criminal Court. Called on Miss Paul of Va. at Jack Johnson's this evening.

April 7th Clear and Pleasant.

Attended the Criminal Court this morning and listened to very able and eloquent speeches from Gov N S Brown—Herman Cox[27] and Andrew Ewing[28] on the case of a negro indicted for burglary with intent to commit a rape upon the daughter of Bartly M Barnes former Sheriff of this county. He was acquited. The morning papers contain a list of appointments agreed upon by Gov Andrew Johnson and Merideth P Gentry[29]—who propose commencing the first of May and speak every day until the last of July—an undertaking calculated to make most men recoil from. The Gazette (Maney[30] editor) and Father Schacht a Catholic priest of this city are at war about the Temporal power of the Pope in this country, occasioned by Maney's advocacy of the Know-nothing or American party—recently sprung into existence.

April 8th Clear and pleasant.

Did not go to church this morning but remained in my office reading. In the afternoon I called at Mrs Tom Smiths.

April 9th Clear and pleasant.

Attended the Criminal Court this morning. Four men on their second trial for robbing Gibson Merritt viz. Graham—Taylor Williams. Went with Sallie Ewing and Mary Bass to hear the Bateman children. Young

---

27 Herman Cox was a member of the board of aldermen in Nashville, 1854 and 1858-1860. He was one of the incorporators of the first street railway company in Nashville, March 1860.

28 Andrew Ewing (1813-1864), lawyer, was born in Nashville, Tennessee. He graduated from the University of Nashville in 1831 and was admitted to the bar in 1835. He was a trustee of the University of Nashville from 1833 until his death; served in Congress 1849-1851; resumed the practice of law; delegate to the Democratic National Convention at Baltimore in 1860; a judge of General Bragg's military court during the Civil War.

29 Meredith Poindexter Gentry (1809-1866), Congressman from Tennessee, was born in Rockingham County, North Carolina. He began the practice of law in Franklin, Tennessee; a Whig in Congress 1839-1843 and 1845-1853; unsuccessful candidate for Governor of Tennessee in 1855; a member of the First and Second Confederate Congresses 1862-1863; retired to his plantation after the Civil War.

30 Henry Maney (1832-1858) was born in Williamson County, Tennessee. He graduated from the University of Nashville in 1850; spent ten months abroad 1851-1852; published an account of his travels, *Memories Over the Water,* in 1854; admitted to the Nashville bar in 1853; editor of the Nashville Gazette 1854-1856; elected to the Tennessee Legislature in 1856.

America was the play in which I was highly amused. After the play I went by invitation to Mrs Tom Smiths where I partook of an elegant supper.

April 10 Clear and very pleasant. No fire.

Recd a charming [letter] from Miss Bonner this morning in which she opens her very soul. Attended the Criminal Court today. Spend the evening at home with Dr. Edgar—and he related a very remarkable story of an old negro belonging to Geo Philips near Maysville Ky—who recently conceived the idea of poisoning all of his posterity to release them as he said from bondage. To accomplish his purpose he collected the heads of venimous serpents—such as the rattle snake—the coper head and put them into a jug of whiskey—and made his family drink it evey morning. One by one they died off—the doctors called it negro consumption—and no one but the old negro knew the real cause. One day this old negro gave his master some impertenance—and his master struck him with his cane. Exasperated to desperation he went into the kitchen—took a heavy draft of the poison—and then came out & told his master the whole story of his poisoning his posterity—and said that he might then beat him as much as he pleased—for he soon would be out of this world.

April 11th Clear and cool.

Attended the Criminal Court today but occuped most of the time reading Bancrofts history of the U. S. Nothing has occured worthy of note—

April 12th Clear and pleasant.

Attended the Criminal Court—but remained in my office most of the day reading.

April 13th Clear and pleasant.

Attended the Criminal Court this morning. After tea I called on Miss Deery—

April 14th Warm and rain.

Attended the Criminal Court this morning. Graham—Taylor Wright and Williams were sentenced for 3 years. Two young men charged with murder were acquited. Called to see Miss Deery after tea.

April 15th Warm and rain.

Did not go to church this morning but remained in my office cogitating on an *affair de coeur.* In the afternoon I called at the City Hotel on Miss Deery also in the evening—

April 16th Clear and quite warm.

Attended the Criminal Court this morning. During the day I have been in quite a stew about an *affair de coeur*. Called to see Miss Deery and Miss Smith today. Miss D went home tonight.

April 17th Clear and warm.

I cast off my winter garments today. The weather is so warm that I find light clothing quite comfortable.

April 18th Clear and very hot. Thermometer 92.

Attended the Criminal Court in the morning but remained in my office most of the day. Rode out on horse-back to see Miss Lytton—and Wm Lawrence and wife. Attended a party at Ellis' this evening.

April 19th Clear, very hot and windy. Thermometer 88.

The papers this morning are filled with rumors of war with Spain—about Cuba. The President has ordered a fleet to the Gulf—and given Commidore McCaule instructions to fire into any Spanish vessel that may offer an insult to our flag. I think it all important that we should possess this island at an early day—and consider the present as the most opportune moment that ever has, or will present itself for the acquisition of that gem of the sea. Passed the afternoon reading Bancrofts history. Attended a party this evening at Jack Johnson's.

April 20th Clear and pleasant. Thermometer 70.

Recd a letter this morning from J S Redfield about the publication of my book last fall. Called on Miss Helm and Miss Rogers from Louisville. Concluded the first volume of Bancroft today.

April 21st Clear — Summer Heat.

B. Mosly was acquited today for the murder of an Irishman. Nothing has transpired worthy of note. The farmers all seem in good spirits at the prospect of a good crop.

April 22nd Clear. Summer Heat.

Young Harding of Ark. was burried at Gen Hardings today and also Mrs Ed Cheatham at her fathers Mark Cockrell.[31] Attended the Presbyterian Church. Dined at the Hotel with Gov Helm and daughter of Ky.

---

[31] Mark Robertson Cockrill (1788-1872), distinguished agriculturalist and pioneer in stock-raising, was born near Nashville, Tennessee. As early as 1814 he brought ten head of imported Spanish merino sheep to Nashville. In 1851 his herd gained the prize for the finest wool grown anywhere in the world. He was also a pioneer in the introduction of imported shorthorn cattle from England into the South and West. As an appreciation of his promotion of agricultural pursuits the Tennessee Legislature of 1853-1854 presented him with a gold medal.

Called after tea on Dr Wm Breckenridge[32] of Louisville whom I travelled with in Europe. Here I met Bishop Otey another old friend. called on Miss Morgan.

April 23rd Clear. Summer Heat.

Attended the Criminal Court today. Called on the Misses Martin of Pulaski in the morning and evening.

April 24th Clear. Summer Heat.

Walked up on Capitol Hill this morning with Miss Helm and Miss Rogers of Ky. Attended the Criminal Court. Dined at 2 o'clock at Dr. Porter's[33] with Dr. Wm. Breckenridge of Louisville and several friends. Called after tea on Miss Smith.

April 25th Clear. Summer Heat.

Attended the Criminal Court this morning. Rode out to see Miss Lytton in the afternoon and called to see Miss Helm and Rogers after tea.

April 26th Clear. Summer Heat.

Attended the Criminal Court. Walking along Cedar St today a boy threw an orange at a large dog which caused him to run against me and throw me flat on my back on the solid stone pavement. The jar was very severe but I sustained no serious damages.

April 27th Clear and quite cool.

The two candidates for Gov. published letters this morning in reply to the interrogations of State Temperance Convention on the subject of a prohibitory liquor law. The Committee does not endorse the views of the two gentlemen—but think it inexpedient to bring out a Temperance Candidate—and recommend Temperance candidates for the legislature. Called on Miss Helm and Rogers of Ky this morning and drove them out to Gen Hardings Park in the afternoon. Called with Jennie Brown on Mrs. J K Polk. Called in the evening on the Misses Martin of Pulaski.

---

[32] William L. Breckenridge (1803-1876), minister, educator.

[33] Robert Massengill Porter (1818-1856) was born in Nashville. He graduated from the University of Nashville in 1836; graduated from the Harvard Law School in 1838; graduated from the Theological Department of Princeton in 1843; graduated from the Medical Department of the University of Pennsylvania in 1845; studied medicine in Paris and visited hospitals in other parts of Europe 1845-1847; was invited to the chair of Anatomy and Physiology at the University of Nashville in 1851, a position which he held until his untimely death, which came as the result of an infection which developed after an anatomical demonstration. Porter was the second husband of McGavock's Aunt Felicia Grundy.

April 28th Clear and pleasant.

Remained most of the day in my office reading. After tea Jno H Smith,[34] Felix Cheatham[35] and Sam Allison—and myself walked out to Matilda Harris where we passed an agreeable evening.

April 29th Clear and warm.

Attended the first Presbyterian Church to day and heard Dr. Breckenridge of Louisville preach. Remained in my room most of the day. Father and Jno arrived today from Ark.

April 30th Clear and pleasant.

Remained in my office all day. In the afternoon I drove out to Jas Foster's with Turner Foster.[36]

May 1st Rain in Murfreesboro. None in Nashville.

At half past eight this morning I started on the rail-road for Murfreesboro to hear the candidate for Gov open the Canvass. We had 15 cars full some six hundred passengers. The crowd in the Public Square numbered between four and five thousand. Gov. Johnson opened in a masterly speech of two hours length. Col. Gentry commenced well but fagged and finally gave out. I was much disappointed in the Col. speech. He did not sustain in his high reputation for talent and eloquence. Reached home before night. Took tea at Mrs. Tom Smith's and accompanied Miss Lydia to the Theatre to see the Booth Family.

May 2nd Quite Warm. Heavy rain in the evening.

Remained most of the day in my office reading. A good deal of excitement prevails today about the efforts of the two Candidates yesterday. A number of young ladies and gentlemen who went out riding this afternoon got thoroughly soaked.

May 3rd Warm and frequent showers.

Went over the river this morning to attend Mr Blood sale of lots in Edgefield—which are situated between the Gallatin Turnpike and Fatherland Street one half mile from the bridge. The average of ten acres was $16 per foot—and some went as high as $20. After tea I attended the Theatre.

---

[34] John Hugh Smith was a Nashville attorney and civic figure. He was Mayor of Nashville 1845 and 1850-1852; a member of the board of aldermen in 1849; a city councilman in 1868; one of the incorporators of the McGavock and Mt. Vernon Horse Railroad Company, February 1860; State Criminal Judge following the Civil War.

[35] Felix R. Cheatham was the son of Leonard Cheatham and the brother of General B. F. Cheatham. He served three terms as County Court Clerk of Davidson County, Tennessee. He was characterized by intimates as "Grand old Felix Cheatham."

[36] Turner S. Foster was a Nashville attorney. On May 22, 1862 he was elected Judge of the Circuit Court of Nashville but afterwards was arrested and sent to the penitentiary. He was one of a group which organized St. Anne's Episcopal Church in 1858 and was chosen as one of the two wardens.

May 4th Cloudy and cool.

Occupied the day in my office reading. Called with Cox after tea on Miss Helm and Rogers of Ky.

May 5 Clear and Cool.

Remained in my office most of the day reading. Went with Miss Jennie Brown to the Theatre.

May 6th Clear and pleasant.

Attended the Episcopal Church this morning. Went out to see Miss Lytton in the afternoon with Rice and called on Miss Helm and Rogers after tea.

May 7th Clear and pleasant in the morn. But quite a storm and heavy rain in the afternoon.

The hotels are crowded today—it is supposed with Know-Nothings. They hold their State Convention to nominate their candidates for State offices. The U. S. Court and the Chancery Court met this morning. Attended the Theatre tonight.

May 8th Clear and quite cold. Thermometer 48 after breakfast.

Attended the Chancery Court today but occupied most of my time in my office. The Know-Nothings Convention has nominated Gentry as their candidate for Gov. and Matt Martin[37] of Bedford for Congress in his District.

May 9th Clear and cold. Thermometer 44 this morning. Frost.

The people from the country say that the frost last night ruined the vegetables and probably injured the wheat. Attended the Chancery and U. S. Court to day. In the latter a young man named Jas Crockett was tried and acquited for embezling a letter from this post office. Grand Jury reported a true bill against Ramsey for the same offence. Called to see Miss Bonner at the Hotel. Attended the Theatre.

May 10th Clear and pleasant.

The papers this morning contain very full accounts of Napoleon and the Empress[38] reception in London by the Queen and Prince Albert.[39] Napoleon made a speech at Guild Hall in reply to the Lord Mayor in

---

[37] Matt Martin, lawyer, soldier, was born in Bedford County, Tennessee in 1812. After engaging in agricultural and business pursuits for some years, he opened a law office in Shelbyville, Tennessee in 1851, continuing practice there until 1861. Near the beginning of the Civil War he was elected major-general of the third division of Tennessee state troops. He was active throughout the war, serving through campaigns in Tennessee, Mississippi, Alabama, and Georgia.

[38] Louis Napoleon Bonaparte, President of the French Republic 1848-1852; Emperor of France as Napoleon III 1852-1870. Eugenie Montijo, a Spanish countess, wife of Napoleon III.

[39] Victoria, Queen of England 1837-1901. Albert of Saxe-Coburg and Gotha, the prince consort; married to Victoria February 10, 1840.

Courtesy Mrs. D. A. Preston

Seraphine Deery McGavock
(1835-1918)
after her marriage to Connally F. Trigg in 1868. She married Augustus H. Pettibone in 1898 and died in Nashville in her eighty-third year.

Courtesy Alfred Leland Crabb

Engraving of Randal W. McGavock,
1856

the presence of a vast audience. Called to see Miss Bonner this morning agreeable to appointment before she started with a bridal party for Gallatin. Ed Ewing and his daughter June and W T Berry[40] of this city started yesterday for Europe to be absent three months. Attended the Chancery and Supreme Courts today and a very pleasant party at Wm Gordons this evening. Dr. D. T. MacGavock had a sale of lots in his addition today—average four or five dollars per foot.

May 11th Clear and pleasant.

Attended the Chancery and U S Courts today and a party at the Wm. Coopers[41] this evening.

May 12th Clear and pleasant.

Occupied the day in the Courts and my office. Stiver Perkins was dangerously shot today in Franklyn by a man named Clay. Called on Miss Bonner after tea.

May 13 Clear and pleasant.

Attended the Presbyterian Church in the morning and took tea with Miss Smith.

May 14th Clear and pleasant.

Attended the Chancery and Circuit Courts this morning but remained most of the day in my office. Called on Miss Bonner after tea.

May 15 Clear and pleasant.

Attended the Courts today. Called on Old Dr. Lindsley[42] and Miss Bonner—

---

[40] William T. Berry (1813-1889), book seller, was born in Georgetown, Maryland. He moved to Nashville, Tennessee in early manhood; opened a book shop which became the best furnished establishment west of the Alleghany Mountains; made two trips to Europe before 1860. Berry's Book Store was the literary center of Nashville, and Berry was probably the best bibliographical authority in the West.

[41] William Frierson Cooper was born in Franklin, Tennessee in 1820. He was admitted to the bar in 1841; moved to Nashville 1845; director of the Bank of Tennessee 1853-1855; elected to the Supreme Court of Tennessee 1861; traveled in Europe during the Civil War; appointed Chancellor of the Seventh, Nashville, district, 1872.

[42] Philip Lindsley (1786-1855), educator, Presbyterian clergyman, was born in Morristown, New Jersey. He graduated from the College of New Jersey in 1804; returned as tutor in 1807; licensed to preach by the Presbytery of New Brunswick in 1810; became Professor of Languages at Princeton in 1813; selected as Vice President of the college in 1817; and was Acting President in 1823. During his teaching at Princeton he declined the presidencies of Transylvania University, Ohio University, Princeton, and Cumberland College at Nashville. He yielded to the Nashville offer in 1824, however, and accepted the presidency of Cumberland College which had been newly chartered as the University of Nashville. His powerful educational missionary spirit led him to devote a quarter of a century to the building of the University and to the spread of higher education in Tennessee. In 1834 he was Moderator of the Presbyterian General Assembly. In 1850 he resigned the presidency of the University to become a professor in New Albany (Indiana) Theological Seminary.

May 16th Cloudy and rain — very warm.

It is said by the farmers that the locust and army worm have appeared in the country. If they become numerous the country will be in a state of starvation and we have no money to supply our wants from other sources. The unprecidented drouth last year produced an entire failure of our crops and another such year will prove disastrous. Attended the Chancery and Circuit Courts today and accompanied Miss Rogers of Louisville to the wedding of Mary Paul Johnson.

May 17 Cloudy, warm and rain.

The General Assembly of the Presbyterian Church of the U. S. assembled here today—about 250 members present. Dr. [Henry A.] Bodman of Phila. the Moderator opened the proceeding with an elegant sermon—followed in the evening by an historical lecture by Dr. Rice of St. Louis. The delegates are entertained by the different members of Dr Edgar's church. The firemen of the city had their annual celebration today. Called to see Miss Bonner after tea—and also Miss Helm and Rogers of Ky who go home in the morning.

May 18th Clear and very warm.

Attended the Courts to day — also the Gen Assembly. Called on Miss Bonner after tea and went with her to church.

May 19 Clear and warm.

Called on Miss Bonner this morning to bid her good-by. Attended the assembly.

May 20 Clear and very hot.

Attended the 1st Presbyterian Church today—and heard an excellent sermon from Dr. Thornwell[43] from S C University. Rice, Allison and myself called on Miss Smith and Miss Lytton this afternoon.

May 21 Clear and intensely warm.

Attended the Courts and the Assembly today and called on Miss Deery after tea.

May 22 Clear. Thermometer 94.

Attended the Courts and the Assembly today. Called on Miss Morgan after tea. City very dusty and disagreeable—

May 23 Clear and Thermometer 96, Storm after dark, a little rain.

Attended the Courts and the Gen. Assembly—the discussion in the latter was very animated. Dr. Smith of Va. and Dr. Plummer of Pitts-

---

[43] James Henley Thornwell (1812-1862), Presbyterian clergyman, President of South Carolina College.

burg made able arguments. Walked from church to Mr. Bass' with Miss Dixon and Plummer where I dined. Attended a small party at Dr. Porters in the evening.

May 24 Clear and pleasant.

Attended the Courts and the Assembly but occupied most of the day in my office. In the evening I called on Miss Dixon of N. Y. and accompanied her to the Presbyterian Church where we heard Dr. Robt. Breckinridge[44] of Ky. preach. He did not come up to my expectations.

May 25 Clear and warm.

Attended the Circuit Court and the Assembly. Dr. Lindsly the former President of the Nashville University died at one o'clock today—

May 26 Clear and very warm.

Attended the Circuit Court and the Assembly. Called on Miss Ophelia Martin in the morning. News of Gov. Wise's[45] election came by telegraph today—Rode out to see Miss Lytton in the afternoon.

May 27 Clear and very warm.

Attended the 1st Presbyterian church this morning and listened to a very long and tedious sermon from Dr. Plummer of Pittsburg. Dined at Mr. Bass' with Miss Plummer and others. Called on Miss Smith in the evening.

May 28 Clear and warm.

Attended the Funeral of Dr. Lindsly in the morning and called on the Misses Martin of Pulaski, Miss Rice and Moore of St. Louis and Miss Krebs of N.Y.

May 29 Cloudy, little rain.

Attended the Circuit Court today. The Gen. Assembly of the Presbyterian Church adjourned this morning after an interesting and harmonious meeting. There were about 300 members in attendance, embracing many of the first divisions in the country. Dined at Dr Porters and went with Miss Rice and Moore of St. Louis to the steamboat. Attended a small party in the evening at Dr Waters.

---

[44] Robert Jefferson Breckenridge (1800-1871), lawyer, Presbyterian clergyman, educational leader, was born in Fayette County, Kentucky. He began law practice in Lexington in 1824; joined the Presbyterian Church in 1828 and entered the ministry; Pastor of the Second Presbyterian Church in Baltimore 1832-1845; President of Jefferson College in Pennsylvania 1845-1847; Superintendent of Public Instruction in Kentucky 1847-1851; taught in the new Danville Theological Seminary 1851-1869. He probably is best known as a leader in public education in Kentucky.

[45] Henry Alexander Wise (1806-1876), congressman, Governor of Virginia. He began the practice of law in Nashville, Tennessee in 1828; returned to Virginia in 1830; held several local offices; served as a Jackson Democrat in Congress 1833-1844; Minister to Brazil 1844-1847; Governor of Virginia 1856-1860. He served in the Confederate Army during the Civil War, later resuming the practice of law.

May 30 Cloudy and warm. Heavy rain after dark.

Attended the Circuit Court after which I passed the day in reading. Took tea at Mr. Bass' with Miss Dixon of Phila.

May 31st. Warm and cloudy.

Attended the Court in the morning and occupied the rest of the day in my office—

June 1st Very cold and clear.

Attended the Circuit Court today—and called after tea on Miss Lizzie Woods with Rice.

June 2nd Clear and cold. Thermometer ranging from 64 to 70.

Attended the Circuit Court in the morning. After tea the democrats of the city fired one hundred guns in honor of Henry A Wise election in Va. and had a grand rally on Broad St. The Know-Nothings were there in great numbers purposely to break up the meeting by crying down the speakers. I made a short speech and was listened to with more attention than the rest—but they kept up a terrible noise even while I spoke. The Know-Nothings went from Broad St to the Square where they were addressed by Temple[46] who has deserted the democratic party and by H Cox and Brian. Three men were shot on the square this afternoon.

June 3rd Clear and cold. 60 to 70.

Remained in my office all day reading. Having heard so much preaching recently I did not go to church.

June 4th. Cloudy, cold and rain.

Attended the Circuit Court. Occupied the most of the day in my office.

June 5th. Cloudy — heavy rain.

Attended the Circuit Court and occupied the rest of the day in my office. The foreign news this morning is particularly interesting. Peace prospects—Vesuvius on fire—Resignation of Canrobert the French Gen in the Crimea—

June 6th Cloudy and warm.

Attended the Circuit Court. Recd an interesting letter from Miss Bonner. The newspapers of the city are making a great to do about the disturbance of the Anti Know Nothing Rally on Saturday night.

---

[46] Lucien M. Temple, a Nashville attorney.

June 7th Heavy rains.

Attended the Circuit Court today—and occupied most of the time in my office reading and reflecting on the predicament I am now in with several young ladies.

June 8th Clear and pleasant.

Attended Court today but remained mostly in my office reading. Wrote to Miss Bonner this evening. Young Haywood an Anti Know Nothing candidate for the legislature made a speech at the Court House and was very much disturbed by the crowd.

June 9 Clear and pleasant.

Attended the Circuit Court—passed the balance of the day reading. Called on Miss Smith and Miss Morgan.

June 10. Clear and pleasant.

Attended the 1st Presbyterian Church from which I went out and dined with Jno Trimble.[47]

June 11th Clear and pleasant.

Went over the river at 11 oc to hear the two candidates for Gov speak. Both made excellent efforts and the friends of both came off satisfied. About 5000 persons present—some ladies. I was informed today that I was the choice of the dem party for Congress.

June 12 Clear and pleasant.

Attended the Circuit Court this morning and listened to a case where Judge Bryan sued Gen Cullum for 500 dollars—fee for defending him for murder. The New York Herald of the 8 which came last night gives the name of the deligates and the first three days proceedings of the National Know Nothing Convention. [They] will find it difficult to make a national platform as there are so many eliments in the body. Remained in my office most of the day. After tea I called on Miss Donelson who has just returned from La.

June 13th Clear and cool.

Received a letter this morning from Miss Bonner. Read the report in the N Y Herald of the proceedings of the Know Nothing Convention at Phila. Mayor Conrad[48] gave them a magnificent banquet at which patriotic toasts and speeches were made. Nothing definite as to

---

[47] John Trimble (1812-1884), lawyer, was born in Roane County, Tennessee. He was Attorney General of Tennessee 1836-1842; a member of the State House of Representatives in 1843 and 1844; a member of the State Senate 1845-1846, 1859, 1861, and 1865-1867; United States Attorney 1862-1864; a Republican member of Congress 1867-1869.

[48] Robert Taylor Conrad (1810-1858), journalist, judge, dramatist.

the proceedings of the Convention. Attended the exhibition at the Female Academy today. Mary[49] my sister graduated and read the best essay "Subject the Mind." Occupied the evening in my office reading political documents.

June 14th Clear and cool.

Occupied most of the day in my office considering the propriety of becoming a candidate for Congress and marrying Miss Bonner or Deery. A dispatch came today announcing that the Phila K N convention had adopted a platform, and that the slavery question is agreed upon satisfactory to the South. Attended a party this evening at Sterling Cockrell's—

June 15th Clear and pleasant.

Remained in my office nearly all day—feeling bad—having various subjects of moment pressing on my mind.

June 16th Clear and warmest day of the season.

This morning I declined being a candidate for Congress and Mr. Torbitt[50] of the Union will take my place. At 11 o c I went to hear F K Zollikoffer[51] speak. The audience was small—his speech long dull and statistical. The suspension bridge gave way this afternoon—one or two persons drowned and 7 horses. Mr Hall of this county went through in a buggy and escaped miraculously. The negro who was driving a waggon loaded with tin escaped but considerably bruised and his leg broken. The timbers that gave way were of new cedar and just placed in.

June 17th Clear and very warm.

Remained in my office most of the day. Nothing of interest transpired.

June 18th. Thermometer 88. Clear.

Remained in my office most of the day. Between three and four o'clock this afternoon a distructive fire broke out in the large furniture

---

[49] Mary Louise McGavock was born in Nashville January 8, 1838. She married James Todd of Louisville, Kentucky May 16, 1865. Todd was a native of Ireland; came to the United States in 1838; became a wealthy merchant and manufacturer in Louisville; died February 9, 1890.

[50] Colonel G. C. Torbett, Nashville newspaper editor. In November 1852 he purchased a half interest in the *Nashville American* and became one of the editors. He was one of the proprietors of the *Nashville Union and American,* which paper was formed in May 1853 by the consolidation of the *Union* and *American.* In May 1858 he sold his interest in the paper to J. O. Griffith of Columbia, Tennessee.

[51] Felix Kirk Zollicoffer (1812-1862), editor, soldier, Congressman from Tennessee, was a native of Maury County, Tennessee. He engaged in newspaper work in Paris, Tennessee, Knoxville, Tennessee, and Huntsville, Alabama 1828-1843; served in the Seminole War in 1836; was owner and editor of the *Columbia Observer* and the *Southern Agriculturalist* in 1837; editor of the *Republican Banner* in 1843; Comptroller of the State Treasury 1845-1849; a member of the State Senate 1849-1852; a State Rights Whig in Congress 1853-1859; served in the Confederate Army as brigadier general until his death.

manufactry on College Hill owned by Messrs Nance Grooms and others. Loss from 75 to 100,000 dollars. No insurance. Called to see Mrs Donelson this evening.

June 19th. Thermometer 86. Cloudy and slight shower.

Remained in my office all day. Called on Miss Woods — Calls — Morgan and Smith. Nothing of interest to note—

June 20th Thermometer 86. Clear.

The wheat crop of Tennessee is better this year than I have ever known it—and the other crops look exceedingly promisng. Occupied the day in my office. Rode with Walter Scott and took tea with him.

June 21st Thermometer 84. Cloudy and rain.

The city papers this morning contain the Platform of the National K N Convention at Philadelphia. After reading it attentively I have concluded that it contains nothing but humbug gotten up for temporary success in the coming elections in the South. Called to see Chas Sumner of Boston today but he had gone to the Hermitage. I hope that he will return to Mass. with different ideas on the subject of slavery. A Mr Thomson of Charleston called on me today with a letter of introduction from Dr. Fraser[52] of that city. Rode out with Bob Brown to Gov A V Brown's to tea where we met Miss Laura Donelson, Miss Zollikoffer, Miss Putnam, Miss Rayburn and Miss Saunders besides several gentlemen. As usual when I visit the Gov there came up a hard rain and we had to stay all night.

June 22nd Thermometer 84. Clear.

Remained in my office all day reading. After tea I called on Miss Morgan—

June 23 Thermometer 80. Cloudy and rain.

Occupied the day mostly in reading. In the afternoon Rice and myself walked out to the Penitentiary.

June 24 Thermometer 78. Cloudy and heavy rains.

The papers this morning state that the K N of this County have nominated Anthony Johnson for the Senate and Lucien Temple and Neil S Brown for the house. The two former are renegade democrats and the later the head and front of the new organization in Tennessee. He was one of the deligates to the Phila convention and has been making speeches since its adjournment at Ratification meetings in N.Y.—Phila—and Baltimore. Brown and Stokes arrived this evening full of

[52] Charles Fraser (1782-1860), lawyer, miniature painter.

consolation for their K N friends. Remained in my office all the day—much troubled about my *affairs de coeur.*

June 25 Thermometer 78. Cloudy.

Occupied the day in my office reading. After tea I called on Mrs. Donelson.

June 26 Thermometer 80. Clear.

Remained in my office nearly all day. I was solicited to be a candidate for the legislature today but declined. This evening I attended the democratic Club room and listened to speeches from Allison and Dr C K Winston.[53]

June 27 Thermometer 88. Clear.

Occupied the day mostly in my office. Nothing of importance occurred.

June 28 Thermometer 88. Clear.

Occupied the day reading. Spent the evening at Wm. Cooper's.

June 29 Thermometer 88. Clear.

At 10 oc I went to hear Philip White on temperance. He disclaimed the charge in the Union and American that he was a K N emissary in disguise. After tea I called with H Fogg on Miss Lizzie Woods.

June 30 Thermometer 88. Rain in the afternoon.

Occupied the morning in my office reading. Sent a note to Miss Bonner—After tea I called on Miss Smith.

July 1st Clear and pleasant.

Attended the Episcopal Church this morning and called on Miss Call of Fla this evening.

July 2nd Clear and pleasant.

Occupied my office most of the day reading town dull except in politics.

July 3rd Clear and warm.

Remained in my office all day reading.

July 4th Clear in the morning, shower in the evening.

I was aroused this morning by the ringing of the city bells in honor of the glorious fourth. The two political parties had their barbecues and speeches at different points in the vicinity of the city. The K N had a very large crowd and made great to do—the crowd at the democratic

---

[53] Charles K. Winston, M.D., was a native of Kentucky, in which state he commenced the practice of medicine; moved to Nashville, Tennessee in 1842; was a leading physician there until 1876; a member of the faculty of the Medical Department of the University of Nashville 1851-1867; President of the faculty 1851-1872.

meeting was respectable and addressed by Andrew Ewing O P Nicholson [54] Dr. Charles K Winston and Wm R Cox.[55] I did not attend the other meeting but understood that A J Donelson[56] presided and that the Vice President and Sec were equally distributed between democrats and Whigs. Gen Call of Fla[57] made a speech—also N S Brown, Collier of Franklin Co and Judge Turner.[58] In the evening the K N who profess to conduct things quietly made a great noise on the Public Square and in the streets. Speeches were delivered by Temple, Bilbo[59] and such like—

July 5th Clear and warm.

Occupied my room all the day reading but my mind was so much deranged on the other subjects that I read without much profit. In the evening I made a visit at Mathew Watson's.[60]

July 6th Thermometer 78. Rain.

Read an abstract of Andrew Ewings speech of the 4th in the Union this morning on KN ism. It is an able document—also in the same paper a communication from Chambliss of Giles Co who was a K N but withdrew. He gives his reasons and urges all true democrats to come out of the order. Remained all day in my office. Called after tea with Henry Fogg on Miss Smith and the Misses Martin—city.

---

[54] Alfred Osborn Pope Nicholson (1808-1876), lawyer, editor, Senator from Tennessee, was born near Franklin, Tennessee. He began the practice of law in Columbia, Tennessee in 1831; editor of the *Western Mercury* in Columbia 1832-1835; appointed as a Democrat to the United States Senate 1840-1842; served in the State Senate 1843-1845; moved to Nashville and edited the *Nashville Union* 1844-1846; President of the Bank of Tennessee in 1846 and 1847; editor of the Washington Union 1853-1857; again served in the United States Senate 1859-1861; Chief Justice of the Supreme Court of Tennessee 1870-1876.

[55] William Ruffin Cox (1831-1919), lawyer, agriculturalist, soldier, was a native of Halifax County, North Carolina. He practiced law in Nashville, Tennessee 1853-1857; moved to Raleigh, North Carolina in 1859; an officer in the Confederate Army; a member of Congress in 1881-1887; Secretary of the United States Senate 1893-1900; spent the remainder of his life in agricultural pursuits.

[56] Andrew Jackson Donelson (1799-1871), soldier, lawyer, was born in Sumner County, Tennessee. He graduated from West Point in 1819; served with General Andrew Jackson throughout the Florida campaign; began the practice of law in 1833; President Jackson's private secretary during both of Jackson's administrations; appointed Minister to Texas in 1844; was afterwards made Minister to Prussia; nominated Vice President on the Know-Nothing ticket with Millard Fillmore in 1856.

[57] Richard Keith Call (1792-1862), soldier, congressman.

[58] Judge W. K. Turner (d. 1864) was made Judge of the Criminal Court for Davidson County and Nashville when the court was created in 1842. He held this position with distinction until his death.

[59] Col. W. N. Bilbo was a Nashville newspaper man and a leader in the Know-Nothing party. He became a member of the editorial staff of the *Nashville Gazette* February 5, 1856. On May 18 he purchased the paper but sold it the following November 11.

[60] Matthew Watson was a Nashville business man. He was chosen a member of board of directors of the Bank of Tennessee in January 1833 and of the Planter's Bank of Tennessee in January 1834. He was one of a small group who aided Rev. James H. Otey in establishing Christ Episcopal Church in 1829.

July 7th. Thermometer . Clear.

The telegraph this morning brings us news of another fight at Sebastipol. Allies repulsed with a loss of about 4000. The English lost 70 officers.

July 8 Clear and very warm.

My name was announced in the Union this morning as a candidate for the lower branch of the legislature in connection with Gen W G Harding for the Senate. Remained in my office all day preparing for the fight. Wrote a note to Miss B and one to Miss D. Called on Miss D in the evening.

July 9th Clear and very hot.

This morning I went out with the candidates to Smith's Springs about 13 miles off on the Murfresboro turnpike. I made a speech of some length and to my satisfaction. After speaking at Smith's Springs I continued the canvass with great earnestness, fighting K N ism with all the abilities I could command up to the day of the election. My opponents were the Hon. N S Brown an old line whig and Lucian Temple a renegade democrat. After I got into the canvass and indeed before I discovered that K N Order was thoroughly organized and numbered on their roll some of the oldest and best democrats of the county. They had been at work for 18 months while the democratic party was asleep. This fact taken in connection with the great personal unpopularity of Gov Johnson in the county caused us to fall behind largely any former vote. We carried the State however by a large majority, which I think will give a quietus to K N ism in Tennessee. After the election was over, and the ebulition of party had subsided I made a visit to Fayetteville in Lincoln Co to see Miss Lizzie Bonner to whom I had been engaged for a year past. I remained there for several days—and she was as ever very kind and affectionate—but she looked so bad and delicate that I was forced against my inclinations to believe that the warnings and advise of my friends was not without foundation. I left her in gloom for I was much attached to her—but my judgement forced me to lay my fears before her.

On my return I went to Alisonia to see Miss Deery—now my wife She was not at home but at Shelbyville. I then went there and the following week—viz. Aug. 23 we were married at Alisonia at 12 o c noon by the Rev John T. Edgar. The whole affair was gotten up and carried out hurriedly without communicating with any one but my immediate family. No one was present at the marriage but her mother and three brothers and my two sisters and brother John. The next day Sallie, Mary, John, and my wife and myself—started in the cars for the North.

At Chattanooga we met with many of our Nashville friends who had been at Catoosa Springs. They were much astonished at my marriage—not having had any intimation of it. From Chattanooga we went direct to Washington City via Atlanta, Augusta, Richmond. We remained in Washington several days—and then went to Baltimore—thence to Phila and thence to N.Y. In New York we put up at the St Nicholas the most magnificent hotel in the world—where we met many of our friends from the South. We remained in the city two weeks during which time we made an excursion up the Hudson to West Point—which furnishes some of the finest scenery in the U. S. We heard Rachel the great French Acress—whom I had heard before in Rome, and also Parodi the great operatic singer. The success of both of these artists was complete. From N. Y. we went to the beautiful city of New Haven and thence to Boston the city of nations. While in Boston we visited Bunker Hill and Cambridge my old Alma Mater, also Mt Auburn, Cushing, and Gordon's.

From Boston we went to Albany, thence to Troy and Saratoga. We remained at Saratoga several days but there were but few persons there, and the weather was quite cold. From Saratoga we went to Montreal by way of Lake Champlayne. From Montreal we ascended the St Lawrence on the Steamer British Empire as high as Ogdensburg, N. Y. The Capt. of the boat to whom I had a letter of introduction from the proprietor of the Dongunna House in Montreal was exceedingly polite—and accompanied us together with another party to Ottawa City on the Ottawa River—an excursion of about 50 miles from the St. Lawrence, by rail from Prescott. Ottawa City has a population of 8 or 10 thousand and is the great lumber mart of Canada. The Falls upon which the city is situated presents a greater variety of scenery than any I ever saw and the scenery about is magnificent beyond description. The English government has made vast expenditures of money here, in the construction of a Canal connecting the city with Toronto on Lake Ontario—through which to convey military stores. Also lumber slides over the falls, through which to carry rafts over the falls in safety, and a suspension bridge of great beauty just below the falls. Returning to the St Lawrence we took another steamer from Niagara Falls. After seeing all on both sides of the river which I had visited several times before we went to Buffalo and thence to Cincinnati via Erie and Columbus. From Cincinnati we went to Louisville by rail — and thence home by stage. Our trip was delightful — and nothing occurred to disturb our pleasure. So much for my bridal trip. Since our return to Nashville we received the congratulations of all our friends. Attended several parties given for us and returned the calls of about 150 persons. We made a visit to Franklin to see my relatives, and to Alisonia to see my wife's family.

[*At this point a section of the original journal has been cut out.*]

Nov. 22 Thermometer 50. Clear.

Last night news reached the city that five spans of the Tennessee River Bridge was distroyed by fire from a spark, while a train was passing over. John Ewing was married last night to Miss Hoard of Rutherford County. Geo D. Prentice[61] of Louisville was there escorting Miss Sue Spence. We had a fire today on Cedar Street but no material damage sustained. Attended the Chancery Court and occupied most of the day reading Story on Equity Jurisprudence.

Nov. 23 Thermometer 50. Clear

This morning I attended the Chancery Court and occupied the most of the day reading—but with a feeling of melancholly—occasioned by a bad dream last night—I dreamed that I went to fr. to see . . . [*Here a section has been blotted out of the original journal.*] She was living in a magnificent palace & surrounded by all the splendors that wealth could give. I occupied a hotel just opposite from which I went to see her. She met me in her parlors with dejected countenance & really seemed the most . . . .

[*At this point the original journal has been cut.*]

Nov. 27

. . . . Before going in a gentleman came into the Anti-room with a mask on his face—& demanded one dollar for initiation fee, which we paid. We were then conducted into a large hall around which were seated a large number of gentlemen with covered faces—& one whom I afterwards discovered to be H.C.—occupied an elevated seat. He had a black robe on, a sword by his side—and plumes in his hat. Those to be initiated were placed in the *proper position* with their toes on a crack in the floor—and were asked the following questions by the Grand Master, as near as I can recollect. Do you come into this Order of your own free will and accord? What is your name? age? country? Do you promise on your honour never to reveal the secrets of this Order. . . . Would you in the absence of a natural opportunity throw yourself upon your own resources?

The G Master then tells you that all is a farce so far but now comes the serious matters[.] Are you in favor of protesting by your influence & money the oppresed & downtrodden of Cuba? Would you be willing

[61] George Dennison Prentice (1802-1870), journalist.

to take command of a company & aid in planting the stars & stripes upon the embattlements of the Moro Castle—provided your own government sanctioned it.

The candidates were then blindfolded & required to take three high steps over sharp swords—with injunctions that if any blood was spilt—it would be ominous of evil consequences. This being over the Grand Surgeon *examined* the candidates & pronounced that no blood had been spilt. The regalia of the Order was then placed on the Candidates . . . .

. . . The G M then gave out a few ridiculous verses in keeping with the whole, which were sung to the tune of Auld-Lang-Zine by members. This being over the meeting adjourned until next Friday night & the newly initiated were informed that they must treat the crowd at Sandy's which they accordingly did. This order is called the A. O. M. C.[62] and is calculated to affect some good—as well as afford much amusement. It shows the absurdity of our attempting to gain the Island of Cuba by fillebustering movements, or in any other way except by population. It also shows the absurdity of Secret Societies—& is well calculated I think to render ludicrous the Know-Nothings—if not break them up. The Order numbers many of our most respectable citizens of both political parties—and I am certain that I am indebted to them for an amount of laughter sufficient to make me *fat* the remainder of my life.

Nov. 28th Thermometer 40. Cloudy.

Passed most of the day in my office reading and attending to business.

Nov. 29th

Attended a public sale of lots in West Nashville today. Property has advanced very much in that direction in the last year.

Nov. 30th.

Passed the morning in my office reading law—the papers. Late in the evening I walked down to the river to see father and Jno. off on the Dr Robinson for Ark. I found a number of acquaintances going down—and among them Mrs. Donelson whom I always admired exceedingly. Father and W. Harding had some mules to carry down and they were so unmanageble that the deck hands had to draw them on with ropes. After the boat left I went once more to the society of the A.O.M.C. knowing that I would enjoy a hearty laughter and sure enough I did. Upon the principle exemplified by the fox when he got his tail cut off. I managed to pass the evening without one moment's cessation of laughter. Among the individuals initiated tonight was A J. Donelson

62 The A. O. M. C. was a fraternal order whose membership was composed of men in Nashville and vicinity. Its aim was primarily social. The initiation ceremony was particularly amusing and hilarious.

and Wm Polk. The former must have perspired one gallon while he was going through the ceremony, and I do not think he answered truly some of the questions proposed.

Late at night there was a large fire broke out in Bells Livery Stable but by the energy of the fire companies it was extinguished.

December 1st.

Occupied myself today in business matters—nothing of note has transpired.

Dec. 2nd

Remained at home all day and did not go to Church.

Dec. 3rd.

This is an important day in Washington. Congress meets and parties are so split up there that it will be difficult to organize the House. News reached here today of great excitement and serious difficulties in Kansas between the Abolititionists and the pro-slavery party. Blood had been shed—the Gov. had called out the Malitia and citizens from the border counties in Mo. were flocking to the Gov. aid. This is a serious question and will cause great difficulties in Congress this session.

The Supreme Court of Tenn met and adjourned this morning. An election was held on Saturday for Supreme Judge in the place of Totten[63] who resigned. Bullock and Harris were the Candidates neither of whom are fitted for the office. The election in this city was a perfect farce and I do not think that one third of the votes in the County were polled, showing conclusively to my mind that the elections of the Judiciary ought never to have been placed in the hands of the people. The Criminal Court met also today.

Dec. 4th

This morning I finished making bridal calls with my wife. While out we called on Jas Maury and lady—who have just arrived from Petersburg Va. She was a Miss Marks. After tea I attended the A O M C and laughed as much as usual. Among the new members was Jas Rice, Jack Read, Tom Smiley.[64]

[63] A. W. O. Totten (d. 1867), lawyer, was born in Middle Tennessee. He began the practice of law in Trenton, Tennessee, but afterwards moved to Jackson. He was appointed one of the Supreme Court Judges under the Constitution of 1835 and served until 1855. In 1861 he was one of the commissioners appointed by Governor Harris to form a military league with the Southern Confederacy.

[64] Thomas T. Smiley was born in Nashville, Tennessee in 1813. He graduated from the University of Nashville in 1833, studied law with Ephraim H. Foster, and was admitted to the bar in 1836. He was Clerk of the Circuit Court 1844-1859.

Dec. 5.

This morning my wife went with Sallie and Mary Manch to Williamson to spend a few days. Occupied in the Criminal Court today.

Dec. 6th

Occupied the day in my office. Attended a large party at Mr. Bass' last night—enjoyed myself very much.

Dec. 7th

Attended the Criminal Court today where I found one of my early schoolmates—the son of Newland Moffett the great Methodist Preacher on trial for obtaining money under false pretences. He was acquitted. After tea I went to the A O M C to see Bob Brown initiated. It was amusing. Afterwards I called on Mr Churchwell and Jas and Bob Deery at the City Hotel.

Dec. 8th

The day has been very windy and dusty. Congress has made no Speaker from last accounts—excitement very great in Washington. No news in Nashville. River low and business quite dull.

Dec. 9th

Remained at home all day quite lonely, all being away but Mother and Mary. Did not attend church.

Dec. 10th

Was most of the day in the warfe, attending to the shipping of things to the plantation. Mother and Mary started for Ark leaving me alone.

Dec. 11

Attended the Criminal Court today—nothing of interest going on. No Speaker yet in Congress.

From the 11th of Dec. up to the first of January 1856 has been passed rather quietly at home. The year is at an end and no Speaker yet in Congress. The Black Republicans or Abolitionist still stick to Banks of Mass.[65] The K N to Fuller of Penn[66] and the democrats to Richardson[67] of Ill. This has been a very eventful year in the history of the world—as well as my own humble history. Rumours of Peace in Europe are current at present, but I give them no credence. The crops in the U S have been abundant and our domestic and foreign relations have been as good as we could wish. I cannot as yet see what is to be the result of my own actions this year—they are in the womb of the future.

[65] Nathaniel Prentiss Banks (1816-1894), congressman, Governor of Massachusetts, Union soldier.

[66] Henry Mills Fuller (1820-1860), Congressman from Pennsylvania.

[67] William Alexander Richardson (1811-1860), Congressman from Illinois.

CHAPTER XVII

"At present I have the promise of a long and useful career." (1856)

The year 1856 did indeed look promising to young Randal McGavock. An alert mind, a fine education, an established social position, a multitude of influential friends — all combined to give a certain brightness and confidence to the future. That McGavock intended to make effective use of each of these attributes is abundantly clear as one follows his daily activities.

1856

January 1

After rather a dull Christmas week I commence the New Year hoping that it may bring additional happiness and prosperity to me and mine as well as the whole country. On last new-years day I was a single man and occupied the day in visiting my friends but today I drank wine only at three places—so much for getting married.

Jan. 2

This day has been occupied mostly in the transaction of my father's business. This evening both he, my mother and Mary arrived on the Cline from Ar.

Jan. 3

This has been such a cold day that nearly every one remains in doors. In the evening I attended the funeral of young Frank Morgan[1] second son of Sam Morgan who died of fever. He was a young man of great promise—and much beloved.

---

[1] Franklin Henry Morgan was the second living son of Samuel D. Morgan (1798-1880), a Nashville merchant, a trustee of the University of Nashville 1844-1880, and chairman of the Commission that supervised construction of the Tennessee State Capitol.

Jan. 4

This morning I got up before day and went to the depot with my wife—who accompanied her brother Robert to Alisonia. It was intensely cold. After breakfast I went with Carrie MacGavock to the St America for New Orleans. The afternoon was occupied in drawing up writs for the next Circuit Court. In the evening I attended the Society of the A O M C where I laughed quite as much as usual in seeing others made Jack-Asses of. Jno R Eakin[2] and Jas Armstrong of Bedford Co. were initiated.

Jan. 5th

Agreeable to a call in the Union the democracy of Davidson met in Convention at the Court House to appoint delegates to the State Convention on the 8th which convention is called to appoint Delegates to the National Convention at Cincinnati next Spring and to nominate electors for the States at large for the coming Presidential Contest. The Message of Franklin Pierce was received last night. It is quite lengthy covering all of our foreign policy as well as domestic affairs in a bold and explicit manner. He also reviews in a masterly and patriotic manner the vexed question of Slavery—showing conclusively that the North has no right to interfere in the domestic institution of the South. This message has elivated Pierce 50 per cent in my estimation and it must meet with the hearty approval of every Southerner.

Jan. 6th

The day has been so cold that I have not ventured out even to Church —but remained at home reading the New-Combs. I heard this evening of a very melancholy affair that took place in this neighborhood. About 18 mo ago a young man who was the cousin of Joseph Ellison daughter —ran off & married her in Chattanooga. The father pursued them & brought them back, when they started to the South accompanied by an older Sister. A few days ago she returned and gave birth to a child by her brother-in law. Hanging is too good for the rascal—he ought to be tared-feathered & burnt—for his wickedness.

Jan. 7

The day has been occupied in attending to business. After tea I attended the Democratic Caucus in the Capitol—for the purpose of making arrangements for the State Convention to morrow. It was largely attended and we had considerable excitement occasioned by the over zealous friends of Andrew Johnson who desired to force the Conven-

[2] John R. Eakin was a member of the board of aldermen in Nashville in 1851.

tion to recommend him for the Presidency to the National Convention. They finally adjourned after perfecting the organization for to morrow.

Jan. 8th

The convention assembled at 11 oc this morning and organized. A committee was appointed to draft resolutions and also a committee to recommend suitable candidates for State Electors and delegates to the National Convention at Cincinnati. Each Congressional delegation retired and voted for their choice.

Wm H Polk of Maury and Isam Harris[3] of Shelby were made Electors for the State at large. The first I consider a bad selection but the last will do very well from all I can learn. The deligates to the National Convention will do—but they might have made a much abler selection. The Platform presented by the Committee on Resolutions was one of the best that I have ever seen offered. In the afternoon A Ewing and A O P Nicholson made several speeches and after tea A V Brown, Andrew Johnson and several old-line whigs who have come over viz. Maj. Lowe of Robertson, Bransford,[4] Haywood and others. The Convention adjourned *sine die* in perfect good humor.

Jan. 9th

It has been intensely cold today—the coldest day of the season. I have remained in-doors all day. Col DeGraffenried of Ga called to see me today. Old Maj. Claiborne[5] died last night. He was one of the oldest residents of Nashville.

Jan 10th

Rose before day this morning and went up on the cars to Alisonia to see my wife. I found her well and glad to see me.

[3] Isham G. Harris (1818-1897) has been described as "the most competent and skillful political leader in the history of Tennessee." He was a native of Franklin County, Tennessee; became a lawyer in 1841, after a few years in the mercantile business; elected to the State Senate in 1847 and to Congress in 1849 and 1851; went to Memphis to practice law in 1853; Governor of Tennessee 1857-1861. On June 24, 1861 he issued a proclamation dissolving the connection of Tennessee with the United States. During the same year he was again elected governor, a position which became merely Confederate Governor after most of Tennessee had fallen into Union hands in 1862. When the war ended he sought refuge first in Mexico and then in Europe; returned to Tennessee in 1867; resumed law practice in Memphis for ten years, elected to the United States Senate in 1877.

[4] Thomas Louis Bransford (1804-1856), business man, was born in Buckingham County, Virginia. He moved to Gainsboro, Tennessee in 1825 and to Nashville in 1856. He had a successful business career, and was at one time President of the Nashville and Cincinnati Railroad Company. He served as a Whig member of the Tennessee Legislature from Jackson County, was twice a presidential elector, and was a candidate for Congress in 1843.

[5] Thomas Claiborne (1780-1856), soldier, lawyer, was born near Petersboro, Virginia. He served as a major on the staff of Andrew Jackson in the Creek War; began the practice of law in Nashville in 1807; a member of the Tennessee Legislature for some years; a Democrat in Congress 1817-1819; resumed practice of law until his death.

Jan. 11th

Remained at Alisonia all day. Went into the factory and saw them make bags for wheat and corn with the new sewing machines. Each machine turns out with the labor of one woman six hundred bags. Great invention.

Jan. 12th

Returned to Nashville this afternoon with my wife. Deep snow on the way.

Jan. 13

The day has been so inclement that I have remained at home reading.

Jan. 14th

The circuit court began today—large docket. Weather cold and very disagreeable.

Jan. 15th

Attended the Circuit Court this morning—finished the 1st weeks docket and adjourned until Monday next. No Speaker yet in Congress. Some talk of a war with England about Central America—but I think it will all end in smoke.

Jan. 16

Weather still continues cold and disagreeable. From the NY Herald I see that they had on the 7th the severest snow storm that has visited them for 70 years.

Jan. 17th

Attended the Supreme Court and the Legislature today—nothing of particular interest going on.

Jan. 18

Remained in my office most of the day reading and attending to business.

Jan. 19th

Nothing has transpired today of any moment. Remained in doors all day.

Jan. 20

It commenced snowing about dark last evening and snowed all night. Last evening my wife received a letter from her brother Robert stating that her brother James was dying and requested us to go up immediately. We reached there about 12 oc and found him much better. The physicians say that he is now out of danger. The snow on the mountain is six inches deep and it is intensely cold.

Jan. 21st

Remained most of the day in the room with Mr. Deery.

Jan. 22

Left Allisonia about two o'clock—found A J Donelson Jr on the cars just from West Point.

Jan. 23rd Intensely cold and clear. River low and coal out.

Attended the Circuit Court today. There is considerable excitement at present in the Know Nothing Councils throughout the state about candidates for County offices. Many men went into the K N organization to secure the spoils, and they are now clamerous on the subject. In nearly every county candidates have come out in opposition to the K N nominees. The Democrats stand off and laugh in their sleaves.

Jan. 24th

Attended Court this morning—but passed most of the day in my office.

Jan. 25th

Remained all day in my office—in the evening I attended the A.O.M.C.

Jan. 26th

Cold and disagreeable—no news—remained in my office all the day.

Jan. 27th

Remained at home today—did not go to church on account of the cold and snow.

Jan. 28

Attended Court today but little doing.

Jan. 29th

We have had the heaviest snow here that I have ever witnessed in Tenn. The cold has been more intense and continuous than I have ever seen it.

Jan. 30

Attended the Circuit Court today—no news.

Jan. 31st

Attended Court this morning—this evening I accompanied Sallie Grundy and wife to a party out at Sterling Cockrells. Before the dance commenced they had tableaues. I appeared in two scenes in my Turkish Costume—and enjoyed myself much.

Feb. 1st

This morning I wrote a letter of thanks as chairman of a committee appointed by the A O M C to Mrs J Watkins and the Misses Cheatham for raising $105 for the Order. I waited on the ladies and presented it in person. Attended the Circuit Court this morning—nothing of interest going on. Gen Harding and Jas McGavock dined with us today. In the afternoon I remained in my office reading.

Feb. 2nd

This morning I went up to Alisonia after my wife. Found her brother James very much improved.

Feb. 3rd

Another snow last night. Remained all day in the house reading.

Feb. 4th

Returned home this afternoon with Seraphine—learned on the cars from Jno Eakin that Banks of Mass was elected Speaker in the House of Rep of U S after ballotting two months. He is what they call a Black Republican and an out and out free-soiler. His election is a great Triumph for the abolitionists of the North, and will induce them to be more insolent to the South and southerners than ever before. He was elected under a plurality resolution. Cullum of Tenn who [was] defeated last summer by Savage[6] because he voted against the Kansas and Nebraska bill was elected Clerk of the House on the first ballot. Strange procedure—strange country this—Whither are we tending.

Feb. 5th

Attended the Circuit Court this morning. The Grand Jury was engaged today in examining the case of Sam Earthman who is charged of stealing a pocket book containing six hundred dollars, and some valuable notes from Wm Cummings. This is the same man that killed James McGavock some years ago. He ought to be hung—for he is a great nuisance to society. Attended the A O M C this evening.

Feb. 6th

Attended the Circuit Court today but occupied most of my time in my office reading.

---

[6] John Houston Savage (1815-1904), Congressman from Tennessee, was born in McMinnville, Tennessee. He was Attorney General of the Fourth Tennessee district 1841-1847; a major and later a lieutenant colonel in the United States Infantry during the Mexican War; a member of Congress 1849-1853 and 1855-1859; a colonel in the Confederate Army during the Civil War; and a member of the State House of Representatives 1877-1879 and in 1887.

Feb. 7th

Remained nearly all of the day in my office reading and transacting business.

Feb. 8th

Attended the Circuit Court today and listened to the argument of Counsel in the cases of a little girl named Samuels against the Corporation of Nashville, in which she claims heavy damages for an injury she sustained some time since by a rock thrown by a blast on the Public Square. Ewing Trimble, Meigs[7] and Houston each made excellent speeches. Verdict $2500 besides the expenses. This will cause the city fathers to open their eyes a little.

Feb. 9th

The democrats of the city and county of Davidson held a meeting today at which I presided. The object of the meeting was to consult as to propriety of nominating County Candidates for the election in March next. The K N have several candidates for each office, and we concluded that it was policy to let them fight it out and we could vote for our men quietly.

Feb. 10th

This morning I attended the Presbyterian Church with my wife. Mrs. Hadley and her son and Robt Deery dined with us. In the afternoon I called on V K Stevenson and lady—also on the Hon Wm Churchwell[8] who took tea with us.

Feb. 11

I was in the Circuit Court a short time this morning. The day has been exceedingly dark and incliment, so much so that I have kept

[7] Return Jonathan Meigs (1801-1891), lawyer, was born in Clark County, Kentucky. He was admitted to the bar in Frankfort in 1822, and moved to Tennessee in 1825; practiced law in Athens for ten years; moved to Nashville; Attorney General of Tennessee 1838-1839; appointed United States Attorney for the Middle Tennessee district in 1841; remained loyal to the Union in 1861; Clerk of the Supreme Court of the District of Columbia 1863-1891. His most important publications were a two volume *Digest of all the Decisions of the Former Supreme Courts of Errors and Appeals in the State of Tennessee* (1848-1850), and, with William F. Cooper, a compilation of the *Code of Tennessee* (1858). Besides his legal duties, Meigs took a prominent part in the educational, cultural, and humanitarian activities of his time.

[8] William Montgomery Churchwell (1826-1862), Congressman from Tennessee, was born near Knoxville, Tennessee. After attending Emory and Henry College 1840-1843, he studied law and was admitted to the bar. He became one of the judges for Knox County and was elected as a Democrat to the Thirty-second and Thirty-third Congresses 1851-1855. During the administration of President Buchanan he was sent on a secret mission to Mexico. During the Civil War he served in the Confederate Army as colonel of the Fourth Tennessee Regiment. He was McGavock's brother-in-law, the husband of Seraphine's sister, Martha Eleanor Deery (1830-1897).

pretty close. The legislature of Tenn has purchased of Andrew Jackson[9] for $48,000 the Hermitage tract of land containing 500 acres. Jackson was compelled to sell it, and I am glad that it has fallen into the possession of the State. Old Hickory was her greatest son, and she may well be proud of him. His fame belongs not to her alone but to the whole nation, and I may say the world.

Feb. 12th

Attended the Circuit Court this morning where I met Jno Marshall[10] of Franklin who informed me that Randal Ewing[11] had been seriously injured by a fall from his horse. His hip-joint is supposed to be crushed. This is melancholy information as he is a young lawyer of promise. Wm is still doing badly and his child was seriously burnt—making Dr Ewings house a perfect hospital. Patrick Otey son of Mr Otey of Franklin, jumped from the steamer Cline just below Clarkesville and was drowned. For the last year or so—his mind has been somewhat deranged. He went to La for his health and was on his return home. Attended the A O M C tonight.

Feb. 13th

Remained in my office most of the day reading. No news.

Feb. 14th

Occupied the day in business, and in reading.

Feb. 15th

Last night and today I have been occupied in drafting a Constitution for a new association that I in conjunction with others have started called the "Robertson Association" in honor of the late Duncan Robertson[12] the Howard of Nashville. This institution is purely charitable and similar to the Howard Association of New Orleans and the

[9] Andrew Jackson (1804-1865), adopted son of General Andrew Jackson and nephew of Mrs. Rachel Jackson, was born near the Hermitage. He lived in Washington during General Jackson's presidency and returned to the Hermitage, where he lived for some years.

[10] John Marshall (1803-1863), lawyer, was a native of Williamson County, Tennessee. He began the study of law in 1824 and in time gathered probably the best law library and the best general library in Tennessee. He served in the State Senate in 1837 and 1839 as a Whig. He spent the remaining years to 1861 in his profession and became one of the outstanding lawyers of the state.

[11] Randal Milton Ewing was born in Williamson County, Tennessee June 1, 1829. He was a lawyer in Franklin, Tennessee for a number of years.

[12] Duncan Robertson (1770-1833), business man, philanthropist, was a native of Scotland. He came to Nashville in 1806 and soon was running a bookstore. He was a member of the City's board of aldermen in 1807, 1809, and 1820-1822, and was one of the initial officers of the Cumberland Lodge (Masonic), No. 60, when it was instituted in June 1812. After his death a monument was erected to his memory by the city of Nashville. Col. Willoughby Williams characterized him as "the most benevolent man who ever lived in Nashville."

Compagnia della Misercordia in Florence. The Constitution was adopted by the members about twenty in number and I sincerely hope that it will be a permanent Institution and affect much good in alleviating the sufferings of the poor, during the prevalence of epedemics in the summer and the cold blasts of winter.

Feb. 16

This morning I drew up a bill chartering the Robertson Association which was presented by Mr Burch[13] of Hamilton and passed.

Feb. 17

Attended the 1st Presbyterian Church this morning with my wife but as it was sacrament occasion I left and went down to see Mrs Tom Smith and her daughter Mrs Farqueharson. Dined with Rice, and passed the afternoon with him at Dr Estherman's house.

Feb. 18th

A telegraphic dispatch reached here today from N Y. saying that the Allies have concluded a piece—upon the strength of which cotton has advanced and bread-stuffs declined. I hardly know whether to credit this intelligence or not. If it be true it will effect very materially the prices of everything in this country and may induce England to take courage and give us a bout for supremacy in Central America. It is supposed that the Steamer Pacific belonging to the Collins line is lost. She has now been out over twenty days and no news from her. I returned from Liverpool in the Pacific and would be pained to learn of her loss. The Waterloo in which I went to Europe was lost the next trip and was never heard of.

Feb. 19th

Remained nearly all day in my office examining Walter Scott's books with Mr. McLaughlin. He left his affairs in a sad condition.

Feb. 20th

The legislature today passed the Omnibus bill, appropriating over one million of dollars towards internal improvements—so much for the K N. It is considered the weakest body that has assembled here for years.

---

[13] John C. Burch (d. July 28, 1881), was a native of Georgia. He graduated from Yale in 1843; moved to Chattanooga, Tennessee in 1852; became prominent in the Democratic Party; elected to the lower house of the Tennessee Legislature in 1855 and to the State Senate in 1857; elected Speaker of the latter body; became editor of the *Nashville Union and American* in 1859; entered the Confederate Army in 1861; purchased controlling interest in the *Union and American* 1869 and again became its editor; appointed Comptroller of the State Treasury in 1873; elected Secretary of the United States Senate in 1879. He is best known for his editorial work, and was a power in Tennessee political circles.

Feb. 21st

Remained all day in my office attending to business and reading. No news.

Feb. 22nd.

This is the birthday of Washington the Father of our Country, and should be celebrated throughout the entire length and-breadth of the land but I am sorry to see that so little is now done to impress the day upon the minds of the rising generation. The country is certainly much larger than it was when he died—and we are more powerful as a nation, but the ligaments that bound us together in his time are loosening and Civil war seems to be gathering its angry clouds in Nebraska and Kansas. May the good sense of the people avert such a catastrophy—and may God still prolong the existence of the nation, as an example for the rising Republics in the Western world. I called with my wife this morning on Jno K Howard Lady and sister of Lebanon at the St. Cloud also on Capt. Williams' family. In the afternoon the Robertson Association met for the election of officers. I was elected President, took the oath of office and upon my enstalment made a short speech thanking the members for the honor conferred upon me—and spoke briefly of the objects and importance of the Association. After tea I attended the exhibition of the literary societies of the University in Odd Fellows Hall. The young gentleman acquited themselves with great credit, and I hope that this beginning after a suspension of six years—will be followed by similar and improved exhibitions.

Feb. 23

Passed the forenoon in transacting business and reading Macauly's History of the rise and progress of the English Church. Dined with the family of Dr Waters'. After dinner Lytton Bostick and myself occupied several hours in making By Laws for the Robertson Association.

After tea I went to the Court House to hear the Candidates for County offices speak. They number about thirty in all and the scene was laughable and amusing in the extreme.

Feb. 24th

This has been a lovely day—after a long and severe winter. I went to church this morning and Dr Edgar delivered a good sermon but I was not in the situation to enjoy it for I was surrounded by old flames. On my right was my wife, on my left was Mrs Maney to whom I was once engaged. In front of me was Miss Lizzie Bonner to whom I was also engaged and just behind me the beautiful Amanda Morgan whom I always admired. What a situation! In the afternoon I walked with

Childress out to see Miss Jane Lytton where we passed an agreeable hour.

Feb. 25th

Occupied most of the [day] in my office—reading and transacting business. Beautiful day.

Feb. 26th

Remained in my office most of the day writing By-Laws for the Robertson Association. News reached here to day by telegraph that the K N Convention had nominated Millard Fillmore[14] for the Presidency and And. J. Donelson of Tenn. for the Vice Presidency. The deligates from Ohio, N.Y, Ct., and Mass., dissented. I consider it a very weak ticket. The K N's here *say* that it is just the ticket, but their countenances indicate differently.

Feb. 27

Occupied most of the day in assisting father to start to his plantation in Ark.

Feb. 28th

I was hard at work today preparing for the meeting of the Robertson Association tonight. The by-laws were adopted, and we are now in a fair way to commence work.

Feb. 29

At work all day making collections for Du Pont and Co of Del.

March 1st

It rained all last night, and the day, making it exceedingly disagreeable. The election for County offices was held today but as the polls are open in each ward of the city, we miss the usual excitement. The result will not be known until tomorrow.

March 2nd

From the papers this morning it appears that the entire K N ticket was elected except Bagley who was defeated by Edmonson. Went to church this morning with my wife and listened to a very good sermon from Dr. Edgar. Lizzie Bonner my old flame was there. In the afternoon I called on Aunt Felicia and Maria Stevenson—then took a walk out to the Penitentiary.

March 3rd

Most of the day has been occupied in business matters. After tea I attended the K N Ratification meeting at the Court House. The crowd

[14] Millard Fillmore (1800-1874), thirteenth President of the United States.

was large but the enthusiasm was evidently forced. Gentry made a beautiful speech, displaying advantageously his oritorical powers. N. S. Brown, Cock, Hatten, Temple, McEwen and Brian also spoke. All endorsed the nominees of the Philia Convention but said little about the Platform. The nominees were good enough without any platform.

March 4th

This afternoon I attended a meeting of the democrats in the Capital—called for the purpose of forming a Club in this City and consulting as to the best method of conducting the Canvass in the coming election for President and Vice President. The day has been mild and agreeable—so much after the long spell of cold that one feels very little like staying in the house.

March 5th

My time today has been given to business matters. In the evening I went to a party at Mrs. Lewis' given to her son who was married this even. to Willo Williams daughter. The party was brilliant. . . .

March 6th

Last night I met Miss Bonner at the party and enjoyed her company much. Today I feel very badly—I did not get up until 12 oc had no dinner, and upon the whole felt rather used up. After tea I attended the Robertson Association.

March 7th

Called this morning with my wife on Mr Lewis and lady and in the afternoon on Miss Bonner at the Academy. I did not see [her] as she was in the country.

March 8th

Attended to business all day—beautiful weather. After tea. I read in the N Y Herald the report of A J Donelson, W N Bilbo and Burton's speeches at a Ratification meeting in N Y.

March 9th

Attended the 1st Presbyterian church today, and listened to a very good sermon from Dr Edgar on foreign missions. In the afternoon I took a long ride, looking at lots in the suburbs. After tea I called at Dr. Porter's and to see Ed Ewing Sr. in his office. His has resumed practice.

March 10th

Remained in my office most of the day attending to business. After tea I attended a meeting of the Robertson Association.

March 11

Occupied the day in business matters, after tea I attended a Concert given at the Odd Fellows by Ole Bull the celebrated violinist. The last time that I heard him was in St. Petersburg—at which time my pocket was picked of one hundred rubles, quite a loss.

March 12

Nothing has transpired today worthy of note. I saw A J Donelson today, who has just returned from the Philia . . . .

March 13th

Most of the day has been occupied in my office. I wrote a letter today at the request of an Irish friend to John Mitchell the Irish Patriot who is now living in Knoxville—inviting to deliver a lecture in our city. After tea I attended the Robertson Association and initiated two members—Henry Maney and Dr Atchison.[15]

March 14th

No news yet of the steamer Pacific—I fear she is lost. It appears from the telegraph today that the city of Gedde in Japan was distroyed last Nov. by an earthquake, 100,000 houses, and 30,000 lives distroyed. I saw a plan of this city at the Hague in Holland and was much interested in it.

March 15th

Occupied the day in attending to business. Nothing of interest occured.

March 16th

This morning I rode out to Gen Hardings on horseback where I dined, and in the afternoon I returned by way of Frank MacGavock's—passed an agreeable day.

March 17th

Occupied the day in business matters. No news worth writing.

March 18

This morning I had a visit from Gov. A V Brown who I hope will be the democratic candidate for the Vice Presidency—with Buchanan. I desired to have a public meeting of the friends for the two men and give expression to our choice—but he thought it best to let matters rest here in Tennessee for the present. The weather today is balmy and delightful after the long and severe winter.

---

[15] T. A. Atchison, M.D., was a native of Kentucky and a graduate of Transylvania University. He practiced medicine many years in Bowling Green, Kentucky and moved to Nashville, Tennessee in 1855. He was Professor of General and Special Therapeutics and State Medicine in the University of Nashville and Vanderbilt University.

March 19

Gov Brown made me another visit this morning, and presented me with a copy of his speeches. Called on Mr. Mitchell whose acquaintance I made last summer in Louisville. After tea I made a visit with Henry Fogg to Mr. Tom Smith's—passed an agreeable evening.

March 20

Went to the warf this morning to see Mrs. Bass off for New Orleans —while there I saw them take off of the boat three corpses who died on the Miss river last summer of yellow fever. This afternoon I met Col Lemar[16] of Miss en route for Ga After tea I attended the Robertson Association. Dr Hoyt[17] and Henry Fogg were initiated.

March 21st

I saw a most painful spectacle this morning. A boy was driving in a buggy and his horse fell into a hole dug by the corporation on a negro man who was digging in the hole—the man was not hurt—but I think the horse will die before they get him out. Sam Allison made me a visit this morning—he has just returned from New Orleans. After tea I attended a meeting of the democrats at Fireman's Hall for the purpose of forming a club for the approaching canvass. B F Cheatham[18] was elected President—and I was selected as one of the Vice Presidents.

March 22nd

Occupied the forenoon in business matters. In the afternoon I accompanied my wife and Mrs. A Porter out to Mr Porters country seat where we passed the night.

March 23

Beautiful day, passed the day at Mr Porters, delightful place.

March 24

I came into the city soon after breakfast this morning with Mr Porter in his buggy. Seraphine came in the carriage with Mrs Porter. I noticed this morning in the Union and American of yesterday a highly complimentary call for me to be nominated for Elector in this Congressional

---

16 Lucius Quintus Cincinnatus Lamar (1825-1893), lawyer, soldier, statesman.

17 Rev. J. W. Hoyte, D.D., was Professor of Moral Science at the University of Nashville about 1859. He was a member of the Nashville Board of Education 1861-1867 and served as secretary of that body. He was pastor of the Second Presbyterian Church in Nashville 1872-1876.

18 Benjamin Franklin Cheatham (1820-1886), soldier, was born in Nashville, Tennessee. He distinguished himself in the Mexican War; appointed brigadier-general in the Confederate Army, May 1861; promoted to major-general in March 1862 and assigned to the army of Tennessee; retired from public life after the War; Superintendent of Tennessee prisons; Postmaster of Nashville 1885-1886. His dash as a military commander won for him the name of the "Ney of the Confederacy."

district. It was written I am informed by my friend Wm Rice. Occupied the day in business matters.

March 25th

This morning I noticed in the Patriot a highly complimentary notice of myself—in connection with the Elector-ship. I hardly expected this from an opposition paper. Passed the day mostly in my office.

March 26th

This has been a most boisterous day—no news worth noting.

March 27

Occupied the day in my office. After tea I attended the Robertson Association where we initiated Gen Darden, Dr Newman[19] and Wm Bernard.

March 28th

Occupied the day in business matters, and reading in my office.

March 29th

Most of the day occupied in business—no news.

March 30

I did not attend church today, but remained in my office reading.

March 31

Occupied the day in business matters.

April 1st

Nothing of importance going on.

April 2

All day in my office reading history, and law.

April 3

Passed the day in writing a speech to deliver at the Convention in Clarkesville next Saturday.

April 4th

About 12 oc I went on board the steamer Clyne for Clarksville accompanied by Gen B F Cheatham, Aaris Brown,[20] Tom Childress and Mr.

[19] John C. Newnan, M.D., (1818-1870) was the son of John Newnan, a prominent Nashville physician from 1810 to 1833. John C. was born in Nashville. He was a graduate of the Medical Department of the University of Louisville and, like his father, was a practicing physician in Nashville for many years.

[20] Aris Brown (1802-1877) was a native of Virginia but emigrated to Davidson County, Tennessee in 1826. He served in public life for more than a quarter of a century as constable, deputy sheriff, and deputy United States marshal. He was director of the Bank of Tennessee, of the Nashville and Chattanooga Railroad, and also the State prison.

Patton. We arrived in Clarkesville about 9 oc and went to the Franklin House. In a few minutes after our arrival Mr Faxon the editor of the Jeffersonian called to see us and invited us to go over to the Democratic Reading room. We went, and were introduced to the deligates from the different counties. Soon after I entered the room I discovered that the deligates from Davidson were considered as outsiders, for Wm Quarles had by letter to the deligates secured the election of a young man named Poindexter. After appointing a committee on resolutions, and organization we adjourned until tomorrow morning.

April 5

At 10½ this morning the Convention met in the Court House—and appointed a committee of five consisting of one from each county to report the most suitable candidate for Elector—the Convention then adjourned until 2 oc. Four counties were for Poindexter—but Davidson cast her votes for me. My name did not come before the Convention. Mr Poindexter was called on to make a speech—which was written out and committed. I do not think that he was a good selection, for he is very small—feeble voice—and poor delivery. I was then called and made a speech and was followed by Quarles, Yancy, Brooks and Rutherford. At 4 oc we started home on a Cincinnati Packet called the Magnolia.

April 6th

Reached home at 10 o c this morning with a severe chill upon me. Went to bed exceeding sick and remained in bed all day.

April 7

Confined all day to my bed—high brain fever.

April 8

Much better this morning. Rode out with Dr Porter. After tea I made a short speech in the Democratic Club Room.

April 9th

Attended the Criminal Court this morning and found Sam Earthman who killed Jas. McGavock some years ago before the Court—indicted for stealing.

April 10

Attended the Criminal Court today. After tea I attended the Robertson Assoc and initiated four members.

April 11

Remained nearly all day in my office reading.

April 12

Occupied the day in my office. No news of note. Weather very pleasant.

April 13

About three o clock this morning our city was alarmed by the fire bells. I got up and went to the public square—where I discovered that the old Nashville Inn was enveloped in flames. The boarders found it difficult to make their escape on account of the rapidity of the flames. Gov. Johnson lost $1200 that was under his pillow. The dome of the Court-house caught from a spark—and in a short time the entire building was consumed. They saved the records of the different Courts—but many valuable books and other things were lost. The next building that took fire was the store of the Messrs Douglass from which the flames spread to the large store of Morgan and Co. The wind blew a perfect hurricane—and the whole city seemed to be covered with fire. The sight was grand beyond discription—but terrible to look upon. I thought at one time that the whole city would be distroyed—but fortunately the devastating flames were assauged by the energy of our firemen. The loss was immense—and I may safely say that it was the most distructive fire that we ever had in Nashville.

Attended the first Presbyterian Church this morning and heard an excellent sermon from Dr Seaborn. In the afternoon I rode out to see Miss Lytton but she was not at home. I then went over to examine some improvements made by Sam Watkins.[21] The whole city seems to be in gloom today.

April 14

Occupied the day in business matters. Those who were burnt out on yesterday are busy getting houses and collecting their scattered goods. Passed the evening at the city hotel with Mrs. Churchwell.

April 15

This morning I attended the Criminal Court in the lower end of the market house. Went over to sale of Putnams edition in Edgefield. Property sold on the turnpike from 15 to 21.65 per foot. Excessively warm today.

---

[21] Samuel Watkins, building contractor, manufacturer, was born in 1794 in Campbell County, Virginia. After the War of 1812 he began to study brick-making in Nashville. From 1827 to 1861 he was the most prominent builder and brick-maker in the city. He was also a large owner of real estate and an official in several business concerns. One of his best known contributions was a public park to the city of Nashville.

April 16

Occupied the day mostly in my office. After tea the members of the Robertson Association assembled at their Hall and went in procession in their robes to the Christian Church, where Jno C Thompson Esq[22] was to deliver a lecture. The evening however was so inclement that we deferred the lecture until next Wednesday evening.

April 17

Attended the Criminal Court today. Bell and Hamilton were on trial for setting fire to the Penitentiary last year. The jury found them guilty—and they were sentenced for seven years additional confinement. The Odd Fellows had a large procession, oration and collation today. This evening I attended the Robertson Association but adjourned early. Mrs. Churchwell passed the evening with us. Dr Waters and lady Dr Edgar and lady and Dr Porter were invited to meet them.

April 18

Passed most of the day in my office—nothing of interest transpired. Called after tea on Mrs. Churchwell at the City Hotel with my wife.

April 19

Occupied most of the day in my office—no news.

April 20

Father returned today from Ark looking quite well. The corpse of Col S P Winder arrived for interment in our city cemetery, also the corpse of Pat Otey who was drowned about 6 weeks since just below Clarkesville. This morning I rode out to the cemetery to procure Duncan Robertson's epitaph. After tea I went with Seraphine to the City Hotel to see Mrs Churchwell.

April 21

Seraphine went up to Alisonia this morning with her sister, and I went to Franklin with Mr. Otey and the corpse of his son. While there I rode out with Jas McGavock to see R Ewing who is still confined from a fall he received from his horse during the winter. Returned to the city.

April 22

Passed the day in my office—transacting business. Thompson's lecture postponed again on account of the inclemency of the weather.

---

[22] John C. Thompson graduated from the University of Nashville in 1846 and in the same class with Randal W. McGavock. He was active in the civic and business affairs of Nashville particularly after the Civil War. In 1872 he was appointed as one of a board of commissioners to forward the construction of a bridge across the Cumberland River.

April 23

Occupied the [day] in business matters. Wm. Armstrong the son of Gen. Armstrong died here today. He killed himself drinking.

April 24th

Passed the day in settling up W Scotts affairs with Sam Watson. After tea the members of the Robertson Association met at their Hall and marched in procession with their robes on to the Christian Church. Mr. Hoyte opened the services with prayer. I then explained the objects of the Association—and J C Thompson followed in a lecture on the "Essential Principle of the Mind." The audience was small—but everything passed off well.

April 25

Occupied the day mostly in my office attending to business matters.

April 26th

Remained all day in my office reading—and looking over cases.

April 27

Did not go to church today—but occupied the entire day in writing a bill in Chancery in the Scott case. Ed Ewing is employed to assist me in the case. It is the first bill I ever filed—although I have frequently answered bills in Chancery.

April 28

The Clerks offices are now all in the Capitol and I find it quite fatiguing to walk up that hill two or three times a day. It will be a long time I suppose before our county magistrates erect another Court House. They are a slow set. For the last few days I have been troubled with a hacking cough and throwing up of great quantities of phlegm.

April 29

Occupied the day mostly in my office reading Macauley's History of England. News reached here today that Walker[23] had gained a great

[23] William Walker (1824-1860), the "grey eyed man of destiny," was born in Nashville, Tennessee. He graduated from the University of Nashville in 1838; received the M.D. degree from the University of Pennsylvania in 1843; continued his studies in Paris for a year; finding medicine distasteful, he studied law and was admitted to the bar in New Orleans; migrated to California in 1850; organized an armed expedition in 1853 with which he attempted to "colonize" Sonora and Lower California with American settlers; landed in Lower California and was proclaimed President of an independent republic; lacked supplies so forced to surrender to United States authorities; acquitted by a sympathetic jury. In 1855 he fitted out an expedition of "emigrants" to Nicaragua, being invited there by a revolutionary faction. With the help of an American transportation concern, the Accessory Transit Company, he brought the revolution to an end and in July 1856 was inaugurated President. His grandiose schemes fell through when he became at

battle in which 600 Costa Ricans were killed besides many wounded. His loss was about 50. If this be true and he succeeds in his hazardous enterprise he will be the greatest hero of his age.

April 30

Remained all day in my office—no news. Walked over to Aunt Felicia's after tea with Sallie.

May 1st

The children of the different schools in the city intended to celebrate the day in the country but the morning was so inclement they deferred it until tomorrow. Jno A McEwin[24] was married this evening in Bedford Co. to Miss Sallie Turner a very hansome woman.

May 2nd

This morning I rode out with Robt Brown to Mr Watkin's grove where the pupils of the high schools had their celebration. I was greatly interested in every thing. The day was lovely—the foliage looked fresh and green, and the children all seemed so happy. They had a platform erected in one of the squares from which the pupils made speeches and sang. After finishing their exercises which were highly creditable they partook of an ellegant collation and then danced until late in the evening. The property holders of Nashville are heavily taxed to support the High Schools but I think the exhibition today will make them all feel satisfied.

May 3rd

This morning I went to depot of the North Western Road to come to some agreement relative to their track through certain property in which I was interested, every thing was amically arranged. Received a letter this evening from Mr Bass introducing the Rev. Dr Baird[25] of the Presbyterian Church who has traveled extensively in various parts of the world and who has considerable reputation as a writer. He proposes delivering a series of lectures here on his travels.

---

outs with a faction of the transportation company headed by Cornelius Vanderbilt. Cut off from reinforcements he was forced to surrender to Commander Charles H. Davis of the United States Navy and brought to the United States May 1857; eluded the federal authorities in November; returned to Nicaragua; again captured; sent back to the United States. In August 1860 he landed in Honduras but was arrested in September by Captain Norvell Salmon of the British navy and turned over to Honduran authorities. He was court martialed and shot on September 12. The best account of Walker's adventures is his own story, *The War in Nicaragua* (1860).

[24] John A. McEwen was one of the leaders in the establishment of Nashville's public school system. Early in 1851 he was instrumental in having the City Council establish public schools in South Nashville. He was a member of the first Board of Education in 1854, served until 1859, and was secretary of the board 1854-1858. He was also editor of the *Nashville Gazette* in 1851.

[25] Robert Baird (1798-1863), clergyman.

May 4th

Attended the first Presbyterian Church today where I heard an excellent sermon from Dr Baird on the Trinity. After tea I went again to hear him lecture on the State and prospects of Christendom—the audience was large and his lecture interesting but rather long. He is not a good speaker.

May 5

The U. S. Chancery Court commenced their sessions this morning—nothing of interest done. A good deal of interest is now felt in the U. S. on Central American affairs. The battle of Rivas—the murder of the Agents of the Transit Company and the attack made by the Costa Ricans upon the cars across the Isthmus all are calculated to arouse the people of this country. My wife returned this evening from Alisonia with her Mother. Attended Dr Bairds lecture this evening on the Russian Empire.

May 6th

Grundy and his wife and Sallie started this morning to Columbus Miss on the cars but were compelled to return on account of the track and several bridges having been carried away by the recent floods. Attended the Chancery Court this morning. Jno McEwen's reception was from 5 to 10 oc this evening. I went with my wife at 8:30—found a large party. The bride of course looked beautiful as all brides do and bridegroom looked made up.

May 7th

Attended the Chancery Court today. At 5 oc I drove out with my wife and Mr. Rice to Jennie Lytton's marriage to Sam Taylor of Tipton Co. It was an agreeable party. Took tea at Dr. Waters' with Dr. Baird, Dr. Edgar and lady, Col. Cave Johnson.

May 8th

After breakfast I accompanied my wife to the study of Mr. [W. T.] Black—a Pastel Artist—who is taking her likeness—after which I called on Mrs. McCready to invite her to give the Robertson Association a benifit on Monday evening next. She accepted. Carrie McGavock and her children arrived today from La by the river. After tea I attended the Robertson Association.

May 9th

This morning I attended the Chancery and U. S. Courts. After tea I listened to a very interesting lecture from Dr. Baird on the Russian Empire.

May 10
Attended the Chancery Court today. Nothing of importance happened today.

May 11th
Attended the 2nd Presbyterian Church this morning. Dr. Baird preached a very interesting sermon. Went to hear him again in the evening.

May 12th
I have been very much occupied during the day in selling tickets for Mrs. Macready's entertainment for the benefit of the Robertson Association. This morning Camille Urn a young french girl who performs exquisitely on the violin fell out with Mrs. Macready and refused to appear tonight. I went up to St. Cloud to see her and prevailed on her to appear at least for this evening. After tea I in company with Seraphine and Mary and found one of the finest houses that I have ever seen in this Theatre. The gross receipts were $300—the Robertson Association received $150.

May 13
Attended the Chancery Court this morning. After tea I attended Dr. Baird's lecture on the late Russian War. His maps of the Crimea and Sebastopol are very fine and I gained a great amount of information from him.

May 14
Occupied the morning in writing a criticism on the lecture last night for the Union and American. After tea I attended Dr Baird's lecture on the Germanic Confederacy. His account of Holland and Belgium was exceedingly interesting. After the lecture I went out to a party at Jno Trimble's with Seraphine, Mary, and Mr McClelland. The crowd was very great—and I did not enjoy myself much.

May 15
Wrote an account of the lecture last night for the Union and American. Attended the Chancery Court this morning where a divorce case was argued by Reid and Meigs. The man's name is Baker and his wife is the daughter of old Tim Dodson near the Hermitage. She alledges cruel treatment from Baker. This afternoon the Firemen had a large procession but not so inspiring as some that I have seen. They have a ball at the Theatre tonight. A dispatch reached here today that President had recognized and received Padre Vigel the new Minister from Nicaraugua. This intelligence will meet with the hearty approbation of the

American people. A meeting will be called in [the]—morning to sympathize with Walker and his cause. Attended the Robertson Association this evening.

May 16th

Attended the Chancery Court this morning and occupied the afternoon in reading.

May 17

Occupied the day mostly in getting up speakers and resolutions for the Nicaragua meeting. After tea the largest crowd assembled in the Market Place that I have ever seen in Nashville on an impromptu occasion. Enthusiastic speeches were made by gentlemen of both parties —among whom was Ed Ewing, N. S. Brown, West H. Humphreys,[26] W. W. Bilbo and myself. The resolutions passed unanimously, but afterwards two of them relating to the Clayton Bulwer treaty[27] were stricken out to give general satisfaction. Some of the K N's thought that it would not do for the resolutions to come from a democrat and they endeavored to resind them and pass others in their stead, but it was no go.

May 18

Did not go to church today but remained at home attending to other matters.

May 19th

The Circuit Court convened this morning at Odd-Fellows Hall. Called this afternoon to see Mr. and Mrs. Churchwell—also James Deery who is exceeding low with consumption. I do not think that he can last many days longer. After tea Seraphine and myself attended Dr Baird's lecture on Italy which was very interesting.

May 20th

Attended the Chancery and Circuit Courts this morning. Dined at Dr. Porter's. After dinner I went to Allisons room and took a nap. Late

[26] West Huges Humphreys (1806-1882), jurist, was born in Montgomery County, Tennessee. He was admitted to the Tennessee bar in 1828; served in the lower house of the General Assembly 1835-1838; served two terms as Attorney General of the state; Reporter for the Tennessee Supreme Court 1839-1851; commissioned United States District Judge of the three districts of Tennessee in March 1853. He became an advocate of secession at the approach of war in 1861 and later accepted a district judgeship under the Confederacy. For this action he was impeached by Congress and found guilty. He reentered the law practice after the war but not in an extensive manner.

[27] The Clayton-Bulwer Treaty was an agreement between Great Britain and the United States, which provided that the two countries should jointly control and protect any canal which might be built across the isthmus of Central America. The treaty was ratified July 4, 1850.

in the afternoon I called on Mrs. Churchwell, Jas. Deery, Aunt Martha and family, and Mr. Bass and family arrived here today from the South—the former by rail—the latter by steamboat.

May 21st

Seraphine and myself rose early this morning and went to the depot to see the Deerys off for Alisonia. Attended the Chancery and Circuit Courts today. After tea I attended Dr. Baird's last lecture—Subject Great Britain and Ireland.

May 22nd

Read President's Pierce's Message this morning on Central American Affairs in which he recognizes the government of Nicaragua and accredits the new Minister. Lord Clarendon[28] in a voluminous reply to Mr Marcy on the questions pending between the two governments refuses to recall Mr Crumpton which will result I hope in his dismissal by our government. Attended the Hall of the Robertson Association this evening, but we had no meeting there being no quorum.

May 23

Attended the Circuit and Chancery Courts today. In the latter an important rail-road case was argued by J Marshall, E Ewing, Meigs and Cooper and F Fogg. Case Field and McIntosh vs N C RR.

May 24

Attened the Courts today. Late in the evening Seraphine and myself drove out to Gen. Harding's upon invitation.

May 25

Soon after breakfast Frank McGavock and family came over and passed the day. We went out to see the blooded stock—some wild elk recently brought from the N W, the water ox, buffaloes. I passed the greater part of the day in a spirited discussion with Gen Harding on railroads and their effects on the country, rail-road tax—general politics. From the telegraph dispatches this morning it seems that the Free Soilers and Border Ruffians as the Missourians are termed had a desperate battle in Kansas. The Black Republicans are holding indignation meetings in the north—at which resolutions were passed denouncing Brooks[29] of S C for his attack upon Chas Sumner recently in the Senate Chamber.

---

[28] George William Frederick Villiers Clarendon (1800-1870), British diplomat and statesman.

[29] Preston Smith Brooks (1819-1857), soldier, politician.

May 26

Cousin Elizabeth brought us to town this morning in her carriage. The Penitentiary case about which so much has been said is now being argued before Judge Baxter by Gardenshire—the Ewings and N. S. Brown.

May 27

Most of the day was passed in making preperations to visit Cincinnati, to attend the Democratic National Convention. At 6 oc in the afternoon two boats left the Nashville warf crowded with deligates from Tenn. and the surrounding States, amid the booming of cannon and the shouts of those on shore. I took passage on the steamer Alionico [?] commanded by Capt Miller a good old democrat.

May 28

Today we have enjoyed the beautiful scenery of the Cumberland—the martial strains of a band on board and the enlivening presence of the ladies. Col. Acklen[30] and lady, Wm Acklen, lady and daughter, E G Eastman[31] and daughter are among the list of 130 passengers.

May 29

Reached Smithland after breakfast this morning where we remained a short time, and proceeded up the beautiful but badly bottomed Ohio.

May 20th

Reached Portland just before day this morning—and left the warf at Lousville in the afternoon, having been all day in getting through the locks. Brother Ed met me at Portland and we rode up into the city and called on some friends.

May 31st

We have had quite an exciting time today—racing with the Eclipse. The two boats ran together for about fifty miles, and we entered Cincinnati at 3 oc running side by side, the passengers walking from deck to deck—drinking champaigne and interchanging jokes. All the first class hotels in the city were crowded, and we all scattered in various

[30] Joseph Alexander Smith Acklen was a colonel in the Mexican War and attorney of some note.

[31] Elbridge Gerry Eastman (1813-1859), newspaper editor, was born in Bridgewater, New Hampshire. He was invited to Tennessee in 1839 by James K. Polk and established the *Knoxville Argus;* given a post in Washington after Polk was elected President; soon went to Nashville, however, as editor of the *Nashville Union;* later became editor of the *Union and American;* served as Clerk of the State House of Representatives 1849-1850; also served a year as Clerk of the Senate. Some of his most significant work was in the organization of building and loan associations in Tennessee and in the promotion of agricultural fairs throughout the state.

quarters of the city thankful to get even moderate accommodation. Ed and myself stopped at the Hennrie House.

June 1st

This morning I went over to the Burnett House which is the head quarters of the different deligations. The city is crowded to overflowing —and many distinguished men are here. The friends of Pierce, Douglass,[32] and Buchanon are all working hard—each claiming the strength of the Convention.

June 2nd

At 8 o c this morning I was in the Tennessee deligation room where —they agreed to cast the first vote of the State for Pierce as a compliment. I agreed to this reluctantly—believing that Pierce had been sufficiently complimented by being made President and by the resolutions of various State Conventions. I was in favor of the State voting from the beginning for the man she wanted, and sticking to him. The Convention met at Nixon's Hall at 12 o c and made a temporary organization. After tea I attended a political meeting at the young men's democratic Association where I heard several excellent speeches.

June 3rd

The Convention was thoroughly organized today. Mr. Ward[33] of Ga was made President. Great commotion during the day among the politicians—and more trigering going on then one who really loves his country liked to see. I was invited to speak tonight, but declined.

June 4th

This morning the platform was read and unanimously adopted. It is the best we have ever had—being purely national in every particular. In the afternoon they commenced balloting for the President—Pierce, Douglass, Buchanan, and Cass were put in nomination. No result today. Buchanon evidently in the ascendent. Dined this evening with my friend and classmate, J. M. Force, who is now a member of the Cincinnati bar. Passed an agreeable evening.

June 5

Called this morning on Thos Benton[34] who is a strong Buchanon man. He said that he came to see how the gander would help. When the Convention met this morning Pierce was withdrawn and soon after Douglass and Cass. Mr. Buchanon was then unanimously nomi-

32 Stephen Arnold Douglas (1813-1861), statesman.
33 John Elliot Ward (1814-1902), lawyer, politician, diplomat.
34 Thomas Hart Benton (1782-1858), statesman.

nated. In the afternoon the Convention met and nominated Jno. C. Breckenridge[35] of Ky for the Vice presidency. His nomination was rather a singular thing. His name was not spoken of previously among the great number of aspirants—but was carried through I may say by acclimation. Every one seems to [be] gratified both with platform and candidates. The people of Cincinnati had a grand ratification meeting in the evening.

June 6th

Left Cincinnati today for home on the same boat and pretty much the same party. Ex Gov A V Brown[36] and family are among the passengers also Thos H. Benton.

June 7th

This morning we put off Mr Benton just above Louisville, and not a soul on board even took off their hats. What a commentary on political life. Passed the day in Louisville.

June 8th

Nothing has occurred today worth noting except the cheering on the shores as we pass along.

June 9th

This morning we got aground—where we remained nearly all day. Late in the afternoon we reached Evansville Ind. which is quite a flourishing town. Here we first heard the cry of "Ten cent Jimmy."

June 10th

Reached Smithland late this afternoon.

June 11th

This morning we changed boats at Eddiville, the river being low. Reached Clarkesville about 12 o c at night and escorted Quarles with our band of music up to the public square where he made us a speech, which was responded to by Mr. Coward of Ga.

June 12

Arrived home just after dinner. My wife returned from Alisonia just fifteen minutes after. In the evening the democrats had a grand ratification meeting on the square. Speeches were made by Cave Johnson,

[35] John Cabell Breckenridge (1821-1875), soldier, statesman.

[36] Aaron Venable Brown (1795-1859), lawyer, Governor of Tennessee, was born in Brunswick County, Virginia. He began law practice in Tennessee as a partner of James K. Polk; a member of the State Legislature almost continuously between 1821 and 1832; a member of congress 1839-1845; Governor of Tennessee 1845-1847; Postmaster-General in President Buchanan's Cabinet. At the Nashville Convention in 1850 his "Tennessee Platform" aroused much comment.

Andrew Ewing, Judge Wright of Ga., Mr. Cowart of Ga., Barckly Martin[37] and others.

June 13th

Today I commenced moving my office from Cooper's block to Vaughn and Fogg's building. Moving is troublesome—one I consider equal to a fire instead of three.

June 14th

The Circuit Court adjourned today

June 15

The K N papers of the city are now trying to prove Buchanon a federalist and hope to keep the old line whigs from his support by saying that he was no friend of Clay's.

June 16th

Attended the first Presbyterian church this morning, weather exceedingly warm.

June 17th

Occupied the day in arranging books in my new office. Called to see Dr Porter who is complaining of being quite unwell.

June 18th

Remained in my office until 12 o c. Attended a Chancery sale, but made no purchases.

June 19th

The weather is extremely warm—so much so that we can do very little here in the city.

June 20th

Wm Polk and Col MacGavock were in my office most of the day making arrangements for the coming canvass.

June 21st

Read political documents all day. Weather very warm.

June 22

Attended 1st Presbyterian church this morning. In the afternoon I went to see Dr Porter who is quite sick.

[37] Barclay Martin (1802-1890), Congressman from Tennessee, was a native of South Carolina. He moved to Columbus, Tennessee, studied law, and was admitted to the bar. He was elected to the Twenty-ninth Congress 1845-1847, after which he resumed the practice of law.

June 23

Occupied the day in reading. In the evening I attended a children's party at Mr. Bass'.

June 24

Great deal of talk today about Fremont being the Candidate of the Black Republicans for the Presidency and fears that the election will be thrown in the House of Rep. as it was in Jackson's time.

June 25

Remained in my office during the day, and called on Dr. Porter in the evening, who is much sicker than I thought he was.

June 26th

Read all day. Attended the Robertson Association, K N meeting at the market house and party at Mr. Williams' all three this evening.

June 27

Weather still continues oppressive. I was nearly all the day with Dr. Porter. Seraphine went out to Col. MacGavock's today with Aunt Martha Winder.

June 28th

All day with Dr Porter who is growing worse every hour.

June 29

Did not go to church today, on account of Dr Porter's illness.

June 30

The Dr is still sinking and I have no hope of his recovery. All they can do for him seems to be of little or not service.

July 1st

Dr. Porter expired at 7 o c this morning, after a painful illness. While sick the whole city seemed to be enlisted. His death is a great blow both to his family and the city. He was an excellent man in every particular and his place will not soon be filled.

July 2nd

This morning at 8 oc Dr. Porter was burried by the Odd Fellows and Medical Faculty. The funeral service was performed at the 1st Presbyterian Church by Dr. Edgar, and he was followed to the grave by the largest procession that I have every known for a private citizen. Well he has gone, and I have lost another dear friend—such is life.

July 3rd

Remained in my office most of the day reading Calhoun's[38] disquisition on government. After tea I attended the Robertson Association also a K N meeting on Broad St. Jas Quarles[39] of Clarkesville the K N elector for this district was the speaker. He made many charges against Buchanon, said he was a Federalist—High Tariff man—and the defamer of Clay's[40] character. His tone on the Catholic question was very much mollified since the canvass last summer.

July 4th

This morning I was aroused by the firing of cannon from Capitol Hill in commemoration of the ever memorable fourth. A party company paraded the Sts. during the day and saluted the K N Press offices. There was a political discussion today at Stuarts Ferry in this county. H. Brien and R. W. Haywood made speeches. The fourth of today is not what it was in the earlier history of the country, the people have lost it seems to me in a great degree that reverence and remembrance that they should keep sacred. It is not uncommon now to [hear] people talk about disunion, civil war. When this Union is disolved the world may bid good by to Republicanism in all time to come.

July 5

There is considerable excitement today about a difficulty that occured yesterday at Stuarts Ferry between R. W. Haywood and an Irish Preacher named Chapman who now edits the Gazette. High words passed and weapons were drawn—no damages.

Andrew Jackson called to see me today and showed some of Old Hickorie's letters about the bargain and intrigue question,[41] and a reply that he had written to a scurrilous article in the Patriot. Went out to Jno MacGavock's this afternoon with my wife and Felix Winder.

July 6th

Attended the Presbyterian church today in Franklin and passed the afternoon at Jno's. It is far more agreeable at this season in the country than in Nashville.

---

38 John Caldwell Calhoun (1782-1850), Representative and Senator from South Carolina and Vice President of the United States.

39 James Minor Quarles (1823-1901), lawyer, was born in Louisa County, Virginia. He commenced the practice of law in Clarksville, Tennessee in 1845; Attorney General of the Tenth Judicial Circuit 1853-1859; a Whig in Congress 1859-1861; in the Confederate Army; moved to Nashville to practice law in 1872; judge of the Criminal Court 1878-1882.

40 Henry Clay (1777-1852), statesman.

41 This refers to charges made by followers of Andrew Jackson that Henry Clay had supported John Quincy Adams in the presidential election, which was held in the House of Representatives in 1824, in return for the office of Secretary of State.

July 7th

Went out to Columbia today according to invitation to attend the Ratification meeting. Gen Pillow,[42] Barkly Martin, Payne and myself made speeches. After tea Haywood and Whithorne[43] spoke. Passed the night with Wm H. Polk.

July 8th

Returned to Aunt Martha's this morning, dined with Aunt Sally Otey and staid all night with Jno.

July 9th

Returned to Nashville on the cars this morning. Late in the afternoon we had a most terrible fire. It originated in the McCombs and Cornelius Cabinet Shop and spread to all the houses adjacent—burning the Masonic Hall and several dwellings—lost [$] 50 or 60,000.

July 10

Occupied the day mostly in my office reading and feel much exhausted from my labours at the fire yesterday.

July 11th

The weather is so warm that it is impossible to do any thing with comfort.

July 12

No business going on—and nothing talked about but politics.

July 13

Attended the 2nd Presbyterian Church today with my wife, to hear Dr Jennings of New Orleans.

July 14

Passed the day in my office preparing for the canvass.

---

[42] Gideon Johnson Pillow (1806-1878), soldier, was born in Williamson County, Tennessee. He graduated from the University of Nashville in 1827 and became a criminal lawyer in Columbia, Tennessee. During the Mexican War he attained a major-generalship due to his friendship with President Polk. When the Civil War broke out he was appointed senior major-general of Tennessee's provisional army. His command was suspended for some months due to his actions at the fall of Fort Donelson. During the remainder of the war he was given no important command. He spent his later years practicing law in Memphis in partnership with Isham G. Harris.

[43] Washington Curran Whitthorne (1825-1891) was born in Lincoln County, Tennessee. He studied at the University of Nashville and at East Tennessee University, graduating from the latter institution in 1843. He began the practice of law in Columbia, Tennessee in 1848; elected to the State Senate in 1855 and 1857; served in the State House of Representatives in 1859; appointed Assistant Adjutant-General of the Provisional Army of Tennessee in the summer of 1861; later appointed Adjutant-General of Tennessee; returned to Columbia after the War; elected to the Forty-second Congress in 1870; appointed by Governor Bate to fill an unexpired term in the United States Senate in 1886.

July 15
All day in my office making up a book of documents.

July 16
Occupied the day in my office reading.

July 17
All day in my office reading.

July 18
Met Michiel Vaughn[44] today before a large crowd in lower Edgefield. We spoke in a beautiful grove and had a fine barbacue.

July 19
The papers this morning on both sides give up that I achieved a triumph over my competitor. Remained all day in my office.

July 20
I did not go to church today, but occupied my time in reading.

July 21
This morning Jno and myself rode out to Goodlettsville where I made a speech against Vaughn.

July 22
Occupied the day in business matters.

July 23
Had an appointment to speak at Hutchinson's Springs today, but it is so far off and the road so bad that I got Wm Cox to fill the appointment.

July 24
Passed the day in my office reading—nothing worthy of note today.

July 25
Occupied myself in reading and transacting business.

July 26
This morning I started to canvass this Congressional District. Made a speech today at Harris' Spring in Cheatham Co. The crowd was very large, consisting of ladies and gentlemen. We had a fine band of music, and excellent barbacue. Passed the night with Geo Sloan.

---

[44] Michael Vaughn was a well-known citizen of Nashville. In October 1861 he raised a company of volunteers known as the "Cumberland Patriots" and served with the group as second lieutenant. Following the Civil War, in May 1866, he was one of the incorporators of the Nashville and Edgefield Street Railroad Company. In 1872 he was a member of a board of commissioners to secure a charter and obtain subscriptions for the construction of a free bridge across the Cumberland River.

July 27

Drove to Sycamore Mills this morning and dined with Sam Watson[45] —after dinner I drove to Clarkesville.

July 28

Occupied the day in conversing with political friends—and after tea I made a speech to a large crowd in the Court house.

July 29

Left Clarkesville this morning for Dover. Dined today with Dr Newell and reached Dover early in the afternoon.

July 30

Today I made a speech at the Court House in Dover to a very respectable audience. The leading democrats of the place are exceedingly polite and attentive.

July 31

This morning Mr Cherry rode out with me some five or six miles to put me in the right road to Charlotte. The Co of Stuart is exceedingly poor in an agricultural point of view and it is a very difficult matter for a stranger to get along—his only guide being the knotches on the trees. In passing through some of these extensive coalings I felt very much as I did in travelling on the Arabian desert. Sometimes I would not see a house, or living creature for ten miles. Staid all night at old man Fentress' in Dixon Co. He is a staunch old democrat, and very rich. He gave me a fine pair of buck's horns.

Aug. 1st

This morning I made a speech on Yellow Creek—and then went on to Shelton's and staid all night at Dr. Moody's.

Aug. 2nd

Drove into Charlotte this morning and made a speech to a fine and enthusiastic audience in the Court House. After dinner I drove down to Kingston Springs, where I found quite a large crowd from Nashville.

Aug. 3rd

Remained all day at Kingston reading the papers and conversing with friends.

---

[45] Samuel Watson (1807-1876), lawyer, was born in New Bedford, Massachusetts. He moved to Nashville, Tennessee in 1849; practiced law; trustee and receiver of the Bank of Tennessee in 1866; appointed trustee of the University of Nashville in 1867; appointed on the Peabody Education Fund Board of Trustees in 1869 and to the State Board of Education in 1875. He was President of the Tennessee State Teachers Association in 1870.

Aug. 4th

Rode 12 miles this morning to Tank to fill an appointment—but found Wm Cox speaking in my place, having promised to do so, if I did not reach there. Returned to Kingston.

Aug. 5

Several gentlemen went to the Narrows of Harpeth today, and caught thirty-seven pounds of most excellent trout. The improvements here are rough but they keep a fare table. The days are warm, but the nights quite cool.

Aug. 6

Occupied the day in playing ucre with the ladies, and rolling ten pins.

Aug. 7

Left Kingston today for Dog Creek—where I filled an appointment with Vaughn. Returned to Nashville tonight.

Aug. 8

Passed most of the day at home with my wife having been absent two weeks.

Aug. 9

Attended the Criminal Court today, but as nothing of importance was going on I returned to my office.

Aug. 10th

This is my thirtieth birth day, just in the meredian of life. At present I have the promise of a long and useful career—but we know not what a day may bring forth. I have often seen men of much stronger frame cut down when they least expected it and why should I count on better things. I have been in a reflective mood all day—reviewing the past and endeavoring to divine the future. My life has been an eventful one, far more so than most men of my age. Many things have happened in my history that I could wish otherwise, but upon the whole I ought to be thankful that I have performed so much of the journey of life without stain upon my escutcheon. Of this I am proud—for I hold a mans good name above all things earthly. I have now been married one year to a beautiful and lovely woman, but as yet we have no offspring which every married person desires.

News reached here today that Ky, N C, Ark, and Mo had gone for the democrats, which is encouraging to every union loving man. From Iowa we learn that the Black Republicans have succeeded. The Fillmore party had no ticket, but fused with the Republicans against the democracy. This looks ominous and I fear it will be the same throughout most of the Northern states. This gives Fremont fourteen States and if it should be thrown into the House it will require only two States more to elect him. If he should be elected I believe it would produce a dissolution of this glorious Union. Every patriot should be on the alert, for if we are once divided no power can bring us together again. I did not go to church today, but remained in my office reading Josephus, and Lelia, the converted Judges.

Aug. 11th

This morning I wrote a letter to the editors of the Republican Banner, in reply to their correspondence at Clarkesville in regard to my speech at that place, in which I charged the Banner of having garbled Gen Jacksons letter, in relation to the bargain and intrigue affair. Attended the Criminal Court at Odd Fellows Hall—nothing of importance going on. Neil S. Brown and Isham Harris have just returned from their canvass, and both make good reports for their respective parties, both claim the State and it remains to be seen which is mistaken.

Aug. 12th

This morning I drove out to Gen Hardings place with Mr. Pochin of Charleston, South Carolina, whose acquaintance I formed on the Rhine. He is a gentleman of intelligence and was much delighted in looking at the Gen.'s fine stock and the pack. Everything in country looked parched this morning but the heavy fall of rain this afternoon will do good.

Aug. 13th

The letter that I wrote on the eleventh appeared in the Banner this morning and the editor occupied two columns and a half in trying to explain out of it. I had an appointment today to speak at Garrett's Mills but the rain prevented me from going believing that there would be no person present. In the Patriot of this date I observe a letter signed Junius, discribing my speech at Dog Creek on Thursday last in which I am represented to have said that the Naturalization laws belonged to the States—a most ridiculous idea. The author cannot distinguish between naturalization and suffrage.

Aug. 14th

Today there is a large barbacue on Yellow Creek in Dixon Co. Gov Johnson and Andrew Ewing went down to make speeches. The great speech of Gov. Johnson's delivered some time since in this city was published in the Union this morning. I think it will tell in the canvass. A man named Cliford was convicted in the Criminal Court today for the murder [of] Spottswood in the second degree and sentenced to ten years imprisonment. A conviction for murder in this degree is quite rare here in Nashville. From the N Y Herald this evening I see that Clayton of Del, Gyer of Mo and Jones[46] of Tennessee have declared in favor of Buchanon and Breckenridge—and it is also stated that the National Intelligencer will come out for them in a few days. The Herald also contains a full account of the Inauguration of Gen Wm Walker as President of the Republic of Nicarauga. His success in that quarter has been truly wonderful.

Aug. 15

Occupied the day in reading, and transacting business. After tea I went to the Market house, and heard a very excellent and eloquent speech from Jno F House[47] of Clarkesville. It was decidedly the best K N speech that I have listened to during the canvass.

Aug. 16th

Attended the Criminal Court today. Andrew J. Donelson called to see me today and said that he had a letter he desired to show me written by my grandfather, in which are expressed his opinions of Mr. Buchanon. A large crowd assembled arround the door to hear us talk. At last he invited me to go home with him, which I declined. After tea I attended the sale of money at the Exchange of one of the Building and loan associations from which I went down to broad st. to hear Mr Sale of Ky. He made a poor speech, so poor that my friends insisted that I must speak or it would be a failure. I did so. Finley followed, and old Bee Clements a K N then got up and as usual made an ass of himself.

News reached here today that Rufus Choate a distinguished Old Line Whig had come out for Buchanon and Breckenridge. I know him personally and believe that his action will have a good effect in Boston and throughout New England.

Aug. 17th

I did not attend church today, as my wife requested but remained in my office reading. In the evening I called on Aunt Falicia and Malvina at the latter place I met the youngest son of Aunt Eliza Mason, named

---

46 James Chamberlayne Jones (1809-1859), Governor of Tennessee, United States Senator, was a native of middle Tennessee. His entrance into public life was as a member of the General Assembly in 1839. He twice defeated James K. Polk for Governor of Tennessee, in 1841 and 1843, being the first native Tennessean to hold that office. In 1850 he became President of the projected Memphis and Charleston Railroad. In 1851 he was elected to the United States Senate.

47 John Ford House (1827-1904), lawyer, was born near Franklin, Tennessee. He was a member of the State House of Representatives in 1853; a member of the Provisional Congress of the Confederacy from Tennessee; served in the Confederate Army; a delegate to the State Constitutional Convention in 1870; served in Congress 1875-1883.

Archer—who Aunt Malvina intends educating. There I also met Mr. Eslin of N C the successor in business of Harry Hill and the gentleman who killed his partner last winter in a duel. After tea I went over to Capt Williams' and passed an hour in reviewing the history of the bargain, entrigue and corruption affair.

Aug. 18th

Nothing transpired today worthy of note. After tea I went with Capt. Williams to Odd Fellows Hall where he reviewed in an able and masterly manner, the whole history of the bargain intrigue and corruption affair. It will be a valuable document for the Old Line whigs.

Aug. 19th

Attended the Criminal Court today. After tea I went to the Democratic Association Room and made a short speech.

Aug. 20

Attended the Criminal Court in the morning. This afternoon I received through the mails, Rufus Choate's letter to the Whigs of Maine, in which he announces himself for Buchanon and Breckenridge. After tea I filled my last appointment with Vaughn in this Co. The crowd was large and enthusiastic and I gained a complete victory over him. I am glad that I have completed this list for now I will have an opportunity to go elsewhere.

Aug. 21st

Read in the Union of this morning a long letter from Watkins of this State (old line Whig) in which he announces himself for Buchanon and Breckenridge. Attended the Criminal Court today. Gov Johnson spoke to a tremendous crowd at Christiana today. Davidson the Irish Orater also spoke.

Aug. 22nd

The K N papers of this morning in giving an account of the speaking at Love's store Wed. night represent Vaughn as having obtained a complete triumph, and the Union gives just an opposite opinion. A. G. Payne of Columbia addressed a large crowd last night on Broad St. His speech was replete with anecdote and sound argument.

Aug. 23rd

This day one year ago I was married, and during the day I have been making preperations to visit my wife who has been absent for two weeks. Left the city on the cars at 4½ and arrived at Alisonia at 11 o c.

Aug. 24

Occupied the day in reading and conversation.

Aug. 25

Went out fishing this morning, but was disappointed in getting minnows and had to abandon it. Left Alisonia at 1 o c with Gen Deery[48] and reached Chattanooga to tea. After Tea I made a speech to a very large and enthusiastic crowd in Concert Hall.

Aug. 26

This morning I went down to Cotoosa Springs and passed the day. Here I met many friends and it [was] really a treat to be once more at a place where I have passed so many happy hours. After tea I went to the station and joined Gen Deery, Robt Deery, and my wife, who are enroute for Knoxville.

Aug. 27

Arrived in Knoxville at 7 o c this morning and came directly to Col Churchwell's house where we propose staying a week or ten days. This afternoon I called on Mr Meek of Columbus Miss who has recently married Miss Cannon. After tea a large crowd assembled in front of the Coleman house to hear democratic speeches. Mr Meek, Mr Swan, Jno Crozier,[49] Churchwell and myself made speeches.

Aug. 28

This morning I was aroused by the firing of canons and the strain of music. This is the day of the Democratic Barbacue. About 3000 persons assembled in the grove and everything passed off well. Watkins M C[50] and O L Whigs spoke first then Payne of Columbia then Jno Crozier and then myself. At night Haywood Lewis and others spoke.

Aug. 29

Remained most of the day at Col Churchwells feeling much fatigued from the labors of yesterday.

---

[48] James A. Deery (d. January 17, 1857) was a native of Sullivan County, Tennessee. He and his brothers established a business house in Knoxville and later established the manufacturing town of Allisona, Williamson County. He was a very successful business man. He experimented with the manufacture of cotton goods on a wide scale in the South and put his enterprise into practice.

[49] John Hervey Crozier (1812-1889), Congressman from Tennessee, was born in Knoxville, Tennessee. He was a member of the State House of Representatives 1837-1839; a Whig in Congress 1845-1849; practiced law in Knoxville until about 1866 after which he engaged in literary pursuits and historical research.

[50] Albert Gallatin Watkins (1818-1895) was a native of Jefferson County, Tennessee. He began the practice of law in Panther Springs, Tennessee in 1839; member of the State House of Representatives in 1845; a Whig in Congress 1849-1853; a Democrat in Congress 1855-1859; later engaged in the ministry.

Aug. 30

Col Churchwell left this morning for New York. Congress adjourned again today, after passing the army bill. Wrote several letters and received a call from Mr McMullen and Miss Noey.

Aug. 31

Attended Dr McMullen church this morning where I heard a pretty good sermon.

Sept. 1st

This morning I walked down town and called into Crow Ramsey's office, where I met Jno Crozier and Judge Harris[51] of the Supreme Bench. Knoxville's has improved wonderfully in the last few years and some of stores and private dwellings would be highly creditable in a large city. The views about the city are superb but the lands look and are very poor.

Sept. 2nd

This morning we drove out to dine with old Mr Churchwell the father of Wm. He is a great talker and a man of fine sense. We had a number of persons to meet us, viz. Judge Harris, Major Lyon, Dr. Lyon, Dr. McMullen, Mr. Moses, Mr. Lewis, Mr. Malery and lady, Miss Noey and several others. The dinner was excellent and we passed the day very agreeably.

Sept. 3rd

Walked down town today and saw Rees Porter—and Petway of Nashville, who report that the K N went on Saturday to meet Gen Haskell[52] and that he made a most eloquent speech but as usual a man was killed. Pacoe an old policeman was shot by Bill Horn. The K N have a grand mass meeting here tomorrow and they are making extensive preperations for the occasion. Old man Churchwell and lady dined with us today. He is one of the greatest talkers I ever heard and at the same time very interesting.

Sept. 4

Passed most of the day at the K N barbacue or conversation. The crowd was very great much larger than ours last week. Gen. Haskell

[51] William R. Harris (1803-1858), brother of Isham G. Harris, was born in Montgomery County, North Carolina. He began the practice of law in Paris, Tennessee in 1827; Judge of the Ninth Circuit 1836-1845; Judge of the Common Law and Chancery Court of Memphis 1851-1855; Judge of the Supreme Court of Tennessee 1855-1858.

[52] William T. Haskell (1818-1859), soldier, lawyer, was born in Murfreesboro, Tennessee. He fought in the Seminole War in 1836; began the practice of law in Jackson, Tennessee in 1838; served in the Mexican War; elected as a Whig in the Thirtieth Congress 1847-1849.

was the orator of the day. He occupied four hours and one half on the stand in the discussion of questions that I considered entirely irrelevant to the issues in the canvass. He was drunk while speaking and I think did his cause more injury than good. After supper Judge Brien, JO Pickett and the Notorious and infamous Brownlow[53] made speeches.

Sept. 5
This has been a very inclement day so much so that I remained in doors. In the afternoon I received a note from Mr. Perry editor of the Standard asking me to come to his room. I went and found him deliberating whether he would challenge, demand a personal explanation or publish a card. Brownlow the night before denounced him in his speech as a liar scoundrel and coward, and without cause. I told him that B. was so low and infamous that I would not consider the two first propositions for a moment and advised the publication of the card—which he did.

Sept. 6
I did not go to church this morning but occupied the day in writing letters.

Sept. 7
This morning I started with my wife and Mrs Churchwell to Va. on a visit to my relations. We passed two weeks delightfully in Wythe, Pulaski, and Montgomery Co.'s. We returned to Knoxville the same way passing through Blountsville the birth-place and former home of my wife. We remained in Knoxville one day and then started home. When we reached Alisonia we found the mill in ruins, having been consumed that morning by fire. The family were in great distress and Mrs. Deery was quite ill in bed. They had only ten thousand dollars insurance and the burning deprives them of every dollar they possess—besides leaving them largely in debt. My wife's money was all in the concern which she will doubtless loose. Such is life—today we are in abundance—tomorrow in poverty. After remaining two days at Alisonia I returned to Nashville and once more entered the fearful arena of politics. The excitement here I found intense, so much so that it was really dangerous. Soon after my return to G Y Poindexter and myself

[53] William Gannaway Brownlow (1805-1877), Governor of Tennessee, United States Senator, was a native of Wythe County, Virginia. His family settled in East Tennessee when he was five. In 1826 he entered the Methodist ministry, serving as an itinerant preacher; became a newspaper editor in 1838, and in 1849 entered upon the editorship of the *Knoxville Whig*. He was a strong Union man, and the *Whig* was the last Union paper in the South. After being the leader of the Unionists in East Tennessee during the War, he was elected Governor by acclamation in 1865 by the Union Central committee. Before the close of his second term he was elected to the United States Senate and took office on March 4, 1869.

went to Gallatin and to Williamson Co where we made speeches. On the day before the election I assisted in naturalizing some sixty foreigners for which the K N's abused us roundly. The election passed here quietly and we carried the state by a large majority which compensated me amply, for my humble labors in the canvass. Old Buck [James Buchanan] as he was familiarly called came out victorious—over the combined forces of KN ism and Black Republicanism. This I consider enough to cause the heart of every patriot in the land to pulsate with joy. The principles of the Constitution have been upheld by the voice of the people, notwithstanding the wild cry of the fanatic and the demon spirit of the K N who sympathized with those who were fighting against every principle of right, honor, and justice.

The election being over I turned my attention once more to my private affairs, which have been neglected for five months past.

Dec. 1st

Great excitement prevails here and in other parts of the State in regard to the Bank of East Tenn which is supposed to be broke. It is believed that the rumour was started by brokers for speculative purposes. I left Nashville this morning for Sullivan Co East Tenn to examine the lands owned by my wife's father.

Dec 2

Arrived in Knoxville this morning. After breakfast I went over to Churchwell's. He thinks that the Bank will be able to sustain itself—but says that the branches will have to suspend. Considerable excitement prevails among the small note holders.

Dec. 3

I staid all last night at Churchwell's. Occupied most of the day with Thos N Nelson talking about filing a bill to enjoin certain trustees in which matter my wife's estate is involved.

Dec. 4

Left Knoxville this morning for Blountville on the cars. At Russelville I took the stage by way of Rodgersville. Found the streams very high and the roads very bad.

Dec. 5

Reached Blountville about three o'clock and put up at Snapps' Hotel. Transacted some business and then retired.

Dec. 6

Started out early this morning on horseback with Mr. Tipton to examine the real estate left by my wife's father. The several tracts are large and valuable, but have been very much injured by yearly tenants.

Dec. 7

Left Blountville this morning homeward. Stopped at Jonesboro and examined a record in Chancery. Staid all night at a miserable hotel in Greenville the home of Andrew Johnson. Went to Russellville where I passed all day at Mr. Nennie's hotel—good natured people but not very agreeable place.

Dec. 8

At 12 o c I left Russelville on the cars, and reached Knoxville about four o'clock. Had an interview with Thomas N Nelson Mr Coke Wm Deery and Churchwell.

Dec. 9

Left Knoxville this morning on the cars for Nashville. At Chattanooga I heard that Frank McGavock had shot two of his negroes dead and wounded two more, which was without the least foundation.

Dec. 10

Reached War-trace before the day this morning where I took a horse and rode over to Shelbyville to attend a trust sale. I bid in the interest of the Deery boys at $5,125. Staid all night in town, and passed the evening pleasantly with Kibble of Murfreesboro.

Dec. 11

Arrived at home after tea this evening and learned that considerable excitement prevailed about an insurrection supposed to be on foot among the negroes of Middle Ten. In Stuart County at several of the iron works some 10 or 11 have been hung and whipped to death. Several white men supposed to have been implicated have also been serverely whipped. The excitement in the lower counties is very great, but I am inclined to think that much of it is without cause. They have increased the police of this city, besides having a strong vigilance committee composed of some of our best citizens.

Dec. 12

Occupied the day in the transaction of business and in attendance on the Supreme and Criminal Courts. Passed the evening at Mr Bass[54] and Col Johnsons room.

---

[54] John M. Bass, lawyer and businessman. He was admitted to the Nashville Bar in 1830, Mayor of Nashville several times, President of the Union Bank, and an extensive planter in Louisiana and Arkansas. He died in New Orleans after having lost much of his wealth during the Civil War. He was the husband of Malvina Grundy, McGavock's aunt.

Dec. 13

Day exceedingly inclement—hard rains all day. Called to see Lum Allison today who has a severe cough, which may terminate into something serious, unless speedily arrested.

Dec. 14

Passed the morning with Mr Steel of Cincinnati and took tea with him at Mrs. Porter's.

Dec. 15

Attended the Supreme Court today, and transacted some outdoor business. Weather intensely cold.

Dec. 16

Left Nashville on the cars this morning for East Ten to attend to my wife's estate which is in a very critical condition being bound up in litigation and vexation.

Dec. 17

Arrived in Knoxville this morning—where I passed the day and night. Called on Mr and Mrs Churchwell who are now boarding at the Lemar House. Mr. C. is in great trouble about the Bank of East Tenn. of which he is President. I think it will go down and leave him in the vocative.

Dec. 18

Left Knoxville this morning for Jonesborough.

Dec. 19

Arrived at Jonesborough before day. After breakfast I walked out to Col Tom Nelsons where I remained all day and night. I have employed Mr. N. as my lawyer to bring suite in equity against Jas A Deery and others for the settlement and adjustment of my wife's interest in her father's estate. Col. N. is a plain, but highly informed man. In the evening I left in the stage for Greenville to procure an Injunction from Judge Patterson. He had retired when I arrived, but kindly got up and granted an Injunction against Gordon and Cox.

Dec. 20

This morning I procured a horse and returned to Jonesborough in company with Mr Neal an Engineer on the East Tenn and [Va.] rail-road. We had a cold and disagreeable ride.

Dec. 21

Today we came on horseback to Blountsville.

Dec. 22

This is decidedly the coldest day of the season. I intended returning to Jonesborough, but defered starting until it moderates. Attended to my business during the day.

Dec. 23

Today I rode 45 miles to Greenville on horseback. Stopped a short time in Jonesborough to see Mr Nelson and the clerk of the Chancery Court.

Dec. 24

Started to Russellville this morning, but missed the connection with the rail-road. The typhoid fever was prevailing in the town and the passengers were compelled to go to a widow ladies in the neighborhood named Gillespie where we remained all night.

Dec. 25

This is Christmas Day. O how I wish that I could be in Rome or Jerusalem today instead of East Tenn. Left Russellville at 12 oc and arrived in Knoxville at 4 oc. Passed the evening with Dr Lyon and Mrs Churchwell.

Dec. 26

Left Knoxville this morning and arrived at Chattanooga at tea. Here I met Aunt Malvina and Mr. Ewing on their way to Mobile. They expect to join Mr and Mrs. Stevenson at Macon. Remained all night at Chattanooga where I had a nice game of ucre with Ky Hooper and Beech.

Dec. 28

Started home this morning. At Deckerd I learned from the passengers on the up train, that they had arrested 10 or 15 negroes in Nashville last night for insurrectionary movements. At Alisonia I saw Wm Deery who informed me that James was rapidly sinking.

Dec. 29

Passed the day in the transaction of business. This is always the busy season, and in the absence of my father who is now in Ark. I have as much as I can attend to conveniently. There is considerable excitement in town in regard to the negroes but I think it all without foundation. They have not the slightest particle of evidence against those they have in prison. Dined today with Aunt Felicia. Passed the evening with Rice.

Dec. 30

A large new building fell on Market St this morning and severely injured two Irishmen, it is supposed that they will die. This evening I went with Mr. McLaughlin up to Alisonia to see if the Deerys would acknowledge service of a subpœna with instructions to have it served if they did not.

Dec. 31

Occupied the entire day in hiring negroes and renting houses. Well This is the last day of a most eventful year, many strange things have happened effecting the great body politic as well as individuals. The dark monster of Know Nothingism has been ingloriously crushed by the National democracy. Fortunes have been made and lost—friends, yes dear friends have passed away—and the old year is full of mingled pain and pleasure. Tomorrow we enter upon a new year, and I hope that it may prove a happy and prosperous one not alone to our own free America, but the whole habitable world. Adieu 1856—long, long, will I remember the events that you chronicle.

CHAPTER XVIII

"Occupied the day mostly in my office." (1857)

Randal McGavock appears to have derived considerable pleasure from his law office. He frequently reports having spent the day there, reading and studying. To infer from this any decline in his interest in social and civic affairs, however, would be a mistake. There are still the friendly associations, the concern for community betterment, and the interest in national political affairs.

1857

Jan. 1st

It is usual with many persons to begin the new year with resolves. Now I have done this frequently myself—but most generally found that my resolutions vanished into thin vapors very soon after made. One can however and ought to profit by the experience and teachings of the past. I have the consolation of knowing that although I have since regretted yet at the time I acted conciously and with pure motives. The day has been occupied mostly in my office in business matters. Heretofore I have made visits on New Year's day to my friends, but I am married now and must do as other married men, else subject myself to the imputation of being called fast. I called a meeting in the morning papers of the Robertson Association this evening in my office, having been compelled to leave our hall on the account of high rent. This is the first call of the members since last spring. The exciting political canvass of last summer and my absence from the city induced us to defer our opperations until things became quiet.

Jan. 2nd

This has been an exceedingly sloppy and disagreeable day. I noticed in the morning paper that Father Mathew the great Temperance

Reformer died at Cork Ireland on the 9th of Dec. He has done more to reform the disipated world than any other man and a monument should be erected to perpetuate his memory. The N.Y. papers are filled with accounts of the trial of Huntingdon the young forger, who kept a running account with the Bank to the amount of twenty millions of dollars. His counsel puts in a novel plea—viz. moral insanity. Mr. McLaughlin who I sent to Alisonia called in today and informed me that he met with a cold reception—and that he was compelled to place the subpœna in the hands of the Sheriff. I have performed my duty—and now let the law perform hers.

Jan. 3

Nothing of importance transpired today.

Jan. 4

Attended the first Presbyterian Church this morning where I heard an excellent sermon from Dr. Edgar and the finest music that I have ever heard in Nashville. My sisters Sallie and Mary are the leaders of the choir. In the afternoon I called on Aunt Felica and Sallie Ewing. Father returned tonight from the plantation in excellent health and spirits.

Jan. 5

Occupied the day mostly in business matters and the evening in reading Dr. Kanes book.

Jan. 6

I had a cow case today—which was amusing. An Irishman and a fellow named Jones both claimed a cow that had been posted in the rangers book. Jones had not seen the animal for two years, but knew her by the ear marks. The old Irishman lost her in Oct last and knew her by her general features—and the amount of milk she gave. The Irishman, my client, got the cow.

Jan. 7th

Attended the Supreme Court today.

Jan. 8th

This morning my wife went up to Alisonia to see her brother James die. This is the anniversary of the Battle of New Orleans—no celebration. Our people have ceased to make memorable those great national days that should be kept in remembrance. Judges Turner and Baxter[1]

[1] John Baxter (1819-1886) was born in Rutherford County, North Carolina. He was a Whig member of the Legislature of North Carolina, being at one time Speaker of the lower house; moved to Knoxville, Tennessee in 1857; remained loyal to the Union during the war; appointed Judge of the Circuit Court of the United States for the Sixth Circuit by President Hayes in 1877.

gave a supper to the members of the bar this evening in Cooper's building. I was present and enjoyed myself finely. I offered the following toast in response to a call—"The Judiciary the most important pillar in the temple of liberty—may its ermine ever be kept pure and free from party prejudice or sectional animosity." After the supper I went to see a friend with whom I passed an agreeable hour.

Jan. 9

Rose early this morning and went with Wm. S. Eakin to Shelbyville. Miss Bonner my old flame was on the cars and quite revived the memory of other times. I had a conversation with her in which I had the consolation of knowing that she had thanked her God for the escape she made. I coincided with her of course. Every thing passed off agreeably. Attended to my business in the town and then walked with Wm. S. Eakin to his mother's where I passed the night. Mrs. E. has a fine farm and lives in very good style. Emmett Eakin and his bride were there, having just returned from New Orleans.

Jan. 10th

Drove in to Shelbyville after early breakfast. After dinner I came home on the cars with Mrs. McClelland under my charge, of Ala.

Jan. 11

Attended the first Presbyterian church this morning—the music was splendid. Handel's Hallelujah was sung excellently well.

Jan. 12

Received two letters from my wife this morning—her brother still lives—answered them. The Circuit Court convened this morning.

Jan. 13

Attended the Circuit Court this morning where I took several judgements and filed a number of declarations. Passed some time in procuring signatures to a letter to Mr Buchanan. This evening I received several letters from my wife, also one from Wm and Robt Deery pressing me to go to Alisonia, as Jas Deery desires to see me before he dies.

Jan. 14

Went up to Alisonia this morning found Gen. Deery much better than he had been yet very low.

Jan. 15

Remained all day at Alisonia attending Gen. Deery. Dr Estell called today and thinks the Gen cannot last much longer.

Jan. 16

Remained all day at Alisonia—the Gen. grows worse, no hope for him. He eats nothing. His mind seems occupied alone on the subject of religion.

Jan. 17

Today Gen. Deery called all the family around his bed and bade them good-by. At 7¼ oc he died as quietly and sweetly as a babe going to sleep.

Jan. 18th

This morning between the hours of 2 and 3 I walked through the snow and cold to Estell's Station where I took the rail for Nashville. Procured during the day a coffin and other burrial articles. Returned to Alisonia in the evening.

Jan. 19

Remained all day at Alisonia. The family are deeply afflicted—particularly the mother, who was much devoted to James.

Jan. 20

At 1 oc today we all started on the cars with the corpse for Shelbyville. Arrived at 3 oc and were met at the Depot by the Odd Fellows who burried the body in accordance with the usage of their honorable order. We passed the night with Mr Alex Eakin.

Jan. 21

Left Shelbyville at 1 oc and reached Nashville at 5 oc. Weather intensely cold—ground covered with a deep snow and the Cumberland river frozen over which I believe is the second time in my reccollection.

Jan. 22

Attended the Circuit Court this morning. Thermometer 12 degrees below zero. Today they cut a canal through the ice in the river to let the coal boats pass. This afternoon I attended the treat given by Gen Clements to his democratic friends. Called a meeting of the Robertson Association but none attended. Passed the evening at the St Cloud with Bill Polk and Maj Ben McCullough[2] of Texas. The Supreme Court sustained Gov. Johnson in his Penitentiary case.

---

[2] Ben McCullough (1811-1862), Texas and Confederate soldier, was born in Rutherford County, Tennessee. He followed his neighbor, David Crockett, to Texas; fought in the Texas War for Independence; gained a reputation for his exploits against the Indians; his rangers distinguished themselves during the Mexican War; Marshal for the coast district of Texas 1853-1859; commissioned brigadier-general in the Confederate Army; commanded the troops in Arkansas until his death.

Jan. 23

Attended the Circuit Court this morning. After tea I went to the hall of the A O M C who have revived.

Jan. 24

I notice in the morning Union quite a complimentary notice of the life and character of Gen Jas A Deery.

Jan. 25

Remained at home all day. Did not go to church this morning, but attended in the evening.

Jan. 26

Attended the Circuit and Supreme Courts today. The Supreme Court decided this morning that the act passed at the last legislature prohibiting all Banks except the Bank of Tenn. from issuing notes under five dollars, was constitutional. They also decided that the stockholders in the old Insurance Co of which Walker was President are liable to the amount of this stock. Called this evening on Mrs. Deery and Mrs Churchwell at the City Hotel.

Jan. 27

Occupied the day in the Courts and at my office. No news. Wrote one letter to Uncle Randal and one to Aunt Polly in Va about their portion of the costs in Uncle Jos' will case.

Jan. 28

Remained all day in my office. Signed a paper recommending Gen. Anderson's[3] re-appointment as postmaster. Received a letter from the Dem State Central Com recommending me as Minister Resident to one of the Courts in Europe. Took tea this evening at the St Cloud with Maj Ben McCollough of Texas. He gave me much information about the country and its history.

Jan. 29th

From the papers this morning it appears that Gen Walker is in a very critical position and likely to be overpowered by the Costa Ricans who are headed by Spencer the agent of Vanderbilt. Mr Brooks of S C who made the assult upon Sumner of Mass. last year in the Senate Chamber, died in Washington a day or two since of croup. This will cause the abolitionists to rejoice in their hearts. I notice quite a com-

[3] Samuel R. Anderson (d. 1883), soldier. He was lieutenant-colonel of the First Tennessee regiment infantry in the Mexican War; appointed major-general of the Provisional Army of Tennessee, May 1861; appointed brigadier-general in the Confederate Army, July 1861; resigned May 1862 and was reappointed; died at Nashville, Tennessee.

plimentary call in this morning's Union upon Lamb of Memphis[4] to become a candidate for Congress in that district. He is a clever fellow and is I understand soon to be united in wedlock with my old friend Miss Lizzie Bonner of Fayetteville.

Jan. 30th

The K N's seem to be hard up for a candidate for Gov next Aug. Some eight or ten persons are spoken of in their papers, all of whom are peculiarly fitted for the position. The weather at present is extremely inclement. Mr. Buchanon has arrived in Washington where he will be surrounded by hungry office seakers for six months to come.

Jan. 31

Attended the Circuit Court today—nothing of interest going on. I notice in the morning papers that the brother of the Engineer on the Nashville and Henderson roads has sold in London a large amount of bonds, which he appropriated to the purchase of a steamer, that he sent to the Crimea, which was left.

Feb. 1st

Went to Shelbyville today.

Feb. 2

Today I had a public sale of the property on the Public Square of Shelbyville. It was largely attended and went off well at good prices.

Feb. 3

Passed the day in Shelbyville, arranging deeds, etc. Learned this evening that Gov Johnson met with a serious accident on the Ga railroad this side of Augusta. His arm was broken near the elbow and his face considerably bruised.

Feb. 4

Returned to Nashville today. Weather delightful.

Feb. 5

Attended the Circuit Court this morning. This evening the Robertson Association met in my office and re-elected me President for one year. After the meeting adjourned Morgan and myself invited the members to partake of a supper at Carter's.

Feb. 6

Occupied the day in business matters, in the afternoon I went to the city Hotel to see Mr Churchwell who has just arrived from N.Y.

---

[4] James B. Lamb was a promising young lawyer and, previously, had served for a time in the Tennessee Legislature.

Feb. 7

Called to see Gov Johnson this morning who is improving. The wind last night and today has blown with great fury amounting almost to a hurricane.

Feb. 8

Went with my wife this morning to Jas Hamilton's to see her mother who is there on a visit. I then attended the 1st Presbyterian church. In the evening I read in the Herald the investigation before the corinor of the mysterious murder of Dr Burdell a dentist in Bond Ct, N.Y.

Feb. 9

Today Grundy and his family left for Arkansas. He intends opening a place there, which I think much better than planting in Middle Tenn. This afternoon at 4 oc my favorite sister Sallie was married to Dr Jno Berrien Lindsley,[5] Chancellor of the University of Nashville. She has married well, yet I was loathe to give her up. I will miss her society, which has brought to me for years past more pleasure than that of any other person. Sallie is the noblest specimen of woman kind that I have ever seen, and my observation has not been circumscribed.

Feb. 10th

Mrs Deery passed the day at my fathers. She is still low spirited and has enough to make her so. Attended the Circuit Court today.

Feb. 11

Attended the Circuit Court this morning. This evening I attended the Theater. The Robertson Dramatic Club. The performance was highly creditable for amateurs.

---

[5] John Berrien Lindsley (1822-1897), physician, clergyman, educator, was born in Princeton, New Jersey. He graduated from the University of Nashville in 1839; studied medicine in Louisville and Philadelphia; and received an M.D. from the University of Pennsylvania in 1843. Turning to theology, he was ordained in 1846 by the Presbytery of Nashville. In 1850 he organized the Medical Department of the University of Nashville and was its dean for six years; became Chancellor of the University in 1855, keeping the Medical Department open during the Civil War; retained his connection with the University after the war, and for four years assumed the added duties as Dean of the Medical School; resigned the chancellorship in 1870 but taught in the Medical School until 1873; took part in the organization of the Tennessee College of Pharmacy in 1873, in which he later became Professor of Materia Medica. Lindsley was also a leader in public health; served through four cholera epidemics; once was Health Officer and Secretary of the State Board of Health from 1876 to 1880. He was a member of the Nashville Board of Education 1856-1860; Superintendent of Schools in 1866; Secretary of the State Board of Education 1875-1887. He wrote widely. A pamphlet, *Prison Discipline and Penal Legislation* (1874), was circulated extensively. His theological publications after 1870 were important contributions to the history of the Cumberland Presbyterian Church. *The Military Annals of Tennessee, Confederate, Series I* (1886), added much to the history of the Civil War.

Feb. 12

Attended the Circuit Court this morning—quite a spicy debate came off in the Court between the Clerk and the Att. Gen. The latter made a motion against the former for not paying over money.

Feb. 13

Attended the Circuit Court this morning. This has been a dull and gloomy day.

Feb. 14

Occupied the morning in Court—and the afternoon in attending the wants of the poor.

Feb. 15

Did not go to church this morning. In the afternoon Seraphine and myself drove out to Cousin Frank McGavocks where we passed the night.

Feb. 16

Came in early this morning from the country. Attended the Circuit Court. Has a full explination of the goosebone theory from Nick Hobson who I believe goes farther with its mysteries than any one else in this neighborhood. They divide the breast bone in three equal parts representing the three winter months.

The goose must be a young one killed in the fall of the first year. It is then cooked and laid aside—and they judge of the winter by the colouring of the bones. If the bone is very dark it indicates cold weather —and if light—fair weather. This looks something like the superstition of the ancients. I learned today that Mrs. Henning and her two interesting daughters had gone to live with the Sisters of Charity in this city which is a most singular freak. They attached themselves about fifteen months ago to the Catholic Church in Paris, which did not meet the approbation of Mr. H. A few weeks since they went to New Orleans to see him, but he sent her word that he never would see them until they renounced their religion. Rather than do this they returned to Nashville, and are now with the Sisters.

Feb. 17

I notice in Brownlows Whig of the 14th a long communication on the Literature of Tennessee in which my work entitled a Tennessean Abroad is spoken of in the highest terms. The writer compares the book to Steven's travels, which I regard as the highest compliment he could have bestowed. This afternoon I took a drive with my wife. Attended the marriage of Dr MacGavock's two daughters this evening. The oldest Elsie to Emmett Cockrell[6] and the next Clay to F K Cheatham. The party was large and delightful.

Feb. 18

Do not feel very well this morning after the disipation of last evening. Attended the Circuit Court and listened to an argument between Demoss and Bob Foster on an attachment case.

Feb. 19

Went up to Shelbyville this morning to attend to some business.

Feb. 20

Left Shelbyville at 10 oc for Knoxville. I met Mr Smith of Macon on the cars who informed me that Ophelia Nisbet had married a young man named Reid of Ga. I was engaged to this lady for a long time and feel some interest in her future happiness.

Feb. 21

Reached Knoxville before day this morning. Called to see Churchwell and lady with whom I dined. Left Knoxville at 3 oc for home. Passed five hours in the night at Dalton. Col Luttrell and Mr Blood of Ga were along, and we had a nice time.

Feb. 22

Took breakfast in Chattnooga and reached the city at five o'clock. Beautiful day.

Feb. 23

Father left today on the Boon for Ark. The two literary societies of the Nashville University celebrated the 22nd which was on Sunday, last night at Odd Fellows Hall.

Feb. 24

News reached here today of the Steamer Humbolt bound from NO to this city, having sunk in the Miss about Vicksburg. Her cargo and many of the crew were owned and a part insured in the office of this city. It will fall heavily and perhaps break up one of the offices. This has been a boisterous day—no news.

Feb. 25

This has been a beautiful day, but for some cause or other I have been low spirited. No news yet about the Cabinet. Gov Brown is in great trouble fearing that he will not get into one of the Departments.

---

[6] Robert Emmett Cockrill (1834-1870), the eldest son of Sterling R. Cockrill. He married Eliza McGavock in 1857.

Feb. 26

Went out visiting this morning with my wife. Read the proceedings of the Ten Historical Society that met in the Capitol yesterday. Mr. A W Putnam[7] and Mr Wales made several valuable presents to the society of early records, letters and relics.

In the evening I attended the largest party I ever saw in Ten at Gen Hardings given to his son John[8] who has recently married the widow Owen. I went with Eastman's daughter and enjoyed myself exceedingly. At the party I learned from Dortch that Gov Brown had received a position in Mr Buchanon's Cabinet. This news will give ease to the old fellow's heart. This is the night of Miss Lizzie Bonner's marriage to Lamb of Memphis. I wish them much happiness.

Feb. 27th

Started this morning on the cars for Alisonia to attend the sale of some personal property. At Duck river just beyond War-trace we were detained some five hours on account of a terrible accident that had just taken place at the bridge to the night train. The bridge was undergoing some repairs and the workmen thought the train had passed and had taken up some of the railing. They say that the proper signal was given to the Engineer, but he paid no attention to it. The result was that the Engineer—fireman, and wood passer were instantly killed—the locomotive ruined and several freight cars damaged.

Feb. 28

Quite a large number of persons attended the sale today and everything went off at high prices. I bought the negroes, not that I wanted them but to save myself, and to keep them in the family. Gov. Brown passed up today en route for Washington.

March 1st

This is the first day of spring, after a long and severe winter. The day is beautiful, but I fear from appearances that the fruit and wheat will be much injured by the white frost. Returned to Nashville today with the negroes I purchased yesterday. Noticed in the morning paper that

---

[7] A. W. Putnam, a citizen of Nashville, was intensely interested in the preservation of Tennessee history. He was chosen vice president of an historical society which was organized in Nashville in May 1849. When the society was reorganized in 1857 he was elected as its president.

[8] John Harding was born in Davidson County, Tennessee in 1831. He studied at Harvard and the University of North Carolina. When his studies were completed he returned to manage and develop one of the finest farms in middle Tennessee. He was especially interested in breeding and training trotting-horses.

Allen A. Hall[9] had retired from the editorial chair of the Banner. He intends I believe to start a neutral paper in the city.

Mar. 2nd

It is quite cold this morning, but I think the day most beautiful. Called early at the Hotel to see Mr Churchwell and lady, who reached here yesterday from Knoxville. Sent some negroes off on the Boon to Ark. Passed the evening in Rice's office.

Mar. 3

I notice in the morning paper that old Mose Singleton has announced himself as a candidate for Congress in this district. This old horse jockey has been a standing candidate for Mayor and the legislature for many years. Called to see Gov Johnson this morning. He is still suffering very much with his arm. This has been a cold cloudy and disagreeable day, a little snow fell in the afternoon.

March 4

This is the day of the Inauguration of Jas Buchanan the fifteenth President of the United States. His election caused every patriot in the land to rejoice, because they believe it saved the Union from the wreck of sectional agitation. May his administration prove a good one, and may he succeed through the exercise of a wise policy, in reuniting the bonds of fraternal feeling—and place the whole country once more in a condition of prosperity and internal happiness. He has had long experience in the affairs of government—thereby enabling him to call into his Cabinet and other important positions the best talent of the country. It is not known here certainly who will constitute his Cabinet but Ten will have one in the person of the Hon A V Brown, who is an old and faithful soldier in the cause of democracy. I saw V K Stevenson this evening who has just returned from Lincoln Co. where he succeeded in getting one hundred thousand dollars subscribed to the Fayetteville branch road which if completed will be an important acquisition to the Chattanooga road and to this city.

---

[9] Allen A. Hall (d. 1868), one of Nashville's outstanding newspaper editors. He came to Nashville about 1825 and became part of the firm of Hall and Fitzgerald. In 1826 they purchased the *Nashville Republican and Tennessee Gazette.* In 1837 he and S. Nye commenced publication of the *Republican Banner,* a daily paper. Hall was appointed Chargé d'Affaires to Venezuela in 1841. When he returned in 1845 he purchased an interest in the *Nashville Whig.* Soon afterward he went to Washington to edit the *Republic,* the organ of President Fillmore's administration. He was editor of the *Republican Banner* 1853-1857. When the *Opposition* was started in 1859 he assumed most of the editorial work. In 1863 he was appointed Minister to Bolivia by President Lincoln, serving in that capacity until his death.

Mar. 5

Nothing of interest has transpired today—occupied my time in my office.

Mar. 6

Received by telegraph this morning an abstract of Mr Buchanons Inaugural and a list of his Cabinet. The Cabinet is composed of sound Union loving men, but not particularly distinguished for talent. Made a fine sale of realty to the Tenn and Ala RR today amounting to $3000. Called to see Mrs. Deery and Mrs. Churchwell this evening. Attended a lecture at Odd Fellows Hall by Mr. Kewen on Nicarauga—and country that I feel deeply interested in. Col Cave Johnson furnished me a very flattering letter to Mr Buchanan today.

March 7

Left Nashville this morning for Washington via Chattanooga. Stopped at Winchester to attend to some business. After tea I called to see Mr Venable[10] and had some good music from his daughter and wife on the piano. I learned during the conversation that he was an applicant for the position of Minister Resident to one of the South American States.

March 8

At Decherd I joined Childress and Kewen of Nicarauga. Reached Atlanta before day this morning.

March 9

Rain all day—took tea in Augusta and proceeded on my journey through So Carolina.

March 10

Took breakfast at Kingsville where I met Col Quitman[11] of Miss. enroute for home. Reached Goldsboro in NC to tea, where we were left by the Conductor. We wrote to the President of the RR and asked his dismissal. Formed the acquaintance of Col Hardee of the Army, now stationed at West Point.

March 11

At 10 oc we again started and reached Weldon for dinner. Passing through Petersburg and Richmond to Acquia Creek we took the steamer for Washington. Arrived at Browns Hotel before day.

---

[10] William Edward Venable (1804-1857), lawyer, diplomat, was a native of Prince Edward County, Virginia. He moved to Winchester, Tennessee and became a distinguished lawyer and teacher of law; served in the Legislature 1847-1848; organized Mary Sharp College in 1850 and laid out the course of study; appointed Minister to Guatemala in 1857, at which post he was striken with cholera.

[11] John Anthony Quitman (1799-1858), lawyer, soldier, politician.

March 12

Met Dr Lindsley and sister Sallie who left this morning for N.Y. having waited for me one week. I accompanied them to the depot and promised to join them in N.Y. Dr. L. handed me a document that I had sent by him to Sam Smith[12] to procure the signatures of our deligation in Congress. Not one of them signed it, having been previously committed to Letherman of Memphis an old line whig and friend of Jas C Jones. This application for a foreign mission I consider the heigth of imprudence, but there is no knowing in politics how matters will turn. The number of applicants for office is not near so great as it was four years ago. Nearly all the Tenn. [applicants] have gone home. The Senate was in Executive Session today and confirmed a number of Minor appointments, and among the re-appointments of many of the local officers in Tenn. After tea I called to see A V Brown who is now the Post Master Gen. Here I met Judge Douglass who invited me to take breakfast with him tomorrow morning at 9 oc. Also met the *immortal* Savage of Tenn., the lady of P.M.G., and Nixon of Ten an applicant for a foreign mission.

March 13

Was invited by Gen. Whitfield the member of Congress from Kansas to call with him and his deligation on the President. There were a number of Indiana among them and I felt a little anxious to see how they would be received. Whitfield introduced them one by one and each man shook hands with him. The President said they did not look like a very bloody set—to which Whitfield replied that they were determined to support his Administration. Old Buck looks badly and I think has gone down very much since I saw him last. I was introduced to him as the Grandson of his old friend Felix Grundy and he seemed glad to meet me. After remaining a few minutes Turner and myself went to the Patent Office where we procured some seeds to send home. I noticed many improvements in the public buildings since my last visit. The Patent Office building is now being extended and when completed will be a most commodious structure. The mechanic's fair is now open in the city, I went in and was much pleased with the many specimens of exquisite home industry. Among the patented articles I was much pleased with an invention for steaming food. It will prove of

---

[12] Samuel Axley Smith (1822-1863), Congressman from Tennessee, was a native of Monroe County, Tennessee. He began the practice of law in Cleveland, Tennessee; District Attorney General 1845-1850; Democrat in Congress 1853-1859; fought in the Confederate Army in 1861.

great utility on large plantations. After tea I called on Jno Bell[13] and family where [they] are keeping house. Here I met Mr Foster[14] the Republican Senitor from Ct. While there Gen. Scott came in and passed an hour. He is looking in excellent health and I was much pleased with his conversation. A deep snow fell while I was at Mr. Bell's. Returning to Brown's Hotel I called on Jacob Thompson[15] of Miss., and Gov. Brown.

March 14

I had an engagement to take breakfast this morning with Judge Douglass, but did not go feeling somewhat unwell. I will call before leaving the city and make him my respects. The Senate adjourned today after confirming a number of appointments and among that of Wm E Venable of Winchester Tenn. Minister Resident to Guatemala and J. A. McNutt of Tenn.[16] to some unimportant place. After tea Gen. Whitfield, Mr. Rusky, Childress and myself went out visiting. Col. Disny[17] the member of Congress from Cincinnati died in this city this morning. Received a letter from my wife.

March 15

This morning I took a stroll on Capitol Hill examining the new wings of the Capitol. The old dome has been removed and the building when completed will present an entirely new appearance. Passed the remainder of the day about Brown's Hotel. The crowd changes every hour, old faces go, and new ones come.

March 16

This morning I went up to the White House and endeavored to see the President but the crowd was so great that I retired. Churchwell arrived this afternoon from Ten. and brought me a letter from my wife. I passed most of the day with Mr W Clusky of this city, who is the correspondent of several leading papers in the country.

March 17

Gave my papers to Gov Brown today with the request that he should deliver them in person. I then went up to the War Department to see

---

[13] John Bell (1797-1869), lawyer, statesman, was born near Nashville, Tennessee. He graduated from the University of Nashville in 1814 and was admitted to the bar in 1816. He was a member of the State Senate in 1817; served in Congress 1827-1841; Secretary of War under President Harrison in 1841; in the State House of Representatives in 1847; a Whig in the United States Senate 1847-1859. He was an unsuccessful candidate for President on the Constitutional Union ticket in 1860.

[14] Lafayette Sabine Foster (1806-1880), Senator from Connecticut.

[15] Jacob Thompson (1810-1885), Congressman from Mississippi.

[16] James Alexander McNutt (1826-1874), teacher, was born in Wythe County, Virginia. He was a talented man with a good education, and was a teacher for several years.

[17] David Tierman Disney (1803-1857), Congressman from Ohio.

Gov. Floyd[18]—but he was in Cabinet Counsel. Called to see Judge Douglass and lady today and then went through the largest printing establishment in the country. This evening I had an interview with Gov. Floyd and he promised to aid me all in his power. Here I met Ruth Floyd and Dr McDowell of St Louis, who is the son of Gov. McDowell[19] of Va. Recd. a letter from Dr. Lindsley today. Wrote to my wife, mother and Sallie.

March 18

This has been an exceedingly boisterous and disagreable day. Occupied the day about the Hotel. After tea Childress, Dixon and Hill of Tenn. called in my room, and we had a game of ucre.

March 19

This has been a real cut throat day. I have not been out of the hotel, but remained in doors, nursing a bad cold and sore throat—

March 20

I went up to the State Department today and found my papers on file. I wanted to see Gen Cass, but he was just going to the White House. Had an interview with Mr. Cobb,[20] Sec of the Treasury, and then returned to the Hotel where I met Benson who invited me to walk up to the Capitol. In the rotunda I noticed a new painting representing the discovery of the Miss. by De Soto. It is a beautiful work of art. We then walked through the new wings of the Capitol. The halls are large and beautiful, and the committee rooms adorned with frescoes representing things American. I also noticed some very good pieces of statuary mostly by Crawford[21] intended to adorn the niches of the building. I never knew until today that the East front of the Capitol was the main front. It was supposed that the high ground east of the building would constitute the business part of the city, but the location of the White House in the West (from which the spoils come) has drawn every thing in that direction.

March 21

Called on Gen Cass this morning, but he was so much occupied that I did not have an opportunity of giving him a talk. I then called on F P Stanton[22] of Ten and enlisted his services to attend to business in my absence. In the evening I called on J Thompson and A S Brown.

---

[18] John Buchanan Floyd (1806-1863), Governor of Virginia, Secretary of War, Confederate general.

[19] James McDowell (1795-1851), twenty-fifth Governor of Virginia.

[20] Howell Cobb (1815-1868), lawyer, politician, soldier.

[21] Thomas Crawford (1813?-1857), sculptor.

[22] Frederick Perry Stanton (1814-1894), Congressman from Tennessee, was born in Alexandria, Virginia. He began the practice of law in Memphis, Tennessee; served as a

March 22

Recd a long letter from my wife this morning. Met a Mr. Fox from Nashville who gave an account of a fugitive negro killing himself on the cars between that point and Chattanooga. He was very bright in colour and had another negro with him as his servant. The Conductor thought he had negro blood in him, and as soon as he was discovered he drew a pistol and shote himself in the belly and then cut his throat with a knife.

Dr. Walter McNairy dined with me today. The New York appointments will be taken up tomorrow and the city will be crowded with office seekers until they are over. These fellows do up the thing very systematically. They have a sweet of rooms in the City which they call their *Ranche* where they meet every day and organize for the purpose of forestalling the President and Cabinet. They have fine liquors and do up the thing brown.

I have formed the acquaintance of several members of the press, since coming here viz. L. Clusky correspondent of various papers, Hope of the Philia Argus, and Punch of the Savannah Georgian. The California appointments were made yesterday, and the disapointed made a terrible to do over it last night.

March 23

This morning Sam Ewing called to see me. He is an applicant for the Consulship to Palemus or Trieste. Hon F P Stanton furnished me a letter this morning to Mr. Buchanon in which he stated that I was better qualified to fill the mission for which I am applying than any other applicant from Tenn. It is a very strong letter, and I filed it in the State Department. Left Washington at 4½ oc for N.Y. Pretty soon after taking my seat in the cars a woman closely veiled took a seat by my side. It turned out that she was a very bright negro. The police carried her back to Washington. No coloured person can leave Washington without entering into heavy bond, well secured by residents of Washington.

March 24

Reached N.Y. about day-light this morning, and put up at the Metropolitan Hotel. After breakfast I strolled Broadway which always presents innumerable attractions for the stranger. I would like to live in N.Y. if I possessed sufficient fortune, but it is no place for a poor man like myself. I would prefer being first in a small village than second here.

Democrat in Congress 1845-1855; Governor of the Kansas Territory 1858-1861; moved to Virginia and subsequently settled in Florida.

March 25

I went to all the principal hotels this morning to see if I would find Churchwell. He has either left the city, or stopping at some private home. Called to see Thos. Eakin also Redfield the publisher who advised me to let my plates remain and not sell them. After tea I went visiting.

March 26

From the papers it seems that the Cabinet have made the N Y appointments—which seem to give satisfaction here. R J Walker[23] has been appointed Gov of Kansas, I hope he will be more fortunate than his predecessor and restore peace to that distracted country.

March 27

Occupied the day in examining fine carriages and other articles. After tea I attended Niblo's where the Ravel family are performing. Dr. Lindsley and Sallie arrived today.

March 28

Occupied the day in shopping and looking about at the different objects of interest. After tea Dr. L., Sallie and myself attended the Broadway Theatre where we witnessed the most wonderful performance of two elephants.

March 29

I did not go to church today, but walked down to the Astor House. The papers of this morning contain interesting news from Europe, California, Nicarauga, and other points. Left N Y at 6 oc this evening for Washington.

March 30

Arrived in Washington about day light this morning. After breakfast I went with Sam Ewing to see Gov. Flag. In the evening I went to a shooting gallery and practiced with the pistol. With some pains I might make a good shot.

March 31

Called this morning with Hulbert to see Stanton. He had an interview with Gen Cass during my absence and reports that the old Gen is favorable to my appointment.

Apr. 1

Went with Stanton this morning to see old Buck. He was engaged, but made an appointment with Stanton at 8 oc this evening. At Stanton's

[23] Robert James Walker (1801-1869), lawyer, statesman.

house I met Mr. Randolph[24] who once pulled Gen. Jackson's nose. He is now in poverty—gave me full particulars about the whole affair. At the Union office I met Mr Poore the man from Mass who wheeled the barrell of apples 30 miles having made a wager of the kind on the result of the Pres. election in that State.

Apr. 2

Occupied the day mostly about the hotel. Took tea with Dr. [Harvey] Lindsley of this city. Returned to Gov. Brown's room where I met Mr Churchwell and Col Pickens.

Apr. 3

Called at the Kirkwood House this morning to see Churchwell. At 2 oc I went to the Court of Claims to hear Stanton on an important case in which one half million of dollars is involved. Called this evening on Stanton and heard a favorable report on my case from Old Buck. Left a copy of my book with Gen Cass to let him know that I knew something about foreign parts. It will do no harm. Made a visit to friend in city. Passed an hour with Gov. Brown who gave me every assurance that he would stand by me to the last in my application for a foreign mission. Took leave of my friends at 12 oc and among them were Mr. W Clusky, D C, Isaacs of Kansas, Judge Williams of Iowa, Nixon of Tenn. and Hulbert.

Apr. 4

At 6 oc this morning Gen. Whitfield of Kansas and myself left Washington for Nashville. About 10 oc the boat passed Mt. Vernon. All boats as they pass are required to toll their bell which I think a very appropriate testimony of the nation's gratitude to the father of his country. At Slash Cottage I purchased a very curious arm chair made by an old negro out of broom-sage straw, wrapped with oak splits. Dined in Richmond and took tea at Weldon, N.C.

Apr. 5

Reached Wilmington for breakfast and Kingsville for supper.

Apr. 6

Left Augusta before day and reached Atlanta about 5 oc. A large fire was raging when we arrived distroying about 50,000 worth of property Duncan the Editor called to see me and gave me much news in regard to my Ga. friends.

---

[24] Robert B. Randolph, a lieutenant in the navy, was discharged for irregularities in his accounts. He felt aggrieved for some words in President Jackson's letter approving the dismissal, so on May 6, 1833 he assaulted Jackson in the cabin of a steamboat at the Alexandria dock.

Apr. 7

Reached Chattanooga before day and Nashville at 5 o'clock.

Apr. 8

This morning the Camollite Church burnt down. I suppose it was the work of an incendiary. The congregation have been dispersed for some time and a great deal of bitterness existed among them occassioned by Mr. Ferguson[25] who had to leave. The fire bells have been ringing all day and the engines running first from one point then another. One year ago our city was visited by one of the most disastrous fires.

Apr. 9

Went to the depot early this morning to [see] Gov Browns family off for Washington. Attended the Criminal Court. Two inches of snow on the ground this morning. After dinner I called on Gov Johnson. He is still suffering from his arm. My wife and myself called on Mrs Deery and Mrs Churchwell. It was not a pleasant visit. We then called on Aunt Felicia who is quite unwell. After tea father and brother Ed reached home from the plantation. A good deal of excitement exists in this Congressional district between the friends of Zollicoffer Quarles and McEwen.

Apr. 10th

Attended the Criminal Court this morning. This afternoon I called with my wife to see Louise Stevenson who has just returned from La. Her health is still bad.

Apr. 11th

It is quite cold this morning, which is unusual at this season. I fear we will have no fruit and that the crops will be injured. A man named Parker alias Jerry Clemons was sentenced to the Penitentiary today for obtaining money under false pretenses. He is a man of great shrewdness and some talent—which was fully evinced in a speech he made to the Court, in which he recounted the history of his life in a very effecting manner.

Apr. 12

Attended Church this morning with my wife. Weather still quite cold.

---

[25] Rev. Jesse B. Ferguson succeeded Dr. William H. Wharton as pastor of the First Christian Church of Nashville. He built up a church membership of 800 and became very popular. His popularity waned due to his differences with many members of the congregation with regard to his acceptance of spiritualist doctrines, together with a litigation over the possession of church property. He was co-editor of the *Christian Magazine,* the organ of the Christian Church, 1848-1852.

Apr. 13

Attended the Criminal Court this morning, and a sale of lots on Broad St. After tea I went to the Union office where I met a number of democrats from different parts of the State who come to attend the State Convention on Wednesday next, and among them J K Walker and Wm Carroll of Memphis, J W Jones and Bright of Lincoln, Nicholson and Whitthorne of Maury, Miller and Helms and Birch of East Tenn, Howard of Lebanon, etc. In conversing with them, they seem not to favor Mr. Buchanon's Pacific R.R. idea.

Apr. 14th

Early this morning I was aroused by the alarm of fire, which was very near—being the stable of Wm. L. Boyd set on fire by some evil one. Occupied the day among the democrats who came up from different parts of the State to attend the State Convention tomorrow. This evening I attended the Caucus in the Capitol. They appointed a committee on organization. An attempt was made on the part of Ewing's friends to have an informal ballot in order to test his strength but failed. Nicholson, Davidson, and Bright made speeches.

Apr. 15

At 10 oc this morning the Convention assembled in the Hall of the House of Rep. and Jonas Thomas of Maury was made President. The Committee composed of one from each county in the State reported the name of Isham G Harris of Shelby and he was unanimously made our candidate for Gov. The Platform was about the same in substance as that adopted two years ago. A resolution was passed inviting Gen Pierce to visit the State—and a committee was appointed to correspond with him. A request was made of Andrew Ewing by the State Con to be a candidate for Congress in this District against Gus. Henry.[26] The deligation of this district met and appointed a committee to waite upon him and see if he would consent. The committee went out to his house, but his child was dying and they did not mention the subject. The deligation met again at 3 oc and fixed the second Monday in May for the District Con. at Clarkesville. Dr. Lindsley and Sallie arrived this morning. Attended a delightful party this evening at Bilbo's. My wife accompanied me.

---

[26] Gustavus A. Henry (1804-1880), the "Eagle Orator," was a native of Kentucky and was educated at Transylvania University. He moved to Clarksville, Tennessee in 1833; was once a member of the Legislature; presidential elector in every election from 1840 to 1852; defeated for Governor by Andrew Johnson in 1853; elected to the Confederate Senate following the secession of Tennessee.

Apr. 16

We did not get up this morning until 11 oc having retired very late. Wm. Polk called very early. Ben Cockrell[27] was married this evening to Sallie Foster. I was invited, but did not go.

Apr. 17

Occupied the day mostly in reading the Statues of the State, and attending to some business matters. Recd an invitation this evening to my brother Edward's wedding. He is going to be married on the 5th of May to Miss Ella Young of Columbus, Miss.

Apr. 18

Occupied the day in my office. This afternoon Gov N S Brown called in and we had a long conversation on the subject of politics. It is reported that Gus Henry will not accept the nomination for Congress, but I do not believe it.

Apr. 19

Did not go to church today but remained at home reading Dr. Anderson's book of travels in the South of Africa which I find quite interesting. This afternoon I took a drive out to McGavock's.

Apr. 20

Attended the Criminal Court today. We now have some prospect of Spring—this is the first mild day we have had this month.

Apr. 21

Another very cold and windy day. We now have March in Apr. I fear the long protracted cold will injure the cotton and corn, as well as fruits and vegetables. Remained in my office all the morning reading the statutes of the State. Attended the Criminal Ct. this evening and found Hugh Scott on trial for whipping a negro in the Market House. The Nashville Union of this morning contains a very fulsome eulogy upon G G Poindexter[28] of Clarkesville calling upon him to be a candidate for Congress. Gus Henry declines the nomination of the K N party for Congress. The Black Republican legislature of N Y have taken the control of the police of the city of N Y and Brooklyne out of the hands of the Mayors because they voted for Buchanon in the late election. This I

---

[27] Benjamin Franklin Cockrill, the son of Mark R. Cockrill, was born November 1, 1832. He married Sallie C. Foster, the daughter of Ephraim H. Foster, and lived in "Richland House," the old home of General James Robertson in West Nashville, Tennessee.

[28] G. G. Poindexter, newspaper man of Columbia, Tennessee. In May 1858 he purchased a portion of the *Nashville Union and American* and became the paper's principal editor. He kept this position until his death November 18, 1859.

consider outrageous. The U S Ct for this district opened this morning—Judge Humphries present, Judge Catron[29] not returned from St Louis.

Apr 22

Attended the Federal and Criminal Courts today.

Apr. 23

Remained in my office most of the day. Wrote a letter to Gov A V Brown. In the evening I attended a little party at Dr Hoyte's given to Dr Lindsley and lady.

Apr. 24

Gen. Zollicoffer announces himself in the morning papers as a candidate for Congress. If Quarles and McEwen come out again we will have some fun, and stand a good chance to run in a democrat. This afternoon Gov Brown, Capt Williams and Bob Brown were in my office and while talking with them I became quite chilly, so much so that I went home where I had a regular chill followed by a raging fever. Just one year ago I had a similar attack just after returning from Clarkesville.

Apr. 25

Remained at home all day nursing myself.

Apr. 26

Did not go to church today but remained at home reading Stevenson's travels in South Africa which I find very interesting. From the northern papers tonight I see that the Black Republicans in the N Y legislature have attempted to pass what they term the liberty bill which I consider high treason. Both the N Y and Ohio legislatures have passed resolutions condemning the decision of the Supreme Court in the Dred Scott case. Brother Edward and Sister Mary started this evening for Columbus Miss accompanied by that faithful servant Nelson.

Apr. 27

Occupied the day mostly in my office—nothing happened worth noting except a disagreeable occurrence that happened in a conversation with Gov N S Brown. I related a little incident that took place while

[29] John Catron (c. 1786-1865), Justice of the Supreme Court of the United States, was a native of Wythe County, Virginia. He came to Tennessee in 1812; was admitted to the bar in 1815; began practice in Overton County; moved to Nashville in 1818. In September 1824 he was elected to the Supreme Court of Tennessee and was the Court's first Chief Justice serving from 1831 until the court was abolished in 1834. He was appointed to the Supreme Court of the United States on March 3, 1837 by President Jackson. At the outbreak of the Civil War he, as Associate Justice, presided over the circuit composed of Missouri, Tennessee, and Kentucky. He made a futile attempt to keep Tennessee loyal to the Union but was forced by the Confederate authorities to leave the state.

we were in London which was evidently distasteful. He used harsh language towards me which I did not much relish, but owing to our intimate friendship I did not resent it upon the spot.

Apr. 28

This morning I wrote a note to Gov Brown demanding an explination and just as I had finished it he came in and I read it to him. He seemed surprised and disclaimed any intention of insulting me, and here the matter ended. Remained in my office all day reading, etc.

Apr. 29

Attended the Federal Ct. this morning where I heard Jo Guild[30] and Ed Ewing make speeches on the case of some La lawyers vs. the Franklin Institute in Sumner Co. for services rendered to Franklin's estate. The fire companies of the city left here today to attend the Rail Road Convention at Memphis. The Mississippi river and the Atlantic Ocean are now connected by rail-way. The Charleston people have sent to Memphis water from the ocean to mix with the waters of the Miss.

Apr. 30

Passed most of the day in my office revising the statues of the State. The city at present seems dull, notwithstanding the K N State Convention meets here tomorrow.

May 1st

Heavy rains today. The grass is just beginning to grow. Attended the Federal Court this morning. At 11 oc I attended the K N Convention. Mr. Hatton[31] of Wilson Co. was nominated as their candidate for Gov. He is a young man without much political character. Gen. Haskell was present and contended for the nomination. He responded to a call after the nomination which was full to overflowing with eloquence. He said that he had passed his boyhood and his manhood in the service of his party and now to be thrust aside was too hard. This is the history of many politicans in this country—up today and down tomorrow. Jo

---

[30] Joseph Conn Guild (1802-1883) was a native of Pittsylvania County, Virginia. He studied law and, in 1821, entered the law office of Foster and Brown in Nashville, Tennessee. He was four times elected to the State Legislature; enlisted for the Seminole War in 1836 and was made lieutenant-colonel of a regiment; Judge of the Law Court in Nashville 1870-1877. In 1878 he published *Old Times in Tennessee,* a book which contains many pictures of men, habits, and customs during the early history of the state.

[31] Robert Hopkins Hatton (1826-1862), lawyer, soldier, was born in Steubenville, Ohio. He began the practice of law in Lebanon, Tennessee in 1850; trustee of Cumberland University from 1854 until his death; member of the State House of Representatives 1855-1857; an American-Party member of Congress 1859-1861; colonel of the Seventh Regiment Tennessee Volunteer Infantry 1861; made brigadier-general in the Confederate Army May 1862; killed in the Battle of Seven Pines.

Pickett, Hickerson and others made speeches. Attended a little tea party this evening at Mr Putnam's.

May 2nd

There is a great deal of dissatisfaction among the members of the K N party about the nomination yesterday. Many of them do not consider Mr. Hatton the man for the times. They had a meeting last night at the Capitol, at which Jno Bell and others made speeches. The party has again changed its name to American Whigs. In the north they call themselves American Republicans and four years hence they will unite and run a southern free soiler for President.

May 3

Did not go to church today but remained at home reading. Hard rain and fire comfortable.

May 4th

Heavy rains all day. I received a letter this morning from Col Thos Nelson in which he states the people in East Ten are actually suffering for want of food. The stock in some counties are dying. The corn crop failed in that section of the State last year, and they sold all of their wheat at high prices and took East Tenn. money for pay, which is not worth anything at present. The K N's of this Co met in convention today and nominated Goff for the Senate and Jos L. Ewing[32] and Mr Vaughn for the House. Passed the evening at Allison's room.

May 5th

This is the day for the meeting of the American Medical Association. They assembled at 11 oc in the Hall of Representatives. Dr. Winston on behalf of the committee on arrangements made a fine speech, welcoming the deligates to our city. Some twenty States were represented this morning, and over two hundred deligates present. Dr. Pitcher of Michigan the President of the last Convention also made a speech in which he gave the Clergy a lick for the active part they take in politics. Paul F. Eve[33] of this city was made President of the Convention and

---

[32] Joseph L. Ewing (d. May 16, 1860), business man, was a native of Davidson County, Tennessee. His only public office was membership in the Tennessee House of Representatives in 1857.

[33] Paul Fitzsimmons Eve (1806-1877), one of the greatest and most successful surgeons that ever practiced in the South, was a native of Georgia. In 1828 he graduated from the Medical Department of the University of Pennsylvania. He studied further in London and Paris and served in a Warsaw hospital for a time. Upon returning to the United States, he was elected Professor of Surgery in the Medical College of Georgia. In 1851 he was made Professor of Surgery in the University of Nashville, a position which he held for ten years. For a short time he was Professor of Surgery in the Missouri Medical College but returned to the University of Nashville as Professor of Operative and Clinical Surgery. In 1877 he accepted a chair in the newly founded Nashville Medical College.

four Vice Presidents. Three elegant parties were given at Dr Foster's, Eve's, and Jennings' in honor of the deligates. I attended Foster's.

May 6th

I did not attend the Convention today but remained in my office most of the day. After tea I went out to Dr. Shelby's[34] with the widow Watkins. The company were at 5 oc and they kept up the dance until a very late hour. The Dr.'s house is better adapted for a fine entertainment than any other in the State.

May 7th

The Convention adjourned today. This afternoon they called in a body on Mrs Polk. Mrs Dr Porter gave a magnificent dinner party to about 30, Dr Lindsley and myself did the honors. This evening I accompanied my wife to the Ball in the Capitol. About 3000 persons were present and every thing went off well. Mr. Touny of Charleston, S C whom I met in Berlin went with us. The ladies were dressed magnificently, the music was fine, the supper good and upon the whole I expect it was the grandest entertainment that ever came off in the South.

May 8th

Left Nashville on the cars this morning for Jonesboro to attend the Chancery Court. Reached Dalton about 9 oc this evening where I will pass the night.

May 9

Left Dalton at 10 oc and reached Knoxville in the afternoon.

May 10

Remained all day in Knoxville at the Lemar House. Passed the day with Crow Ramsey and the Lyons. After tea I called on Mrs. Churchwell.

May 11

Started this morning on my journey. At Russellville the stage was crowded with drunken boatmen, and a woman of doubtful character which made it very disagreeable of course. We reached Jonesboro late in the night.

May 12

Attended the Chancery Court today but nothing was done in my case. The Messrs. Deery, and young man named Baily sent from Nashville

[34] John Shelby, M.D., (1786-1859) was born in Sumner County, Tennessee. He graduated from the University of Pennsylvania and practiced in his native county for some years before moving to Nashville 1820. He retired many years before his death, and was Postmaster of Nashville 1849-1853.

by Gordon are here. Payne of Memphis is here to inspect the work on the East Tenn RR which is progressing very slowly. It is the impression up here that if they do not get more aid soon from quarter, they will have to stop opperations.

May 13
Attended the Chancery Court again today. The lawyers in the case had a consultation, but did not arrive at any thing definite.

May 14
Today the parties in the case agreed on a decree to sell the property in Sullivan Co. on the 15 and 17 of Sept. next. All the interests together with the dower will be sold and the purchaser will get a clear title. An account was ordered of the personalty. Started home after dinner. At Greenville a number of rough N Carolinans got in the Stage.

May 15th
Reached Russellville at 9 oc after a very bad night's ride. Reached Knoxville this afternoon where I staid all night.

May 16
Started from Knoxville at 8 oc and reached Chattanooga to tea. Here I staid all night. Met Knox Walker, Birch, Key, Correy, and McCall. Dr Chandler of N C who was enroute for Texas gave me a fine imported Pointer. I noticed in the Union today the marriage of my brother Edward on the 5(th) inst to Miss Ella Young of Columbus Miss. Also that the Democratic Convention at Clarksville had nominated And Ewing for Congress—and myself for Floater which I shall decline.

May 17
Left Chattanooga this morning, and arrived in Shelbyville this evening.

May 18
Occupied the morning attending to business matters in Shelbyville. Reached home at 4 oc. Andrew Ewing has declined the nomination for Congress.

May 19
Attended the Circuit Court today. Received a letter from Clarkesville informing me of my nomination by the Democratic Convention as a candidate for joint-Representative.

May 20
Attended the Circuit Court today. The Shelby Guards paraded today, and have a ball tonight. After the parade they started round the city

with a mammoth cake with a pyramid on top. The pyramid broke to the delight of the boys.

May 21st

Attended the Circuit Court this morning. Called on Dr Lindsley after tea.

May 22

Attended both the Circuit and Chancery Cts. Called with my wife on Capt Williams' family.

May 23

I dreamed last night that the Hon A V Brown was dead, and that he was burried in the night. He was burried with military honors and the horses attached to the hearse ran away scattering the coffin into fragments, and rolling the deceased statesman in the dust of the street. I do not believe in dreams, but it may be that this may prove ominous of the light that I may hereafter regard him. Attended the Circuit and Chancery Courts today.

May 24

Attended the first Presbyterian Church this morning, and heard a very indifferent sermon from Dr. Elliott.[35] In the afternoon I called to see Mrs Polk who is highly indignant at the reports now going the rounds of the papers in regard to her marrying Mr Buchanan. She says that she has no idea of ever marrying anyone—she has too much respect for the memory of her husband ever to change her name.

May 25

Attended the Federal Chancery and Circuit Courts today.

May 26th

Today they took up in the Circuit Court the case of Mayfield vs McCombs and Overton which involves a new principle in our Ten Courts. Overton owned the lot on the corner of Cherry and Spring streets, which was leased by McCombs for the purpose of carrying on the Cabinet business. Sometime in [18]54 he placed a steam engine in the establishment which was entirely frame for the purpose of turning, etc. In [18]56 the whole establishment was consumed by fire, which spread to other buildings in the vicinity, and among others that of Mayfields—who now sues for damages.

[35] Rev. Collins D. Elliot was Principal of the Nashville Female Academy jointly with Rev. R. A. Lapsley from 1838 to 1844. In 1844 he became Principal and continued until the close of the school in 1866.

May 27

News reached here this morning by telegraph that Gen. Walker of Nicarauga had capitulated to Capt Davis[36] USN and was in New Orleans. Ten thousand persons turned out to meet him and he made two speeches in which he said all was not yet lost. Strange man and still stranger history. News also reached here today of the death of Senitor Butler[37] of South Carolina. About nine o'clock this evening the Nashville Manufactury establishment was burnt—loss $100,000.

May 28

Attended a sale of lots in Edgefield today, and found builders few and figures low. Attended the Circuit Court today.

May 29

Attended the Circuit today and listened for a while to the argument in the case of Mayfield vs Overton and McCombs.

May 30

This has been quite an exciting week among the sporting men. The Spring races closed today, every race was a good one, and a great deal of money has changed hands. From all accounts there is a great scarcity of provisions throughout the whole country and in some of the States the people are actually starving. Corn is selling here now at $4 and $5 per lb. and glad to get it at these rates. In the North Western States they seem to be suffering more than elsewhere. The wheat crop generally promises well and the corn in some sections, but the latter is unusually backward. Col Jno McGavock Miss Winder and family, and Mary Bass arrived today from La also Dr Waters and family from Ark.

May 31

I did not go to church today. In the afternoon I called on Mrs Polk, Mrs. VK Stevenson, Mrs Porter and Jno McGavock.

June 1st

Attended the Circuit Court today—and listened to the very able argument in the case of Mayfield vs McCombs and Overton. Jno. Marshall and E H Ewing both made speeches of marked ability.

June 2nd

This morning Judge Baxter charged the jury in the case of Mayfield vs McCombs and Overton and they found for the defendant. This after-

[36] Charles Henry Davis (1807-1877), naval officer, was a native of Boston. He did scientific work in the United States Navy; helped to organize and plan the work of the Union Navy during the Civil War; later assumed command of the upper Mississippi River gunboat flotilla; served for a time as Superintendent of the Naval Observatory following the War.

[37] Andrew Pickens Butler (1796-1857), lawyer, politician.

noon I accompanied my wife out to Billy Watkins' where we passed the night. The old fellow is a great democrat and has an elegant place on the bank of the Cumberland.

June 3rd

This morning we called to see Ben Cockrell and lady, but found them absent. We then drove over to Gen Hardings where we took dinner. J Geo Harris[38] and his two children, Miss Armstrong and Frank MacGavock's family were there. After dinner we drove over to Jno O Ewing's place.

June 4

Rose at 4 oc and went out fishing with little John Bass in Big Harpeth which is in a few hundred yards of the house. We had no luck. After breakfast I walked with Mr Ewing over his place and looked at his fine stock, etc.

June 5

Left Mr Ewings after breakfast and took dinner at May Graham's. Stopped at Gen Hardings and Frank McGavock's on our return. Edward and his wife and Mary reached here today from Columbus.

June 6

I notice in the morning papers the appointment of Gen. B F Cheatham Consul to Aspinwall. Occupied the day mostly in my office.

June 7

Attended the first Presbyterian Church this morning. In the afternoon Edward and myself drove out to Dr. Hadley's where we had a nice mess of strawberries and cream. After tea I called on Mr Thos Eakin of N.Y.

June 8

Attended the Circuit Court this morning, but passed most of the day in my office. After tea I called on Lavender and wife of NY, Blewett of Miss and Mr Bass' family.

---

[38] Jeremiah George Harris was born in Croton, Connecticut October 30, 1809. He entered the field of journalism as soon as he became of age, as associate editor of the *Political Observer* in New London; served on three other New England papers, *New Bedford Daily Gazette, Bay State Democrat,* and *Boston Post;* was influenced by James K. Polk to come to Nashville, Tennessee in 1839; took control of the *Nashville Union* with the purpose of weakening the Whig power in Tennessee; worked with Polk to organize the Democratic party more thoroughly than it had ever been before; was sent abroad in 1843 with a commission from Daniel Webster, Secretary of State, as a commercial agent of the United States; returned in 1844 and resumed his editorial duties on the Union; became a disbursing officer in the Navy in 1845 and served in that capacity until his retirement in 1871.

June 9

The convention at Clarkesville nominated Wm Quarles for Congress. In the morning papers I notice the message of Gov Walker from which I infer that Kansas will be a free State, he favouring the idea of submitting the Constitution to the people for radification after its adoption —Gen Walkers speech at N.O. is also published this morning. He says that he intends returning to Nicarauga and carry out his mission of Americanizing Nicarauga.

June 10

Attended the Circuit Court today. Nothing of importance to note, Wm Quarles and Dr Menees[39] of Robertson are in town. The latter has consented to run for the Senate in his district. Bob Haywood is a candidate for Floater in this district.

June 11

This morning I attended the annual Commencement of the Nashville University. The speeches were all highly creditable, and every thing passed off to the entire satisfaction of the trustees and faculty. In the afternoon the Alumni had a meeting and elected Judge Wm Yerger[40] of Miss to deliver the next annual address. The students had a fine ball at the College building this evening.

June 12

This morning Edward and myself rode out to Jno O Ewings to look at some stock. It was very warm and we suffered exceedingly. Father and Jno McGavock left Ark this evening on the Huntsville.

June 13

This morning I was invited to deliver a Fourth of July oration before the Swiss Relief Society.

---

[39] Thomas Menees, M.D., was born in Davidson County, Tennessee in 1823. He graduated from the Medical Department of Transylvania University in 1846; elected to the State Senate in 1857; a member of the Confederate Congress throughout the war; resumed the practice of medicine in Nashville in 1865; elected Professor of Materia Medica and Therapeutics in the Medical Department of the University of Nashville in 1873. When the Medical Departments of the University of Nashville and Vanderbilt University fused in 1874, he became Professor of Obstetrics and Dean of the Vanderbilt faculty.

[40] William Yerger was born in Lebanon, Tennessee, the son of a prominent Dutch family. The family moved to Mississippi about 1838. William studied law and settled in Jackson, Mississippi, where he became a well-known judge. He was described as "a well read and able lawyer; a ripe and accurate scholar; a profound judge of men and affairs . . . ." See Henry S. Foote, *The Bench and Bar of the South and Southwest.* St. Louis: Soule, Thomas and Wentworth, 1876.

June 14
Did not attend curch today. In the afternoon I called to see Jno M Hill[41] and took tea at Mr Bass'.

June 15
The dabblers in politics are all agog this morning about a reported difficulty at Fayetteville between Harriss and Hatton. The story goes that Harriss Knocked Hatton off of the stand. Attended the Circuit Court today. In the afternoon I had quite a spirited game of ucre with Allison, Rice and Childress. This is the day that the comet was to appear, but the predictions of the philosophers have not been verified, and the inhabitants of this sub-lunary sphere are permitted to exist yet a little while longer.

June 16th
Occupied the day mostly in assisting for a large party given at my father's this evening in honor of Ed and his wife. The evening is inclement—but the young never stop for the weather.

June 17
The party last night passed off very well. The rooms were crowed and the ladies looked charming. They danced until 3 oc this morning. Attended the Circuit Court today.

June 18
Occupied the day in writing a speech for the 4th of July.

June 19
Attended the Circuit Court this morning and instituted suit against the Ten and Alabama RR for damages to some lots belonging to my father. Sent some stock off on the Huntsville by Ed to Ark.

June 20
Occupied the day in my office. No news.

June 21
Did not go to church today but remained at home reading and writing.

June 22
I had a severe attack of colera-morbus last night and have felt very much debilitated all day.

---

[41] John Melchour Hill (1797-1870), business man, was born in Lancaster, Pennsylvania. He migrated as a young man to Giles County, Tennessee; settled in Nashville in 1819; accumulated a fortune in the auction and commission business and retired in 1845. He was a shareholder and director in numerous banks and insurance companies and was active in many manufacturing enterprises.

June 23

Remained most of the day in my office. After tea I called on Wm Quarles who is now making the canvass with Gen Zollicoffer. The papers of this date contain a long letter from Wm. Walker to President Buchanon in relation to his imprisonment by Capt Davis USN.

June 24

Occupied the forenoon in my office. In the afternoon I went up to Odd Fellows Hall and listened to the discussions between Quarles and Zollicoffer candidates for Congress in this district. They both made exceedingly dull and uninteresting speeches. I do not think any thing was gained or lossed on either side—as it was a pretty dead pull between them. I took tea at Aunt Falicia's.

June 25

Remained all day in my office reading and writing.

June 26

Occupied the forenoon in my office reading and writing. In the afternoon I played ucre with Rice.

June 27

This day has been occupied pretty much as yesterday. Heavy rains all day and night which I fear will injure the wheat crops.

June 28

Did not go to church this morning, but occupied myself in committing my speech for next Saturday.

June 29

From the papers this morning it seems that the people of Memphis have taken the law into their own hands. A man named Able, a gambler, shot a fellow gambler and the people held a public meeting—and they went to the prison and took Able out and were about to hang him, but some of the citizens interfered and they carried him back. Beautiful weather for harvesting.

June 30

AOP Nicholson's speech at Centerville is published this morning. He wants to go to the US Senate and made this speech I suppose to off-set Gen Pillow's letter on the issues of this canvass. Father and Ed reached home today from Ark.

July 1st

Occupied the day mostly in my office, nothing worth noting.

July 2

Remained all day in my office reading and attending to business. Some gentleman in Charleston sent me the Mercury which I received this evening, containing the funeral obsequies of Langdon Cheevis[42] one of South Carolina's great sons.

July 3rd

The thermometer is down to 60 this morning which is too cold for the cotton plant and the corn. Occupied most of the day in committing my speech for tomorrow.

July 4th

The procession this morning was small, but respectable. Fehr was in his glory, being mounted on a large cream-coloured conostooga horse, with a Mexican sadle and a bridle. Fogg and myself went in a carriage together. Reached the ground about ten o'clock. Fogg made a short speech before reading the declaration. We both got through to our satisfaction. After the speeches were over they commenced the dance, rifle shooting, etc. Lager beer was passed around freely—and every one seemed to enjoy themselves. It was the first celebration of the 4th of July by our foreign born citizens in Nashville.

July 5th

Attended the Episcopal Church this morning with my wife. Did not go out in the afternoon.

July 6th

Occupied the forenoon in my office reading, etc. This afternoon Gen Wm Walker reached the city. It was not known until thirty minutes before his arrival that he was coming, yet a very large crowd assembled at the depot to receive him. He was conveyed to the city Hotel where he made a speech to the crowd—in which he said that he and his movement had been meligned and that the north was against [him] and then appealed to [the] south to give him their moral countenance and encouragement. I wrote letters to a number of gentlemen today inviting them to deliver lectures next winter for the benifit of the Robertson Association.

July 7

The papers of this morning are teeming with high [praise] on my speech on the 4th. Remained in my office all day, reading, etc.

---

42 Landon Cheves (1776-1857), lawyer, politician, farmer.

July 8th

Dr Jno. S. Young[43] and old and valued citizen died last evening. He was an excellent friend and working democrat. The papers of this morning announce the death of the Hon Wm L. Marcy of NY who was one of the greatest statesmen of the country and decidedly the best diplomat of the age. In his death the democratic party and the nation loose one of its brightest ornaments.

Gen Wm Walker made a fine speech at the Capitol this evening in which he vindicated himself against the aspersions of those who called him a filly-buster—a tyrant—and a man unacquainted with the science of war. The crowd was very large and his speech was received with great applause. The Shelby Guards escorted him from the hotel.

July 9th

Gen Walker and Capt Fapace left for New Orleans this morning. Received this evening a package of 50 vol of Clusky's Political encyclopedia.

July 10

This is decidedly the warmest day of the season. Occupied the day in attending to business matters. The speech that I made on the 4th July was published in the Gazette this morning. The Rev. Charles Tomes,[44] Rector of the Episcopal Church died this evening leaving a large and interesting family. He was truly a christian who practiced what he taught, and was one of the most charitable, social, and worthy gentlemen I ever knew. I have no doubt but that the recent division in his church contributed in a great measure to aggrevate his disease.

July 11

Occupied the day mostly in my office reading—nothing new.

July 12

Attended the funeral of the Rev Chas Tomes this morning at the Episcopal Church. The church was much crowded and he was burried with Masonic Honors—being a Knight Templar.

July 13

I notice in the papers of this morning that they had terrible riots in NY on the 4th between a party living in Five Points, and calling them-

---

[43] Dr. John S. Young, Nashville physician, was a native of Augusta County, Virginia. He settled in Warren County, Tennessee about 1830; served as Secretary of State of Tennessee 1829-1847; superintended the erection of the Lunatic Asylum and was one of the building commissioners of the state capitol.

[44] Rev. Chas. Tomes became rector of Christ Episcopal Church in Nashville in October 1848 and continued until his resignation May 1, 1857. During most of this period he also helped supply the pulpit of the Church of the Holy Trinity. In 1857 he organized the Church of the Advent as a result of an unsuccessful attempt to introduce the free pew system into his church, and accepted the rectorship in June, but died the following July 10.

selves Dead Rabbits and the Bowery boys. A good many were killed and the military had to be called out to quell the disturbance. This is a sad commentary upon that city. In the last few years riots have been on the increase in the large cities, both in the North and South. What they will lead to is yet to be seen.

July 14

Occupied the day mostly in my office preparing a placard of the Deery lands in East Tenn. Gen Zollicoffer's wife was burried today. She was ill but a short time and died while her husband was away—canvassing in the lower part of the district.

July 15

Remained in my office most of the [day]—but little fitted for business, having a severe attack of flux or something akin to it.

July 16

Remained at home all day—sick and troubled with heat. After tea Seraphine and myself spent the evening at Mr. Bass'.

July 17

I believe this is the warmest day of the season—the thermometer being 90 degrees in my office which is one of the coolest places in town. Occupied the day in looking over some of my wife's stor acc' [accounts] while a girl—preparing for the settlement in Sept.

July 18

Remained in my office most of the day. Jno. Bell commenced his speech of the canvass this evening. The burden of his song was Distribution—his favorite hobby.

July 19

The different pulpits of the city are occupied today by an unusual amount of talent—but being unwell I had not the pleasure of hearing any of them. Bishop Elliott of Ga. at the Episcopal, Dr Huston at the Presbyterian, Mr Fall[45] at the Camolite, Dr Howell[46] at the Baptist, and J. Ferguson at Odd Fellows Hall.

---

[45] Rev. Philip S. Fall was an Englishman by birth. He came to Nashville from Louisville, Kentucky in 1826 to occupy the pulpit of the First Baptist Church. His leadership was largely responsible for the establishment of the First Christian Church of Nashville, of which church he remained as pastor until 1831. He entered educational work in Kentucky; returned to the Nashville church 1858-1876; later became president of a school in Frankfort, Kentucky. While a minister he established a private seminary in Nashville in 1828.

[46] Rev. R. B. C. Howell, Baptist minister, was a native of North Carolina. He came as pastor to the First Baptist Church of Nashville in January 1835 after eight years in Norfolk, Virginia; organized *The Baptist* in 1835 and edited it for thirteen years; resigned

July 20

Occupied the day in my office—reading, etc.

July 21

Remained in my office all day. Mother and Seraphine went out to Franklin this evening. Jno. Bell concluded his long winded speech at the Market House tonight. He was exceedingly bitter—and poured his vials of wrath upon Gov Johnson and the democratic party generally.

July 22

This morning the Hatton Club, the Shelby Guards and a few citizens on foot and in carriages went out to meet "Bob Hatton." It was a sorry display for the K N's of Davidson. The speaking commenced at Watkins Grove at 12 oc. Gen Harris opened in an able and masterly effort satisfying all of his friends. Hatton made a complete failure and I could see disappointment depicted on the countenances of all his friends. Gen Harris gives encouraging accounts of his prospects throughout the State, and thinks that his majority will exceed ten thousand if the poll is any thing like a full one.

After tea I called on Harris—old Joe Miller and Mrs. Donelson.

July 23rd

The Candidates for Gov went up to Murfreesboro this morning accompanied by friends. From the papers of this morning it seems that Gen Walker of Kansas has issued a proclamation calling out the US troops to quell the disturbance in Lawrence occasioned by the free State party in attempting to carry out the Topeka Constitution. Since writing the above I learn that the candidates have agreed to close the canvass—both being phisically exhausted. I regret this exceedingly as the principles of democracy have nothing to lose by discussion.

July 24

Hon A V Brown of this State has recently been honored with the degree of L.L.D by the University at Chapel Hill NC where he graduated. [George D.] Prentice of the Louisville Journal was shot a day or so ago by Mr Durrett[47] of the Courier but unfortunately was not killed.

Went out to Williamson Co this afternoon on the cars and staid all night at Aunt Martha's where Mother and Seraphine have been passing several days.

---

the pastorate in 1850 and moved to Richmond, Virginia; returned to the Nashville church in July 1857 where he remained until 1867. He died April 5, 1868. He was one of Nashville's outstanding religious leaders.

[47] Reuben Thomas Durrett (1824-1918), lawyer, historian.

July 25

Drove into Franklin this morning with Cousin James McG. and called on Dr Ewing's family. The jury brought in their verdict today in the case of Perkins vs Shy—they found him guilty only of an assult. Dined at Col McGavock's and staid all night at James McGavock's.

July 26

Came into the city this morning—but did not go to church.

July 27

Occupied the day mostly in my office reading. Received a letter from Mr. W. Clusky enclosing a notice of my 4th of July oration. He states that Tennessee will not receive another foreign mission.

July 28

Occupied the day mostly in my office reading—Young's American Statesman.

July 29

Occupied the day in business matters. At 5 oc I left the city for Winchester. Staid all night at Deckerds.

July 30

Walked over to Winchester this morning. During the day I took the depositions of Dr Wallace Estill and Mr W Garner to use in case I have in Jonesboro. The Circuit Court is now in session in Winchester. Gen Pillow made a visit to this place a few days since—with the view of feeling the popular pulse in regard to his prospects for the US Senate. Like Gid, he distributed his likenesses through the country. Left Winchester for home at 10 oc.

July 31

Reached Nashville at 10 oc this morning. I met two of my college class-mates on the cars—Philip Gillchrist of Ala and David Spence of this State. This city is usually dull at present. A great number of our citizens are out of town, many of them at Bersheeba and Tyree Springs. Father returned from Franklin today, and says that mother is somewhat better than usual.

Aug. 1st

I regret very much to learn this morning of the death of my young friend Duncan Claiborne.[48] He died last night after a lingering illness.

[48] Duncan R. Claiburne (1831-1857) was well-known throughout Tennessee. He edited a Democratic paper in Winchester 1854-1855. In 1855 he was elected Principal Clerk of the Tennessee House of Representatives.

He was a clever gentleman—and excellent companion. Jas Rice left this morning for Va to be absent until the first of Oct. Two Irishmen were killed today at the Reservoir by the falling of a derrick.

Aug. 2

Attended the Baptist Church this morning to hear my old friend Dr Howell—but he was in the country and another gentleman filled his pulpit. In the afternoon I attended the funeral of Duncan R. Claiborne. Mr. Ferguson delivered an excellent discourse, in which he enunciated several ideas that were somewhat original. He is without doubt a Universalist in his sentiments.

Aug. 3

Heard this morning that Hopkins L. Turney[49] of Winchester died on Saturday last of a disease of the heart—while on his way home on the road side. I was with him all day Friday, taking depositions, and he appeared perfectly well. How true is that sentence of the bible, that in the midst of life we are in death. He filled a high place among his constituents altho he had lost to a considerable degree his influence. Also learned today that Knox Walker's oldest son was killed in Memphis by being thrown and dragged by a horse.

Aug. 4

For the last three or four days we have had an unusual quantity of rain—which will injure the cotton—and I fear cause the wheat that is now shocked in the fields to sprout. Aunt Falicia left this morning for Philia. taking all of her children with her. Beverly Tucker of Va. has just published a very able letter vindicating the course pursued by Gov Walker in Kansas. He says that those in the south cannot afford to be wrong when our cause is just. I think this letter will do much good. The telegraph brings us news of the elections in Ky Clay[50] is elected to Congress in the Ashland district. Democrats have 8 out of 10 Congressmen—and have carried the legislature—which will give them a US Senitor next winter. This is glorious news from a State that has so long stood out in the front rank of opposition to the democratic party.

Aug. 5

The news from Ky is confirmed today. Attended the Criminal Court today. A man was on trial for stealing a jar of pickles.

---

[49] Hopkins Lacy Turney (1797-1857), Congressman from Tennessee, was born in Smith County, Tennessee. He practiced law in Jasper and Winchester, Tennessee; a member of the State House of Representatives 1828-1838; a Democratic member of Congress 1837-1843; United States Senator 1845-1851.

[50] James Brown Clay (1817-1864), lawyer, congressman.

Aug. 6

The election went off more quietly today than I ever saw it in Ten. The vote in this Co. has falled off large and the gain democratic. The intelligence from the out Cos. indicates the election of Harris by an increased majority, and the legislature is probably democratic.

Aug. 7

A good deal of noise was made by the K N's yesterday because I presented an Irishman at two ballots to vote. He was refused at the first because his papers were not six months old and a majority of the judges were K N's. At the other ballot where his vote was received a majority of the judges were democrats. There is a difference of opinions on this subject between the two parties. The democrats contend that a man is entitled to vote as soon as he receives his final papers, and the K N's contend that he should remain in the Co. six months afterwards.

Aug. 8

Occupied the day in taking depositions and making preparations to leave for East Ten.

Aug. 9

Left Nashville with my wife at 8 oc and reached Chattanooga at 4 oc and then came to Look-out mountain where we propose passing several days. Col. Whitesides has built a new hotel and a number of cottages facing the eastern brace of the mountain near the Lenora Spring. A large number of visitors have been here during the season but they do not stay long.

Aug. 10

This is the day that the Southern Commercial Convention meets in Knoxville. A large crowd is expected there, Nicholson, Pillow, and Polk passed up today on their way to Knoxville—with the view of making Senitorial capital. I took a walk this morning to Point Lookout and enjoyed the magnificent panorama of mountain scenery. In the afternoon Miss Kate Williams called up to see us—and I returned with her to their cottage.

Aug. 11

The Williams called to see us today and I returned with them and took a game of ucre.

Aug. 12

Today we went in company with the Williams to the Rock fields and the Rock City which are on the eastern brow of Lookout Mt. about 3 miles from the hotel. Mrs. Williams had prepared an elegant lunch—

and we passed the day most delightfully. The Rock fields are a number of huge boulders in various shapes scattered over the surface of the ground—and the city is a succession of narrow caverns intersected with each other. We intended going to the lake, but it is 9 miles over a rough road and we gave it up.

Aug. 13

The views from Lookout are superb—and it is one of nature's grandest works—but the company come and go so fast that one has no opportunity of forming acquaintances and it becomes very very lonely. This evening we left the Mt. accompanied by Miss Kate Williams for Cotoosa Springs in Ga. Gen. Bynum joined us at Chattanooga and we reached there at 9 oc.

Aug. 14th

Last night we found a great crowd here. The ladies were put in the attic with three or four others and I was sent over to Buzzards Roost where I remained seperated from my wife about one week, annoyed to death every night by the infernal noise kept up by Dr Oliver and his drunken associates. At the end of one week we were placed in better quarters in the hotel. I met a number of old acquaintances, viz. Dr Collins and family of Macon Ga Capt Smith Mrs. Boykin and the Nisbits. I also formed a number of agreeable acquaintances, viz Mr Stovall and lady, Augusta, Gen McKee, Ala, Mr Weavers and ladies, Ala, Miss Legard, Ala, Mrs Gibson and Miss Crawford, Ga, Mr Montgomery Cummings and Dr Howard, Savanah, the Neily family of Savanah, Battey family, Augusta, Capt Orne and Col Tillman, Memphis, Miss Thompson, Atlanta, Miss Thompson, Macon and many others. Recd. a letter from home while here in which I was pained to learn the death of Harriett, an old family servant. The company at Catoosa has diminished very much since we arrived and I think the grand fancy ball which is published will be a failure, as the guests do not seem to take much interest in it and the proprietor looks only to the money part of it.

[*There is an unexplained break in the Journal at this point.*]

Aug. 31

This morning we took leave of Catoosa and our friends amidst the waving of handkerchiefs—and kissing the girls which I found quite agreeable. I placed Kate Williams under the charge of Judge Cole with directions to see [her] off this evening. Mr. Warren and family of Augusta accompanied us to the depot—and as far as Dalton where we seperated. We reached Knoxville at 5 oc and stopped at the Lamar House.

Sept. 1st
Robt Deery was to be here today by appointment, but disappointed me as he has frequently done before. Knoxville looks dull—and I understand there is very little business doing here now. Wheat is down and it seems to regulate every thing in this region.

Sept. 2nd
I met Judge Swan today who informed me that he and Jno Mitchell was about to start a democratic paper here in Knoxville to be called the Southern Citizen. I subscribed for it—and think it will be a good paper.

Sept. 3
Occupied most of the day in taking depositions in the case I have in Jonesboro.

Sept. 4
Occupied the day as yesterday in taking depositions. Maj. Ramsey acted for me and Mr Cocke for the Deerys. The testimony of the different witnesses in regard to the cost of maintaining a school girl here in Knoxville differ widely. Mr Legard, Mrs Jno P Erwin and daughter and Dr. Percy arrived here this evening.

Sept. 5
This morning I walked out about a mile from town to see a drove of negroes belonging to Franklin, a negro trader. Most of them had chains about their necks and rists, which arroused my sympathies. I then went over to Sloan's marble yard to see them working the beautiful marbles of East Tenn. At 6 oc we left Knoxville in company with Dr Percy of Miss, Mr Legard of Mobile, Mrs Jno P Erwin and daughter of Nashville. Reached Bull's Gap the terminus of the rail road about 10 oc. Some of the passengers remained all night at a rude tavern but we continued on to Greenville. When we reached there the hotel keeper had to go over to a neighbouring house and borrow a candle. Having no matches he went into the kitchen to blow up a coal. Having no room in the house he colonized us over the street.

Sept. 6
Soon after breakfast Mr Wm Williams[51] and Miss Erwin called to see us and invited us to dine. We accepted and passed the day most

[51] William Williams (1776-1862), lawyer, was born in Halifax County, North Carolina. He graduated from Harvard University in 1799; came to Nashville in 1804; practiced law for a quarter of a century. He was a member of the Tennessee Legislature for a time and was a magistrate for a number of terms. He was a trustee of the Robertson Academy, the Craighead Academy, and the University of Nashville.

agreeably. The family of Williams living here have been distinguished for many years for their wealth and aristocracy. Dr Williams was an officer in the revolution (I saw his sword) a great whig and an inveterate enimy of Andrew Johnson. They regarded him as a low mechanic —and during the Dr.'s life time a fierce and bitter warfare was carried on between them. Lowery and Sevier called to see us today. At 3 oc we left Greenville and reached Jonesboro at 9 oc. The rail road is now running to this place. We stopped at the Eaton House kept by Dr. Kinney, an old democrat who represented Washington Co in former years in our State legislature. Miss Chester a pretty young lady died here this evening of consumption. Franklin Deadrick's wife is also expected to die of the same disease. Jonesboro is a low place—with but one long street—and nothing in it to invite a stranger.

Sept. 7th

Occupied the day looking over the clerk and Master's acc in my case against the Deerys, which I find long, tedious, and uninviting.

Sept. 8

Mrs. Deadrick died last night. I saw a negro boy carrying round her funeral notice—which was written on a sheet of paper with a piece of crape attached to the top and handed to the passerby to read. I saw an amusing scene on the street today between an old lady who is a pensioner and her son. They had a small waggon—filled with articles which they had purchased in a store. The conversation between them was truly rich—the old lady contending that the articles were dearly purchased by the blood of her beloved husband and she would have the control and benifit of them. I took a walk out to Thos A R Nelsons this morning and had a long conversation with him on business. On my return I met Landon C Haynes.[52] A large party reached here this evening from the Va. Springs—among them Mrs Dawson, son and two nieces, Tom Martin and two daughters, Ophelia and Octavia, Sam Vance, Mrs. Tate and Mr. Mumford of Memphis.

Sept. 9

Attended the funeral of Mrs. Deadrick this morning. Mr Legard passed through today with Mrs Erwin en route for North Carolina.

---

[52] Landon Carter Haynes (1816-1875) was born at Elizabethton, Tennessee. He was educated at Washington College, East Tennessee; read law in the office of Thomas A. R. Nelson; admitted to the bar in 1840; elected to the lower house of the State Legislature in 1849 and was chosen Speaker of that body. The reputation he had gained as a speaker and debater was largely instrumental in his election to the Confederate Senate in October 1861. After the war he moved to Memphis and engaged in the practice of law until his death.

Sept. 10th
I was occupied today in looking over acc. [accounts] and taking depositions. The deposition of my wife was taken and as usual on such occasions she made herself extremely rediculous by flying into a kind of hystirics—which I believe she cannot control. We left the Eaton House in a jiffy for Blountville. I feeling very bad of course. Wm Deery and myself got off at Union and organized the lands belonging to the estate in that neighborhood which are very fine. Borrowed horses and went over to Snapps tavern in Blountville.

Sept. 11
Occupied the day in examining the lands about Blountville.

Sept. 12
Robt Deery and myself went out today and examined the knob lands in the neighborhood of Blountville.

Sept. 13
Being no church today in Blountville, Mr. Davenport and myself rode out to examine the Beaver Creek Estate which contains over four thousand acres. We dined with an old iron man named Shipley. Returned to Blountville same day.

Sept 14
Passed the day quietly at Snapps tavern. A number of Seraphine's old acquaintances called to see her today—and among them a very clever old man, named Gregg—and Robt. Allison her cousin.

Sept. 15
This is the day of the sale. Gordon of Nashville and Franklin Deaderick arrived this morning. The people began to come in early this morning. We commenced the sale in the Court House after dinner. The town lots sold beyond my expectations and the farm back of the town which I purchased brought a fine price, but the other lands sold very low.

Sept. 16
We left Blountville after breakfast this morning and reached the Magnolia House in Bristol for dinner.

Sept. 17
This is the day of the sale here. After dinner the crowd assembled in the Ten. rail-road depot and the remainder of the estate of Wm Deery was disposed of. Wm H Gordon and myself purchased the Beaver Creek Estate and Davenport purchased the Union property as agent for Churchwell. The outside tracts were taken by others.

Sept. 18

Today Wm Deery and myself drove in an old shackling buggy down to the Beaver Creek farm which I am more pleased with every time I look at it. I procured sealed bottles filled with mineral waters of the place which I consider very fine. It is about 25 minutes drive from the boundary line of this tract to Bristol by a circuitous road. Left Bristol this evening, and reached Jonesboro for tea. Received letters from Scudder of Shelbyville, Wm. S. Pickett of Memphis and father.

Sept. 20th

This morning we went to Dr Cunninghams where we met Dr Lyons of Columbus Miss who accompanied us to church and delivered a most excellent sermon. We dined at Dr Cunningham's and attended curch again after tea.

Sept. 21

Occupied the day in the Clerk and Master's room going over the Acc [Accounts] etc. This evening the cars ran eight miles below Jonesboro and it was really amusing to witness the struggle between the hotel agents and the proprietor of the RR eating house. The hotels and stages gained the day, but their time is soon at hand and they will have to give up the ghost.

Sept. 22

Occupied the forenoon in the office of the Clerk and Master, and in the evening we took our leave of the "Gander Grass" town which is the oldest berg in East Ten., for home.

Sept. 23

We had quite an agreeable company in the stage today, viz. Mrs Jas Wilson and two sons, Bob Brown and sister, and young Franklin of Jefferson Co. who are on their return from the Va Springs. Reached Bull's Gap for supper and staid all night.

Sept. 24

Took the cars at day light this morning, and reached Chattanooga for supper—where we passed the night.

Sept. 25

Reached Nashville at 4 oc this afternoon—and found the streets very dusty.

Sept. 26

Our Mayors election came off today—and there was more than ordinary interest felt in the result. Jno A. McEwen was the candidate of the

K N party and Gen. B F. Cheatham of the opposition. The majority of the former was only 75 votes. The money market here and throughout the country is very tight. The banks of Philia and Baltimore have suspended specie payment—and it is anticipated that our banks will do the same. They have been doing nothing for some time past—consequently money is exorbitantly high, and exchange cannot be had at any price. Cotton and negroes are still very high—but grain has declined. Mr. Gadsden[53] of So C who we met on the cars called to see us tonight.

Sept. 27th

I attended church this morning, and this evening. Accompanied Mr Gadsden up to Mr Bass' where we met Miss Lowery of La, a very pretty, and agreeable lady.

Sept. 28

The Bank of Nashville suspended this morning, which has created quite a panic. The old banks refuse to take any of the Free Bank notes today and the consequence has been that every holder of free bank notes is trying to get rid of them. This bank is owned by [N] Hobson and [W] Wheless and they have done a more extensive business than any other bank in the city. The note holders are safe, but the depositors are in a bad bag and they are numerous. They have made an assignment. A monetary crisis seems to extend over the whole country particularly the northern cities—all of which is the result of over-trading—the balance of specie shipment for the last fiscal year being largely in favor of Great Britain. The country has also run wild in land speculations and other operations of a hazardous character. The merchants and other business men of this city held a meeting today, and passed a resolution requesting the State, Union, and Planters Banks to suspend but they very prudently (I think) declined.

Sept. 29th

Information reached here today that the Exchange Bank, Bank of Shelbyville and one or two others had suspended which has increased the excitement occasioned by the suspension of the Bank of Nashville. The country is in too good condition to be hurt much.

Sept. 30th

The Bank excitement has subsided somewhat today, and more confidence manifested. I attended the Circuit Court today. Several members of the legislature have arrived.

---

[53] James Gadsden (1788-1858), railroad promoter.

Oct. 1st

Attended the Circuit Ct today, and was much amused at the examination of some witnesses in a dog case brought from Williamson Co. It seems that one man killed another's dog for killing sheep—and a neighbouring magistrate gave a judgement to the owner for 10 and the case was brought here on account of there being too much excitement in Williamson. Bank matters are a little more quiet today.

Oct 2nd

Attended Ct. today. Read Gen Scotts letter in reply to Gid Pillow's publication which is one of the best things the old Gen ever wrote and places Pillow in a very unenviable position.

Oct. 3

The town is swarming today with people who have come to attend the meeting of the legislature and the fairs that are to come off soon.

Oct. 4

Attended the first Presbyterian church today. Geo D Prentice of Louisville delivered a lecture at Odd Fellows Hall last night on the Politics of the day. Those who heard him say that it was very fine.

Oct. 5th

This morning I went up to the Capitol to see them organize the two branches of the legislature. The democrats caucused before the body convened and of course having the majority their candidates went through without any difficulty. Gen Danl Donelson[54] of Summer was made Speaker of the House and Robt W. Haywood of Davidson Chief Clerk. [J. C.] Burch of Hamilton was made Speaker of the Senate and Chas. Stone of Davidson Chief Clerk. Mrs Donelson was married today at the Episcopal Church to Mr Lapice of La. and started on the cars south this evening. A telegraph dispatch reached here this evening announcing the death of Maj Venable of Winchester Tenn who recently went out as Minister to Guatemala. He died pretty soon after his arrival there of colera and leaves a large family at home in a destitute condition. He was a man much liked at home, a good scholar—and a perfect gentleman. The Capitol was illuminated tonight by order of the Sec of State. A J Donelson came out this morning in another letter against his brother

[54] Daniel S. Donelson (1801-1863), soldier, was born in Sumner County, Tennessee. He graduated from West Point in 1825; served many times in the State Legislature and was at one time Speaker of that body. Early in 1861 he selected the site and built Fort Donelson on the Cumberland River. In July, 1861 he was made brigadier-general in the Provisional Army of the Confederate States. He saw much service with General Bragg's army in Kentucky and Tennessee.

Gen D Donelson which I consider disgraceful—and will consign him to everlasting disgrace. I passed the evening at Rice's room with a party of friends.

Oct. 6th

The two branches of the legislature completed their organization today—and fixed upon Thursday to elect a U. S. Senitor in J C Jones' place. And Johnson will be elected without any struggle.

Oct. 7th

Attended the Circuit Ct today. Hon Henry Edminson,[55] Mr C from Va called to see me also Churchwell of Knoxville. Dined today with Burton Lee of State. Attended the annual Mechanics Fair.

Oct. 8th

I went up to the Capitol today to see them elect Andrew Johnson US Senitor. He was nominated in Caucus and every democrat voted for him. The opposition voted for NS Brown. The elevation of Johnson to the Senate shows what talent and determination will do. He started in life a poor tayler in the little village of Greenville, East Ten and has gradually risen to the Senate having been a member of the legislature, member of Congress and Gov of the State. He was serenaded tonight at his hotel, and responded in a brief and pertenant speech. Gov Harriss reached the city today but will not be inaugerated until next month. I attended the Mechanics Fair at Evans store on the square this evening where I found a large crowd. It is an improvement on last years. I entered a chair made of broom-straw and wraped with oak splints from Stark Cottage, Va. made by a negro 90 years old—also a pumpkin of great size, grown on Dr. Hadley's farm, 7 ft. in cir., weight 170 lbs.

Oct. 9th

Occupied the day mostly in my office writing a bill for Mr Bass. In the afternoon I attended the Circus with Gen. Smith, Anderson, and Clements. The horses are all jaded, but the acting was very good. The novel fete of rolling a wheel barrow up a wire that was extended on the outside of the canopy from the ground to the top of the pole was performed by a man that looked like a Frenchman—and followed by a lady who balanced herself with a long pole. After tea I called on Aunt Felicia and Cave Johnson.

---

[55] Henry Alonzo Edmundson (1814-1890), lawyer, soldier, was born in Blacksburg, Virginia. He commenced the practice of law in Salem, Virginia in 1838; a Democrat in Congress 1849-1861; served in Confederate Army throughout the Civil War; resumed the practice of law and also engaged in agricultural pursuits.

Oct. 10th

Passed the day mostly in my office. After tea I went to the Theatre with Gen Dunlap[56] Dortch and Churchwell. Mr and Mrs. Drew were inimitable in Black-Eyed Susan and Handy Andy.

Oct. 11

Did not go to church today, but remained in my office writing. Brother Grundy came down today with his family. His wife is looking better than I ever saw her—and her child is a large and good looking red-headed girl. Called to see Maria Stevenson this evening.

Oct. 12

The legislature adjourned today for the week—in order to give the members an opportunity to attend the fair which commenced this morning. I drove out and passed several hours on the grounds but was disappointed in not seeing a larger contribution. I noticed several beautiful quilts—a pair of fine blankets made by Mrs. Barnes of Sumner Co. and a picture worked cruel by a young lady of Campbell Co. Gov. Johnson made a speech at the opening. I did not hear it but was informed by several that it was a poor affair. Passed the evening in Rice's room playing ucre with Allison, McMurry and Rice.

Oct. 13

Occupied the day in my room writing.

Oct. 14

News reached here this morning of the suspension of the NY banks which caused a considerable run on the State Bank this evening. In fact the whole finance of the country is in a awful condition. The crops were never better, but we have no money to get them to market. How long this state of things will last no one can say.

Oct. 15

This morning the State Bank suspended after saying that no emergency could force them to suspend. I presume that Union and Planters will soon follow. This policy meets with the approval of many—but I doubt its expediency very much. I attended the State Fair today. There were about 5000 persons present and the exhibition of blooded stock was highly creditable to the State and the exhibitors. The premiums offered

[56] William Claiborne Dunlap (1798-1872), lawyer, soldier, was born in Knoxville, Tennessee. He began the practice of law in Knoxville in 1819; served in the Indian campaigns in 1818 and 1819; moved to Bolivar, Tennessee in 1828; a Democrat in Congress 1833-1837; Judge of the Eleventh Circuit Court of Tennessee 1840-1849; member of the State Senate 1851, 1853, and 1857; member of the State House of Representatives 1857-1859.

this year are unusually fine, and the competition greater than in former years showing that a spirit of rivalry is abroad in the country. Rice and myself called to see the widow Bass this afternoon at the St Cloud.

Oct. 16th

The Union and Planters Banks suspended specie payment today. I have never witnessed such times before, and the end is not yet. Passed the evening at Alison's room playing ucre with Rice, McMurry and Alison.

Oct. 17

Went out to the State Fair early this morning with Churchwell and Dunlap. The crowd in attendance was very large—and the exhibition of animals very fine. The proceedings of the day wound up by a sale of horses sheep cattle and buggies imported from the north by the Live Stock Co. I did not think much of these animals.

Oct. 18th

Did not go to church today, but remained at home reading.

Oct. 19th

The Fair was continued today—but the weather was so inclement that but few persons were present. Jas M. Davidson delivered the agricultural address in the Hall of the house of Representatives. His delivery was very fine but he was evidently out of his element on the subject of agriculture.

Oct. 20th

Occupied the day mostly in my office—the weather has turned quite cold. The Free Banks have all suspended specie payment—money market still growing tighter.

Oct. 21st

Did not make my appearance today until after dinner, when I went up to the Capitol and listened to the discussion on the resolution to elect another US Senitor.

Oct. 22nd

Attended the debate in the legislature today. At the instance of one of the Profs. in the University of Nashville I took some pains to defeat the charter of another medical school in this city. Called with Dr Lindsley to [see] Wm H Polk and others on the above subject.

Oct. 23

Occupied the day in my office, and at the Capitol. Quite an interesting case is now up in the Federal Court for damages for false imprisonment. A man named Wheeler from Ky was arrested some time since in the town of Charlotte on suspicion of horse stealing—and it turned out that he owned the horses. The circumstances of the case were sufficient in my opinion to ground the arrest. Mr Clarke from Ky is one of the counsel for Wheeler.

Oct. 24

The resolution passed today after a long struggle on the part of the K N against it to elect a US Senitor on Tuesday next in the place of John Bell.

Oct. 25

The pulpits of the city were occupied today by baptist preachers. I did not go to church, but passed the morning with Rice Allison and Childress. In the afternoon I remained at home reading. After tea I called to see JM Davidson on the subject of the new medical college.

Oct. 26th

Occupied the day at the Capitol attending the session of the legislature and the Federal Court. Tonight I attended the democratic caucus to nominate a candidate for US Senitor. On the 16th ballot AO.P Nicholson received the nomination. On the first ballot Pillow received 22, Nicholson 21, Ewing 6, Dunlap 5, Guild 5. Ewing ran as high as 11—Dunlap and Guild was dropped after 3 or 4 ballots. Nicholson's gain was on Pillow. Geo. W. Jones received 3 votes during the evening. Ewing and Pillow are very much disapointed and say that it was Andrew Johnson's influence that decided the matter, and I am decidedly of the same opinion. After the caucus adjourned I went down to Nicholson's room at the Verandah and found Johnson there. Brother John reached here today from Ark and reports fine crops, but no money.

Oct. 27

This morning I listened for a while to Clark' speech in the Federal Court—and then went up into the Convention of the two houses of the legislature. Whitthorne nominated A O P Nicholson and Richardson nominated John Bell. The K N desired to postpone the Convention until next Tuesday in order to give Nicholson and Bell time to answer certain interrogatories they had published. Some of the K N['s] thought that the election was unconstitutional and by one subterfuge and another they prevented an election in the morning. Several very bitter speeches were made by the K N's. The convention adjourned until 3 o'clock, when Mr. Whitthorne read Mr. Nicholson's reply to the interrogatories. The K N's then wanted to adjourn until Thursday in order to give Mr Bell time to answer, but the democrats informed them that they did not care to know Mr Bell's views—and therefore went into an election. All of the democrats voted for Nicholson. One K N took his hat and left the hall. Goff and Vaughn asked leave to be excused from voting. Nicholson was elected.

Oct. 28th

The Banner of today contains a long and scathing communication in reply to Gen Pillows communication in regard to the Mexican War. It is supposed that a gentleman named Buckner[57] who recently moved to this Co is the author. He was an officer in the Regular Army in Mexico—and appears to be perfectly familiar with the whole matter. I think Pillow occupies a very unenviable position and I would not be surprised if he involved himself in a serious personal difficulty. He must feel very sore after defeat and then to have all these men down on him.

My wife returned today from Williamson Co. where she has been for a week.

Oct. 29th

Occupied the day in my office attending to business matters. Recd a copy of the bill filed by Churchwell as Trustee in which he wishes to hold me responsible for the ten thousand dollars that I drew from the Insurance office for the benifit of the Messrs. Deery. I think it very unbecoming a brother-in-law and he will find himself mistaken when it comes to trial.

Oct. 30th

Nothing has transpired today of much importance—except the election of Dunlap for Comptroller, and [W. F.] McGregor for Treasurer of the State. Both democrats.

Oct. 31st

In this morning's Banner another scathing piece was published against Gen Pillow. He (Buckner) fixes it down pretty tight on the Gen about the howitsers found in Pillow's camp. It is thought by some that Pillow will fight him, but I doubt exceedingly whether he will

---

[57] Simon Bolivar Buckner (1823-1914), Confederate soldier, Governor of Kentucky, was born near Mumfordsville, Kentucky. He graduated from West Point in 1844; fought with distinction in the Mexican War; resigned from the army in 1855 and became a successful business man; commissioned a brigadier-general in the Confederate Army; was taken prisoner at the surrender of Fort Donelson and sent to Fort Warren in Boston Harbor; exchanged in August, 1862, and was active throughout the remainder of the war; engaged in newspaper work and in insurance business after the war; elected governor of Kentucky in 1887; active in the Kentucky Constitutional Convention in 1891 and in the national election of 1896.

notice him in any other way but through newspaper editorials. I have been occupied all day in business matters.

Nov. 1st

I did not go to church today—but remained at home attending to matters of business.

Nov. 2nd

The next few days will be trying upon our merchants—most of them having payments falling due—and the banks being suspended they will find it difficult to procure Eastern Exchange. Left Nashville at 5 o c this evening for East Ten.

Nov. 3rd

Arrived at Chattanooga to breakfast and took supper at Bulls Gap.

Nov. 4th

Reached Jonesboro ("Gander Grass") to breakfast after a very fatiguing nights travel in the stage. In the afternoon I went (to?) the Clerk and Master' Office and took out the papers in the case of McGavock and wife vs Deery et als for examination.

Nov. 5th

Occupied all day in examining the C and M Rept which is very voluminious being over 100 pages. The more I see of the transactions of the Deerys the more I am convinced of their rascality. It is painful for me to reflect that I am in anywise connected with them.

Nov. 6th

This morning I read in the Union and American the Inaugural Speech of Gov Harris—also Gov Johnson's farewell speech. Both are short and common place. All day examining report.

Nov. 7

Occupied all day in examining Report in which I find instead of the Deerys being in my debt—they bring me in debt—by a multiplication of charges. We will see what we will see. We have had a great deal of rain here the last few days—but yesterday and today have been like summer—too warm for fire and delightful out-doors.

They still drag along slowly with the R.R. They run now ten miles below Jonesboro, leaving 30 miles of awful staging.

Nov. 8th

I did not go to church today, but remained at the hotel reading the book of Job and conversing with a merchant from Baltimore named Kemp. This evening we had quite a storm and heavy rain, and one of the most remarkable peals of thunder I ever heard. It sounded like a rapid succession of cannon shots. At first I thought it was the reverbration among the surrounding hills, but all the citizens of Jonesboro say they never heard the like before.

Nov. 9th

The Chancery Ct met today, and all the lawyers from the surrounding counties are in attendance. I met Judge McKinney[58] today. This afternoon and this evening Judge Nelson and myself have been engaged in taking Exceptions to the Clerk and Master's Report. I went out and staid all night with him.

Nov. 10th

I occupied most of the day in the Chancery Ct. My case was called but the lawyers were not ready, I presume it will be taken up tomorrow. Pleasant day—after the heavy rains.

Nov. 11th

The second child born in Ten is now living in Washington Co and is above 80 years of age. Her maiden name was Miss Robertson and the first child born in Nashville was Dr. Robertson.[59] This is quite a coincidence. Gen. Jackson and Hugh L White[60] held Court in this county in early times. Their signatures are on the records of the Circuit Court. My case was taken up today, and the Exceptions argued on both sides. Most of my exceptions were sustained and most of the opposite side overruled. Thos A R Nelson appeared for me, Jas Deaderick, L C Haynes and Mr. Haynes for the Deerys, Milligan, Maxwell and Coke for Churchwell and the Bank of East Ten and Barton for Gordon.

Nov. 12

Occupied all the day in the Chancery Court. Passed this evening at Dr. Cunningham's house. The 3 son of F. Deaderick was married tonight to a daughter of Gen Jackson's.

---

[58] Robert J. McKinney (1803-1875), lawyer, was a native of Coleraine, North Ireland. His father, Samuel, brought the family to Philadelphia in 1809 and finally settled in Hawkins County in East Tennessee. Robert was admitted to the bar in Tennessee in 1834; began practice in Greenville; Justice of the Tennessee Supreme Court 1847-1861; one of the peace commissioners sent to Washington by Governor Isham G. Harris in 1861.

[59] Felix Robertson, M.D. (1781-1865) was born in Nashville, the sixth child of General James Robertson. He graduated from the Medical Department of the University of Pennsylvania in 1806; returned to Nashville and secured a large practice which he retained for many years. He was a public-spirited citizen participating in numerous welfare activities.

[60] Hugh Lawson White (1773-1840), Senator from Tennessee, was a native of what is now Knox County, Tennessee. He was Judge of the Tennessee Supreme Court 1801-1807 and 1809-1815, and a member of the State Senate 1807-1809 and 1817-1825. He was elected to the United States Senate to fill the vacancy caused by the resignation of Andrew Jackson and served from 1825 to 1840. He received the electoral votes of Tennessee and Georgia in 1836 for president.

Nov. 13

Judge Lucky pronounced a decree this morning in my case. It was satisfactory in some particulars—and not at all so in others. The Report was referred again to the Clerk and Master.

Nov. 14

Occupied all the day in the Chancery CT. Most of the lawyers left today for Blountville.

Nov. 15th

I intended going to Blountville today but could not procure a horse in Jonesboro. I find that there is quite a number of Quakers and Dunchards in this portion of East Ten. The former have a meeting now going on at Reytown just below Jonesboro. I made the acquaintance of Mr. Atkinson of Baltimore, a merchant and quite an agreeable gentleman. After dinner I was invited up to young Cunningham's room where we chatted, eat apples, and boiled chesnuts. Attended the Presbyterian church this evening. Dr. Wells preached and Mr. Sullins methodist prayed excelently well.

Nov. 16th

This morning I went on the cars as far as Union where I fell in with several gentlemen and went over to Blountville and put up at Snapps tavern in the room with Col. Nelson. The Circuit and Chancery Cts. are in session, and the same set of lawyers that I met in Jonesboro I find practicing here. I was introduced to Jno Netherland[61] of Rogersville today and am much pleased with him. He told me that he was in the legislature at the time of the Senitorial election in which Eaton[62] Foster[63] and Mr. [Felix] Grundy were candidates and that he voted for the later all the time.

---

[61] John Netherland (1808-1887), lawyer, was born in Powhatan County, Virginia. He settled down to practice law in East Tennessee in 1832; State Senator in 1833; representative from Sullivan County in 1835; representative from Hawkins County in 1851; defeated as the Whig candidate for Governor against Isham G. Harris in 1859; a member of the Constitutional Convention of 1870. He was a most successful jury lawyer, and a Union man during the Civil War.

[62] John Henry Eaton (1787-1856) was one of the most conspicuous figures in nineteenth century Tennessee history. He was in the United States Senate 1818-1829; Secretary of War in Jackson's cabinet 1829-1831; Governor of Florida 1834-1836; Minister to Spain 1836-1840.

[63] Ephraim Hubbard Foster (1794-1854), lawyer, Senator from Tennessee, was born near Bardstown, Kentucky. He graduated from Cumberland College in Nashville, Tennessee in 1813 and began the practice of law in Nashville in 1820. He served in the Creek War and in the War of 1812; was a member of the State House of Representatives 1829-1831 and 1835-1837; appointed as a Whig to the United States Senate to fill the vacancy caused by the resignation of Felix Grundy 1838-1839; was re-elected to the Senate for a full term in 1839 but resigned; was elected to the Senate in 1843 to fill the vacancy caused by the death of Felix Grundy; unsuccessful candidate for Governor in 1845.

Nov. 17

This morning I listened to the argument in the divorce case of Crockett Rutledge and wife. The divorce was granted. After disposing of this case they took up the felony docket and I was really surprised to find so many jail birds and such odd cases for this remote and mountainous region. One fellow was indicted for burglary—another for perjury, another for open and notorious lewdness, and a woman with a bastard child in her arms was arraigned for stealing a pair of breeches. Poor creature she must belong to the womens Right Party and ought to be banished to New England.

Nov. 18

I have been occupied all day in business matters, trying to get an overseer for my farm next year and also trying to sell my farm near Blountville—but I can find no purchaser, neither a man suited for an overseer.

Nov. 20th

This morning Col. Nelson rose as is his custom, made a fire and commenced his work but it being rather cold he took a drink of apple brandy and before breakfast he took five drinks which made him drunk, and he was unable to attend his business. I was much pained to see this, for he is a man of the first order of intellect and an ornament to the State. I left Blountville after dinner and rode on horseback with Love and Logan to the Tank at old man Rhea's where I took the cars for Jonesboro. Mr. Rhea is upwards of 70 years of age—and was a prisoner in Canada for 5 months during the war of 1812. He was under Gen Harrison.[64] This has been an intensely cold day and the Iron Mt is covered with snow.

Nov. 23

This morning I ran a mile in mud knee deep for my trunk rather than be left by the R.R. Reached Chattanooga for supper and continued my journey homeward.

Nov. 24

Reached home about 8 oc this morning—and found father complaining seriously with rheumatism in one of his shoulders. Attended the Chancery Ct, the legislature, and called on Gov Harris.

Nov. 25

This is the day appointed by the lower branch of the legislature for the discussion of the restoration of the old license law which will doubtless pass. Called this evening to see Allison.

[64] William Henry Harrison (1773-1841), ninth President of the United States.

Nov. 26th

This is Thanksgiving day—and we had service in most of the churches, and business was suspended. The recent news from England is rather startling. The bank of England has raised the interest to 10 per cent—a thing unprecedented—and many large failures have taken place in the banking and commercial community, which of course produces a depressing influence in this country.

Nov. 27th

Attended the Chancery Court, and the legislature today. Nothing transpired worthy of note.

Nov. 28th

The bill chartering the Centre University—A Methodist College at this place, passed the Senate today. If they succeed in getting it through the house it will be unfortunate as I regard it as a rival school to our present University, which is now in a flourishing condition. Father still suffers much with pain in his shoulder. Took tea with Allison and Hennie Cockrell at Mr Bass'.

Nov. 29

Did not go to curch today, but remained at home reading. Called on Allison and Aunt Felicia this evening. The telegraphic news from Europe is alarming. Their financial condition is worse even than ours. What is to be the end no man can tell.

Nov. 30th

Attended the Chancery Ct. and the legislature today. Passed the evening at Crozier's room playing ucre and eating oysters.

Dec. 1st

The last steamer from Europe brought news of the suspension of the Bank of England. A very able letter appeared in the National Intelligencer a few days since by Old Bullion [Thomas Hart Benton] on the subject of Banks and Banking which I hope will have some influence on the action of our legislature which is now discussing that subject.

Dec. 2nd

Attended the Chancery Court and the legislature this morning. Met with my old friend and room mate at Cambridge Robt. Lyon Rogers whom I was very glad to see—as it brought to mind many pleasant recollections of the past. In the afternoon I had quite an exciting game of ucre with Jno Thompson and Jno Hugh Smith in Rice's room. The Robertson Association held a meeting tonight. Went to a party with my wife at Mr. Bass'.

Dec. 3rd

This morning I went to the Methodist Book concern to get an estimate of the cost of publishing a course of lectures to be delivered for the benifit of the Robertson Association. Called at the hotel on Rogers and his wife also on Gov Helm of Ky. who is very low with an affection of the kidneys. Also called on Mrs. Churchwell and then went to the Academy to see Dr Elliott about getting the girls to attend the lecture tonight. Called on Mrs Jas K Polk and Mrs Knox Walker. Attended the lecture by Jas. M. Davidson for the benifit of the Robertson Association in company with Mrs. Knox Walker of Memphis. The crowd was the largest and most fashionable that I ever saw assembled to hear a lecture in this city and the orator delivered one of the most beautiful, appropriate, and eloquent lectures that it has ever been my pleasure to listen to. After the lecture was over I returned with Mrs. W to Mrs Polk's where I met Lizzie Young, V K Stevenson and Speaker Burch of the Senate.

Dec. 4th

Attended the Chancery Court—and the legislature today.

Dec. 5

Father, Mother and Mary left for Ark today on the Jas Johnson.

Dec. 6

I did not attend church today, but remained at home reading.

Dec. 7

For the first time in ten years I rose before day and attended the market. In the absence of the family, Seph. and I are keeping house. The Supreme Court met this morning. The legislature is still occupied on the Bank question. The democratic party are divided, some are in favor of putting all the banks into immediate liquidation and have an exclusive metalic currency. Others are for giving them ample time to wind up and favor a mixed currency—or rather a paper currency over ten or twenty dollars based on coin.

Dec. 8th

From the dispatches this morning I see that Orr[65] of South Carolina has been made Speaker of the House. Allen[66] of Ill Clerk and Clusky PM. Grundy arrived here today on the cars from Ark. Attended the Criminal and Supreme Courts today.

[65] James Lawrence Orr (1822-1873), statesman, diplomat.

[66] William Joshua Allen (1829-1901), lawyer, was a native of Wilson County, Tennessee. He practiced law in Illinois; State Senator in 1855; Circuit Judge 1856-1861; a member of Congress 1862-1865; United States District Judge for the southern district of Illinois 1887-1901.

Dec. 9

We have had heavy and constant rains for six days—the R.R. tracks are washed up in many places, and the river promises to be as high as it was in 1847. The people living in the submerged portion of the city are suffering very much. Abstracts of the President's Message came to hand today. He recommended a bankrupt law to be applied to corporate bodies—and an additional force to be sent to Utah. He is down on Gen Walker and his expedition.

Dec. 10th

I had announced in the morning papers that Wm H. Polk would not lecture this evening. He disappointed us very much having broken the link of the series. The fact [is] I do [not] think that he would have done much any how. Gen Benum of Chattanooga Rice Allison Dr Lindsley and Sallie dined with me today, Gen. Benum staid all night.

Dec. 11

Occupied most of the day in my office. No news worth nothing. Weather fair and beautiful, making one feel better.

Dec. 12th

Attended the Criminal Court today. Young McNid son of an old Scotch gunsmith on Deaderick St was sent to the Pen for two years for burglary. This evening Miss Kate Williams came over and passed the evening with us, and we had a merry time.

Dec. 13

Attended the first Presbyterian Church this morning. A young missionary preached a poor sermon. In the afternoon I went with Miss Williams, Gen Benum and Seraphine to hear Mr. Ferguson in Odd Fellows Hall. It was crowded with all classes among whom I noticed several gamblers. Mr F is a strange man, and preaches a strange doctrine.

Dec. 14

I met White of the Chancery Ct this morning. He has just returned from Washington and informs me that J C Jones Capt Williams Poindexter Churchwell Leatherman, Hawkins, and several other Ten are there asking for foreign appointments. We shall see what we shall see ere long. Wrote a letter to father today, also one to W O Vance of Clarkesville, relative to inviting Jno G. Sax to lecture here.

Dec. 15

I notice a card in this morning's Union taken from a New Orleans paper from Mr Jno Bass, relative to a suite instituted against him by

James Dick Hill for a supposed mal-administration of his father's estate. The papers of New Orleans it seems are taking Hill's side of the question. The NY and Boston banks resumed specie payments yesterday after a suspension of sixty days. The Senate of Ten refused yesterday to recognize the suspension of the State Bank.

Dec. 16

Attended the funeral of Jimmy Henning this morning. He was just 15 years old—and was the companion of my dear little brother Hugh. Being an only child—his parent will miss him very much in their old age. Aunt Malvina and Mary Bass started for New Orleans today. Mr. Stovall who I met at Catoosa last summer called to see me today. He is from Augusta Ga. Gen. Bynum, Seraphine and myself went over to Capt Williams and passed the evening.

Dec. 17

All the bills on the bank question were killed in the legislature today. Gov Harris sent in a message on the subject of banks, which is very much the same that Gov Johnson sent in, which will induce them to resume the subject after the Christmas Hollydays. Attended the Supreme Ct this morning. The New Orleans Opera Troupe appears this evening in the Bohemian Girl. There was no lecture this evening on account of the few persons in attendance.

Dec. 18

Gen Bynum left on the cars this morning for Chattanooga. He intends going to Havana for his health. Attended the Supreme Ct and legislature hall today, nothing going on of interest. Passed the evening at home reading Tucker's new History of the U.S.

Dec. 19th

Read a long and interesting letter in this morning's paper giving an acc of Walker's arrival in Nicarauga. If [he] does not succeed this time he may as well give it up as a bad business. I hope that he may succeed, for I consider the population and regeneration of Central America by our race, as one of the great moves of this progressive age.

Dec. 20th

Did not go to church today but remained at home writing a letter to father. Grundy and his family came down today.

Dec. 21

This is the day that the people of Kansas are to determine wether [whether] they will or will not have slavery. Attended the Supreme Court, and the legislature today.

Dec. 22

The legislature adjourned today for two weeks. A very important case is now being argued in the Supreme Court, viz. Weakley vs. Childress in which the power of the Chancery Ct to decree the sale of an infant's property is involved. Gen. Haskell and family reached town today. He still appears crazy.

Dec. 23rd

I attended the Supreme Court today and listened to a very able argument in the case mentioned in my notes of yesterday by Jno Marshall and E H. Ewing. This evening I attended the Opera with Rice and Childress. It was crowded but I thought that Durand the Prima Dona was poorly supported.

Dec. 24th

Mr Meigs concluded the argument in the case commenced on the 22nd today. The speeches of all the counsel were lengthy and able. The decision is looked forward to earnestly, both by the members of the bar, and the people. The city presents quite a scene of activity today, and every one appears to be busy, making preperations for tomorrow. Oysters, fruits, confectionaries, fire crackers, sky-rockets, premium beff and good things generally seem to be in vogue.

Dec. 25

Passed the day quietly in my office. Christmas in my early life was a joyous day, but now it is very dull. I went out in the suberbs to see some young men play Cricket, but they did not come up to what I have seen frequently before. The Club is a new one, and they may improve. The old license law has gone into operation and the effects are visible on every street.

Dec. 26

I attended the Supreme Ct this morning. Met Lert Claiborne on the street. He is just from Washington and says that Douglass is a dead man, and that the Adm. will be sustained.

Dec. 27

Did not go to church today, but remained at home reading.

Dec. 28

Attended the Supreme Ct this morning. Mr Savage, member of the legislature from DeKalb died at Smithville yesterday. News reached here yesterday of the capture of Gen Wm. Walker on the San Juan

River in Nicarauga by Comedore Paulding[67] of the U.S.N. The Gen. and 150 men were brought to N.Y. He is on parole, and has gone to Washington. A great deal of excitement prevails in N.O. and the south generally about. It is understood that Gen. Cass and Gov. Brown are on the side of Walker. I think Comedore Paulding transcended his instructions, unless he had secret instructions that we know nothing of. Gen. Walker was not only a citizen, but her highest citizen, being the President.

Dec. 29

Attended the Supreme Ct today. The News from Kansas is that free soil and pro slavery men are fighting like all the world. In the election on the 21st instant they voted in favor of slavery. The free soilers kept away from the polls.

Dec. 30

Attended the Supreme Court today. Nothing transpired worthy of note.

Dec. 31

Attended the Supreme Ct. this morning. This evening J. L. Bostick lectured before the Robertson Association. The audience was very small. His lecture was very fine. Subject "An Ethnological View of the Negro Races"—after the lecture Bostick, Fogg, and myself went to Thompson's room to play ucre and watch for the incoming of the year 1858.

67 Hiram Paulding (1797-1878), naval officer.

CHAPTER XIX

"What Esau is this?" (1858)

In addition to his law practice, Randal McGavock had business interests that centered chiefly in the ownership and operation of sizable landholdings. This combination of activities becomes particularly apparent during his journal entries for the first half of 1858. Then, in the late summer of that year, a new interest is induced by a bite from the political bug. He is encouraged to run for mayor of Nashville, and, after a brief but vigorous campaign, is elected to this office.

1858

Jan. 1st

I have been occupied all day in hiring negroes and attending to business. The first of Jan. is always a busy day—accounts are due and to be paid, moving,—visiting, etc. The new year has set in most gloriously. The sun shines brightly—and atmosphere is as balmy as a spring day. I hope that it may so continue.

Jan. 2

The rain has again set in, and the streets are sloppy, and disagreeable. I have been occupied all day in business matters. This evening I attended a lecture by Jas E Rains[1] before the Robertson Association—which was very fine, reflecting great credit upon the lecturer. His subject was "The Greatest Productions in Art, as Testimonies to what is Right, and Just, and Good."

---

[1] James Edward Rains (1833-1862), lawyer, soldier, was born in Nashville, Tennessee. He graduated from Yale in 1854; studied law; became City Attorney of Nashville in 1858 and Attorney General of his judicial district in 1860; elected colonel of the Eleventh Tennessee Infantry in 1861 and saw the greater part of his service in East Tennessee; commissioned a brigadier-general in November 1862, but was killed shortly afterwards in the battle of Murfreesboro.

Jan. 3

Did not go to church today. The evening was spent in visiting the poor of the city.

Jan. 4

This is a trying day with those who have notes to pay in Bank. Attended the Supreme Ct today.

Jan. 5

I have occupied the entire day in attending to business. Grundy and his family left today on the Josephine Savage for Ark. He intends making it his home. This is the mildest, and most inclement winter I have ever experienced in Ten. It is fortunate for the poor that the winter is mild, for the times are so hard they would suffer much.

Jan. 6

I read a speech of Sam Smith of Ten. recently made in Philia at a mass meeting in support of the Administration on the Kansas question and in opposition to Mr Douglass and his adherents. It is not a speech of much ability. Gen Granville P. Smith has been appointed Mail Agent in Barkley Martin's place—he having been displaced because he supported Nicholson over Pillow in the late Senitorial election.

Jan. 7

I have been quite unwell all day—and remained closely in doors. This evening I attended the lecture before the Robertson Association by the Rev J B. Ferguson. Subject "Democracy: its nature and issues." He discarded all party and treated the subject in a purely philosophical way. His audience was large—and well pleased.

Jan. 8

This day used to be celebrated as a national hollyday but there is no demonstration here today, every one seems to be pursuing their usual business matters. I had a call again this morning for relief from Mrs Wright, the daughter of old Maj Gillman. This evening I called to see Mrs Tom Smith and Lydia where I met Sam Parke that used to live here when I was a boy. He is quite an exquisite in appearances ———

Jan. 9

Occupied the entire day in business matters, and visiting the poor of the city.

Jan. 10th

Today I dined with Mrs Porter and Dr Blackie and Sister Sallie. The Dr I found to be a good Mason—and we occupied several hours alone in the smoking room discussing the principals of the fraternity.

Jan. 11th

Attended the Circuit Court this morning. Occupied the day in arranging my business so as to be able to get off for East Ten. tomorrow. I learned through Alex Porter today that Wm Walker was rejected when he applied to be admitted to the bar in La—a piece of information that I never knew before. Mr Clark[2] of Ky has been appointed Minister to Guatemala which cuts out Estleman, Newman, and Jones of Tenn.

Jan. 12

Filed my declarations in the Circuit Ct this morning. Left the city at half past two on the cars for Sullivan Co. Eastman and Gen. Smith are on their way to Washington City, the latter to fill the place vacated by turning out Barkley Martin. The locomotive gave out a few miles east of Murfreesboro, and we had to go back and telegraph to Nashville for another. We took supper at Lyttles Hotel. At Stevenson old Mr. Longstreet[3] of Miss. got on the cars with his family. He is the author of the Ga. scenes and other amusing works. . . . He is highly intelligent and very companionable.

Jan. 13

We missed the connection at Chattanooga. In the afternoon I went to Dalton where I am at present.

Jan. 14

Left Dalton early this morning, and reached Bulls Gap—which is the meanest place in East Ten. Stopped at Esq Patsey Kite's.

Jan. 15

Remained all day at Bulls Gap. No stages, roads in a terrible condition, and no conveyance. Mrs. Mills with whom I had some correspondence relative to her negroes called to see me today.

Jan. 16

Put my negroes in a waggon this morning and took a mule for myself, and started on the Balls Mill road for Reytown, where the RR terminates. Passed the night at a house on the way.

Jan. 17

Met Tom Nelson and Mr Cunningham on the road today. Reached the terminus about 4 oc in the evening, requiring two days to come 25 miles.

---

[2] Beverly Leonidas Clarke (1809-1860), lawyer, politician, diplomat.

[3] Augustus Baldwin Longstreet (1799-1870), lawyer, minister, educator, writer.

Jan. 18

Started at five oc this morning, and reached Bristol at 8 oc. Here I hired a waggon and carried my negroes down to the farm. Mr. Hughes reached here about the first of Jan., and has commenced operations. Ben Shipley who lived on the place last year played sad havoc with every thing.

Jan. 19

Occupied the morning in looking over the farm. Mr. Hughes and myself went into Bristol—and purchased some small articles for the farm, all the heavy utensils we ordered from Lynchburg.

Jan. 20th

This morning I went into Blountville to see Mr A J. Brown on business, but he was not there and I had to go to Union. Staid all night at Mr. McClelland's.

Jan. 21

Called to see Mr Brown this morning and sold my Blountville farm to him. I then went up to Andrew Bogels and purchased one mare, one pair of oxen and a dog. I then went down in the Fork and staid all night at James Cole's.

Jan. 22

This morning I purchased a large Black mare from Miss Cole, and then went on to Blountville. In the afternoon I purchased a mare from Ned Taylor. Passed the night at Sam Snapps.

Jan. 23

Occupied the morning in business matters. In the evening I rode out to my farm.

Jan. 24

This morning Mr Hughes and myself rode out to Beech Grove meeting house, where I heard a very good sermon. In the evening Mr Hunt and several of the neighbours called to see me.

Jan. 25th

Occupied the day on the farm giving directions to the overseer how to proceed in the year's work—and in trying to get off some troublesome tenants.

Jan. 26

Remained all day on the farm.

Jan. 27

This morning I rose early and went into Bristol where I took the cars for Mac's Meadows in Wythe Co, Va. Reached Uncle Randal's[4] soon after dinner where I found all the family well.

Jan. 28

This morning Uncle Randal and myself rode over to Fort Chiswell where we took dinner. The day has been quite cold, and the ground covered with snow. Cloyd returned with us, and I passed a very agreeable evening.

Jan. 29

Wishing to purchase some stock for my farm I went over Uncle Randal's place, but I found but one animal that I wanted, and that was a bull, which he could not part with.

Jan. 30

I returned today to my farm in Sullivan Co Ten.

Feb. 1st

This morning I rode into Blountville to attend the Co court with the view of getting the road changed through my farm, and having Mr. Hughes appointed overseer. Returned to the farm this evening.

Feb. 2

Occupied the day in making contracts with labourers, renting the Forge to old man Shipley, and other matters before leaving.

Feb. 3

Today I started home, but missed the connection at Bristol and have to lay over until tomorrow. Attended the concert of Prof. Rives this evening. He is a blind man who was educated in Nashville, and is a very fine pianist. He was assisted by two young brothers named Clary from Baltimore. As I was going to the concert a gentleman pointed out in a cluster of trees the grave of Gov Issac Shelby.[5]

Feb. 4

Left Bristol at 1½ oc on the cars, and reached Henderson's at 5 oc. Here I took the stage and came to Greenville. The night is so bad and the roads so heavy that I have concluded to lay over until tomorrow. After supper I went over to the Court house and listened to a discussion in a debating society on that old and worn out question, "Whether

---

[4] Randal McGavock (1803-1890), farmer, was born at Max Meadows, Wythe County, Virginia. He lived at his father Hugh's homestead at Max Meadows, and engaged in agricultural pursuits.

[5] Isaac Shelby (1750-1826), soldier, first Governor of Kentucky.

capital punishment ought to be abolished." It was not a very interesting debate.

Feb. 5

This morning I procured a horse from Mr Vance and left my valise with him, to be sent on with the mail tonight. It took me all day to reach Bulls Gap where I passed the night.

Feb. 6

My valise was not sent, and I am compelled to be detained two days more. Feeling so vexed with Vance I walked down to Masten's which is a very good house where I passed the day and night. Mr. Masten has a splendid bottom farm, and some good blooded stock.

Feb. 7

This afternoon two stages came along filled with Cadets from the College at Lynchburg, Va. I got on, and we went to Esq. Patsey Kite's in Gap where we staid all night.

Feb. 8

This morning we made an early start on the cars, and reached Chattanooga for late supper.

Feb. 9

Reached home at 9 oc this morning and found my wife and the family all well.

Feb. 10

Went up to the legislative hall today and talked with some of the members about a bill for the purpose of giving aid to the Robertson Association. They passed the resolutions instructing our Senitors in Congress to vote for the Lecompte constitution. The resolution granting Gen. Walker the use of the Capitol to make a speech was negatived. I called to see the Gen this evening. He is looking very well, and seems to be in good spirits.

Feb. 11th

Passed the day in the Circuit Ct room and in my office attending to business.

Feb. 12

I notice in the Banner of this morning another severe piece by Mr Buckner against Gen Pillow. Gen Santa Anna[6] has also written a strong letter denying the charges of bribery made by Pillow in his first publi-

[6] Antonio Lopez de Santa Anna (1795-1876), Mexican general and political leader.

cation. Poor Pillow—he is in a made fix, but he does not deserve the sympathy of any one. We had a heavy snow last night, and some sleighing today. Took tea this evening at Mrs. Porter's with some of her Shelbyville friends.

Feb. 13

Occupied the day in business matters.

Feb. 14

This morning I was engaged in Cooper's office where he was writing a demurrer and answer to Churchwell's bill at Winchester, in which I am a party defendant. At 2½ I left the city on the cars for Manchester in Coffee Co. Miss Kate Williams was on the cars, en route for Constantinople. She gave me a sweet kiss when I bade her farewell at Tullahoma. Reached Manchester about 9 oc and put up at Dr. Holt's house.

Feb. 15th

The object of my visit to Manchester is to attend to a suite of Bass and McGavock Esq vs. Dr. Thos Anderson in which I am retained as counsel. My bill was demurred to but Chancellor Ridley overrided the demurrer and they are required to answer. I am very much pleased with Judge Ridley. He is a fine looking and very agreeable gentleman. I walked out with Mr. Isobel to see the Old Stone Fort and the Falls just below Manchester. The Fort was very large, but its history is unknown. The Falls are very beautiful, and excel many such curiosities in the country of great celebrity. Mr A B Robertson of Nashville has a fine flouring mill and distillery near Manchester.

Feb. 16th

Occupied the early part of the day in the Ct room. At 4 oc Judge Ridley, Collier, Keeble, Col. Anderson, and myself left Manchester for Winchester. We took tea at Tullahoma. While here Col. Anderson walked us over the town and showed us Madame Catrous' summer residence. Reached Winchester at 9 oc and put up at Mrs. Sims'. F B Fogg, Houston, and Sneed[7] came up on the train from Nashville.

Feb. 17

Today the case in which I am interested came up—and the demurrers very ably argued. The Judge sustained my demurrer, but over-ruled the rest.

---

[7] William Henry Sneed (1812-1869), Congressman from Tennessee, was born in Davidson County, Tennessee. He began the practice of law in Murfreesboro, Tennessee. He began the practice of law in Murfreesboro, Tennessee in 1834; a member of the State Senate 1843-1845; moved to Knoxville in 1845; a representative of the American Party in Congress 1855-1857.

Feb. 18th

Occupied the day in the Chancery Ct. Randal Ewing came up last night and we called to see our mutual friend Mrs Carter. In the evening I called to see old Maj. Venable's family for whom I feel great sympathy. He died recently in Guatemala where he was sent Minister by the government.

Feb. 19th

I intended leaving Winchester last night, but the omnibus left me. Today I spent some time in the Ct room. This evening I performed a fete that was worthy of my younger days. Two young ladies, the Misses Claiborne of Nashville, were standing in the upper porch of Mrs. Sims' tavern, and said they would kiss me if I would climb the post and get up to them. In the twinkling of an eye I handed a gentleman my hat and went up the post, and they gave me my reward.

Left Winchester in company with old Dr Baird the great traveller and lecturer, Mrs. Carter, Col Sneed, and Coke of Nashville.

Feb. 20th

Left Decherds before day this morning, and reached Shelbyville to breakfast. Occupied the day in Shelbyville in business matters. Returned to War-trace this evening, where I passed the night.

Feb. 21st

Reached Nashville at 9 oc this morning and found on my arrival another niece. Ed is now a father and I suppose he feels quite proud. Gen Walker made a fine speech last night in Odd Fellows Hall to a large crowd.

Feb. 22nd

Today I have been occupied in business matters.

Feb. 23

Nothing has occurred today worthy of note.

Feb. 24

Remained in my office most of the day. Paid several visits to the poor. Attended Dr Baird's lecture this evening. Mr Hockett appeared tonight in Fallstaf.

Feb. 25

I commenced reading Blackstone again today. Visited a number of the poor of the city. No news worth noting.

Feb. 26th

Occupied the day mostly in my office. At 9 oc this morning I attended the exhibition of the High Schools of the City at the Theatre which is highly creditable to the teachers, and gratifying to our citizens. This evening I attended the commencement of the Medical School in Odd Fellows Hall. They turned out on the world tonight 109 Drs. Dr. Crawford of Greenville Ten. made an excellent speech on behalf of the faculty to the graduating class.

Feb. 27th

Occupied the day mostly in my office—and in visiting the poor.

Feb. 28

It was so inclement today that I did not go to church, but remained at home reading. I read Mr. Hunter's speech delivered in Richmond on the 22nd Feb. at the celebration of the erection of the bronze equestrian statue of Washington by Crawford. It is one of the most beautiful tributes ever paid to the "Father of our Country"—Gen. Scott was present, and received by the two houses of deligates with marked consideration. The papers are full of accounts of the difficulty at Washington between J B Clay of Ky and Gen Cullom of Ten. It originated in a bar-room, a challenge passed, and the friends of the parties interposed, and as usual settled matters.

March 1st

This is the coldest day we have had this winter, and if it continues we may yet have some ice. Occupied the forenoon in business matters. This afternoon I took two girls to the Orphan Asylum named Margaret and Leenore Brogure. Won two barrels of apples from Estherman at euchre.

March 2nd

Passed the day in my office reading, attending to business and the wants of the poor.

March 3

Occupied the day in reading, etc.

March 4

Remained in my office all day. Tonight I went down on Lower market St. to hear the Candidates for County offices speak. For County Ct Clerk the contest is between F R Cheatham and Wm. Foster,[8] although

[8] William Lytle Foster, lawyer, was prominent in the civic and political affairs of Nashville. He raised a company for the Confederate service, which he led in the battle of Fishing Creek.

there are three other candidates. Foster made a party question and speaks in the most absurd manner, among other expressions he said that the democracy were crying aloud for his blood, because he was the son of the Hon E H Foster. C Nance is a candidate for Circuit Ct Clerk and made a very earnest and amusing speech.

March 5

Today I went out to Jno O Ewing's and James Rains' with Ed to look at their Jack stock.

March 6

Today our County elections came off, and the excitement ran very high. F R Cheatham was re-elected over Foster by a small majority, which is regarded as a great triumph by the democrats.

March 7

I did not go to church today, but remained at home reading.

March 8

I went up to the legislative hall this morning and called to see Gov. Harriss. After tea Rice and myself called to see Mrs Tom Smith.

March 9

Passed the forenoon in trying to get up another democratic paper. This afternoon I went up to the Capitol, and listened to the discussion on the Bill to increase the capital of the Bank of Ten. A wide breach has been made among the democratic members on the Bank question by the injudicious policy of the Union and American, which I fear will run into the next canvass and cause our defeat.

[*At this point a section of the original journal has been cut out.*]

March 17th

Passed the day in my office reading. This evening I attended an oyster supper at the Traders Bank. Col Johnson, Gov Harriss, Dr Estherman, Mr Correy, Volny Stevenson, Crozier, and Blood were present.

March 18th

The legislature today passed a Bank Bill establishing branches of the State Bank at Memphis and Knoxville. About noon I went down to the steamer Savage and took off a destitute family, who lost every thing they had on the Princess. I sent the mother and the little children to the city hospital—and carried the oldest girl to our house. This evening I attended a very pleasant party at Mr Vaughn's given to his friends in the legislature.

March 19th

Passed the day mostly in my office reading. This afternoon I went up to the Capitol where I found them wrangling in the House about who and how the Code shall be printed. After much discussion they gave it to the Union and American.

March 20th

Occupied the early part of the day in reading. Passed the afternoon and evening in the legislative halls. This is the last night of the sessions, and they held on until 12 oc rushing things through in great haste,

March 21st

Attended the 1st Presbyterian church today, and heard Dr. Stiles again. He is really a man of fine talent and superior intelligence. The congregation was unusually large, and the attention perfect for nearly two hours. This evening I went again to hear him.

March 22nd

This morning I went up to the Capitol to witness the closing scene of the session. At 12 oc both houses adjourned sine die. Mr Burch the Speaker of the Senate made a beautiful validictory. Speaker Donelson also made a good speech. After the adjournment the members had a convival entertainment in library room, where speeches were made and toasts were given by different gentlemen. Most of the members left today. This evening I attended the first lecture of J G Sage of Vt who has [a] great reputation. He is a fine looking man, but his articulation is bad. His poem was on Yankee Land—and abounded in much good wit and humor. After the lecture I went to E G Eastman's by invitation to meet Mr Sage. Barry, Walker, Stockell, McKenzie, Torbitt, and Burch were present. Mr. Sage I found much more interesting in social converse than as a speaker. He repeated some of his poetry with effect.

March 23rd

This morning Mr Aris Brown called and asked me to take his son into my office, who recently graduated in the Law School at Lebanon. To please the father I agreed to take the son. In the afternoon Seph and myself drove up to Mrs Bostick's and passed the night.

March 24

Went over to Jim Bostick's and purchased a Jack to send up to my farm in East Ten. He has a beautiful daughter who walked over to Mrs. B.'s and spent the morning with us. After dinner we returned to the city.

March 25th

Passed the entire day in business matters. J G Harriss called to see us today. He is as fat, awkward, and full of flattery as ever.

March 26th

Rose early this morning and went down to the Chattanooga depot to ship a Jack to my farm in East Ten. Occupied the day in my office reading.

March 27

We have received intelligence that the Lecompton Constitution for Kansas has passed the Senate by a majority of eight. Its fate in the House is extremely doubtful; Douglass, Bell and Crittenden[9] are all against it.

March 28th

The Union and American contains a long letter of A. V. Brown on the Pacific railroad. He favors the southern route, as the most practicable, and less liable to obstructions from snow drifts, and other difficulties. Attended the Presbyterian Church this morning and heard a sermon from Mr Mack of Columbia. Dined with Ann Waters, took tea with Jno O. Ewing.

March 29th

Occupied the day in my office reading Blackstone. Miss Cushman[10] appeared at the Theatre this evening as Romeo. I did not attend, but remained at home reading Tucker's history of the U. S.

March 30th

Passed the day mostly in my office reading. This evening I attended the Theatre in company with Rice to see Miss Charlotte Cushman as Queen Catherine in the play of King Henry the Eight. She is without doubt the greatest living actress, but is growing quite old now. Ah, it is a great treat to see her in her favorite pieces.

March 31st

This morning I went with Davidson to see O'Kane who met with a serious accident having fallen through a hatch way into a barrell. Passed the day in my office reading Blackstone and Tucker's History of the U. S.

---

9 John Jordon Crittenden (1787-1863), lawyer politician.

10 Charlotte Sanders Cushman (1816-1876), a native of Boston, was one of the greatest American actresses. Her reputation in Europe was equally famous.

Apr. 1st

The papers throughout the country are filled with accounts of the great religious excitement that is now spreading over the land, unprecidented in extent and the number of converts. It is not the result of the labors or power of any one man or set of men—but seems to be the spontaneous outpouring of religious enthusiasm from the hearts of the people. Some think that the Milenimum is close at hand. I am glad to see the work going on, as there is much sinfulness and wickedness in the country that this movement may eradicate in a degree.

Passed the forenoon in my office reading Blk. Commentaries. In the afternoon I went over to the Traders' Bank and entered into a game of set back ucre with Dunlap and Dortch. This evening I went to the Theatre to see Miss Cushman in Guy Mannering. The house was crowded and I never saw Meg Merriks better presented.

Apr. 2nd

From the Telegraph this morning it appears that the Kansas Bill that passed the Senate was amended and passed yesterday in the House. I do not know whether the Senate will concur in their amendment. We will see the result of this protracted discussion in a few days. The papers this morning announce the death of my old friend Sam Allison. He died at his uncle's, Mr Perkins, in Williamson Co night before last of Consumption. Poor Sam. I little thought that he would have been so soon numbered among the dead. We have been intimate friends and companions for many years and before my marriage we passed much time together. He was not a popular man, on account of his austere manner, but was liked and admired by his friends. He had a fine solid intellect, and was well educated, but I doubt whether he would have ever attained much in the profession, or a as politician. Peace be to his ashes. The members of the Bar held a meeting this evening to take into consideration his death. Neill S. Brown was called to the Chair and I offered some resolutions, which were adopted, and ordered to be published. I went to the Theatre again this evening to see Miss Cushman in Rosalin.

Apr. 3

This morning I attended Allison's funeral. The service was read in Christ's Church, and he was burried at the new cemetery, Mt Olivet.

Apr. 4

This morning I went to hear Alex Campbell[11] preach. His sermon was very good but not equal to some that I have heard from him. A

[11] Alexander Campbell (1788-1866), one of the founders of the Disciples of Christ.

young man named Brown, who staid at Johnson's and Weavers', died this morning from the effects of swallowing some false teeth in sleep. A few days ago O'Kane fell through a hatch way into a barrell head foremost and was not killed, showing that we are all pretty much creatures of distiny. Sometimes a cannon ball will not kill a man, and again a tack will send him into eternity. Bob Brown went up to be prayed for tonight at the Methodist Church and professed religion.

Apr. 5

The Criminal and County Courts met today. Henry Maney died about 12 oc after a lingering illness. Poor Henry, he is gone and his bright countenance and sweet companionship will no longer rejoice the hearts of those who were intimate with him.

Apr. 6

Passed most of the day in my office. Wrote an obituary notice of Henry Maney for the Robertson Association. This evening I went out and sat up with the corpse until 12 oc. His sister Bettie remained until I left leaning on the coffin and gazing intensely through the glass into the face. She looked like a statue. I never before saw such an evidence of absorbed grief.

Apr. 7th

This morning I attended the funeral of Henry Maney. The members of the Robertson Association, the bar, and a secret literary society attended in a body. He was burried at Mt Olivet, and a large number of persons were present. This evening I remained at home reading Dr Halsey's new work on the bible which I find exceedingly interesting. I met old Maj. Blewett today of Columbus, Miss. I think he is looking about for another wife.

Apr. 8th

The Kansas Bill has been defeated in the House, and she will remain out of the Union, furnishing fuel to keep the Slavery agitation. Dr Jas Kent of Montgomery Co, Va reached here today, and I have been with him all the afternoon and evening.

Apr. 9

Occupied most of the day in my office and in showing Dr Kent the attractions of the place. Passed the evening at Aunt Felicia's with Maj Blewett, J G Harris and Dr Kent.

Apr. 10th

The Daily News which has been suspended for a week or so—came out this morning under the wing of new parties. It is now in the hands of printers, who are likely to make it go. Passed the day in my office in reading and attending to business.

Apr. 11

From the telegraph this morning we learn the sad intelligence of the death of the Hon Thos H Benton. He died at Washington yesterday. His death was not entirely unexpected having been suffering for some time past with an internal cancer. He was truly a great man—being classed with Clay Webster[12] and Calhoun. He has been in public life ever since his youth, and has rendered much service to his country. At the time of his death he was at work on his abridgement of the Congressional Debates—several volumes of which have already appeared.

My sister Mary joined the 1st Presbyterian Church of this city today.

Apr. 12th

Passed the day mostly in my office reading Blackstone. This evening I went over to Rice's room and he showed me the pistols and ring that Allison left him in his will. While there Dr Furquharson came in and the conversation turned on the revival now going on in the churches. Dr. F. though that it was all nonsense and said that the best of the people in the world would not go to heaven, but that it would be filled up with a few weak minded. . . . that this class of people, generally professed religion while the better class set up their morality against the church. After tea I read Halsey's new work on the Bible with great interest. He points out the beautiful passages of poetry and eloquence in the bible and in such a manner as to induce one to read the bible with renewed interest. He says that the poetry, eloquence and philosophy of the bible is unequaled by any writing in the world.

Apr. 13th

Passed the day in my office and the Criminal Court room. From New Orleans we learn that the Miss river is unundating every thing, and producing much damage—plantations, cities, and railroads are submerged.

Apr. 14th

Went up to the Criminal Court and staid a short time—and then returned to my office and passed the day reading. G G Poindexter, and F Dunnington[13] reached the city today, from Washington.

---

[12] Daniel Webster (1782-1852), lawyer, statesman.

[13] F. C. Dunnington was a resident of Maury County, Tennessee. Early in 1856 he bought an interest in the *Nashville Union and American.* He sold half of this interest to G. G. Poindexter in 1858. The paper was suspended during the war. In October 1865 Dunnington and Ira P. Jones purchased the paper and resumed its publication in December.

Apr. 15th

Occupied the day in my office reading. Jno Bostick and Lucy reached here today from Ark and report the river very high. Dr Jas Kent left for home today, having disposed of all his negroes. The Odd Fellows of the State had a celebration today in this city. Dr W K Boling[14] delivered the oration in the Theatre in which he presented briefly the history and benefits of the order. He said that Odd Fellowship came up to Bancroft's idea of an ideal democracy.

Apr. 16th

Last evening I went over to Capt Williams' and played whist with Mrs W and Mary—and a little French woman who is there teaching french. Passed the day in my office reading. At 2 oc Dr. Lindsley started to the north by way of St Louis with Mary, Miss May Lindsley, Miss Eve and Miss McEwen. They are going to Washington to attend the Medical Convention.

Apr. 17

Passed the day in my office—nothing of moment has occurred.

Apr. 18

Attended the 1st Presbyterian Church this morning with my wife. Took a walk this afternoon through west Nashville which is now decidedly the most beautiful and agreeable part of the city for private residences.

Apr. 19th

There was a large fire before day this morning on Market St.—near Broad—some three or four store houses were destroyed. Rain most of the day, no news.

Apr. 20th

This afternoon I went up with my wife to Dr Hadley's[15] near the Hermitage—where we staid all night.

---

[14] W. K. Bowling, M.D., was born in Virginia in 1808. He attended the Medical College of Ohio, at Cincinnati, and graduated from the Medical Department of Cincinnati College in 1836. He first practiced medicine in Logan County, Kentucky. He was a member of the Kentucky Constitutional Convention of 1849, and was in a large measure instrumental in giving public education in Kentucky constitutional status. In 1851 he founded the *Nashville Journal of Medicine and Surgery* and sustained it for a quarter of a century. In the same year he assisted in the founding of the Medical Department of the University of Nashville, and was elected Professor of the Practice and Institutes of Medicine.

[15] John L. Hadley (1788-1870) was the son of John and Margaret Livingston Hadley of North Carolina, and the grandson of Colonel Thomas Hadley. He attended the University of North Carolina in 1806-7 and graduated from the Medical School of the University of Pennsylvania in 1812. During the War of 1812 he served as surgeon in the army. He married his first cousin Amelia, daughter of Colonel Joshua Hadley, in 1815, and moved to Tennessee, where in 1826 he purchased 1,171 acres of land in Jones's (now Hadley's)

Apr. 21st

This morning I rode out in the woods to look at the Dr.'s stock with the view of buying some mares, but they were so small and indifferent that I did not get any. This evening we drove over to Aunt Maria Masterson's and passed the night.

Apr. 22nd

Returned to the city this morning and stopped on the way to see Mt Olivet the new cemetery which I think susceptible of being made a most lovely spot.

Apr. 23

Passed the day in my office and in the Courts.

Apr. 24

This morning Gen Bynum called to see, and introduced a Mr Tupper from Charleston. The Gen has just returned from Cuba—where he passed the winter for his health. Dined today at Aunt Felicia's with Dr Boardman and lady of Philia.

Apr. 25th

Attended the 1st Presbyterian Church this morning with Mrs Boardman. Mr Park of Knoxville preached an excellent sermon. The evening was so cold and inclement that I remained at home reading Halsey's new book on the Bible.

Apr. 26th

Filed a bill in Chancery this morning against the Bank of Commerce for Gordon. Bought a lot of large brood mares today for father from a German who brought them from Ohio.

Apr. 27th

Occupied most of the day in writing for father. The heavy frost last night injured the wheat and the fruit very much.

Apr. 28

I attended the trial of a young man named Rodgers—of Clarksville for forging a check on Hardy Brien—and he was acquitted because Brien had no money in the bank—altho the evidence was clear that he intended to deceive. The spirit of the law was lost sight of and the felon acquitted on a tecnicallity.

Bend, east of Nashville. About 1830, he stopped practising medicine, turned his energies to farming and livestock, and built "Vauclause" where he lived as a neighbor to Andrew Jackson. In addition to his agricultural pursuits, he served as a member of the Board of Trustees of the University of Nashville. Of his thirteen children, two sons survived him: John, Jr. inherited the house and land called "Gretna Green"; Robert the "Vauclause" mansion. A portion of the Hadley property has now become Old Hickory, Tennessee.

Apr. 29th

This morning I had a visit from Miss Mary Williams and a very sprightly little French woman who is now staying with her, learning her to speak French before going to Constantinople. Occupied the day mostly in my office reading. This afternoon I had a game of whist with Blood, Walker and Williams. After tea I attended a meeting of the AOMC's at which 12 candidates were initiated.

Apr. 30th

Passed the day in my office, attending to business—nothing new worth noting.

May 1st

News reached here this morning of the passage of the amended Lecompton bill—which I hope will now quiet this long vexed question. We had a celebration today here in Nashville of the anomalous government founded here 85 years ago. The crowd in the procession and on the ground (Watkins' Grove) was very great. Mr. Elliot on behalf of the young ladies of the female academy—made a speech in which he returned the flag used in the Mexican War by the 1st Ten Reg to Col Campbell.[16] Mr Elliot asked Col Campbell to defend the Regiment from the aspersion recently thrown upon them in the U. S. Senate by a Senitor from Ga which he did in a very happy manner saying that there was no regiment that acted better or with more bravery than this Regiment. After Col Campbell's speech Mr. Putnam the President of the Historical Society received the flag to be deposited in the Capitol. Mr Thos Smiley then read a statement written by Maj A Heiman[17] of the movement and doing of the 1st Tenn. Regiment. The oration of the day was then delivered by James M. Davidson which every body thought was a bad

[16] William Bowen Campbell (1807-1867), the last of the Whig Governors of Tennessee, was born in Sumner County, Tennessee. He began the practice of law in Carthage, Tennessee about 1829; elected Attorney General for his circuit in 1831; elected to the State Legislature in 1836; resigned the same year to serve as Captain of a company of volunteers in the Creek and Seminole Wars; served in Congress 1837-1843; colonel of the First Regiment of Tennessee Volunteers during the Mexican War; elected Governor of Tennessee in 1851; voluntarily retired in 1853 and accepted the position of President of the Bank of Middle Tennessee; remained loyal to the Union at the outbreak of the Civil War and on July 22, 1862 accepted the office of brigadier general in the Federal Army; forced to resign in September of the same year because of ill health; again served in Congress 1865-1867. He is regarded as one of Tennessee's best and most competent soldiers.

[17] Adolphus Heiman (1809-1862), a native of Potsdam, Prussia, was well known both as a soldier and an architect. He was a first lieutenant in the "Harrison Guards" and adjutant of the First Tennessee Regiment during the Mexican War. He was appointed the architect of the Tennessee Hospital for the Insane in 1848 and also planned the construction of the suspension bridge across the Cumberland River at Nashville which was completed in 1850. Another architectural work was a building which was first used by the University of Nashville and, in recent years, has housed the Nashville Children's Museum. During the Civil War he was colonel of the Tenth Tennessee Regiment, succeeded at his death by Randal McGavock.

selection. They should have taken some of the decendents of those old pioneer settlers, instead of a man born in a foreign country. This selection seemed to mar the entire proceedings of the day. The children and negroes consumed the things prepared for the table before the speaking was over, and the crowd had to go without meat or drink.

May 2nd

I did not go to church this morning. The Methodist Conference is in session and all the pulpits of the City are occupied by methodist preachers. This afternoon I attended service in the Theatre by Dr. Wharton (Campbellite) also service in the Market House by a methodist preacher. After tea I went with my wife to the 1st Presbyterian.

May 3rd

Occupied the day in my office.

May 4th

Passed the day in my office. Called this evening on Mr. Boardman and lady of Philia.

May 5

Attended the Chancery Ct this morning, also the Methodist Conference now in session at the State Capitol.

May 6

I started at 5 oc this morning for Bristol—reached Chattanooga for dinner, and Cleveland for supper. Col J Geo Harris accompanied me as far as Dalton. He is en route for N.Y. where he will take the Frigate Wabash for the Mediterranean.

May 7th

This morning Gen C. Ramsey placed Mrs Gen Milligan of Greenville and children under my charge to Greenville. She is a sister of Jno. K. Howard. Dined at Jonesboro and reached Bristol at 2 oc.

May 8th

Passed the day on my farm which I found to be in a much better condition than I expected. Mr. Hughes, my overseer, has done a great deal of work since he commenced operations. He is now planting corn, having already put in all of his small grain.

May 9th

Occupied the day in going through the knob lands of the farm, which I have never seen before.

May 10th

The Magnolia hotel at Bristol was burnt to the ground last night, the work of an incendiary. My baggage was in it, but most of it saved. Occupied the morning in riding over the farm, and the neighborhood. At 3 oc I left Bristol for Jonesboro, where I am at present likely to remain several days.

May 11th

Occupied a part of the forenoon in making out exceptions to the Amended Report of the Clerk and Master. The remainder of the day was passed about old Kenney hotel, and Tom Nelson's law office. I met a man today who lives in Ashville, N.C. and has a patent for making the most remarkable soap I ever saw or heard of. You can take a white pocket handkerchief and draw it through the hub of a wheel, and with this soap and cold water you can take out the tar or grease in a few minutes. The soap can be made, he says, in three minutes, and any where, requiring only a large kettle, and plenty of water, into which he throws some substance that converts the water into soap. I tried the soap in washing my hands, and it is certainly equal to any I have ever seen. This evening I attended an amateur concert in the Court House given by some of the young men of Jonesboro. The music was highly creditable for an inland place like this.

May 12th

It was quite cool this morning—and an old gentleman from Greasy Hollow remarked that "we had *very searching ar.*" In a conversation with Mr. Love of Carter Co. on the subject of politics he said the south ought to insert the 25th chapter of Leviticus into their platform on the subject of slavery. I read the chapter and found that it was very strong on that subject.

May 13th

This morning I heard a most ludicrous comparison. Two gentlemen, a whig and democrat at the Va Springs were comparing the relative merits of Clay and Polk, the Whig contended that Clay was his superior in every respect, the democrat on the other hand contended that Polk was his equal in every respect. . . . I have been all day occupied in the Chancery Ct of Jonesboro and I think I have pretty well got through with my case.

May 14th

This morning I rode out in the country about seven miles to attend a sale of some stock. I did not purchase any thing. The last spike of the East Ten and Va RR was driven today. A large number of persons were present when it was done—each director took a lick at it. It occupied seven years and forty two days in building—almost as long as the the Revolutionary War.

May 15th

This morning Mr. Nelson presented his second decree in my case. I think I have pretty well got through with the matter. At noon I got on the cars and went up to Johnson's Station where I found a horse for me to go over to Col. N G Taylor's in Carter Co. I stopped at Hon L C Haynes' on the way. The battle of Franklin was fought on his farm and he now lives in the old Tipton house. Col Taylor lives on Buffalo creek—near Buffalo Mt.—and his farm is the picture of beauty. His wife is a very clever lady, and he is the prince of hospitality.

May 16th

This morning Col. Taylor and the boys and myself walked to the very sumitt of Buffalo Mt. to hear an old negro named Harry preach. The scenery from this Mt is magnificent.

May 17th

This morning I left Col Taylor's home and went with him up to his farm on the Wautauga. The valley of the Wautauga is very rich and beautiful. I passed the night at Carter's Station.

May 18th

Left Carter's Station at 3 oc this morning on the cars, availing myself of the first through trip after the completion of the rail-road. Took breakfast in Greenville, and supper in Chattanooga. Gen Twiggs[18] and Fred Stanton were on the cars.

May 19

Reached home at 9 oc this morning and found all well. The city is all agog—about some defalcations that have come to light. It is rumoured that Burton,[19] the Sec. of State, is a defaulter for over one hundred thousand dollars worth of bonds. A young man named Mosely—and Luttrell the late Comptroller are implicated. The Investigation Committee appointed by the legislature are at work, and we will pretty soon know the whole matter. Today I have been engaged in preparing declarations for the Circuit Court.

May 20

Nothing has transpired today of moment.

---

[18] David Emanuel Twiggs (1790-1862), soldier.

[19] F. H. W. Burton, Secretary of State of Tennessee 1855-1859.

May 21
Passed the day mostly in my office reading.

May 22
I notice in this morning's paper that Gen Persiffer F Smith[20] who had command of the Army at Utah is dead. My old friend, Gen. Harney, will now take the command. I purchased a negro girl today for my wife's waiting maid. After tea I went over to Capt. Williams' and had a game of ucre with the ladies.

May 23rd
The Union of this morning has a strong editorial on the defalcations recently perpetrated by some of the State officers, and the Banner has one against the gamblers who are about to take the town. I went to hear Mr Pearce, the father of the Bishop, preach this morning in the 1st Presbyterian Church. He did not come up to my expectations. In the afternoon I heard a sermon in the Market Place.

May 24th
The British cruisers in the Gulf of Mexico have in the last three weeks boarded and over-hauled some ten or fifteen vessells belonging to the U S and fired into several. It is thought that the President will send the Home Squadron there.

May 25th
It appears from intelligence recently received from Utah, that Brigham Young[21] has abdicated, and the Mormon imbroglio is at end. Attended the Chancery and Circuit Courts today.

May 26th
Mr Spence the President of the Exchange Bank is out in a card this morning in reply to Cave Johnson's card of yesterday, in which he intimates pretty clearly that Mr Morton, the Cashier of the State Bank, is at fault and should be held responsible for the missing bonds belonging to his bank. It appears that there will be another over-flow in the Miss. This is the third over-flow this year.

May 27
This morning I went down to the Theatre and had a great rush to get tickets for the Concert this week. Burton, the Sec of State, reached the city today, and publishes a card in which he states that a great wrong has been perpetrated by the investigating committee upon him,

---

[20] Persifor Frazer Smith (1798-1858), lawyer, soldier.
[21] Brigham Young (1801-1877), second President of the Mormon Church and colonizer of Utah.

and that he hopes public opinion will be suspended until he proves his innocence, or is proved guilty. His card is very manly, and he talks like an innocent man.

May 28

Occupied the day mostly in my office. This afternoon I took a game of ucre in the State Bank with Geo Harris, Cave Johnson and G G Poindexter.

May 29

Burton resigned the office of Sec of State yesterday, and Gov Harris has appointed Mr Ray of Memphis his successor. The Great Southern Mail will come through East Ten after the 1st of July. This will be a great thing for that road. Dr Lindsley and Mary returned home this evening, after an absence of six weeks in the north.

May 30

Hon J M Davidson repeated his lecture last night on "The Jewels of a Commonwealth" for the benifit of the Robertson Association. Bishop Cavenaugh[22] of Ky preached a very excellent sermon in the 1st Presbyterian Church this morning. I called on Mrs Polk, and at Mr Bass' this evening.

May 31st

Most of the day has been occupied in my office reading. The weather is very sultry and it is much more agreeable in than out doors. A man named Bell and his horse were killed this evening by lightning in South Nashville. Went over to Capt Williams' this evening and played cards with the ladies. They leave tomorrow for East Ten, before going to Europe.

June 1st

Occupied most of the day over at Capt Williams' sale of furniture. Mr David Stewart and two sons from Liverpool arrived here today. He is the best specimen of an "Irish Gentleman" that I ever saw.

June 2nd

Today I dined at Mrs Porter's with Mr. David Stewart and his two sons and a number of guests invited to meet them.

June 3rd

The morning papers announce the death of Wilkins Tannehill,[23] a very old man and one of the oldest citizens of Nashville. He was for

---

[22] Hubbard Hinde Kavanaugh (1802-1884), Methodist minister, educator.

[23] Wilkins Tannehill (1787-1858) was born on the outskirts of Pittsburgh, Pennsylvania. He moved to Nashville, Tennessee in 1810; developed into a commercial leader; ceased

many years connected with the press of this city, and was a man of high literary attainments. For several years past he has been entirely blind, and has been confined to the house. A telegraph dispatch reached here today announcing the death of my friend and class mate, J B Hulbert. He was a gentleman of the highest acceptation of the word, and I know of no one whose death I regret so much. He leaves an interesting wife, and several children. In cleaning the reservoir out yesterday they found seven babies, and one old negro woman. This speaks well for the morality of Nashville.

Mr. Tannehill was burried this evening with Masonic honors. He was a true Mason and belonged to the "Knight Templars." The members of the Nashville Bar held a meeting this evening in my office, and passed resolutions of respect for J B Hulburt who was a member of our Bar. A telegraphic dispatch reached here this evening announcing that eight hundred citizens were under arms, and had formed themselves into a "Vigilance Committee" to suppress the rioters, burglars, and murderers of that city [New Orleans]. It seems that it has become dangerous for a peaceable citizen to go out in the streets after dark. The Att Gen entered a nole prosequie in the case of the government vs Gen Walker.

I accompanied Sallie and my wife to the great Concert tonight and it was certainly the best I ever attended here. Thalberg performs on the piano exquisitely, but not with as much expression as some others that I have heard. Vientemps I think quite equal to Ole Bull as a violinist but is not so imposing in his appearance as the great Swede. Perring has one of the best tenor voices that I have ever listened to, and Madame D'Angri is a charming vocalist. The Theatre was crowded to overflow by the elite and fashion of the city and the neighbouring counties.

June 4th

This morning I called with Gov N S Brown on Ex Sec Guthrie[24] of Louisville. He is the Vice President of the R R between this city and Louisville. He is a large man with a good head but he looks cold, impassive, and dull. The Chancery court decided a case in my favor today which I feel proud of—as it involved new points in regard to the Free Banking Act of 1851 and '52. Father and Mother started to the

---

commercial pursuits due to his interest in Masonry and in writing; became the section's outstanding Mason; engaged in writing and newspaper work 1818-1855. He was an outstanding leader in educational affairs and in many other activities connected with civic welfare. Besides his newspaper editorships, he wrote some creditable works on Greek and Roman literature.

[24] James Guthrie (1792-1869), statesman, businessman.

plantation in Ark. this evening at 4 oc on the Jno Runyan. I expect they will find the place submerged, as the river is represented as being higher than usual.

June 5
Attended the Circuit and Chancery Courts today.

June 6
I did not go to church today, but remained in my office writing an essay for Maria Masterson to read at her examination at Lebanon. Subject "What is true nobility?"

June 7
Passed the day in my office attending to business and reading.

June 8th
It seems from a dispatch received here today that the Know-Nothing candidate for Mayor was elected in N. Orleans, and that the "Vigilance Committee" has disbanded and order restored. Accounts of the flood on the Miss are terrible, nine tenths of the planters are deep under water—being forced many of them to abandon their places. Of course, a great deal of the stock must be distroyed and no chance for a crop this year. Those who are in debt will suffer a great deal, and it will cripple even those out of debt. The families of Col Jno McGavock[25] and Mrs. Winder reached here this evening from La.

June 9th
Nothing has transpired today of any importance.

June 10th
Mosely was bailed today—bond five thousand dollars.

June 11
Attended the Circuit Court this morning. Recd. a letter from Mother—river very high and the plantation suffering from back water.

June 12th
The Gov makes a proclamation this morning for Burton, the Sec of State. Reward $500. Mrs. Meigs, the wife of Return J Meigs Sr died very suddenly last night.

June 13th
One or two cases of small-pox are in the city, but there is no apprehension of its spreading.

[25] John McGavock (1815-1893) was a native of Tennessee. He married Caroline Winder, the daughter of Van P. Winder and Martha Anne Grundy and the grand-daughter of Felix Grundy. He was a successful farmer on a large scale.

June 14th

Occupied the day in business matters. A dispatch reached here this evening, giving an account of the distruction of the Steamboat Pennsylvania, about 70 miles below Memphis. Over one hundred lives were lost. I witnessed a street fight this evening between Dr Morton, and Alex Nichol about a pen-knife. N claimed that M had his knife, and called a witness to prove it. M. denied that it was his knife, and a fight ensued. After a round or so the beliggerents were separated, and no body hurt. Took tea at Mr Bass' where I met Mr Conner of N O who is soon to be married to Mary Bass.

June 15th

Passed the day in my office and the Court Room.

June 16th

Remained nearly the entire day in my office reading.

June 17

Nothing of moment has occurred today. I attended the exhibition at the Female Academy. The graduating class was very large, over 40—and the young ladies acquitted themselves hansomely in music, the reading of their essays, etc. This is unquestionably one of the finest female institutions in the U S—reflecting great honor upon our city, and the Rev C D. Elliott who is at the head of the Institution. I saw my old flame Lizzie Bonner, now Mrs. Lamb. She looks as delicate as ever.

June 18

I received a letter from the Hon H S Foote accepting the invitation to deliver a lecture next fall for the benifit of the Robertson Association. He is now in the city.

June 19th

Yesterday afternoon Mary, Seph, and myself drove out to Alex Porter's in my new carriage. Alex lives like a prince, but the health of his wife, it seems to me must mar his happiness very much. He undertook to learn me how to play billiards, but I expect he found me rather a sorry beginner. We had quite a severe thunder storm this evening.

June 20th

News reached here last night that Judge Harris was dead. He died from the effects of being scalded a few days ago, when the steamboat Pennsylvania exploded. His brother the Gov will now have to perform the unpleasant duty of appointing his successor.

I did not go to church this morning but remained at home writing up the minutes in my father's Court for the Judge to sign tomorrow. Man should not work on the sabbath day, but I frequently do things that my concience reproves.

June 21st
Occupied the day mostly in my office reading Goldsmith's works.

June 22nd
Passed the early part of the day in my office. In the evening I called with my wife to see Mrs W H. Gordon and Miss Kate Polk of La.

June 23
This has been decidedly the warmest day of the season. This evening I attended the wedding of Mary Bass to Mr Conner of N. O. It was quite an elegant affair and the ladies looked beautiful notwithstanding the heat was so oppressive. I devoted myself principally to the married ladies, and especially those from Charleston. The widow Bass was the finest looking woman in the room, and was escorted by Gov Foote of Memphis. Mrs Acklen looked well, and her diamonds are the largest single stones that I have ever seen in the country. Mr. La Piece and lady were present, and both looking well. Among the young ladies I was attracted by Miss Maggie Lindsley, Miss Sallie Acklen of Ala., etc. The supper was very fine, and I enjoyed it much—particularly the hot venison steak—and water—ice.

June 24th
This morning it was so excessively hot that I bought some ice, and eat it up to cool the inner man. Father and Mother, Grundy and family reached the city this morning from Ark. Remained most of the day in my office reading etc.

June 25th
The weather still continues oppressively hot. A dispatch from Memphis today states that A Wright[26] will serve on the Bench of the Supreme Court if elected—to fill the vacancy occasioned by the death of Judge Harris. There was a sale of the Petway lands yesterday on the Nolinsville turnpike, about 6 miles from town, and the average price was 208 dollars per acre. Some went as high as 250 per acre. This is the greatest sale of lands in this county that I have heard of, considering their quality and locality.

[26] Archibald Wright (1809-1884), lawyer, was born in Maury County, Tennessee. He was reared in Giles County; studied law; was admitted to the bar in Pulaski in 1832; served throughout the Florida war; moved from Pulaski to Memphis in 1857; served on the Tennessee Supreme Court Bench 1857-1861; continued the practice of law after the Civil War.

June 26th

Passed the day mostly in my office reading. Called on Mr Watsons family this evening.

June 27th

Attended the 1st Presbyterian Church this morning where I saw the new organ, which I expect is the finest in the western or southern country. I notice today in the Washington Union—that the Black Republicans of Philia held a meeting recently at which they ignored the slavery question. This I consider the work of Bell and Crittenden who are preparing for a grand coalition between their portion of the American party south and the Black Republicans.

June 28th

Attended the wedding of Dr Blacke[27] this morning at the Episcopal Church to Miss Martha Cheatham. He is a native of Edenburg and at least 10 years younger than she. At 2 o c I went down with my wife to the Chattanooga depot to see her off to Shelbyville where she goes to see her mother. Blackie and bride and Conner and bride were on the cars, going north. After tea I played ucre until 12 o c with Cooper, Rice, and Thompson. Game 25 to 11. Cooper and myself winners.

June 29th

Remained all day in my office reading.

June 30

Occupied the day in my office. This evening I attended the Commencement Exercises of the University of Nashville. There were only two graduates. The Alumni held a meeting after the exercises and I do not think that more than eight were present.

July 1

Occupied the day in my office reading. This evening I rode out with Dr Morton[28] to witness a post mortem examination on a Scotchman that was found dead in Harding's Woods from the effects of mania perta. His head was swollen to an enormous size and his whole person was as black as a hat. He evidently died several days ago as putrifaction had taken place and [he was] full of maggots. A negro dropped dead in front of my office today.

---

27 George S. Blackie (d. June 19, 1881), M.D., was a native of Scotland. He studied medicine at the University of Edinburgh, the University of Bonn, Berlin, and Paris. He practiced medicine in London and Kelso, Scotland before coming to Nashville in 1857. He wrote extensively in the field of the natural sciences.

28 Dr. J. W. Morton was a practicing physician in Nashville. In 1866 he was selected by the Nashville Board of Health to do sanitary work. He was City Physician of Nashville in the early 1870's and Health Officer 1874-1878.

July 2

Occupied two hours in the Recorder's Court this morning, attending to two cases. Mrs Quinn for keeping a disorderly house and her son for selling liquor to negroes, both fined.

July 3rd

The Union publishes a long account of the celebration of the 4th of July in 1827 here in Nashville at Vauxhall Gardens, at which Gen Jackson, Felix Grundy and Jno Bell figured. Bell was then a great Jackson man, and the object of re-publication is to contrast the position he then occupied with his present position. The 4th was celebrated at Franklin today, but no demonstrations were made in this City. Passed the day in my office reading.

July 4

This morning I was arroused by the firing off of cannons in honor of our Independence day, notwithstanding it is the Sabbath. Did not go to church today but remained at home reading the Auto Biography and Lectures of Lola Montez.

July 5

Remained all day in my office reading. One of the young men engaged in the Post Office has the small pox and I fear very much that it will spread over the City.

July 6

Passed the day in my office reading, weather very warm.

July 7th

Occupied the day in my office reading.

July 8th

There was a large Picnic at Gen Hardings Park today. I did not go, but remained at home copying a bill for father.

July 9th

Jno came up today from the plantation and reports that the river has fallen within its banks. The Union and Planters' Banks now refuse to take on deposit—the money of the State Bank. Today I have been engaged in writing for father.

July 10th

The Union Bank this morning commenced taking State Bank paper again, the officers having come to some understanding. The City of Memphis was visited yesterday with the greatest rain that has ever been known to fall there, which filled Bayou Gayoso—washed up the bridges —and flooded the streets of the whole city.

July 11th

I did not go to church this morning, but remained at home. This evening I attended the Presbyterian Church and heard a very good sermon from Mr Mack.

July 12th

Passed the day in my office reading. The City is remarkably dull, no business going on—and the streets pretty well deserted.

July 13th

During the forenoon I was engaged in reading, and playing ucre in the afternoon. Gen Anderson, and Wm L. Foster had a fight this evening on the street. Foster made the attack, no damage done. They go before the Recorder's Court at 9 oc tomorrow.

July 14th

Engaged in reading all day. Severe accidents happened today on the streets. Some ladies were thrown from a barouche, and two of them very much mutilated. Mr Scovel was thrown from a buggy, and considerably injured.

July 15

The Convention of Bishops at Bersheba Springs confirmed the location of the University of the Episcopal Church South at Sewanee in Franklin Co. They already have one half million of dollars to commence on, and they purpose raising five and one half. If their views are carried out, it will be the greatest literary institution in the U S. One or two more cases of the small pox have appeared in the City, but no especial alarm seems to prevail among our citizens. I rose very early this morning, and took a ride on horseback for exercise. Received a letter from my Overseer in East Ten. He gives a good account of things up there.

July 16th

Occupied the day in my office reading. My wife got home from her visit to Bedford this evening. Attended the sale of Building Asso money this eveng.

July 17th

Remained all day in my office.

July 18th

Called to see Jno McGavock and family who have just arrived from Ark. He is in bad health. On my way home I met M. Clusky of Washington—and Wright[29] the member of Congress from Ten.

July 19

Today I drove up to the Hermitage with Clusky and Wright. It was intensely hot, and the horses suffered greatly. These gentlemen took tea with us.

July 20th

News reached here today of the death of Gen Quitman of Miss. He died at his residence near Natchez, from the effects of the National Hotel diseases. No man stood higher in Congress as a gentleman and statesman. He was the head and front of the southern fire eaters or fillibusters. News also reached here today of the failure of the Ocean telegraph experiment. A V Brown and family reached home yesterday from Washington. Other democrats may call upon him, but I will not because of his duplicity in certain matters in which I felt an interest.

July 21st

Passed the forenoon in my office reading and went out to dinner at Bilbo's with Wright and Clusky. We intended going to Gen Harding's —but it was too late when we rose from the table.

July 22nd

I have passed the day mostly in my office reading. This evening I called with my wife on Mrs J K Polk—and Jno O. Ewing and wife.

July 23rd

The papers of this morning are filled with extracts from other papers in the State condemnitory of the management of the State Bank and their refusal to resume specie payment. In Memphis a public meeting was held—at which resolutions were passed condemning the owners of the Citizens Bank—and also the State Bank.

July 24th

Occupied the day in writing letters, and attending to business matters.

---

[29] John Vines Wright (1828-1908) was a native of McNairy County, Tennessee. He served as a Democrat in Congress 1855-1861; a colonel in the Confederate Army; elected to the First and Second Confederate Congresses; Judge of the Circuit Court of Tennessee; Judge of the State Supreme Court; practiced law in Nashville 1865-1866; Chairman of the Northwest Indian Commission in 1886; appointed to the law division of the General Land Office in 1887 and served until his death.

July 25

Attended the church of "Holy Trinity" at Odd Fellows Hall this morning. Dr Quintard[30] preached a very good sermon, and the music of the choir was excellent. Passed the evening at home.

July 26

Passed most of the day in my office reading. Crozier and Dortch sold out the traders Bank today to Porterfield. Cave Johnson has signified his intention to the Gov that he would resign the Presidency of the State Bank in a few weeks, which I think will meet the approbation of all good democrats.

July 27th

Occupied the morning in my office reading. In the afternoon I went over to the Post Office and played ucre with Anderson, Clements and Brown. Miss Annie Nichol, one of the beauties and belles of this city, was married this evening to David Dunn of Memphis.

July 28th

Passed the day in my office reading.

July 29th

Remained all day in my office reading.

July 30

Occupied the day in my office reading.

July 31

Attended the Presbyterian Church today.

Aug. 1st

Dr Edgar preached a very good sermon. In the afternoon I remained at home, until late when I took a ride in the directions of the Race Course. Cave Johnson dropped in after tea, and we had an agreeable conversation on banks, etc.

Aug. 2nd

Attended the Criminal Court this morning in the new Court House which is a very plain and unattractive building, and inferior to the old

[30] Charles Todd Quintard (1824-1898), physician, Episcopal Bishop of Tennessee, was a native of Connecticut. He received the degree of M.D. from the University Medical College in New York in 1847. After a brief practice he became a professor in The Memphis (Tennessee) Medical College. In 1854 he began to study for the ministry and was ordained priest in 1856. He was a chaplain and surgeon in the Confederate Army during the Civil War. In 1865 he was elected Bishop of Tennessee serving in that capacity for thirty-three years. His most important educational work was the second founding of the University of the South in 1868.

one. There is about seven hundred cases on the docket, out of which they are about thirty felony cases.

[*At this point entries for six days are omitted without explanation.*]

Aug. 9th

Attended the Criminal Court this morning. Passed the day in my office reading.

Aug. 10th

This is my thirty-second birthday. Remained in my office all day reading.

Aug. 11th

About 1 oc this morning I had a most desperate attack of colera-morbus—occasioned by eating water-melons yesterday. About daylight I sent for Dr. Martin. Remained in bed all day. Mother wrote to father from Mrs Bosticks in which she stated that Lucy Bostick had run off from a camp-ground and married a young man named Josordern. I regret this exceeding both on her account and her mothers.

Aug. 12th

Remained most of the day in my office reading. I see in the Southern Citizen that Mr. White, late member of the Ten. legislature was arrested at Chattanooga upon the charge of forging land warrants.

Aug. 13

Occupied the day mostly in my office reading. The Criminal Court still occupied on felony cases. Nearly all convicted.

Aug. 14th

Passed the day mostly in business matters.

Aug 15

At 2 oc I started on the cars for Manchester in Coffee Co.

Aug 16

Attended the Chancery Court today.

Aug. 17

Attended Chancery Ct today. After tea I started with Mr Stubblefield for McMinnville, the most ambitious little town in the state. They have an excellent hotel, college, fine Court House, the finest law offices in the State, and plenty of gass.

Aug. 18th

I met Harvey H. Watterson[31] this morning who seems to be the chief man of the town. After breakfast I started in an excellent stage coach in company with Mr Grey and lady for Beersheba Springs in Grundy Co. On the way we passed along the base of Ben Lomand which was sold yesterday by Col Rowan to a young man named Pickett of La who intends expending seventy five thousand dollars in improvements for a summer resort. Reached the Springs about 2 o c.

Aug. 19th

Beersheba is certainly the most attractive watering place now south of the Va Springs. Col Armfield has expended a large amount of money here, and has succeeded in collecting around him in the private houses some very agreeable people. The foundation is well laid and I have no doubt but that it will be in a few years, one of the most inviting summer retreats in the U S. They have over four hundred persons here at present. Neither the view or the water equal several other points in the State. I went into the ball room tonight and waltzed with Miss Key of Ky who is one of the fastest girls I ever saw.

Aug. 20

Got up rather late this morning, having run too long last night. Passed the day mostly playing euchre. Called to see Dr Waters, Harding, Bass, and Armfield families. Went into the ball room again tonight. Mr Sessions of Miss who has a fine voice contributes largely to the amusement of the Co.

Aug. 21st

Occupied the day in talking to the ladies—playing cards, etc.

Aug. 22

Attended divine service this morning in the ball room. Bishop Green of N C preached a very good sermon. In the afternoon James Wilson drove me out in his carriage to what is called the "Old Mill," which is about 5 miles from the Spring, and one of the most secluded and romantic places I ever saw. It is situated in a deep basin formed by Laurel Creek—surrounded by tall cliffs. The dam is of solid rock formed by nature. After the water of the creek falls over the dam it

---

[31] Harvey Magee Watterson (1811-1891), lawyer, editor, Congressman from Tennessee, was born in Bedford County, Tennessee. He served as a Democrat in Congress 1839-1843; sent by President Tyler on a diplomatic mission to Buenos Aires; a member of the State Senate 1845-1847; editor and proprietor of the *Nashville Union* 1847-1851; editor of the *Washington Union* 1851; practiced law in Washington, D. C. for fourteen years; moved to Louisville, Kentucky, becoming a member of the editorial staff of the *Louisville Courier-Journal.*

falls over a high cliff. While here we met Mrs. Prince and a young man named Chambers from Miss. They were in the grist room under the bluff, and seemed much confused when they discovered us. I called to see Miss Ophelia Martin this evening, and as usual she attempted her sarcasm upon me. "What Esau is this?" turning to Mr. Fogg, and alluding to my beard. My reply was "The same that knew you in your younger days and who like the illustrious hunter wears hair of his own, and not that put on by woman for deception." She backed down at once.

Aug. 23rd

I rose very early this morning and went out with some gentlemen on a fox chase under the mountain. After breakfast I went out with Mr Wilson, his mother and Miss Hardeman to see the New Mill and the Stone Door. The New Mill was built by Col Armfield at spot almost as romantic as that of the Old Mill. There are several very pretty falls here, and a vein of coal about twelve inches in thickness. The mill is propelled by steam, and cuts all the lumber used at the Springs. The view from the stone door is very fine, and the formation of the point rather peculiar. Mrs. Virginia French has written a very pretty story of an Indian Legend.

Aug. 24th

Dined today with Mr Philips of New Orleans. Attended the Calico Ball this evening. Lemira Eakin dressed me up as Abou Gosh the robber of the Holy Land and I entered with Mrs. Galloway of Miss who was dressed as an Indian Queen. Many of the characters were amusing, as well as ridiculous. I enjoyed the evening finely, and laughed enough to last me a month.

Aug. 25th

Many of the gentlemen from Nashville left this morning. The day has been passed in lounging about the premises conversing, and reading news-papers.

Aug. 26

Passed the day in playing cards, rolling ten pins, and dancing. This evening Mr Bibb of N O furnished considerable amusement to the company by dragging a dead fox around the Springs, and then placing the hounds on the trail. The amusement was novel, and all seemed to enjoy it.

Aug. 27th

The great disideratum at Beersheba (water) has been supplied by a water-witch, who has found bold streams all over the mountain and a very short distance from the surface. Attended the ball this evening.

Aug. 28th

Started home at 5 o c this morning by way of Tracy City. We had a full load and my fellow passengers were Thos Martin, lady and daughter Ophelia of Pulaski, my old mother-in-law, Mrs. Crutcher, S Cockrell and lady, Henry Fogg, Ive Webster. We passed through Altemont the County seat of Grundy, a new and very uninteresting place. Tracy City is a new village recently laid out by Col Tracy at the terminus of the Sewannee coal road. We did not explore the mines although I wished to do so. I had conceived that the railroad up the mountain was exceedingly dangerous, but found it no more so than roads ordinarily. The cars stopped as we were descending to give the passengers a view of the location of the University of the South recently selected by the Episcopal Bishops assembled in Convention at Beersheba Springs. The view is magnificent—and I was told that there was plenty of water on the spot. They propose raising three and one half millions of dollars, which will erect a structure superior to any in the United States. At Cowan we took the train for Nashville and reached home about 7½ o c where I found Judge Dickinson and family from Miss.

Aug. 29

Did not go to church today, but remained at home.

Aug. 30

Started at 5 o c this morning and reached Shelbyville at 9 o c where I went to attend to a case in Chancery which was tried—and which I lost. The bill was to enforce the purchasers at a public sale to take their bids, but the Chancellor decided the case upon the Statute of frauds—alledging that the book kept on the day of sale, did not discribe the property sufficiently.

Aug. 31st

Occupied the forenoon in attending to business. Left for home at 3 o c in company with Jno Marshall.

Sept. 1st

Occupied the day in business matters. Attended the sale of money of the Building Association this evening. The State Capitol was illuminated tonight in honor of the completion of the Atlantic Cable.

Sept. 2nd

This is the day of election of Supreme Judge of the State to supply the place of Judge Harris—also to determine whether we will hold a Convention to change our Constitution. The K N or American party are attempting to defeat Judge Wright—by secretly voting for Walker—a Circuit Judge in Hardin Co. I hope they will not succeed in their mean trickery. The people take very little interest in the election, and the poll throughout the State will consequently be very small. The Robertson Association held a regular meeting at my office this evening at which two members were initiated.

Sept. 3rd

Occupied the day in my office reading, etc. Received a communication today from President Buchanan.

Sept. 4th

I have been solicited today by numerous individuals of both parties to run for Mayor of the City but declined. The cars ran off the track today near Bell-Buckle and injured a number of passengers.

Sept. 5th

Attended the 1st Presbyterian Church today. Dr Mac preached. This afternoon I went to the St Cloud in company with Judge Dickinson to call on the Blewetts of Miss. I have met a good many persons today, whose acquaintance I formed this summer at Beersheba Springs.

Sept. 6th

This morning the Committee appointed by the Robertson Association visited the jail and Work House of this city. The jail we found in a bad condition—and an unwholesome place. The Work House is well kept, although the Coperation has not furnished sufficient room. The building is very small, and the inmates both male and female, black and white all sleep together. . . . At the request of Mr. Bostick I set today for my whiskers at Mr Cooper's studio, for Halbert's portrait—they being of the same colour of his. Called today with my wife and sister Ann on Mrs. Galloway of Miss, Mr Prince of Miss., and Mrs Bibb of La. Witnessed a game of Boston this evening at the State Bank. Old Cave lost $2.50. It was his first attempt at the game.

Sept. 7th

The legislative committee are out this morning in a long communication in which they bear down pretty heavily on Arthur Crozier the former Comptroller of the State. They made several grave charges, which if he does not explain pretty satisfactorily will place him in an unenviable position. This evening a number of persons were at our house to meet Maj Blewett and family.

Sept. 8th

Nashville is improving more at present than I ever knew it before, notwithstanding the complaints about hard times, and the stringency of the money market. Dwellings and business houses of a superior quality are going up in all directions. The fall trade has set in unusually brisk, giving promise of a good time for our merchants. What we need here is a large first class hotel which I hope to see erected soon.

Sept. 9

Passed the forenoon with Judge Dickinson—who left for Columbus with his family at 2½ oc. Randle Blewett, Tup Cheatham and myself drove out to Gen Harding's Park to see his collection of animal curiosities.

Sept. 10th

Occupied most of the day in my office. Walked out with Houston to see his new house in West Nashville.

Sept. 11th

Mrs Winder reached the city last evening from the Va Springs, very much improved in health. Gen Zollicoffer is out in a card this morning in reply to a card from the legislative committee, in which he endeavors to exculpate Crozier from the charges therein made.

Sept. 12th

Attended the 1st Presbyterian Church this morning. In the afternoon I went up to the St Cloud to see Randle Blewett, and Elias Fort of Columbus Miss.

Sept. 13th

The Circuit Court met this morning, I procured the final papers of a young man named Corrigan, who I sent to this country from Dublin in 1851. This evening the Committee appointed by the Robertson Asso, Dr Lewis, Hawkins, and myself, visited the Poor House about four miles on the north side of the river. The Co has about 80 acres of land, which produces enough bread for the establishment, but not enough bacon. The houses are wholly insufficient for the purposes, and the men and women are kept together. The expense of keeping up the establishment over and above what they make on the farm is about 1500 dollars.

Sept 14th
Attended the Circuit Court this morning. No news worth noting.

Sept. 15
Attended the Circuit Court today.

Sept. 16
Occupied the day mostly in my office, and in business matters.

Sept. 17
I have been called upon today by many Americans and solicited to run for Mayor—and I promised to take the matter into consideration.

Sept. 18
I attended the funeral of R O'Kane[32] this morning. The St. Patrick Club, and the Robertson Association turned out. He was killed on the RR near Cowan. A cleverer man never lived. He was charitable, honorable, and agreeable. Mr G M Fogg[33] declined running for Mayor today, which determined my mind to be a candidate.

Sept. 19th
Attended church this morning. This evening I went round the City and blazed my way for the race this week.

Sept. 20th
Out all day electioneering. I find most of the workers in both parties committed to the other candidates, some size in number.

Sept. 21st
Out all day talking to the people. This evening the Candidates spoke on the corner of Cedar and Spruce streets.

Sept. 22nd
Out all day and night among the people. Made a speech tonight on the corner of Broad and College streets. My prospects now begin to brighten.

Sept. 23rd
My phisical powers begin to weaken by extraordinary exertion, but I still go on in the work. Made a speech tonight in South Nashville

[32] R. O'Kane was one of Nashville's most popular and successful merchants.

[33] Godfrey M. Fogg, Nashville business man and civic leader. He was a member of the board of aldermen in Nashville 1849-1852 and 1856-1857. As Chairman of the City Finance Committee in 1847 he was instrumental in helping Vernon K. Stevenson secure a subscription of $500,000 from the city of Nashville to aid in the building of the Nashville and Chattanooga Railroad. He was chosen President of the Nashville Cotton Mills when the mills were established in 1881, and was President of the Union and American Publishing Company in 1887 and 1888.

where I got decidedly the advantage over Clemons who I consider the man that I have to beat. Godshill is the next strongest man. etc etc.

Sept. 24th

This has been a day of extraordinary labor. At 3 oc this morning the Revolution in my favor commenced among the masses. The candidates made speeches tonight at the Market House, where the largest crowd assembled that I ever saw in this city. Mr Horn declined tonight. But little attention was given to any of the speeches except those of Clemons and my own. Clemons made a real low down bull ragging speech that disgusted every one, and lost him many votes that he would have received. After the meeting adjourned I went to Mrs O'Sullivan's Irish boarding house on Front street where I found Godshill and his friends ahead of me but it made no difference as I am confident of every vote in that house. From this point I dashed over Capitol Hill to another grocery, then to Jno Dolin's on Market St. Here I met Godshill again and I proposed that he should ride behind me, but my horse would not carry double and we had to ride and tie. We went to a Germain Ball on College Hill, and then to an Irish ball near the depot. We were out all the night.

Sept. 25

This is the day of the election. The first thing that I done this morning was to dash over the City and get my friends ready for the battle. At 9 oc I had them all with my tickets at their post. During the day I dashed on horseback from poll to poll urging my friends on—and keeping up the fires as well as I could. When the votes were counted out I was 93 ahead of Clemons and then came Godshill, then Hale, then Singleton. Tonight I was serenaded by the Germain Band and a large number of my friends called to see me. Refreshments were prepared and every thing passed off finely, I made a speech to the crowd, in which I thanked them for the honor bestowed upon me.

Sept. 26th

Attended the first Presbyterian Church this morning. In the evening I went over to see Mrs Porter.

Sept. 27th

Occupied the day mostly in my office listening to the suggestions of older heads about the Corporation Affairs.

Sept. 28th

Passed the forenoon in my office. At 3 oc I went out to Jos Acklin's to dine by invitation with Gen Wm Walker and Col Nothurst. It was the finest dinner I ever sat down to and the company enjoyed it finely. Walker is now on his way to Nicarauga where he expects to be successful.

Sept. 29th

I felt rather heavy this morning but I went to work and wrote out my Inaugural and arranged the Standing Committees of the Corporation. I was serenaded tonight by a negro band of the City. The negroes are highly delighted with my election.

Sept. 30

Very much occupied all day in acquainting myself with Corporation matters.

CHAPTER XX

"I did not think she would forget the Mayor of Nashville soon." (1858-1859)

Randal McGavock served as mayor of Nashville, Tennessee from October 1, 1858, through September 30, 1859. Although one of the youngest mayors in the city's history, the accomplishments of his brief administration compare favorably with any up to his time. Because of his splendid service, many citizens solicited him to run for a second term. He resolved not to be a candidate, however, and retired from office without seeking re-election.

Oct. 1st

At 11 oc today the two bodies of the City Council met, elected their Presidents and then appointed a committee to waite upon me, and inform me that the two houses, were in Convention and ready to receive me. I was conducted into the Hall, received the oath of office, and delivered my Inaugural. The board is the best I have ever seen, and I think we will move on harmoniously and peacably. Attended the sale of money in the building Asso this evening, and bought out my stock.

Oct. 2

Remained in the City Hall from 9 oc to 12 AM attending to Corporation affairs. In the afternoon I remained in my office.

Oct. 3

Attended the Presbyterian church this morning and heard a very good sermon from Dr Edgar.

Oct. 4

Attended the Circuit and County Cts this morning—also passed most of the day at the city hall. Several cases of small pox have appeared in the City in the last day or so.

Oct. 5th

The comet last night looked beautiful. Young James Hadley was burried today; he was thoroughly educated and died before entering upon the active duties of life. Passed the day mostly in my office at the City Hall attending to Corporation matters.

Oct. 6th

The corner stone of the new Masonic Temple was laid today with the usual ceremonies on such occasions. I did not turn out having so much business to attend to.

Oct. 7th

From the papers this morning I see that the Cristal Palace at NY was distroyed by fire, loss about twenty five thousand dollars. The difficulty between the two editors in this city, viz W H Smith[1] and Poindexter, has been settled satisfactorily. Occupied most of the day in attending to Corporation affairs. This evening I attended a Concert with Thompson and Rice given at Odd Fellows Hall for the purpose of raising means to purchase an organ for the church of the Advent. Jim Craighead was the leader, and I think made himself ridiculous. The young ladies acquited themselves with credit.

Oct. 8

The KN papers have been filled the last few days with the speeches of Forney[2] against the Adm.

Oct. 9

Attended the Circuit Ct this morning, but occupied most of the day in Corporation Affairs. Published a card this morning asking the citizens to close their houses on Monday next in honor of the opening of the State fair. Called the City Council together this evening, and they passed a resolution to attend in a body the opening ceremonies on Monday.

Oct. 10

Did not go to church today. This evening I called on Mr. Conner and lady who have just returned from their bridal tour.

Oct. 11th

About 10 oc today the Shelby Guards, Agricultural Bureau, and City Council went out in procession to the Fair Grounds. The weather was exceedingly inclement, and but few persons were in attendance. Gov

[1] William Hy. Smith was editor of the *Nashville Gazette* 1845-1850; assisted F. K. Zollicoffer as editor of the *Republican Banner* 1851-1856; retired in 1856 to become one of the editors and part owner of the *Nashville Patriot* (formerly the *True Whig*); became one of the editors of the *Nashville Daily Union* in 1863.

[2] John Weiss Forney (1817-1881), journalist.

Harris delivered a short and appropriate speech, and the exhibition of blooded cattle was very fine. Mr Dodge was there with the finest specimens of apples I ever saw. They were grown on his farm in the mountains. I also saw some excellent Catawba wine made in Knox Co by Mr Armstrong.

Oct. 12th

I occupied the day in raising $11,000 to pay the interest due in NY on our Corporation bonds, which I succeeded in doing and which re-established our credit with the bond-holders. A most bloody fight occurred today at the Fair Grounds, between the Owens of Williamson and the Cowens of Davidson. One of the Owens was killed on the spot, and another very badly wounded. One of the Cowens was also badly injured. It was a desperate fight and happened in the crowd of ladies and gentlemen.

Oct. 13th

After attending to some Corporation business this morning I went out to the Fair where I passed the day. I saw the greatest curiosity I believe that is now in the world—viz. two negro girls about seven years of age in one. They have two heads, four arms, and four legs, but one body. They dance, talk intelligently on different subjects at the same time. . . .

Oct. 14

Attended the Fair this morning. The City Council met this evening and I sent in a message on a bill that they passed at a previous meeting. The Common Council construed it into a veto—and passed the bill over my head—but it was killed by the Alderman. A compromise bill was then offered which I did not like but gave it my signature, with the view of producing harmony. They then went into the election of officers. Jno M Bright delivered a beautiful lecture tonight at Commercial Hall for the benifit of the Robertson Asso.

Oct. 15th

Went out to the Fair this morning where I found a tremendous crowd assembled. The children of the High Schools were there by invitation—1600 in number, and I marched in front of them as Mayor of the City around the ampitheatre. A silver cup was awarded to Mr Pearl[3] the superintendent of the schools.

Oct. 16

I went to the Fair again today, but there was a small crowd, and the stock sold of an indifferent character.

[3] Joshua F. Pearl, Superintendent of Schools, Nashville, Tennessee 1854-1861 and 1865.

Oct. 17

Did not go to church today. In the afternoon I called on Mrs. Polk, and took tea at Aunt Felicia's.

Oct. 18th

The City Council met at 10 oc this morning to swear in the officers—and take bonds. I went out to the Penitentiary this evening to examine some beat rock for the streets of the city, where I saw Holmes whose term expires in Dec. He threatened my life when he went in, but I suppose he has abandoned the idea ere this. Five years imprisonment at hard labor is enough to drive such thoughts out of a mans mind.

Oct. 19th

Nothing of interest has occurred today. Mrs Winder and family started to La. this evening. I think she is running a great risk as the yellow-fever is so bad.

Oct. 20th

Passed the forenoon in the City Hall. And the afternoon in my office attending to business.

Oct. 21

Occupied the day in business matters. This evening I attended the lecture of Dr Quintard for the benifit of the Robertson Asso. His subject was Jerusalem. After the lecture I walked home with Wm S. Eakin and lady where I passed an agreeable hour.

Oct. 22

Occupied the day in business matters, nothing worth noting except that I attended the most brilliant amateur concert at the Female Academy that I ever heard. It was given for the benifit of the Orphan Asylum. One of the performers (a Germain Teacher) has one of the most exquisite voices and sings with more effect than any one I ever heard except on the stage.

Oct. 23rd

Passed the forenoon in the City Hall and the afternoon in my office.

Oct. 24th

Attended the Theatre this morning, where the Rev J B Ferguson preached to a crowded house. Every seat was occupied. Grundy and his family left for Ark this evening.

Oct. 25

Attended the Circuit Court this morning after which I went to the city hall and remained until 12 oc.

Oct. 26th

Occupied the day in business matters. This evening I had a plesant game of cards at Rice's room.

Oct. 27

Judge [Elijah] Walker of Wayne Co publishes a card in this morning's Union disclaiming any knowledge of the use of his name in the late Judicial election. This places the KN party in rather a bad light. Dr May[4] of Washington has just arrived here to take his chair in the new Medical College. I think he will be sadly disappointed, as I believe the college will prove a failure.

Oct. 28th

Occupied the forenoon in the Circuit Court Room and the city Hall. The City Council met tonight and my Police bill was rejected. Whitmore showed me a calculation this evening showing that Dr D T. McGavock was worth one million of dollars.

Oct. 29th

This evening I started with Seraphine on the cars to Col Jno McGavock's in Williamson. His carriage met us at the depot.

Oct. 30

This morning Jno and myself went into Franklin which has improved very much since I visited it last. Called to see Aunt Eliza Ewing who now lives in the country, also called at Cousin James' who has grown so fat that I hardly recognized him.

Oct. 31st

Attended church in Franklin this morning, and heard a very good sermon from Mr Morey. Dined at Mr Otey's with the Bishop. Took tea at Cousin James'.

Nov. 1st

Returned to Nashville this morning and occupied the day in business matters. This evening I attended at Douglass' Hall the Introductory lecture to the Eighth Course in the Medical Department of the University of Nashville by Dr Lindsley. Dr May of Washington also delivered a lecture.

Nov. 2nd

Attended the Chancery Ct this morning and occupied the balance of the day in attending to Corporation matters.

---

[4] John Frederick May, M.D., assumed the chair of Professor of Surgery and Clinical Surgery at the Shelby Medical College after it was founded in Nashville in 1857.

Nov. 3

Occupied the day in corporation matters.

Nov. 4th

Occupied the day in business matters.

Nov. 5th

From the telegraph dispatches this morning it appears that Douglass has carried Ill. but the Black Republicans have swept most of the states in the north. What is a little remarkable the Democratic candidate for Gov in Mass, has carried the city of Boston.

Nov. 6th

Attended the Chancery Ct this morning, and occupied the day in business matters. This evening Capt Davis called to see me and said that he had been told that I had said that I considered the men composing the present police as all a set of thieves. Some evil disposed person gave it currency with the view of prejudicing them against my Adm. I told him, and also Capt Petty that it was false, and that if I believed it I would have suspended the last one of them.

Nov. 7

I started this morning for East Ten but missed the cars. Did not go to church this morning, but heard that the prayers of the Presbyterian Church was asked for Jno A McEwen, who is very low with consumption. Old Joe—the favorite and faithful body servant of Grandfather (Felix Grundy) died on Thursday last. He has been owned for some years past by Robt Rains who was not very kind to the old man. At 2½ oc I left Nashville for East Ten. Passed the night at Chattanooga.

Nov. 8th

Walked out this morning to a mill in the vicinity of Chattanooga to ascertain the price of frames for building. Left on the evening train.

Nov. 9th

Reached Jonesboro for breakfast, occupied the day in the Chancery Court.

Nov. 10th

Passed the day in the Court Room.

Nov. 11th

This morning my case was taken up and argued. Judge McKinney came in and was admitted on affidavit a party defendant in the case.

Nov. 12th

Occupied the day in Court Room.

Nov. 13

Staid all night with Col Nelson.

Nov. 14

Started to Bristol this morning. Walked out to the farm where I found all well. In the afternoon I went down to the White Sulphur Spring and found the water delightful. The turning of the creek from the Spring has improved the water greatly.

Nov. 15

Occupied the day in going over the farm seeing what Mr Hughes has been doing during the year. He has done a great deal of work but his expenses have been heavy. His crops are better than any one else in the County and he took six premiums this year at the Fair.

Nov. 16

This morning I rode to Blountville. Occupied the day in attending to business and in the Court. The Chancery and Circuit Courts are both in session. I saw in the Court Room to day for the first time in my life a man that had been tared, feathered and rode on a rail. A young fellow living over the line in Va—was caught by a party in Ten and so treated for keeping a . . . . list as he termed a paper exhibited in Court—in which the fair name of about thirty young girls in the vicinity of Bristol was impugned. He indicted the party, and the jury brought in a verdict of guilty (they having submitted) and fined the party one dollar each and costs.

Nov. 17

Occupied most of the day in Col Nelson's room—drawing up an answer to Tipton's Bill. After dinner I returned to the farm on Beaver creek.

Nov. 18

Attended a sale of stock in the neighborhood but occupied the day mostly in going over the farm.

Nov. 19

Occupied the day in settling Acc. up with Mr Hughes. I paid him all the notes he held on the farm but not yet exactly at the state of our Acc. during the year. Left the farm late this evening for Bristol where I met at the hotel Cousins Hugh Ewing and James McNutt on their way to Nashville from Wythe Co Va. They are both looking excellently well —weighing over two [hundred] each.

Nov. 20

Left Bristol at 1 oc this morning and reached Chattanooga for supper.

Nov. 21

Reached Nashville early this morning and being somewhat fatigued I did not go to church.

Nov. 22nd

The accumulation of two weeks work has left me very much occupied today at the City Hall, and in the Court Room.

Nov. 23rd

Occupied the day in business matters. The board of Aldermen met this evening and adjourned over until Thursday night.

Nov. 24

Nothing has occurred today worthy of note.

Nov. 25th

Passed the day at the City Hall and at the Chancery Ct.

Nov. 26

I purchased a new book today by Holmes[5] called the Autocrat of the Breakfast Table, which I find quite a readable book.

Nov. 27

Occupied all day in attending to Corporation affairs. This evening I went to hear Geo D. Prentice lecture on American Statesmanship. He delineated fully the corruption of the times, and the degeneracy of our public men. He said with much truth that the first thing a member of Congress done after reaching Washington was to thrust his hand as deep as possible into the public Treasury, and that if their ears were as long as their hands, they would all be Jackasses. I suppose there is no man in the country half so corrupt as Prentice himself and I was strongly reminded while he was speaking of the old adage, "that it took a thief to catch a thief." He had a full audience.

Nov. 28

Attended the first Presbyterian Church this morning.

Nov. 29

Occupied the day in business matters. Wm Cox lost his child today. Mary Jones Polk was married this morning to Joe Branch of Ark. She has been on the carpet a long time and is quite an elegant girl.

Poor Bob Brown! I fear he will grow crazy now.

---

[5] Oliver Wendell Holmes (1809-1894), essayist, poet, teacher of anatomy.

Nov. 30th

Attended Hardin P. Bostick's sale this morning. The house and 3¾ acres of ground brought $13,050 and some of the lots at 16 per foot. The streets of the city are in a terrible plight.

Dec. 1st

Occupied the day in business matters.

Dec. 2

Nothing of importance has occurred today.

Dec. 3rd

The Robertson Asso. had a meeting last night and the Charity Committee went out today and raised several hundred dollars.

Dec. 4

Jno A McEwen died last night about 7 o c of consumption. He has been in feeble health for 18 mo past. His loss will be severely felt by his family this community and the State. We were boys together. He was my Tutor in college and my friend. The citizens had a meeting at the Court House at which N S Brown, F B Fogg, A Ewing, C K Winston, Jno G Ferguson and myself made speeches. I called the City Council together who passed resolutions on the subject of McEwen's death. The members of the Bar and the Robertson Asso. also passed resolutions. We have had a great many false alarms of fire the last few days.

Dec. 5

Attended the 1st Presbyterian Church this morning. After dinner I went out to Mt Olivet to see Jno A. McEwen burried. There were a large number of his friends in attendance. After returning from the funeral I went up to see Aunt Malvina Bass, where I passed the evening.

Dec. 6

Occupied the day in attending to Corporation affairs.

Dec. 7

We received this morning in the papers a synopsis of the President's Message, and the Post Master General's (A V. Brown) Report. The increase of the postal expenditures has been very great, and an increase to 5 cts on letters is recommended.

Dec. 8

Occupied the day mostly in my office and in attending to the poor of the city.

Dec. 9

The City Council met tonight, and a good deal of excitement prevailed on the subject of the Chattanooga R R. V K Stevenson the President—and E H Ewing both made lengthy speeches.

Dec. 10th

The Council held another meeting Tonight—and passed resolutions of a stringent character as to the management of the Chattanooga R R. Messrs Hollingsworth and Rhea were appointed to cast the proxies of the City on the 15th instant at Murfreesboro for the Corporation.

Dec. 11

This has been a very inclement day. Nothing of importance has occurred. I attended a jubilee of the printers last night, and made them a speech.

Dec. 12

Father and mother started for Ark at 10 o c on the Runyan. Attended the Presbyterian Church this morning.

Dec. 13

Occupied the day in the Courts, at the City Hall, in my office, etc.

Dec. 14

The President's Message is very long, and very good. He recommends the purchase of Cuba, a Protectorate over Mexico, and several very important measures. I have been engaged all day in business matters.

Dec. 15th

Occupied the day in attending to business matters. This afternoon I acted as Clerk in the Federal Court in the absence of father. I wrote out a number of depositions in two cases where a man named Arnold and one named Wright of the District are charged with forging land warrants. This evening I attended a grand amateur concert given for the benifit of the Robertson Asso. The house was full, and every thing went off well. Miss Page from the Nashville Female Academy was the principal singer, and she acquited herself admirably. After the Concert was over I accompanied Mad-sell [Mademoiselle] Sehosia to the Academy.

Dec. 16

The election at Murfreesboro yesterday resulted in the success of V K Stephenson over the combination that was brought against him. The Corporation of Nashville cast her vote against him. There was a good deal of excitement among them and some feeling exhibited. Wm Barry was burried today.

Dec. 17th

Occupied most of the day in the Federal Ct room taking depositions in the case of the United States vs Willis N Arnold for forging land warrants. He was committed to jail for trial. Attended the Theatre tonight for the first time this season. Miss Maggie Mitchell had a benifit—and the house was crowded to overflow.

Dec. 18

Occupied most of the day in the Federal Court taking depositions in the case of the United vs Henry Wright for forging land warrants. Mr Wright is a lawyer in Henderson Co, Ten of extensive practice and has quite a Websterian looking head. He feigned to be deranged and cut up a good many pranks, but the Judge had him examined by two physicians who pronounced that he was possuming. The trial proceeded and he was committed for further trial.

Dec. 19

Attended the 1st Presbyterian Church this morning—and remained at home reading the remainder of the day.

Dec. 20

Occupied the day in business matters, nothing of interest transpired.

Dec. 21st

Passed the day mostly in my office.

Dec. 22

Passed the day in attending to business matters.

Dec. 23

The Council met this evening, and some of the members in imitation of the invested thirteen took their hats and withdrew from the Hall.

Dec. 24

Passed the day in business matters.

Dec. 25

At 9 o c I went over to Mrs Porter's to see the children's Christmas Tree. I enjoyed seeing them so happy. The day passed off quietly and pleasantly.

Dec. 26

Did not go to church today, but remained at home reading, etc. In the afternoon I took a walk.

Dec. 27

Occupied the entire day in business matters. The Board of Aldermen met this evening and concurred with the Common Council on the Huxter Bill, about which there is a good deal of interest in the City.

Dec. 28

Passed the day mostly in business matters.

Dec. 29th

Nothing of importance has occurred today.

Dec. 30

I have been occupied all day in business matters.

Dec. 31

Tonight Rice and myself went out masking, and had a great deal of fun. We closed the old year in real jolly way.

[*1859*]

Jan. 1st

I signed the Huxter Bill as it has been termed this morning, and rented the Market House under it. Passed the evening very pleasantly at Dr Martins.

Jan. 2

Did not go to church this morning, but remained at home reading, etc., etc.

Jan. 3

Very busy all day in business matters. This evening I attended Shackosh's Grand Concert and was highly entertained. Madam De Willkamp brought a letter of introduction to me from Col De Graffenried of Macon, Ga. She is a charming little creature—and has quite a romantic history, being the daughter of a wealthy N Y Banker and ran off with a German Count.

Jan. 4

Occupied the entire day in business matters. Attended the Concert again to-night.

Jan. 5

Business, Business, Business all day. Concert again this evening.

Jan. 6

Called a meeting of the City Council this evening to mature a bill to govern the night police, but the two bodies could not agree.

Jan. 7

Occupied the day in business matters. In the evening I accompanied Sallie and my wife to Shackosh' last Concert.

Jan. 8

Andrew Ewing delivers an oration in Memphis today upon the occasion of the Mempheans having procured a bust of Gen Jackson. *Ha, Ha, Ha.* The steamer Cumberland made an excursion trip up to the Hermitage today. The Germain and Medical Students formed the principal list of passengers. I attended a house warming at the Union and American Building this evening and made a short speech.

Jan. 9

Did not go to church today. About 9 o c this evening I had a tilt with a burglar who was attempting to get into our house. I think he is in colleague with Holmes who has recently served out his term in the Pen for the same offense.

Jan. 10

Maria Louisa Stevenson died about 4 o c this morning of consumption, after a lingering illness of several years. She was a most excellent woman. We travelled together in Europe and of course there are many pleasant reminicences connected with our association. She married young, and to a man entirely too old for her. I do not think she had much happiness after marriage.

Jan. 11

I attended Mrs. Stevenson's funeral this morning and the remainder of the day was occupied in business matters.

Jan. 12

Occupied the entire day in attending to business.

Jan. 13

Father and Mother reached home today from Ark in good health. I attended the City Council this evening for the purpose of seeing them elect their night police. The whole thing was a perfect farce.

Jan. 14

Today I have been occupied in business, nothing worth noting.

Jan. 15

Passed most of the day in the City Hall and in the Circuit Court room.

Jan. 16

Attended Dr Quintard's church this morning but did not hear the sermon on account of the allarm of fire.

Jan. 17

Attended the Circuit Court this morning, and remained most of the day at the City Hall attending to business matters.

Jan. 18

Occupied all day in my office.

Jan. 19

Nothing has transpired today worthy of note.

Jan. 20

About noon today a very respectable young girl appeared at the City Hall and from her appearance I thought her deranged and carried her to the Sewanee House where she remained all night under the care of an Irish girl.

Jan. 21

This morning I went down to see the girl that I placed at the Sewanee House but I could not see any change in her. I sent her out to the Asylum where she will be well treated. Grundy and his wife arrived yesterday from Ark.

Jan. 22

Passed the day in the Circuit Court room, and in the City Hall.

Jan. 23

Attended the 1st Presbyterian church this morning, and the Episcopal this evening.

Jan. 24

This morning I received a note from B F Miller stating that Caroline Waters, the girl that I sent to the Asylum on Saturday was an imposter. I called to see the [girl] and from his discription she must be the same. Dr Cheatham[6] called today and says that the lady is not crazy, but has met with some great misfortune, which oppresses her mental faculties. Occupied all day in business. Dined with Rice at the "Shakespeare House" and after dinner we called to see Mrs Bankhead and her daughter.

---

[6] W. A. Cheatham, M.D., was a native of Tennessee and a graduate of the University of Pennsylvania. He began the practice of medicine in Nashville in 1845. He was Superintendent of the Tennessee Hospital for the Insane 1852-1862.

Jan. 25

This morning I went up to the Supreme Court Room—but as nothing special was going on I returned to the City Hall.

Jan. 26

Occupied the day in business matters. Tonight I had another flare-up with S—who causes me great trouble and unhappiness.

Jan. 27

Occupied the day mostly at the City Hall. Ed Cooper[7] was to have delivered a lecture this evening before the Robertson Asso but it was so inclement that no one attended. The Council met this evening and elected Mr J A Hayden Civil Engineer of the City. I received a letter today from Mr. Reed of Londonderry Ireland, inclosing a carefully drawn up pedigree of the McGavock family in county Antrim Ireland. From this document I ascertain that there are yet a number of the descendants of Randal McGavock living near Scarryhill. They are all small farmers, but bear an excellent character for good sense, honesty, and industry. Randal McGavock the ancestor of the stock now in Ireland, was the brother of James who was the ancestor of the stock in America. I sent a hack out to the Asylum today at the suggestion of Dr Cheatham after Miss Caroline Waters, who feigned derangement. The driver brought her to my office and she looked as well as any body and conversed freely. I told her that I did not think that she would forget the Mayor of Nashville soon. She replied that she would not.

Jan. 28th

Occupied the day in business matters. Josie Southall died last night of consumption after a lingering illness.

Jan. 29

Attended Josie Southall's funeral this morning. She was burried at Mt Olivet, the new cemetery, which will soon be made a most beautiful place.

Jan. 30

I did not go to church today, simply because I did not feel like listening to sermon. I occupied the day in visiting the warf, the Work House, and the quarters.

[7] Edmund Cooper (1821-1911), lawyer, Congressman from Tennessee, was born in Franklin, Tennessee. He studied law at Harvard and commenced practice in Shelbyville, Tennessee. He was a member of the State House of Representatives; a Union delegate to the State Constitutional Convention of 1861; a member of the Thirty-ninth Congress 1866-1867; Assistant Secretary of the Treasury 1867-1869; resumed the practice of law.

Jan. 31

Wrote a number of letters today, and was quite busy in attending to Corporation affairs.

Feb. 1st

Occupied the forenoon in business matters. In the afternoon I attended a meeting of the Historical Society. Here I met a gentlemen from NY who is collecting material for the life of Gen Jackson. Called to see Gov Harris where I met Jas Lamb who has recently moved from Memphis to Fayetteville having been attracted there by old Bonner's wealth.

Feb. 2nd

Passed the forenoon principally at the City Hall. In the afternoon I drove out to Gen Harding's with Aunt Felicia and a young man named Sidney Clay of Bourbon Co Ky. He is my 3rd Cousin, and the grandson of Aunt Reid, deceased. He is both hansome and intelligent. Took tea at Aunt Felicia's.

Feb. 3rd

Passed the day at the City Hall and in my office. Read a speech this morning of Atkins[8] our member from the Western District on the present condition of parties which I think very good, certainly much better than I expected. Also read the speech of Gov Johnson in the Senate of the US on the subject of the Pacific Rail Road. He opposes National Conventions for the purpose of nominating candidates for the Presidency. Jeff Davis[9] responded to him, and said that if he wanted a pony race such view might do, but he would not say that he would vote for the gentleman even in such an emergency.

Feb. 4th

Nothing of importance has transpired today.

Feb. 5th

Occupied the day in the Circuit Court and at the city hall.

Feb. 6

Last night Caroline Walters, the girl that I sent to the Lunatic Asylum last week returned to the City on the Minatonka, having been to Paducah

[8] John DeWitt Clinton Atkins (1825-1908), agriculturalist, politician, was born in Henry County, Tennessee. He was a member of the State House of Representatives 1849-1851; served in the State Senate 1855-1857; served a brief period in the Confederate Army; elected to the Confederate Provisional Congress;; served in Congress 1873-1883; chosen United States Commissioner of Indian Affairs 1885-1888. He was active in agricultural pursuits throughout his life.

[9] Jefferson Davis (1808-1889), President of the Confederate States of America.

where she played the same game that she did here. Today she went to a house of ill-fame.

Feb. 7

Did not go to church today. This evening Caroline Walters left the house of ill fame and passed the night at the St Cloud, having rigged herself out in Mary Combs fine clothes. She is a perfect mystery to me, and I am unable to say whether she is deranged or not.

Feb. 8

Occupied the day in my office, and at the City Hall, David McGavock of Va took dinner with us today. The City Council met this evening, and transacted a good deal of business.

Feb. 9

Nothing of interest has occurred today.

Feb. 10

Passed the day in going over the streets and superintending work. This evening I attended a meeting of the Council, at which V K Stevenson made a speech on the subject of increasing the tax of the city for four years to aid in the construction of the North Western R.R., of which he is the President. The Council passed a resolution, ordering an election.

Feb. 11

Attended the Circuit Court this morning where I met Tom Marshall[10] of Ky who has come here with view of lecturing. He is rather rowdyish in his appearance, and looks like he drank a good deal.

Feb. 12

Occupied the day in my office, the Circuit Court, and at the City Hall. Nothing has transpired today worthy of note.

Feb. 13th

Attended the 1st Presbyterian Church this morning. Attended the funeral this afternoon of Capt Gordon, one of our oldest, and most respected citizens.

Feb 14

Passed an hour very pleasantly this morning with Tom Marshall. He was lying in bed at the St Cloud with a cigar in his mouth. He has been on a spree for some days, and is just getting over the effects. He said some good things, and among others he said that whiskey was the only

[10] Thomas Alexander Marshall (1794-1871), lawyer, politician.

true democrat. Recd a dispatch today from the Mayor of Petersburgh stating that Caroline Walters was there deranged. I replied, stating that she did not belong to this State and City, and that I believed her an imposter. From the NY Times I see that Wm M Churchwell of Ten has been appointed by the President on a secret mission to Mexico. Mr. Forsyth[11] has resigned.

Feb. 15

The Capt. of Police shot a man this morning who resisted an arrest. Went down with St Clair Morgan to test some fine imported wines at a house recently opened on Market Street by Messrs. Riva, two Italian gentlemen. They were very polite, and their wines are excellent. Occupied the day mostly in my office at the City Hall, and at the Circuit Court Room.

Feb. 16

Passed all the forenoon in the Circuit Court Room. At 2 oc Gov N S Brown and myself had a case of forceable detainer before two magistrates. Thomas Farrell Irish vs. Levy, a Jew. The Jews as usual swore every thing for their man, and the case was decided in his favor.

Feb. 17

Occupied the forenoon in the Circuit Court Room—and the afternoon at the City Hall. Mallie Waters died this evening of scarlet fever, after a very brief illness. This is a most melancholy death, being a lovely child, and only daughter.

Feb. 18

Occupied most of the day with Mr Hayden, Civil Engineer of the City. In the afternoon I attended the funeral of little Mallie Waters. Mary reached home this evening from La with Col Jno MacGavock.

Feb. 19

Nothing has occurred today worth writing about.

Feb. 20

Attended the 1st Presbyterian Church today. Dr Edgar delivered quite an eloquent discourse on the subject of foreign missions. He spoke feelingly of the many privations that our pilgrim forefathers endured in order to plant the light of the gospel in this continent. This afternoon I rode out to see Bob Brown who has been quite sick for several weeks.

Feb. 21

Occupied the day at the City Hall, and my office.

---

[11] John Forsyth (1812-1877), editor, publicist.

Feb. 22

The military companies of the city celebrated Washington's Birthday. They gave me a salute at the City Hall.

Feb. 23rd

Nothing of interest to note.

Feb. 24th

Passed the day in my office attending to business matters. Attended a meeting of the Council this evening.

Feb. 25

This evening I went to Odd Fellows Hall to hear Tom Marshall lecture on the French Revolution. He was just drunk enough to be eloquent. His subject was the French Revolution. I introduced him to the audience at his request.

Feb. 26

Occupied the day in business matters.

Feb. 27

Attended the Presbyterian Church this morning. After dinner I went over and played a while with Sallie's baby (Louise)[12] then called on Dr Waters who has just returned from Ark and who is much grieved at the loss of Mallie. I then went to see a poor woman on Front St who I found quite sick in bed. I then called to see Tom Marshall at the hotel where I passed two hours very agreeably. I found him lying in bed with the stump of a cigar in his mouth and every few minutes he would get up and take a drink of whiskey. He showed me the place on his hip where he was shot in a duel by Jno Rowan, Jr of Bardstown. He gave me a full history of the whole affair, and indeed of his life.[13] He spoke eloquently and feelingly of his mother, also of Jno J

[12] Louise Grundy Lindsley, daughter of John Berrien Lindsley and Sallie McGavock, lived in Nashville until her death in 1944. Her interest in the history of her family and native city continued unabated through the years. She exercised great care in preserving the manuscripts of her family, including the journals of her Uncle Randal.

[13] It is interesting to note that the will of John Rowan, Sr. contained the following passage:

> My duelling pistols I bequeath to my son John, and at his death to his oldest son. They are never to be used by either but when their honor imperatively demands it, and in that case I know they will be held steadily.

"Young John" Rowan was, like his father, a dead shot. The duel, an outgrowth of the sarcasm and ridicule which Rowan and Marshall had heaped upon each other during the course of a political debate, was initiated by Marshall. Marshall was well-known as a cool, experienced duellist. In the duel, however, Rowan fulfilled his intention merely of putting a ball in him "so that he would not sit down for a while." An ironic note was struck some years later when Rowan saved Marshall from drowning in the Kentucky River. "That is the second time Rowan has saved my life," Marshall is reported to have declared grimly. See Young E. Allison, *The Old Kentucky Home, Its Song and the Story* (Bardstown, 1923).

Crittenden. He said that Henry Clay was a great orator, but a mean man, lacking the elements of a gentleman. Leaving The Hotel I went to Aunt Felicia's and took tea. After tea I attended the Episcopal Church at Odd Fellows, from which I accompanied Mademoiselle Schoshet to the Academy.

Feb. 28

Occupied the forenoon in business. After dinner I rode over to Dr Shelby's to look at his fine stock and then went over to the City. After tea I attended Tom Marshall's 3rd lecture.

March 1st

The month has opened beautifully. The telegraph brings us news this morning of the destruction of a fine steamer on the Miss near Baton Rouge over 200 lives lost. Mr Sickells M C N J—killed Mr Key on Sunday in Washington on account of intrigue with his (Sickles wife). Mr Key was District Attn, for the District of Columbia.

March 2

Nothing worth noting.

March 3

Occupied all day in attending to Corporation affairs. The Police force of the City appeared today with their silver badges. The night force have stars, the day crescents. Attended the Theater tonight. Miss Logan appeared.

March 4

Congress adjourned last night—nothing of importance has been accomplished during the session, and a great deal of wrangling among partisans.

March 5

Walked up to the Water Works this morning. Saw Grundy off for Ark etc.

March 6

Attended the Presbyterian Church this morning.

March 7

Occupied the day in Corporation matters.

March 8

News reached here this morning by telegraph from Washington that Post Master General A V Brown of Ten died at 8 oc of pneumonia. This is a great calamity to his family and the country. He was a man of great social qualities and powers, a fine speaker—more than ordinary ability, and untiring energy. His greatest fault was his want of sincerity, and phisical courage. The absence of these qualities retarded his progress and elevation in the political world. Attended the meeting of the board of Aldermen and afterwards went to the Theater to hear young Edward Booth. The play was over before I reached there, and I did not see him. The house was full to overflow.

March 9

The papers of the City are all draped in mourning this morning for Gov Brown.

March 10

Occupied the day in Corporation matters.

March 11

Edwin Booth, the second son of the old tragedian, is now attracting a good deal of attention here.

March 12

Occupied the day mostly at the City Hall.

March 13

Did not go to church today, being on the Committee of Arrangements to receive the remains of Gov Brown tomorrow.

March 14

At 9 oc the Chattanooga train arrived bearing the remains of Gov Brown. A large procession both civic and military escorted it to the Capitol where the Episcopal service was read by Dr Quintard, and a prayer by Dr Summers. The body was then conveyed to Mt Olivet Cemetery where the Masonic Fraternity burried him. The bells of the City were tolled, and the business houses closed for one hour.

March 15

Occupied the forenoon at the City Hall, and the afternoon at my law office attending to private business. The "*Oppositions*" Convention met in this city yesterday and nominated James Quarles of Montgomery, a renegade democrat for Congress, and Dick Cheatham a notorious gambler—What is to become of the morals of this city?

March 16th

The City is pretty full today of delegates to the Democratic Convention tomorrow. I attended the Caucus tonight where I found considerable difference of opinion on the currency question and the doctrine of squatter soverignty. And Ewing brought in a set of compromise resolutions which created much discussion, but were finally recommended to be passed in Convention tomorrow. Nowles, Nicholson, Ewing, Whithorne, Walker, Manees and others made speeches.

March 17

Quite a diabolical affair took place on our streets last night. Capt Dismukes was going home from the Theater with his wife, and was knocked down by one of four men with brass knuckles and badly shot. The Police was on hand pretty soon, and exchanged shots with the rascals, but made their escapes. The Convention for this District met at 10 oc and nominated Dr Mennees of Robertson for Congress. He accepted. The State Convention met at 11 oc. Jno Howard of Wilson in the Chair and appointed some on a committee on Resolutions. Andrew Ewing then offered some resolutions in regard to the death of Gov Brown which were unanimously adopted. Nicholson made a short speech in which he narrated the dying scene. The convention then adjourned until 3 oc at which time a platform will be presented. At 3 oc the convention met and adopted a platform that seemed to give general satisfaction. Hon Isham G Harris was renominated without opposition. Dr Menees was nominated for Congress in this District and young Merritt of this City for Floater. Attended a supper tonight at the St Cloud given by the St Patrick's Club. Every thing went off well, I made several little speeches.

March 18

Occupied the afternoon at the City Hall. This evening I went to hear Dr Robt Grundy of Memphis preach at the 2nd Presbyterian Church. He is the nephew of my grandfather, and a very considerable man. I was delighted with his sermon.

March 19

Passed the day in attending to the business of the Corporation. This evening three men were arrested on suspicion, supposed to be engaged in the attack of Dismukes.

March 20

Attended the 2nd Presbyterian Church this morning and evening. Dr Grundy is without exception the best divine that I have heard in years.

March 21

Occupied most of the day in business. Dined with Dr. Grundy and Aunt Felicia and went to hear him preach again tonight. He took tea at our house.

March 22

I was occupied nearly the whole of the afternoon in [moving] about with the City Engineer in the Alleys of South Nashville to define boundaries, etc. This is one of the pleasant duties attached to the office of the Mayor. About 1 oc today the hardest rain and hail storm fell that I almost ever witnessed. Attended a meeting of the Board of Aldermen this evening, where I heard the North Western R R question discussed again by Mr Hamilton. Action on the question was deferred.

March 23rd

Occupied the day mostly in the Mayor's office. Dr Grundy left on the cars for Memphis today. I went down to see him off. He has made quite an impression on me.

March 24th

Nothing has occurred today of interest. The City Council met this evening, no business transacted of moment.

March 25

Passed the day in my office.

March 26

Quite an unfortunate occurrence took place this evening at the 4th Ward poll. Ira Stout, who was a candidate for Constable was insulted—by Mr. Feltz and stabbed him with Feltz' own sword cane. I appeared for Stout, and advised him to go to jail and not offer to give bail. It is thought that Feltz will die. Gower was elected. Attended a meeting of the board of Aldermen this evening.

March 27

Did not go to church today, but went this morning down to the Work House where I found Mr Dix the Keeper playing cards in the public room. I said nothing to him at the time, but intend doing so. This evening I went to see a sick Irishman and sent him to the hospital. I then called on Sallie Ewing and Mrs Polk.

March 28

The trial of Stout came off this morning, before three Magistrates, and he was acquited. A woman was arraigned before the Recorder this morning dressed in man's clothes. Her hair was cut short and she said she was from Allen Co Ky. She was sent to the Work House. Mr J B White called to see me today and brought Mr. Laneus, the preacher in Edgefield, who is recently from La. The Council met again tonight, but as usual accomplished but little.

March 29

A very severe storm passed over the City last night, blowing off the roofs of houses, chimneys, etc. The tin roof of the 1st Presbyterian Church and the Court House were blown off, and the rain ruined the plastering. The Opposition Convention met at the Capitol this morning and nominated Jno Netherland of East Ten for Gov. I went up this evening and heard Gen. Foote[14] of Miss., House, and Quarles speak. Foote had a black wig and his whiskers were died black, giving him a very singular apperance. This evening Jno Bell and others made speeches. I did not attended but told that it was an enthusiastic meeting.

March 30

Occupied the day mostly at the City Hall—nothing transpired of interest.

March 31st

The Council met tonight and passed the gravel Bill, also the Topographical bill in which I was much interested. Recd a letter from Cloyd MacGavock of Fort Chiswell, Va.

Apr. 1st

The month opens beautifully. This evening I went out to the Water Works to examine a rail-way being constructed by the Engineer to haul coal from the boats up on the banks.

Apr. 2nd

Occupied the day in business matters.

Apr. 3

The river is rising very rapidly, so much so that many of the boats above the bridge will be unable to get under. Attended Dr. Quintard's church this morning—and again this evening. Accompanied Mademoiselle Schosa to the Academy.

Apr. 4

This morning I am troubled with the rheumatism—and fear that it will cling to me through life.

Apr. 5

The City Council met this evening and appropriated [$]30,000 toward building the Howard School House—also the bill relating to graveling the streets. Recd a very flattering letter from my farm today. The crops look well and every thing moves on well.

---

[14] Henry Stuart Foote (1800-1880), lawyer, United States Senator, Governor of Mississippi.

Apr. 6
Suffered a great deal today from rheumatism. Weather quite cold. I fear the fruit and wheat are much injured.

Apr. 7
Geo Bradford and Mr Brien Sr had a fight in the Court room this morning—no damage of consequences.

Apr. 8
Passed the forenoon in the Criminal Court Room and the City Hall. Occupied the afternoon in my law office.

Apr. 9
Col Netherland the Opposition candidate for Gov arrived in the city this morning and has been closeted all day with his K N friends. Tonight he made a speech to a large crowd in the Court House. He reviewed the platform of the democratic party, and told some pleasant anecdotes which pleased the crowd. I expect he is about the best man they could have selected for the occasion.

Apr 10
Did not go to church today. This evening I took a walk, and called to see Aunt Felicia.

Apr 11
Occupied all day in drawing up an abstract of Mr Grundy's character for Jno M. Bright[15] of Fayetteville, who is to deliver an oration in May on his life and character. This evening I had the street committee convened to consider the propriety of purchasing a tug and boats for bringing gravel to the city.

Apr 12th
Occupied most of the day at the City Hall. The board of Aldermen met this evening and passed the resolution ordering an election to be held for a subscription by the city to the North Western R R

Apr 13
Met Geo W. Jones[16] and Wm Polk in town this morning. The day has been exceedingly sultry, so much so that I actually suffered from heat in my office.

15 John Morgan Bright (1817-1911), lawyer, Congressman from Tennessee, was born in Fayetteville, Tennessee. He graduated from the University of Nashville in 1839 and from the Law Department of Transylvania University in 1841; a member of the State House of Representatives in 1847 and 1848; a general on the staff of Governor Harris 1861-1865; a Democratic member of Congress 1871-1881. When not engaged in political pursuits he was active in the practice of law.

16 George Washington Jones (1806-1884), Congressman from Tennessee, was a native of Virginia. He was a member of the Tennessee House of Representatives 1835-1839;

Apr 14

Passed the forenoon in the Criminal Court Room, where two women were on trial for stealing goods out of Douglass' Store. Attended a meeting of the City Council and a Musical party at Aunt Felicia's.

Apr. 15

Occupied the forenoon in business matters. This afternoon my wife and myself accompanied Carrie McGavock to Williamson.

Apr. 16

Early this morning Jno and myself went out fishing. Pretty soon after we reached Hughes Mill, Jim Craighead and Thompson came out from the City. Craighead was well equipped, having water boots, rod, minnows, bucket, etc. He was the only one of the party who had any luck. We were fully compensated however, in a most excellent dinner at Jno.'s.

Apr. 17

Went to the Presbyterian Church this morning and heard a very good sermon. Dined at Mr Otey's. Made a visit this afternoon to Aunt Eliza Ewing.

Apr. 18

Returned to the City this morning, and occupied the day in attending to Corporation matters.

Apr. 19

Occupied the day in business.

Apr. 20

All the day at the city Hall.

Apr. 21st

The Candidates for Gov. have agreed upon a list of 65 appointments, extending over the three divisions of the State. At 6 oc A. M. I started on the cars for Duck river in Maury Co., having an appointment with John Marshall and Jno McGavock to go a fishing. Marshall disapointed us, but Jno and I went out and passed the entire day in fruitless endeavors. We met three gentlemen from Nashville, viz. Ed Ewing, Dillon, and Nevins. Ewing got turned over in a canoe, and wet all over. I do not think Rutherfords Creek or Duck—and this point good places to fish.

---

served in the State Senate 1839-1841; Clerk of the Lincoln County Court 1840-1843; a Democrat in Congress 1843-1859; a member of the First Confederate Congress 1862-1864; appointed a member of the board of trustees of the Tennessee Hospital for the Insane in 1871 and reappointed in 1877.

Tom Brown of Pulaski and Miss Pillow, daughter of the Gen. were married this morning.

Apr. 22

Occupied the day in business.

Apr. 23

This afternoon my wife and myself went out to pay Cousin Lysander's family a visit. I have not been there before since his death.

April. 24

I was very sick last night, so much so that I did not get up until dinner time. In the afternoon we all walked over to Mr Hayes' and made a visit. Here we met Wm Lawrence and family and Mrs Hayes from Nashville.

Apr. 25

We returned to the City today, after a most delightful visit. Occupied the entire day in attending to Corporation affairs.

Apr. 26

News reached here today of the explosion and distruction of the steamer St. Nicholas just below Memphis, some sixty lives lost and among them it is believed that G J. Pillow Jr is lost. Attended the board of Aldermen this evening.

Apr. 27

Occupied most of the day in Corporation affairs. An Irish Woman from Me called at my office with a boy six years old who could not speak or walk. She wanted him provided for, stating that she was unable to do so. A young man who called with a bone fellon on his thumb and wanted me to send him to Cincinnati. In the morning papers I notice a most horrible attempt at murder, etc. Some one supposed to be a negro went to Dr May's in Maury Co. and cut the throat of a very fine Jack, and then cut the animal up. Not satisfied with this brutal act he got into the room where the Dr and his wife were sleeping and with the blood of the Jack upon his hands came very near choking the Dr to death. His wife gave the alarm and a gentleman in the house came to the rescue. The villain made his escape, after stealing two watches, and other valuables.

Apr. 28

Occupied the day at the City Hall. The two boards met in Convention this evening and elected a watchman and appointed me to cast the proxies of the Cor for Directors of the Winchester and Ala R R

Apr. 29

Passed the day at the City Hall.

Apr. 30

Appointed two Spring Keepers today one a democrat, and one an American or opposition.

Apr. 31

The democrats of the Murfreesboro Congressional district held a Convention today and nominated Bate by acclamation for Congress. He was present and declined the nomination, the whole matter being previously arranged so that Ready might run independent against the regular nominees of the Opposition.

May 1st

The candidates for Gov spoke today at the Capitol. It was the opening speech of the Canvass, and consequently many persons of both parties from a distance were present. Gov Harris opened the discussion in an able and dignified speech. Col Netherland's speech was filled with anecdotes and humorous sayings, but not very sound. The democrats were much gratified with Harris, and the Opposition pretended to be pleased with Netherland.

May 2nd

Occupied nearly the whole day in making preparations for the presentation of Hon Felix Grundy's likeness to the State Historical Society. At 8 oc this evening I went to the City Hotel and escorted Jno M. Bright, the Orator of the occasion to the Capitol, where I found assembled the largest crowd that has ever yet congregated in that spacious building. At least one half of those that went failed to get in. I presented the picture in a few brief remarks, which were responded to by Col Putnam. Mr Bright then delivered an oration upon the life and public services of Felix Grundy. It was truly a splendid production and delivered in a masterly manner. Every one seemed pleased, and the whole affair went off well.

May 3rd

I started at 4½ oc this morning on the cars for Winchester, having been delegated by the City Council to cast the proxies of the Corporation in the election of the Directors of the Winchester and Ala R R. I reached Winchester about 11 oc and was made Chairman of the meeting. After tea I called on my old friend, Sallie Carter, and went with her to an amateur theater in the town.

May 4th

Joined my wife at Decherds, and proceeded to East Ten. Between Chattanooga and Dalton the rear car was thrown off the track, and we missed the connection. Dalton is a very unpleasant place having poor hotel arrangements.

May 5

Left Dalton this evening and proceeded on our journey.

May 6

Arrived at Bristol at 10 oc and proceeded at once to the farm on Beaver Creek. I found every thing going on well, and the crops looking promising.

May 7

Occupied the day in going over the farm examining the stock, and the crops.

May 8

Passed the day on the farm. Late in the evening I went to Bristol for the purpose of taking the cars to Jonesboro.

May 9

Reached Jonesboro before day, and passed the day in the Chancery Ct room. Met Nelson and Hayes, the opposing candidates for Congress in this District, both are sanguine of election. Also met young Rees and Cooke of Knoxville. The former is a candidate for Atto Gen of the State.

May 10

Returned to the farm this morning.

May 11

All day on the farm, hard at work.

May 12

" " " " " " " "

May 13

Mr Jno King's wife and niece called to see my wife this morning and carried her home with them. Late in the evening I rode up.

May 14

All day on the farm.

May 15

The foreign news by telegraph this morning shows that a bloody European war is inevitable. The Sardenian and Austrian Armies have already had a battle. Breadstuffs have risen greatly in this country.

Attended the Methodist church this morning in Va. Mr. Mooring was the preacher, and he gave a very beautiful and pathetic discription of the City of God. In the afternoon I went to hear Parson King preach. He was very dry, but sensible.

May 16

Passed the day on the farm.

May 17

A great deal of rain fell last night and today, causing the creeks to overflow, and the heavy wheat to bend. Occupied the day in making a settlement with Mr Hughes. Went into Bristol late in the evening to go home.

May 18

All day on the cars.

May 19

Reached home at 9 oc this morning. The firemen had a magnificent parade today. Attended five balls tonight.

May 20

Dr. Shelby, one of our oldest and most influential citizens, was burried on Monday last. The old man drank a great deal for several years past.

May 21st

Father, mother, and Mary left on the Johnson today for Ark.

May 22

Attended the first Presbyterian Church this morning. Dr Bardwell[17] of Aberdeen, Miss preached. He has come to supply Dr Edgar's place for several months.

May 23

Occupied the day in the Court Room and the City Hall attending to business.

---

[17] Rev. Joseph Bardwell became the pastor of the first Presbyterian Church October 1, 1859, due to Dr. Edgar's advanced age and increasing feebleness. He was regularly installed the following January and served until February 16, 1862, when the Federal Army moved on Nashville.

May 24

Attended Bostick's sale this morning. Lots went off slowly and low. The board of Aldermen met this evening.

May 25

Our streets have become quite animated recently in the shooting way. A few days since Mr Poindexter and Mr Beaumont[18] editors, exchanged shots on Cedar St about an article that appeared in the Banner. The latter was shot in the leg, no serious injury. Today Col Matt Martin and a Mr Brown of S C exchanged four or five very wild shots without and any damage being done. This was a Sickles case. The wife of the former being seduced by the latter.

May 26

Dined today at Aunt Felicia's. Mr and Mrs Thayer of N Y were the honored guests. The party consisted of Col Acklin and lady, Judge Catron, Dr Buchanon[19] and lady, Dr Martin[20] and lady, and Mrs D T McGavock. My wife was present.

May 27

Occupied the day mostly at the City Hall. Another shooting affair in the streets tonight, both parties badly wounded.

May 28

Purchased a steamboat this morning for the Corporation, to be used as a tug in towing gravel boats from the upper Island. Passed the day in business matters.

May 29

Attended the first Presbyterian Church this morning. This evening I went down to the work house.

May 30th

This evening I accepted the invitation of Mr Thayer of N Y and went out to see a mower cut a field of clover. It was the first exhibition of the kind that I ever saw—and I was perfectly delighted. There was quite a row this evening at the machine shop of the Chattanooga depot. Some

---

18 Thomas W. Beaumont of Clarksville, Tennessee, editor of the *Republican Banner* from May 12, 1858 to March 18, 1860.

19 A. H. Buchanan (d. 1863) was distinguished surgeon and teacher of medicine. He was a native of Virginia, and a graduate of the Medical Department of the University of Pennsylvania. He practiced for many years in Columbia, Tennessee and moved to Nashville in 1842. He was one of the original faculty of the Medical Department of the University of Nashville.

20 R.K.C. Martin (d. 1870), M.D., was a native of Tennessee and a graduate of the University of Pennsylvania. He began the practice of medicine in Nashville in 1833, and was one of the city's leading physicians until his death.

men came from Ill and were employed in the shop, which offended the old hands. The foreman shot one man, and a boy by accident. This incensed the workmen and they assembled together, and threatened to take the foreman out of jail and hang him. (The foreman gave himself up.) I was sent for to quiet the mob—but being out of town, the police officers went down and dispersed them. Late in the evening a hand-bill was circulated calling upon the mechanics of the City to rise and expel the abolitionists from the city, but it resulted in nothing.

May 31

Attended a sale of lots this morning belonging to Frank McGavock—in the free territory, back of Grundy's Hill. They sold well, ranging from $20 to $47.50. Passed the afternoon in the City Hall.

June 1st

Occupied the day mostly in the Chancery and Circuit Ct rooms. Went out this morning and laid off the Howard School House in South Nashville. There was an amateur Concert tonight at the Capitol, gotten up by Mrs F B. Fogg, Vice Regent of the Mt Vernon Asso., for the purpose of raising funds to purchase the home of Washington. About 800 were present.

June 2

Passed the day at the City Hall. This evening I attended the R R meeting at the Market House. J S Craighead, I. Jones and Rea made speeches against the tax for the NW R R and Jno H Smith responded to them very happily. After the speaking was over I attended the firemen's Ball at Odd Fellow's Hall.

June 3

Passed the forenoon in the Chancery Ct room. This afternoon there was speaking on Broad St., tonight at the Market House. The City is quite excited on the subject of the tax and if the citizens believe that the [$]300,000 asked for would build the road, they would vote for it, but they have but little confidence in the subscriptions in the lower counties and the second mortgage of the road.

June 4th

The election was carried today after the most vigorous effort on the part of the friends of the road. I noticed one remarkable feature in the election, viz. That those most active in favor of the subscription were either now property holders in the city, or property holders in the suburbs.

June 5

Attended the 1st Presbyterian Church this morning. Went to the Work House this evening.

June 6

Called to see Gov Harris this morning. He is in fine spirits and thinks that if the democrats will only make the proper exertions, that he will be re-elected by an increased majority.

June 7

Went out to Franklin today to hear the candidates for Gov. speak. Harris, I thought made decidedly the best speech.

June 8

Occupied the day in the City Hall.

June 9

Passed most of the day in attending to the affairs of the Corporation.

June 10

Occupied the day in the City Hall and on the streets.

June 11

This morning the citizens held a meeting at the Court House at which I presided and passed resolutions requesting the City Authorities to make the Chatham Artillery of Savannah, Ga. (who are expected here on Wednesday next) the guests of the City. I called the Council together this evening and they passed a resolution authorizing me to entertain the company at the expense of the City.

June 12

Did not go to church today, but remained at home reading etc.

June 13

The Board of Aldermen met this morning and adopted the resolution of the Common Council. Passed the day in the business of the Corporation.

June 14

Occupied the day at the City Hall.

June 15

The Chatham Artillery reached here this morning on their own train 40 m. past eight—and were met at the depot by the military of the City and immense concourse of citizens. Sam Godshall received them at the depot on behalf of the City. In the afternoon the Artillery fired salutes from Capitol Hill. After tea they called in a body on Mrs. Polk and gave her a serenade. Also gave a serenade at our house and then a number of beautiful rockets.

June 16th

This morning the Chatham Artillery accompanied by the military of the City—and a number of citizens made a visit to the Hermitage. I had two steamers lashed together and the party passed from one boat to the other. When we arrived at the Hermitage Dr Lawrence welcomed them. After examining the tomb and house the company fired minute guns and then returned to the boats, where Mr Dix had prepared a most bountiful lunch. We reached the City just before dark and were received by an immense concourse of citizens and saluted by Bill Cole, with his big gun. After supper we went to a ball given by the Germain Fargers at Harmonice Hall.

June 17

This morning the Artillery practiced and went through their various evolutions before an immense concourse of citizens. Returning to the city, St Clair Morgan had them at his home. At 3½ oc we all set down to a sumptuous dinner given at the City Hotel by myself as mayor of the City.

June 18th

Last night the Capitol was illuminated. I had the Chatham Artillery at my house last night. Went up with them this morning as far as Murfreesboro—and returned to city. Thus has terminated a succession of the most pleasant entertainments that we have ever had here in Nashville. I felt quite fatigued today.

June 19

From the telegraph today, it seems that another great battle has taken place near Mellan. The Austrians have evacuated that beautiful city. The losses on both sides estimated at over 35,000, greater than the whole population of Nashville. I did not go to church today but remained at home resting, etc.

June 20

Today I commenced to work in earnest on the streets, hauling gravel, etc. Mother had a very severe congestive chill today which alarmed us very much. She was delirious for six hours but we finally succeeded in relieving her.

June 21st

Dr Wm Nichol's wife was burried this morning. Mother is decidedly better today and I now hope that she will recover. Occupied the day in going over the city, and in sending Bright's oration on the life and character of Mr Grundy over the country.

June 22

Passed the day mostly on the streets. No news.

June 23

All day on the streets, and at the City Hall.

June 24

News reached here today that Grundy was very sick

June 25

This morning I called on Gen Burnett of N Y who has come out to get Gen. Jackson's snuff box[21] This evening my wife and self went up to Triune to see Grundy. Found him very sick with congestive fever.

June 26

This is an excessively warm day. Remained in doors nursing Grundy who is quite sick. Dr C Winston came up today from Nashville.

June 27

Dr Winston and my wife went home this morning, Grundy being decidedly better.

June 28

Occupied the entire day with Grundy who I think is now out of danger.

June 29

Started home this morning in the stage. At 3 oc I dined with Capt R C Foster.[22] Col Burnett of N Y was the honored guest. A merry crowd was around the board, and we had a delightful evening. The

---

[21] General Andrew Jackson was presented with a gold box by the city of New York in 1819. The gift so impressed Jackson that in his will he stipulated that at the close of the next war the box should go to the New York patriot "adjudged by his countrymen, or the ladies," to have been "most valiant in the defense of his country." The award was not made until August 18, 1859, the legatee being General Ward B. Burnett.

General Burnett entered West Point in 1828; became a second lieutenant; quit the army in 1836; returned to service at the outbreak of the Mexican War as colonel in command of the Second New York Volunteers; severely wounded; brevetted brigadier-general by President Polk.

[22] Robert Coleman Foster (1818-1871), soldier, was the son of Ephraim H. Foster. He commanded the Harrison Guards in the Mexican War; they being a part of the First Tennessee Regiment; appointed brigadier-general in the Tennessee military establishment during the Civil War; a bitter enemy of Jefferson Davis; Recorder of Nashville in 1866.

Commencement exercises of the Nashville University took place at the Capitol this evening. I was not present but understood that every thing went off well.

June 30

We had quite a storm this morning and a fire in the midst of it.

July 1st

Passed most of the day in the City Hall financeering to meet [$]11,000 that falls due in the different Banks tomorrow. Dr. Lindsley, Sallie and Mary started this morning for Europe. They sail from Boston on the 13th on the Steamer Arabia—and expect to be absent three months. I should like exceedingly to be in Europe myself at this time.

July 2nd

Received this morning by express from Savannah, Ga from the Chatham Artillery a handsome silver pitcher and waiter accompanied with a very complimentary letter. I succeeded in saving the Corporation from protest today.

July 3

Did not go to church today, feeling very bad from the effects of the dinner at St Clair Morgan's yesterday. I always feel bad after a regular dinner—not that I drink or eat too much, but the heated room and other things connected with a set dinner cause me to feel bad.

July 4

July 4th was ushered in by the merry peal of all the bells in the city, which rang again at noon and sunset. A great many excursion parties left the City, the business houses were all closed, and we had fire works at night.

July 5

Occupied the day at the City Hall. Tonight Fire Co No 1 received a splendid new engine which they escorted from the depot by a torch light procession. I went down to their Hall and made them a short speech, and gave them a toast. I left the company in a fine glee. Gov N S. Brown made a speech to the Netherland Club last night but was very much interrupted by the firemen's procession.

July 6

Occupied the morning in going over the city and the evening in my office.

July 7

All day in my office—no news.

July 8

Gen Zollicoffer comes out in a long letter this morning in response to a letter signed by a few foreigners, and opposes the doctrine promulgated by Gen Cass in his late letter on the subject of naturalization and perpetual allegiance.

July 9

Occupied the day in attending to the affairs of the Corporation.

July 10

Attended the 1st Presbyterian Church this morning. Drove out to Bosley's Spring this evening.

July 11

Occupied the forenoon in going over the City looking after the different hands at work for the Corporation. The election of the Directors of Nashville and North Western R R. came off today—and the old Board were re-elected, the County and City voting for Bird Douglass[23] for President, in the place of V K. Stevenson who triumphed over them. Indeed I consider Col Stevenson a remarkable man—particularly on R R subjects and in the management of men. He possesses an extraordinary degree of energy. This evening I called with my wife on Mr Conner and Mary who have just reached here from Charleston.

July 12

Jno G. Ferguson, a member of the bar, died very suddenly and unexpectedly this morning. The members of the bar held a meeting at the Court House. Several speeches were made, and resolutions adopted. Attended his funeral this evening. I heard today of the death of James Garvin of Louisville. He died in Philia, was enroute for Europe. He was my friend, a noble spirit, and a perfect gentleman.

July 13th

I went out to Franklin this morning for the purpose of appearing in horse case for Jno Bostick. The case was not reached. I returned home in the evening, after passing a most disagreeable day. The weather for several days past has been disagreeably hot.

July 14th

Father is quite ill today with an attack of bloody flux. Day is so intensely hot that it was impossible to do much.

---

[23] Byrd Douglas became an important figure in the business affairs of Nashville. In 1886 he was chosen President of the Tennessee Manufacturing Company. He was a member of the board of directors of both the Fourth National Bank and the American National Bank.

July 15

Detailed accounts of the battle of Salfereno have been received. The loss on both sides very great. Jas Woods,[24] Esq was burried today. He was a young man of some promise. The members of the bar held a meeting at the Ct House and passed resolutions, made speeches touching his memory. Called to see Sam Carpenter of Memphis, formerly of Bardstown Ky this evening.

July 16

Remained all day in my office, weather so intensely hot that it was disagreeable to be on the streets.

July 17th

Attended the 1st Presbyterian Church this morning. Dr Edgar has returned from Ky much improved in health.

July 18th

The weather continues intensely hot. Persons are sun struck every day in our streets. Laborers have ceased to work except in the cool of the evening and morning.

July 19

Occupied the day in matters pertaining to the interest of the Corporation. Weather continues very hot—many persons have died from the effects of the sun.

July 20

Occupied the day in business matters. Mr Young, father of Ed's wife, reached here today from Columbus Miss.

July 21

Occupied the day mostly in my office.

July 22

All day in attending to business. Heard Quarles speak at the Market House—and Menees on Broad St. Large crowd on Bd St I would not be surprised of Menees was elected.

July 23

St Clair Morgan made a speech tonight to the foreigners on the subject of naturalization the duty of the U S towards adopted citizens etc.

July 24

Col Bransford made a most excellent speech last night at N & C R R Depot on the subject of the currency. Attended the 1st Presbyterian

[24] James Woods (1825-1859), lawyer, was born in Davidson County, Tennessee. He graduated from the University of North Carolina, studied law in Lebanon, Tennessee, and began practice in Nashville in 1854.

Church this morning. Went out to the Mt. Vernon Gardens this evening in company with J K Howard, Dunnington, Poindexter. We remained until 9 o'clock.

July 25
Occupied the day in going over the City—and with committees. News reached here today that peace had been concluded—no particulars given.

July 26
I went last evening to hear And Ewing speak at the Chattanooga Depot on the currency and the foreign question. He had a large crowd, and made a good speech. Occupied the day in attending to the affairs of the Corporation.

July 27
Col Sandy Young left this morning for the Va Springs.

July 28
And Ewing, Nicholson and Geo Massey made speeches tonight to a large crowd on Bd St. The latter has heretofore acted with the Whig Party but finding out that he would likely be in a minority through life, abandoned the Whig ranks and proclaims himself a democrat.

July 29
Occupied the day in corporate affairs. House of Clarksville made a speech for the Opposition tonight—and Torbitt for the democrats. The excitement is getting quite high throughout the State.

July 30
Occupied the day mostly in my office. Jno C Burch of Chattanooga made a speech to the democrats tonight, and Ed Cooke of Franklin to the opposition.

July 31
I went out to Gen Harding's today with my wife, and remained all night.

Aug. 1st
Came to town this morning and occupied the day in business, returned in the evening to Gen Harding's

Aug 2
Occupied the day in business and returned again to Gen Harding's.

Aug 3
Passed the day in business—returned to Gen Harding's at night. Jno Bell made a speech tonight.

Aug 4

This is election day—great excitement. Opposition made desperate efforts in the City but gained only 46 votes.

Aug 5

The news comes in favorable to the Opposition, who have made large gains in nearly every county heard from.

Aug 6

News conflicting this morning. Difficult to say who has the day.

Aug 7

Attended the Presbyterian church this morning. Dr. Edgar gave out that the congregation would meet on Tuesday next for the purpose of electing an assistant clergyman. Dr E is getting too old and infirm to discharge the duties of the church.

Aug 8

Occupied the day in business matters. This afternoon I went out to Gen Harding's with Randal Gibson of La. The opposition party had a great gloryfication tonight over their recent victory. They have elected seven members of Congress. Democratic Gov elected by about nine thousand, both branches of the legislature democratic.

Aug. 9

Occupied the day in the affairs of the City. Board of Aldermen met this evening.

Aug. 10

Occupied most of the day in reading. This is my 33rd birthday. Times pass away rapidly. I am now in the meridian of life.

Aug. 11

Attended a meeting of a committee at the Court House this morning for the purpose of making preparations for a barbecue to be given to the people of Bowling Green, Ky. The R R is just completed to that point, and our citizens calculate on reaping benifits from the trade of that region.

Aug. 12

Occupied the day in attending to the affairs of the Corporation. The subscribers to the new hotel met this evening and appointed Jno

Kirkman[25] and S D Morgan Commissioners to act on their behalf. I presume the work will soon be commenced.[26]

Aug. 13

The election for Attorney Gen and Rep of the State was held today. There are eight candidates, and it is hard to say who will be elected.

Aug. 14

Attended church this morning at the 1st Presbyterian, and this evening at the Work House. Rev J B McFerrin[27] preached a most effective sermon to the inmates of that establishment.

Aug. 15

Godfrey M. Fogg and S N. Hollingsworth[28] are announced as candidates for Mayor this morning. I understood that Bee Clements will be a candidate in a few days. Occupied the day in going over the city, and attending to my official business.

Aug. 16

Passed the day in my office. Bee Clemons is again a candidate for Mayor, also W P. Downs.[29] The Opposition papers talk of making a party question—holding a convention and having only one candidate.

Aug. 17

Occupied the day in the Criminal Court Room where the Battles are being tried for the murder of young Owen of Williamson last fall at the Fair Grounds. I presume they will be acquited.

---

25 John Kirkman (d. 1888) was a Nashville banker. He was a director of the Third National Bank. In 1884 he became President of the American National Bank. His generosity caused him to allow the congregation of the Church of the Advent to meet in the Odd Fellow's Hall, which he owned, before they erected a church of their own. He was killed on Broad Street in Nashville by a runaway horse.

26 The Maxwell House.

27 John Berry McFerrin (1807-1887), Methodist preacher, was born in Rutherford County, Tennessee. He was admitted to the Tennessee Conference in 1825; ordained deacon in 1827, and elder in 1829; became editor of the *Southwestern Christian Advocate* in Nashville in 1840; assumed charge of the publishing interests of the Methodist Episcopal Church, South in 1858; in charge of Methodist missionary work in the Army of Tennessee during the Civil War; elected Secretary of the Board of Domestic Missions in 1866, and from 1870 to 1878 directed the work of both domestic and foreign missions. During the period from 1878 to 1887, through careful management, he placed the finances of the Methodist Publishing House on a sound basis. His most notable literary contribution was a three volume *History of Methodism in Tennessee* (Nashville, 1869-1873).

28 S. N. Hollingsworth, Nashville politician. He was a member of the board of aldermen in 1858 and Mayor of Nashville in 1859. In 1859 he was one of a committee which edited the *Opposition,* a weekly campaign paper published in the interest of Colonel John Netherland in his struggle for the governorship against Isham G. Harris.

29 W. P. Downs was member of the board of aldermen of Nashville in 1850, 1853, 1855, and 1857.

Aug. 18

Occupied most of the day on the streets attending to official duties. I intended going to Fayetteville tonight, for the purpose of attending a barbecue to be given there tomorrow—upon the completion of the R R to that place but something turned up to prevent my going. The gold snuff box presented to Gen Jackson by the City of N Y was in compliance with his will awarded to Gen Burnett of N. Y today at the City Hall. I presided over the meeting. Dr Jno M Lawrence represented Col Andrew Jackson, and Gen Gideon J Pillow represented Gen Burnett. Speeches were made, and the crowd all took a pinch of snuff out of the box. I believe there was some pepper in the snuff, from the amount of sneezing, etc.

Aug. 19th

From the official returns it appears that Jno. W. Head[30] of Sumner is elected Attorney Gen and Reporter of the State.

Aug 20

Occupied the day in Mayor's Office and in attending to official duties.

Aug. 21

Attended the 1st Presbyterian Church this morning. This evening I went to hear Dr Quintard at the Work House.

Aug. 22

Passed the day in going over the City examining the work I have going on.

Aug. 23

No news today.

Aug. 24

All day on the streets.

Aug. 25

Occupied the day in reading, and attending to business.

Aug 26

All day in my office.

Aug. 27

Occupied the forenoon on the streets. This afternoon I made a visit to Col MacGavock's with my wife, where I found Mrs Young of La., formerly Harriett Guin, an old flame of mine. She looks very well, and I think will marry again.

---

[30] John W. Head served as Attorney General of Tennessee from this date until the outbreak of the Civil War.

Aug. 28

The day has been so inclement that we did not go into church. This evening Cousin Jno and myself went over to Cousin James'. He is one of the fattest men I ever saw and suffers much with croup.

Aug 29

Returned to the City this morning. Occupied the day in business matters. This [afternoon] I attended the funeral of Mr Ellis' child, an infant about one year old.

Aug. 30

This is the day of the Opposition Jubilee. I went out to Watkins' Grove in company with Gov Harris, Jno K. Howard, and Dunnington. There were about 4000 persons assembled. Emerson Etheridge[31] was the lion of the occasion. He made a speech of about two hours in length. I was disapointed in him, having heard so much about him. I consider him a third rate man. Jno Netherland followed and then N S. Brown. They had a large bell drawn through the streets on a wagon, which was rung most violently all the day and all night much to the annoyance of every one. Jno Bell is their man for the next Presidency, but they will be disappointed—the Black Republicans will want a man of their own. Tonight they had a torch light procession and speaking at the City Hotel. This is the first jubilee over a defeat that I ever heard of.

Aug 31

Occupied the forenoon in going over the City—examining the work going on in different directions. My official term as Mayor of Nashville expires in one month, and I wish to accomplish as much as possible on the streets.

Sept. 1st

Occupied the day in attending to the affairs of the Corporation.

Sept 2nd

Passed the day mostly on the streets, overlooking work etc.

Sept 3rd

All day attending to business matters.

---

[31] Emerson Etheridge (1818-1902), orator and statesman, was a native of North Carolina. He began the practice of law in Dresden, Tennessee in 1840; a member of the State House of Representatives 1845-1847; elected as a Whig to the Thirty-third, Thirty-fourth and Thirty-sixth Congresses; served as Clerk of the National House of Representatives 1861-1863; a member of the State Senate 1869-1870; Surveyor of Customs in Memphis 1891-1894.

Sept 4th

Attended divine service at the Work House this evening—service by Dr Hayes.[32]

Sept 5th

Mr S N. Hollingsworth, one of the candidates for Mayor, is out this morning in a card calling for a Convention to nominate a candidate. He is getting alarmed and thinks that if he can secure the nomination he can walk over the track without difficulty.

Sept. 6th

This is the day for the grand R R Jubilee given by the citizens of this county and city to the people of Ky upon the completion of the road to Bowling Green. At 9 oc the procession moved over the bridge to depot and escorted the Ky-ans to a beautiful grove in Edgefield. There was at least 10,000 persons present. The barbacue was the best I ever saw, and every thing went off well. Gen Barrow made the welcoming speech —and was followed by Gov Helm, the President of the road. Mr Thomas L Bransford and a gentleman from Ky [John Finn of Frankfort] whose name I did not hear, also made speeches. In the evening there was mass ball in the Court House. The business houses around the square were illuminated, also the Capitol.

Sept. 7

This morning the Mayor of Louisville,[33] several members of the City Council and some ladies arrived. I called to see them and accompanied them to the Capitol, State Prison, and Col Acklin's. In the afternoon they drove to Gen Harding's. After tea I had a wine party at my house, and invited our City Council to meet them.

Sept. 8

The Louisville delegation returned home this morning, much gratified with their visit. Occupied the day mostly at the City Hall.

Sept. 9

Occupied the entire day in business matters.

Sept. 10

The opposition Convention met this morning and nominated S N. Hollingsworth as their candidate for Mayor. The names of G M. Fogg, Gen Zollicoffer, and Thos Smiley were in nomination. The nomination does not give satisfaction and I think will be defeated.

---

[32] Rev. John S. Hayes, pastor of the Second Presbyterian Church of Nashville, Tennessee, 1857-1861.

[33] Thomas H. Crawford, Mayor of Louisville in 1859 and 1860.

Sept. 11

Did not go to church this morning, but remained in my office, reading and writing. Attended service at the Work House this evening by Dr T O. Summers.[34]

Sept. 12

Occupied the day in attending to the affairs of the Corporation.

Sept. 13

Passed most of the day at the City Hall and in going over the streets examining work etc.

Sept. 14

Today there was another call upon me to run again for Mayor, and numerous persons of the opposition party have solicited me to run, but after weighing the whole matter deliberately, I resolve not to become a candidate.

Sept. 15

It is generally understood today that Jno Hugh Smith will run against Hollingsworth. I went out tonight to Slade's in the 7th Ward to hear them speak. The crowd was small and seemed to be for Hollingsworth.

Sept. 16

Occupied the day in business matters. Tonight I went out to hear the candidates speak in the 8th Ward. While Hollingsworth was speaking, a man on the opposite side of the street called for me, and said that I had made the best Mayor Nashville ever had, and he intended voting for me anyhow.

Sept. 17

Passed the day mostly in my office. Took a game of ucre with Rice, Thompson, and Bostick this evening.

Sept. 18

Attended the first Presbyterian Church this morning and service at the Work House this afternoon. At 8 oc I started on the cars for Fayetteville to attend a R R meeting.

[34] Thomas Osmond Summers (1812-1882), Methodist clergyman and editor was born near Corfe Castle, Isle of Purbeck, Dorsetshire, England and emigrated to the United States in 1830. He entered the Methodist ministry in 1835; ordained elder in 1839; Secretary of the General Convention which met in Louisville, Kentucky in 1845, which organized the Methodist Episcopal Church, South; moved to Nashville, Tennessee in 1850 as Book Editor of the Church; editor of the *Sunday School Visitor* 1851-1856, of the *Quarterly Review of the Methodist Episcopal Church, South* 1858-1861 and 1879, and of the *Christian Advocate* 1868-1878. In 1878 he became Dean and Professor of Systematic Theology at Vanderbilt University.

Sept. 19

Passed the night at Decherd. Reached Fayetteville at 11:30 oc. There was quite a large number of the stockholders of the Winchester and Ala R R present and the object of the meeting was to take into consideration a proposition to lease the road for ten years to the Nashville and Chattanooga R R Co. A great deal of feeling was manifested about the matter, and I think they were almost unanimous against it. Frank Estille, Jno Bright, and myself made speeches. I cast the vote of the Corporation for the lease. I saw my *old friend,* Dr Bonner and Geo W. Jones. I sat down to the meanest quarter dollar dinner I ever saw and what made it worse the hotel keeper is the Mayor of the town. I felt a little mortified that he did [not] extend to me the freedom of his town. About half way between Fayetteville and Winchester my attention was directed to a slate bank just under the R R road which has been burning for six months. The smoke and smell arising from it is exceedingly disagreeable. An Irish laborer dropped his pipe there which produced the ignition. Reached home about 12 oc tonight.

Sept. 20th

All the papers are filled with articles about the Mayorality. The excitement is growing warm. Dr Lindsley, Sallie, and Mary reached New York from Europe yesterday. I saw Dr Jno Foster of New Orleans this morning. He is looking well.

Sept. 22

Occupied the day at the City Hall and on the streets looking after the work going on for the Corporation.

Sept. 23

The canvass is getting quite warm and the contestants very bitter.

Sept. 24

Hollingsworth was elected today over Smith by a majority of only twenty two. Smith and Mat Brown had a fight just after the polls closed about some remark Smith made in his speech last night at the Market House.

Sept. 25

I did not go to church today, but remained at home reading.

Sept. 26

Occupied the day mostly at the City Hall.

Sept. 27

The Board of Aldermen had a meeting this evening. Occupied most of the day in my office writing my last message to the Board, giving a brief history of the past year's work.

Sept. 28

All day in my office writing, and attending to business.

Sept. 29

Passed the day in my office writing.

Sept. 30

This afternoon the two boards met in convention for the last time, and I read them quite a lengthy message, giving a summary of the year's work. The board passed a resolution thanking me for the manner in which I had discharged the duties of the Mayoralty.

CHAPTER XXI

"The scene was most impressive and distressing to an old Democrat." (1859-1860)

Once he had been relieved of the responsibilities of the Nashville mayorship, Randal McGavock began to take a more active part in national political affairs. In April, 1860, he was a delegate to the Democratic national convention in Charleston, South Carolina. The following June he was again a Democratic delegate, this time to the national convention in Baltimore. In this section of his journal, covering the period October 1, 1859, through September 30, 1860, McGavock's political feelings were alternately those of hope and frustration. He senses the development of the secession movement and provides many interesting insights into the gathering clouds that threaten national unity.

Oct. 1st

The new Mayor and Board were sworn in today and the inaugural of the Mayor read. I thought it a poor affair. This is the day for the greatest democratic Jubilee, but the weather is so inclement that we have given it up. The barbacue was given to me this morning, and I had it distributed to the Poor of the City. This afternoon we had [a] speaking in the third story of the Court House. Gov Harris made the first speech, which was nothing more than a rehash of his canvas speech. He was followed by Gov Guild Thomas Avery, Finn of Ky and Haynes of Memphis. After tea a large crowd assembled at the Capitol where we had fine music and fire works. A O P. Nicholson made a most able and statesman-like speech which was listened to with great attention. He was followed by Geo W. Jones, Watterson, and others.

Oct. 2nd

Did not go to church this morning but remained at home. This afternoon I walked out with G M Fogg to R Houston's place in West Nashville. After tea I attended prayer meeting at the 1st Presbyterian Church.

Oct. 3rd

The legislature of the State convened this morning and made their organization. Whitthorne of Maury was elected Speaker of the House and Newman of Franklin, Speaker of the Senate. The ancient order of A.O.M.C. had a torchlight procession tonight. There was three or four hundred in the procession—all dressed in white gowns and black cowls, except three—one of whom was in black—one in a spangled uniform, and one with a sythe on his shoulder was dressed very uniquely. The transparences were very beautiful and the whole city turned out to see them.

Oct. 4th

Attended the Circuit Court today. Wm Ewing and wife dined at our house today. She is quite an accomplished lady.

Oct 5th

Attended the Circuit today.

Oct 6th

Gov Harris' message was sent in to the Legislature this morning. His position on the Banks is extremely hard. He wants to throw around the Charters all the restrictions possible. Some of the democrats are opposed to him on this matter and an effort is being made to establish another democratic paper here.

Oct. 7

Attended the Circuit Court this morning.

Oct. 8th

Nothing worth noting today. I attended the Circuit Court.

Oct. 9

Attended the 1st Presbyterian Church this morning and heard a very excellent sermon from Dr Bardwell, who has been employed to assist Dr Edgar. This evening I heard an excellent discourse from Mr Rhea, a Missionary in Persia. He is a native of Sullivan Co Ten and has been in Persia eight years.

Oct. 10

Went out to the State Fair this morning and stayed all day. The exhibition of horses and cattle was very good but the crowd was small. After tea I attended the Planters' Convention at the Capitol. The object of the convention is to create a common interest among the planters of the South, and the several States to send delegates to a Convention annually. Four or five States were represented, and several very important subjects discussed—among others was some resolutions offered by Mr Sterling Cockrell requesting the President of the U S to send Lieutenant Maury[1] with a corps of Engineers to the Miss Valley and make a survey from the mouth up to St. Louis—for the purpose of ascertaining the character of the winds and currents on the river and the practicability of reclaiming the bottoms of that great valley. After leaving the Convention I went with Knox Walker to his room at the St Cloud and discussed the matter of starting another democratic paper in Nashville.

Oct. 11

Went out to the Fair again today. The crowd was very great, assembled principally to Lieutenant Maury' address. The exhibition of stock was very fine, but the chief attraction to me was the Floral Hall, which has been recently erected. A beautiful fountain occupies the centre and the floor was filled with exquisite—and rare flowers. In the second story there were numerous articles of art and virtue. Dr Lindsley returned with Sallie and Mary from Europe last night, after an absence of three months. They say that they had a delightful trip. This evening I called on Col Cave Johnson with Mr Faverly of Memphis and urged him to withdraw his declension to act as President of the Bank of Tennessee. He consented.

Oct. 12

Occupied the day mostly in business matters. Attended the Circuit Court and the legislature this morning. Attended the Theatre this evening. [James E.] Murdock appeared as Richlieu.

Oct. 13

I went out to the Fair this morning and staid a short time. The crowd was greater than on Tuesday, and I think the greatest I ever saw on the grounds. This evening I attended the Fair given by the ladies of the

[1] Matthew Fontaine Maury (1806-1873), naval officer, scientist, was a native of Virginia but moved with his family to Franklin, Tennessee at the age of five. He was given the rank of lieutenant in the navy in 1836, after having experienced considerable sea duty. His extensive oceanographic observations culminated in 1855 in the publication of *The Physical Geography of the Sea,* the first textbook of modern oceanography. Through this work and countless other writings he gained a world wide reputation. During the Civil War he was a commander in the Confederate Navy, but spent the greater part of his time representing his government in England and experimenting with electric mines. He remained in England until 1868, returning to accept the Professorship of Meteorology in the Virginia Military Institute at Lexington.

Orphan Asylum. I also attended the City Council being interested in the elections held. All of the old officers were retained.

Oct. 14th

Occupied the day in attending to business, and in endeavoring to buy out the Daily News—expecting to convert it into a democratic sheet.

Oct. 15

Went out to the Fair and passed most of the day. The exhibition of stock I did not think very much of. The bull stock and some few horses were quite creditable but taking the whole affair it was not equal to what the county ought to have, let alone the State.

Oct. 16

Attended the 1st Presbyterian Church this morning.

Oct. 17

Occupied the day mostly in my office reading. This afternoon I went out to Elliston's and acted as a juryman to change a road.

Oct. 18

The telegraph brings news this morning of an insurrection at Harper's Ferry, Va. A man named Brown[2] of Kansas noteriety was at the head of it. A number of negroes were engaged in it. Most of them were arrested and some killed. The US Circuit Court is in session at the Capitol. This evening I went with my wife and Miss Josephine Porter to the Theater. Murdock appeared as Othello—and Mr Keeble as Iago. Both played their parts well. I attended the sale of the Balch property today—all of which is under water at high tide. The prices were several times greater than I expected, ranging from 15 to 50 dollars per foot. I saw a calliope on wheels today belonging to a circus. The music was anything but agreeable, being harsh and unmelodious. Being a novelty it attracted much attention.

Oct. 19th

Occupied the day mostly in my office reading.

Oct. 20

Attended the sale of property in Balch's Addition yesterday. Every foot of the ground is under water at high tide, yet the prices ranged from 15 to 50 dollars per foot. This owing to the fact that three railroad depots have been recently located in that vicinity.

[2] John Brown (1800-1859), of Osawatomie, one of the most rabid of the abolitionists.

Oct. 21

Occupied the day mostly in my office. No news.

Oct. 22

Occupied the day mostly in my office, reading etc.

Oct. 23

Attended the 1st Presbyterian Church today, and heard a very good Sermon from Dr Bardwell. This evening I heard a very good sermon from Philip Thompson—one of my early friends. He studied and practiced law for a while, but has recently turned preacher. I hope that he may succeed. I always feel a deep interest in the success of my early friends and associates.

Oct. 24th

Occupied the day mostly in my office reading. Recd. a Columbus paper from Judge Dickinson tonight containing a very able exposition of the territorial question now agitating the public mind. He is now purely in the democratic ranks—and I hope he may be elevated to a position commensurate with his abilities and his deserts.

Oct. 25

Passed the day mostly in my office. Gov Harris sent into the legislature today an entirely new Board of Directors. All of them are democrats, but not so good a board as the present one. I think the Gov has taken upon himself a great responsibility in turning out Col Johnson and placing over him a man that has no claims upon the democratic party. After tea I heard an Irish Wake just back of the Post Office. The women made a great noise. Gov Harris, Eastman, Watterson and myself had a game of ucre.

Oct. 26

I went up to the Capitol today and remained a short time—nothing of interest going on there.

Oct. 27

Occupied the forenoon in my office reading. This afternoon I rode over to Edgefield—which is improving rapidly. The first train from Louisville reached here this afternoon. A large number of the citizens of Louisville came over.

Oct. 28th

Called this morning on Mayor Crawford of Louisville, Jas Guthrie, Wm Garvin and others. This evening Mr Bass gave an entertainment to the gentlemen from Louisville. I was present and enjoyed myself very much. The democratic portion of the delegation are warm for Guthrie for the next Presidency.

Oct. 29

The Louisville delegation left for home this morning. I occupied the day mostly in my office. Hon Jas C. Jones died today at his residence in Memphis.

Oct. 30

Attended the 1st Presbyterian Church today. Dr. Edgar was unusually animated and delivered an excellent discourse. I saw Alex Porter this evening who has just arrived from Philia where he intends living for several years. I regret that his wife's health compells him to leave here, as he is one of the most companionable gentlemen we have.

Oct. 31

The legislature adjourned today on account of the death of Gov Jones. I received tonight through the mail a copy of Mangan's Poems with a preface by Jno Mitchell. I ran through it, and found several interesting pieces.

Nov. 1st

Occupied the day mostly in my office reading.

Nov. 2

Passed the day in my office. Wrote a piece for the Gazette about turning out of the Bank Directory.

Nov. 3

Passed the day in my office. Went out to Alex Porter's to dinner. Rice, Cooper, and a young gentleman from N Y were there. Drove in late in the evening. Gov Harris was inaugurated this morning at the Capitol and an attempt at Fire Works was made this evening in honor of the occasion.

Nov. 4

Brown, the insurrectionist was sentenced to be hung on the 2nd of Dec next. Sold my mares today to McMurry for 80 feet of ground in Harding's Addition and gave him [$]350 besides. I commenced reading Randall's Life of Jefferson today.

Nov. 5

Grundy started to Ark today with his family on the Jno Fisher. Occupied the day mostly in my office.

Nov. 6

Attended the 1st Presbyterian Church this morning—service by Mr Bardwell. We have delightful weather now.

Nov. 7

The Chancery Court met this morning. The Medical School of the Nashville University held their commencement this morning at the Theatre—lecture by Dr Winston. The school opens with 340 students, the largest number ever in attendance at the beginning of the session. A young lawyer named Eastman from Concord N H. came into my office today. I passed the evening very pleasantly at Ann Waters'.

Nov. 8

Occupied the day mostly in my office reading.

Nov. 9

Attended the Chancery Court this morning, and passed the remainder of the day in my office.

Nov. 10

All day in my office.

Nov. 11

At ten o'clock today Wm H. Gordon and myself left Nashville for our farm in Sullivan Co Ten carrying with us a pair of Cootswool [Cotswold] sheep and a pair of Essex pigs.

Nov. 12th

Reached Bristol at 10 oc where we met Mr Hughes, our overseer, who went with us to the farm.

Nov. 13

Occupied the day in going over the farm with Gordon. He never saw it before, and is very much pleased.

Nov. 14

Went to Bristol this morning and took the train for Jonesboro.

Nov. 15

Occupied the day in the Chancery Court Room. Our case was continued until the next term. This evening Gordon started for Nashville, and I returned to Bristol.

Nov. 16

Passed the day in going over the farm looking at the stock which are all in good condition, and watching the hands splitting rails.

Nov. 17

Mr Hughes started out this morning in search of young mules, wishing to increase our stock, having a surplus of food for the winter.

Nov. 18

Occupied the day on the farm.

Nov. 19

Occupied the day in selecting sites for barns, orchards, and dwellings.

Nov. 20

Passed the day in reading Randall's Life of Jefferson, which I find very interesting.

Nov. 21

I rode into Blountsville this morning with Mr Rhea. I found the Chancery and Circuit Courts both in session. Judge Gaut[3] of Athens was presiding in the latter. The Court Room was crowded to overflow to witness the trial of Billy Waters, a dwarf who killed a man named Cup last May at Union. Waters and his brother and two old sisters were all in the room, and I am certain that I never saw such a collection of lilliputians before. The case is a very agrevated one and I would not be surprised if the jury found him guilty. Billy Water's wife is a large fine looking woman and has two children that Waters says are his. I met Geo R. McClelland of this county who is just from Nashville and who informed me of the death of Geo Poindexter. He was shot on Friday last in the street by Allen A Hall with a double barrelled shot gun. The difficulty arose out of a newspaper controversy. This is sad news indeed. Poindexter was a young man of promise and ability and his loss will be seriously felt by the Democratic party of Ten. There is a great deal of excitement in Va about the Harper's Ferry insurrection. Companies are forming all over the state and I fear something serious will result yet. I returned to the farm this evening.

Nov. 22

Passed the day on the farm.

Nov. 23

Went into Blountsville again today and found the case of Waters still up. I heard Deaderick's speech and Matt Harper opening. I should have liked very much hearing L Hayes and Thos Nelson as they are both very able and eloquent, but it was necessary to return to the farm.

---

[3] John Conaway Gaut, attorney, was born in Jefferson County, Tennessee in 1813. He studied law in Athens and began practice in Cleveland, Tennessee in 1838; Circuit Judge of his district 1853-1865; resumed practice of law in Nashville. He was a leader in the building of the East Tennessee and Georgia Railroad.

Nov. 24

Occupied the day on the farm.

Nov. 25

Mr. Hughes and myself went down on the Holston today in search of mules but we had a hard days ride and no success.

Nov. 26

Went into Bristol this morning, and learned from the Postmaster that E G. Eastman, Editor of the Union and American, was dead. He died last Tuesday night of apoplexy. This is truly a lamentable loss. He was one of the most useful men in the State. The democratic party loses one of her oldest and best editors, the cause of agriculture one of its main supporters, the city of Nashville one of its most enterprising men, and his family a kind and good father and husband. The death of the two Editors of the Union and American in such rapid succession will cause a material change in the paper.

Nov. 27th

This morning I took two negro boys and a man named Gadsey, who is working on the farm, and explored a Cave on the place. I found two domes, several avenues, and some very pretty formations. The day has been so inclement that I have remained indoors.

Nov. 28

Occupied the forenoon on the farm. This evening I went into Bristol, and left on the cars at 11 oc tonight for Mac's Meadow Wythe Co Va.

Nov. 29

Reached Uncle Randal's at 3½ oc this morning, and woke Hugh Ewing up, who conducted me to a room, where I had a good nap. I found all of the family well. Gordon Kent came over soon after breakfast, and invited me to dine with him. After dinner Hugh and myself rode over to Fort Chiswell and returned to Uncle Randal's after dark.

Nov. 30

I left Mac's Meadow before day this morning for Washington. At Liberty I met Jno V Wright and lady of Ten. The country of the Roanoke valley is very beautiful and rich, a great deal of meadow land. Lynchburg is not a very handsome town. The situation is lofty and rugged and the houses look old. After leaving Lynchburg the lands become poorer and I saw many fields turned out or abandoned, being grown up in pine. At Lynchburg the canal crosses the river, and the railroad the canal, one above another. Nearly every village through which we passed today I heard the drum and fife, and saw men with guns in hand. They are holding themselves in readiness in case of an invasion on the part of the abolitionists. It is supposed that an attempt will be made on Friday next to rescue old Jno Brown, but I apprehend that no man has entertained a serious thought on the subject. All Va is thoroughly aroused and I think it very well, as she has been asleep on the subject too long already.

Dec. 1

Reached Washington before day this morning and stopped at Brown's Hotel. Wm Churchwell and M McClusky called to see me. I have met during the day a great many members of Congress and old acquaintances. Called on Dr Harvey Lindsley.[4]

Dec. 2

Jno Brown of Harper's Ferry notoriety was hung today at Charlestown. Everything went off quietly, and was conducted with the most perfect military precision. I understand that Gov. Wise had some fifteen hundred or two thousand men under arms. His body was given to his wife who carried it to N. Y. The abolitionists are holding prayer meetings in the northern States today. A great deal of excitement prevails all over the country. I called to see Mr and Mrs Churchwell today. They are living at the Lafayette House. Passed the evening at the National Hotel in Mr Wm Duran's room of Philia where I met a number of Pennsylvanians and among them a gentleman named Jno H Filler of Bedford, Penn B R who was taken out of the cars at Harper's Ferry while on his way to Charlestown to see old Brown hung. His account of the attentions that he received from the military was highly amusing.

Dec. 3

Most of the members have arrived, and a great deal of caucassing and bargaining going on among the different parties. I went over to the Smithsonian Institute to see Prof Henry in regard to having some sulphur water I brought from the farm analyzed. Met with E J Morris[5] of Philadelphia who was Minister to Naples while I was there. The democratic members nominated Mr Bocock[6] of Va for Speaker tonight, but made no other nominations. I passed the evening with Mrs Jno V. Wright who I find a most charming lady.

---

[4] Harvey Lindsley, brother of Philip and V. S. Lindsley. He was a prominent physician in Washington, D.C.

[5] Edward Jay Morris (1815-1881), Congressman, diplomat.

[6] Thomas Stanley Bocock (1815-1891), lawyer, Congressman.

Dec. 4

This morning was so very inclement that I did not go to church but remained in Col Nelson's room. Took dinner with Churchwell and wife. This evening I met Jas Guthrie and Geo Caldwell[7] of Louisville. The latter is a member of the National Democratic Committee, and is decidedly for Jas. Guthrie for President. We went together over to the National to see Mr Pratt,[8] the member for Ct. He gives a good account of the sentiments of the conservative people of the North in regard to the Jno Brown affair—and thinks if the thing is properly managed it will break down the Republican Party of the North.

Dec. 5

Congress met this morning at 12 oc. The Black Republicans nominated Jno Sherman[9] of Ohio for Speaker. The democrats, Mr Bocock of Va and the Opposition South, Mr Gilmer[10] of N C. Mr Clark[11] of Mo offered a resolution, the purport of which was that no man who endorsed the Helper book[12] was fit to be Speaker. The excitement was very great. No election.

Dec. 6

Congress met again this morning, excitement very great. The battle is between the Black Republicans and the democrats. The Opposition South have but little to say, occupying as they do an awkward position. They cannot vote with the B R since the Jno Brown foray, as that would be political suicide, and they cannot go with the democrats as that would be giving up everything. Clark's resolution was under discussion in the House and Mason's Resolution in the Senate.[13]

---

[7] George Alfred Caldwell (1814-1866), lawyer, soldier, Congressman from Kentucky.

[8] James Timothy Pratt (1802-1887), business man, politician.

[9] John Sherman (1823-1900), statesman.

[10] John Adams Gilmer (1805-1868), lawyer, Congressman.

[11] John Bullock Clark (1802-1885), lawyer, soldier, Congressman.

[12] Hinton Rowan Helper, *Impending Crisis of the South,* published at New York in 1857, was an economic appeal to the non-slaveholders of the South. The author, a North Carolinian of the small-farmer class, used the census reports of 1790 and 1850 to contrast the Northern and Southern states, thus showing that the South, with slave labor, was unable to keep pace with the "free" North. It was widely circulated as Republican campaign literature, and its endorsement by John Sherman was a factor in his defeat for the speakership.

[13] Representative John B. Clark of Missouri offered the following resolution December 5, 1859; "Resolved, That the doctrines and sentiments of a certain book, called 'The Impending Crisis of the South—How to meet it,' purporting to have been written by one Hinton R. Helper, are insurrectionary and hostile to the domestic peace and tranquility of the country, and that no member of this House who has indorsed and recommended it, or the compend from it, is fit for Speaker of this House."

Senator James M. Mason of Virginia introduced a resolution requesting the appointment of a committee to examine the facts, character, and extent of John Brown's raid at Harper's Ferry, Virginia.

Dec. 7

The debate on the two resolutions continued today. The Southerners threaten disunion if a Black Republican President is elected. The conservative men of the North have begun to move in view of the impending dangers, and are calling Union meetings in the principal cities. The Democratic National Committee met at 12 oc at Willard's Hotel, and adjourned until 7½ this evening, at which hour they assembled. All of the States were represented except Ga Ala and Md. The 23rd of April was fixed upon as the day for holding the Convention at Charleston SoC. Nearly every man expressed an opinion as to the condition of things in his own State, and from what I could gather the democratic party is yet sound in all the great questions, and if we only manage things rightly we can carry the next Presidential election—and thereby bring quiet to our distracted land.

Dec. 8

I attended the debates in both branches of Congress today. No Speaker and no probability soon. I went up to Capitol with Mr Morris of Philia whose acquaintance I made in Naples in the year 1851.

Dec. 9

I went up to the Capitol with Mrs Wright of Ten Nelson[14] of Ten and Pryor[15] of Va had some sparring today, in which the latter got worsted.

Dec. 10th

Attended the debates in Congress today. No speaker—excitement still up at the highest point. We had a fire at Brown's Hotel tonight which alarmed the inmates very much.

Dec. 11

I did not go to church this morning on account of the inclement weather. I started home this evening, by way of the Baltimore and Ohio R R. When we reached Harper's Ferry I went out and examined the bridge, the Armory, and the Engine House that old Jno Brown took possession of. I had a good night's rest in the sleeping car.

Dec. 12

Stopped this morning at the Louisville Hotel where I met Geo Caldwell, Mr Steel and family. May Crawford called to see me and we

[14] Thomas Amis Rogers Nelson (1812-1873), lawyer, Congressman from Tennessee, was born in Kingston, Tennessee. He served two terms as Attorney General of the First Judicial District; elected as a Unionist to Congress 1859-1861; reelected, but captured by Confederate scouts while en route to Washington and not allowed to serve. He was a Union sympathizer and was one of the counsels who defended President Andrew Johnson in his impeachment trial in 1868. He was Judge of the State Supreme Court 1870-1871.

[15] Roger Atkinson Pryor (1828-1919), lawyer, congressman.

went together to see the great Artesian Well, which is 2200 feet deep. The water tastes brackish, and is much used for bathing. It is certainly a great curiosity. Dined with Geo Caldwell and took tea with Levin Shrivers—where I passed a delightful evening.

Dec. 14

Started to Nashville on the cars at 5 oc with Mrs. Baker and two children in charge from San Francisco. Met Ballie Peyton[16] on the cars who is just from California after a long absence.

Dec. 15

Found my wife and the family all well. Occupied the day in my office.

Dec. 16

Passed the day in my office. Tom Craighead had a reception at Carter's today. He was married to Puss Carter Thursday night. Mrs Porter reached home today from Columbus.

Dec. 17

Occupied the day in my office. Dined at Mrs Porter's with Dr Humphries[17] of Danville, Ky. and Mr Bardwell.

Dec. 18th

Attended church at the 1st Presbyterian. Dr Humphries preached. Went this evening to see Mrs Bass and family.

Dec. 19

Occupied the day in business matters. A very deep snow fell this evening.

Dec. 20

I notice that they have not made a Speaker yet in Congress. Mr Bocock of Va withdrew yesterday. I attended a party this evening at old Mrs Craighead's given to Tom and his bride.

Dec. 21

Occupied the day in my office reading, and attending to business.

Dec. 22

Passed the day in my office.

---

[16] Bailie Peyton (1803-1878), lawyer, soldier, diplomat, was born near Gallatin, Tennessee. He served as a Whig in Congress 1833-1837; practiced law for a time; moved to New Orleans in 1841; United States Attorney for the eastern district of Louisiana 1841-1845; served with distinction in the Mexican War; Minister to Chile 1849-1853; moved to San Francisco in 1853; practiced law; returned to Gallatin, Tennessee in 1859; a member of the State Senate of Tennessee 1869-1870.

[17] Edward Porter Humphrey, Presbyterian clergyman.

Dec. 23
Passed the day in my office reading.

Dec. 24
Occupied the day in business matters.

Dec. 25
Attended the 1st Presbyterian Church this morning. Dull Christmas.

Dec. 26
Passed the forenoon in my office. This afternoon I passed with a party of gentlemen playing ucre, and drinking wine.

Dec. 27
Passed the day in attending to business.

Dec. 28
I rode out this morning to examine a piece of land belonging to Wm H. Gordon with the view of making a trade. The balance of the day has been passed in business matters.

Dec. 29
Occupied the day in business matters.

Dec 30
Remained in my office all day reading, etc.

Dec. 31
The weather is so cold that every one remains indoors. This is the last day of the year 1859. It is hard to say what the year 1860 will develop in our Republican institutions.

[*1860*]

Jan. 1st
Attended the Episcopal Church this morning where I heard Dr Smith[18] read a letter from Bishop Otey, giving an account of the condition of the church in his diocese. The new year set in clear and intensely cold.

Jan. 2
Democrats of this county held a meeting at the Court House today and appointed delegates to the State Convention on the 18th instant. I have been occupied all day in making out rent notes for this year. The weather continues intensely cold.

---

[18] Rev. Leonidas Smith of Warrenton, North Carolina. He served as Rector of Christ Episcopal Church in Nashville from June 1857 to January 1, 1862.

Jan. 3

Occupied the day in business matters.

Jan. 4

This morning I went up to the Capitol but there was no quorum. Passed the day in my office attending to business. I intended calling at Mrs Tom Smiths this evening but was prevented by a little difficulty at home between certain parties, unnecessary to mention.

Jan. 5th

Occupied the day in my office reading and attending to business.

Jan. 6

Passed the day in my office. This evening I attended a lecture at the Capitol by Mr Baldwin on the subject of the African Race. He took the position that the negro was intended by nature to be a servant, that the free negroes of the South ought to be sent to Africa to civilize that country—that they were a nuisance here. Considered slavery a great blessing to the negro and the white man. He had a good audience, who gave him strict attention.

Jan. 7

This morning I went down to the river and engaged father's and mother's passage to Ark on the Jas Johnson. Occupied the day in my office reading etc.

Jan. 8

Attended divine service at the church of the Advent this morning. Dr Quintard is the Chaplain of the Rock City Guards and the company was present in uniform.

Jan. 9

This afternoon I attended a handsome collation given by Capt Robert C. Foster to his company, the Rock City Guards. Gov Harris, Gen Foote and a number of gentlemen outside of the company were present. Several speeches were made and toasts drunk.

Jan. 10

Father mother and Mary left today for Ark. I was engaged during the afternoon at Gordon's store taking depositions for a case in East Ten.

Jan. 11

Attended the Supreme Court this morning and heard a number of opinions delivered. The weather has been so very inclement that I have remained indoors nearly all day.

Jan. 12

The House of [Rep.] at Washington have not effected an organization yet. The Pemberton [Mills] in Lawrence Mass fell yesterday and destroyed some two hundred persons.

Jan. 13

Occupied the day in my office. The weather is very inclement.

Jan. 14

Occupied the day in my office reading.

Jan. 15

Attended the 1st Presbyterian Church this morning. Dr Bardwell preached a very good sermon. This afternoon I walked down to the suspension bridge to see the river which is very high and rising rapidly. I then called to see Aunt Felicia and Aunt malvina. The latter has just returned from New Haven where she went after Jno her son. He was at an abolition school and she took him away. After tea I remained at home reading the book of revelations.

Jan. 16

The delegates to the Democratic State Convention are pouring in, and the purport is that we will have a very large attendance.

Jan. 17

Occupied the day among the politicians. This evening I attended the Caucus at the Capitol. The organization was made before the time, and trickery used in the beginning.

Jan. 18

The Convention met at 11½ oc and Geo W Jones was made President, and ten Vice Presidents, myself among the number. The committee on resolutions made a report which was not accepted—but recommitted for alteration. The object of recommittal was to show that the democracy of Ten endorse the views of the Administration on the subject of slavery in the territories, and not Mr Douglass. There was much excitement but every thing quieted down finally. Landon C. Haynes and W C. Whitthorne were selected as delegates for the State at large. The former I consider a very good selection the latter very bad. The delegates to Charleston are upon the whole very good—much better than usual, although not so good as could be wished. Resolutions were passed expressing a preference for Andrew Johnson for the Presidency, and complimentary to Gov Harris. Landon C Haynes made a most brilliant and eloquent speech tonight. It was the only speech made in the Convention worthy of notice.

Jan. 19

I have been quite unwell all day, so much so that I have been unable to do anything.

Jan. 20

Passed the day at home nursing myself.

Jan. 21

All day at home, suffering with piles.

Jan. 22

Attended the 1st Presbyterian Church this morning and remained at home all evening.

Jan. 23

Occupied the day in my office.

Jan. 24

Started before day this morning for Louisville on the RR to attend the Grand Festival there this evening. About 75 of the members of our legislature accompanied us, also the Mayor and several members of the City Council. We reached Louisville about 4 oc and were received by a committee who escorted us to different hotels. I came to the Louisville Hotel in old Mr. Garvin's carriage. At 9 oc the members of the Ky and Ten legislatures, the executive officers of La, and a committee of the Ohio legislature assembled at Mozart Hall where we found one of the most eloquent and sumptuous entertainments that I ever sat down to. It was understood when we left home that we were invited to a R R celebration but it was converted into a Union meeting of the most enthusiastic character. The Mayor of the City presided. Speeches were made by Gov Magoffin[19] T Newman who represented Gov Harris of Ten Gov Wickliffe[20] of La Jas Guthrie Payne of Memphis Stokes of Ten Whitthorne of Ten and others. Payne made the speech of the evening. Brown,[21] the member of Congress elect who is too young to take his seat, made a very good speech. Prentice was drunk and made an ass of himself. Everything went off well, and all were pleased.

Jan. 25

This morning I called to see Mrs Steel in the hotel, where I met Watson Andrews and wife of Fleming Co. He is a great wag, and an old politician. Dined at Mr Wm Richardson's where I met Judge Storer[22] of Cincinnati and a number of friends. This evening the whole

---

[19] Beriah Magoffin (1815-1885), lawyer, farmer, Governor of Kentucky.
[20] Robert C. Wickliffe (1820-1895), thirteenth Governor of Louisiana.
[21] John Young Brown (1833-1904), congressman, Governor of Kentucky.
[22] Bellamy Storer (1796-1875), lawyer, Congressman.

party left Louisville for Cincinnati on the splendid steamer Jacob Strader. Capt. Shirley made himself very polite and treated us very kindly. When we passed Madison we were greated by a large crowd, amid the beating of drums and the booming of cannon. Payne made a speech at this point. We had a number of ladies on board, and the evening was passed most agreeably.

Jan. 26

Before reaching Cincinnati this morning we were met by two magnificent steamers filled with gentlemen from the City—and with a fine band of music. They lashed to our steamer and approached the City abreast. As soon as we got in sight we were saluted from both sides of the river by the firing of cannon. The manufacturies were crowded with the operatives who gave us a hearty welcome from the tops of the houses. The Mayor had the full police force out in uniform to keep the crowd from the visitors. We went immediately to the Little Miami R R for Columbus. Pretty soon after we started Longworth's Sparkling Catawba commenced flowing and every man and woman got their fill. We were saluted at every point on the way by the firing of cannons and the enthusiastic welcome of a generous people. At Columbus the military were out and indeed the whole population was out and escorted us to the Capitol where we had several speeches. After tea there was a banquet at the Odean Hall, and a hop at the Neal House. I did not hear the speeches tonight, for I was worn out and went to bed early.

Jan. 27

This morning we left Columbus for Cincinnati through the Big Miami Valley by way of Dayton. When we reached Dayton Gov Dennison[23] received a dispatch from Gov Morgan[24] of N Y inviting the party to visit Albany. The Gov and Ohio legislature accompanied us to Cincinnati. We reached the city about 4 oc and were received most magnificently at the depot and escorted to Pike's Opera House which is the finest building of the kind in the U. S. The guests were placed in the parquet—the distinguished gentlemen on the stage, and the ladies above. At a certain signal from the Mayor all the ladies rose and waved their handkerchiefs, and the gentlemen below their hats. It was a soul stirring scene. The Mayor made a short speech of welcome —and was followed by Judge Storer on behalf of the citizens in a beautiful speech. Gov Magoffin, T Newman, and Gov Dennison also made speeches. This evening we had a magnificent banquet at the

[23] William Dennison (1815-1882), Governor of Ohio.
[24] Edwin Denison Morgan (1811-1883), Governor of New York, United States Senator.

Burnett House where many speeches were made and much good feeling prevailed.

Jan 28

The guests assembled according to invitation this morning at Mr Longworth's residence where they were received in the most hospitable and sumptuous style. The party drank 1200 bottles of Catawba, besides other liquors. The affair must have cost him $5000 at least. At 1 oc I left Cincinnati in company with Eugene Underwood for Lexington, Ky having been invited by Gov Magoffin to make him a visit at Frankfort. Every village that we passed on the way we were greeted most enthusiastically. At Lexington they had bon fires and the whole town turned out to receive us. I made a speech from the balcony of the Phoenix Hotel and another at the banquet. James Clay, Wickliff, and a number of gentlemen made speeches, and everything went off well.

Jan. 29

At 10 oc we left Lexington for Frankfort where we went immediately to the Gov mansion.

Jan 30

This morning I went to the Capitol where I met many of the gentlemen whose acquaintance I had formed on the Journey. I afterwards visited the Penitentiary, the Arsenal, and the Cemetery. Frankfort is most remarkably situated and a very pleasant little town. This evening the Gov. held a Levee where we had an opportunity of seeing the beauty of this portion of the State. Gov Magoffin treated us like Lords. He has an interesting family. I shall never forget his kindness.

Jan. 31

Left Frankfort at 7 oc this morning and reached Louisville at 11 oc. Received calls from Gov Alfred Caldwell and James Guthrie. Left Louisville for Nashville at 8 oc.

Feb. 1

Reached home at 7 o'clock this morning after a cold night—the ground covered with snow. Father mother and Mary reached home today from Ark. A telegraphic dispatch was received today that Pennington[25] of N J had been elected Speaker of the House of [Rep.] He belongs to the People's Party but voted for Banks and Sherman.

Feb. 2nd

Attended the Supreme and Circuit Courts this morning. Passed most of the day in my office.

---

[25] William Pennington (1796-1862), Governor of New Jersey, congressman.

Feb. 3

I notice today that I have been placed on the democratic Central Committee which means that I must work myself to death, and receive no pay or thanks for it. Called to see J G Harris, U S N, who has just returned from a long cruise in the Mediterranean on the U S Frigate Wabash. He is looking in fine health.

Feb. 4

Occupied the day mostly in my office attending to business. The Branch of the State Bank at Clarkesville was robbed night before last of $18,000.

Feb. 5

I did not go to church this morning feeling unwell. I remained at home all the day.

Feb. 6

Attended the Supreme Court and Circuit Court today. Judge McKinney delivered an opinion in the case of the Bondholders of the Alisonia Manufacturing Co vs the creditors of the Misses Deery. The decree of the Court below was confirmed which I consider just. I suppose the bondholders will now sell the Mill property.

Feb. 7

I went to the Capitol today to look after a bill chartering the Avoca Spring Co. Occupied the balance of the day in my office.

Feb. 8

The Supreme Court adjourned today.

Feb. 9

Passed the day mostly in my office visiting, and attending to business.

Feb. 10

I read in the morning's paper the Speech of the Queen of England to Parliament. As usual it is quite short and to the point. Mr Pennington has made Mr Sherman Chairman of the Committee of Ways and Means and Corwin[26] Chairman of Foreign Affairs. The Circuit Court adjourned today. Passed most of the day in my office attending to business.

Feb. 11

I went up to the Capitol today and found the members busy doing nothing. I examined a patent today, which I think will be very useful to the whole world. It is an invention of Dr McKean of this city for

---

[26] Thomas Corwin (1794-1865), statesman.

lifting ships or boats over sand bars or shoal places. The vessel is lifted by means of large balls placed on either side of the ship, and made of gutta-percha. The balls are placed under in a collapsed condition, and then inflated with condensed air which is obtained by means of pumps.

Feb. 12

Attended the 1st Presbyterian Church this morning and heard a long sermon from Mr Bardwell. This afternoon I called to see Mrs Polk with Aunt Felicia.

Feb. 13

Passed most of the day in my office. This evening Bostick, Rice and myself took a game of ucre, and had a good supper.

Feb. 14

Passed the day in my office reading. Jno reached home today from Ark.

Feb. 15

Occupied the day almost entirely in my office. Went up to the Capitol and listened to some windy speeches on the subject of conventional interest.

Feb. 16

Passed most of the day at the Capitol. This evening I went up to Gov Mansion (the little brick on the side of Capitol Hill) and had a game of cards with the Gov—Howard, and Whitthorne.

Feb. 17

Passed the forenoon in my office reading. This evening I dined with Jno C. Thompson—J D Porter,[27] our old classmate was the honored guest.

Feb. 18

Occupied the day in my office and on the streets. The candidates are all in town today, and I never saw so many before. I think it a bad sign for the country to see so many men seeking a lively-hood without labor. If they would go to work at some honest calling it would be much better for them and the country.

---

[27] James Davis Porter (1828-1912), Governor of Tennessee, educator, was born in Paris, Tennessee. He graduated from the University of Nashville in 1846; began the practice of law in Paris in 1851; served as chief of staff to General B. F. Cheatham throughout the Civil War; Judge of Twelfth judicial circuit of Tennessee 1870-1874; Governor of Tennessee 1875-1879; Assistant Secretary of State of the United States 1885-1887; Minister to Chile 1893-1894; President of the N. C. and St. L. Railroad 1880-1884; Chancellor of The University of Nashville in 1901; President of the Peabody Normal College in 1902; merged the two institutions forming George Peabody College for Teachers, of which he was President until 1909.

Feb. 19th

Attended the 1st Presbyterian Church this morning. Took tea at Mr Bass'.

Feb 20

Went up to the Capitol today for a short time. Passed the remainder of the day in my office reading and attending to business.

Feb 21

It is rumored in the city today that Jas Newman of Knoxville who is a delegate to the Charleston Convention has been arrested for forging land warrants, and that his brother Tux Newman (Speaker of the Senate) will be arrested. Dr Clark of Bristol is here with Nixon's new patent for a hand-loom, which I consider a good thing. I attended the funeral of Mrs. Wm Gleaves today. She was the oldest daughter of Jos P. Clark and died in childbirth.

Feb. 22

All the military companies of the city were on parade today in honor of the birth-day of Washington. The Opposition Convention met today at the Capitol. A long string of resolutions were passed—speeches made and Jno Bell recommended for the presidency. Henry, Brown, Peyton, and Clemmons were the principal characters who figured in the Convention. Bell made a short speech this evening.

Feb. 23

At 12 oc today I left the city on the steamer Minitonka for Paducah. Henry and H Allen of Monterey were on board, and we had a pleasant game of ucre.

Feb. 24

Reached Paducah about noon, and took a Cincinnati boat for Cairo where I passed the night at the new brick hotel on the point.

Feb. 25

Left Cairo at three oc this morning and reached the Macon Station in Macon Co on the Ill Central R R at 4 oc. Here I procured a horse and rode five miles out on the prairie to the farm of Robt and Wm Deery, where I found Mrs. Deery and the boys well.

Feb 26

The prarie at this season when the grass is dead looks to me very much like the desert. The winds are very severe and the mud intolerable. The lands are very rich, the soil being as black as my hat. It is a great corn and wheat country. I like its productiveness, but do not like the absence of the negro, the scarcity of wood and water, the terrible winds and the monotony of the scenery. It is very lonely looking on the prarie.

Feb. 27

This evening I bid Mrs Deery good-bye and went with Robt to Decatur where Wm Deery is sick at the hotel.

Feb. 28

Left Decatur before day this morning and reached St Louis to dinner, passing through Spring field and very rich and highly cultivated country. This evening I attended a military ball at one of the Theatres in company with Wm Hynes. The ball was a failure. I stayed all night with Hynes.

Feb. 29

Occupied the day in going over the City of St Louis in the street R R cars which have been recently extended over the city. Also visited the slave market and the dog market. St Louis is the greatest city in the west—and will, I think, before many years be one of the greatest cities on this continent. I left St Louis this evening on the Ben Lewis for the mouth of the Forkideer river.

March 1st

All day reaching Cairo.

March 2

Reached the Dyersburg landing just after the little steamer had left. Went to bed in a log cabin, with hogs under the floor.

March 3

This morning I started to Dyersburg in a skiff in company with two gentlemen of that place. Reached the town at 11 oc. Distance 35 miles. The whole country on the river was covered with water, and we had a very disagreeable trip.

March 4th

I was so much fatigued from the labors of yesterday that I did not get up until 12 oc. This evening I went out to M Burton's who formerly lived in Nashville and staid all night.

March 5

Attended to business this morning and returned to Dyersburg landing on the little steamer, where I got a good steamer in a very short time, and proceeded down the river to Pecan Point which I reached before day.

March 6

Jno and Dr Erwin and myself went down to Ed's and took dinner. Both Jno and Ed are well advanced in plowing.

March 7

All of us went down to pay Grundy a visit today. He lives at Shawnee Village—seven miles from Pecan Point. All of the boys have good places and are comfortably fixed. Took tea at Ed' and left for Memphis tonight—on the Packet.

March 8

Reached Memphis before day [and] stopped at the Given House. Occupied the day in going over the city, attending the Courts, visiting friends etc. Memphis has improved very much since I was here eight years ago, and I think will be, in a very few years, ahead of Nashville.

March 9

Occupied the day in going over Memphis pricing property etc. Everything is very high here. I left at 4 oc on the cars for Nashville.

March 10

While the passengers were at their breakfast this morning, I ran up into Huntsville to see the Big Spring, and take a bird's eye of the town. The spring is very large and the water good. The town is small, but pretty. At Stevenson I got a fish and some eggs for my breakfast. Reached home about dark—and found my wife at Gen Harding's.

March 11

I did not go to church today, but remained at home.

March 12

Occupied the day in my office, and on streets attending to business.

March 13

Passed the day in my office. This evening I attended Dr Boynton's lecture on electricity. He had a crowded house and his experiments were very interesting.

March 14

I attended the legislature this morning. They are rushing business through rapidly.

March 15

Passed the day in my office reading etc.

March 16

The newspapers are filled with speculations in regard to the Presidency.

March 17

All day in my office attending to business.

March 18

I was a good deal alarmed this morning by the explosion of some Vespar Gas in the room next to my office and the fire which ensued. I thought at one time the Colonade building would be destroyed, but the firemen succeeded in extinguishing it. This Vespar Gas has been recently introduced here, and [I] think the owners may as well take it away, as every one will be afraid to use it in their lamps. I attended church both this morning and this evening. Dr Cunningham of Shelbyville preached.

March 19

Occupied the day in my office.

March 20

News reached the city this morning that we were likely to get into a war with Mexico. Two vessels had been captured and brought into New Orleans.

March 21

Passed the day at the Capitol engineering bills through the legislature.

March 22

Occupied the day in my office attending to business etc.

March 23

Most of the day in the legislative halls.

March 24

Passed the day in my office. No news.

March 25

Did not go to church this morning, but remained at home nursing a sore throat.

March 26th

I read this morning a very able and interesting speech delivered in Congress by S S Cox[28] of Ohio on Mexican affairs. He reviews the history of Mexico since 1824—under the various governments and favors a protectorate over Mexico and the acceptance of the McClain treaty. The legislature adjourned today at 12 oc after a session of five months. The two Speakers, Newman and Whitthorne, made speeches and adjourned their respective bodies. Some important laws have been

[28] Samuel Sullivan Cox (1824-1889), lawyer, diplomat, Congressman from Ohio and New York.

passed, but take their legislature all together, I do not think they have accomplished much. Many of the democratic members came here as hard as pot mettle on the subject of banks, and they have passed more bank charters than any previous body, and their appropriations have been more extravagant. A few good men occupied seats in the body, but as a whole they were excessively weak.

March 27th

Occupied the day at the City Hall, valuing City property, having been appointed by the Mayor (Hollingsworth) in conjunction with Ex-Mayor Castleman[29] and Mr Hale to re-value the realty of the City.

March 28

All the day at the City Hall.

March 29

All the day at the City Hall.

March 30

All the day at the City Hall. Dr Cason was shot dead today at the Commercial Hotel on Cedar St by a man named Trewett from Sparta, White Co Ten. It was supposed that Trewett was laboring under mania at the time. Dr C was called in professionally and was killed while writing a prescription. He did not move from his chair, but was found sitting with pencil in hand. Mr Trewett was committed to jail. Sally, my sister, gave birth to boy child last night. She is doing very well.

April 1st

Being an inclement day I did not go to church, but remained at home reading. I went over to see Sallie and her baby, both of whom were doing well.

April 2nd

Occupied the entire day at the City Hall valueing the property of the City.

April 3rd

All day at the City Hall.

April 4th

All day at the City Hall.

April 5th

All day at the City Hall.

29 Robert B. Castleman was Mayor of Nashville in 1854 and 1855. He was Clerk of the Davidson County Court 1840-1850.

April 6th

All day at the City Hall. The trial of Thomas Millington for shooting at Dr Briggs[30] is creating a good deal of sensation in the City just now. Mr Taylor and Andrew Hamilton had a street fight this evening about a freight bill. I separated them. Taylor is from Ky.

April 7

Occupied the day in valuing property.

April 8

Attended church both this morning and this evening. Made a visit to Aunt Malvinas this evening.

April 9

Occupied the day in valuing property.

April 10

There was a large fire last night on Union Street, which destroyed the four brick tenements opposite to our house. We came very near being burnt up, but fortunately the wind shifted, and we were saved. I worked all night.

April 11

Occupied the day at the City Hall.

April 12

All day at the City Hall valuing property.

April 13

All day at the City Hall.

April 14

Occupied the day at the City Hall mostly. Attended the funeral of Jno Trimble's son, aged 19 years.

April 15

Attended church this morning.

April 16

Occupied the day mostly at the City Hall at work—assessing property.

---

[30] William T. Briggs, M.D., was one of Nashville's most distinguished surgeons. He graduated from the Medical Department of Transylvania University and practiced for three years in his home town, Bowling Green, Kentucky. He moved to Nashville in 1854 to teach in the Medical Department of the University of Nashville. In 1868 he succeeded Dr. Paul F. Eve as Professor of Surgery in the University. He was President of the American Medical Association, and was one of the delegates to the International Medical Congress at London, England. He contributed extensively to medical literature and, himself, owned the largest medical and surgical library in the South.

April 17

All day at the City Hall. We finished our work today except the Wilson Addition which Castleman and Hale will do up.

April 18

I left Nashville this morning for Charleston with the delegates to the Democratic Convention. Reached Atlanta, Ga about twelve oc tonight where we put up at the Trout House. Mr Alick Moore of Williamson Co got his pocket picked at the depot tonight.

April 19

Left Atlanta this morning, and took tea at Augusta.

April 20

Reacher Charleston this morning about day-light and stopped at the Mill's House. Some of the delegates from the different States are here, but the crowd will be very much smaller than usual on such occasions owing to the exorbitant charges of the hotels. Ewing, Howard, Jones, and myself were all put in one small room.

April 21

Occupied the day in aiding Mr Smally, the Chairman of the National Committee, in issuing tickets of admission to the different delegations. The National Committee held a meeting this evening at the Masonic Hall, but adjournd without doing anything. I took a walk this evening on the Battery, which is one of the most beautiful and inviting places about Charleston.

April 22

I did not go to church this morning, but attended the negro church this evening, which is regarded as one of the attractions of the city. The church is very large, and I never saw as many negroes assembled together before. They were all well dressed, and looked very happy. Many of the northern delegates were present, and I could see from their expressions that they were very much astonished.

April 23

At 12 oc today the National Convention assembled in the Hall of the Institute. Mr Flourney[31] of Ark was called to the chair temporarily and the Hon Caleb Crushing[32] of Mass made permanent Chairman. A

[31] Thompson B. Flourney remained at the convention and was one of the two Arkansas delegates who refused to withdraw. Following the adjournment of the convention to Baltimore he became the leader of the Douglas faction in Arkansas. He was also present at the Baltimore convention.

[32] Caleb Cushing (1800-1879), lawyer, diplomat.

committee on credentials and on the platform were appointed and the convention adjourned.

April 24

The Convention met at 10 oc this morning but accomplished nothing, as the committee on resolutions were not prepared to report. Dined this evening at Mr Conner's.

April 25th

I attended the investigation before the Committee on Credentials of the contested seats of the New York delegations. Mayor Wood's[33] delegation, and the Albany delegation were the contestants. Each produced affidavits, and there was any amount of vituperation indulged in on both sides. The Albany delegation were finally admitted.[34]

April 26

The Convention assembled at 10 oc; the galleries crowded, and the floor. The committee brought in a majority and minority report, which gave rise to a great deal of discussion. I attended a party at Mr Conner's this evening.

April 27

The Convention met at the usual hour this morning, and resumed the discussion on the resolutions reported by the committee. The Douglass men, and the southern delegates differ widely on the resolutions, neither are disposed to yield, and the result looks disastrous. Speeches are made from the balcony of the Mills House every night.

April 28

The Convention met at the usual hour and the discussion continued. No result. Prospect gloomy.

April 29

This evening I attended St Michael's Church where I heard an excellent sermon. After service Mrs Conner invited me to walk through some of the church yards of the city, which are beautifully arranged, being laid off with much taste, and the tombs and monuments kept in good condition.

April 30

The Convention assembled at the usual hour this morning, and the minority resolutions adopted, the entire south voting against them.

---

[33] Fernando Wood (1812-1881), Congressman, mayor.

[34] The significance of the seating of the Albany delegation headed by Dean Richmond soon became apparent. The Douglas platform was adopted, instead of the Southern-rights platform, by a vote of 165 to 138. The seating of the Wood faction would have caused the adoption of the Southern-rights platform. For further details of this contest see Dwight L. Dumond, *The Secession Movement, 1860-1861* (New York, 1931).

The following States withdrew from the Convention, and protested against the adoption of the minority report, viz. South Carolina, Georgia, Florida, Ala, La, Texas, Arkansas, and Delaware. It was a solemn sight to see these States leave the Convention. All was silence, and the scene was most impressive and distressing to an old democrat, who believes that the salvation of the country depends upon the perpetuity of the party.

May 1st

The Convention assembled again this morning and the remaining South States presented two resolutions. One was that it was necessary for the nominee to get two thirds of the entire electoral vote, which was adopted. The other resolution was laid on the table. This evening the convention commenced ballotting for President. The following names were put in nomination, viz. Douglas, Guthrie, Johnson,[35] Lane, Dickinson,[36] Pierce of Md, Hunter[37] etc.

May 2nd

The Convention balloted all day, without result. I took a drive this evening about the suburbs of the city which are beautiful.

May 3

This morning the Convention met, and adjourned to meet at Baltimore on the 18th of June. The seceding delegations did nothing, but will meet at Richmond on the 11th and await the action of the Baltimore convention. I left Charleston at 2½ oc in company with several of the delegations.

May 4

All day on the cars, and very much crowded.

May 5

Reached home at 8 oclock this morning, and was beset on all sides by inquiries from persons interested in the action of the Convention.

May 6

Attended the 1st Presbyterian Church this morning and heard a very good sermon from Dr Mullin of Clarksville. This evening I called on Mr Wm Garvin of Louisville, V K Stevenson, Mrs Bass, and Mrs Polk. I took tea with Mrs. Polk.

---

35 Andrew Johnson's name was presented by the Tennessee delegation in accordance with the prior action of the state convention held at Nashville.

36 Daniel Stevens Dickinson (1800-1866), lawyer, Senator from New York.

37 Robert Mercer Taliaferro Hunter (1809-1887), Congressman from Virginia.

May 7

Occupied the day mostly in my office. The Typographical Society of the United States met at the Capitol this morning. About fifty members present from different parts of the country. This evening I attended a very large and handsome party at Aunt Felicia Porter's given to Gov Magoffin of Ky., who was not present, having been disappointed by the adjournment of the Charleston Convention, which made it necessary for him to go to Washington.

May 8

I did not get up until very late this morning, having been kept up until a late hour last night. This evening I attended the funeral of Mr Beal Bosley,[38] one of the oldest and most estimable citizens of this community. He was in his ninety sixth year, and left a large estate.

May 9

Attended the Chancery Court this morning. Mr West's paintings were sold at auction this morning and some of them brought very high prices. They were taken in Italy, but not very desirable.

May 10th

News reached here today of the nomination of the Hon Jno Bell for the Presidency by the "Constitutional Union" party at Baltimore. This organization is composed of the remains of the old whig party and late K N. American or Opposition party. Their platform is the Union, the Constitution, and the execution of the laws. They hope to come in on the discussions of the democratic party, but they are doomed to disappointment. The City Hall bell and the cannon gave utterance to the feelings of Mr Bell's friends in this city. At 4 oc I went over to dinner given by Gen Barrow in honor of his birthday. The Rock City Guards were in attendance and looked very well. I was called upon for a toast among others and gave the following: "Our Host and Hostess, the Prince of Hospitality, and the Queen of the Reception," which was well received. Gen B said that nobody but a red-headed man could have given such a toast. A splendid banquet was given at the Capitol tonight to the Typographical Union Society. I was not present—not being invited.

May 11

Attended the Chancery Court this morning. This evening I went up to Dr Hadley's.

[38] Beal Bosley was one of Nashville's pioneer settlers, coming to the region with James Robertson and his band.

May 12

Passed the day very pleasantly at Dr Hadley's. They are very kind people, and it is an agreeable place to visit.

May 13

Attended church this morning in a little brick school house near Dr Hadley's. Mr Ragsdale, a Methodist, preached a very sensible sermon. This evening I visited "Soldier's Rest" now owned by Dr Hadley. It was formerly the residence of Gen Thos Overton, who was the second of Gen Jackson in the duel with Dickinson.[39] He is burried in a field opposite the house.

May 14

Started from Dr Hadley's pretty soon after breakfast and made Dr Lawrence a visit. His wife is a charming woman, and he has an interesting family. Called at the Hermitage, which is now unoccupied, and visited the tomb. Dined at Jno Harding's and called at David McGavock's.

May 15

Occupied the day mostly in my office. I met Gov N S. Brown in the Chancery Ct. He has just returned from Baltimore and reports that there was great harmony in the Convention. Minorities always harmonize.

May 16

Passed the day in my office reading and attending to business. The Chicago Convention meets today and its action is looked to by the country with great interest—and will doubtless have some bearing on the Baltimore Convention next month. Passed the evening at Aunt Felicia's.

May 17

Rose very early this morning, having been arroused to see Miss Mary Ready who had a spasm in the front room. She was sleeping with Mary, and was quite insensible when I reached her. I gave her a good drink of Berbon whiskey and rubbed her wrists and ankles with it, which brought her to. The Chicago Convention met yesterday and organized by the unanimous election of David Wilmott,[40] as temporary chairman. Some distraction seems to prevail as to the choice of men. Abstracts of Douglass' speech in reply to Davis in the Senate was received this morn-

[39] Charles Dickinson was killed by Andrew Jackson in a duel which took place May 30, 1806. The duel grew out of a disagreement over a horse race which served to aggravate the already sensitive relations between the two men.

[40] David Wilmot (1814-1868), Congressman from Pennsylvania.

ing in which he charges the South of having changed positions on the subject of S Sovereignty. The Firemen of the city had their annual celebration today, which was quite an imposing sight. A company from Memphis was in the procession with an engine and hose carriage. Many of the houses in the city were decorated and devices of various sorts hung out. They had a magnificent banquet tonight at the Theater. I was present and never saw men behave so shamefully in all my life. They got drunk very early, and carried off wine, cakes, turkey and everything by the wholesale.

May 18

This morning I went up to Jos L. Ewing's place to attend his funeral. Jno Bell arrived today at two o'clock, and was received at the depot by a large number of his friends, who escorted him to the City Hotel where he made a short speech. N S Brown and E H Ewing also made speeches. Grundy and his family reached Nashville today from his plantation in Ark.

May 19

Passed the day mostly in my office.

May 20

Heard a very good sermon this morning by Mr Davis, a Cumberland Presbyterian. The Assembly of this church is now in session.

May 21

The St Cloud Hotel was on fire this morning, just after day light, but was extinguished. It is the general belief that it was set on fire by the proprietors, the furniture being insured for a large amount, and the hotel closed. The Sewanee House burnt up ten years ago under the same circumstances, and the same proprietor. Occupied the day in my office, and in the Courts.

May 22

All day in my office. There was quite a terrific storm here last night, but no damage. The same storm passed through Louisville Cincinnati and Memphis and very destructive in all these places.

May 23

Occupied the day in my office.

May 24

An election was held today for Atto General for this district and Magistrates for the city. Jas Rains' majority in this city alone was about sixteen hundred. He is of course elected. Passed most of the day in my office.

May 25

I read Davis' and Douglass' speeches in the Senate on Davis' resolutions. Both are very able. Occupied the day mostly in business.

May 26

Occupied the day in the Courts, and in my office.

May 27

Attended the 1st Presbyterian Church this morning.

May 28

Occupied the day in the Courts—and in my office.

May 29

All day in my office.

May 30

All of the forenoon in my office. This afternoon I called with my wife on Mrs and Miss Acklin who have just got up from La.

May 31

Passed the day in my office.

June 1st

Attended the sale of the Sewanee furniture today. It was sold for the purpose of re-furnishing and refitting. I have been occupied all evening in a conversation with Dunnington in regard to purchasing an interest in the Union and American office.

June 2nd

This evening I drove out to Gen Harding's park with my wife to a picnic given by the young gentlemen of the city. The company was select and the affair well gotten up. Fenton's Silver Band was in attendance. Miss C Bankhead returned with us.

June 3rd

I attended the 1st Presbyterian Church this morning. Dr Robt Breckenridge of Ky delivered a sermon to the students of the University. The cadets and the Rock City Guards were in attendance in uniform. The sermon fell short of the reputation of the man. Everyone was disappointed. W M Churchwell has been appointed by the President, Minister to Guatemala and Honduras. Not a very desirable place.

June 4th

Attended the Circuit Court this morning. This evening I went to the College to witness a review of the Cadets—and the Rock City Guards.

It was a pretty sight and both the Cadets and Guards acquitted themselves well. Many ladies and gentlemen were present. I understand that hereafter they propose to have an annual review, and will invite companies from all parts of the state. This is a good idea and will tend very much to keep the taste of our people for military discipline, which, from the present condition of affairs in the country, will be very much needed by the South—before many years.

June 5

This morning I went to Williamson in company with my wife and Sallie to attend the wedding of Sallie McGavock, the second daughter of James McGavock. She was married by Mr. Cunningham to Mr. Frierson of Shelbyville. The bridal party came to Nashville this evening, and left immediately for Missouri.

June 6

Occupied the forenoon in the Circuit Ct room, and in my office reading. This evening I attended the Commencement of the Nashville University at the Capitol. The crowd in attendance was very large, and the exercises very interesting.

June 7th

Dr Lindsley, Aunt Felicia, and her children started for the north this morning. Mr Everett's[41] letter of acceptance as a candidate for the Vice Presidency was published here this morning. It is quite lengthy and very patriotic in its tone.

June 8th

Occupied the day mostly in my office reading. The city is unusually dull and great complaints made about the hard times. The failure of the crops in this region for the past two years is the cause of the present strengency. This city and indeed the farmers of Middle Tennessee have been buying food for man and beast for six months past, which of course drains us of our specie and fills the coffers of the North West.

June 9th

Occupied the forenoon in my office. My old flame, Lizzie Bonner, called to see my wife today. She is looking very well.

June 10

Attended the 1st Presbyterian Church today. Dr Elliott preached. He has given up the Nashville Female Academy, over which he has presided for the last twenty years. Mr Everhart of Huntsville, Ala has taken charge of the institution. I attended church again this evening.

---

[41] Edward Everett (1794-1865), statesman, educator.

June 11

Occupied the day mostly in my office. I took tea this evening at Mr Bass' and with the Hon James Guthrie of Ky. He conversed very freely about Presidential matters. If he could be nominated and elected he would make a good president. The Richmond Convention met today.

June 12

I have been quite unwell all day. Mr Allen of Texas, the grand-nephew of my father, stayed all night with us. The Richmond Convention adjourned today to go to Baltimore but will return to Richmond if they do not get what they want.

June 13th

Passed the day in the Circuit Court—and in my office.

June 14

This morning I left Nashville in company with my wife for the Baltimore Convention by way of Chattanooga.

June 15

Passed the farm and Uncle Randal's this morning but did not stop. At the Montgomery Springs depot Wm S. Eakin and wife got on the cars en route for the north. Passed Lynchburg about dusk. Wm Carroll and several other acquaintances are on the train.

June 16th

Reached Washington before breakfast this morning and being very much fatigued we passed the forenoon in sleeping. The city is crowded with politicians on the way to Baltimore. Congress adjourned today. The Senate will hold over for several days in Executive Session.

June 17th

I did not go to church today but remained at Willard's, which I think the best hotel in the city.

June 18th

This morning our party in company with Mr Churchwell, Geo W. Jones, and others made a visit to Mr Buchanon in the White House. The old gentlemen is very grateful now for any attentions as he has been so much abused and neglected of late. This afternoon I went over to Baltimore. My wife went on to Philia in company with Wm Eakin and wife. Col Cave Johnson and myself stopped at a private boarding house, being unable to procure lodgings either at Barnums or the Eaton house. The convention assembled today but no business transacted.

June 19

I attended the Convention today in the old Theatre. The crowd was very great. No business was transacted. The committee on credentials not ready to report. We had speaking tonight on Monument Square from two stands. The friends of Douglass from one, and his opponents from the other. The excitement was very great on both sides. I see no hope of harmonious action in the Convention.

June 20

The Convention met again today, but nothing done. The Committee still not ready to report. Speeches at night.

June 21

I attended the Convention again today, nothing done, but a few bitter speeches made. I met my old Cambridge classmate today, Robt Lyon Rodgers. We went together to see the city work house, which is one of the finest and most complete buildings of its kind that I ever saw.

June 22

The Committee on credentials reported this morning, adversely to admitting the seceding delegates, and in favor of the bogus Douglass delegates, which will cause a dissolution of the convention and I fear the Nationality of the party. I left Baltimore this evening for Philia.

June 23

I met with Dr Lindsley, Aunt Felicia, and family, and Grundy this morning at the Continental. News reached here today of the dissolution of the Convention and the nomination of Douglass by one, and Breckenridge by the other.

June 24

This morning we attended Dr Wordsworth's church in company with Mr Hooper. The sermon was excellent. Passed the remainder of the day in the Continental Hotel which is the most complete establishment that I ever saw.

June 26

This morning I went out to Germantown to see Sue Dixon, an old friend, but missed the place. I do not regret going as I had an opportunity of seeing that city and the country. Dined today with Wm S. Eakin; Mr and Mrs Hooper were present. This evening we went out to Laurel Hill and after tea we amused ourselves riding through the city on the street rail roads.

June 26

We left Philia this morning and reached Washington this afternoon. Stopped at Brown's Hotel.

June 27

Occupied the day in going over the city, gathering political items. Called on Cave Johnson. Left the city at 5 P.M.

June 28

Reached the Montgomery White Sulphur Springs at 11 oc this morning where we found about 250 visitors. The place is magnificently improved but I do not admire the situation or the water. I met Cousin James Kent—and his son-in-law, Mr Otey.

June 29

Today Cousin James Kent offered me his carriage, and we took Mr Senator Clay[42] of Ala and lady over to the Yellow Springs about four miles distant.

June 30

We left the Montgomery Springs this morning and reached Uncle Randal's at Mac's Meadow to dinner.

July 1st

Occupied the day mostly in the house conversing.

July 2

Today Hugh Ewing and myself went over to Fort Chiswell and passed the day.

July 3

Passed the day at Uncle Randal's.

July 4

We left Mac's Meadow today in company with Cloyd McGavock, and reached Bristol this evening. Quite a storm came up just as we arrived and there was more electricity in the atmosphere than I ever saw before.

July 5

Cloyd and myself went down to see the farm today. He advises me to sell the place.

July 6

Cloyd and myself occupied the day in rolling ten pins, playing black gammon etc. We dined with old Parson King.

[42] Clement Claiborne Clay (1816-1882), statesman, diplomat.

July 7
Cloyd left for home this morning and then we came down to the farm.

July 8
Passed the day in walking about, looking at stock etc.

July 9
Occupied the day on the farm. The stock all looks well, so does the corn and oats and hay, but our wheat crop is a failure.

July 10
All day on the farm.

July 11
All day on the farm.

July 12
All day on the farm.

July 13
The young folks in the neighborhood had a picnic at the Sulphur Spring today. I went down and enjoyed myself very much.

July 14
All day on the farm.

July 15
Passed the day mostly in the house.

July 16
This morning I rode over the knolls to Blountsville, it being Circuit Court day. Hon Thos A R Nelson made a speech, giving an account of his stewardship—and then branched out in general politics. He agrees with the Southern democrats on the subject of Squatter [Sovereignty] but supports Bell and Everett.

July 17
Had a visit today from Mr and Mrs King and a preacher from Abingdon. All day on the farm.

July 18
Occupied the day in making up accounts with the Overseer, and in going over the farm. The overseer has entirely too much company and I intend putting a stop to it.

July 19
Passed the day on the farm. The wheat is all in, also the oats, the corn laid by, and on Monday we will be ready to commence plowing

for wheat. I have been engaged all day in making up the accounts of the farm.

July

My wife and myself after leaving the farm in East Ten passed several days at Parson King's and one week at the hotel in Bristol. While in Bristol I occupied my time in getting subscribers to stock in the Avoca Springs Co. The Cumberland Gap R R is terminated at Bristol. While here the party in Savannah owning lots here had a sale and everything went off well. We went from Bristol to the Allegany Springs where we passed one week very pleasantly. It is a quiet place, but well kept, and the water superior for medical purposes to any establishment of the kind in the mountains. We met and formed some agreeable acquaintances here. From the Allegany we went over to the Montgomery White and stayed some ten or fifteen days. I met at least twenty five or thirty Cousins here, Kents and Cloyds. Col Cave Johnson and party reached here just before we started, and we remained several days on their account. From the Montgomery Springs we came to Lookout Mt where we passed three days very pleasantly.

Aug 28

Our party left Lookout Mt. at 6 oc this morning, and reached Nashville this evening at 5 oc.

Aug. 29

I have been a good deal on the streets today and heard something said about politics. I find some Douglass men here and a good deal of feeling between the two wings of the party. The Bell party are in fine spirits and say they expect to elect their party by the people. I read Yancey's[43] speech delivered at Memphis and I regard it as an able affair.

Aug. 30

Passed the day mostly in my office attending to business.

Aug. 31

All day in my office

Sept. 1st

Employed the day in business matters.

Sept. 2nd

I did not go to church this morning on account of the rain, but remained at home reading a new book called Nemeses which I find quite interesting. Attended the Prayer meeting tonight. Went to see and relieve a poor woman this afternoon.

[43] William Lowndes Yancey (1814-1863), Congressman from Alabama.

Sept. 3

Attended the Circuit Court this morning and took judgements in a number of cases. Passed most of the day in my office attending to business.

Sept. 4

Occupied the whole day in my office.

Sept. 5

Mr Breckenridge made a speech at Lexington today which I think will be of great importance in the canvas. It will do him much good or great harm. A company from Louisville is now on a visit to our city. This evening they went through the Zouave practice on the Public Square. They are well drilled, and made a good appearance. Judge Dickinson and family are now in the city and all in fine health.

Sept. 6

Occupied the day mostly in my office

Sept. 7

Called this morning to see E J Dawson and brother of Ga Occupied most of the day in sending documents over the State from the Democratic State Central Committee, of which I am a member.

Sept. 8

Most of the day in my office. This evening Jno H Crozier of Knoxville made a speech on Broad St. He made several good points but wound up too much on the fire eating order. I was then called on and made a short speech in favor of Breckenridge and Lane.[44] Bob Haywood followed me, and the meeting adjourned.

Sept. 9

Attended the 1st Presbyterian Church this morning and heard a sermon from Dr Bardwell on the doctrine of election.

Sept. 10

The fair commences today near this city but I did not go out, being too busy. I was appointed today by the Mayor to go to Cincinnati and see if we could not get a direct R R from that city to Nashville but declined. Mr Alexander, the great stock raiser of Ky, has two magnificent bulls here on exhibition. They are the same that took the $1000 premium at St Louis. They took the premium and certificate today.

---

[44] Joseph Lane (1801-1881), Delegate and Senator from Oregon.

Sept. 11
Attended the Circuit Court this morning. Called this evening at the St Cloud to see Judge Guin and family of La.

Sept. 12
I attended the State Fair today, but became very tired of it before I left.

Sept. 13
Attended the Fair again today. Alexander of Ky beat Gen Harding and David McGavock on the best stallion. The exhibition in the Floral Hall was very good. I noticed a patent today, filtering and purifying water, which I think very good. The water first passes through a sponge, then through layers of carbon and gravel into a stone vessel in the bottom of the filterer and is thrown off through cocks. I also noticed a shingle machine that is capable of making one hundred thousand per day of an excellent quality. The new steam fire engines belonging to the city were on the grounds and performed well. The exhibition of blood stock was very good.

Sept. 14th
Occupied the day in the Circuit Court and in my office.

Sept. 15
All day in my office. I have been very much interested in a book recently published called Nemeses. The scene is laid in Va.

Sept 16
Attended the 1st Presbyterian Church this morning.

Sept. 17
All day in my office and in the Circuit Ct Room.

Sept. 18
The telegraph this morning reports that Walker and 70 of his men had been captured by a British man of war and handed over to the authorities of Honduras, who had given the men liberty to return to the U S—but had ordered Walker and one other to be shot. Mr Jas Walker is very much troubled about his son; I saw him today on the street. N S Brown and Baillie Peyton made speeches tonight on the Square. The latter was quite drunk.

Sept. 19
News reached here today that Gen Wm Walker and Col Ruckler were certainly shot by the government of Honduras. Two Douglass Electors published a card this morning in the Union and American proposing a fusion. And Johnson, And Ewing, and Gov Harris are in

favor of accepting their proposition. The Nashville Democrat of this evening comes out in an article two and one half columns in length written by Gov Foote opposing the proposition. We expected this but the acceptance of the proposition made by their own Electors will give us the whip hand in the race. The State Central Committee, of which I am a member, will publish a card tomorrow recommending the Breckenridge Electors to accept the proposition. I had an interview with the Chairman of the Douglass State Central Committee tonight, and he refuses to fuse, or have anything to do in the matter.

Sept. 20

Occupied the day mostly in Dem State Committee Room sending off documents etc.

Sept. 21

Judge Dickinson and Gov Harris went out today to Mt Pleasant to make speeches. Occupied the day in my office.

Sept 22

All day in the Committee Rooms.

Sept. 23

Attended the 1st Presbyterian Church this morning and this evening. Dr Lyons of Columbus preached. Called to see Aunt Felicia and Aunt Malvina today.

Sept. 24

Several political companies reached the city this morning on the trains for the purpose of attending the Bell and Everett Meeting here tomorrow. Mr Crittenden of Ky, the big gun of the occasion, reached the city today.

Sept. 25

The procession today fell far short of their demonstration in [18]56, [18]52, [18]48, or [18]44, and the crowd on the ground very small and the enthusiasm smaller. Crittenden, Maynard Golladay and Stanton were their speakers.

Sept. 26th

Occupied the day mostly in my office. This evening I went down to the Public Square to hear Gov Foote make a political speech. He is the head and front of the Douglas wing of the democracy of this State. I never in the whole course of my life heard such an effort. He poured out his vials of wrath copiously upon the Administration, the delegates to Charleston from Ten, the Union and American, Breckenridge and Lane, Gov. Harris, Johnson, Ewing, Yancey, Davis, and the whole world. Detailed private conversations with great men, etc. His laudations of Douglass were fulsome, and his remarks about Bell very respectful. He had a large crowd to hear him.

Sept 27th

Passed the day in my office, and the Committee Room. This evening I went to Broad St to hear Gov Johnson. He spoke over two hours and with great effect. I did not like his speech altogether, but I suppose it answered a good purpose. He brought in his Homestead Bill which I thought was unnecessary—particularly as it was killed by the President's veto—and is not popular in the South. He gave Jno. Bell the devil and Know Nothingism particular h. . . . The crowd was immense and gave him all attention. Jas M Davidson, the Irish orator, followed in an incensing rallying speech. Then came Mr Leech of Ky.

Sept 28

Called this morning on Maj Blewett, Mrs Harrison and daughter of Columbus, Miss, and Mrs Ward of Texas. The Electors for the State at large spoke at the Court House today. Wm Polk was absent and Dick McCann represented him. Peyton and Haynes both made good speeches. The candidates for Mayor spoke this evening, and each man is confident of his election.

Sept. 29

The up train on the Chattanooga R R ran off this side of Laverne this morning. One man named Smith of this city was killed. Geo Hooper the mail agent was badly hurt. Gov Johnson, L C Haynes, Jas Davidson, Farguharson, and Burch were on the train, but not hurt. The election for Mayor came off today. S. N. Hollingsworth, Richard B. Cheatham,[45] Jno. H. Smith, and Action Young are the candidates. Cheatham was elected and I think he will make the best Mayor of the four, although the moral effect of electing such a man is certainly bad. We had a little company at our house this evening to meet Maj Blewett and others from Columbus, Miss.

Sept. 30

Attended the 1st Presbyterian Church this morning and heard a very good sermon from the Rev Dr Lyons of Columbus, Miss. Old Leslie Combs[46] of Ky. made a speech at the Ct House yesterday to a large crowd. He is now very old, but amused the crowd very much telling anecdotes—etc.

---

[45] Richard B. Cheatham was very active in the civic affairs of Nashville. He was a member of the board of aldermen 1858, 1859, 1865, 1866, and 1873, and Mayor of Nashville 1860-1861.

[46] Leslie Combs (1793-1881), soldier, politician.

CHAPTER XXII

"In sorrow, humiliation, and anger I marched my regiment back to their quarters." (February, 1862)

It is at this point that an unfortunate gap exists in the McGavock journals. As related in the initial entry below, his journal, embracing the period October, 1860, through January, 1862, was lost when Fort Henry fell into the hands of the Union army. It is possible that the journal was not destroyed and may still exist. Efforts to locate it, however, have been fruitless. In it he doubtless chronicled many of his reactions and those of his fellow Nashvillians to the outbreak of hostilities. It must have included also an account of the organization and early activities of the "Bloody 10th" Tennessee Infantry which McGavock organized among the Irish of Nashville, a group he dubbed the "Sons of Erin." The account which follows is that of the fall of Forts Henry and Donelson and includes some of the most graphic eyewitness reporting available in the literature on the Civil War.

Feb 4, 1862

Having lost my journal of two years at Fort Henry, I propose writing from memory up to this 12th of March, while every incident is fresh in my mind, and the ample leisure of a prisoner's life within the walls of Bastile Warren affords me an opportunity of mature reflection on every point of moment. My Journals together with trunk, camp equipage, etc. were left in my shanty in Fort Henry where the federals entered and plundered me of everything. They rifled my trunk, drank my whiskey, and will, I suppose, publish my journal, and sell it to help pay the expense of the war.

This morning at about 3 o'clock I was aroused by the quick and successive firing of guns on the Ky side of the river. I got up and ascertained that the firing was by Capt Paggett's[1] cavalry pickets who reported that three or four gun boats were coming up the river and were then but eight or ten miles distant. I immediately awoke everybody, and we soon commenced preparations to receive the long looked for, and much dreaded monsters of the North-Western waters. Col Heiman immediately sent a messenger to Fort Donelson to convey the news to Gen Lloyd Tilghman[2] who was in command of the defenses of the two rivers. Sure enough our information proved correct, for at 12½ oc four gun boats came up and fired twenty two times at the Fort which was responded to by our batteries by an equal number of shots. The enemy evidently have good artillerists and longer range guns than we have. They threw their shot and shell with great precision, but without damage. The boats then retired behind the point below the island. While the firing was going on the infantry were removed back, so as to be out of range of the gun boats. Our pickets this afternoon report that eight gun-boats and nine large transports are three miles below at Marburry and that they were landing forces. This evening we could hear plainly the music from their brass band. They regaled us with Yankee Doodle, Hail Columbia, The Star-Spangled Banner, and St Patrick's Day in the Morning. The latter was for the benefit of the Irish Reg. at Fort Henry. At 11½ oc Gen Tilghman arrived in company with Maj Gilmer[3] from Ft Donelson and with three companies of Gantt's[4] Cavalry.

Feb. 5

We have been working hard most of the day in the Ft. making ready for a regular engagement. The gun boats came up again this morning and threw a few shot and shell without effect. Gen Tilghman had the infantry today in the inner line of rifle pits showing us our position and the ground that each company was to occupy. This afternoon he took

---

1 Captain Paggett's cavalry was a part of Col. Joseph Drake's Second Brigade at Fort Henry. His company was engaged chiefly in spying activities.

2 Lloyd Tilghman (1816-1863) was a native of Maryland. His first commission was that of colonel in command of the Third Kentucky Infantry. He was promoted to brigadier general in the latter part of 1861 and placed in command at Fort Henry. He later served in Mississippi with Gen. Joseph E. Johnston, and was killed in the battle of Baker's Creek during the seige of Vicksburg.

3 Jeremy Francis Gilmer, soldier, was born in 1818 in Guilford County, North Carolina. He graduated from West Point in 1829 and was active in the engineer corps until the Civil War. In 1861 he was appointed Major of Engineers in the Confederate Army and served on General Albert Sidney Johnston's staff. He was later appointed Chief of the Engineer Bureau in Richmond, and in August 1863 was promoted to Major-General. After the war he became engaged in a number of business enterprises.

4 Lieutenant-Colonel Gantt commanded the Ninth Tennessee battalion of cavalry at Fort Donelson.

one half of the 10th Reg and one half of Col Drake's[5] 4th Miss Reg and went out to make a reconnaisance but returned without gaining any information. Our pickets today had a brush with the enemy's pickets in which we lost one man belonging to Capt Millner's Cavalry Co. This evening all of our forces at Ft Heiman were brought over to Ft Henry except the sick and three companies of cavalry. Our forces at Ft Henry amounted to about twenty six hundred, excluding the Artillery Company in the Fort, which was divided today by Gen Tilghman into two Brigades. The 1st Brigade commanded by Col Heiman of the 10th Tenn Reg and the 2nd by Col Jos Drake of the 4th Miss Reg. Col Heiman sent out three pieces of light artillery and two companies of infantry to our outer works at the point where the Dover road comes in, with instructions for them to remain all night.

Feb. 6

Last night Gen Tilghman stayed as usual on the steamer Dunbar, which lay about one mile and a half above the Fort on this side. About 8 oc the Dunbar landed at Ft Heiman and about 10½ oc Gen Tilghman with Maj Gilmer and others crossed over to Ft Henry in a small boat. Before his arrival it was evident from the smoke of the gun boats that this was the day for the regular bombardment. Very soon after they moved up in full view of the Ft. Gen Tilghman then ordered the Commanders of Reg to take their men out of range of shell and shot of the boats, and had all things made ready for an engagement with the boats. At about 12½ oc the bombardment opened on both sides, and grew fiercer and fiercer every minute. The gun boats which were four in number continued to advance step by step and finally got right up to the Ft. The river was very high and the Ft surrounded entirely by water. The guns of the boats and those of the Ft were nearly on a level, giving them every advantage. Three gun boats were in the rear of those engaged. The engagement lasted one hour and twenty minutes, when our flag was struck and the Fort surrendered with all in it including Gen Tilghman—numbering in all fifty two men. Some who were in the Ft and who did not belong there properly escaped. Our rifle gun bursted after firing with great effect about ten times, killing several of the gunners. The 128 pounder was rendered useless by the vents becoming stopped. We had to fire thirty two lb ammunition out of the 42's. We had but a small company of artillerists and most of them recruits with no reliefs—and really but two or three good gunners. Such was the condition of things at the time of the surrender. Col Heiman

[5] Colonel Joseph Drake, a member of the Fourth Mississippi Regiment, was in command of the Second Brigade during the engagements at Forts Henry and Donelson.

From The Historic Blue Grass Line

Nashville Inn — City Hotel

Court House, built in 1802, as it looked in 1832

Cumberland River Bridge
From Harper's Pictorial History of the Civil War

Courtesy Library of Congress

View of occupied Nashville, looking north along the Cumberland River, from the roof of the University of Nashville.

remained with Gen Tilghman in the Ft during the bombardment. While the fight was going on the boats would frequently throw shell to the rear of the Ft, evidently to reach the infantry. We moved our position from place to place, until we reached the point where the Dover road comes in and where seven pieces of our light artillery were placed. Very soon after we reached this point one of our cavalry pickets came in and reported that the enemy were approaching in large force, and within one half mile of us. I immediately communicated with Col Drake who was in command of the 2nd brigade and suggested that he place his men in the rifle pits on the right of the artillery and that I would in the absence of Col Heiman place the 1st brigade on the left and that we would give them battle right there. This was immediately done. I then sent my Adjutant R McG Southall[6] post haste to the Ft to inform Gen Tilghman of the approach of the enemy—and to ask him if, out of two Gen's in the Ft, the forces outside could not have one and to say to him that we awaited orders. The message brought back was that the Ft had surrendered, and that I must take command of the forces, and march them southward. I at once informed Col Drake of the intelligence and order and the whole force moved at once in the direction indicated. To march southward we had to go through one of the Ten river bottoms which was full of mud and water. The horses drawing the artillery were very indifferent. They fell and floundered and the wheels went down over the hubs in the mire. I ordered the drivers to take the horses out, spike the guns, and leave them. The infantry behaved well throughout the day but Gantt's Cavalry acted most shamefully and disgracefully. Instead of remaining in the rear to protect the infantry they rushed by us, some without their hats and were all evidently panic stricken. I got in front of them, and endeavored to stop them, but my efforts were without avail. On, on they went, and I lost sight of them entirely. Pretty soon after leaving McCuchens which is about three miles from the Ft Col Heiman overtook us, much to our joy, and said that the enemy's cavalry were attacking our rear. He thereupon drew up the whole force in line of battle to receive them. We remained in this position for about one half hour and then proceeded in the direction of Dover, where we were ordered to go after crossing the bottom before mentioned It is fortunate that we took this road, for if we had gone the regular Dover road we would have been cut to pieces, as the enemy's forces under Gen Grant[7] numbered over

[6] Randal McGavock Southall (1827-1866) was the son of Joseph Branch Southall and Mary Cloyd McGavock.

[7] Ulysses Simpson Grant (1822-1885), General of the Union armies, eighteenth President of the United States.

twelve thousand. We marched at least twenty miles over a very bad road—and high creeks. In crossing some of the creeks the men had to go four abreast and hold each other up and with their cartridge boxes hung on their muskets to keep them dry. We reached Ft Donelson in safety, about 12 oc at night and went into the cabins of the Regiments stationed at this Post. Some twenty men were cut off by the enemy's cavalry—among them the Maj of Col Gee's[8] Ark Reg. Thus ended the day's work—and we came off better than I anticipated. I always knew that we would be defeated here whenever the enemy came in force. I so expressed myself frequently to Gov Harris, the Military board at Nashville and even to Gen A S Johnston,[9] who I went to see expressly on the subject at Bowling Green. The authorities, both State and Confederate, are to blame for this disaster to our army for Col A Heiman, the Commandant of the post four months before the surrender, informed them of the weakness of the position in an able and elaborate report. He constantly urged the necessity of strengthening the post but no attention was given to it. Indeed they seemed to regard the defenses of the two rivers as not very important. About three weeks ago a letter addressed to Gen Tilghman was received and contents immediately telegraphed by Col Heiman to Gen Polk,[10] Gen Johnston, and Gov Harris. Copies of the letter were also sent by Col Heiman to these gentlemen. This letter was written by a gentleman in Paducah and sent by his son who had it sewed up in the lining of his boot. He stated that Gen Smith[11] would start on a certain day up the two rivers with 60,000 men with the gun boats and the federals expected to make a junction with Gen Buel[12] at Nashville on the 22nd of Feb. Gen Tilghman had every confidence in the correctness of the statements in this letter, and he again sent dispatches to the proper authorities and asked for reinforcements. But no help came. I understood from Col Heiman who was in the Ft during the bombardment that Gen Tilghman

---

[8] Colonel Gee commanded the Fifteenth Arkansas Regiment during the engagements at Forts Henry and Donelson. His regiment was part of the Second Brigade.

[9] Albert Sidney Johnston (1803-1862), soldier.

[10] Leonidas Polk (1806-1864), minister, soldier, was born in Raleigh, North Carolina. He graduated from West Point in 1827; resigned his commission; entered the Episcopal ministry in 1830; appointed Missionary Bishop of the Southwest in 1838; made Bishop of Louisiana in 1841; instrumental in founding the University of the the South; Major General in the Confederate Army; killed at Pine Mountain, near Marietta, Georgia.

[11] Charles F. Smith (1807-1862), brigadier (later major) general of volunteers in the Federal Army. A native of Philadelphia, he was graduated from West Point in 1825, taught there for several years, and helped train many of the officers who fought in the Mexican War and on both sides in the Civil War. After having served as commandant at West Point, he was put in charge of a light battalion in the Mexican War and was later in command of the Red River expedition. At Fort Donelson, Smith's division advanced on the left, at a position nearest the river below the fort. In the center was Lew Wallace, with John A. McClernand on the right.

[12] Don Carlos Buell (1818-1898), Union soldier.

conducted himself nobly and he held the Ft as long as it was possible. When he was satisfied that he could not hold it and before stricking his flag, he gave orders for the forces outside of the Ft to retreat to Dover. Before closing this sad day's work I must here bear testimony that the 10th Ten Reg never broke their lines during the long march and that they picked up many guns left by others and brought them safely to Ft Donelson. Some of them had as many as half doz guns, some swords, and some overcoats, etc.

Feb. 7th

I stayed last night with Capt Dortch. This morning I felt very well considering the exposure yesterday. My Regiment borrowed some tents and pitched them according to Capt. Dixon's[13] orders opposite the Dover grave yard. We are bad off for cooking utensils and blankets. Having no overcoat or blankets my men suffer very much. I observed a very strong feeling here today against Gen Tilghman for surrendering Ft Henry, but as soon as the facts were properly presented they all agreed that he had done right.

Feb. 8th

I am now staying at Brandon's hotel which is very close to my camp and to headquarters. It is very much crowded, but I managed to get something to eat, and a place to sleep. In addition to the three regiments that I left here the first of Jan., viz. Sugg's,[14] Head's,[15] and Bailey's,[16] I notice Gantt's six companies of Cavalry from Maury Co and Col Abernathy's[17] Reg from Giles Co.

---

[13] Captain Dixon was a member of the engineers in the Confederate Army. He was cited by General Leonidas Polk for his action at the battle of Belmont. Of his work General Lloyd Tilghman wrote: "To Captain Dixon, of the engineers, I owe . . . my special acknowledgements of his ability and unceasing energies. Under his immediate eye were all the works proposed by myself at Fort Donelson and Heiman executed, while his fruitfulness in resources to meet the many disadvantages of position alone, enabled us to combat its difficulties unsuccessfully."

[14] Colonel Cyrus A. Sugg commanded the Fiftieth Tennessee Regiment at Fort Donelson. He was later seriously wounded at the battle of Missionary Ridge in November 1863. He commanded his regiment at the Battle of Chickamauga where he was cited for gallantry.

[15] Colonel Head commanded a regiment of Tennessee volunteers.

[16] James E. Bailey (1822-1885) of Clarksville, Tennessee, attended the University of Nashville, read law in Clarksville, and was admitted to the bar in 1842. He was a member of the State Legislature in 1853 and was appointed by Gov. Isham Harris to the Tennessee Military and Financial Board in 1861. On Christmas Day, 1861, he was elected Colonel of the Forty-ninth Tennessee Regiment. After being exchanged as a prisoner of war, he served as a member of the Military Court in Hardee's Corps. After the war he was appointed special judge of the State Supreme Court and was elected U. S. Senator in 1877 to fill the vacancy created by the death of Andrew Johnson.

[17] A. H. Abernathy commanded the Fifty-third Tennessee Regiment at Fort Donelson.

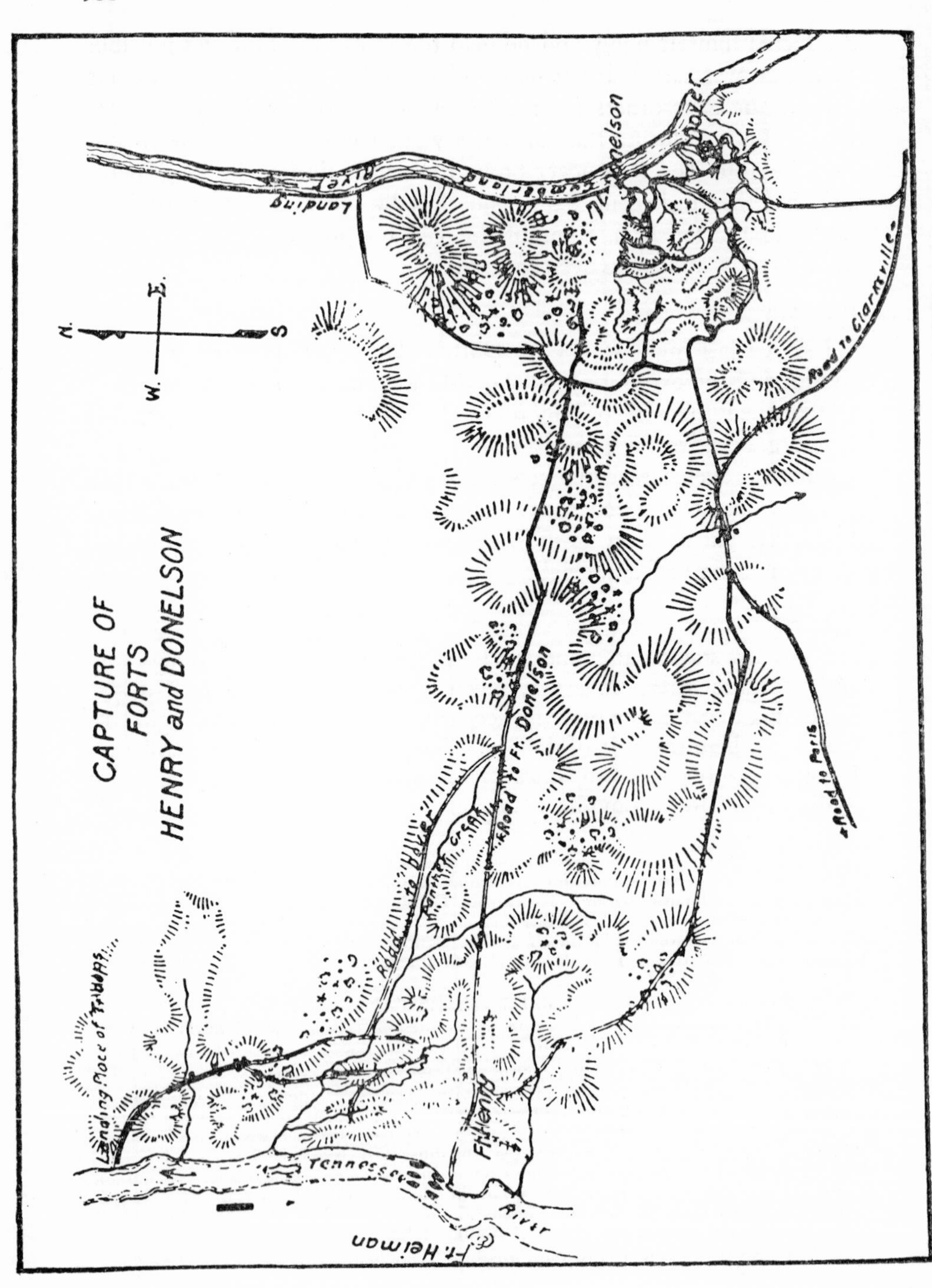
CAPTURE OF
FORTS
HENRY and DONELSON
N.
S
W.
E.
Road to Clarksville
Road to Paris
Road to Ft. Donelson
Road to Dover
Ft. Henry
Tennessee
River
Ft. Heiman
Landing Place of Troops
Landing
Dover

Feb. 9th

Gen Gideon J Pillow arrived here today and assumed the command of the forces. Troops are now beginning to come in from Hopkinsville and from Bowling Green. I regret very much that Gen. Pillow has been placed in command, as I have no confidence in him as an officer and if I am not much mistaken we will require ere many days all the skill and talent that we can bring into the field. I received some boxes of clothing today from my wife. Anticipating my wants and those of my men, she sent me blankets, comforts,—and every thing that a denuded soldier might need. These articles came in good time, as the weather is quite cold and disagreeable.

Feb. 10th

Today Gen Pillow ordered that Capt Morgan's company of my regiment be assigned to duty in the Fort as heavy artillerists. The men of the company did not want to go, saying that they had no practice in artillery and that they did not wish to separate themselves from their Reg. Upon being informed by their Capt of their disinclination to go, Gen Pillow rode out to my encampment, had Capt Morgan's Company drawn up into line, and made the following speech: "You are Irishmen and I know you will prove true to your adopted South. I come here to drive the Hessians from this neck of land between the rivers, and to replant the stars and bars upon the battlements of Fort Henry. I will never Surrender! The word is not in my vocabulary! I had Irishmen with me in the Mexican War—and at Belmont where they proved themselves equal to any of our soldiery. Many of you know me personally, *certainly all of you by reputation* and I want you to go now when I command you." Like good soldiers they went, although they knew nothing about artillery. For some cause or other they returned to their Reg the same evening. We moved our encampment today to a position on the east side of the valley leading to the Ft. and about the centre of the line of Rifle Pits laid out by Maj Gilmer. Gen Simon Bolivar Buckner reached here last night from Bowling Green with a portion of his brigade. I do not know how he and Pillow will get along together, considering the dressing the former gave the latter several years ago, when Pillow was trying to get into the Senate of the U S. Pillow is a vindicative man, and not likely to forget the matter. It is very evident that the enemy will make an attack upon us very soon. Our line of rifle pits are very extensive, but we are getting them up rapidly. The parapets are made of logs and brushwood, covered over with dirt.

Feb. 11th

Troops are still coming in slowly from the direction of Hopkinsville and Bowlingreen. Forrest's[18] Cavalry went out on a scout today in the direction of Ft Henry and brought in several prisoners. Col Brandon also went out with a pretty strong force of picked men belonging to this county and who were acquainted with the hills and valleys. They met the enemy and were repulsed, losing several men.

Feb. 12th

Col Forrest's Cavalry were driven in this morning by the advanced guard of the enemy who they reported as approaching in large force from Ft Henry. About morn they arrived and commenced investing our lines. The gun boats came and threw a few shot and shell this afternoon without effect. Gen Floyd reached here tonight and being the senior officer took the command. He brought his brigade with him.

Feb. 13th

The ball opened this morning by the firing of a gun from Porter's Battery, which was on the hill next below the valley that leads to the Ft. The enemy during the night had planted their batteries on hills to command our centre. Firing pretty soon became general from the batteries on both sides, and was kept up all day. The position occupied by my Reg was a high hill above the valley leading to the Fort about the centre of our lines and very much exposed to the batteries of the enemy. Three batteries played upon us all day. Maney's Battery occupied the summit of this hill and it was at this battery that the enemy directed his fire. About two o'clock the enemy attempted to storm our position. The 49th 47th, and 17th Ill. Regiments made a charge upon us and came up within a few feet of our entrenchments but were repulsed with a terrible loss. Maney's Battery and Porter's Battery did good work here and the firing from our rifle pits was terrific. My Reg behaved nobly and was as much as I could do to keep them in the pits, they were so anxious to get out and charge them. The fight lasted fifteen or twenty minutes but was terrible while it lasted. They report 40 killed and two hundred wounded but it must have been much greater, as our men went out and brought in at least 60 muskets. Unfortunately the leaves of the woods were fired by our shell—and most of the enemy's dead and wounded were burnt up. Maney's battery suffered very much during the day. His

[18] Nathan Bedford Forrest (1821-1877), Confederate general, was a native of Bedford County, Tennessee. He became wealthy as a cotton farmer prior to 1859; enlisted in the Confederate Army as a private in June 1861; soon began a career of cavalry raiding which made him famous; returned to his cotton plantations at the close of the war; was involved in the early activities of the Ku Klux Klan, but did not keep his connections long. For some years he was President of the Selma, Marion, and Memphis Railroad.

first Lt was killed, besides about fifteen others. The balance of his lieutenants were wounded, and three of his horses killed. I lost only one man in this engagement and several wounded slightly. This afternoon the gun boats, four in number, came up and engaged our water-batteries and after a long and fierce struggle were driven back. Capt Dixon who had command of our guns was killed in the engagement. A ball struck one of our pieces, and knocked a nut off which struck him in the head, and killed him instantly.

Feb. 14th

The batteries have been busily at work all day, also the sharp shooters. The balls from the latter came whizzing by us as thick sometimes as hail stones, and we can hear no report of their guns. They have the guns, but not the marksmen. The gun boats came up again this evening and engaged our batteries. They came up to the branch just below the Ft and were so close that every shot took effect. Our fire was more than they could stand. They fell back, nearly all of them in a crippled condition. It was intended by our Gens to make an attack on the enemy today and our forces were actually drawn out for the purpose but Gen Pillow concluded it was too late in the day to bring an attack (12 oc). Our Generals had a consultation tonight about 11½ oc and it was agreed that we should attack the enemy outside of our rifle pits and on our left wing by five o'clock in the morning. The forces under Gen Buckner which occupied the pits on our right were to be withdrawn and placed on the left with Pillow's forces. The Brigade commanded by Col Heiman was to remain in their pits. Col Head's Reg was to take the place of Buckner's men in the pits on our right and the two Regiments in the Fort were to remain there. The plan was to make the attack on our left and open the way for our retreat. As soon as the plan was laid before me, I objected to it because I saw plainly that Col Heiman's Brigade together with the Reg. in the Ft were to be sacrificed and I believe that every military man will condemn it in the future.

Feb. 15th

Our troops for some cause or other did not move as early this morning as was agreed upon last night. Gen Buckner did not cross the valley leading to the Fort until sometime after daylight and the attack was not made until at least one hour after sunrise. The fight continued on the left wing until late in the evening. We drove the enemy from their position and gained at this point a signal victory, which if it had been followed up would have resulted in a complete rout of the enemy. While they were retreating and just as they were about crossing the ridge leading into the Central valley, a battery and several Reg's came to their aid. The battery opened upon us and caused our troops to falter. At this point our forces were ordered to fall back into their pits. Late in the evening the enemy charged our works on our right and succeeded in getting possession of them. The fight here was long and terrible resulting in an immense loss of life on their side. Our forces finally succeeded in driving them back. The firing from the batteries was kept up very briskly on both sides until after dark. As soon as the firing ceased I got on my horse and rode into Dover to learn the result of the day's work. Knowing Gens Floyd and Pillow intimately for years I went at once to headquarters, where I found the two Gens seated alone. Floyd was writing at the time. He soon finished and read aloud the paper, which was a telegram to Gen Johnston giving a statement of the battle. We then entered into a conversation about the battle, and I suggested that if the battery that opened while the enemy were fleeing had been captured (which could have been easily done by Col Heiman's Brigade) the rout would have been complete, and the enemy driven entirely away. Pillow replied that if Buckner had have been up in time according to his promise, the enemy would have been routed. In a few minutes Gen Buckner came in and I retired, with the impression on my mind that the battle would be renewed tomorrow with greater vigor. I then went to the telegraph office, and sent a dispatch to father, giving him the result of the battle. Our loss in killed and wounded was about four hundred and that of the enemy at least four thousand. After some conversation with Dr Morton of Nashville, I returned back to my encampment and communicated to Col Heiman the sum and substance of my conversation with the two Gens. We eat a box of salmon sent to us by Mrs Gregg from Nashville and retired.

Feb. 16th

At 1 oc this morning I was aroused by Col Heiman who informed me that an order had been received from Headquarters to the effect that our forces were to retreat before day, and that every Reg must be ready to march by 4 oc with provisions in their haversacks, blankets, etc. Agreeable to order I had my regiment ready and we marched beyond the town of Dover where we were halted. The morning was cold and disagreeable. After standing here about one half hour I became impatient and began to smell a rat. I accordingly went to Col Heiman and asked him why the delay. If we expected to make a successful retreat we should be moving, that we were burning time, etc. He replied that he did not know that he was awaiting orders. I then inquired for Gen

B. R Johnson[19] who is in command of the division. After some delay and difficulty I found him and he seemed to be profoundly ignorant as to what was going on and said that he was waiting for orders. He then went to Head Quarters where he remained for some time. Great activity seemed to prevail at the Dover warf where there was two steamboats. Lights were moving about in every direction and some movement was evidently going on of an important character. I noticed that the forces assembled where I was were becoming demoralized and were going off by ones, twos, and threes up the river. Gen Johnson then returned and reported that Generals Pillow and Floyd had turned the command over to Gen Buckner and that they had gone up to Nashville on the boats, and that Gen Buckner had surrendered the whole army, that white flags were then floating from the Ft and our breast works. I was perfectly shocked and so were my men. I asked Gen Johnson if there was no chance of making our escape. He replied no, that the enemy was three times as strong at our right as they were yesterday morning, that Floyd and Pillow had taken all the transports and that escape was hopeless. My first thought was to cut my way through with my regiment, but I reflected and concluded that if I made the attempt and got my men butchered, every body would say that I attempted to do with one Reg what Gen Buckner would not attempt with the whole army. I then thought of getting a flat and crossing my regiment over the river—but no flat was to be had. I then thought of swimming the river but the water was high and the morning cold, and many of the men could not swim. Here all expedients for retreat was at an end, so I determined to share the fate of my men, rather than desert them as some officers did in their hour of trouble. In sorrow, humiliation, and anger I marched my Reg back to their quarters. I then rode over to the Ft where the white flag was flying. Very soon after, the gun boat came in sight and threw several shot and shell at the Ft evidently not aware of the surrender. I then went back to my encampment and took breakfast with some of the men, after which I rode back to Dover. As I was going in I could see the Hessians coming into our lines and could hear plainly their exultant shouts. Oh! how these shouts sank into my heart. They came into our encampments, bursted open the trunks of officers and robbed them of everything. While I was in my room at Brandon's Hotel they stole Tenth Legion, my saddle horse, to which I was much

---

[19] Bushrod Rust Johnson (1817-1880), soldier, teacher, was born in Belmont County, Ohio. He graduated from West Point in 1840; served in the Seminole and Mexican Wars; Superintendent of the Western Military Institute of Kentucky at Georgetown, commissioned a brigadier-general in the Confederate Army in 1861; promoted to major-general in 1864. After the war he became Superintendent of the Military College of the University of Nashville.

attached. He was hitched in front of the hotel and I think was taken by a field officer. I made complaint to Gen Grant—and he told me that if I could find the horse he would make the man give him up, but that he would have to be turned over to his Quarter Master. Of course I gave myself no further trouble about him. I passed the afternoon and evening mostly in my room in the hotel with some of the officers of our Reg. The men of the Reg and some of the officers left Dover on a steamboat this evening. Several of the gun boats started up to Nashville this evening. A portion of Floyd's Brigade and Forrest's Cavalry escaped.

CHAPTER XXIII

"I am heartily tired of confinement." (March July, 1862)

The surrender of the Confederate forces at Fort Donelson gave 14,000 prisoners to the care of the North. Randal McGavock was one of this group. He was to spend the next five months in a Northern prison. The Confederate officers at Fort Donelson were sent first to Camp Chase in Columbus, Ohio. They remained there only a few days and were then transferred to Fort Warren in Boston Harbor. McGavock has left a rather full picture of prison life at Fort Warren. The prisoners had access to numerous newspapers and other periodical literature. This enabled them to follow the conflict closely. McGavock read widely, and the enforced leisure of the prison gave him much time in which to record his observations.

Feb. 17th

This morning the full realization of the sad disaster to our army and our cause is painfully presented to my mind. Some 12,000 of our best troops are to be incarcerated in northern prisons, the Capitol of Ten to be attacked in a few days and properly destroyed, if not evacuated, the heart of the Confederacy penetrated, and a blow stricken that will cost much blood and treasure to retrieve, if ever done. Oh! how sad it is to see so fair a country inhabited by the northern hordes. Can it be that this will last always? No—no—no—the God of justice, truth, and mercy will in his own good time hurl the oppressors from power and restore once more the blessings of peace amongst a people fighting for liberty, constitutional rights, and their property. I have not been out much today, wishing to avoid as much as possible the supercilious stare of the Yankees, who hold their heads aloft in the air, as if they had accomplished something by their valor—not thinking for a moment that they were badly whipped at every point on Saturday, and that our surrender was for the want of bad Generalship on our side—and not bravery or great deeds on theirs. They outnumbered us at least four to one, and really deserve no credit. This evening Col Heiman and myself together with a number of officers from our Reg came on board the steamer Tecumseh where we found six or eight hundred rebel prisoners, and two companies of Yankees to guard us. The boat did not leave the warf until late in the night.

Feb. 18th

We passed Smithland and Paducah during the day, but saw nothing at either place to attract particular attention. At Smithland they have fortified a high hill back of the town and have a small garrison. They also have fortifications at Paducah and Cairo. We reached the latter place early in the night and remained all night on the boat.

Feb. 19

This morning the ice is running heavy in the Miss. After taking on some coal—and some commissary stores we proceeded up the Miss en route for St Louis. The boat is very much crowded, and very disagreeable to me. We occupy our time in fighting over our battles, playing cards, etc. We passed Cape Girardeau today and were saluted by a battery at that place.

Feb. 20th

We reached the City of St Louis today, and was received with great cordiality by the citizens who came down to see us. They seemed disposed to do all in their power for us, and contributed to our comfort very much by furnishing articles of necessity. After remaining here for a short time the boat went over to the Ill shore, where we lay along-side other boats containing rebel prisoners.

Feb. 21st

Today quite a number of citizens came over from St Louis to visit acquaintances among the officers. Col McClarren called to see me and presented me with a box of fine shirts and drawers—which I distributed. Wm Haynes gave me thirty five dollars in currency, and Mr Logan in Hillman's Ten Iron House handed me three dollars. Geo Marshall came over and made a great splutter and offered to do anything for me, but did nothing. Tom Yeatman also made great promises, but did nothing. Henry Hitchock[1] actually sent my note back to me by Horace Berry. All of these gentlemen came from Nashville and were friends of my youth. Hitchcock and myself graduated together. This evening we left for Alton, Ill.

[1] Henry Hitchcock (1829-1902), lawyer, soldier.

Feb. 22

Pretty soon this morning we had the pleasure of seeing some of our old Ft Henry friends who are on parole—viz Gen Tilghman—McConnico[2]—McLaughlin—Taylor[3]—and others. Truly it was happy meeting. They remained with us all day. Henry Southall (Colored) also joined us here. He was very glad to see his master Randal as well as myself and others. The men were marched off of the boat and conveyed to the cars, where they will be sent in boxes to Chicago to Camp Douglass. It seems to be the policy of the Government to separate the officers from the men, in order to break all ties existing between them, and to prevent any future organization. It was a sad sight to see them have men marched away from their officers. Here we changed boats and the officers returned to St Louis or the place opposite.

Feb. 23

Owing to the heavy fog we did not reach St Louis until about 9 oc this morning. We remained on the Nebraska all day, where the crowd, the filth, and the stench made it exceedingly disagreeable. I had no idea that the South could furnish so many dirty men among Field officers. A number of ladies came over today from St Louis with baskets filled with eatables. They were not allowed to come on the boats. An officer arrested the husband of a lady who waved her handkerchief at the prisoners. Several little boys were also arrested for giving apples to us. Surely freedom has fled from this land.

Feb. 24

Our party was shipped today on the steamer Southwestern where we are much more comfortable. Col Bailey, Col Quarles, Col Simonton, and Capt Ross were paroled today in St Louis. Why they should be paroled and not the balance of us is a mystery. Tom Yeatman wrote a note to Lt. Kirkman today in which he stated that he was trying to get Kirkman and myself paroled. Gen Tilghman arrived here today, en route for Ft Warren.

Feb. 25

I noticed a steam boat today with more prisoners from Ft. Donelson. She also had a large quantity of tobacco on board, which I supposed was seized at Clarksville. We are doing much better today than usual on our boat. I was appointed Field officer of the day, and I had every-

---

[2] W. Lafayette McConnico of the Tenth Tennessee Regiment served as acting assistant adjutant-general under General Tilghman at Fort Henry. He was given honorable mention for this work at the battle of Forts Henry and Donelson.

[3] J. Walker Taylor commanded a detachment of guides at Fort Donelson. He was commended for gallantry by General Buckner.

thing kept clean and our meals and regular time and together. No news from Yeatman about the parole.

Feb. 26th

Remained on the boat all day.

Feb. 27

This morning we were informed pretty soon after breakfast that we were to be sent to Columbus Ohio. Randal Southall was so unwell that he remained on the boat, and went to the hospital in St Louis. Before starting my old friend and classmate at Cambridge, Mass, Lt Col J M Force of Cincinnati called to see me. He belongs to the Reg that is to guard us to Columbus. We were all marched off of the boats, with soldiers on each side, with packs on our backs to the R R Depot. I was unfortunate enough to be placed in a box car with fifty men, negroes and all, without any stove and nothing to eat or drink. I stood it as long as I could and finally jumped out and accosted the officer in charge and told him that I wanted a seat in one of the passenger cars. Seeing that I was a Field Officer and knowing that I was an acquaintance of his Lt Col he procured me a seat.

Feb. 28

We passed through Terre Haute early this morning, where I was disposed to halt and see my old uncle the Rev Mr McNutt, but being a prisoner I had to move on. This evening we passed through Indianapolis, the Capitol of Ind. I saw Jno Hall of Nashville standing at the door of a hotel. Dr Wood of Nashville was also here. The Irish of this place were very kind to us and really sympathize with us every where we have met them in the north. Their true and generous nature always inclines them to take sides with the oppressed.

March 1st

We arrived this morning at the Depot in Columbus, where Col Moody, an ex-Methodist preacher, took charge of us, and marched us with much pomposity through the principal streets of the town and thence four miles distant with our packs on our backs to Camp Chase, which has been represented to us by the Yankees as being a beautiful and charming place. Oh! what vicissitudes flesh is heir to. Two years ago I was escorted by the magnates of Ohio from this same depot in company with the Ten and Ky legislatures to their Capitol—where fine speeches were made, and where we feasted and made merry with our *friends,* who *loved* us *more than* language could tell. Now I am a Rebel Prisoner too poor and mean for even their dogs to bark at. When we reached Camp Chase we were examined closely and deprived of all our side arms—and then marched into a pen or high enclosure containing some rough and filthy shantys where vermin and all manner of creeping things infested. The mud was over our shoe tops—and thirty-six men were placed in a room 12 by 24 including the bunks. Three of us occupied a bunk four feet wide and not long enough to straighten our limbs in. The smell from the pit is intolerable, and I predict that if these men are kept here until warm weather, they will die like sheep with the rots. Oh! what a shame that in the name of liberty, the descendants of the brave men who gave them their heritage should be so treated, simply because they wished to protect their Constitutional rights and to preserve their homes, their property, their wives and their children from the ruthless hand of the invader.

March 2nd

I rested badly last night, having to sleep on the hard plank and not room enough to turn over in. The more I see of this dirty and loathsome prison, the more outraged I feel. There is no farmer in Ten that calls himself respectable that would permit his hogs or cattle to stay in such a place. Today there was a meeting of the Field officers to select a Superintendent, and a Commissary out of our own officers for the prison. This was done by order of the Federal Authorities. At the meeting I made a little speech urging the necessity of selecting for the first position some man of activity and energy, who would pay strict attention to the sanitary condition of the prison, as the health of the officers absolutely required it. They selected a physician for the place and I suppose he will do all in his power.

March 3rd

Our mess got along finely considering all things. It is composed of the officers of my own Reg and six officers of Col Suggs' Reg with whom I am intimately acquainted, having formed the Reg. We have one negro (Haywood) a faithful servant who does our cooking aided by two officers detailed every day. I took as much exercise today as was practicable in the small muddy pen. Col Moody, the Commandant of the concern, accosted me today and inquired if I was comfortable. I looked at him a moment and replied: "*Comfortable did you say?*" He went on and made no response.

March 4th

This morning we were informed by the same Col Moody that the Field officers must be ready to start to Ft Warren, Mass by twelve o'clock. When the hour of separation arrived it was truly a painful and heart rending sight. Company officers were parting with those whom they had followed for many months, with those who had led them into battle, and who had fought side by side together in defense of Constitutional liberty. There was not a dry cheek in the whole party—and I could see from the firm grip of the hand and the determined expression on each countenance that neither separation or incarceration could obliterate the memory of the past or dampen our ardour in the great and common cause which brought us together, and which will reunite us sooner or later though the powers of all the earth may combine against us. We feel that God is on our side, that our cause is just and righteous, and that we only have to be patient to witness the realization of our most sanguine hopes.

At 12 oc our baggage was carried out and then we were marched out in solemn procession. Quite an effecting scene occurred soon after leaving the gates of the prison. Two free negroes who followed us out were stopped and ordered back by Col Moody to the prison. They replied that they wished to go with their Cols and share their fate. The dictatorial and haughty ex-Methodist preacher in a Col's uniform—ordered them to go back, that they would not be allowed such privileges. I was standing close by and seeing how unhappy the poor creatures were, my very blood ran cold, and I involuntarily exclaimed: "The Lord reigneth, blessed be the name of the Lord." After this exhibition this same pharasaical Col went into the omnibus where there was a few invalid officers, and burst into a flood of tears saying that he hoped that the war would soon be over and that he never heard of a victory on his side without weeping. Oh! most vile and God-forsaken reprobate. If justice is ever meeted out to you, your portion will be the execration of all good men upon this earth—and a hot place hereafter. We were marched four miles to the depot and left the Capitol of Ohio at 3 oc P M, never again to see it, I hope. This evening we stopped at a little town where the R R cross and they handed us in some weak coffee, stale bread, and pork that was perfectly raw. I gave my portion to a little boy who was selling apples and pies and told him to carry it home to his mother and tell her to cook it for him.

March 5

We passed through Cleveland in the night and reached Buffalo early this morning. The snow is very deep on the ground, and everything looks dreary without. We passed through Rochester, Utica and other places during the day. At each point where we stopped we were subjected to the idle gaze of the curious and the inquisitive. I neither asked or answered any questions relating to public affairs. We reached Albany late in the afternoon and crossed the Hudson on the ice. Maj Granberry[4] of Texas had his wife with him, a small and delicate woman, but she waded through the shock on the ice like a heroine, and seemed determined to cling to the fortunes of her husband. At Springfield, Mass we got the best supper that we have had since leaving Ft Donelson.

March 6

We reached the depot in Boston about 2 oc this morning and remained in the cars until about 8 oc. Maj Smith, an army officer who had charge of us, after eating his breakfast and smoking his cigar at the Revere, came down and kindly permitted the large crowd that had assembled to escort us several blocks off to the warf where a little [boat] called Charles Fremont was ready to convey us to our place of destination. Ft Warren is situated on a small island outside the Boston Harbor, from which there is a good view of the city, Bunkerhill Monument, Charlestown Navy Yard, etc. The Ft is substantially built of Quincy granite and I expect is one of the best belonging to the old government. When we landed they marched us up within the enclosure and drew us up into line. Col Dimmick[5] the Commandant of the Ft, an old and very polite officer of the Regular service, was then presented and we were counted and recounted and counted again to see if they had the number they started with. When this was over we broke ranks and took by the hands our two Gens, Buckner and Tilghman, who preceded us several days. Very soon we were surrounded by a number of political prisoners from Md who received us with a great deal of cordiality and immediately ordered breakfast for us and I must say that it was the best meal I have set down to since entering the army. Our Gens and these gentlemen were so kind to us that I really forgot that I was a prisoner, but fancied that [I] was in the select society of congenial minds who had happened together by some freak of fortune in this inhospitable latitude. Very comfortable rooms were furnished us and iron cots, with mattresses and blankets—which with the fervid heat from an anthracite fire rendered our condition very comfortable. Gen Tilghman, Col Heiman, Col Gregg[6] of Texas, and Lt Col Jackson of Ala and myself occupy the same room.

---

[4] H. B. Granbery was commander of the Seventh Texas Regiment. His regiment was prominent at the battle of Missionary Ridge, November 1863 and the battle of New Hope Church, May 1864.

[5] Justin Dimick (1800-1871), soldier.

[6] John Gregg (1828-1864), later promoted to General. He was in command at the Battle of Raymond when McGavock was killed.

March 7th

Today I have occupied myself in fixing up our room, ordering such articles as we need from Boston and making our mess arrangements. The occupants of our room, together with four others have accepted the invitation to join the Baltimore mess, which has been formed for some time and have every thing properly arranged. We have French cooks and waiters, and as well served tables as can be found at any first class hotel in the country.

March 8th

All day in room.

March 9th

This morning I read several chapters in the Bible and attended service in Commodore Barron's room. Major Brown of Baltimore read a sermon and Mr Farrison of Baltimore the Episcopal service. Today the prisoners of War were paroled upon their signing the following document:

Head Quarters Ft Warren
Boston Harbor, Mass. March 8/62

"We the undersigned having been granted the limits of this Post (excepting the Barracks, the Warves and the beach beyond the sea wall, as far as that extends, and beyond the limits of the grass on other parts of the island) do solemnly bind ourselves upon our honor, that we will not take advantage of the privilege thus granted; that we will not converse nor have any communication whatever with the sentinels or other soldiers of the Post, except as required by their duties in connection with us, or with citizens; that we will not attempt to communicate with nor connive at any attempt to communicate with the shore, nor utter any language militating against the Government of the United States in public or in a position to be heard by any of the soldiers of the Command or by citizens; and that between "Retreat" and "Reville" we will not leave the *sets* or *Quarters* assigned to us."

This was signed by all of the Ft Donelson prisoners, and we now have the liberties therein specified. I wrote a letter to Thos Eakin of N Y today asking him to make me a remittance. I also wrote to my wife.

March 10th

Today Gens Buckner and Tilghman were placed in solitary confinement by order from the War Dept at Washington. Col Dimmick sent for them at his room and never permitted them to return. They have been on parole, and for what reason they were placed in solitary confinement, we cannot imagine. This summary procedure on the part of the Government cast quite a gloom over the prisoners in the Ft. I wrote a note to Judge Parker today of Cambridge—my old law professor, asking him to use his influence to get me paroled in Boston and Cambridge and to send me some books to read. I also wrote to Chas Woodburry of Boston—an old friend, letting him know that I was here. I ordered a suit of clothes from Jno Earle and Co, my old tailors in Boston.

March 11th

I have become pretty well acquainted and very much fascinated with some of the political prisoners from Md. Geo P Kane, the Marshall of Baltimore, is a fine looking, very intelligent and agreeable gentleman. He seems to delight in making every one comfortable about him. He figured largely in Baltimore during the riots there last spring—and is a true type of southern character. Dr Chas Macgill of Hagerstown, Md looks like an old Roman. He, too, is very kind and devotes himself to the sick. Mr Wm G Harrison, a member of the House of Deligates from Baltimore, is an old gentleman whose character is without spot or stain. He devotes himself to the sick and occupies his time constantly in administering to all their little wants. He is a good man and will have his reward. Commodore Barron[7] who was captured at Hatteras is a man of fine intelligence and a most worthy representative of our Navy Dept which is yet to build up. Mr Henry W Warfield, a member of the Md Legislature from Baltimore, is an exceedingly clever gentleman and has assisted the Fort Donelson prisoners very much by giving them current funds at par for southern money.

March 12th

I received a letter from Tom Eakin today remitting me $150 which is very acceptable. Col Heiman received a letter from Mrs Thayer of N Y in which she desires to be remembered to me. Pillow's official report has been received and commented upon by the officers. It is all Pillow—and we are unanimously of the opinion that it is not a fair statement of facts, and that President Davis did exactly right in suspending he and Floyd from their command. Floyd makes a better and more truthful statement—yet he does not extricate himself from the great responsibility of surrendering the army at Ft Donelson.

March 13

We arrived here just one week ago today; it does not seem so long, because we have been so much entertained by conversations with each

[7] Samuel Barron (1809-1888), Confederate naval officer.

other about affairs in the South. My tailor sent my clothes today, but took care to get Chas Woodburry to guarantee payment, notwithstanding I patronized him for years and always paid my bills promptly. I referred him to my friend Woodburry to let him know who I was, and Yankee like because I was a prisoner, he gets a guarantee before he sends the clothes.

March 14th

Judge Parker of Cambridge did not answer my note, but sent a message by one of the officers of the Ft that if I wished any thing to let him know. I suppose he feared to commit himself to paper. I saw his speech in one of the Boston papers today which was delivered at the opening of the Law School on 3rd Inst—in which he alludes to the fact that some of the graduates of the Law School are engaged in "this unholy war" and that he is certain that they did not learn the doctrine of rebellion there. I could in truth say that it was there that I learned what my constitutional rights are and that rebellion to that instrument never appeared in southern states, but alone in the North and more particularly in Mass, which has always been violating the constitution and was the first State in the Union to secede. If I had seen the old man's speech before writing to him, I never would have written.

March 15th

I have occupied the day in reading, walking around the Ft viewing the shipping, etc.

March 16th

There was a service today in Commodore Barron's room but I did not attend.

The northern press are very much puzzled about the falling back of the Confederate forces from the Potomac. The N Y Tribune is down on Gen McClelland[8]—who has just issued a flaming proclamation to his army telling them that the period of inaction is over and that he intends to make an advance movement at once and do some fighting. Col Heiman received a beautiful letter from Mrs Thayer this evening. She is a noble woman. I wrote letters tonight to my wife—Dr Lindsley and Mrs Blood of N Y.

March 17th

This is St Patrick's Day. Oh! how I wish that [I] was with my Irish Reg at Chicago to celebrate the day and cheer them up in their imprisonment. Mrs Thayer sent a box to Col H and myself today, containing

[8] George Brinton McClellan (1826-1885), soldier, Governor of New Jersey.

fine whiskey, brandy, cigars, cheese, sardines, etc. We had some of our friends to visit us this evening and help us enjoy it. I have commenced collecting the autographs of the prisoners in Ft Warren, which will one of these days be quite interesting to me or some one else.[9] The weather for the last three or four days has been very windy and unpleasant, so much so that I have had no disposition to venture out-doors.

March 18th

Today it has been clear and pleasant. I took a walk around the Ft this morning but the wind was too keen for a southerner without an overcoat. Some young ladies came over from Boston today to see Miss Dimmick. It is a novel sight to see a female within these walls and it cheers one up notwithstanding we are not allowed to speak to them. The papers today are barren of news. They are filled with surmises in regard to the falling back of our forces from the Potomac. I read some three or four letters today in the N Y Herald from Nashville giving an account (Union) of things in Ten. I do not know the author, and really do not care to know.

March 19th

This morning the weather was much pleasanter than usual. The papers today contain accounts of a battle at Newe Berne, N C in which it is represented that the Federals gained a victory. They also claim another victory at Salem, Ark. and at 10th island. The Federal government has evidently succeeded in gaining many small victories, but I do not think they will amount to much. The great results must be determined before many days in the great conflicts that must take place on the Tennessee or Rapahannock Rivers. I called to see today several gentlemen who have been kind enough to show me a great deal of attention in the way of supplying many little wants. Col Jackson was visited today by Mr Hunt, his brother-in-law from Louisville. Col Dimmick came in the room with him, but withdrew and permitted an interview of some thirty minutes. This evening I was very much disgusted with the comments of a certain individual on the subject of the "Retreat from Ft Henry." He claims every thing and no body done anything but himself. He was Col of a Reg—which he commanded together with his brigade. He was Col of *"my Reg"* and acting Brig Gen of *"My Brigade."* He seems jealous of every one who figured with him, when in truth no one thinks or cares much about it—because they

[9] McGavock's autograph book of the prisoners at Fort Warren has not come to light. John Calvin Brown's collection is on deposit at the Tennessee State Archives. In it McGavock wrote: *"I was surrendered* at Fort Donelson, Feb. 16." There is another collection in the Confederate Museum, Richmond, but it is not likely that this one was McGavock's.

are willing for him to carry as much of the Ft Henry and Ft Donelson affair as possible.

This evening I enjoyed very much the music of the brass band, which is very good. They play mostly old national airs, some of which I admire very much.

March 20th

This has been the pleasantest day we have experienced here. I took advantage of this morning and walked round the ramparts. For the last two days there has been constant firing of cannon either at the Charlestown Navy Yard or South Boston. I suppose they are testing guns or practicing in artillery. I received a letter today from my friend, Chas L Woodburry of Boston, in which he offers to send me any thing I desire. Letters were received by some of the officers from Camp Chase today, in which we learn that they had considerable sickness among the officers there and two deaths. I notice in the Louisville Journal of the 15th an amusing letter from this place written by Gen Buckner to the Editors, enclosing two dollars, asking them to send their paper with a lengthy poscript about Roger Hamon and etc. The Editor takes occasion to write a long editorial on the subject in which he tries to be very facetious. I would not read such a dirty sheet as the journal and I would not give them an opportunity of making merry over my misfortunes. The Editor suggests that the Rebel prisoners be made useful on the public works—in building bridges—etc.

It is absolutely impossible to gather any reliable information relative to the movements and results of the war, from the northern press. They are either prevented from publishing but one side, or they purposely avoid doing it.

March 21st

This has been a boisterous and rainy day, so much so that I have not been out of my room except to meals. My friend, Woodburry from Boston, sent me another package of newspapers today. I notice that the President of the U S has appointed Gen Dix[10] and Mr Pierpont commissioners to examine the cases of certain political prisoners. Some were released upon their taking the oath of allegiance and others sent back to prison. The latter refused, I suppose to take the [oath.] This is equal to the Star Chamber—or the scenes enacted in Venice under the old Doge. The papers are filled with maps and one side descriptions of the battle at Newbern, N C, the re-taking of the forts on the eastern shore of Fla, the bombardment of Island No 10 in the Miss, the

---

[10] John Adams Dix (1798-1879), statesman, soldier.

advance of Gen Smith up the Ten, and the victories of Gen Curtis[11] in the western part of Ark. The issue of London Times received by yesterday's steamer contains a very correct view of the battle and surrender at Ft Donelson. Indeed the English and French seem to understand this war much better than the northern people. I notice in the Boston papers of today the speeches of Andrew Johnson and Horace Maynard[12] made at Nashville on the 14th. They are both characteristic. When such men are permitted to retake the reins of government in Ten. I have but little hope for restoration of that peace and quiet that seems to be so much desired by the Federal Adm. The embittered hatred entertained by all good men throughout the State of every party towards these political demogogues will render their stay there any thing but agreeable.

March 22nd

I have remained close to my room today reading a novel called "A Strange Story" by Bulwer. It is quite interesting and exciting sofar as I have gone. I had a very pleasant game of euchre today with some of the prisoners. I wrote to my friend, Woodburry of Boston, today who sent me another package of papers. I made the acquaintance today of a Mr Winder, who built the Winder block of buildings in Washington. He is a political prisoner, and is related to Van P Winder[13] of La.

March 23rd

This morning I read several chapters in the book of Exodus. Twenty seven prisoners arrived here today from Key West. They were sailors taken on the Privateer Beauregard. The Boston papers today announce that the city of New Orleans has been taken by Federals. I place no confidence in it.

March 24th

The day has been occupied reading the Strange Story by Bulwer. The following passages struck me so forceably that I here copy them: "Ah, what a mockery there is in that grand word, the world's fierce war-cry, Freedom!" "What a lovely bridge between old age and

---

[11] Samuel Ryan Curtis (1805-1866), soldier, congressman.

[12] Horace Maynard (1814-1882) was one of the leaders of the Union party in East Tennessee. He was a native of Massachusetts and graduated from Amherst in 1838; came to Knoxville, Tennessee in the same year and began the study of law; made Tutor and afterwards Professor of Mathematics in East Tennessee University; first appeared in politics in 1852 as a Whig Elector; elected to Congress in 1857 and re-elected in 1859 and in 1861; Attorney General of Tennessee while Andrew Johnson was Military Governor of the state; again elected to Congress in 1865 and served continuously for ten years; Minister to Turkey 1875-1880; Postmaster General of the United States under President Hayes.

[13] Van Perkins Winder attended the University of Nashville, graduating in 1834. He then married Martha Grundy, McGavock's aunt.

childhood is religion!" "How intuitively the child begins with prayer and worship in entering life, and how intuitively on quitting life the old man turns back to prayer and worship, putting himself again side by side with the infant." This evening I wrote to the following persons, Mrs Dr Boardman, Philia, Mrs Sam Colt, Hartford, Mrs Alice Richardson and Mrs M Steel, Louisville, Capt Thompson, Camp Chase, Maj McConnico, Alton, Ill.

March 25th

The papers today contain an account of a battle at Winchester, Va. in which a victory is claimed by the Federals. Gen Shulls was wounded, and the loss said to be very great on both sides. It is also stated that President Davis is going West to visit our armies. His presence will have great effect towards inspiring our people and our soldiery. Col Heiman received a letter from Col Bailey today who is on parole at Columbus. Dr Hoyt of Nashville has visited Columbus. I think it strange that he did not write to me from that place, telling me the condition of things at home. I have occupied the day in reading mostly. This evening I went into Col Brown's and Hanson's room where I heard the orators of Ten, Ky and Miss discussed in full. Lt Col Jackson who has been very low in our room ever since our arrival is now convalescent. He walked out today for the first time. The prisoners who reached here [a] day or two ago, and who have been confined to their room, were permitted today to walk about. Two of the prisoners have some prospect of an exchange. They are highly elated of course.

March 26th

This has been a most beautiful day. After breakfast I walked around the Ft and inhaled the fresh air from the sea. I finished the "Strange Story" today. The book is well named.

March 27th

This morning I walked out on the parapets and met a very good looking woman, who I ascertained was the wife of the man who kept the boarding house for the laborers employed in the Ft. She broke the ice and I pitched in. She was very voluble and seemed disposed to play the agreeable, but said that she was restrained by orders. While talking with her I noticed that the eyes of the whole Ft was upon us, even old Col Dimmick, the Commandant, whose age ought to exempt him from such an imputation, made his appearance and seemed to dislike my attentions, altho brief and casual.

March 28

I received letters today from mother and Aunt Felicia, the first intelligence that I have received from home. Of course every word and every line was weighed. Col Kane of Baltimore had a party of the prisoners in his room just before dinner and we made merry over an excellent ham, some good Holland Gin—whiskey—ale—etc. Old Capt Berry who has [$]25,000 in the Nashville made himself particularly interesting, particularly as the telegraph today brings the news that she has run the blockade and made her escape from Beaufort, N C. I answered the letters received tonight.

March 29th

This morning I walked for the first time entirely round the little island upon which Ft Warren is situated. It contains about twenty five or thirty acres. I am inclined to believe that the Federals did not achieve so great a victory at Winchester as they made out—or at Pea Ridge in Ark. I received letters today from H. T Boardman and lady from Philadelphia, also from Wm Underwood and Co, Boston. All are anxious to administer to my comfort while in prison.

March 30th

This morning I walked round the island in company with Roger B Hanson[14] of Ky., and he showed me a very amusing letter from G D. Prentice. I attended service in Commodore Barron's room. This evening Cols Hanson and Farqueharson[15] came into our room and drank ale and made themselves very amusing. They are very different in character, one is all wit and humor and the other just about as dry as they make them. Both are good drinkers, but the effects of the liquid is quite different upon the two individuals, producing a contrast quite amusing to those around.

March 31st

This has been a real wintry day, a snow storm, and etc. I received a number of papers from Nashville, the latest being the 15th. The Banner, Patriot and Times are among those sent. All printed on inferior paper and some only half sheets, showing that the papers are in keeping with every thing else there since the surrender. Col Brown[16]

---

[14] Roger Weightman Hanson (1827-1863), Confederate general.

[15] Robert Farquharson was a Nashville business man. He was a member of the board of directors of the Bank of Tennessee in 1817 and of the Nashville branch Bank of the United States about 1833-1834; alderman of Nashville 1829; trustee of the Nashville Female Academy; commander of the Forty-first Tennessee Volunteers at Fort Donelson in 1862.

[16] John Calvin Brown (1827-1889) was born in Giles County, Tennessee. He began the practice of law in 1848; an officer in the Confederate Army attaining the rank of

received a letter today from his brother, N S. Brown, from Nashville. He gives a gloomy account of things there. The people have lost confindence in Gen A S. Johnston, and he thinks that he will be whipped at Corinth and that the star of the Confederacy is set. He also says that the Fed officers and soldiers are very insolent to the citizens. It is a gloomy letter, and coming from a man who is acquainted with matters in Ten, it is calculated to make one feel very badly. Cols Farquharson and Hanson have been on a hearty bust today. This evening they signed a pledge not to drink any thing more during their imprisonment here. I think this a good resolution on their part.

April 1

A good deal of amusement was had today among the prisoners in playing off tricks of one sort and another, it being April-fool's day. It seems that Gen Gov Andrew Johnson has made another speech. Yesterday's N. Y. Herald has it in full, and like all the speeches that he made, he holds himself up as a master, as the peculiar and chosen friend of the people—and invites every body to lay down their arms, and come to him. The soldiers who protected him in the Capitol while he was making the speech were their friends, and come to protect and not destroy. He said that there were more abolitionists in Ten. than in the Fed army. The papers of today contain no news relative to the war. I walked round the island four times today for exercise. The distance round is about three quarters of a mile.

Apr. 2

In a conversation with Dr MacGill of Md on the subject of horse raising he said that a horse intended for the saddle or work ought not to be fed on green grass—but alone on dry food, from the time of weaning of the colt. This he says, hardens their limbs, prevents splint and other formations on their legs. Their food should be changed often from oats to corn, chops etc. When a horse gets very cold or warm pour a tumbler of whiskey in the bucket of water. After reading several chapters in the bible, I took up Halleck's[17] Elements of Military Art and Science, and Rob Roy. I received a letter today from my wife dated at Alisonia, Ten. on the 15th March. This is the first letter that I have received from her since leaving Ten. I also received a letter from mother in which my wife's was enclosed and postmarked Louisville

major general in 1864; in Tennessee legislature in 1869; Governor of Tennessee 1870-1874; President of the Nashville Railway; Vice President of the Texas and Pacific Railway in 1876; made General Solicitor of the Gould railroads west of the Mississippi in 1881; Receiver of the Texas and Pacific in 1885, President in 1888; President of the Tennessee Coal, Iron, and Railroad Company in 1889.

[17] Henry Wager Halleck (1815-1872), soldier, author, lawyer, business man.

Ky. My friend, Miss Sue Dixon of Philia, wrote me a long and very pleasent letter, which was received today. Chas B. Woodburry of Boston sent me a present today of one dozen bottles of superior pale brandy and one box of cigars. How kind this was in him. Eight of the political prisoners from Md were offered a release today, upon the condition that they would not give aid and comfort to the enemies of the U S government. Most of them I understand will accept the terms, but some refuse. As Md has never seceded, I do not see how thy can compromise themselves by so doing.

Apr. 3

Five of the gentlemen who were offered a release yesterday went home today, the balance would not accept it, saying that they were arrested with process being served for no alledged cause and in an extraordinary manner, and they would not go out [of] prison unless they went as freemen. I admire their spunk. Some of the old time grit still lives in Md. An amusing incident occurred here today. A catholic priest from Baltimore visited one of the political prisoners from that city, and was accidentally left by the boat. Col Dimmick when he found it out was in a great stew. They hailed the boat and fired off small arms, but it was of no use, the wind was in the direction of the Fort and they could not hear. The old Col however was determined that the priest should not remain in the Ft all night, not knowing [what] devilment he might do, so he brought in a small schooner and sent the priest to Boston. I wrote letters tonight to my wife, Miss Sue Dickson of Philia and C. Woodburry of Boston.

Apr. 4

I received a letter today from Mr Steel of Louisville in reply to one I wrote to his wife. Three of the Ft Donelson prisoners who came in with us went to Richmond today on a parole of fifteen days. They go for the purpose of effecting an exchange. Their names are Col Baldwin[18] of Va., Maj Brown of Miss., and Maj M. Alexander of Ala. (Col B. was not at Donelson.) I am glad they have gone, as they may be able to do something for the balance of us, and they will also have an opportunity of presenting to the proper authorities the conduct of Floyd and Pillow at Donelson—and the universal execration in which they are held by every officer and soldier that was arrested, for their disertion, and unmilitary conduct of affairs at that Post.

[18] Colonel William E. Baldwin commanded the Second Brigade in General Buckner's division at Fort Donelson.

Apr. 5

The papers today contain no news. Dr. MacGill received a letter from his wife, in which it is stated that we gained great victories at Fredericksburg and Gordonsville. This is a real God-send if true, as we have met with so many disasters recently. Stocks have been falling for the last three days in N Y which is a pretty good sign that they have met with some reverses. As the northern press are not allowed to publish any bad news from their army, I look to the stock market as my index. This has been a real winter day, cold wind and snow. I am suffering very much from hoarseness.

Apr. 6

It is just one month today since our arrival here. No news in the papers of interest except that Andrew Johnson had arrested the Mayor and city council, because they had refused to take the oath of allegiance to the U. S. Brannon and another gentleman were also arrested for manufacturing cannon, swords, etc. for the Confederacy. Mrs. Granburry, the wife of a Texan Maj now here, writes from Hagerstown, Md that we have gained a great victory at Gordensville Va and that we have taken over seven thousand prisoners. It cleared off during the day and the snow melted that [fell] yesterday. I have confined myself to my room all day, being very much troubled with cold, especially in the head and chest. My roommates try to make fun of being sick. They say that I ought to take some medicine and not drink so many cock-tails. I tell them that I have studied my own system, and understand the treatment of colds in my own case very well. Col Hanson read a reply to Prentice's note, in which he turns the whiskey over to Col Dimmick and writes him a very tart rebuke for bringing him before the public so prominently as a drunkard.

Apr. 7th

I remained all day in my room nursing myself.

Apr. 8

Today I felt well enough to go to my meals and take a little exercise. The evening Transcript contains dispatches to the effect that Island No. 10 had surrendered, and the Federals were defeated at Corinth.

Apr. 9

I got up early this morning and answered letters from my sister, Mrs Lindsley and Jas Todd of Louisville. I also wrote one to Wm Quarles at St Louis in regard to some money left there by Dr Hoyt.

The dispatches this evening indicate that we obtained a victory at Pittsburg [Landing], altho they claim the victory. The loss is represented as being 60,000 on both sides. Gen A S. Johnston reported killed, and Beauregard[19] wounded. Gen Prentice[20] was made a prisoner by the Confederates. Twenty six prisoners reached here this evening mostly Fort Donelson prisoners who have been at Camp Chase. Amongst them are Col Bailey, Major McConnico, Lt Col Carter, young Foote, etc. McConnico spent the evening in our room with Col Kane and Dr McGill of Md. We had a fine time together. These prisoners say that we gained a great victory at Pittsburg.

Apr 10th

There is no additional news from the fight at Pittsburg Landing, altho I am inclined to believe from the sudden fall in U S securities that they have not gained a victory. Their papers concur in the statement that we whipped them badly the first day and that Grant's army was demoralized, and that had not Gen Buel come up to his relief he would have been cut to pieces. They also admit having lost five batteries, and that some two thousand of their men were taken prisoners with Gen Prentice. They admit further that our army retreated in good order. Our Gens evidently made a forced march from Corinth with the view of surprising Gen Grant before he was reinforced by Gen Buel. This fight, I think, will delay their forward movement on Corinth sufficiently long to enable our Gens to strengthen their position. The prisoners here all seem confident that we have gained a victory. I received a letter from Dr Boardman of Philia today, in which he promises to use his influence to obtain a parole for me at Washington.

April 11th

There is no additional news from the battle. They fired salutes in honor of a victory today on Boston Common, but it was ordered upon the receipt of the first telegram. It was reported in Boston this evening that Gen Banks was killed. McConnico moved his trunk into our room this evening. He is fine company and will amuse us very much singing, telling stories, etc. Any thing to kill time, as we are running against time.

Apr. 12th

The papers today are softening down a little on the Pittsburg Landing fight. I think they begin to see that they sustained a defeat there

19 Pierre Gustave Toutant Beauregard (1818-1893), Confederate general.

20 General Prentice was a division commander in the Union Army. He was captured at Shiloh.

instead of a victory. A telegram this evening announces that Gen Mitchell[21] with his division has taken possession of Huntsville Ala. having marched from Nashville to Shelbyville, thence to Fayetteville, thence to Huntsville. I hope this is not true, as it would cut off our R R communication between the army of Corinth and the army of East Ten. and Va. I joined in a game of draw poker this evening for amusement at one cent ante and lost fifty seven cents during the sitting. We dismissed the Italian servant who has been attending our room today and secured the services of "Little Jack" a Scotch boy, who was captured on the privateer Beauregard—and who is now a prisoner.

Apr. 13th
Not feeling very well today, I did not attend service—but remained in my room reading the bible, and Halleck's work.

Apr. 14
Occupied the day as usual, nothing new.

Apr. 15
Nothing transpired today worthy of note except the arrival of Gen Mackall, Maj Davidson, and four other prisoners taken from Island No 10. They report that the Federals captured 2500 at No 10 instead of 6000 which they claim, and that 1200 of them were sick.

Apr. 16
The weather has been quite pleasant for several days past. I noticed today one of the Cunard steamers going out with a good number of cabin passengers. I wish very much that I could have been one of that number.

Apr. 17
Col Dimmick issued an order today that no more liquor be brought into the Ft. He has been very kind to the prisoners and some of them have abused his kindness by getting drunk and acting in an unbecoming manner. I think he has done perfectly right and have no doubt of its good effects.

Col Bailey and myself took a walk around the island this morning. I saw the Baltimore News Sheet this morning which contained a good many interesting extracts from Southern papers and among them the southern version of the battle at Pittsburg [Landing]—and President Davis' message to Congress announcing the death of Gen Johnston. Our side claims a victory as well as the Feds. The President speaks in highly complimentary terms of Gen Johnston who was shot in his

[21] Ormsley McKnight Mitchel (1809-1862), astronomer, soldier.

leg and died from loss of blood, having remained on his horse during the battle. Many in the south have blamed Gen J for the fall of Henry and Donelson—and its results, but I do not think he is so blamable, because he did not have forces sufficient to defend such a long line, and so represented to the authorities at Richmond. Lincoln[22] has approved the emancipation bill, and the bill to abolish slavery in the District of Columbia. What will the people of Ky do now, and what will the *conservative* element in the north do? Nothing in my opinion but prove false to all their professions and tamely submit to the rule of the powers that be. The South is evidently going through the fiery furnace now and many days will not elapse before the question of her independence will be determined. Fts Henry, Donelson, Island No. 10 and Pulaski have fallen. The main artery of communication between our army at Corinth and in Va. has been cut by the occupation of Huntsville. The gun boats will certainly take Ft Pillow and then Memphis and there is nothing to keep them from going even to N.O. The seige at Yorktown cannot last many more days and the safety of Richmond depends upon our success there. I received two letters today from Nashville—one from Aunt Felicia and one from Sallie Ewing, from which I learn that Gov Gen And Johnson has confined Generals Barrow and Harding in the State Penitentiary and that my wife has gone with her mother and brothers to Marietta, Ga. I heard Col Hanson of Ky read a letter today from Prentice in reply to one he recently wrote in regard to some whiskey that Prentice sent to him and P's comments about the matter in his paper. I think P rather got the gentleman down in the correspondence.

Apr. 18th

Two gentlemen from Baltimore were here today and gave us glowing accounts of things in the South. They say that they have direct intelligence and that there is no doubt but that we gained a great victory at Pittsburg Landing. The city of Richmond was illuminated upon the reception of the news. They say that our Gens have confidence that they will gain a victory at Yorkstown—and that several vessels have run the blockade with arms and ammunition recently and that at least 150,000 men have volunteered since the fall of Ft Donelson. This is too much good news to be good. I received a letter today from J B Lindsley, but it contains no news. I passed the evening at Mr Harrison's room, where a number of prisoners were assembled to eat oysters, and hear McConnico sing.

---

[22] Abraham Lincoln (1809-1865), sixteenth President of the United States.

Apr. 19

Today Col Dimmick relaxed his rules somewhat in regard to Generals Tilghman and Buckner. Since their solitary confinement they have not been allowed to go out even for exercise—but today they were permitted to walk on the ramparts separately. They are not allowed to speak or to recognize any of their fellow prisoners. Two more prisoners reached here by a merchant-ship from Cadiz. They were captured at Algeria, Morocco, opposite to Gibralter—and carried to Cadiz and thence brought in irons to this place. One of them, Mr Myers of Savannah, Ga was officer on the celebrated steamer, Sumpter, belonging to the Southern Confederacy. The other—Mr Tunstall of Ala, was Consul at Cadiz for six years, having been appointed by Gen. Pierce. They were arrested by order of the U S Consul at Algeria. I received a very interesting letter from mother today giving me the names of some of the [men] killed and wounded at the battle of Shiloh. Many of my acquaintances from Sumner, Wilson, and Davidson counties were among the number. I was sorry to hear of the ilness of my dear old father. The troubles of the country weigh heavily upon him, and I have no doubt is the cause of his illness.

Apr. 20

I did not attend service today, but remained in my room reading. I took the usual exercise in walking.

Apr. 21

Letters have been received here in the last day or so from Camp Douglass near Chicago and from Camp Chase near Columbus Ohio, to the effect that some officers and many men are about to take the oath of allegiance, and return to their homes. I am sorry to hear this because we have already enough to exchange them and I do not like the effect it may have upon them in the future. I have no doubt but that many of them prefer taking the oath to remaining in prisons that may endanger their health; many have families at home who are suffering—and dependent upon them—and many will take the oath, disregard it, and reenter the army. I think from what I hear that some of the Field Officers in this Ft would take the oath if they had an opportunity. Nothing has occurred today worthy of mention.

Apr. 22

The Federal papers for the past day or so are not so jubilant about their victory at Pittsburg Landing as they were in the beginning. They now admit that their loss in killed and wounded was immense and that their army is demoralized. Great fault is found with the Gens in

Photo by J. T. O'Toole

Courtesy Max Straw, Metropolitan District Commission, Boston

View of Fort Warren, George's Island, Boston Harbor, 1958. The Civil War fort is the pentagon-shaped structure with the parade ground in the center.

Courtesy Margaret Lindsley Warden

Officers of the Tenth Tennessee

COL. RANDAL W. McGAVOCK

CAPT. LEWIS R. CLARK — CAPT. THOMAS GIBSON

COL. ADOLPHUS HEIMAN

CAPT. ST. CLAIR M. MORGAN — DR. JOS. M. PLUNKET
Asst. Post Surgeon at Ft. Henry command. News reached here today that we had taken 4000 prisoners from Burnside expedition and 1500 from Gen Banks. Yet to be confirmed.

Apr. 23

Below I furnish Col A Heiman's Report of the battle at Ft Donelson in verse. Its chief merit is lost to those who do not hear him read it.

Pillow and Floyd, two Generals of might
Came to Donelson the Yankees to fight.
Pillow said he is a Hero
And would drive them back to Cairo,
The Cumberland and Tennessee
From Hessians I will free—
In fact I am the man for the crisis
If you only follow my advices—
With Johnson on my left, and Buckner on my right
I shall give them a Devil of a fight—
Gideon, said Floyd, I'll make you understand
That these troops here are under my command,
Besides you are too big for your britches,
This you have shown by your ditches—
Ah! cried Pillow, do you mean at Camargo
On this unkind hint I shall lay an Embargo—
But let this pass, we must have no contentions now,
Or we will not gain fresh laurels for our Brow.
With pick, shovel, and spade
Lines of rifle pits were made.
And a consultation was held of Cols & Gens wise
On the 15th of Feb by daylight in the morning
The Rebels gave them a *Hell* of a storming,
They were driven back from their position
And our affairs were thought to be in the best condition—
Now our Generals put together their wits
And ordered the troops back to their rifle pits—
Said it was no use to hold out any longer,
The enemy is by great odds the stronger—
They will cut off our communication
And that will be followed by starvation.
Gideon said Floyd, I cannot, I will not surrender
And he felt his neck and pulled his suspender—
Ah Ha! said Pillow, you are afraid of the halter—
Now did you ever know me to falter—

But like yourself, surrender I will not,
Let us try and fix up a great plot—
Give the command over to Buckner and let us be smart,
Let him surrender while we depart—
And so they did,
With kin and kith
And during the night
They took to flight
Said now all is over
We are the Heroes of Dover—
Make defences, that was the order given
That the enemy from our lines may be driven.

Apr. 24th

I received another very nice letter today from Miss Sue Dixon of Philia. She did not receive my reply to her first. I also received a letter from Miss Rebeccah Murdock of Baltimore in reply to one that I wrote to her when I sent the carpet that I used for a blanket at Donelson. She says that she will use it for a piano cover—and keep it through life in remembrance of me. Col Dimmick would not let me have the letter, altho I was allowed to read it. He thought that it contained treasonable sentiments. News reached here today by letter that Gens Harding, Barrow and Jos Guild were coming here as prisoners, sent by And Johnson and that it was thought that Gen Harding would lose his mind. I regret this very much, not only on his own account—but his wife and children. News was also received that Hollins with fourteen gun boats was at Ft Pillow. I do hope that he will be able to drive Foote[23] and his flotilla clean out of the water. Messrs. Myers and Tunstall who recently arrived here from Africa as prisoners were carried into Boston today by the U S Marshall to undergo an investigation before a commission sent from Washington. How strange that citizens in this *free country* should be brought three thousand miles in irons with no charges preferred by the government and a Commission sent to ascertain *from them* the cause of their imprisonment. This is worse than the days of the Doge in Venice.

Apr. 25

Before breakfast this morning Col Bailey and myself walked around the island and counted the steps, making the circuit of our path 1765 paces. I noticed the largest merchant ship that I have yet seen here going into Boston. Like all other vessels now she had no cargo. This

[23] Andrew Hull Foote (1806-1863), naval officer.

war will ruin the Yankees engaged in the shipping interest. The insurance in foreign ports for shipment on vessels belonging to the U.S. is so high that shippers prefer patronizing other bottoms. The telegram from Yorktown today states that Gen McClellan has caused a canal to be cut connecting the two rivers, which they think will give them a great advantage, also that their fortifications are now one thousand from our lines and that they now occupy positions that command us completely. This is their version. The Boston Courier which is the most liberal paper that I have seen in this region contains a long editorial today on the recent municipal elections in the West and copies from several Western papers and showing that the democratic party north is beginning to speak out against the policy of the administration, and will ere long produce a revolution in sentiment in regard to this war here in the north. I occupied the day in reading and in playing cards. Tonight I managed to swallow down two of Dr McGills celebrated "belly scrapers," which I expect to hear from by times in the morning.

Apr. 26th

I received a letter this morning from mother dated the 4th inst., in which I learned of the death of James McGavock, Betsy McGavock and Martha McGavock.[24] I learned through the papers that Gens Barrow and Harding had been sent to Ft Wayne. I regret this as I wanted them to come here. The Boston paper this evening contains a piece from the N O Crescent to the effect that Andrew Johnson had been assassinated. This news if verified will give great joy to the inmates of this Ft.

Apr. 27

Another sabbath day has come but we hear no church going bells and we see none of those loved ones that we are accustomed to go to church with. The day although beautiful has been long and dreary—and devoid of incident. Occupied my time in reading the bible and papers.

Apr. 28th

I commenced reading Motley's History of the Dutch Republic this morning—which I find very interesting. News reached here today that the fleet of the enemy had passed the Fts at the mouth of the Miss and were in front of the city of New Orleans, that there was a great panic in the city. Martial law had been proclaimed, all the cotton burnt—and the steamboats excepting those necessary to carry off the coin and the ammunition. If this news should prove true it will be a terrible blow

[24] Martha W. McGavock (1849-1862) was the daughter of John McGavock and Caroline Winder.

upon the Confederacy. We cannot afford to lose New Orleans. I received a letter from Aunt Felicia in which she states that she is not allowed to leave the city, because of her connection with the hospitals in Nashville for taking care of the sick and wounded soldiers. This is a great outrage. Gov Andrews[25] and Staff made a visit to the Ft this morning. Col Dimmick was out in full uniform. The Battalion is composed of fishermen from about Capes Ann and Cod—and shoemakers from Linn. They are well drilled. They volunteered with the understanding that they were not to go South but remain here to defend the Fort.

Apr. 29th

About three o'clock this morning Col Thomas J Davidson of Ripley Miss died in the room adjoining ours. He was convalescent, but owing to some imprudence in eating and drinking he relapsed. His body will be sent home in charge of Col Wells of the same regiment. The news today does not confirm the taking of New Orleans altho the papers contend that the information of the intelligent contraband is reliable. This evening I attended a party given by Cols Hanson and Kane. We had pickled oysters and bread from Baltimore, ham and dried beef from Va. and Bourbon whiskey from Ky. The evening passed off pleasantly. McConnico, Tunstall and Warfield entertained us with songs.

Apr. 30

The news today from N.O. is rather better than it was yesterday. The forts below are still in our possession and in good condition. The federal fleet was before the city and had demanded its surrender which was refused. The commanding officer informed the Mayor that if the Confederate flag was not hauled down from the City Hall that he would fire upon it. His vessel was placed in position for that purpose but had not fired. Gen Lovell[26] telegraphed to the Sec of War that he had moved his forces back to Camp Moore—that the citizens were loyal, and that the enemy had not forces sufficient to occupy the city. All the cotton in the city and the boats in the river and lake had been destroyed. Mr Smith, one of the political prisoners here from Va. and son of Extra Billy, was exchanged and left here today. I received a letter today from Dr Boardman of Philia in which he states that he had made arrangements with Gen Wool[27] through Mr Tucker, assistant Sec of War at Washington, to effect my exchange. I wrote to Gen Wool, also

[25] John Albion Andrews (1818-1867), twenty-first Governor of Massachusetts.
[26] Mansfield Lovell (1822-1884), soldier and civil engineer.
[27] John Ellis Wool (1784-1869), soldier.

to Mr Randolph[28] Sec of War of the C S A and enclosed them in a letter to Dr Boardman to be forwarded. I also received a long and very interesting letter from Father Brown, who is at Nashville. He was the Chaplain of our Reg. Wm Quarles of Clarkesville has played a shabby trick upon me. My father sent two hundred dollars in gold to me by Dr Hoyte, who left it with Quarles at St. Louis to bring it to me. I never would have known it, had not my mother have written me. I wrote to Quarles at St Louis and Columbus, but he did not answer my letters. Today he sent me *through* Col Bailey *one Hundred* and *fifty* dollars in Federal Treasure Notes and stated that balance would be sent to me from Louisville. He sent it by Express and I had to pay $1.27 charges on it. My father paid heavily for the gold in Nashville and I will have to do the same thing over when I get out of here.

May 1st

How unlike is the 1st of May here, and in the South. There the flowers are blooming and the birds singing and here we have a cold, dark, and disagreeable day. I received letters today from my wife, and sister Sallie. This evening I wrote to Father Brown—and mother.

May 2nd

The news this morning is very discouraging. Ft Macon has been surrendered. New Orleans is in the possession of Commodore Farragut[29]—and Corinth evacuated. The letter of Mayor Monroe of N O to Commodore Farragut is a noble production and places the Commodore in a very awkward position. I received a letter today from father, in which he states that Judge Catron offered him the Clerkship of the U S Court —and he declined. I am glad of this because he is too old to hold the office, and under the circumstances his acceptance might reflect upon his children hereafter. I saw a letter today from Col Guild from Detroit. He will be sent to a Fort on Lake Huron, together with Barrow and Harding.

May 3rd

I received a letter today from Willie Eakin in which it is stated that Jas Rice was taken prisoner at Shiloh. The evacuation of Corinth and the occupation at Fredericksburg Va is denied in today's dispatches. It is stated that the members of Congress from the border slave states, and some of the conservatives members from the north are meditating a withdrawal in body on account of the action of the extremists of the

[28] George Wythe Randolph (1818-1867), lawyer.

[29] David Glasgow Farragut (1801-1870), naval officer, was born a few miles from Knoxville, Tennessee.

Federals or Republicans on the confiscation question. They evidently have trouble in their camp and I hope that it will end in a revolution here in the north.

May 4th

This has been a most charming day, making it far more delightful out on the island, than indoors. I answered letters today from Gordon and Co Louisville Father Sallie, my wife—and Willie Eakin. The news this evening is that it is thought that Napoleon [III] will interfere in our affairs and recognize the Confederacy. A proposition comes from Ten. that all the 12 . . . . men who will take the oath of allegiance and return home and be quiet citizens will be released. I have no doubt but that many will avail themselves of the opportunity. Those who entered the service for motives other than that which actuates the man of principle will certainly do so, and they are not a few.

May 5th

The telegrams this morning state that our forces evacuated Yorktown in the night without the knowledge of the enemy, that some seventy odd guns were left spiked, and a large amount of ammunition and camp equipage. From the position of Yorktown I have no doubt but that it would have been impossible for Johnston to have held it, having to contend against superior guns, and the gun boats. I think it a good military move under the circumstances. McClellan in his dispatch to the War Dept says that he is pursuing with cavalry, supported by infantry and intends pushing us to the wall, so by tomorrow we may expect to hear of some fighting. I notice in an extract from the Knoxville Register that Col W M. Churchwell is Provost Marshall of that place—and that the conduct of the Union men in East Ten. is giving great trouble. The evacuation of Corinth by Beauregard is reported, but not believed. We have here another disagreeable day, I never experienced at this season a more fluctuating climate. It seems to me that we have some half doz changes during the day.

May 6th

The evacuation of Yorktown is confirmed this morning. Our rear guard and the enemy had a fight near Williamsburg yesterday. Heavy loss on the Federal side, but particulars not received. I answered Mrs Sullivan's letter from Baltimore today and wrote to my friends, Robt Lyon Rogers of Baltimore and Anthony Kimmell of Frederick, also to my wife.

May 7th

Our forces have passed Williamsburg. Gen McClellan in his official report seems to think that we have a superior force and rather intimates that he will have a tough time before reaching Richmond. Gens Dix and Pierpont were here today in the capacity of Commissioners from the Government to investigate and act upon the cases of the political prisoners now confined here. Some four or five N C seamen were released and others refused to go without a pass, saying that they were brought here by the government and should be sent back by the government and [not] thrown out without money or friends. Mr Millner of Va was released, Mr Bigger and Gordon of Baltimore, and Capt Berry of Charleston. Mr Catsell of Baltimore refused to shake hands with Gen Dix. A number of other gentlemen were examined, but not released. All refused to take the oath of allegiance. Mr Gordon went out unconditionally but I believe he took the oath when first arrested and was afterwards for some cause or other arrested again. The others were let out on parole. I received a long letter today from Miss Sue R Dickson of Philia, also one from my wife, and my mother. My wife is still in Marietta Ga.

May 8th

The fight at Williamsburg appears by today's papers to have been more serious than at first supposed. They admit a loss on their side of three hundred killed and seven hundred wounded. Our forces are retreating beyond the Chickahominy river in the direction of Richmond. McClellan has sent 60,000 men by transports up York River with the view of making an attack on our rear. There will be some very hard fighting before they reach Richmond, but I fear they will do so very soon. It is stated in the dispatches that Beauregard has evacuated Corinth and gone to Pocahontas, a little place in Ten on the line of the M and C R R—between Corinth and Grand Junction. Old Capt Berry left here this morning much to [the] pleasure and regret of all his fellow prisoners. He is a real jolly old Irish Gentleman—and was arrested in N Y because, as he says, he was considered a dangerous man. His parole does not allow him to go South until regularly exchanged. He is a sea faring man. Built the Nashville-Columbia, and other steamers belonging to that line. He says that he is going to England very soon and expects to be able to render to the South some service yet. Lt Col Jackson's sister, Mrs Hunt of Louisville, and daughter was here today to visit him. I wrote to mother today and sent a ring of my own make to my friend, Miss Sue R. Dickson of Philia. Received a letter from young Malone of Columbus Miss, stating that he was out of money and suffering.

May 9th

This day one year ago I was sworn in together with my company "The Sons of Erin" as a soldier to serve the State of Ten. for twelve months, and consequently my term of enlistment expires, but if I could be released from this prison I would return to the south—and serve for the war as a private if I could do no better. My whole heart is in the cause of the Confederacy, because I believe that the perpetuity of Republican principles on this Continent depends upon our success. If we are overpowered and subjugated it will require a much stronger government than that of the U.S. A Senator has already announced from his seat that the Constitution was suspended.

We have no additional news today from the seat of war. I received a long letter from Aunt Felicia giving me a great deal of interesting news from Nashville. Also received a very long letter from my friend, Miss Sue Dickson of Phila. She is a noble woman, and although born and brought up in the Quaker City—and having a brother in the northern army, she is a rebel—and her heart is with the cause of the South.

May 10th

The Federals claim a great victory at West Point on York River—and say that we are evacuating Norfolk and that the government archives are being moved from Richmond. Received a long letter today from Aunt Malvina Bass, who is now in Nashville. Mr B. and nearly all the family are south. This has been so disagreeable a day that I have remained in doors and been deprived of the usual amount of exercise. The wind has been blowing very hard all day—and the waves running quite high.

May 11th

Col Dimmick and another officer of the garrison attended service this morning in Commodore Barron's room. This has been a charming day and most of the prisoners have enjoyed walking around the island—and basking in the sun. I wrote two long letters today, one to Miss Sue R Dickson of Philadelphia and one to Mrs Jno M. Bass of Nashville. When the mail boat came over this evening she had a flag flying—and those on board were very jubilant over the news just received. Capt. Pearson handed me an extra which contained intelligence of the distruction of the Merrimac by the Rebels, the capture of the Yorktown and Jamestown, the evacuation of Norfolk by Gen Hayes—and its occupation by the Federals. They state that our army retreated in good order, carrying with them their provisions forage etc.

May 12th

This is the day of the meeting of the reconstruction party in Ten. The call is signed by one hundred and thirty seven names—a majority of whom are Yankees and their immediate decendants who have settled there. Very few of them have any status in society or influence—and many of them are entirely irresponsible. I hardly think that Gov Gen Andrew Johnson will be able to vote the State back again into the Union. I saw a letter today from E Etheridge to Miss Sue Spence in which he says that Col Palmer[30] and other prisoners here from Ten. will be released upon their taking the oath of allegiance—and renouncing Jeff Davis and his crew. I do not think that Col. P. will accept Miss Sue's proposition. She is very anxious for him to take the oath and go home. Mr. Tuntstall who was Consul at Cadiz—and brought here a prisoner in irons, was released today on parole. A letter was received here this evening stating that Capt St Clair M. Morgan, Sam Cowan, and Capt Maney had effected their escape while going from Camp Chase to Johnson's Island. I hope that they will land safely in Dixie. We have had another beautiful day. This afternoon most of the prisoners were out on the island—enjoying the pleasant air, and looking at the smacks running through the narrow passage by the Ft.

May 13

The news this morning is decidedly better for the cause of the Confederacy than any thing I have heard since I have been in this Ft, but it may be changed tomorrow, and I will not allow myself to exult. The news from Va is that our forces fell back in the direction of Richmond in good order and that they distroyed the Navy Yard at Norfolk before evacuating that place. Gen Halleck admits that the rebels are gaining strength at Corinth every day, and that they are strengthening their position. Gen Lovell has joined him with thirty thousand men.

The news from England and France indicates that those governments will soon interfere in our affairs and endeavor to stop the war in this country. Negotiations were going on between the two governments on the subject during the month of April. A U S war-brig came here today,

[30] Joseph Benjamin Palmer (1825-1890), lawyer and soldier, was a native of Bedford County, Tennessee. He was admitted to the bar in 1848; was actively engaged in politics as a Whig 1851-1861; elected Colonel of the Eighteenth Tennessee Regiment at the outbreak of hostilities in 1861; was captured at Fort Donelson and sent to Fort Warren; exchanged in May 1862 and reelected Colonel of his old regiment; made brigadier-general in 1864. After the war he again entered his profession and continued to have an active interest in politics.

but I have not learned the object of her coming. The fine brass band that belongs to the post discoursed most excellent music this evening in the Court of the Fort. I received letters today from Mrs Sam Colt and her sister, Hettie Jarvis of Hartford, Ct., also one from my old classmate, Mellen Chamberlain of Boston. Charlie Woodburry sent me a fine box of cigars, and I sent half of them to Gen Tilghman.

May 14th

I wrote to my friend Woodburry today thanking him for his kindness. The news today is good. The correspondence from Europe confirms what was published in the telegraph yesterday in regard to the interposition of England and France in American affairs. Foote's Flotilla have failed to do any thing at Ft Wright. Two of his gun boats were sunk. I commenced reading "My Novel" today by Bulwer. This afternoon I went out on the island and looked at some of the prisoners playing "Bull-pen." It was quite amusing to see some old fellows running after the ball, and their endeavors to avoid a blow.

May 15th

There is no special news today except from Foote's Flotilla. It seems that we sank two of their best gun boats with our fleet. I saw today in the N.Y. Herald the proceedings of the presentation of the flag of my old company "The Sons of Erin" to the sixty ninth (Irish Reg) N.Y. Mr Chapman, the correspondent of the Herald, wrote a letter from Cairo giving a history of the flag, which is false from beginning to end. My friend, C. Woodburry, was here day before yesterday and was very anxious to see me, but was not permitted. I did not even hear of it until this morning.

May 16th

I have been a prisoner now just three months today, and I think it high time that some steps were taken to release me. Although I am quite comfortable, and doing well, yet there is nothing like one's liberty. The steamship, Niagera, went into Boston today from Liverpool, and we will get in tomorrow's papers some correspondence relative to the question of intervention. I received a letter from Jno B. Lindsley, in which he represents the feeling between the Unionists and Secessionists as very intense. I also received copies of the Nashville Union and the Nashville Dispatch. The former is a vile and filthy a little sheet as I ever saw. Col Dimmick and some of the officers stationed here went to Boston today to attend the funeral of Gen Peabody who was killed at Shiloh. He broke his parole—and deserves his fate.

He was captured and paroled by Price[31] in Mo. This is the day set apart by Jeff Davis for humiliation and prayer for the Confederacy. Col Wells—one of our prisoners, is a preacher and it was proposed by some that he preach a sermon in the dining hall. Application was made to Col Dimmick but he objected saying that he did not care what we done in our case-mates, but a public demonstration would not be allowed.

I wrote a letter today to Maj Hugley of the Sixty ninth reg N Y correcting the statements published in the Herald on the 14th inst. relative to the flag of my old company "The Sons of Erin." It was left in the Company's headquarters at Ft Henry from which it was taken and not captured at Donelson from the Reg as represented. Mr Chapman, the Special War Correspondent of the Herald from the army in the west, is the greatest liar I ever read of or after. I think more lies can be found in his letter than was ever before compressed within the same limits. I hope that he will go where he properly belongs.

May 17th

No news by the boat this morning of interest. I received a letter from Aunt Felicia, who gives me a very gloomy account of the condition of society in Nashville. The reign of terror has been inaugurated by Andrew Johnson—and there is no telling what the future will bring forth there. The weather here now is beautiful and the spring is fairly opened.

May 18th

Attended service this morning in one of the Mess Rooms. Lt Col Wells of Miss preached a very good old-fashioned, country, camp-meeting, Methodist sermon. Cols Hamilton and Voohries are also preachers and they propose having two sermons a week—which I think just one too many for those who attend. Col. H. said after the sermon that Col W had introduced steam on the old ship of Zion. A great many pleasure yachts passed by the Fort this evening and some of them very beautiful. I noticed that most of them stopped at a house on an island opposite. I suppose to take refreshments. The news this evening is that we repulsed the gunboats on James river below Richmond, also at Ft Wright on the Miss. The proclamation of Gen Hunter[32] freeing the slaves in So C. Ga. and Fla has created great excitement in Washington and a rupture in the Cabinet. Hunter, it is stated, will be superceded, and his proclamation modified by the President. The great East-

[31] Sterling Price (1809-1867), soldier, tenth Governor of Missouri.
[32] David Hunter (1802-1886), Union soldier.

ern has arrived in N Y. The N H of the 17th contains the proceedings of the Union meeting at Nashville on Monday last. Geo Campbell presided and Ed Cooper was chairman on resolutions. Speeches were made by Geo Campbell, Gov Johnson, Wm H. Polk, Jno S. Brien, the two Stokes, the two Coopers of Shelbyville and Wisener. All the speeches were very poor—and certainly not creditable. If I mistake not—the time will soon come when these men will be detested by every true Tennessean. McConnico was in a great singing mood tonight and he entertained us until bed time with songs rather of a sentimental character.

May 19th

Recd the Nashville Union today of the 13 and 14, one of which contains a list of deligates to the Union Meeting held there last Monday—and the proceedings of the same. Very few names that I recognized as men of influence and position. This evening I participated in a game of football which is pretty severe exercise to one unaccustomed to much. I received a book of poems by express from Miss Sue R Dickson, called Lucile by Owen Meredith. I read it nearly half through last night and was much pleased with it.

May 20th

I finished Lucile today and must say that it is one of the pleasantest little stories I have read for years. It is full of freshness, and written in excellent style. No news today of interest.

May 21

I received a letter today from mother and heard indirectly from my wife. All are well and doing well. I notice the death of Abraham Caruthers[33] of Lebanon. He died at Marietta, Ga. N S Brown has been arrested at Nashville by order of Andrew Johnson—besides a number of other prominent citizens in Middle Ten. Abe Lincoln is about to call out one hundred thousand more troops to be held as reserves. I suppose the government apprehends some danger from abroad.

May 22

The papers today contain no news of interest except the approval of the Homestead Bill by the President. Private letters from Ten. state that County Judge—Trustee—Sheriff of Williamson Co. has been

[33] Abraham Caruthers (1803-1862), lawyer, was born in Smith County, Tennessee. He began the practice of law in Columbia, Tennessee in 1824; Judge of the Circuit Court of the Third Circuit 1833-1836; elected Judge of the Fourth Circuit 1836-1847. He resigned his judgeship and, in October 1847, founded the Law School in Cumberland University at Lebanon, Tennessee. In 1861 he was a member of the Legislature from Wilson County.

arrested but had given bail to [make] their appearance. I felt very indignant today upon hearing a whole company while drilling with their Capt. at their head singing "Old Jno Brown" which is an Abolition Song published soon after the execution of that scoundrel, and which is very insulting to a southerner. No gentleman would be guilty of such conduct.

May 23

Col Rogers Hanson of Lexington, Ky left here today for Fortress Monroe. He expects to be exchanged for Col Cockran of N.Y. I received a long and very beautiful letter this morning from Miss Sue R. Dickson of Philia. Forty one prisoners reached here this evening from Ship Island. They are mostly officers of the Southern Navy—and they give a very deplorable account of the management of things on our side. Gen Mansfield Lovell they regard as a humbug. The two gun boats which were nearly completed, and one of which cost the government eight hundred thousand dollars might have prevented the Fed fleet from ascending the river and saved New Orleans. Somebody is certainly culpable but who I will not pretend to say. One thing is certain the President and the Sec of War should have seen that so important a point was placed under the control and management of competent and reliable officers. This evening I participated in a game of football but I found the exercise so severe that I retired and engaged in a small game of draw poker.

May 24

I was arroused this morning by the firing of salutes from two men of war—which was responded to from the Fort. They belonged to the U S and have gone in, I suppose, for provisions and repairs. The notorious scoundrel and liar, Parson Brownlow of East Ten made a visit to the Fort today on a special boat in company with Gov Andrews and staff. The battallion passed in review before the Gov. Brownlow sent for Lt Col White of Hamilton Co East Ten and offered to parole him having I suppose, obtained authority from the government. He also sent for Col Lillard and Lt Col Odell of East Ten and made the same offer to them. They are not required to take the oath but to go home and not take up arms again. Brownlow delivered a pay lecture at the Music Hall in Boston last night, to a large audience which was published in this morning's papers. Like all of his speeches it is full of low slang, villinous abuse of reputable persons—and talk about himself. I did not see him to-day, and I am glad that all of the prisoners showed the disposition to give him the go-by. Col Dimmick and all the officers of the Ft, even the Surgeon, turned out in full uniform to meet Brownlow and Gov Andrews. Salutes were fired upon their approach. Oh! what is this country coming to? I received a very interesting letter today from Aunt Felicia Porter, from which I learned that it is intensely hot in Nashville, while we are sitting by fires here, that Andrew Johnson is still making arrest in Ten. David McGavock and Jno Harding have been put in the work house. Our friends in Nashville are hopeful and expect a gain of a victory at Corinth. At a judicial election there T S. Foster (secession) carried the city. The telegraph this evening states that our army is now beyond Richmond, which I do not believe. I have occupied myself today in reading my usual number of chapters in the Bible and "My Novel"; took a game of poker. Did not go out on the island at all today.

May 25th

I occupied the day in writing letters to Miss H H Jarvis of Hartford, Ct.—Miss Sue R Dickson of Philia—Mrs Mellen Chamberlain of Boston—Aunt Felicia and my mother. In walking around this morning I could hear the church bells in Boston distinctly—a distance of nine miles. This Revolution has brought about a strange state of things. Today we had two sermons going at the same time among the prisoners. In one room a Methodist preached, assisted by a Presbyterian, and in the other a sermon written by an Episcopalian clergyman was read by a Unitarian who does not believe in the Trinity. Men of all denominations in the South have been brought together in one common brotherhood. Lt Col White of East Ten left this evening. The Boston paper says that he was a good Union man but joined the Confederate Army to save his own life. (Boston Journal)

May 26

About 1 oc last night the boat came over from the city—and brought some news of an important character. Three companies of the Battalion stationed here left before day. When the boat arrived it brought the news of Gen Bank's defeat and retreat together with the proclamations of the Governors of Penn—NY—Mass—calling upon the militia of the several states to march to Washington. A very ridiculous letter by Gov Andrews of this State to the Sec of war also appeared. He says that the young men of the State are otherwise engaged—but if the President means to carry out Gen Hunter's proclamation he thinks he can be ready in 40 days. The NY papers make great ridicule over the letter. Great activity prevailed about the Fort all day. The battallion here has been raised to Reg. and started this evening for Washington. Three volunteer companies came in to take their places to guard the prisoners. They are a much more genteel looking set of men than those who left. One company is composed of young men about Boston—and is quite a fancy company. We learn also from the papers today that there is great excitement in Baltimore between the Secessionists—and the Unionists—and probably some blood spilt. I have occupied myself all day reading "My Novel."

May 27th

This has been an exceedingly disagreeable day. Rain all day and dense fog. I have been amused at the Fancy company on guard duty. They do not look like they like their new duties very much. The prisoners have annoyed the Corperal very much in going to the privy. I notice in the evening paper that the Fed Congress (lower branch) has passed a confiscation act. I think it will pass the Senate, and will be approved by the Executive. An Artillery company in Boston refused to go to Washington and were disbanded by the Gov. It has been reported here that Gen Harding was dead, but I think it a mistake, as Col Heiman received a letter this evening from Gen Barrow dated the 20th and no mention is made of it. They are both at Ft Mackinau. I received a letter today from sister Sallie, and she informs me that father's health is improving and that the family are all well.

May 28th

An unusual number of large sized vessels went out this morning. The steamer Niagera went by the Ft with a large number of passengers—but stopped outside—where she remained all day. The Boston Journal states that she was stopped by Lord Lyons for the purpose of sending dispatches of an important character. The defeat of Gen Banks and the recent movements about Washington may induce his government and France to do something. I received a letter today from my wife dated Marietta Ga May 6th. She is well—and doing well—and is using all efforts to procure my exchange. Poor creature, I fear she will hope without hope for some time to come. Occupied myself most of the day reading "My Novel" which grows more interesting the further you proceed in the story. I also took a game of poker today.

May 29th

Four prisoners went South today—having secured an exchange, viz. Maj Crosby and Capt Shipley of Ky—Col Baldwin of Columbus Miss and Capt Shelea from N O—No news in the papers today. I was a good [deal] amused today seeing the fancy gents from Boston removing the refuse from the Court. They touched it lightly with their spades. Each man had on white gloves—and a five cent cigar in his mouth.

May 30th

I received a letter from old Col Anthony Kimmell this morning. He traveled with me in Italy about ten years ago and is now a strong Union man. I read his letters to the Baltimoreans here—who say that he is an old fool—and dislike him very much. Also received a letter from mother—who informs me that arrests are still being made daily by Andrew Johnson in Davidson and the surrounding counties. Several young girls came over from Boston to spend the day, and the brass band gave us plenty of music for their benifit I suppose. The paper this evening brings us intelligence of the evacuation of Corinth. They say that our forces have fallen back on Ocalona on the Mobile and Ohio R R. I do not credit this information as Ocalona is situated in the pararie where there is no water. The same paper states that Roger Hanson has returned from Fortress Monroe to Washington for the purpose of taking the oath of allegiance. I do not believe this. Thirty two prisoners (Privateers) left here this evening for Fortress Monroe to be exchanged for the crew of the Cumberland. Some of them have been in prison eight or nine months.

May 31st

Maj Grace remarked this morning that prison was the best place in the world to find out human nature—and I believe he is correct. The minutia of character is here developed—which is ordinarily kept from the world—and I am certain that such contact does not give any one any better opinion of mankind. The thoughts of most of the prisoners, particularly those that have no taste for reading seems to run upon women chiefly—which can be plainly gathered from their conversations and anecdotes which frequently decend very low. Even those that have a taste for reading read nothing but light, trashy, yellow back literature. . . . In regard to the disposition to those that read light literature, I presume our minds are too much occupied with the affairs of the country at present. I know this to be the case with me . . . . The evacuation of Corinth is confirmed this evening. It is supposed that our army has gone to Grand Junction. This is a good move in some respects —as it gets Halleck farther away from the river—and the siege guns that he has mounted there also away from his fortifications. The Miss Central R R is also better for provisions, and there is more water than at Corinth. There is a report in the paper this evening of the evacuation of Richmond but I do not believe it. The same paper has a telegram from Fortress Monroe stating what we heard before in regard to Roger Hanson of Ky.

June 1st

I did not attend service today but remained in my room writing letters. I wrote to sister Sallie—Wm Nevins of N Y and Ellen Thurston of Brookline NY.

June 2nd

We heard today of the engagement near Richmond, and although they claim a victory—I think we gave them thunder. They admit the entire rout of Gen Casey's[34] division, and the loss of twelve batteries and all the camp equipage. Lt Col Jas Jackson of Florence, Ala. left us this evening for Fortress Monroe. He is to be exchanged for Lt Col Neeff of the 2nd Ky. He was our room mate and we slept side by side for three months. He was shot badly at Mannassas—and was surrendered at Ft Donelson. His whole heart is in the cause. I expect he will participate in the battles soon to be fought near Richmond and Corinth. This evening we had a big game of poker (eight hands) but few coppers changed hands.

June 3rd

News reached here today that NS Brown had made a speech at the Union meeting in Columbia—and it created a good deal of commotion among the prisoners from Ten. His brother, Col Jno Brown, does not believe it—but I do. I expect he considers that the revolution is a failure—and it is best for him to look out for himself. Col B. is very much mortified. No additional news from Richmond. I saw a letter today from Col Roger Hanson to Capt Stoke. He says that we will all be exchanged very soon. Both governments have agreed upon the terms and he saw the documents. Maj Davidson received two gallons of fine whiskey today from Scudder at Shelbyville, Ten. and we all got on a spree. Col Dimmick came in late this evening with a bottle of Kimmell from old Col Kimmel of Md. It was marked 1851 and purchased in Sweden by Col K. I was asleep when he came in and some of my friends told him that I was sick. We heard today of the death of old Capt Berry, who was recently released from this place. He died in Brookline NY of apoplexy. He was an Irishman by birth—but his home was in Charleston SC. He was a sea captain and built the Nashville, and the Columbia. He was a very fat and short man, drank a great deal, and was full of fun and frolic.

---

[34] Silas Casey (1807-1882), Union soldier.

June 4th

The papers to day contain no war news—but they admit a loss of over three thousand instead of three hundred at Richmond on Saturday last. I received a letter from Gen W. G. Harding from Ft Mackinaw—so it seems he is not dead as reported. Col Heiman bought a pineapple today and sliced it up. Instead of pouring sugar over it he poured salt by mistake. Gregg then took it and mashed it up in a jelly—washed the salt out—and then poured a sugar over it. Col Lillard from East Ten. came in and pitched into it—and thought it just about right. It has been raining hard all day—and we have fires in our rooms it is so cold. I had a game of single handed euchre with Myers of Ga at 25 cents a game.

June 5th

The telegraph this morning brings us astounding news if true. Gen Halleck, in an official communication to the War Dept, states that Beauregard's army has become utterly demoralized and that Gen Pope[35] had taken ten thousand prisoners and fifteen thousand stand of arms. I have no doubt but that upon the evacuation of Corinth a great many stragglers were left behind—and I think it more than likely that many of the twelve month men—whose time has expired have determined to go home and attend to their interest and see their families. The Tennesseans have probably been influenced by the position of some of the leading men in the State. I received a letter from Dr Lindsley today and answered Gen Harding's letter.

June 6th

I received letters today from Wm Nevins and Jeness of NY—and Miss Sue Dickson of Philia. We have had a very dense fog all day, the wind driving it from the ocean. Maj Doss received a letter today from the US Sec of War stating that a general exchange has been agreed upon by the two governments. From all accounts the battle at Fair Oaks or Seven Pines was a pretty severe one. The northern press admit that they were badly whipped on Saturday but they claim to have regained all the ground lost on Sunday and Monday. The carnage on both sides was heavy. The papers contain whole columns of the killed and wounded.

June 7

From the papers today—and a letter from Lt Col Jas Jackson written at Baltimore—it seems that there is another hitch in the exchange of Prisoners—and there is no telling when we will be released. Thurlow

[35] John Pope (1822-1892), soldier.

Weed[36] has just reached NY from Europe on the Peoria. He was received by the City Authorities—and made a speech—in which he said that England and France would not interfere in our American affairs—that it was considered that the U.S. was fully able to crush out the rebellion. Ft Pillow on the Miss is reported by the telegraph to be evacuated—and our forces have fallen down to Ft Randolph. I have no confidence in our ability to hold any Ft on the river and consider that the Federals virtually have possession of the entire country on the rivers, and the sea-board. It is also reported that Gen Joseph Johnston[37] was seriously wounded near Richmond on Saturday by a Minie ball in the groin. If this should prove true, it will be a great loss to the Confederate service—Gen Smith is next in command. The Nashville Union was received here this evening, containing the address of the Committee recently appointed at the Union Convention held in Nashville. It sets out in a picture drawn of Ten. at the time of the passage of the ordinance of Secession—then a picture of her present subjugated and unhappy condition—and finally concludes with an exhortation for the people to return to their allegiance. Signed by Wm·B Campbell, Jordan Stokes,[38] Rupert Houston, A A Hall, and others. The same paper contains the speech of N S. Brown made at the Union meeting in Columbia. I heard his brother, Col Jno C Brown read it—and he was very much troubled and mortified. Gov Brown considers that the rebellion has played out—and it is best for Ten to return to the old government. I received a letter today from Mrs Jno O. Ewing from Nashville, in which she states that her father had 1400 bails of cotton burnt up by the agents of the government.

June 8th

This has been an exceedingly cold day. A high and fierce wind blew all day—the sea ran unusually high. I sat by a large fire most of the day writing letters to Miss Sue Dickson and others. I did not attend service. Received two Nashville papers this evening, one of which contained the official report of Gen Beauregard of the battle of Shiloh I was asked to read it—and while doing so, Col Gregg of Texas overlooked the paper—and undertook to correct me as I went along. I handed him the paper and told him to read for himself—that I did not consider his corrections very polite. He has been a school teacher in his time, and

[36]Thurlow Weed (1797-1882), politician, journalist.

[37] Joseph Eggleston Johnston (1807-1891), soldier.

[38] Jordon Stokes, lawyer, was born in Chatham County, North Carolina in 1817. He began the practice of law in Carthage, Tennessee in 1838; elected to the Legislature in 1839; moved to Lebanon about 1841; served in the Legislature 1851-1852, and elected Speaker; elected to the State Senate in 1859. He was a consistent and conservative Union sympathizer throughout the Civil War.

he has been in the habit of overlooking boys while reading. The papers contain intelligence today of the evacuation of Fts Pillow and Randolph —and the occupation of Memphis by the Federals. This gives them entire possession of the Miss river. I fear very much that my father and brothers will suffer very much as their plantations are between the Fts and Memphis on the Ark side of the river. Some letters were received here today from the Sec of War—which rather threw a damper over the exchange question.

June 9th

We have no news today from the armies. A letter written to a gentleman in Baltimore states that President Davis claims in a published proclamation a great victory at Richmond—took eight thousand prisoners and seventy guns. It is announced that Count Pusigny is coming to this country. His mission must be of an important character. Maj Davidson of Ten left here today for the south, having succeeded in effecting an exchange. He is a good soldier, having been educated at West Point—and participated in the Mexican War—and in the battles of the old army on the frontiers. I am glad that he has gone—because we need the services of such men in the Confederacy, altho we all regret to part with him because of his great good humor and fun. He was the life of the prison. The last words he said when he went on the boat was "Bully for the mocking-bird," a favorite expression his. I received a letter today from my mother in which she states that my negro man, Martin, had left Nashville and—gone with the Fed army. He is not a valuable or reliable servant—and certainly an ungrateful dog. She also states that brother Edward has removed his negroes to Col Young's plantation in Miss for safety, has heard from my wife at Marietta who is anxious to get back to Nashville.

June 10th

No news today and nothing happened worthy of note.

June 11

The Europe went out today from Boston. W F. Cooper of Ten was a passenger. He did not even drop me a line. He ought to be ashamed to leave the country at this time—when the services of every man is needed at home. The position taken by his brothers in Shelbyville and his own course must blast them hereafter. The Swedish man of war went out today.

June 12

I remained in my room all day. News was received here this evening that the Moniter has been taken in James River—and that Gen Jackson[39] had obtained a victory over Freemont and Shields,[40] also some information from Ten—to the effect that Gen Durmont has asked for re-enforcements and fears that Gen Smith will come over the mountains from East Ten and attempt to retake Nashville.

June 13

I forgot to mention that one of the prisoners from N O was placed in close confinement yesterday for using harsh language to-wards one of the sentinels. The sentinel was discharging his duty, and the young man cursed him. Col Dimmick told him that if he would say to the sentinel that he intended no offense it would be looked over. He refused to do so. I think the young man entirely to blame. I read Hon Alfred Elys' "Journal in Richmond" which is simply a diary of his experience while a prisoner of war. The book is not interesting. He evinces great egotism—and no genius. The U S ship Niagera went in to Boston today for repairs. She is the largest vessel in the service—drawing 26 ft and over three hundred ft in length. The same that carried the Japanese Ambassadors home. I walked down to the play-ground and witnessed a game of football by the young men, and pitching quoits by the old gentlemen. We received no news today either by the papers or by letter.

June 14

In looking over the papers this morning I see that gold has gone up from 3½ to 5½ premium, which is rather a good omen for the South. Chas Sumner has published a letter which is calculated to create some stir among the conservatives of the north. He claims to have the ear and confidence of the President—and intimates pretty clearly that he is an abolitionist in sentiment, and will ultimately take full ground for abolition sentiments. He advises the abolitionists to sustain the administration. I received a letter from my wife today from Marietta, Ga. of the 24th of May. She speaks of going to Cassville which is about twenty miles north of Marietta on the R.R I do wish she was here in Boston with some of my friends. This separation from her makes me perfectly miserable. I have felt gloomy all day. Mother wrote a note in which she stated that Currin McNairy, Wm Stockell,[41] and Jno O. Ewing had

[39] Thomas Jonathon "Stonewall" Jackson (1824-1863), soldier.

[40] James Shields (1806-1879), lawyer, politician, soldier.

[41] William Stockell, chief engineer of the Nashville, Tennessee fire department, was born in Malton, Yorkshire, England in 1815. After living a number of years in Baltimore and in Cincinnati, he moved to Nashville in 1846. He was thereafter connected with the Nashville fire department and became nationally known, being President of the National Association of Chief Engineers in 1878.

left the city for fear of being arrested. The officers of the Planters and Union Banks have taken the oath of allegiance—except Orville Ewing[42] who is sick.

June 15th

This morning I made my appearance in a new suit of black—which attracted much attention and comment among my fellow prisoners. Attended service—by Col Wells of Miss., assisted by Cols Voorhies and Hamilton. Major Brown and Mr Harrison from Baltimore also had divine service. I received letters today from Carrie McGavock and Miss Sue Dickson of Philadelphia. The former writes under a great state of gloom, having recently lost a charming daughter and her brother-in-law, Jas McGavock. Her husband's health is also very bad. Miss D.'s letter is quite lengthy and highly interesting as usual. Col Heiman and myself received a joint letter from our friend, Mrs Medora Thayer of N Y. She says that her husband starts in a few days for Europe—and she intends writing to Sec Stanton[43] and get him to parole us—and allow us to spend the summer with her at Hussac's Falls, which would be very delightful. Col H answered the letter today. He writes a good letter, but not being very familiar with the English language, he amuses me asking his room mates how to spell words that he is not very certain about. "Do you put an e behind so and so"—is a very common enquiry with him. Col Jno C Brown received a letter today from his brother in which he rather apologizes for making a Union speech—and says that the paper does not represent it properly. Ah! This will not do. The fact of his making a speech at all—at such a meeting is sufficient, d—— him. Col Bailey received a letter from Gen Harding—who says that he, Barrow, and Guild are getting on quite well—but he fears that he will freeze there this winter. One man told him that the thermometer at Ft Macinac in winter was sixty or seventy degrees below Cairo. No news by the papers this evening, except that there was a strange movement of troops at Richmond yesterday.

June 16th

Four months today we were surrendered at Ft Donelson and our prospects of being released is as remote as the day we came here. Commodore Barron received a letter today from Sec Stanton saying that general exchange would take place in a few days, but we have been

[42] Orville Ewing, Nashville lawyer and business man. He was admitted to the bar in 1829; a member of the board of aldermen in 1841; Treasurer of the Nashville, Chattanooga, and St. Louis Railway, Secretary-Treasurer after 1851; elected President of the Planter's Bank in 1856; one of the incorporators of the Church and Spruce Street Railroad Company in 1866.

[43] Edwin M. Stanton (1814-1869), lawyer; President Lincoln's Secretary of War.

hearing this for several weeks past. The papers contain no news today. The Bavaria and China have arrived off Halifax—but bring no news from Europe. I wrote a long letter to Jno McGavock's wife to-night in reply to one received yesterday. Maj McConnico and Dr McGill received a supply of ready-made cocktails today from a man named Alvey in Hagerstown, Md who has great celebrity for mixing liquors. He certainly understands his business—as I can willingly testify. We drank his health in deep potations.

June 17

This is the anniversary of the battle of Bunker's Hill which is one of the holy-days in Boston and Charlestown. Flags were floating during the day from the monument and every public place. The bay was crowded with small boats filled with pleasure parties—who assemble on Gallop island and other little islands and enjoy themselves—in an irrational manner. Most of the islands in the harbor belong to the State and General government. Upon Deer island there is a large establishment for the correction of prostitutes sent from Boston. The graves are some small islands that rise up just a short distance from Ft Warren on the outside of the harbor. No news today from the armies. Some letters were received from Ten stating that the Federals were withdrawing their troops from the towns in Middle Ten and concentrating them at Shelbyville where they apprehend an attack from Kirby Smith.

June 18th

The telegraph reports this morning that a petition was sent to President Lincoln signed by a large number of Senators and Representatives praying for an exchange or release of the prisoners now held by the Confederate Government. I do hope that something will be done, as I am heartily tired of confinement. In taking my usual walk this afternoon around the island my attention was drawn to the collection of myriads of fish under the sea-wall. Most of them are what they call Hard-heads here. The wind has been blowing very stiff all day—and the sea running high. I suppose these fish were driven in by the storm—or assembled there to catch minnows. The habits of fish are very illustrative of the world, the large fish eat up the small ones—and so on in turn they are eaten up by still larger ones—until they reach the whale where the matter stops. This evening I took a game of whist with Commodore Barron Gen Mackall and Lt Cassel. The Commodore was my partner and we beat them two rubs. Gin todies were introduced during the setting and a delicate dish sent in by Col Kane—who has a great character for mixing up good things. McConnico gave us a treat for tea—of nice strawberries and cream—and cake. The strawberries were very large and came in small split baskets holding about one quart which were purchased at the sutler for eight cents—basket and all. By returning the basket you are allowed two cents. There is no news from the armies today. Gold is now up to 7½ premium in N Y. The higher it gets the better for the South.

June 19

. . . I received a letter today from Col Anthony Kimmel from Longmore, Md. who tells me that he is using his endeavors to have me exchanged for Col Kinley of Md. I answered his letter immediately also wrote one to Miss Sue Dickson of Philia. No war news today.

June 20

Nothing has happened during the day of any moment. The papers are entirely destitute of news. The U S gun-boat South Carolina—passed here today for Port Royal. Her deck was crowded with men. The cadets had a mock dress parade this evening which was very amusing. They were dressed in all sorts of fantastic style. The Adjutant had a pole in his hand about ten feet long instead of a sword, a tin bucket was used for a drum—and orders of an amusing character was read out. My young friend, Tho. Morton, promised to procure a copy of them for me. I commenced reading Macauley's England today.

June 21st

Soon after breakfast this morning I went out alone on the ramparts and took a seat—and quietly enjoyed the pure, balmy atmosphere—and the scenecy around. I noticed some cattle and horses standing in the water cooling on the point of a small island, presenting a beautiful picture for a painter. News reached here today of the evacuation of Cumberland Gap by our forces. This will give up East Ten and South Western Va to the enemy. Gen Mitchell is marching on Chattanooga and will make a junction, I suppose, with the forces going through the Gap. I received a letter from Aunt Felicia this evening, full of local news about Nashville.

June 22

I attended service this morning. Mr Harrison read the Episcopal service—and Major Brown read a sermon by Dr Robertson. The Federals also had service today in a couple of tents stretched outside of the Ft. After service I occupied myself writing a letter in answer to Aunt Felicia's received yesterday. The boat this evening brought no news—except that Beauregard had gone to Richmond and left Bragg[44] in

---

[44] Braxton Bragg (1817-1876), Confederate general.

command—and that Price had also gone to tender his resignation. I place no confidence in either statement. A young man named Singleton was brought here this evening as a prisoner. He was captured at Post Republic—where he commanded a battery by Freemont. We had a splendid dinner today for a prison. Fresh salmon—roast and boiled mutton, macaroni—fresh cheese—green peas—Irish potatoes—radishes—lettuce—dessert—etc. A large merchant ship that anchored near the Fort this morning was towed in this evening by *our* "Uncle Sam's Tug"; Uncle Sam will never know any better, and the Yank must turn his *honest* penny. Col Heiman and myself were taking a walk as she passed by, and we bet five cigars on the heighth of the main mast. He said that it was nearer two hundred ft in heighth than eighty. I took the bet. We met old Mr Howard from Baltimore and agreed to leave it up to him—and he said it was about seventy five. We then met a Federal soldier and he said it was about three hundred and fifty. Finally we agreed to leave the matter to Lt DeBru who belongs to the Navy—and he decided that it was about one hundred and sixty feet. So Col Heiman won back his five cigars. The weather for the last few days has been charming for New England. All of the prisoners now pass the day out on the ramparts or on the island outside the Ft.

June 23rd

This morning a nettle fish was brought in and placed on the door step. Col Lillard asked me what it was. I told him that it was a Yankee poultice used for colic. I told him if he would lay on his back—I would apply it to his belly and he would see its effects. He replied that he could not wave his rank but that I might apply it to his Lt Col [Odell].

I was very much amused today at a little romance related to me by Maj Grace.[45] The scene was in Dover on Monday previous to the fight at Ft Donelson. Mrs McLauflin, an Irish woman that was the wife of a private "Sons of Erin" 10th Reg Ten Vol. and who left the camp at Ft Henry a few days before the bombardment went to Dover to be confined. When she arrived everybody was busy making ready for the approaching battle—and had no time to look after her. Two officers however of the 10th tendered their services. Capt Ellis got a room for her and some whiskey which is considered indispensable by an Irish woman on such occasions—and Jimmy Kirkman *two minutes* after the little "Son of Erin" made his appearance had it tied up in a rag and walked up and down the floor with it in his arms until relieved by the woman's husband. I admire the conduct of these two officers on the occasion—and would have liked very much to have witnessed the scene.

[45] William Grace, of Nashville, major, Tenth Tennessee Regiment.

News reached here today of a battle on James Island near Charleston in which the Confederates obtained a victory. This evening the Cadets had a party and a dance. Some of the men were dressed up as women —and they danced old-fashioned reels, cotillions, etc. Col Dimmick came into our room this evening to hear McConnico play on the guitar and sing. His performances as usual were excellent. I think he exerted himself a little more than ordinary to please the old Col and he succeeded. Col Lillard volunteered to assist Mc in singing The Grave of Napoleon—much to the annoyance of Mc and those present—as his voice was any thing but concord and sweetness. Some of my fellow prisoners in this casemate got on a bust after one o'clock last night and went round serenading those who have preferred sleeping to hearing their music.

June 24th

This morning I received a letter from mother containing photographic likenesses of her and father. She informs me that father—Harrison—the Fed clek—AVS. Lindsley,[46] Litton and others have been summoned to appear in Washington this week to give evidence against Judge Humphries before the Senate of the US upon the charge of treason. Father proposes coming here to see me if he will be well enough, with Dr Lindsley. I am truly sorry that father has to go to Washington to give evidence in this case—but I cannot see how he could have avoided it—without running off and leaving every thing which he could not well do. I wrote a letter to father at Washington. Many of our citizens in Nashville are taking the oath by compulsion. No man is allowed to transact business of any character unless he takes the oath—and if he refuses he is sent below the lines not to return under penalty of being punished as a spy. A man known to be southern in sentiment is held responsible for any thing marauders or guerrillas may take from Union men. This is going back to the ages of barbarism. The old Normans practiced these things in England. This has been a dark, rainy, blustering, and cold day. I have been hovering around a fire all day.

June 25th

Recd another very interesting letter from Miss Sue R. Dickson—and the Nashville Union—in which I see that Andrew Johnson summoned all the preachers of Nashville to appear at the Capitol. He told them that they could not continue in their pulpits without they took the oath

[46] A. V. S. Lindsley (1814-1885) was born in Princeton, New Jersey. He came to Nashville in 1824; President of the Mt. Olivet Cemetery Company and the Nashville and Lebanon Turnpike Company; trustee of the University of Nashville 1852-1855; Postmaster of Nashville 1862-1867; State Senator from Davidson County 1867-1868.

of allegiance. They asked for several days to consider the matter. The same paper contains an account of a Union meeting at Pulaski Ten at which Thos Martin presided and N S. Brown made another speech. One thousand troops have been sent out to Gen Harding's farm to eat up his substance. Rain all day. The proclamation of Gen Butler is severely condemned in the British Parliament—and by the press of England.[47]

June 26

Judge Humphries of Ten was tried today before the US Senate, and impeached. My father was one of the witnesses. It made me feel bad to see his name associated with such as W H. Polk—Brownlow—Scovall—and others but having been the clerk of Humphries Court and remaining in Nashville I do not see how he could well avoid it. I hope he did not take the oath of allegiance to the U.S. Judge Humphries is in the Confederate States and would readily plead guilty to all the charges preferred against him. Every body is now on tip-toe expecting a general engagement at Richmond which will decide the fate of that city, and probably the war. President Lincoln has just paid a visit to Gen Scott at West Point—and there are a great many speculations in the papers about it. Gen Pope accompanied him.

June 27th

The President has formed a new military division in Va. and placed Gen Pope in command of it. This will make Freemont, Banks, Shields, McDowell,[48] and other Gens in that quarter subject to Gen Pope's command. Gen Beauregard says that Gen Pope's statement about taking 10,000 prisoners at Farmington is false—and that he, B., took more prisoners at that place. I regard the placing of Pope in his present position as virtual condemnation of the other Gens. The papers concede this evening that the Feds were whipped in the recent fight on James Island. A small and very hansome yacht ran around the island this evening close to the shore, with ladies and gentlemen on board. I was

[47] Benjamin Franklin Butler was a member of the Massachusetts legislature in 1853 and 1859; an officer in the Union Army during the Civil War; a Republican member of Congress from Massachusetts 1866-1879, except for one term; elected as the twenty-ninth Governor of Massachusetts in 1882.

Butler's proclamation, issued while he was in command of affairs in New Orleans in 1862, reads as follows:

> As the officers and soldiers of the United States have been subject to repeated insults from the women (calling themselves ladies) of New Orleans, in return for the most scrupulous non-interference and courtesy on our part, it is ordered that hereafter when any female shall, by word, gesture, or movement, insult or show contempt for any officer or soldier of the United States, she shall be regarded and held liable to be treated as a woman of the town plying her avocation.

[48] Irvin McDowell (1818-1885), soldier.

seated on the parapet and they waved their handkerchiefs which I returned—although it is contrary to rules. The subject of a general exchange still continues to keep up considerable talk and speculation. Col Dimmick told Col Bailey today that he thought we would all be off in less than ten days. Col B upon the strength of it wrote to his wife in St. Louis to join him in Baltimore. Col Heiman received a letter from Mrs Thayer enclosing him a check for seventy five dollars, loaned money—which he sent for, at her request if he needed it. Very kind in her.

June 28th

Lt Col White wrote a letter from Knoxville to Col Odell informing him of the death of Col Lillard's wife. Poor man, I feel sorry for him. It is bad for a man to lose his wife under any circumstances—but while he is away from her in prison—it is awful to think of. He is very much troubled. Another prisoner arrived here today in the person of Thos Clay of Ky, one of Gen Buckner's staff. He was captured at Ft Donelson but paroled at Camp Chase on the ground of ill health. He is the son of Col Henry Clay who was killed at Buena Vista—and grandson of Henry Clay. Sitting by him at table, I was forceably struck with the coincidence of the grandsons of two men who were contemporaries in the early political history of Ky. should now be prisoners together.[49] The news from Europe per last steamer indicates very clearly that England and France will offer their mediation very soon to settle this war. The British press and the members of parliament are down on Gen Butler's proclamation in regard to the ladies of NO. It has been very warm today and the bay as smooth as a mirror—and the vessels standing still without a breath of air in the sails. Lt Whittle of Va got his collar bone broke this evening while playing foot-ball. Col Lyon ran against him and knocked him down. We have an English servant from the Revere House to attend our room now and I am very much amused at his pronunciation. He invariably gives the letter I the sound of H. Ice he calls hice. Quite a number of ladies were here today on a visit. They are the wives of the officers, and as none of them were good looking, I did not give myself any concern about them. We had quite a frolic in our room this evening. Lt DeBru brought in a bottle of gin upon which several of the party got quite merry—or rather tight. The party

[49] Felix Grundy and Henry Clay became antagonists early in their political careers. As a member of the Kentucky Legislature in 1802 Grundy opposed and Clay, still comparatively unknown, supported the chartering of a banking corporation. The following year Clay was elected to the Legislature in a contest against Grundy. Both entered the Twelfth Congress in 1811 and cooperated in bringing on war with Great Britain. Their actions in this crisis gained for them the title of "war hawks."

consisted of Marshall Kane, Lt Myers, Lt DeBru, Col Jno Brown, Col Bailey, McConnico, Col Gregg, Col Heiman, and myself. Col Heiman was very tight and quite happy and felicitous in his remarks and singing. Just before retiring Myers returned and insisted that Col H should sing the "Old Tom Cat." Both were undressed. The Col commenced the song several times but without success. Finally he said he would be d——if he did not sing it. So he took one breath and went through it rapidly without stopping. I do not think that I have laughed so much in an age—as I did at his appearance and singing.

June 29

The papers this evening bring the news of the defeat of the House Confiscation Bill in the US Senate. I received a letter from Sister Sallie conveying the painful intelligence of the death of sister Mannoah—brother Grundy's wife. She died at the Gayoso House Memphis. Had been sick for several weeks but was pronounced by her physician as out of danger the day before the bombardment of that city. The excitement caused her to relapse and she died the day after. She had been dead three weeks before the family heard it at Nashville. She was a noble woman and leaves three beautiful children. Poor Grundy—I feel so sorry for him. His loss is irrepairable.

June 30

This morning's telegraph brings the news of the capture of Richmond—but the papers of this evening indicate pretty clearly that McClelland was whipped. It is very difficult to get the true state of the facts from the papers, as the government prohibits them from publishing the truth. I see that Gov Johnson has sent to the Penitentiary some of the preachers because they refused to take the oath of allegiance. The Catholic clergy were not interrupted because they are considered loyal—when Father Brown was the Chaplain of our Regiment. Mr Wallace of Baltimore handed me a copy of the Globe today, containing a full account of the proceedings of the trial of Judge Humphries of Ten. before the Senate. My father was the first witness examined, and they interrogated him pretty long and closely.

July 1st

The prisoners within the walls of this Ft were highly excited and overjoyed this morning at the news from before Richmond. Our accounts of the battle are as yet all from the northern papers, but enough has leaked out to satisfy us that the Federal Army has been repulsed—and has fallen back from their position—and got under the protection of their everlasting gunboats without which they could do nothing. They have every advantage of us on the water—but when they come to a hand to hand fight we have proved more than equal match to them. I received a letter today from Dr Lindsley written from Philia. He and father will be here to-morrow. I also received a letter from Miss Sue Dickson of Phila. This has been a clear and pleasant day, after the rain. I could see the city, and the towns on the bay more distinctly than anytime before.

July 2nd

This morning Col Heiman and myself dressed up in our best bib and tuck to receive father and Dr Lindsley. We walked down to the boat—but were disappointed. The general tenor of the news this morning indicates that we gained a great victory before Richmond. The papers try to smooth it over—and soften the pull of public speculation here in the north—by calling it a great strategic movement on the part of Gen McClelland—but the truth cannot be kept back long and we will soon learn the whole story. There is a call by the President this morning for three hundred thousand more troops "having been advised so to do by the Governors of the several northern states in view of their recent great victories—and to put down the rebellion at once." Now this call is for one or two purposes—to reinforce the army in Va. or make ready for a conflict with England and France which now seems unavoidable. Mr Seward[50] is in Boston today having an interview with Gov Andrews on the subject of Mass furnishing her quota of the 300,000. The Gov made his proclamation this evening. We have news today that Gen Curtis in in a very critical situation, and the prospects are that the Fed army will soon be driven entirely out of the State of Ark. We also have news that Gen Mitchell is falling back, and that the Federals are fortifying Nashville, Ten. The Boston Cadets left here today and were mustered out of the U.S. service this evening on the Boston Commons. They have been on duty here about five weeks, having come down to take the place of the Battalion that was sent to Washington. The Cadets were composed of men of substance in Boston, and they became heartily tired of guarding prisoners—so much so that they gave out of their pockets the sum of thirteen hundred dollars and their camp equipage to some *roughs* in the city to take their place. The roughs came over today and many of them are boys not over fourteen years of age. The Cadets upon leaving drew up in front of Col Dimmick's quarters and gave the old man three times three cheers and after they reached the quay—they cheered considerably, all of which I thought very unmilitary. I received a long and very interesting letter today from Gen W G.

---

[50] William Henry Seward (1801-1872), lawyer, statesman.

Harding at Fort Mackinaw. He writes in good spirits and says that Barrow, Guild, and himself get along very well there. Each have separate rooms, the scenery beautiful and the climate charming in *summer.* I also received a letter from Gen A Kimmell of Md—enclosing me a letter from Col. Kenly who was taken prisoner by Stonewall Jackson at Front Royal. The Col desires me to exchange for his Lt Col. Before leaving Fort Warren I want to be well assured that I am checked through to Dixie.

July 3

Father and Dr Lindsley came over this evening on the boat. Col Heiman and myself went down to meet them. Father was greatly affected upon meeting me but after he discovered that I was comfortably situated he became more reconciled. Col Dimmick was very kind and carried us round through all the Casemates and magazines. I saw more of Ft Warren today than I have done during my imprisonment of four months. Father and Dr L. dined with Col Dimmick. I am truly delighted that they came. They left this evening on the boat—and will leave Boston in the morning for home. They expect to pass Sunday at Niagera Falls. The news today from the seat of war is highly important —and it is now clearly evident from Federal Authority—that the Confederates achieved a victory.

July 4th

This is the anniversary of the Independence of the US. Altho not a citizen of the U.S. now, yet I feel that we of the South are more entitled to celebrate and hold sacred the day than the people of the north. The declaration was the product of [a] southern mind, and it was for the principles contained in that instrument that induced me to take up arms. I told Col Dimmick yesterday that we were better entitled to celebrate the day than the people of the north—because we had always preserved the principles embodied in the Declaration, whereas they had set at naught every principle contained in it. They fired a national salute from the Ft today at noon—and this evening it was rockets in the city—and the various towns that skirt the harbor— embracing a distance of about sixty miles. Col Dimmick was very kind to let the prisoners go out on the parapets and witness the exhibition. We have no additional news from the seat of war. I received a letter today from mother. She states that the city authorities of Nashville have requested every house in the city to display the U. S. flag on the 4th of July, that Andrew Johnson has imprisoned seven of the Clergymen of the city—leaving the Catholics untouched. Edward, my brother, took the young negro men from the plantations to Col Young's plantation near Columbus Miss—leaving the old men and the women and children there to make a corn crop.

July 5th

I forgot to mention yesterday that several balloons were sent up yesterday. The one that went up from Boston Commons turned an eagle loose after it had ascended. The noble bird turned its course southward, where it properly belongs. The news today from the recent battles are rather meager. Several private letters were received today from Baltimore—stating that it was believed there that McClelland was surrounded—and that he would have to surrender and Gen Lee[51] would not accept anything but an unconditional surrender. The news from Europe today is important. France sends a fleet at once into American waters—in view of an anticipated conflict with the U.S. and also sends an additional force to Mexico. The English press is getting clamerous for intervention in our affairs. Cotton has taken a sudden and heavy rise—market excited. American securities falling rapidly. This taken in connection with the fact that gold and exchange has gone up very high within the past ten days in N.Y. shows very conclusively to my mind that a great financial crisis is impending which may involve the whole world in difficulties—and complications that no man can unravel, and time alone can determine its results both in the old and the new world.

July 6th

This been an exceedingly warm and sultry day. I took a walk around the island this morning, and it was so unpleasant that I returned to my room. Mrs Mayor Brown of Baltimore attended service this morning and it was a treat to hear the sound of her voice. I wrote letters today to Miss Sue Dickson—and Mrs Jno O. Ewing. This evening we have news that Richmond was illuminated on last Wednesday night—in honor of the triumph of our arms in the series of battles before that city. The Boston Herald—a Republican paper, in an editorial this evening pitches into Lincoln, Stanton, McClelland—and everybody generally. Old Jno Hugh Smith, the present Union Mayor of Nashville—who was a witness in the Humphries case before the Senate—arrived on the boat this evening. He sent for some of [his] old acquaintances. Heiman-Davis-McConnico-and myself passed the evening with him and ragged him pretty hard about his present associations—and position. Cols Bailey and Brown refused to see him—because he is Union.

[51] Robert Edward Lee (1807-1870), Confederate general.

July 7th

Occupied a good part of the day with Jno H. Smith who left this evening for home. Tonight Clay and Lyons invited several of [us] into their room to drink some good whiskey. During the evening McConnico and Brown got into a discussion about our going to see Smith. I remarked that my record on the Southern Question was as good as anybodys. Maj Chairs who had just come into the room said that I was a liar. I told him that he was a G—d— liar and scoundrel—and made at him. Those present jumped in between us and he was carried out the room. His conduct was wholly unjustifiable and if he is a gentleman he will make the amend honorable to-morrow morning. Another fight is reported to have taken place on James River last Thursday. As usual they claim a victory.

July 8

Young Jones of Pulaski is quite sick in the hospital. Col Dimmick went over to see him today and read some religious book to him. This has been an exceedingly hot day—and the heat haze was so thick that I could hardly see the islands around. I noticed today a dog following Gen Buckner. He is with him every day and seems to know his hour for walking—and watches regularly and earnestly for him to come out of his room. The dog seems to know that he is a prisoner, and evidently sympathetic with him. The papers contain no additional war news but the NY Herald has one or two editorials on the subject of intervention—indicating that the north now fully believes that England and France will intervene, as soon as the news of the battles before Richmond reaches there. Commodore Barron had a letter from Norfolk today, giving an account of the recent battles—but Col Dimmick would not let him have it—because it was contraband. The servants in one of our Mess rooms—got on a drunk tonight and they all landed in the Guard House. Some of the gentlemen will have to go without their breakfast to-morrow morning.

July 9

One hundred additional prisoners arrived here this morning—forty-five of whom are officers, field and company, and some of them wounded. They are Virginians,—North Carolinians,—and Louisianians, taken in the recent battles before Richmond. They give a glorious account of those battles and say that we gained a great victory—and have over ten thousand prisoners. Jeff Davis was on the field, Beauregard was not there with any of his forces from the West as represented by the Federal Papers—and Stonewall Jackson was not killed. They state that Gen Joe Johnston is so far recovered from his wounds as to be able to ride on horseback. The Steam-ship Arabia passed out this morning from Boston—having on board the French Princes who attached themselves to Gen McClellan's Staff about twelve months since. Their names are the Prince de Joinville and his two nephews, Comte de Paris, and Duc de Chartres. Their sudden departure after the recent disasters to the Federal army before Richmond is rather significant, altho the papers say that they intended leaving two weeks ago—being compelled to return to attend to matters of a private character. The money market in NY yesterday shows that gold is sixteen per cent premium—and exchange one hundred and twenty eight. I do not think they can stand this long. Stocks will certainly commence tumbling down very soon. Col Bailey received a letter today from Tenn. stating that Calvin McNairy and others who have taken the oath there now regret it. I passed the evening at a game of cards at Mr Winder's room.

July 10th

Two or three yachts and a steamer came to the quay this morning loaded with ladies who desired to come ashore and see the Rebels but Col Dimmick would not permit it. They waved their handkerchiefs and seemed much excited. The soldiers returned the compliment but they received "nary wave" from the rebels. I went into the hospital to see young Jones from Pulaski who is quite sick. Here I saw Mr Granburry, a Chaplain of one of the Va Regiments. He was shot just over the left eye and is doing well. . . . Wm H Polk, the traitor of Tenn, is now in Boston. The object of his visit is to release Major Porter of Maury Co, Ten, who is a prisoner here. Mayor Smith said when he was here a few days since that Polk obtained the release from Lincoln by telling him a dirty anecdote—for which the President is said to be very fond. . . . Old Abe was so much delighted that he jumped up—took Polk by the arm and escorted him down to the Sec of War's office where a release was made out by order of the President for Major Porter. Gold and exchange continues to go up, the former is quoted today at 17¼ and the latter at 130. I received a very long, and very interesting letter today from Aunt Felicia.

July 11th

Nothing has transpired today worthy of moment. In this evening's paper there is a telegram to the effect that the War Dept had agreed upon a general system of exchange of prisoners with the Confederate States. I hope that this may be so—but really I have heard so much on the subject that I have become tired—and shall await quietly the coming event.

July 12

No news today from any quarter of importance. There was a meeting at Faneuil Hall today—called by the Mayor of the city for the purpose of working up the people to the point of enlistment—in compliance with the call of the President for three hundred thousand troops. Edward Everett, Chas G Loring[52] and others made speeches, which I think wholly unequal to their reputation and the occasion. They are experiencing considerable difficulty in raising troops. In the state of Maine many men are fleeing to Canada to avoid going into the army. Mr Gordon and his sons—who have a large jewelry establishment in Boston were arrested day before yesterday on the charge of treason. Cols Bailey and Pendleton came into our room this evening and quite a discussion arose in regard to the Yankee character. Bailey was very bitter and contended that in their religion, literature, and morals they are wholly corrupt. The orators—statesmen and authors were taken up and handled pretty roughly. Someone remarked that Prentice was a great orator, and that he was from New England. McConnico said that Prentice deserved no credit for his oratory for when he was drunk he had no . . . control of his mouth. . . . Several Nashville papers were received this evening containing the proceedings of the celebration of the 4th there and the speeches of J Stokes—Houston—Johnson—Campbell—etc.

July 13

This has been a most charming day. The atmosphere here is far more delightful than even in Boston and there is no comparison with any point south of this in this season. The Rev Mr Granburry a methodist preacher from Va—who was a Chaplain in one of the Regiments there—delivered a beautiful discourse today to the prisoners under the shade of a tree outside of the island. After the service I returned to my room and wrote a long letter to Aunt Felicia. I received a long and highly interesting letter by the mail this evening from my friend, Miss Sue Dickson of Philia. It contained a great deal of contraband news in regard to the recent battles, but Lt Parry gave it to me—under the promise that I would not communicate its contents to any one.

July 14

The news by telegraph this morning is very important. Forrest with 2800 cavalry has captured an entire regiment at Murfreesboro—and two Generals, and will likely capture another Regiment there. The Federals were shelling the town. The probability is that Forrest will go

[52] Charles Greeley Loring (1794-1868), lawyer.

on to Nashville. Van Dorn[53] has retaken Baton Rouge and captured 1500 prisoners. Gen Custis is reputed to have been captured with his army in Ark. Jno Morgan[54] is again in Ky, waking them up. Gen Butler publishes a letter trying to explain away his Proclamation in regard to the ladies of New Orleans and he only makes the matter worse. Gen Mitchell is in Washington under arrest for some of his infamous conduct in North Ala. The Confiscation Act has passed both houses of the Federal Congress, and it is thought that the President will approve it. An order was published today in the Ft limiting the letters of prisoners to three sides of a sheet of note paper. I think this very well, for some of them write outrageously long letters. A bark ran upon the rock near this island this evening, but I suppose she will get off without much injury when the tide rises.

July 15

Nothing has occured today of interest. It seems that Forrest instead of marching on Nashville as expected went back in the direction of McMinnville.

July 16

The exchange question has broke out again here and it is generally believed that a general exchange will take place very soon. I was appointed today on the carving committee in our Mess. Wrote to Miss Sue Dickson today.

July 17th

There is no news of any importance today. The President has approved the Confiscation Act, just what the friends of the southern cause desired. The Congress of the US is about to adjourn and [by] their acts the present session has tended more to arrouse and keep up the fires of the Confederacy—than all else besides.

July 18

This has been a beautiful day. I received a letter this morning from my wife written from Tunnell Hill Ga. and dated the 26th of June. She had heard from me by letter from Maj Davidson who went from here on the 9th. Received a letter this evening from Mother stating that father and Dr Lindsley had reached home safely. Lt DeBru of the Navy did a good thing today. He had one thousand dollars in English sovereigns deposited with Lt Pearson, the Post Commissary. He demanded his money—and Pearson opened his eyes in amazement, having sold the gold some time since in Boston at 2 per cent. DeBru

53 Earl Van Dorn (1820-1863), soldier.

54 John Hunt Morgan (1825-1864), Confederate cavalry leader.

made him pay eighteen, the present price of gold. So the Yank was out Yankeed. From the papers I gather that the Federals will be compelled to resort to a draft before they can get the 300,000 troops. I saw a long list in the Nashville Union of persons who have taken the oath —but I recognized but few of them.

July 19th

This morning I was standing down at the quay watching the arrivals by the boat—when Col Dimmick passed—and called me aside and handed me a letter which he said was contraband—but that I might read it—and hand it back to him. It turned out to be a letter from Robbie Porter written by his mother and containing photographs of the whole family. The mother of young Singleton—(Mrs. King of Washington) was here today visiting her son. She had Miss King with her—a very attractive young woman. Lt Dimmick left here this afternoon to join Gen McClellan. Some of the officers, myself among the number, gave him a letter, setting forth how kind and polite he and his father had been to the Confederate prisoners, and asking the same treatment extended to him in the event he should be captured. We had a telegram from the North America this evening off Cape Race. News of the battles before Richmond had reached England—but no particulars given as to its effect.

July 20

I attended service today under the willow-tree outside the Ft. Mr. Grandburry preached—and Mr Martin prayed. I noticed several Federal officers present. While at service Cols Hanson Baldwin and Jackson arrived on a little steamer from the City. They are just from Ft Delaware, having applied to be sent here in preference to remaining there. They report that the chance for exchange is rather slim. Jackson got on a spree late in the evening—and emptied the chamber all over himself. He was then washed off—put in clean under-clothes—and got into my bed—where he slept all night.

July 21st

I read in this morning paper President Lincoln's address to the members of Congress from the Border Slave States—and their reply. Lebanon Ten is now in the possession of the Confederates, and the Federals are receiving large re-inforcements at Nashville. Gen Twigg died a few days ago in Ga. The Confederate Ram—called the Arkansas made an attack on the Federal Fleet of gun-boats at Vicksburg—doing them much damage. I wrote a letter this evening to Aunt Felicia.

July 22

The news from Europe by the Asia shows that they have the particulars of the battles before Richmond and regard them as disastrous to the Feds. The Unionists in Nashville have had a panic and fear the Confederates will re-take the city.

July 23

I had a message today from old Mrs Moses Stevens—who now lives in Salem. I went to school both to her husband and son when quite a small boy. After the death of her husband she returned to the place of her nativity—after living in Ten. for thirty or forty years. President Lincoln publishes an order today dated the 11th making Gen Halleck Gen in Chief over the entire land forces of the U.S. to remain at Washington. This I consider a severe slam on Gen McClellan. The telegraph this evening brings intelligence of an agreement between Gens Dix and Hill on the subject of exchanges, which goes into operation immediately. It created quite a stir among the prisoners here. Some of them commenced packing their trunks. The Evening Traveller contains some extracts from English papers on the subject of the battles before Richmond—and they are very severe upon the US. Lt DeBru after reading them remarked very earnestly that the English understood their people well—and know that they were not fighting for Constitutional Rights but to get the fine farms of the South, upon which to settle branches of their families.

July 24

I took a walk before breakfast this morning as is my habit when I get up early enough. When I reached the water my attention was attracted by the congregation of thousands of Jelly Fish—or Nettle Fish as some call them and it was really interesting to watch the various shapes and forms they assumed. The variety was very great—and the sight highly interesting. Passing along I came to [a] pen containing four pigs, six months old, which have been fed upon the offall from the kitchens of the Fort and I think they would average two hundred weight gross. Wm H. Polk of Ten. came and returned on the boat this morning. He enquired for Maj Porter and Cols Gant and Voorhies. The former went home with him, having authority from the government to do so. The latter refused to see him. He did not ask for me, and I am glad of it—as it places him in [the] future just where I want him, so far as I am concerned. When such men as Polk and Brownlow can procure the release of prisoners—where good men have failed, it speaks bad for the government. The steamer Asia from Liverpool passed into Boston this morning with a large lot of passengers. A Federal soldier died in the hospital today and was escorted with military honors to the boat this evening and sent to his home. I saw him several days ago in the hospital—and thought then he would die. He was a fine looking man. Several southern ladies from Washington and Alexandria were here today—visiting their relatives who are prisoners. Another order came here today from Washington for a list of prisoners here. I suppose this is another evidence that there is an exchange to take place soon. Another report is published today from Gen Pope giving an account of the extraordinary doings of his Cavalry in Va. He is famous for his reports and the great beauty about them is that there is no truth in them. The Boston papers today give a wonderful account of the exploits of the Ram Arkansas on the Miss—and state that she distroyed nearly their whole fleet. The speech of Mr Sennott, a Boston Lawyer, was published today in the Courier. It was made before the US Commission in case against the Gordens—for treason. It is the finest specimen of satire that I have seen in a long time and will give him great reputation. He gives it strong to the Adm, the Republican party—and many leading men in the north. I wrote a letter today to Miss Sue Dickson in reply to one received yesterday. I also wrote to mother—and to my tailor in Boston ordering a military suit—in anticipation of going to Dixie soon. I read a book today called The Attic Philosopher—giving a history of life from an attic window in Paris. It is a very readable and interesting little book. A dense fog came up late this evening—enveloping the whole bay in darkness. I could not see the islands adjacent.

July 25

I see from a dispatch today that Gov. [W. B.] Campbell of Ten. has accepted the position of Brig Gen in the US service, and will take command in Ten. His course in this war will disgrace him through all time in the eyes of all good men. In Memphis it is stated that a large number of citizens have taken the oath. Those who refuse are sent nolens volens south of the lines. I read some accounts from a Chicago paper giving an account of the Ram Arkansas that has just run through the Federal fleet at Vicksburg. This account makes it the most extraordinary vessel for war purposes ever constructed. Several US war vessels have been lying close to the Fort during the day.

July 26th

Nothing has transpired today of any particular interest except that the telegraph states that the Confederates have crossed the Ten. river at Chattanooga in force and are moving on Nashville. An Irishman—who is a private among the prisoners had an attack something like colera. Dr McGill placed a hot mustard plaster all over him. Thinking he was about to die he called for help and mercy in his wise: Oh holy Virgin Mary have mercy upon me. Oh father—son and holy ghost and the Virgin Mary have mercy upon me. God dam that blister. Take it off or I will be dam if it don't burn a hole in my belly.

July 27th

This has been a very hot day. We had two sermons today—but I did not attend because—I felt very blue all day thinking about the condition of the country. The paper today states that the Confederate Cavalry captured a steamer on the Ten. River—destroyed a great deal of cotton near Florence captured sixty waggons—burnt a vast amount of quartermaster and Commissary stores. Col Dimmick extended our privilege this evening—and we were permitted to walk in front of our quarters until 9 oc. This is a great relief—and much pleasanter than being cooped up during a hot evening in a room with half doz persons.

July 28th

This has been a glorious day for the prisoners in Ft Warren. This evening Col Dimmick received an order to have the prisoners ready by Thursday to start for Richmond on the splendid steamer, Ocean Queen. He immediately turned Gens Tilghman and Buckner out of close confinement and the scene of the meeting between them—and their fellow prisoners was wonderful. Many of them shed tears of joy. The Federal soldiers gathered around perfectly amazed at the feeling exhibited. They remained until 11 oc in our casemate talking over their experience in close confinement. The paper this evening states that there is reason to believe that Vallandigham[55] of Ohio will be arrested for treason.

July 29th

This has been a busy, bustling day in the Ft. Every one is packing his trunk and procuring as far as their means will allow all those little articles that they may require. The Sutler has done a brisk business—also the express men that run to Boston. Lt Pearson, the commissary of the post, and who keeps the money of the prisoners, told me today that over twelve thousand dollars had been checked from him in the last sixty days. I really think that the prisoners here in the last six months have expended over twenty five thousand dollars in clothing and one thing and another. I received the last letter today from my

[55] Clement Laird Vallandigham (1820-1871), politician.

friend, Miss Dickson—that I expect to receive until the war is over. Since my imprisonment she has written to me regularly every week, and has contributed more than any one else to cheer my lonely heart.

July 30

We had quite a storm today, and one of the heaviest rains fell that I have ever seen. Occupied myself today in writing letters to those who have been most kind to me since my imprisonment. I wrote to Miss Sue Dickson—Dr J B. Lindsley C L. Woodburry—Aunt Felicia and Mother. Every one has been exceedingly busy today, packing up—and procuring such articles as they need. I leave a small box with Lt Pearson containing two quilts—one given to me by Gen Tilghman and one by Ann Waters. I leave them with him for safe keeping until sent for. There is no news today of special interest.

July 31

This is the day of our departure from Ft Warren—having been here for five months lacking only a few days. Our little boat this morning brought over the Misses Dimmick and a number of ladies who came to see us off. Charlie Woodbury also came over to see me and take leave—having obtained permission to do so from Washington. At 11 oc the steamer, Ocean Queen, cast anchor in the channel—and the little boat carried over our baggage—and a company of federals to guard us en route. The prisoners were then drawn up in line in the shade of the Ft—and the roll called. We then took leave with the Baltimore prisoners, and Col Dimmick—which was very effecting. This being accomplished we bid a final adieu to Ft Warren amid the sweet strains from the band—and the waving of handkerchiefs from the ladies, and even the federal soldiers. As soon as we all got snugly fixed in our berths the steamer started off for Fortress Monroe. The day was beautiful and the sea smooth, consequently not many suffered from sea sickness. Our steamer is one of the largest vessels afloat—having been built for the Pacific trade. She is 3000 tons burden, 1300 horse power—but very slow. She is now used for a government transport—the owners receiving two thousand dollars a day for her.

Aug. 1

We had a dense fog all last night—and until noon today, being off the banks. The fog whistle was blowing constantly. No incident of note.

Aug. 2

This has been a beautiful day and the sun-set this evening was one of the most magnificent that I have ever seen at sea. Several steamers, and ships were in sight today.

Aug. 3

We cast anchor this morning just below Fortress Monroe—from which point we had a good view of the Ft—Old Point Comfort—and the village of Hampton—that Gen Magruder[56] distroyed—also of the Rip Rapes—and other noted places. In a short time a transport called the Knickerbocker came along side—and took us off—and then moved to a point above the Ft where several other transports were lying loaded with prisoners. While here some five or six transports came down loaded with federal troops—and we all came to the conclusion that a feint was to be made at some other point—or that these troops were being sent to relieve Gen Pope. Late this evening we started up the James but did not go more than ten miles—when a blue light appeared and we dropped anchor. We were now near Gen. Burnsides'[57] encampment and we could hear the drum beating, the Assembly, and see the camp fires bright at 2 oc showing that a movement of some sort was on foot.

Aug 4th

We remained at anchor out in the stream nearly all day—when we again started. During the night we passed Commodore Porter's[58] fleet of Morton boats which look quite formidable—and before day we cast anchor again right in the midst of the gunboats. We lay here nearly all day and had a fine opportunity of seeing the celebrated Moniter, Galena etc.

[56] John Bankhead Magruder (1810-1871), soldier.
[57] Ambrose Everett Burnside (1824-1881), Union general.
[58] David Dixon Porter (1813-1891), Naval commander.

CHAPTER XXIV

"The men were all exceedingly glad to see me." (August-October, 1862)

Life in a military prison, even the restful existence at Fort Warren, did not appeal to Randal McGavock. He was much more interested in returning to the scene of battle. As soon as he was exchanged, he went to northern Georgia to visit his wife and to Columbus, Mississippi, to see members of his family. From there he proceeded to Clinton, Mississippi, where his old regiment, the Tenth Tennessee, was reorganized.

Aug. 5th

Today we landed at a point called Eakin's landing some 15 miles below Richmond. No examination of trunks was made. The debarkation was as rapid as possible, as we were all anxious to get off the hot and crowded boats and put our feet on old Va soil. Nearly every man as he stepped off the boat—seemed to draw a long breath—and evidently looked like he felt better and happier. We were badly fed on these transports, having nothing to eat but hard sea crackers and concentrated coffee. The Commissary, like most government officials, charged the government but pocketed the rations. Four or five men died on the boats for want of proper nourishment and attention. Soon after getting off of the boat I met Mr Langhorn from Western Va—who came down to obtain a permit from Gen Thomas[1] to go after his son—Jas, who is in the insane hospital there. He was wounded and taken prisoner and sent to Ft Delaware and his derangement resulted therefrom. Capt Scott took his horse which was hitched up and rode him to Richmond without leave, which I consider a very dirty trick. Our government officials are very culpable for not having any transportation for the prisoners to Richmond or any one to receive us. The privates scattered off by themselves—and many—and I may say nearly all

[1] George Henry Thomas (1816-1870), Union soldier.

of the officers had to walk to Richmond. Fortunately, I procured a seat in an ambulance and rode to the city in company with Gen Buckner and others. We stopped on the way at Gen Longstreet's[2] Head Quarters —where Gen B stayed all night. The Gens troops had a fight today and lost Malvern Hill and some twenty of his men. Commodore Barron and myself reached the Spotswood Hotel at 3 oc. We were put in a room with Col Caldwell—who opened a bottle of brandy and gave us a treat.

Aug. 6

I slept nearly all the morning—being very much fatigued. In the afternoon I walked round to the Exchange Hotel where I met Gov Foote—Buck McNish—and several other acquaintances. Nearly all of the prisoners got up from the landing today, and they looked tired, worn, and mad.

Aug. 7

This morning I called with Gen Tilghman and the officers of Brigade to see the Sec of War Mr Randolph—who informed us that we must proceed to Vicksburg and reorganize our Regiments. He informed us that the Confederacy had abundance of arms, having received three ship loads recently from Europe, and that we had captured over thirty thousand stand of arms in the recent battles near this place. He answered all questions asked with great promptness and clearness. All Richmond seems to be a hospital—and the sick and wounded must suffer very much during this very hot weather. Prices of every thing here are exhorbitantly high. Hotels charge three and four dollars per day—second handed Colts pistols from [$]50 to [$]100 a piece—a double reined bridle eighteen dollars—melons from two to three dollars, apples one dollar per doz., and every thing else in proportion. Col Heiman—Maj Grace, Maj Clark, and myself went to the Theatre tonight, but was very much disappointed, as it was a very poor affair—and in an old church converted into a Theatre. We then went down to Gen Tilghman's room and stayed until bed time.

Aug 8th

Gen Tilghman and myself called today on the President—but he was engaged with the Sec of State on important business and we did not see him. I met his aid, Col Johnston son of Gen Sidney Johnston who appeared to be a very nice gentleman. Just as we went in Gen Buckner came out, in company with Cols Hanson, Brown, and . . . whom he has recommended for Brig Generals. I think we have more Gens than

[2] James Longstreet (1821-1904), soldier, businessman, diplomat.

Brigades and I think the President might find better material than either of those gentlemen—but after appointing Jos Rains, Geo Maney and others, I do not know what he may do. I dined at the Exchange with Gen Tilghman. During the day I drew my back pay—procured my transportation ticket to Vicksburg and my passport. News reached here today that ten thousand men on their way to reinforce Gen Buell had been cut off. That Gen Caswell[3] of East Ten. had been assassinated —and that the Arkansas had been blown up by its commander. Some of it is believed—but not all.

Aug. 9th

During the forenoon I was occupied making purchases. This evening I wrote my report of the battle of Ft Donelson and handed it in to Col Heiman, my Brigade Commander. I called to see Capts Williamson and Allen of Ten. who were wounded in the recent battles. The mother and sister of the latter are with him. He is confined to his bed, but Williamson is walking about. After tea I walked with Col Bailey over to the Exchange to see Gen Tilghman and others.

Aug. 10

This is my thirty-sixth birthday. I left Richmond this morning at 8 oc in company with Col Bailey. The cars were so crowded that I found it very difficult to get on at all. Finally I got into a box car filled with negroes going to Jefferson Co Ten. They were mostly children purchased in Richmond at very high prices—for an investment. I suppose that the man considers it safer than holding Confederate paper. Just before reaching Lynchburg we met a train of cars containing some federal prisoners who have been there for some three months—and are now on their way north. I also saw some twenty five prisoners just taken by Gen Jackson's army. Reached Lynchburg and put up at the Norvelle House—and five of us were put in a room with one window and it was so hot that I did not sleep a wink during the night.

Aug. 11

Left Lynchburg before day this morning. At Liberty I met with Dr Otey who gave me full information relative to my relatives in Pulaski and Montgomery Counties. Reached Mac's Meadow about 2½ oc and found Aunt Polly, who is looking very well for a woman of 74. She is as much like father as any brother and sister I ever saw. Uncle Randal was up at Wytheville when I arrived but came down this evening on a hand car. Eight thousand pounds of lead is shipped from this depot every day for the use of the army.

[3] Brigadier General W. R. Caswell, Commander of the Department of East Tennessee.

Aug. 12

I had an excellent night's rest. There is more hay on the meadows in Western Va than I ever saw and the corn crops look better. Cloyd McGavock[4] and Cousin Cynthia came over to see me this morning. Left Mac's Meadow at 2½ oc and reached Bristol at 8 o'clock and then proceeded to Knoxville.

Aug. 13

Reached Knoxville early this morning and proceeded to Dalton Ga. where I was fortunate in meeting a train loaded with troops—and I proceeded at once to Tunnell Hill, seven miles distant where I met my wife, her mother, and brothers. They were rejoiced to see me, and I was happy to meet my wife once more after a sore separation of seven months. They are comfortably situated in a private boarding house close to the depot where there is a number of Ten. Refugees from Ten.

Aug. 14

I have occupied the day in the house talking with my wife. This evening Cols Bailey—Abernathy—Sugg—and Brown passed down en route for Vicksburg. Col Byers of Gallatin returned from Chattanooga this evening and reports that Gen Cheatham will cross the Ten. river tomorrow with his division for Nashville. The army will move in three columns on Nashville and they expect to bag Buell's entire force. Gov Harris and Staff are at Chattanooga. He is trying to raise a State force —and has made Gen Anderson Commander. I hope he will succeed but have my doubts.

Aug. 15

Remained all day with my wife talking over to her my experience as a prisoner of war. News reached here this evening of the disertion of large numbers of Kentuckians from Buell's army.

Aug 16th

This is an exceedingly dull little place—and I miss very much the daily papers that I was accustomed to read at Ft Warren and which gave me the news of the whole world but I am willing to do without this, and have my freedom and the society of my wife. Gen Tilghman passed down this evening en route for Vicksburg.

Aug. 17th

I notice in an Atlantic paper of today that Gen McCook[5] was killed a few days ago in North Ala. by the guerrillas, while riding out in an

[4] Joseph Cloyd McGavock (1813-1886), the son of James McGavock II of Fort Chiswell, Virginia.

[5] Robert Latimer McCook (1827-1862), lawyer, soldier.

ambulance. The Federals to revenge themselves hung several citizens in the neighborhood. His remains were carried to Nashville and thence north. Andrew Johnson called to see his remains and was much affected, so said. The same writer states that a number of prominent secessionists were shot in Nashville by the Unionists in revenge of McCook's death. Bishop Hughes[6] of N Y. made a speech recently in Dublin Ireland in which he says that this country can never be divided and that if the Rebels succeed he will transfer his allegiance to them meaning—I suppose that the whole north would adopt our form of government and—take the Constitution of the Confederate States instead of their own.

Aug. 18th

This morning I went up to Chattanooga in company with R E Deery and Gen Pope Walker[7] on a freight train. At Ringold Dr Houston, Mr Stratton, and Mr Leiper of Middle Ten. got on the cars. As soon as I reached town I procured a pass to walk about the place and another to go out. I then went to the State Bank where I met Fisher—the Cashier — Lytton Bostick — Geo Maney — Judge Humphries — Judge Baxter — Dunlap — Dr Quintard — and other friends. The latter and myself then went up to Gen. Sam Anderson's quarters, where I met Gen Smith, Jno K Edmonson, and others. Anderson looks badly. We then went over to Geo Maney's quarters where I took dinner. After dinner I drove with him in an ambulance to the Crutchfield House and called on his wife, who has just arrived from Marietta. She looks very fat, and weighs 150 lbs. I met Gen Cheatham here. He looks very fat and coarse. I am told he is very popular with the army. The troops here are crossing the river every day—and the column moves this week in the direction of Nashville. All that I conversed with seem sanguine about re-conquering Ten. in a very short time. They will have some hard fighting before they do it. I returned this evening to Tunnell Hill. At Catoosa Station I met Col Lockhart who stopped there a few days to recruit—also met Al Ewing, and Mr Sheppard of Nashville. They report that there is a large and agreeable party there. I met on the train Maj Granburry and wife, Col Browder, and Lt Dunlap all enroute to Vicksburg to join their commands.

Aug 19th

Robert Deery came from Chattanooga this morning and brought a telegraphic dispatch from Mrs Churchwell—who states that her hus-

[6] John Joseph Hughes (1797-1864), Roman Catholic prelate.

[7] Leroy Pope Walker (1817-1884), lawyer, Confederate Secretary of War.

band is expected to die. Robert and my wife started up to Knoxville this evening. Gen Buckner reached Chattanooga last night—and it is supposed that he will take command of one of the divisions there. Col Smith's battallion of Cavalry passed through here this morning en route for Loudon. They have been encamped here for some time at Gordon's Springs about ten miles from here. They are generally well mounted and equipped. I left Tunnell Hill this evening for Vicksburg.

Aug. 20

Reached Atlanta before day this morning but did not go on because the train left for West Point before I could change my trunk. I met Judge Ridley—Geo Cunningham and several other acquaintances here. Col Lockhart and myself left on the train for West Point this evening.

Aug. 21

Reached Montgomery this morning and met at the hotel A O P Nicholson—Judge Martin Mr Sykes en route for Chattanooga. Montgomery is one of the most beautiful inland towns in the south. The streets are wide—and all diverge from a common centre. The Capitol is on an eminence—but does not look very fine. The store houses and residences are substantial and some of them costly. Col Lockhart and myself went out shopping. There are no goods in the town to speak of—and what we saw were in the hands of Jews—who ask enormous prices for everything. Twenty dollars for a common white felt hat. Twelve dollars for a pair of common ladies shoes. Five dollars a bottle for execrable whiskey. Fifty five dollars for a common saddle with wooden stirrups, and everything else in proportion. At night they have no lights in the cars, because they can procure no oil. Indeed there seems to be a general scarcity of everything. The corn crops along the road look badly. This is no country for corn. Left Montgomery for Mobile this evening.

Aug. 22nd

Reached Mobile about 9 oc this morning where I met Gen Tilghman—Maj Barbour—Maj Ellis—Col Heiman—Maj Grace—Col Murphy—and several other Ft Warren acquaintances. A steamer called the Alice ran the blockade here yesterday, and brought a large cargo of powder and salt-petre. The weather here today is excessively hot and disagreeable. There is no business here to speak of—and the city looks dead. They have obstructed the ship channel leading into the harbor and have a number of batteries leaning upon it. They have about five thousand troops here—and the citizens feel safe. I met Mr Lewis here

Courtesy Library of Congress

View from the South Steps of State Capitol during the Civil War, looking east. The Davidson County Courthouse is seen in the center. Note the barricade at foot of steps.

Courtesy Library of Congress

View of South Nashville, December, 1864. In the foreground, buildings and campus of the University of Nashville. Fort Negley, built by occupying Federal troops, is atop the nearest hill.

today, from Knoxville, and he told me that Churchwell died on Monday evening last. Gen Tilghman and staff left this evening for Jackson Miss.

Aug. 23

The prisoners have not been delivered yet at Vicksburg—and I would not be surprised if the President's Proclamation in regard to Gen Pope's order caused the Federal Government to disregard the Cartel—and not deliver the prisoners. Mr Dun called to see me this morning—and invited me to spend several days at his house. I met Flippen today from Nashville. He looks as fat as ever. When I saw him he was sitting on a box—leaning against a store door with his pants rolled up to his knees—and a negro blacking his shoes, and he reading a paper, presenting a picture for Punch. I left the city this evening on the Mobile and Ohio RR for Meridian in Miss., in company with Lt Col Murphy.

Aug. 24

Reached Meridian before day this morning but learning that the prisoners had not reached Vicksburg I proceeded to Columbus to make a visit to Sister Ann and family. At Artesia I met Judge Dickinson and Mac and brother Edward—who had been up to pay brother Jno a visit at Tupelo. Reached Columbus at 4 oc and found all well at Judge Dickinson's. Sister Mary has been here ever since the fall of Donelson.

Aug. 25

Dr Lyons Mr Harrison—and Davidson Cross called to see me today. Brother Edward when he left the plantation in Ark. brought all of his negroes—and the men from father's place. Eight or ten of the men have run off since he brought them here. Judge D and myself called over to see old Maj Blewett today. He is very much troubled about the death of his son Randal who was killed in one of the recent battles before Richmond. I met Sis Harrison there. Sister Ann gave a little tea party this evening and invited a few of her friends to meet me.

Aug. 26

We have news here today that Pope and Buell are both falling back—also that Gen Butler has been relieved of his command in New Orleans—and his place taken by Gen Dix. Butler is going to Charlestown. Gen Pope, in his official report of the battle of Cedar Run—claims a victory as usual, but correspondents to the N Y Herald and Tribune show the contrary. Edward and myself called this morning on Mrs Dr Malone—Dr Lyons—Mrs Lamar Whitfield. This evening Sister Ann and myself called on Mrs Hamilton—Mrs Barry—Mrs Cannon. The weather here during the day is excessively warm—but the nights are pleasant.

Aug. 27

This has been another intensely warm day, so much so that I have remained all day in the house.

Aug. 28

We have had two dispatches today containing good news. The evacuation of Nashville Clarksville and Ft Donelson. A fight between Morgan and Gen Johnson in which the latter was repulsed and taken prisoner. The forward movement of our army into Ten. I think the conscript law will operate badly where overseers are taken from plantations. It is unsafe to leave negroes on plantations by themselves. They will not work, and there is great danger in their rising and doing some evil. The application of the law should except overseers. Mrs Laura Whitfield gave me a little party this evening which was very pleasant. I met Judge Milton Brown and his son, Col J A Brown, there. Judge Dickinson and myself visited the Government works which have been established here since the evacuation of Nashville. They are quite extensive—but mostly of frame and temporary in their character. I noticed four brass pieces taken at Shiloah—and made in Mass. No news yet from the prisoners that were to be delivered by the Federals at Vicksburg. From present appearances I think there will be a number of Cols without any commands.

Aug. 29

I called this morning on my friend Miss Annie Fort who is just recovering from a severe spell of sickness. She is a most interesting and accomplished lady. Also called on Laura Whitfield and her sister, Mrs Sykes. Received a beautiful wreath and bouquet of flowers this morning from Mrs Wm R. Cannon with the following note. "I hope Col MacGavock will accept the meagre remnant of flowers sent, (that have survived the excessive drouth) as an evidence of my warm appreciation, not merely of his high toned character, and captivating gifts, but likewise of the high testimony given his country of his patriotism." Occupied the remainder of the day at home, on account of the excessive heat. Capt Billups and lady called to see me this evening.

Aug. 30

Mr Meaks called this morning. He is just from Price's army at Tupelo—and reports that Col Faulkner with 800 cavalry make an attack on the Federal cavalry 1500 strong near Riensi—and was repulsed losing two of his companies. I read a long and very able communication in the Memphis Appeal on the subject of Martial Law—which I think will open the eyes of some of our military men. The object is to show that the military is subservient to the civil law under our Constitution. Judge Dickinson and myself sat up tonight with Col A H Young who is dying. I do not think he can last much longer.

Aug. 31st

Col Young died this morning. I attended Dr Lyons' church this morning where I met Col Baldwin who has returned from Jackson. He has no tidings from the prisoners—but I see in a dispatch this evening some of them left Camp Martin in Indiana on the 23rd inst.

Sept. 1st

At 9 oc I attended the funeral of Col Young. Dr Lyons preached the sermon, and gave him a most excellent character. At the cemetery I saw a beautiful monument erected by brother Edward in memory of his wife. I met Mrs Hamilton today, formerly Miss Abert for whom I entertained a very tender feeling about fifteen years ago, when I first visited Columbus. She is decidedly the finest looking woman that I have ever seen here. This evening Sister Ann and myself returned the call of Capt Billups and lady. Mrs B is quite elegant—and they live in style.

Sept. 2nd

This morning Judge Dickinson—Sister Ann and myself drove out to "The Oaks" the residence of Judge Perkins, about nine miles from Columbus. It is quite a princely looking place for this country and reminds me very much of some of the old English county seats. The mansion is large and well furnished; the grounds or park around the house is large and of native growth interspersed with beautiful cedars. Near the house is a flower garden, in the center of which is a bowling alley. Judge Perkins is now eighty two years of age but well preserved. He is very tall and erect and is evidently a man of very marked character. He has accumulated a vast fortune which he has given chiefly to his son in La. Mrs Henry, his niece lives with him, but the old man carries the keys and is his own housekeeper—and a good one at that. He is a man of great system and economy in all things. He says that economy is sweet. We returned late in the evening. At two points on the road we were stopped by guards and required to exhibit our papers. One of them asked me if I was thirty five years of age. They arrest every man they find as Conscripts under thirty five. A dispatch reached here today containing glorious news. Gen Lee telegraphed to President Davis on the 31st of Aug—that after three days hard fighting on the plains of Manassas he had obtained a signal victory over the combined forces of Pope and McClelland. The enemy are falling back in Ten, and Buell's army is now in a very critical condition. It is the best day's news we have had in a long time—and I hope it may all be confirmed and that victories may continue until we drive the Vandals beyond the Ohio. This evening there was public thanksgiving in the Baptist church. The number present was large—mostly ladies. Dr Teasdale—Dr Neilly —and Dr Stanback officiated. The Music on the organ and from the choir [was] good and the ceremonies very interesting.

Sept 3

This morning I walked down town with Judge Dickinson and obtained papers for myself and brother Ed to go to Jackson. I afterwards met Mr Hamilton who called to see me yesterday and Dave Armstrong. The latter is just from Guntown where brother Jno is encamped. Col Otey invited us to his room and gave us an excellent drink of whiskey and some fine soft peaches. I called and bade Mrs Young and Mrs Whitfield goodbye. Left Columbus at 10 oc tonight.

Sept. 4

The country between Columbus and Jackson is very thin, and the crops burnt up. Met with Freeman of Memphis—formerly of Nashville, on the train. He is manufacturing shoes at Canton. Edward bought a pair from him and gave him fifteen dollars. Reached Jackson at 4 oc and stopped at Bowman House—a large four story house but a very bad table. Gen Tilghman and Staff are here.

Sept. 5th

The news this morning is glorious. Bull Nelson's command numbering 10,000 captured—all his artillery, small arms, and stores captured; Gens McClelland and Pope mortally wounded—Dan Sickles killed—and capture of large number of prisoners and valuable stores. Preparations to evacuate Washington. Long Bridge blown up. Nine thousand prisoners paroled on the Field. The rout surpasses that of 21st July. Our army in possession of Arlington Heights. Now if all this be true, or only half of it—we are certainly in good condition. Col Heiman and Maj Grace reached here today from Mobile. Boyd Cheatham and Lt McMurry of our Reg are here. They made their escape. The former from Ft Donelson and the latter from one of the Northern prisons. The straglers are encamped near the town. No news from the prisoners yet. The gun-boat Epy fired one gun at Vicksburg this morning and retired. I am very much disappointed at the appearance and size of Jackson. It is not half so large as Columbus. The houses indifferent—and no business of any consequence seems ever to have been transacted here. The State Capitol is a poor affair. I received a letter from my wife this evening written at Knoxville on the 21st of Aug. She encloses an obituary notice of Mr Churchwell written by Mr Ramsey the historian.

Sept. 6th

The communication on Judge Shaskey on the subject of Martial Law has had a good effect—as Gen Van Dorn has suspended it in this State and discharged all of the Provost Marshalls. Also set at liberty the political prisoners. The civil authorities now take cognizance as before of all offences not military. Maj McConnico went down to Vicksburg this morning with about two hundred Federal prisoners. One of them had no pants on—but his blanket wrapped around him. This was a shame. He should have been furnished with pants. Gen Breckinridge's command moved today in the direction of Memphis. I wrote letters today to Uncle Randal—Mrs Churchwell—and my wife.

Sept. 7th

I attended the Presbyterian church this morning in company with brother Ed. I read the report of the Sec of War—and a correspondence between Mr Seward and Mr Hughs, the Chairman of the democratic State Central Committee of Ten. The Sec cuts him off very summarily. Three thousand prisoners reached Vicksburg this evening. It is reported that all of Col Abernathy's Reg but one took the oath. His Reg was formed in the counties of Giles and Marshall in Ten. This is the work of Gen Wm B Campbell who visited the prisons north a short time ago. Col Browder has just reached here from Tipton Co Ten. He reports that the Dutch soldiers are playing the wild with negroes of that county. Tom Craighead and eighty of his negroes were arrested and carried to Memphis. He was put in irons. Ed and myself took a walk around town this evening. The residences are mostly built on squares and are of an indifferent character. George Yeiger's and Col Withers' places are the handsomest in the town. The Gov's Mansion is large and occupies a whole square, but looks very delapidated. Jas Price of La called to see me today—also young Mason of Nashville. I met Dr Jno Foster[8] of N O this evening.

Sept. 8th

News reached here today by telegraph that Gen Kirby Smith had taken Cincinnati—that Gen Jackson was marching on Baltimore, that Gen Buell was falling back on Nashville, and Gen Bragg pursuing. That Gen Grant was evacuating Corinth and Gen Price following him.

[8] John Dickinson Foster, M.D., was the son of Ephraim H. Foster. He graduated in medicine in Philadelphia, and later became physician in charge of quarantine in New Orleans. He died a martyr's death in New Orleans while fighting an epidemic of yellow fever.

Most too good to be true. I went out to the encampment this evening near town where some of the returned prisoners are staying. I went in bathing in Pearl river—in company with Capt Cheatham—and Lt Roscoe. Took supper in camp with Col Sugg. Capt A. J. Polk[9] arrived here this evening from Cooper's Wells. He is not now in the service. Dr Voorhies arrived from Vicksburg and says that there is no news of the prisoners.

Sept. 9

A petition was presented to me this morning for signature, addressed to the President, asking him to re-instate Gen Wm Carroll[10] who has been under arrest for some time past for drunkeness. I signed out of regard to his family and for past associations—but do not regard it as a military proceeding. I called this evening to see the wife of Col Withers. He is at Vicksburg—and has command of a Reg. of Artillery. Met Mrs Gen Wall of Texas and Mrs. Freeland of this vicinity. In the Mobile paper I see that Gen Beauregard has been assigned to command at Charleston—Gen Joe Johnston West of the Miss Generals Pillow and Lovell have been reinstated. Chas J Ingersoll[11] of Philia has been arrested for a speech he made in that city which was considered treasonable.

Sept. 10th

Gen Tilghman received a dispatch from Vicksburg this morning that 4000 of our prisoners had arrived. He has issued an order for all officers to go there at once. News reached here today that Stonewall Jackson had gone into Md. His forces have crossed the Potomac and his cavalry reached the Relay House. Jeff Davis has taken the field.

Sept. 11th

At 7 oc this morning I started on the train for Vicksburg. On the way we met two long trains filled with returned prisoners from Camps Morton and Chase. The balance will be here in a few days. It is my first visit to Vicksburg and I hope my last, as it is an ugly, dirty, and disagreeable place. I met with Felix Winder there. He is Capt of a company in La Reg—and is looking well. Three privates of my Reg. arrived. I met a large number of Field officers who went there to meet their Regiments. I returned to Jackson this afternoon.

---

[9] Allen J. Polk (1824-1897), lawyer, was born at Farmville, North Carolina. He practiced law in Columbia, Tennessee and at different times resided in North Carolina, Tennessee, Kentucky, Mississippi, and Arkansas. He held a major's commission during the Civil War, but was never in active service.

[10] William H. Carroll was appointed brigadier-general in the Confederate Army October 21, 1861, in command of the District of East Tennessee and the forces therein. He resigned his command February 1, 1863.

[11] Charles Jared Ingersoll (1782-1862), lawyer, congressman.

Sept. 12th

Occupied the day at the Bowman House. Brother Ed left for Columbus this evening. I thought it best for him to go there, and await the return of the prisoners, and avoid the heavy expense of staying here.

Sept. 13th

I left Jackson this morning in company with little Lida Pickett for Cooper's Wells, which is thirteen miles distant. I found quite a number of ladies here from N O mostly—but few gentlemen. Among the ladies were Mrs Ward of Texas, Mrs Freeland of this county—Mrs Violett of N. O., Mrs. Woodlief and daughter, Mrs Kennedy, and among the gentlemen—A. J. Polk—Tom Polk—Gen Crittenden[12]—Mr Hilliard of Ark—Gen Patrick Henry—etc. The improvements are on an eminence overlooking the surrounding country. The water is both sulphur and calcium. It is a cool and pleasant place.

Sept. 14

Occupied the day about the wells—talking etc.

Sept. 15

Dr Jno Foster and myself had a nice game of whist this morning with Mrs Freeland and a lady from La. I took a drive this evening. Mrs Kennedy entertained the company this evening in singing operatic songs. She has a magnificent voice. There was a dance in the ball room this evening.

Sept 16

I intended returning to Jackson this morning but it rained so hard I postponed it. This has been a dull day here. Passed my time conversing.

Sept. 17

Left the Wells this morning in company with Mrs Pickett, Mr Woodlief and returned to Jackson. This evening Dr Foster and myself went out to Mrs Freeland's in her carriage. She lives 10 miles from Jackson—and has a beautiful place. She is a widow with two children. I think Dr F has an idea of addressing her. She is a charming woman.

Sept. 18

Passed the day in reading and conversing. This evening we drove over to see Mrs Perkins and Mrs Gale—and took tea there.

Sept. 20

This morning we returned to Jackson. My Reg has not arrived yet. We have news today of another battle and victory for us near Harper's

[12] George Bibb Crittenden (1812-1880), soldier.

Ferry. I hope it may be confirmed. I went down to Col Sugg's camp this evening to see some of his officers. Abner Gale called to see me today. I met Donelson today who was an old classmate at Moses Stevens'. He lives in Yazoo River. Also met Mr Haywood—who married Miss Irwin.

Sept. 21

This evening I accepted the invitation of Mr Donelson and accompanied him to his home in Yazoo Co.

Sept. 22

Met a son of Jno C McLemore's at Mr Donelsons. Rode over to Mr King's to look at horses.

Sept. 23

Mr. L P King and myself drove to Benton today to look at some horses. Here I met Mr Tom Clark a merchant—who is a great character. I took quite a fancy to him. We returned to Donelson's to dinner—and this evening I came in the stage to R R Station.

Sept 24

Reached Jackson this morning at 10 oc. The 50th Tenn Reg organized today by the election of Col Sugg—Lt Col Beaumont—and Maj Robertson. Passed the night in Joe Pickett's room.

Sept 25

I left Jackson this morning for Clinton to meet my Reg—which is now encamped about one mile and one quarter from this place. The men were all exceedingly glad to see me, which was very gratifying. The Reg numbers about 450 privates. Some 200 joined the Federal army at Camp Douglas—and I notice that they were mostly the young men of the Reg. I understand that they all deserted the Federal Army as soon as they got a chance.

Sept 26

Occupied the day at the camp. Capt Ellis—Capt Handy—and Randal Southall—have been discharged from the Reg for disability.

Sept 27th

Remained at Camp all day. News reached here today of another great battle in Md on the Potomac in which we were victorious.

Sept. 28

This evening I went to Jackson to carry the rolls of the companies—to the Adj Gen. Sam Walker and wife and daughter—Knox Walker's daughter—Miss Pickett—and Miss Crowdus have just arrived here from Memphis. I was in the parlor of the Bowman House with [them] this evening—and we had quite a feast of music. News reached here tonight that Bragg and Smith had made a junction some twenty miles from Louisville. Major McConnico and Capt Wallace serenaded the ladies tonight.

Sept. 29

Received a letter from Brother Ed and Sister Ann today. I telegraphed to Ed to come at once to Clinton—also wrote letters to Ed and my wife. Passed another very pleasant evening in the parlor.

Sept 30

Left Jackson this morning in company with Gen Tilghman and others for Clinton. Went out to my camp about 10 oc. Gen T made speeches to three Regiments encamped here. The burden of his remarks to my Reg was in regard to their reorganization. He said that we had some good officers, but many very bad ones—and recommended some half doz of his Ky friends for Capts. He then told them that he had provided everything for them—from a tenpenny nail to a locomotive if they needed such a thing and if they did not get everything that they were entitled to—it would be the fault of the Regimental officers and not his fault. In his speech to Quarles' Reg he pitched into Gen Pillow pretty severely—and charged him with having caused all our misfortunes at Ft Donelson. He is quite a demagogue—and lets off a great deal of gas.

Oct. 1st

Brother Ed reached here this morning from Columbus. Passed the day at my camp. Col Heiman made speeches to all of the companies today and read a letter from Gen Tilghman recommending six gentlemen that he spoke of yesterday for Capts. The weather has been intensely hot today.

Oct. 2nd

Today the companies in the 10th Tenn Reg were re-organized—and I think the organization better than ever before. None of the gentlemen that Gen Tilghman recommended received a single vote. Two young gentlemen that I recommended were made lieutenants without opposition. I am very much pleased with the organization thus far—with one or two exceptions. Some ten or twelve of the old officers who were present were left out. News reached here today that Capt Sumner with the No 290 and other vessels had whipped out the Federal Fleet at the mouth of the Miss. river, and had taken Commodore Porter and Gen Phipps prisoners. The day has been intensely hot.

Oct. 3rd

Today we held an election in our Regiment for Field officers. Col Heiman Maj Grace and myself were elected without opposition and several lieutenants were elected to supply vacancies. Lt Dorsey reached here today from Nashville, having left there on the 18th of last month. He reports six thousand federal troops there and says there is great scarcity of provisions. Brother Ed was elected second brevet lieutenant in Capt Morgan's company. I desired him to be with me, and selected this place for him in preference to taking a higher position which he could have obtained without difficulty. This evening he and I went to Jackson.

Oct. 4

Had an interview with Gen Tilghman this morning—and he expressed great dissatisfaction because my Reg did not elect any of his Ky friends. I have come to the conclusion after mature deliberation that he is a humbug. I wrote a long letter to my wife today. This evening brother Ed went to Columbus on leave, and I returned to Clinton.

Oct. 5

Remained all day at Watts' House in Clinton. Did not go to camp or church. Wrote a letter to President Davis recommending Col Heiman for a Brig General's place.

Oct. 6th

I occupied most of the day at camps assisting the Q M in obtaining the receipts of the men on the pay rolls. I noticed that many of the men are sick from eating too much fresh beef—without any salt meat. The latter is very scarce and difficult to procure. News reached here today that Price has been fighting ever since Friday last, and that he was inside entrenchments at Corinth, and that he had distroyed the R R between Corinth and Grand Junction—which cuts off Gen Grant's communication with the Miss River.

Oct. 7th

Occupied the day at the camps. The Reg was paid off, and some clothing distributed. I appointed a board of Survey and had some of the blankets condemned. The shoes were of very indifferent quality. The men said that after Gen Tilghman's speech—they expected better things. An order was issued today to have our tents struck and ready to go into Jackson at 8 oc. The news from Corinth is unfavorable today —and I would not be surprised if we were badly whipped.

Oct. 8th

Maj Grace came very near being killed this morning by a horse he purchased yesterday. The horse kicked until he jumped off. He was then thrown down, and the horse broke away, and ran up the R R and fell in a culvert—and was badly hurt.

The Journal ends with this entry. His regiment was so busy during the months which followed that McGavock had little time to record his activities. It is presumed that he intended to write the story later from memory, as he had done in a few previous instances. His death at Raymond, Mississippi, on May 12, 1863, removed that possibility.

INDEX

This index was compiled by Josephine Murphey. Inasmuch as the Journals present several discrepancies in the spelling of proper names, every reasonable effort has been made to use the generally accepted spelling here. It should also be noted that a number of names are listed for which there are no identifying footnotes accompanying the text.

A NOTE ON THE TYPE
IN WHICH THIS BOOK IS SET

Claude Garamond, Parisian designer of the printing types which bear his name, died three years before Shakespeare was born. His royal Greek type imitated the Greek writing of a scholar of his time. His roman and italic forms were innovations, being designed as metal types, not as imitations of hand writing.

His roman letter forms won general acceptance in France and elsewhere and were a chief influence in establishing the roman letter as standard in place of the gothic or black letter.

The Garamond used here is a modification of the original letter as conceived by the Intertype Company.

The type was set by Joe K. Terry; the typography by Aubrey M. Hamilton. The title page and dust jacket were designed by Walter Diffee.

McCowat-Mercer Press, Inc.
JACKSON, TENNESSEE